Reprinted from the editions of 1902-1905, New York and London
First AMS EDITION published 1969
Manufactured in the United States of America

Library of Congress Catalogue Card Number: 70-86377

70-8582
AMS PRESS, INC.
New York, N.Y. 10003

The EMPIRE OF THE TSARS

AND THE RUSSIANS

BY

ANATOLE LEROY-BEAULIEU

TRANSLATED
From the Third French Edition
WITH ANNOTATIONS

PART I

THE COUNTRY AND ITS INHABITANTS

AMS PRESS
NEW YORK

A WORD FROM THE TRANSLATOR.

IT is not for the modest translator to preface by any words of personal appreciation a work such as this, which, as a Russian, I feel it an honor and a great privilege to be allowed to present in English garb to the nation of all others whose friendly, enlightened, and unbiassed judgment of us and our country we all are most anxious to secure. But inasmuch as my work is not altogether merely a literal translation, I may be permitted to point out in how far a slight amount of editing has been called for.

It was thought desirable by the publishers to let a moderate thread of annotation accompany the text, so as to bring into yet stronger light the masterly pictures of Russian life—historical, social, popular,—which Mr. Leroy-Beaulieu unfolds before the reader in a series as varied as that life itself. I gladly take this opportunity of answering the many questions which I have been asked during my twenty years of life in America, among Americans, and try to tell them not only what I know they want to know in the way of characteristic details, but also, as far as the necessarily limited space at my disposal will allow, some of the things which I think they ought to know and do not as yet. I imagined myself reading the book with a circle of interested friends, and from time to time laying it down to discuss some point, to elucidate some historical allusion, to illustrate some description, and sometimes—very rarely, very respectfully—to offer some slight objection. Where I was drawn into a discussion or narrative too long to be placed at the bottom of a page, I gave the note at the end of the chapter, in the form of an appendix. To distinguish my annotations from the author's own, I adopted the simple expedient of marking them with figures, while the usual signs—stars, daggers, etc.—were retained for the author's notes, thus doing away with the cumbersome initials or "Translator's note" at the end of each annotation.

However sparingly I made use of the latitude left me in the matter of annotation, this addition to the original work threatened to swell the English volume to a more than reasonable bulk. It became necessary, therefore, to have recourse to condensation. This delicate and responsible operation being necessarily left to my discretion, caused me more care and anxiety than all the rest of the work put together. Very rarely, very cautiously and lightly, with a fear on me as of committing sacrilege, I proceeded to abbreviate a paragraph here and there. Not so much by elimination—for it is but seldom that several lines or as much as half a page at once have been omitted—as by persistent compression, on the same principle as a pound of down, when compressed, is a pound still, though its volume is diminished. "What will the author say to this passage?—or this?—or this?" was the test question always present before my mind, and it was my standard that he should not be able to detect the abbreviations at the first reading unless he knew where they were made.

After long and careful deliberation, it was thought advisable to depart from the ordinary custom of having but one index for a work of so great compass, and of placing this complete index at the end of the last volume. Every student knows how utterly unpractical and disconcerting such a system is, and will thankfully welcome an innovation which places all the references within easy reach and frees him from the necessity of cumbering himself with a big book otherwise unneeded, not to speak of the discomfort of doing without an index at all until the publication of the third volume, which naturally cannot take place for some considerable time after the first appears. The innovation was the more appropriate in the present case that the three volumes of Mr.

Leroy-Beaulieu's work are in a great measure independent of one another, as they treat three entirely separate divisions of his immense subject,—the first volume being devoted to " the Country and People," the second to " The Institutions," and the third to " Religion " and Church matters.

In the preparation of this first index, I have classed the items more according to subjects than to names and words, with the exception of the ethnographical chapters. This subject being the most unfamiliar and bewildering, from the great number of races, peoples, and tribes, with their strange, hard names, I took particular care to include all these names in the index, in a manner to facilitate immediate reference and cross-reference.

The transliteration of Russian words and names, I believe, to render the original sound as nearly as the writing of one language *can* render the pronunciation of another. This result will be helped by the system of accentuation I have adopted, using both the accents—' and '—in this way, that the first marks a short vowel, and the second a long one. Take, for instance, *o* in "hot" and in "hole." In "hot" it would have a ', so : "hòt," and in "hole" a ', so : hóle;—' on *i* makes the sound short, as in "fin " ; ' makes it long, as in "eat," "beet." The ^ gives the vowel a very open sound, as that of *a* in "hand," "man." A few simple rules for the pronunciation of the different vowels, some consonants, etc., are given in notes, as the need of them occurs.

Z. A. RAGOZIN.

NEW YORK, April, 1893.

AUTHOR'S PREFACE.

WRITTEN EXPRESSLY FOR THE AMERICAN EDITION.

THE work herewith offered to the English-reading public is forbidden in Russia. The English or American reader will wonder at this : he should not. The Anglo-Saxon who wishes to judge of Russian matters must begin by divesting himself of American or British ideas. For a book to become officially naturalized in the domains of the Tsar, it is not enough that it should breathe the spirit of sympathy with the great Slavic people and respect for its sovereign. Autocracy, like faith, has its *noli me tangere.* It cannot allow either its acts or its principles to be discussed. And this is just what this book does, with a freedom obviously incompatible with the autocratic system. It would, therefore, be unreasonable to complain of the ostracism decreed against these volumes ; it rather claims the author's thanks, as being tribute to his sincerity from the Russian censure. Indeed, he can boast a rare good fortune—that of being able to freely express all his friendliness towards Russia and her people, without a doubt being cast on his independence of spirit.

One thing I cannot too much impress on my readers, and that is that we are not justified, we Westerners, in applying to Russia the same notions and the same rules as to Europe or America. To do so would be the height of ignorance and unfairness. Yet this is the very error into which most foreigners fall. They suffer themselves to be imposed upon by the geographers, who assure them that Europe extends to the flat-topped ridge

vii

of the Ural and to the peak-crowned steeps of the Caucasus. All this college ballast must be thrown overboard, these conventional limits be done away with. Russia is neither Europe nor Asia ; she is a world by itself, situated between Europe and Asia, and, in a way, belonging to both. The Russian Empire—I trust I have succeeded in demonstrating thus much—is indeed, in a sense, a European state, as it is a Christian one ; but it is not a state of our time. If it does belong to Europe, it is to a Europe of another age, not to our modern Europe. If one would really understand Russia, one should, to look at her, recede some three or four centuries into the past. To imagine, on the faith of the almanacs, that Russia as she is and the Emperor Alexander III. belong to the end of the nineteenth century, is, in spite of all chronological tables, a gross anachronism. The Tsar Alexander Alexàndrovitch, crowned in the Kremlin of Moscow, is not so much the contemporary of Queen Victoria as of Queen Isabel of Castile. The uprightness of his intentions, the loftiness of his character are beyond all doubt, but neither he nor his people live in the same intellectual atmosphere with ourselves. He can with a good conscience sign *ukàzes* that *our* conscience condemns. If, at the distance of four centuries, the Russian Tsar takes against his Jewish subjects measures which recall the edicts issued in 1492 by *los Reyes Católicos*, it is because Orthodox Russia is not unlike Catholic Spain of the fifteenth century.

Between this "Holy Russia" and the democratic republics and constitutional monarchies of the West there lies, for any mind trained to observe, an interval of several hundred years. Even tourists, as, with their habitual presumptuous flippancy, they steam by express across the Russian plains, are struck with this anomaly. What makes it so very hard to understand Russia is that, modern as she is if we look to dates, to the external side of her civilization, to all that she has appropriated of our mechanical sciences, to her army and her bureaucracy, she is mediæval still in the manners and spirit of her people. Urban or rural, the Russian masses have not felt the breath of either Renaissance, or Reformation, or Revolution. All that has been done in Europe or America for the last four centuries, since the time of Columbus and Luther, Washington and Mirabeau, is, as far as Russia is concerned, non-existent.

Not that she kept entirely aloof from the West or never tried to enter into closer relations with it : all her history ever since Peter the Great, and even before him, may be described as one continuous effort to "catch up" with Europe. I have shown in what sense Peter and his descendants succeeded and in what sense they failed. No, the Russia of the Románofs certainly never stood still. She has advanced since Peter the Great ; at times even her rulers, in their haste to get ahead, attempted to push on the ponderous and compact empire at an accelerated pace which the heavy popular masses could not keep up. Contrary to all that we have seen in Europe, the initiative, the impulse has always come from above, from those in power, and never had monarchs, or ministers such a weight to lift.

But, if Russia kept progressing in all directions, Europe, too— the West—was advancing at an increasing pace, into all sorts of new roads, so that Russia, massive and slow, instead of "catching up," always found herself at a great distance behind. Another thing, at which we should surely not wonder : our nimble West (Europe and America both, which to remote Russia are all one)—our unstable West, in its precipitous race for that which it calls Progress, ended by arousing a feeling of uneasiness in the religiously attuned soul of old Russia. As far back as the time of Peter the Great, there were the so-called "old Russians"—hardened Moscovites, who were scandalized at the overt imitation of Europe—the Europe of Louis XIV. and of Queen Anne. With what feelings, then, must such men, in our days, view our republics and our parliaments, our class strifes, our governments and our parties, which give to our political life the semblance of a

perpetual civil war, in which the weapons are lies and slander?
Our liberties, too often meaning oppression of the weak, and our
license, spreading itself to the destruction of all tradition and
reverence ; our democracies with their thirst for novelty and their
appetite for wealth, too often inspired by a gross and unblushing
materialism ; our incessant agitation, similar, from afar, to the
idle plashing of the waves of the sea—all our restless instability, in
short, have alarmed Russia and the Tsar. After having long
believed, with a childlike faith, that to be civilized meant
to resemble us, imitate us, numbers of Russians, even of the
thin cultivated "upper crust," have come to ask themselves
whether the wide road to "progress" opened out by our politicians
and our thinkers does not end in a precipitous cliff. And so, after
placing all her pride and vain-glory in copying us and standing
by our side, Russia became distrustful, disturbed in spirit at the
excesses produced within her domains by our imported ideas, and
her government stopped her with a jerk. She is no longer anxious to resemble us, nor to keep up with us. She thinks it safer
to remain herself, to retain—or to recover—her own individuality.

Such is the prevailing feeling in the surroundings of the
Emperor Alexander III. For the last two centuries. his country's
history has been that of a pendulum drawn alternately towards
two opposite poles. It oscillates between European imitation and
Moscovite tradition. Just now, the attraction of Moscow and the
Russian pole prevails, as it did at one time under Nicolas. The current is no longer, as under Catherine, Alexander I., and Alexander
II., set towards Europe. Alexander III. prides himself in being,
first and foremost, a national ruler. He is the Orthodox Tsar of
popular tradition. Russian, and nothing if not Russian. He
seeks for no glory save that of embodying in himself his people.
To him, the Russian Tsar is Russia incarnate. With whatever
feelings we may regard certain of his acts, it is impossible to
deny the dignity of his personal character. Never, perhaps,
has Russia had a ruler more profoundly imbued with his

duties, more earnestly thoughtful for the welfare of his people. His qualities as a sovereign, his virtues as a man, are his own ; his government methods are not. They are the outcome of the soil, of the autocratic system of which he is the representative and which he deems it his mission to maintain in its integrity. This man, invested with the omnipotence which breeds the Neros and the Caligulas of the world, is an upright, honorable man. He is brave, simple, modest ; he is calm and patient. He has shown a quality most rare with those possessed of absolute power : self-control. The protracted resistance encountered by his policy in Bulgaria has not goaded him into one act of passion. This auto-crat who, with one sign, can put in motion ten millions of men, is a lover of peace. He has made war, and he dislikes it ; he has seen its horrors too closely in the Balkàn. It is repugnant to his conscience as a Christian and as a ruler of men. If Europe, all brist-ling with bayonets, is still at peace, the merit thereof lies, in a great measure, with the Emperor Alexander III. Self-constituted warder of the peace of the world :—a grand *rôle* for an autocrat, and we in France wish that he may long continue to enact it.

Whatever the future may bring, whatever the results the Tsar's policy, domestic and foreign, may be,—whether Russia is weak-ened or strengthened thereby,—whether the sovereign's authority is shaken or confirmed by it in the end, one thing is certain, and that is that this huge country will remain, in any event, one of the three or four great states of the globe. It will, in our hemisphere, balance the United States in the other. That alone should suffice to arouse on behalf of the Empire of the Tsars, the interest of whoever is a passionate student of the destinies of the human kind. However remote this ponderous Russian people may appear to us, however backward its civilization and institutions may seem to us, this new-comer among nations has already manifested an original genius in all branches of human activity—in arts, in science, in letters. Therefore, even while noting its defects or even vices, we have not the right, we Occidentals of Europe or

America,—we, its elders, to deal contemptuously with it. Its youth may have many surprises in store for us. Let us then, whether we call ourselves Neo-Latins or Anglo-Saxons, beware of the inane race-pride which is too often aired by the Teuton, on the Elbe and the Visla, towards the Slav. The Slav has by no means had his final say—indeed he has scarcely yet lisped his first words. Because he is different from us, and because nature and history have retarded his development, we are not to pronounce him doomed to everlasting inferiority. Such presumption may bring its own punishment To show us that he has in him the stuff that goes to make a great people, all the Russian Slav needs is a chance and a couple of centuries' credit.

January, 1893.

CONTENTS.

BOOK I.

NATURE, CLIMATE, AND SOIL.

CHAPTER I.

CHAPTER II.

CHAPTER III.

BOOK II.

RACES AND NATIONALITY.

CHAPTER I.

CHAPTER III.

CHAPTER IV.

BOOK V.

THE SOCIAL HIERARCHY : THE TOWNS AND URBAN CLASSES.

CHAPTER I.

CHAPTER II.

CHAPTER IV.

BOOK VII.

THE PEASANT AND THE EMANCIPATION.

CHAPTER I.

CHAPTER II.

CHAPTER III.

CHAPTER IV.

BOOK VIII.

MIR, FAMILY, AND VILLAGE COMMUNITIES.

CHAPTER I.

CHAPTER II.

CHAPTER III.

CHAPTER IV.

CONTENTS.

CHAPTER V.

CHAPTER VI.

CHAPTER VII.

PART I.

THE COUNTRY AND ITS INHABITANTS

NATURE, CLIMATE, AND SOIL.   RACES AND NATIONALITY
THE NATIONAL CHARACTER AND NIHILISM
HISTORY AND THE ELEMENTS OF CIVILIZATION
THE SOCIAL CLASSES
THE PEASANTRY AND THE EMANCIPATION
THE MIR

THE EMPIRE OF THE TSARS

AND

THE RUSSIANS.

BOOK I.

NATURE, CLIMATE, AND SOIL.

CHAPTER I.

Difficulty of Knowing Russia—Description of the Land—In What does it
Differ from Western Europe?—In What is it European?

IGNORANCE of all that is foreign has always been one of France's
chief blemishes, one of the chief causes of her disasters. This
vice of our national education we are at present seeking to remedy :
we are making up our minds to let our children learn the languages of our neighbors ; but, if it is effectually to benefit us in
our politics, our knowledge of foreign things must not be limited
to those nations only who actually touch our boundaries. Like
ancient Greece, modern Europe forms one family, the members of
which, even in the midst of their quarrels, keep mutually dependent on one another. The interests of external politics are common to all ; not much less so are those of internal politics.

There is, amidst the European states, one which, notwithstanding its remoteness, has more than once weighed heavily on Western Europe. It is backed up against the East, and, between it
and France, there is only Germany. It is the largest of European

states, the one which has the greatest number of inhabitants, and it is the least known ; in many ways the Mussulman East and the two Americas are known better.   Distance no longer can separate Russia from the West ; it is Russia's manners, institutions, language, which keep up the high barriers that rise between her and the rest of Europe ; political and religious prejudice raise up others.   Liberals or Democrats, Catholics or Protestants, all alike find it difficult to keep their Western ideas from imparting a false coloring to the pictures they draw of the Empire of the Tsars.   The pity aroused by the victims of her official politics has for a long time warped our judgment of Russia.   She was seen only through Poland and was mostly known only from the pictures drawn by her adversaries.

Russians are fond of saying that only Russians are competent to write about Russia.   We should be perfectly willing to leave to them the task of depicting themselves, could they bring to it the same earnestness, the same sincerity, the same interest that we bring to the study of them.[1]   Moreover, if foreigners are prejudiced, so naturally is each nation on its own account.   To national prejudice are added party views, school theories.   Nowhere have I heard a greater diversity of judgments on Russia than in that country itself.

How can we expect to understand a nation that is still endeavoring to read its own riddle, that moves on with jerky, unsteady gait, with no well-defined goal as yet, that—to quote one of its own sayings—has left one bank, but has not as yet reached the opposite one !   In these successive transformations we must discriminate between what is superficial, external, official, and what is deeplying, permanent, national.   No people known to history, possibly no country in the world, has undergone so many changes in the

[1] Earnestness and especially *sincerity* have hardly been until now the distinctive qualities of foreigners' study of us,—if the name "study" may be applied to what has always been more like a blind, hostile arraignment. It is only, so to speak, since yesterday that things have begun to mend in this respect.

course of one or two centuries ; not one, with the exception of Italy and Japan, has seen similar ones in the course of a score of years. The reforms of all sorts have been so numerous that the most attentive observer finds it difficult to keep track of them. The application of them is still so recent, at times so incomplete and so much disputed, that it is not easy to appreciate all their effects. Old-time Russia, the Russia of which we had some kind of a knowledge, has perished with the abolition of serfdom. New Russia is a child whose features are not yet fixed, or, better still, a youth at the critical age at which face, voice, and character are in the act of being moulded for life.

Does this imply that in studying contemporary Russia we should forget the past? By no means : the past everywhere shows through the present. All the institutions, all the characteristics peculiar to Russia, all that makes her different from Western Europe, has deep roots which must be exposed to the light, or the troubles under which she labors will remain incomprehensible. Whatever violence the hand of a despot gifted with genius may seemingly have done to her destiny, her people were not exempted from the laws which regulate the growth of every society. Her civilization is bound up in the land, in the people's life-blood, in its historical training of centuries. As is the case with all states, and in spite of seeming breaks, the present of Russia is the outcome of her past, and the one is not to be understood without the other. If we wish to gain a profitable knowledge of this people, at once so similar to and different from their European brethren, the first thing needful is to realize the grand physical and moral influences which ruled its growth and helped fashion it, which, even in spite of itself, will for a long time yet hold it under their sway. The real bearing, the probable results in the near future of all the changes which are going on in Russia escape our grasp if we remain in ignorance of the conditions under which labor the development and capabilities for civilization of the country and the people.

This is a great, an immense question, and, as though not yet sufficiently swathed in darkness, it is further obscured by inveterate prejudices. It is, in fact, the first and last problem, and if *that* is unsolved, any study of Russia must remain both baseless and barren of results. In order to appreciate her genius and resources, her present and, still more, her future, it is imperative to know the soil which nourishes her people, the races that compose it, the history she has lived, the religion to which she owes her moral training. Let us begin with nature, soil, and climate ; let us see what kind of moral and material development they allow of, what is the population, and what the power the promise of which they hold out to her.

The first thing that strikes one at the first glance at a map of the Russian Empire, is its extent.* It covers over twelve million square miles ; of these, something over three fall to the share of Europe, *i. e.*, about eleven times the size of France in her mutilated condition, fifteen or sixteen times the size of united Italy, or the three United Kingdoms.† These colossal dimensions are so much out of proportion with the smallness of the so-called "great European States," that, in order to bring it fairly within the grasp of our imagination, one of this century's greatest scientists sought the help of astronomy.   According to Alexander von Humboldt, the portion of our globe which owns the sway of Russia, is larger than the face of the moon at its full.‡   In that empire, the vastness

---

* I would remind the reader that all this description of Russia and the people who inhabit her was written *before* the volume of the *Géographie Universelle* of Mr. Élisée Reclus, devoted to Scandinavian and Russian Europe, saw the light. (See *Revue des Deux Mondes*, 15th August, 15th September, 1873.)

† It is no longer correct to say that the Russian Empire is the most extensive in the world.   The British Empire, continually enlarged as it is by annexations in Asia, Australia, and especially Africa, surpasses it in acreage ; as to its population, it nearly trebles that of the Northern Empire, but to the latter remains the twofold advantage of compactness of territories and greater homogeneousness in the population.

‡ *Central Asia*, vol. iii., p. 34.

of which can be realized only with the help of the stars, the land has no visible boundaries. Its plains, the hugest on our planet, stretch on into the heart of the old continent until they reach the mountain masses of Central Asia ; between the Black and Caspian Seas they are barred by the gigantic bulwark of the Caucasus, the foot of which lies partly below the level of the sea, while its summits rise near on 3,000 feet above the height of those of Mont Blanc. To the northwest Russia owns the lakes Làdoga and Oniéga, the largest of Europe ; to the northeast, in Siberia, that of Baïkal, the largest of Asia ; to the south, the Caspian and Aral Seas, the largest lakes in the world. Her rivers are in proportion with her plains ; in Asia she has the Obi, the Yenisséÿ, the Lena, the Amoor ; in Europe, the Dniepr, the Don, the Volga, that central artery of the country, a river that, with its sinuous course, measuring nearly 2,400 miles, does not altogether belong to Europe. Nine tenths of the Russian territory are as yet almost untenanted, and Russia already numbers over ninety million souls, twice as many as the most populous of European states.

If we look only at European Russia, from the Glacial Ocean down to the Caucasus, we ask ourselves : Does this country really belong to Europe? Are only the proportions laid out on a larger scale and is nothing changed but these ? or is not rather this prodigious expanding of land sufficient to separate Russia from Western Europe? Are not the conditions of civilization modified by the ungainly enlargement of the stage which is to be filled by man ? The contrast of size alone would make out between Old Europe and Russia a difference of capital importance, but is this difference the only one ? Do not other and no less important contrasts flow from this primeval contrast ? Russia's climate, her soil, her geographical structure—are all these European ?

Instead of being, like Africa, attached to the common trunk of the Old World by a narrow joint, Europe is shaped like a triangular peninsula, the whole broad base of which leans against Asia and is one body with her. There is only a slight ridge between them, a mountain chain remarkable neither for width nor height, and below this chain which is really no partition at all, there is nothing but a gap wide open and unprotected. Thus soldered on to Asia, Russia is similarly shaped.

Two main features distinguish Europe amidst all the regions of the globe : in the first place, her piecemeal structure—"*all cut up into small pieces*" by the sea, to use the words of Montesquieu ; "*peninsular articulate*," to use those of Humboldt ; in the second place, a climate temperate as no other under the same latitude— a climate which is in a great measure the consequence of this very structure. Russia, on the other hand, adhering to Asia by her longest side, bordered to the north and northwest by ice-bound seas which yield to the shoreland but few of the advantages usually enjoyed by littorals,—Russia is one of the most compact, most eminently continental countries on the face of the globe.

Differing thus from Europe in structure, Russia also lacks Europe's climate—temperate, softened by the encompassing waters. Russia's climate is continental, *i. e.*, almost equally extreme in winter-cold and summer-heat. Hence the averages drawn from the varying temperatures are deceitful. The isothermal lines rise up towards the pole in summer ; sink low down southward in winter, so that the greater part of Russia is comprised, in January, within the frigid zone, and within the torrid zone in July. The very breadth of her lands condemns her to extremes. The seas that bathe some of her boundaries are either too distant or insufficient in extent to be to her what they are to other countries by turns—reservoirs of warmth and breeders of coolness. Nowhere in the west of Europe, do we see winters so long and severe, or summers so hot. Russia remains excluded from the influences which temper the cold to the rest of Europe, from the Ocean currents as well as from the winds of the Sahara. The long Scandinavian peninsula, which stretches out between her and the Atlantic, turns away from her shores the great stream of warm water, the gift of the New World to the Old. Instead of

these mild influences, it is the polar ices, Siberia, the Arctic region
of Asia, that hold Russia under their sway. Against that proximity, the Ural chain is but an apparent defence, neutralized by its
inconsiderable elevation and by its position, nearly perpendicular
to the equator. Vainly Russia stretches down to the latitude
of Pau and Nizza, she must go down all the way below the
Caucasus to find a bulwark against the north wind. The bulk of
the land being perfectly flat, is open to all the atmospheric currents,
to the arid breath from the deserts of Central Asia no less than
to the winds from the polar circle.

This absence of mountains and consequently of valleys is
another of the broad distinctive features of Russian nature, as
opposed to European nature. This horizontality of the soil, we
may say, is not merely a superficial characteristic, it is an essential
feature of the geology as well as the geography of the country.
The flattening of the outer crust is only a result of the parallelism
of the underground stratification. Instead of frequently rising
to the surface, as in the West, and offering a rich variety of landscape, soil, and culture, the divers geological tiers remain hori-
zontally stratified, presenting immense tracts of identical soil, requiring identical agricultural treatment. On the greater part of
this vast expanse, one would think that the crust of the earth has
been spared the commotions which have everywhere left so many
traces in the other half of Europe. The most ancient formations
are there found without a break, apparently unaltered by either
fire or water. Slowly emerged out of the sea, the land pre-
serves its marine aspect in its immense, slightly undulating plains,
which easily carry fancy back to the relatively recent period when
across this depression the Baltic blended its waters with those
of the Black Sea and possibly the Caspian with those of the Arctic
Ocean, separating Europe from Asia. The mind's eye has no
difficulty in figuring to itself the Glacial period, when the floating
icebergs carried into the heart of Russia, even to Vorònej on the
Don, the erratic blocks of Finnic granite with which the centre

of the empire is to this day thickly studded, down to, if not beyond, the line of the Black Mould zone.

Another great blessing of European nature is almost lacking
in Russia—the proper degree of moisture, which the Atlantic
brings and the Alps store up for the West.   Russia, debarred from
her share in this blessing by the remoteness of seas and want of
mountains, is thereby deprived of a principal source of wealth.
The winds from the ocean reach her almost totally robbed of their
water-vapors ; those from Asia have lost all theirs long before
they touch Russian soil.   From west to east moisture goes
steadily decreasing until it is reduced to the barest minimum in
Central Asia.   The wider the continent expands the poorer it
becomes in rain.   At Kazàn already it rains only half as much
as in Paris.   Hence, over a vast region in the south, the two
principal factors of fertility, warmth and moisture, are dis-
joined ; hence, in part at least, those woodless, arid steppes, so
un-European to the eye, that cover the entire southeast of
the empire

If in all that concerns the physical conditions—structure, climate, moisture—Russia stands in complete opposition towards
Western Europe, she is in all of them narrowly related to the
Asiatic countries she touches on.   If we go by natural landmarks, Europe proper begins at the narrowing of the continent between the Baltic and Black Seas ; and Russia fits better the thickset
bulk of Asia, of which she is a prolongation and from which the
geographers' fictitious boundaries cannot separate her.

In the southeast there are no natural boundaries at all, and
that is why geographers have by turns proposed the Don, the
Volga, the Ural or Yaïk, or even the depression of the Obi, as
frontier landmarks.   The desert steppes that make up the centre
of the old continent stretch into Russia by the wide gap opening
between the Ural chain's southern links and the Caspian.   From
the lower course of the Don to the lake of Aral, all these low
steppes that lie on both sides of the Volga and the Ural River,

form a peculiar region, the dried up bed of an ancient sea, of which the shores are quite distinguishable, and of which the vast salt lakes known as the Caspian and Aral Seas are the remnants. By a hydrographic freak which has exercised a considerable influence on the destinies of the Russian people, it is into one of those locked-up seas, decidedly Asiatic as they are, that the great artery of Russia, the Volga, debouches, after turning her back on Europe nearly from her very source.

North of the Caspian steppes, from the 52d degree of latitude to the uninhabitable polar regions, a long chain of mountains, the longest meridian chain of the ancient continent, seems from a distance to place a wall between Russia and Asia. The Russians of old used to call it "the stone belt,"—indeed the word "Ural" means "belt"; yet and in spite of its name, the Ural marks the end of Asia on one side, only to mark its fresh start nearly unaltered on the European slope. Slowly descending in terraces into Europe, the Ural is not so much a chain as "a table-land crowned with a line of moderately high summits." Most of the time it presents only low-rounded ridges covered with forests, like those of the Vosges and the Jura. The central portion is depressed to such a degree that in the principal passes from Siberia into Russia, for instance from Perm to Yekaterinbùrgh, the eye vainly seeks for summits, and that in order to conduct a railroad through the pass, the engineers had neither tunnels nor any other great works to execute. In this high latitude, where the plains remain seven or eight months under snow, none of the summits of this long chain reaches the line of everlasting snows, none of its valleys encloses a glacier. The Ural really does not separate either the climates or the floras or faunas of its two sides. Owing to its direction which runs nearly perpendicularly due south, it allows the winds from the pole to blow almost equally unhindered along both its opposite slopes. Russia is the same on both, or rather Siberia is only an exaggerated edition of Russia, or Russia a toned down edition of Siberia. The Russian plains start afresh east of the Ural, as vast, as monotonous in the basin of the Obi as in that of the Volga ; offering the same uniform platitude, the same horizontality of the soil and geological sediments.   On both sides the vegetation is identical.   One solitary tree,—the *arole* of the Alps, *Pinus cembra*—scarcely marks the difference between the forests on the respective sides.   Not until one reaches the heart of Siberia, the Yenisséÿ in its higher course, and Lake Baïkal, does one encounter, springing from a different soil, a new flora, a new fauna.   The upheaval which raised the Ural was not suffi-cient to disjoin the two regions separated by the ridge in all that concerns appearance and real unity.   Instead of being a boundary or bulwark, it is to the two Russias only the reposi-tory of precious mineral wealth.   The rocks of eruptive or metamorphic origin bear ores which were lacking in the regu-larly stratified subsoil of the wide plains.   The Ural chain no more separates the two than does the river to which it gives its own name, and one day when Eastern Siberia will be more densely peopled, the Ural will be looked upon as the central axis, the spinal column equally belonging to both great halves of the empire.

Considered thus as a whole, consisting of two similar halves, Russia proves herself decidedly different from Europe.   Shall we therefore pronounce her part and parcel of Asia ?   Shall we, in the name of nature, cast her back on the Old World, in one lot with the sleeping or stationary peoples of the Far East ?   Far from it.   Russia is no more Asiatic than she is European.   By her soil and her climate, by the bulk of her natural conditions, she differs no less from historical Asia than from Europe proper ; it is not by mere accident that the Asiatic civilizations have all been wrecked on her.   Astride on the Ural, Russia, by herself, forms an isolated region, with physical characteristics peculiar to herself, a region enclosing all the northern plains of the old continent, descending too low down to be called boreal, but which the name of " Russian Region " would suit well, and which, from the deserts of Central

Asia to the "*tundras*"[2] of the polar circle, from the estuary of
the Danube to the sources of the Yenisséÿ and the Lena, comprises
nearly the whole of the colossal depression which covers the north
of the ancient world, Humboldt's "Lower Europe" and "Lower
Asia." "Russia is a sixth part of the world," the Emperor
Alexander III. is reported to have once said—and geography has
nothing to object to the haughty utterance.[3] Russia's natural
affinities point to North America rather than to old Asia or Western Europe—to that America towards which she reaches out by
her eastward stretching dependence, Siberia. With her climate
always in extremes and her viewless expanses of territory, she
was too rough a land, constructed on too wide a scale, ever to
have been the cradle of civilization, but was one of the countries
most admirably fitted for its reception. Like North America, like
Australia, Russia, short of her extreme parts, offers to Europe an
assimilable soil, a field where human activity can unfold itself on
the very widest scale.

With her unkind climes, her meagre forests and woodless
steppes, with her lack of stone and building materials, Russia may
seem but a poor shelter for the gorgeous plant of European culture.
But what man needs is less the spontaneous yield of a given soil,
than the facility to master it, bend it to his requirements, to domes-
ticate it, if we may so word it. Many countries externally better

[2] The Russian *tundra* forms a belt of varying, but always considerable,
width, skirting the polar sea across the north of European Russia and Siberia, that may be described as the arctic Prairies. Only in lieu of tall,
waving grasses—clinging lichens on low rocky knolls, and wet mosses that
softly yield under the reindeer's dainty hoof, cover the level ground.
Here and there a clump of the dwarf shrub-birch, the kind that does not rise,
but spreads, crawling on the ground with thin, sapless, serpentine limbs,
twisted and gnarled. And this is summer. Nine months out of the twelve
this comparative variety disappears under a brittle crust of frozen snow, which
the reindeer finds it easy to break with short, dry raps of his nervous and
vigorous little foot, to get at the fodder kept fresh and juicy beneath. Lapp
and Esquimau villages are sparsely scattered over the face of the Siberian
tundra, with their relays of dogs for travelling.

[3] See Appendix to Chapter I.

endowed, offer to civilization a less secure field.   There is, in the New World, a state to which the forests and savannahs of Southern America open a career nearly as vast, as boundless as Russia. The sun of the tropics, rivers the largest on our globe, the moisture brought to it by the trade winds, give to its vegetation and animal life, in all their forms, a matchless vigor.   Its flora and fauna rejoice in the most marvellous variety and vitality ; but this very bounteousness of nature is hostile to man, who knows not how to conquer it.   Grasses and forests, wild beasts and insects alike strive with him for the possession of Brazil.   Nature there is too rich, too independent and powerful, to easily accept the post of handmaiden, and even when, as in India, man will have materially mastered the soil, he will still be in danger of morally bending under the yoke, enervated by the climate, enslaved by deteriorating influences.

Not such is Russia.   If the forests cover very nearly the same area, there are none of those creepers, of those beautiful parasites of all shapes and colors, which turn tropical forests into inextricable tangles.   Like the flora, the fauna, too, is poor for so vast a land ; but then there are few insects, no snakes, no wild beasts, if we except a few wolves in the woods, a few bears in the wastes of the North.   Barring the great deserts, there is, perhaps, not another such wide expanse on the face of the earth where the manifestations of life present so little variety and so little power. Inanimate nature alone, only the earth is great in size ; animate nature is puny, not abounding in species, not robust in its births, quite incapable to cope with man.   From this point of view, of such capital importance as it is, Russia is as European as any part of Europe.   The land is docile, easily made subservient.   Unlike the most magnificent countries of both hemispheres, it seems made for free labor.   The Russian soil does not require the toil of the slave ; it needs neither the African negro nor the Chinese coolee. It does not wear out him who tends it, does not threaten his race with degeneration, it gives no half-breeds.   Man there encounters only two obstacles—cold and space. Cold, which is less difficult to conquer than extreme heat. Space, in the present the already half-tamed foe of Russia, and, in the future, her greatest ally.

APPENDIX TO BOOK I., CHAPTER I. (See p. 11, note 3.)

The same conclusion—practically amounting to this : that Russia is and ought to be herself and not somebody else—is arrived at by Mr. N. Danilef-sky in his remarkable book, *Russia and Europe*, an exhaustive investigation of the questions implied by the title in all their phases and bearings. He contends, however, that the question, "Is Russia Europe?" does not admit of a categorical answer, inasmuch as the question, "What is Europe?" would first have to be answered, which it is not by saying it is "a part of the world," since the division of the world—especially the Old—is purely arbitrary, disjoining regions which have the greatest natural affinity, such as the south of Europe and Asia Minor, Lybia and Arabia,—and bracketing others which having nothing in common, such as Central Asia and India (with the Himâlaya, too, between), Italy and Norway, Sahara and the Cape. But Africa at least is a separate continent, almost an island; so are America, Australia. But Asia and Europe are essentially one, or rather "Europe is only the peninsular western portion of Asia, at first differing from her less strikingly than her other peninsulas, then more and more, as it becomes more dismembered and attenuated." Geographically, then, the question, "Is Russia Europe?" answers itself: it is and it is not ; it is in part. How much? that depends, and greatly, on personal views. But Europe is a reality after all ; it represents something definite : "Of course it does! Something very real and weighty. For Europe is not a geographical, but an historical and cultural term. Europe is the stage of the Teutono-Roman civilization, neither more nor less,—indeed 'Europe' is that civilization itself." Not by any means a "universal culture," for no such is possible ; nor yet the old Greco-Roman culture, which had its roots and affinities in Asia, and its own very definite area : the shores and isles of the Mediterranean basin, Asiatic, European, and African alike, thus bringing geography and cultural history into beautiful agreement. No. Teutono-Roman culture built up on the ruins of the Greco-Roman, and on another stage ; just that and nothing more. But that is a great deal. Now again in *this* sense, "Is Russia Europe?" "To the questioner's sorrow—or pleasure, for Russia's woe—or weal, NO," answers our author. "She was not nourished on one of those roots by which Europe absorbed the wholesome as well as the baleful saps of the ancient world first destroyed by her,—nor on those roots which brought up nutriment from the depths of the Teutonic spirit." I shall have to refer more than once to Mr. Danilefsky's book, and it is a pity it should have been unknown to Mr. Leroy-Beaulieu, for had he known of it he could not have ignored it, and it might have modified some of the views of so conscientious an inquirer.

BOOK I. CHAPTER II.

The Two Great Zones—The Zone of Forests and the Woodless Zone—Subdivisions of the Latter—The Black Mould Zone—The Steppe Region—Accidental Steppes—Primeval Steppes.

RUSSIA'S chief characteristic is unity in immensity. At the first glance, while comparing the ice-bound *tundras* of the North to the scorched wastes that skirt the Caspian, the lakes that sleep within their granite banks in Finland, to the warm terraced slopes of the Crimean shore, one is struck with the grandeur of these contrasts. The impression conveyed is that between these boundaries—between Lapland, the reindeer's domain, and the Caspian steppes, where the camel is at home—lies a space so vast as to need many widely differing regions to fill it up. Nothing of the kind. Russia at all her extremities, even where she touches on Europe, yields specimens of all the climates. Yet the territories that bear the most marked aspects—Finland, Caucasus, Crimea—are merely annexations, natural appendages, though greatly differing from Russia proper. In the interval, between the projecting spurs of the Karpathian Mountains and the Ural chain, there spreads a region unmatched, on any like area, for similarity of climate and sameness of nature's aspects. From the huge Caucasian bulwark to the Baltic, this empire, surpassing in size the rest of Europe put together, really offers less variety than western countries, owning an area ten or twelve times smaller. This comes from the uniformity of the plain-structure. The west of the empire is more temperate, more European ; the east more barren, more Asiatic ; the north is cólder, the south warmer. Yet, the south, being unprotected against the polar winds, cannot differ from the north, either in landscape or vegetation, as markedly, abruptly as France from Italy or Spain.

At the same time, under the fundamental unity through the homogeneousness of structure and climate, Nature has stamped several regions with singular clearness and precision. These regions, offering each a number of well defined special characteristics, split into two great groups or zones which, between them, cover the whole of European Russia. Both equally flat, with a nearly equally extreme climate, these two zones, mutually analogous as they are, present the most singular contrast. As concerns the soil, vegetation, moisture, indeed most physical and economical conditions, their differences amount almost to complete opposition. Setting apart the uninhabitable northern extremity, the two regions divide the empire into nearly equal halves, cutting through it diagonally, from west to east, and both cross the Ural, projecting their prolongation into Asia. One is the region of forests and peat-swamps, the other is the woodless zone of the steppes.

From the opposition of these two zones, from the natural antithesis of steppe and forest, has proceeded the historical antagonism, the strife of many centuries, which has divided the two halves of Russia,—the warfare between the sedentary North and nomadic South, between Russian and Tatar, and, later on, between the Moscovite state, founded in the heart of the forest-region, and the sons of the steppes, the free Cosacks.[1]

The forest zone, although steadily reduced by excessive cutting, still remains the vaster of the two. Taking in all the north and centre, it goes tapering from west to east, from Kief to Kazàn.

At the northern extremity beyond the polar circle, as on the summits of high mountains, no tree can withstand the intensity

---

[1] In the case of this name as of most others, mispronunciation in the mouth of foreigners led to mis-spelling. The "free sons of the steppes" are named *Kazàk*, a form much easier to eye and tongue than the faulty, generally accepted *Cossack*. But any correction of the kind is apt to bewilder foreigners, and is therefore, as a rule, to be avoided.

and permanency of the frost. On both sides of the Ural there is nothing but the *tundras*, vast and dreary wastes, where the earth, permanently hardened by frost, is clothed with moss. In these latitudes no culture is possible ; there is no pasture but lichens, no cattle but the reindeer, who knows no home but these arctic regions. Hunting and fishing are the only pursuits of the inhabitants, few and far between, of these ice-bound tracts.

The forests begin about the 65th or 66th degree of northern latitude, the atmosphere being slightly warmed by the neighborhood of the Atlantic and the deep gash cut into the shore by the White Sea. From here the forests, interspersed with boggy clearings, descend beyond Moscow, as low down as Kief. From north to south, the kinds of trees succeed one another much in the same order as in the Alps from summit to base. The fir and larch come first, then the forest pine and the birch. The birch, the pine and the fir, the three trees most common in Russia, mingle with the willow and the aspen. Further southward grow the linden, the maple, the elm, and towards the centre the oak at last makes its appearance. There are in these regions, especially in the northeast, immense forests virtually primeval from lack of thoroughfares, but they are sparse, rambling, broken up by large fallow tracts, where nothing grows but meagre brushwood.

The soil that bears the greatest portion of these forests, at least in the northwest, from the White Sea to the Niémen and the Dniepr,[2] is a low plain, spongy and abounding in peat, intersected with arid banks of sand. The highest tableland, the Valdaÿ Mountains,[3] scarcely reaches 1,000 feet. This region abounds in water

[2] Consonants preceding the *n* in the beginning of a word or syllable in Russian words and names should be clearly sounded. Thus " Dniepr" must not be read " *Niepr*," or "Dniestr" " *Niestr*," but " *D-niep-er*" and " *D-niest-er.*"

[3] The short or truncated *y* with which so many Russian words and names end, and which will be rendered by *ÿ*, always follows a vowel and offers no difficulty in the pronunciation, being exactly similar to the same sound in the English, "toy," "boy" (ex.: *Tolstòy*). The difference is that in Russian it is combined not with *o* alone, but with all other vowels. And here it

and springs ; here lies the starting-point of all the great rivers, the chief tributaries of Russia's four seas.   The little relief of the soil frequently robs the various streams of a clearly defined watershed.   No ridge separates the basins, and at thaw-time the future tributaries of the various seas sometimes get mixed and produce huge swamps.   On a very slightly inclined soil the rivers' course is sluggish and hesitating ; the waters, ignoring the uncertain slope, lose themselves in endless marshes, or flow together into numberless lakes, some of which form immense expanses, like the Làdoga, a real little inland sea, while the vast majority resolve themselves into miserable ponds, like the eleven hundred lakes of the government of Arkhangelsk.

All over this zone winter, whose sway lasts through half the year, leaves little room for vegetation and culture.   The earth frequently lies over two hundred days under snow ; the rivers do not cast off their icy fetters until May or the end of April.   But for the impetuous northern spring, which carries all before it, and at whose touch vegetation springs into life as by a sudden explosion, tilling the ground would be simply useless.   Barley and rye are the only cereals that will thrive in that stingy soil.   Wheat is seldom raised and does not pay ; flax and buckwheat are the only plants that really prosper under that severe sky.   The soil, indeed, in all this region does not provide sufficient food for the population, which, dispersed though it be over vast tracts, and never averaging over fifteen to the square mile, and frequently falling below even this figure, can never force from the soil a sufficiency of bread.   Small crafts have to eke out the livelihood refused by agriculture.   Sparse as it is, the population of these poverty-stricken countries increases but imperceptibly ; it has, so to speak, reached the point of saturation.   From this whole northern half of her European territory, Russia can hope for some

should be remembered that the Russian vowels have the same value as in all European languages except English : *a* like *a* in *far, star ; e* like *e* in *grey,* or the letter "*a*"; *i* like *ee* in *eel,* or *i* in *bit, whip ; u* like *oo* in *boor, moor* (not *door* and *floor*).

increase of population and national wealth only by favoring industrial pursuits, which flourish especially in the region of Moscow
and that of the Ural.[4]

Very different as regards promise for the future is the woodless
zone—the most peculiar, un-European of all. Originally less extensive than the forest zone, it is constantly gaining ground in
consequence of reckless tree-felling, a proceeding which by de-
priving the earth of moisture and shelter makes the climate even
worse than it naturally is. Stretching over the whole south, it
broadens from west to east, crosses the Ural and extends far into
the desert waste of Asia. This zone is flatter still than the forest-
bearing one ; on an area several times the size of France it cannot
show one hill 350 feet in height. In the west the Karpathians
throw out a spur of granite rock which turns off the course of
rivers, some of which, like the Dniepr, it encumbers with falls, without the aspect of the country around being in the least altered.
Now it stretches into undulating plains, now again relapses into
the horizontal monotony of the sea in repose. At times it slowly
grades down towards the Black Sea and the Caspian ; at others
it lapses abruptly in tiers or terraces of uneven height, but all
equally flat. There is no boundary to these viewless expanses, save
the horizon line, into which they hazily merge. Not the slightest
swelling, save in certain parts innumerable small artificial knolls,
known under the name of "*kurgàns*" (mounds), or "*moghili*"
(tombs), rounded in shape, from twenty to forty or fifty feet in
height, at times apparently disposed in regular lines, as though
to mark a road through these wastes—they are tombs of extinct
peoples, or landmarks along obliterated highways, from the tops
of which the herdsman of the steppes can survey his flock at a
distance.*

[4] See Appendix to Chapter II., No. 1.

* Such *kurgàns* or *moghili* are met with in the north, in Siberia as
well as in Russia. Numerous diggings made within the last few years
leave no doubt whatever concerning their destination.

No mountains, no valleys. The rivers skirting the outline of the above mentioned terraces mostly flow along at the foot of a sort of downs, which, however, in obedience to a general law, accompany the course of the rivers,—the Don, the Dniepr, the Volga—and are, as a rule, nothing more than the supports of a higher tier, and just as even, just as flat on the top as the low plains on the opposite bank, which the overflow of the river in spring converts into a marsh. The small rivers and rivulets born of the thaw dig their beds in the ground, but do not form valleys any more than the great rivers do. They usually roll along in deep ditches, fissures, or ravines, with abrupt banks, under which villages seek shelter from the winds that sweep the plains.

The absence of trees is the distinctive feature of this entire zone. In the northern portion of it, that is undoubtedly brought about by man's own hand, often quite recently, or even in our own time. Farther southwards, on the contrary, in the steppes properly so called, nature alone seems responsible. Soil and climate, and, above all, lack of water and of shelter, are the causes of these steppes being entirely bare of trees. Such few as do spontaneously grow there keep to the ravines, which, at the proper season, become beds for the rivulets. The plain is frequently covered with a layer of fertile earth, somewhat too loose, and certainly too exposed to every wind that blows for trees to take root there, while the subsoil, being generally chalky, does not favor the growth of forests. In other parts, again, we find the soil too much impregnated with saline substances, where nothing grows but meagre tufts of grass. It is drought which everywhere impedes the growth of woods, while, on the other hand, the want of woods increases the drought ; so we find ourselves moving in a circle from which there is no escape.

This region, then, through which course the greatest rivers of Europe, suffers from want of water. Heaven grudges it rain, earth grudges it springs. This evil goes on growing from north to south, from west to east. The rainfalls, frequently separated by long intervals and always irregular, at least as to quantity, come only in spring and in autumn. All through summer the denuded earth, parched by such a sun as Asia knows, yields up all her moisture to an atmosphere which in no shape returns it, for the clouds keep at an elevation which does not allow of their condensing into water. In certain districts of the farthest south such a thing as a whole year, nay, eighteen months, without a drop of rain, is not unknown. The penury of water in summer is often such that in many villages the peasants, lacking spring or brook, are reduced to drink the liquid mud of the blackish pools wherein they have tried to keep the spring waters.

This southern zone, too, which would seem entitled to a more temperate climate, is, on the contrary, the very home of abrupt contrasts. It passes, within the year, through arctic cold and all but tropical heat, swayed by turns by the atmospheric influences of Siberia and Central Asia, the icy wastes of the north and the sandy wastes of the southeast. Under the latitude of Paris and Vienna, the countries north of the Black and Caspian Seas have in January the temperature of Stockholm, in July that of Madeira. Two extreme seasons, with next to no transition, scarcely a few weeks of spring and of autumn. In this southern zone the winters are shorter than in the north, but scarcely less severe. The vicinity of Siberia and Central Asia robs the Caspian of the property usually belonging to vast sheets of water, that of moderating the temperature. Along the shores of this continental sea, almost at the foot of the Caucasus (44° northern latitude, which is that of the south of France), the thermometer descends to 30° below freezing point (Centigrade),* while in summer it rises to 40° above. On the confines of Asia, in the parched Kirghiz steppes, *i. e.*, under the latitude of Central France, the mercury at times congeals and remains congealed through several days, while in July the thermometer may burst in the sun. It is in the interior of

---

* The temperature is given throughout according to the Centigrade measurement.

the continent, in Siberia and Turkestan, that these excessive temperatures attain their maximum. Round about the Aral the difference between the greatest cold and the greatest heat amounts to 80° and even to 90°, so that the Russian troops in their expeditions to Central Asia have had to face by turns the extremes of both winter and summer. Even to the north of the Black and Azof Seas the seasons are markedly exaggerated. There also the difference between the hottest and coldest day of the year sometimes exceeds 70°. The Crimean peninsula itself, though bathed by two seas, does not escape these terrible contrasts.

These extremes of temperature are among the obstacles that civilized life has to battle with in Russia, but they nowhere amount to an insurmountable barrier. It should not be forgotten that of all the privileges enjoyed by Western Europe her temperate climate is the one most rarely found even in the finest of her colonies. The other continents frequently, and from analogous causes, labor under the same disadvantages as Russia. The climate of the Northern States of the North American Union greatly resembles in this respect the south of Russia ; the most populous States, those of New England, New York, Pennsylvania, pass through very nearly the same extremes of temperature as the steppes of the Black Sea.

If denuded of trees, Southern Russia is far from lacking vegetation. Over a great portion of this vast territory the richness of the soil makes up for the scantiness of water, and in such places as do not suffer from too hostile atmospherical conditions its fertility is really marvellous. As concerns soil, cultivation, and population, the woodless zone naturally falls into three different regions, into three strips or bands, which tend from northeast to southwest. They are : the region of Black Mould, that of fertile steppe land, and that of sandy or saline steppes.

The Black Mould belt, one of the most fertile as well as most extensive arable plains on the globe, occupies the upper part of the woodless zone, immediately below the zone of forests and lakes. Deriving still some moisture and shelter from the latter, the Black Mould region is placed in much less unfavorable climatic conditions than is the steppe region of the farthest south. It owes its name (*tchernoziòm*) to a layer of blackish humus, varying in thickness from, on the average, one foot and a half to five. This mould consists chiefly of loam, and, in lesser proportion, of oily clay mixed with organic matters. It dries up rapidly and becomes pulverized in the process ; but it becomes, with equal rapidity, impregnated with moisture, and, under the action of rain, returns to its original condition of a sort of dough as black as coal. The formation of this layer of wonderful fertility is attributed to the slow decomposition of the steppe grasses, accumulated in the course of many ages.

The *tchernoziòm* stretches in one long band across the whole of European Russia. Starting from the provinces of Podolia and Kief in the southwest, it ascends towards the northeast to Kazàn and beyond ; after the break occasioned by the Ural, it reappears in Siberia, in the southern part of the government of Tobolsk. On its upper edge, the *tchernoziòm* still shows some woods. As we advance towards the south, these woods get sparse and stunted in size, until they gradually vanish. In the midst of boundless plains, the last clumps of oaks, aspens, or elms look like small islets lost in space. The trees grow single, even the brushwood disappears. Nothing remains save arable lands, one vast plain to which no end is seen, uniformly stretching away into distance for hundreds of miles.

Notwithstanding its faulty cultivation, by means of rather primitive implements, this region together with the Mississippi valley, is one of those immense storehouses of grain which bid our modern world defy *any* famine. The fertility of this soil, which may even yet be called new, till very lately seemed inexhaustible, and the agriculturist has long had reason to believe that it would never need manure or any fertilizer. Just now, however, it is not only conceded that this fertility should be entertained artificially, but there already are complaints about exhaustion, and experts foretell that, unless there is a change of method, ignorance will have achieved the feat of ruining the richest soil in all the world.' This part of Russia, as a consequence of its fertility, is the most populous. On an average it already numbers from sixty to sixty-five inhabitants to the square mile, and in certain western portions of it, over seventy-five. And the population increases as new issues are opened by the railways, and as agriculture progresses in its conquest of the neighboring steppes.

Between the *tchernoziòm* and the southern seas lie the steppes properly so called, as distinct from the Black Mould fields, which are frequently so designated, so that at last any treeless plain comes under that name. It is in these steppes that the flatness of the soil, the absence of all tree-vegetation, and the summer droughts reach their maximum. Slightly inclined towards the Black, Azof, and Caspian Seas, they take in the lower basins of the Dniepr and the Don, the Volga and the Ural. Left to itself, with little or no cultivation, the steppe is a desert plain, without trees, or shade, or water. For days and days the traveller looks in vain for a shrub, a hut ; still it is not always the barren waste for which the word stands in the Western mind. These immense tracts, covering in European Russia alone over half a million square miles, include lands of very different qualities, which, therefore, notwithstanding a certain outward likeness, are called to widely different uses in the future. Steppes are of two kinds, two types clearly defined : the steppe with productive soil, not unlike the *tchernoziòm*, and the steppe made up of sand, stone, and salt. The former, much the most extensive in European Russia, are ready for cultivation and full of rich promise ; the latter, apparently, will ever be unfit for it. The former are steppes only accidentally, owing to the absence or scarcity of man. The latter are everlasting steppes, by nature's own decree.

The fertile steppes fill the greater portion of the space that

⁵ See Appendix to Chapter II., No. 2.

lies between the *tchernoziòm*, of which they are a continuation, and the Black and Azof Seas. They include the lower course of all the rivers that flow into those two seas, from the Dniestr and Bug to the Don and Kubàn; they stop a long way short of the delta of the Volga, but turn up towards the northeast, where they spread between the great river and the southern spurs of the Ural chain. The subsoil generally consists of a layer of vegetable humus, identical with that of the Black Mould belt. Left to themselves, these steppes bear splendid witness to their natural fertility, in the shape, not of forests, but of a gorgeous garment of grass and flowers all their own, so they have nothing to envy the richest forests. Such a steppe is to be likened not to an African desert, but to an American prairie. The exuberance of life shown there by nature is marvellous. The grass shoots up to a height of five or six feet, even higher in rainy years. Well may the legends of Ukraïna tell how the Cosacks, in their venturesome expeditions, used to hide in the grass-thickets, horse and all. This excessive vigor of grass-vegetation may be accounted as one among the causes of the lack of woods : the tall grass, in its rapid growth, would smother young saplings. It is, however, not the gramineous tribe, or grass properly so called, that yields the bulk of steppe-vegetation, nor do they lend it that look of vigor ; the steppe owes those to other and taller plants—umbelliferous, leguminous, labiate, composite—which abound in springtime, and whose blossoms clothe it with a thousand colors. The species, too, are few, just as in the north the forests offer no great variety. They are mainly of the so-called " social " species, growing in large patches, and mostly annual plants, as others find it rather hard to weather a climate which combines Baltic winters with Mediterranean summers. Besides, the steppes are not wholly wanting in ligneous plants : a few shrubs are to be met with, trees even occasionally, though small and stunted ; among others, the wild pear, which the Cosack ballads have made the emblem of slighted love.

During the brief spring of this region, the vegetation of the steppes, like that of Northern Russia, unfolds with prodigious rapidity. The spring rains supply it the wherewithal to resist the intense summer heat ; but if the rains fail to arrive in time, it fails too, a victim to drought. In certain districts, or certain years, all this gorgeousness lasts only a few weeks : in July all is gone,—wilted, parched. The blaze of the sun, untempered by shade, scorches everything, and the tall plants, which converted the steppe into an ocean of verdure, now raise their bare stalks, spikelike and ghastly ; the steppe is transformed into a dried up *pampa*, yet, even in this shape, this once beautiful wealth of vegetation is not wasted. These grasses, scorched by the sun in the fulness of their ripeness, yield to the flocks a sort of naturally cured hay, on which they feed through the rest of the season. Each year the entire vegetation disappears at the approach of winter : whatever has survived the sun, perishes under the snow.

This primeval steppe with its spontaneous wealth of flowers, the steppe of history and the poets, gets narrowed every year, and will soon vanish before the encroachments of agriculture. The Ukraïna of the Cosacks and Mazeppa, with all her legends, has already lost her wild beauty. The plough lords it over her ; the wilderness where Charles XII. and his army could lose themselves, is now under regular cultivation. Gògol's steppe, like Cooper's prairie, will soon be a memory ; it will join the confining *tchernoziòm*. It is difficult to draw an exact boundary line between the two zones, one of which is steadily increasing at the expense of the other, and must end by absorbing it altogether. For the causes of so unequal a development we must question history as much as nature. For hundreds and thousands of years, these steppes have been the great thoroughfare followed by all the migrations from Asia into Europe ; as lately as the end of the eighteenth century they were exposed to the inroads of nomadic tribes from Crimea, the Caucasus, and the lower Volga. But for the submission of the Crimean Tatars, the Nogaÿs that dwell on the shores of the Azof Sea, and the Kirghiz of the Caspian region, these steppes never could have been opened to agriculture, under whose yoke they will soon have completely passed, thus becoming assimilated to the Black Mould territory of which they have for centuries been the neglected prolongation.

Two things, besides the scarcity of working-hands, have delayed the breaking of these grassy steppes,—two things partly connected with each other : drought and want of wood. Against drought it is difficult to find a remedy ; from lack of water, the most fertile of these plains will always be exposed to an alternation of good and bad years. Hence frequently recurring dearth, sometimes actual famine, in provinces which, at other times, might be regarded as the granaries of the empire.

The want of trees is perhaps a greater drawback still to the inhabitants, whom it affects in twofold guise—lack of fuel and building materials, since stone also is not to be had most of the time. For cooking and heating they have nothing but the dry stalks of the tall steppe-grasses and the dung of the flocks, of which they rob the soil. Such resources cannot suffice a population at all dense ; but the opening of roads and railways, of coal and anthracite mines, will gradually remedy these discomforts, by bringing in wood or substitutes for wood and restoring the manure to its proper agricultural uses. One great advantage these steppes possess in their geographical position : the vicinity of the great rivers' estuaries and of the Black Sea opens out to them the greatest facilities for trade with Europe. It is the only region in the empire that has access to a sea free from ice at all seasons. [6]

Between the arable steppe and the *tchernozióm* proper, the mode of culture and the density of the population are the only

[6] Mr. Beaulieu forgets the Baltic provinces, which possess a first-class harbor, Libava (Germanized into Liebau), which never freezes, on a deep gulf of the Baltic, open to navigation all the year round. The immense importance of this fact to commerce secures to Liebau a great future, of a different kind of greatness from that of Cronstadt of course, which owes more than half its glory to its military qualities.

distinctions to be drawn with any degree of accuracy. In the steppe the population is scant, the culture still nomadic. With only 35 or 36 inhabitants to the square mile, the culture by triennial rotation—the farming system in general use all over the Black Mould region—must soon prevail. Thus the annexation of the steppe to the *tchernoziòm* is effected easily, without hurt to anybody, without martyrs to civilization. The fertile steppe, covering 300,000 or 400,000 square miles, is still nearly as extensive as the Black Mould region now under regular cultivation. In the near future both will form one agricultural region, occupying, in Europe alone, from 600,000 to 800,000 square miles, about double the total area of France. The American prairie, which is passing through analogous phases, will probably be the only cereal-bearing country that may outdo it, and if its development is more rapid, it will be owing to the abundance of capital and to European immigration.[7]

South and east of the fertile steppe come the barren steppes, forever unapt for cultivation. No vegetable layer there—nothing but sand, or a soil impregnated with salt, still more forbidding. Such is the vast Uralo-Caspian depression, the bottom

[7] Sheep-breeding is carried on in the south of Russia on nearly as large a scale as in Australia or New Zealand. It is a pity, for that is the resource of tracts that are not good for much else. But while the hands that should put them to their proper use are not forthcoming—kept busy, most of them, in the north scratching the earth for a sustenance which, less fortunate than the barnyard fowls, they do not obtain from it,—this immense region must be made to yield income of *some* sort. But unless this makeshift industry soon yields the place to the legitimate one of agriculture, there may be danger of that gorgeous wheatland permanently deteriorating. The huge tracts of plain and hill-land on the east side of the Adriatic used as sheep-walks by the ancient Roman non-resident landlords, and those in the south of Italy which continued to be so used by the various foreign kings and feudal lords down to almost modern times, are made forever unfit for culture, or if they *can* be reclaimed it would be at a cost which well justifies the hesitations of closely ciphering financiers. Sheep-breeding is the surest and quickest mode of enriching the present to the destruction of the future, and should be confined to unproductive, poor-soiled steppeland, which still grows natural fodder of a quality sufficient for that most easily contented and most close-nibbling of browsers—the sheep.

of a sea but lately desiccated, where the evaporating waters have left behind a deposit of salt, and which, here and there, is still studded with small salt lakelets,—remnants of an inland sea of old, now reduced to the proportion of the Caspian. This is as genuine a desert as the Sahara itself, with but few oases. Starting from Tsarítsin, on the lower course of the Volga, which they include, these salt deserts mingle with or join the immense Kirghiz steppe, a region of stone and sand, and stretch on and on into the very core of Turkestan. Part of these salt steppes lies below the level of the sea, and the Caspian itself, of which they were once the bed, lies about eighty-five feet below the surface of the Black Sea.

This Uralo-Caspian steppe is, of all European Russia, the driest, most denuded, most exposed to excessive seasons. It is a decidedly Asiatic country, by virtue of its soil and climate, by its flora and fauna, by the race of its population and their mode of life. If there is, in these parts, a natural boundary line between Europe and Asia, it should be sought for, not in the Ural River, (the Yaïk), but at the western end of that Caspian hollow, the prolongation of the deserts of Central Asia; around the point where the Don and the Lower Volga come nearest each other, though art has not yet contrived to unite them, so very marked is the physical boundary of the two regions.

A glance at the other side of the Azof Sea, shows us the northern half of Crimea and the neighboring shoreland, that lies between the Isthmus of Perekop and the mouth of the Dniepr, forming a little region of itself, scarcely less unfit for agriculture— a bit of Asia dropped north of the Black Sea. Here the sandy and rocky steppes predominate. Even where we catch a glimpse of vegetable land, the scarcity of springs and rain would seem to doom to sterility, for a long time to come, this upper half of Tauris, of which such great things were expected in the time of Catherine the Great. From the mountains of Southern Crimea and the coast of the Caspian to the fertile steppeland, the barren steppeland, this side of the Ural River, covers nigh on 300,000 square miles which cannot show as much as a million and a half of population. On all this area it seems hopeless to attempt growing trees, an operation already very difficult in the Black Mould region and the adjacent fertile steppes. Unfit for agriculture, indeed for life in permanent settlements, these vast tracts, like the neighboring portions of Asia, appear to be good for nothing but cattle-raising and nomadic life. Hence these are the only regions of European Russia still held by Asiatic tribes—Kalmÿk and Kirghiz and, until quite lately, the Crimean Tatar and the Nogaÿ. They feel as much at home on these steppes as in their original Asiatic homes. They lead the same life, driving their flocks to pasture on the scant grass that grows on sand, and the meagre plants impregnated with salt which stud in tufts the arid soil.

At this southeastern extremity of European Russia we meet with the same mode of life that we observe in the extreme north, amongst the Lapps and Samoyèds: a nomadic existence under the tent made of hides, only substituting the camel for the reindeer. But then, these two regions are the least populous of the entire empire this side of the Ural. Including the numerous fishermen on the Volga, and the laborers in the salt works, the steppes of the southeast cannot show an average of six people to the square mile. In certain portions of the Kalmÿk steppe in particular, there are *not quite two* inhabitants to the square mile. Not until we reach the mouths of the Dvina in the government of Arkhangelsk do we find another as scanty population. The northern coast of the Caspian is not much better off than the ice-bound coast of the White Sea, nor has it a much more promising future to look forward to.

This review would be incomplete did we not mention one more region, less extensive and but lately annexed, which, from its mountainous soil and southern climate, holds a peculiar position. This region comprises the Caucasus and the southern coast of Crimea, which, with its abrupt steeps, is merely a prolongation of the Caucasian chain. Nature, which nowhere marked out a boundary for Russia, neither towards Europe nor towards Asia, appears to have raised at least one very efficient barrier in this one direction, between the Black and Caspian Seas. What boundary could be better carried out than this ridge, measuring from 14,000 to 18,000 feet in height, towering between two seas? It is as though another Pyrenees had been heaped up to twice the height of the chain that separates France from Spain. And yet this barrier, which seemed to stand athwart Russia's way, has been crossed. Nature herself, indeed, even while raising, furnished the means to defeat it. Thrown across an isthmus, between two inland seas, fated to be subjected to Russian influences, the Caucasus, in the logical order of things, had to be entered from both sides, and could not but easily succumb to a back-handed stroke of strategy. This bulwark of Asia could not hold out against the necessity for Russia to step over it in order to reach the South, that everlasting allurement of all Northern nations.

The Caucasus and the southern coast of Crimea cannot be accounted a new region of the Russian soil,—Russian nature ends with the plain ; they are an entirely different country, as varied of aspect as the regions of Russia proper are monotonous. There, on the steep sides of the mountains, we find forests, the counterpart of those that have vanished from the centre of the empire downward, not meagre, sparse, and monotonous as in the north, but dense, vigorous, displaying a vegetative power unknown to Moscovia proper. There, too, fruit-trees thrive, along with that variety of plants and culture which Russia would vainly look for on her plains, from the shores of the glacial seas to those of the Euxine,—the vine, which on the banks of the Don still enjoys but a precarious shelter, the mulberry, the olive-tree. It appears as though the various zones of culture characterized in other countries by these three trees, unite into one on the slopes of these mountains, as though to compensate Russia for the monotony of her plains. Few are the varieties of fruit not acclimated in these Crimean hanging gardens suspended above the sea, or in Transcaucasia, where Russian merchants, not content with having succeeded in the cultivation of cotton and sugar-cane, are discussing the introduction of tea plantations.

APPENDIX TO BOOK I., CHAPTER II.—NO. 1. (See p. 19, note 4.)

The misery is increased and made wellnigh hopeless by the prohibition laid on the peasants to leave the land allotted them at the time of emancipation. The Emperor Nicolas took pride in proclaiming that Russia was "an agricultural country." So agriculture was "encouraged" at the expense of everything else, and the fiction was kept up during the great crisis which was to decide Russia's economical future. The unfortunate peasants of the north, while nominally set free, were given over to a bondage worse than the last. An intelligent landlord could and would allow numbers of his people, for a moderate yearly payment, to go to any place where they could earn a good living. Now they were made bond-slaves, not to men, but to a soulless thing, a soil incapable of rewarding their most assiduous toil with enough of mere rye alone to last the family to the year's end, not to speak of the seed grain for the following season. So they were burdened over and above the taxes, with a considerable purchase sum for the land allotted them, and placed in the impossibility of paying either, even at the cost of half-starvation to themselves, by being "fastened" to a soil absolutely unfit for cultivation under any conditions whatever. The reason given is that "had they their will, they would rush down *en masse* to the south, south-west, and southeast,—(which, *nota bene*, are as good as uninhabited!)—and the north would become a waste." As if that argument did not work precisely the other way: will people—and such conservative people as the Russian peasants—rush away from their homesteads to unknown lands unless they have nothing left to lose and all change is gain? Why, that is just what the North ought to be. The forests should be nursed back to their former richness and re-stocked with the wild beasts whose extermination has robbed the country of a real and bountiful source of national wealth. When one thinks that the forests about Nòvgorod and Pskof, all cut up by streams and interspersed with lakes, teemed with beavers only a century and a half ago! Then the whole great North is undermined with ores—copper, lead—so rich that huge lumps of pure metal crop up under the plough and are taken to cities by the peasant-wives along with their flax or eggs, carefully hidden under their aprons, and sold for a few coins with fear and trembling—for it is forbidden to take notice of such things, as they might be to the prejudice of the administration pet—agriculture ! Besides, the share demanded by the exchequer on all such finds, and the charges for licenses to extract ore are so exorbitant that no native company can stand them, not to speak of individual effort, which is totally inadequate. So that, with wealth untold under one's feet, it is cheaper for Russian manufacturers to import their raw material, even though we by no means rejoice in free trade. Then a German or American syndicate comes along, goes into things, makes an offer, and lo ! all doors open before them, and though red tape and "to-morrows" are not spared even to them, favors, privileges, exemptions are showered upon them. They go to work, and make colossal fortunes, which they carry out of the country—and sneer at the Russians for a set of im-provident, narrow-minded, short-sighted sluggards, too ignorant and lazy to pick up the wealth which is simply wasted on them. There is no doubt that this state of things, especially the mistake of maintaining compulsory settlement and culture, have much to do with the present disaster. The liberal press cried itself hoarse at the time, foretelling the logically impend-ing ruin, which has come to pass, for logic does not deceive as statistics sometimes do. The present emperor, Alexander III., has come to the relief of the peasantry in every way ; remitted arrears, paid up large instalments of the so-called "redemption certificates" (the purchase money for their lands, paid out to the proprietors in a lump), distributed large quantities of grain against seeding time, fed thousands of families, rebuilt burned-up villages. His great heart is ever open to their needs, his hand never closes—all in vain ! A column of figures can add up in only one way. And until the evil is struck at the root, and the grown-up men of Russia are officially acknowledged capable to discriminate what is best for them and to know their own minds, and allowed to act accordingly, there is no salvation. This compulsory coupling of man and earth is unnatural, and has come to be like the binding of a living body to a corpse. And all the time there lies the immense South in the sun, wide open, awaiting only hands to treble the wealth of the empire, and that for all times, inexhaustibly.

APPENDIX TO BOOK I., CHAPTER II.—NO. 2. (See p. 24, note 5.)

Not ignorance entirely. When it is the Russian people that are in question, the word comes glibly to the lips or pen of even our friends, when "poverty" should stand instead,—and other things. If the peasants could have afforded more cattle and horses through all these years, and if the few poor beasts they did manage to keep had not been so often sold off for arrears of taxes and to satisfy the claims of the local bloodsucker, the ruth-less usurer, known under the graphic nickname of "village fist" (*kulàk*), to whom they are fatally driven by the absolute necessity of procuring grain against seeding time, or money for the collector or something as vital,— things might be different.   The reason why the exhaustion of the soil has been progressing at so frightful a rate of late years is that freedom has come to the peasant weighted with the taxes which did not concern him under the old *régime*, besides the obligation of paying for his land to the State, which had advanced the money to buy off the former landlord.   He has succumbed under the load, that's all.   And the land, which was to a certain extent looked after by the landlord, has simply gone to rack and ruin because its present owner is not allowed to keep a sufficient percentage on the produce of his labor upon it to secure a bare sustenance to himself and his, let alone improving the soil.   This is one of the reasons—which I have not seen mentioned anywhere—why the present famine is not only so universal, but so permanent, a phenomenon not to be explained by a couple of bad seasons in *such* a land.   It is the general deterioration of one of the granaries of the earth.   It would take millions for fertilizers and years of rest to restore the soil to its natural richness.   So where is there hope?   It *might* be done, if the people were freed from compulsory residence on their lands.   They would gladly pay the taxes for them and—rush into the glorious South, which is virtually virgin soil and is being wasted for lack of hands.   The Government might then take in hand the temporarily half-deserted region, which would fill quickly enough once it became its old self again.   It is a simple plan, and, Heaven knows, feasible enough with the untold millions of vacant acres, but—it won't be done!   "Igno-rance" is easily said, but so conscientious an inquirer, so good a friend, as our author should not be quite so quick with the word.   What, then, shall we say of the New England farmers as a body, who, with nothing to hamper or hinder them, have allowed land throughout their States, ever since they first took possession of it, to go down to nominal value and deteriorate till it is impossible for an ordinary family to make more than a bare living out of a hundred-acre farm with unceasing toil and the plainest of fares—just in the same way : by taking and taking from the soil without putting enough in—and that originally not from lack of means, but from the thrift that hates to lay out to-day a dollar that is to bring a return, and an ample one, not to-morrow, but in a year or perhaps two.   *Now* of course it is different : the means *are* wanting, and the farms to be had for the asking.

BOOK I. CHAPTER III.

Homogeneousness of the Country—Its Vast Plains were Destined to Political Unity—Uneven Population—How, for a Length of Time, it was Distributed after an Utterly Artificial Manner—Relative Importance of the Various Regions—Vital and Accessory Parts—Russia a Country Born of Colonization—Her Double Task and Consequent Contradictions.

THE physical diversity of the various regions of the country must not blind us to their homogeneousness. Russia is so naturally one, that, short of an island or a peninsula, no country in the world is more clearly stamped for the dwelling-place of a nation. Through all their differences, all their physical and economical oppositions, the two great zones of North and South belong together like two halves that complete each other and cannot be separated. In the first place they have in common the soil, the plain, which admit of no barrier, no possible boundary ; in the second place, the climate is common to both ; the winter, which for weeks and weeks gathers them under one mantle of snow. In January you can sleigh it from Arkhangelsk or Petersburgh to Astrakhan. The absence of snow would be for the South as dire a calamity, and nearly as rare as for the North. As in the southern steppes, so in the forests that skirt the polar circle, the rivers are ice-bound for months. The Sea of Azof freezes just like the White Sea, and the northern half of the Caspian just as the Gulf of Finland. The Black Sea is the only one of Russian seas the ports of which are not all closed by ice in exceptionally severe winters [1] ; but the *limans*, or broad estuaries of the great rivers, do freeze up almost regularly. As a rule, the navigation on the Black Sea is not in-

[1] See preceding Chapter, note 6.

terrupted ; but under the breath of the north wind, along the
coast of Crimea just as along that of Canada, vessels not unfrequently have their rigging hardened by frost, and their hulls
coated with a congealed crust, which make them heavy and
stiff, and seriously imperil them.

With no mountains to part them, the two zones, with their
forests and steppes, are linked together by their rivers. Of these the
greatest have their sources in the one, their estuary in the other.
The different natural regions do not correspond to the various
basins : that of the Arctic Sea holds only the extreme north, that
of the Baltic only the western provinces ; the entire centre and
the east incline southward, as represented by their rivers, the
Dniepr, the Don, and, above all, the Volga, the Russian Mississippi, which carries to the Caspian the melted snows of the
Ural, together with the waters from the lakes of the low table-
land of Valdaÿ.

It is not only by what they have in common, but just as
much by their discrepancies that the two great zones are united.
The more widely their soil, their products differ, the more exclusive the call which they seem to have received from nature, compelling each to seek assistance from the other. The central region
alone, where forests and cultivated fields touch and mingle, the
principality of Moscow of old, might be all-sufficient to itself.
Neither the North nor the South could. The North needs the
grain of the South, the South wants the wood and timber of the
North. If ever nature herself traced the outline of an empire, it
was when she drew the lines from the Baltic to the Ural, from the
Arctic Ocean to the Black and Caspian Seas. The frame was
clearly marked, history had only to fill it out. These vast regions
were as fatally doomed to political unity as countries ten or twelve
times smaller, like France or Italy ; and not only that, but the
plain was to make the process both easier and more rapid.

In this respect Russia has the advantage of another colossus
of the modern world. In the general flatness of the soil, in the

relative sameness of the climate, she has more solid guaranties for
her unity than the United States of North America, the North and
South of which are, indeed, also strongly linked together by a
great river, but where contrasts of every kind are more accentu-
ated, and could be still increased by territorial acquisitions to the
North and to the South.

In Asia, as in Europe, it is nature that has marked out the
field for Russia's sway. From the high tablelands of the Ural
her rule spreads over the Siberian plains ; from the low flats of
the Don and the Volga, over the depressed basin of the Caspian
and over Central Asia. Asiatic Russia, especially Western Siberia,
is not to the Russians an alien colony, impossible to assimilate,
difficult to keep ; it is a prolongation, a natural continuation of
their European territory. Far from resembling the ephemeral
creations of the Asiatic conquerors, the Russian Empire is a solid
structure, of which Providence itself has laid the foundations.
There may be some uncertainty about its definitive boundaries,
more especially towards the West, the line of contact with Western
Europe, where history has created live forces independent of
physical conditions. But, no matter whether she win or lose a
few provinces between the Baltic and the Karpathian Mountains,
Russia is sure to remain one whole, with her two grand zones,
sure to keep her sway over the low and cold region of the old
continent, an immense region created for unity and therefore
doomed for a long time to centralization and absolutism

Nature drew the plan of the Russian Empire even before Peter
the Great ; when and how will that immense frame be filled out ?
How many hundreds of millions will be accounted subjects of the
Tsar ? What figure will the population of this empire reach, the
vastest on earth, and so far, in proportion to its extent, the least
populous ?

One fact strikes you at the first glance: it is the uneven density
of the population. Even in Russia proper, situated in Europe,
there are districts which have, to the same area, a hundred times

the population of others. The influences which have been at work to regulate this uneven distribution are twofold—historical and physical : the latter, essential, permanent ; the former, accidental, transitory, and consequently bound to yield to the others in the end. History, owing to their geographical position, has for a long time shaped the two zones' destinies, but little in accordance with the nature of the soil and the climate. Confining with the steppes of Central Asia, the woodless zone was the first exposed to the inroads of the Asiatic nomads, and the last wrested from them. Hence an abnormal development of the two regions and a distribution of the population to some extent artificial. Leaving out the West, which, being far away from Asia, worked out a destiny of its own, the most fertile regions were the last to be inhabited, the last to be cultivated. Agriculture, hence wealth and civilization, could not for centuries thrive and blossom on the spot marked out to them by nature. Repelled from the south by the inroads of the nomads, the Russians were relegated to the regions of the north, incapable as these are to support a numerous population, a great civilization.* The effects of this anomaly, which were still keenly felt in the eighteenth century, are now rapidly vanishing. The southern half of the empire already holds a far greater number of inhabitants than the north ; there are certain tracts of the Black Mould region which lay in great part waste a century or two ago, and are now counted among the most populous. Population still crowds chiefly around the two historical centres of old Russia—Kief and Moscow. But old habit is no longer the principal cause of this. At Kief the attraction lies in the soil and the climate ; at Moscow it is the central position and industry that detain and draw people, while the fallen queen of the North, Great Nòv-

---

* Nothing but the utter ignorance of Western Europe concerning Russia could warrant the saying that "the Russians must be sent back into their steppes, whence they never should have issued." Far from coming out of the steppes, it is only at a comparatively recent date they set their foot in them.

gorod, sees around her forsaken *kremlin*[2] a sparse sprinkling of inhabitants as poor as the wretched resources of her surrounding fields.

Physical conditions being identical, the population of a country increases in proportion to its civilization. Every transition from one stage of culture to another : from pastoral and nomadic to settled agricultural life,—from purely agricultural to commercial and industrial life—every step even from one way of working the ground to another, more productive one ; for instance, from such desultory agriculture as is practised in the steppes to the method of triennial rotation, from *ex*tensive to *in*tensive farming—every such step enlarges the field for population. In Russia, where, even in the European part of it, can be found all the modes of existence from that of the nomad hunter, the only regions capable of considerable increase in the population are those which can pass from one stage of culture to another. But there are several that are debarred by nature from such an advance : the extreme north is set apart by nature for fishing and the chase, as the Uralo-Caspian steppes for pastoral life.[3]

As industrial life is only just budding in Russia,[4] it is to agri-

[2] *Kremlin* (more correctly *kreml*), the thing and the word, is the exact equivalent of the Greek *akropolis*. Every old Russian city had its *kremlin* It is the central fortified enclosure, always on an elevation, however slight ; the place of shelter in danger, of safe-keeping of the city's treasury and shrines in peace.

[3] The trouble is that nature is systematically thwarted, at least in the case of the north, with results that go widening in their effects as the circle in the water. See preceding chapter, appendix.

[4] Industrial life would be much more than "budding," the decided *forte* of the Russian genius being applied science, if things and people were let alone. But one cannot open a laundry or lunch-room without a special license. Red tape and the exorbitant dues and percentages, not to mention the "sundry" cost item, devour the possible future profits before work has begun, in a country where capital is not yet equal to such drains. They may, in the end, not amount to more than advertising comes to in this country ; but then advertising is a voluntary outlay, under the enterpriser's control, and materially helps his business, while the disproportionate tribute levied at every step by the Russian exchequer yields no return whatever to the undertaking which it cripples beforehand.

culture we must look for nearly all the development of population to be expected in the near future.   But then agriculture is, more than industrial enterprise, immediately dependent on physical conditions, therefore the increase of population in Russia is almost entirely controlled by climate, the degree of moisture, the geographical situation, and, above all, the fertility of the soil. Were it not for the delay which history has imposed on the southern regions, the density of the population would be in almost direct ratio to the fertility of the soil.

This tendency gives the key to a curious phenomenon in statistics.   Take European Russia with Poland, and you will see that two thirds of the entire population do not occupy quite one third of the territory, and, more singular still, it is in the most populous region that population increases most rapidly.   This seeming anomaly is easily explained : the zone where population is densest and increases most includes the most productive portions of the empire.   It comprises the two regions which own the best lands, the Black Mould belt and the arable steppes ; it takes in the great industrial tract around Moscow, and, lastly, along the western frontier, a mixed region, at once agricultural and industrial, composed of the quondam kingdom of Poland, and a portion of the adjoining provinces—a country whose rise was favored both by its geographical situation and ancient civilization. The industrial region of Moscow owes its numerous population not so much to historical causes as to its central situation between the two great river thoroughfares, the Volga and its affluent the Okà, and to the twofold vicinity of the finest forest lands of the north and the richest Black Mould lands.   Put together, these four regions cover, this side of the Ural, not more than about 1,000,000 (one million) square miles out of an area of over three millions, while they number 55,000,000 or 60,000,000 people out of a total population of about 90,000,000.   It is at their point of junction, near the meridian of Moscow, that Russia's natural centre of gravity may be located.   *There* lie the vital parts of

the empire. The other regions, covering two thirds of its European territory, are only more or less necessary appendages; their
degree of importance is determined by their relations with the
central nucleus, some linking it to one or other sea by means of
long rivers, which open to it the issues on Europe and Asia,—
others presenting it with the precious mineral wealth hidden in
their mountains,—others again, the largest number too, keeping
for it in their forests immense reserves of timber, while some few
in the south are its gardens, hot-houses, and orchards.

The uneven distribution of inhabitants over the various provinces affects the statistical averages in a way to greatly mislead
on the subject of the real relation between the population and the
area it covers. If the empire, as a whole, has only eight inhabitants to the square mile; if European Russia herself numbers only
twenty-eight or thirty, the most productive parts, the industrial
region of Moscow, the agricultural one of Black Mould, are very
nearly as densely peopled as Central Europe, and already have
got ahead of Spain. Instead of being sprinkled over immense
areas till they are almost lost to sight, two thirds of Russia's
entire population are concentrated within an area scarcely more
than thrice the size of France. Now, in Russia as everywhere
else, the compactness of the population gives greater facilities to
civilization, more power and cohesion to the people, more means
of action to the government.

From one half of her European territory and from three quarters of her Asiatic possessions, laboring under the curse of either
extreme cold or extreme drought, Russia cannot expect any notable increase of population. Asiatic Russia, although three times
the size of European Russia, seems incapable of feeding even an
equal population. With eighty millions, Siberia, Turkestan, and
Transcaucasia put together might be comparatively as well off as
the Russia this side of the Ural with a hundred. Taking into
consideration the physical and economical conditions of the empire, also the demands of life as to food, clothing, warmth, Russia

seems fated to drop behind the United States in regard to population, and even, it may be, in two or three centuries from now,
behind Brazil.   Notwithstanding the vastness of her domain, she
is not at all sure ever to exceed India's 250,000,000, or, consequently, China's half milliard.   Indeed, it is not impossible that
innumerable hordes from the latter country may at some future
time push up northward and strive to wrest from the Russian
colonists the possession of Siberia, if not of Central Asia itself.

Whatever may be the probabilities for or against these remote
prospects, Russia already has 115,000,000 of inhabitants, and about
the year 1950 she will have 180,000,000 on one continuous territory,
a thing not to be thought of for any other European nation, unless
the Germans, with their persistent "eastward push" (" *Drang
nach Osten* "), succeed in extending their rule, at the cost of the
Slavs, over the greater part of ancient Poland, on Austro-Hungary,
and possibly over the Balkan peninsula.

In Europe as well as in Asia it is principally to the soil and
agriculture that the Tsar must look for an increase, in the near
future, of the number of his subjects.   Field labor, however, is
far from being their only resource.   In many a district, notably in
the central region, industrial enterprise already contributes to the
increase, not only of wealth, but of the population too.   Russia is
already far better equipped in this respect than she was ever
thought to be.   Industry will sooner or later take a vigorous
start, and even now is progressing rapidly.   Should they ever be
allowed to draw their means of sustenance from abroad, the
number of inhabitants might, on the strength of this one item,
multiply indefinitely.

Russia not only finds within her own boundaries the raw
material for almost every possible fabrication—thus, for instance,
Russian cotton factories use scarcely any cotton but that grown in
Turkestan—but nature has endowed her with the two great agents
of modern labor—iron and coal.   It is not half understood what
immense coal mines underlie the Russian plains.   They keep

showing up on all sides, every kind and quality—in the north, in
the centre, around Moscow ; the southeast (basin of the Donèts) ;
in the southwest in the governments of Kief and Khersòn ; in
Poland and on both sides the Caucasus ; in Asia itself in the
Kirghiz steppes ; in the basin of the Amoor and the isle of Sak-
halin. To coal and anthracite the Caspian coasts add naphtha and
petroleum. After being trammelled in the north by the lack
of openings, in the south by the lack of combustible materials, the
industrial development will soon be quickened, once the railway
lines are completed and some of the coal mines are worked. And
industry will open the way to agriculture by opening out regions
now lying waste and enticing the tiller of the earth to follow.
Thus the mines of the Ural lead to the fertile plains of Western
Siberia ; those of the Altaÿ and Amoor Mountains will draw culture into the very heart of Asia, just as, in California and Australia, culture came at the heels of the goldseekers.

If Russia's mineral wealth has long slept inactive under the
grass of the steppes or the trees of the forests, the reasons have
been many ; the most bountiful stores unfortunately lie at the
confines of Asia, in places of difficult access, some of them half-
desert still or insufficiently connected with the centre of the empire ;
then there are the distances and the high cost of transport ; then,
again, the scarcity of the population, and worse still, their poverty
and ignorance—all serious obstacles to industrial development.
The nature of the soil, the rigor of the climate, history, the habits
of the people, even to the social conditions—these were so many
drawbacks which condemned the eastern plain-land of Europe
to remain stationary a long time as an essentially rural and
agricultural country.

In order to gain a proper appreciation of the economical condition of Russia we must not lose sight of the fact that, under
Peter the Great she had not quite fifteen millions of inhabitants ;
that as late as the middle of last century her population did not
yet equal that of France under Louis XV., and at the beginning

of the present century that of the German Empire of to-day.*   If we take up the successive censuses and examine into their statistics it will be seen that Russia is a country in the process of making up its population.   She is, in many respects, just a colony ; and this is a fact of capital importance to any one desirous of seriously gauging both her resources and her difficulties.   Yes, Russia is a colony, and her history is really that of her colonization.   The first turn was the west's, then came the north and centre, and now the turn has come to the south and the east.   The lower basins of the Dniepr, the Don, the Volga can be, in this respect, compared to those of the Missouri and the Mississippi, the Russian East to the American West.   The colonial character shows in the dates of the foundation of cities, as well as in the rapidity of their progress, and their very looks.   Sebastòpol, Khersòn, Nicolàÿef, Khàrkof, Taganròg, Rostòf, Sarátof, Samára, Perm, Orenburg, the greater part of the capitals of governments or districts in the south and east, are younger than the capitals of the Atlantic States in North America.   Odessa, a creation of the Duc de Richelieu, is not quite a century old, and already holds as many inhabitants as Rouen and Hâvre put together.   The region named New Russia, of which Odessa is the capital, is as felicitously named as the New England of the United States, and the colonization of it is far more recent.   This country, wellnigh a desert at the beginning of the century, has actually increased its population tenfold within less than a hundred years.   The growth of the towns and the rural districts on the banks of the Don and the

* The so-called " revisions," operated at irregular intervals, for the single purpose of ascertaining the numbers of the taxable population, took in only the males of the classes subject to the capitation tax, and can, consequently, furnish only approximative data.   These revisions *suppose* the entire population, in its successive increase, to amount to the following figures in the given years : 14 or 15 millions in 1723 ; 16 or 17 in 1742 ; 19 or 20 in 1762 ; 28 or 30 in 1782 ; 36 in 1796 ; 41 in 1812 ; 45 in 1815 ; 65 in 1835 ; 68 in 1851 ; 75 in 1858.   See Schnitzler's *Empire of the Tsars*, v. ii., pp. 5 ff.   In 1889 it was calculated that the population had already reached the figure of over 110 millions.

Volga, in the latitude of Vorònej and Saràtof, has scarcely been less rapid.

The aspect of all these cities in the south and the east is just what would be expected from their recent origin. As in the Far West of the United States, they are all built on a large scale, all one like the other, with no feature of interest, without individuality, with no other difference than that of site. Like those of America, they cover far more space than European cities with an equal number of inhabitants. One feels that they were constructed less for the present than for the future, in view of an indefinite growth which has not always progressed as fast as it was hoped. With their huge public buildings, their ambitious boulevards, and their broad streets to be filled by coming generations, the most prosperous have an unfinished look, temporary yet pretentious, which is not pleasing to travellers. As in America, the cities, instead of following in the track of agriculture, have preceded it ; but then more than one of these presumptuous cities has been, on the morrow of its foundation, forsaken in favor of a better situated rival, and left with its huge square and mute avenues which no crowd will ever enliven.

It is curious to measure even at this early hour the conquests of Russian colonization, to calculate how many parallels of latitude, or how many degrees of longitude, from north to south, from east to west, it has won from nature or from barbarism : there is all the vast region of the steppes and the Black Mould, the haunt of the horseman of old, Scyth, Tatar, or Cosack, there are the shores of the Black and Azof Seas, where in the beginning of modern times the Genoese still held fortified counting-houses, such as the French keep along the coast of Guinea. This is the greatest, possibly the only conquest of the West from the East, of Europe from Asia ; it were more correct to say that Europe, thanks to the Russians, has nearly doubled her area at the expense of Asia.

Have we not there a grand result ? And with what resources,

what elements has this immense and rapid colonization been achieved; is it going on still? With the Russian people, who, to effect this great work, have received from abroad none but inefficient, insignificant assistance. The two Americas, Australia, all the colonies of both hemispheres, receive every year a considerable contingent of emigrants and European capital. Russia has been compelled to colonize herself without anybody's aid, either in men or money. A colonization carried on without immigration, by a country itself deficient in population, by a nation itself only half civilized—such has been the task accomplished by Russia.

If Russia has colonized herself it is not that she did not ask Europe for emigrants. Many did come from two sides—first from Germany, then from the Greek-Orthodox provinces of Turkey and Austria. These two classes of colonists, who arrived in the middle of the eighteenth and the beginning of the nineteenth century, played an unequal part, but both had only a secondary local share in the immense work. The Germans are the most numerous. Russia in modern times has offered the first opening to Teutonic emigration, which has not worked as well there as in America. Called in by Catherine II. and other Russian sovereigns, settled on the choicest lands, sprinkled a little all over, from Peterhof at the gates of St. Petersburgh to beyond the Caucasus, but especially in New Russia and along the Lower Volga, these Germans have kept well together in separate groups, alien patches in the midst of the native population, not mixing with it nor exerting any influence over it.*

At the present day they number many hundred thousands, that preserve their religion, their language, their manners and customs, bearing the name of *colonists*, and forming under this designation a separate class which, until very lately, enjoyed particular privi-

---

* Besides these German colonists, there are the Germans of the Baltic provinces, about 160,000 of them, then the tradesmen and craftsmen of German or Austrian origin, dispersed over the various cities.

leges,—exemption from military service in the number.* Living as foreigners in the state whose subjects they are, these colonists are distinguished by many essentially Teutonic qualities, such as the spirit of order, of economy, of family solidarity. In the isolation of their small communes, they have made for themselves a small civilization of their own, a domestic civilization so to speak. They have formed agricultural colonies, very curious for the politician and the philosopher to observe. They have achieved a moderate competence without being able ever to rise any higher. Hence it is that their influence on the Russian people, which in material things is almost naught, is still less morally.† Whatever share Germany has had—and it is a large one—in the development of Russia, she has owed it much less to these rustic colonies, self-centred as they are, than to the German nobility of the Baltic provinces and the German scientists invited to settle in Petersburgh.

Rather different has been the part played by the Greco-Slav immigrants. If they have not yet quite become merged into the Russian people, they do not, like the Germans, form a separate body within the empire. The kinship of language where Slavs are concerned, the unity of faith which is a bond between all, or nearly all, have been powerful links between these immigrants and their adopted country. Among them are to be met all the Christian tribes of the East : Greeks, Rumanians, Serbs, Dalmatians, Bulgarians, Armenians, Ruthenians, former Turkish or Austrian subjects, attracted of old to Russia by political and religious sympathies. This emigration, co-temporary with their first national awakening, gradually ceased parallelly to the political emancipa-

* The suppression of this exemption in 1874, by the law introducing universal military service, has caused a number of these colonists to emigrate. Many, however, after unsuccessful attempts at settling in Brazil and elsewhere, went back to Russia.

† When we come to the study of Russian sects, we shall have, in dealing with the *Stundists*, to quote a recent exception to this rule. See vol. iii., book iii., ch. ix.

tion of the small oriental nations on their native soil. Most of these colonies, organized like the German ones, in villages and districts, have settled preferably in the south and in Crimea. The region around Odessa, before it bore the name of New Russia, received from its Serbian colonists that of New Siberia. Many of these Orientals took in Crimea and the adjacent coast-lands, the place vacated by Tatar or Nogaÿ emigrants, so that between the two empires—the Russian and the Turkish, a double current was established of emigration and immigration, the one drawing to itself the Christians, the other the Mussulmans. These small oriental colonies, some of them scarcely inferior to the German ones in the matter of agriculture, have given their first impulse to the navy and to commerce ; they furnished to them both merchants and sailors. The ports of the Black and the Azof Seas—Odessa, Khersòn, Mariòpol, Taganròg, are so many former Greek cities, and remain partly Greek still.

Neither Germans nor Orientals, however, no matter how great their services, can claim any large share in the millions of inhabitants and the millions of acres of cultivated soil which have been added in less than a century to the wealth of Southern and Eastern Russia. The great colonizer of the Russian land is the Russian people, the *mujik*.[5] How many difficulties, what inferiority in every branch are implied in this seemingly so simple fact, if closely looked into ! Instead of the most enterprising men from the most advanced European states, as in America or in Australia, the agent is a people that has long been kept back by nature and history, serfs but yesterday ; instead of all political and civil liberties, of the independence and almost royalty of the individual —an autocratic state, a meddlesome and nagging administration, the solidarity of the commune, which binds man to man and the laborer to the soil.[6]

<hr/>

[5] The *j* to be pronounced as in French : *je, joli ;* the *u* like *oo* in *moor*.

[6] This paragraph can scarcely be accepted unconditionally, at least as applied to the Russian people. It is doubtful whether too much culture,—

The Russians have had a twofold task set them, of apparently irreconcilable elements : to borrow civilization from Europe on one side, and on the other to carry civilization to desert lands. They have had a nation to educate, all but virgin lands to break. This task they had to accomplish under conditions the most repugnant to colonial growth, burdened with standing armies and a long term of military service, under a system of strict centralization and an omnipotent bureaucracy. It is owing to these inconsistencies much more than to the inferiority of soil and clime, if their development has been less rapid, and, above all, less productive than that of Northern America ; that is what has kept European emigration away from the steppes and will keep it away for ever. No matter that Russia owns on both sides the Ural admirable land, which but awaits the plough—colonists from the West will not look that way. Even her neighbors of the Scandinavian North prefer the American " Far West " and the wastes of Canada.[1]

developed liberties, ready-made institutions, the "royalty of the individual," —is a good thing in the beginnings of colonies. Colonies founded in this way are born old, like the Chinese philosopher Lao-tze, of whom the legend has it he was born eighty years old with a flowing white beard. And they do not aggrandize or strengthen the mother country. They are separate organisms from the first and very soon assert their independence,—if necessary, with armed hand. See the ancient Greek colonies and the American colonies. Or else such colonies, if even outwardly thriving, are consumed by a blight at the core, they bear a curse of moral depravity, of lack of vitality, of restlessness and inability to settle down to the wholesome, normal, work-a-day routine which builds up a solid nation as well as a healthy, prosperous individual. See the South American Republics of Latin race. For, planting in rows full-grown trees with ripe fruit on them will never make a forest or an orchard. While the kind of colonization of which Mr. Beaulieu speaks so slightingly is the only kind that gives to the state not an insecure dependence, but a vigorous offshoot, fed on the same sap, living the life, growing the growth of the whole. Secession is an impossibility : can a limb secede from its trunk?

[1] Be it so and may it remain so. Therein lies the country's future, and it does not matter if we do not live to see it. The American States cannot dispense with immigration ; but for immigration they would not exist, and their vital principle was, from the beginning, under a great show of gentle-

4

Russia, then, is a recently colonized country. This is a fact which should not for a moment be lost sight of. Many of her peculiarities, many of her faults, private and public, come from this simple fact. This partly explains a certain remnant of crudeness in so many cultured Russians ; for instance, the puzzling mixture of hyper-refined tastes and savage instincts, and a certain superficiality in all but the mere luxury of intellectual culture and civilization.[8] Such inconsistencies are more or less noticeable among the Americans and in all "new" countries, where civilization, being too young and hasty, still has about it something unbalanced.

Russia is a colony one or two centuries old, and at the same time an empire of a thousand years.[9] She has some affinities with America and some with Turkey. This opposition alone gives

ness and moderation, Conquest,—the most ruthless conquest that ever Europeans perpetrated : taking possession of a continent by exterminating the only landlord, the native race. The case is different where a homogeneous, compact race owns an area of land too extensive for its present use ; it naturally considers it a precious safeguard for future times ; for the race has vitality and it will increase and expand and cover its own land, never fear. The times are gone by for offering "inducements" to foreign immigration, and our experience with our German colony is not such as to make us call for more. And do not the American States begin to look apprehensively on the human tide that keeps rolling in across the Atlantic and already take active measures to stem it ? If Russia continues unattractive to emigrants, she will at least have no Chinese question to face—and solved such questions can never be, only cut, more or less cruelly.

[8] A word concerning which it were desirable to come to a generally accepted mutual understanding. As commonly understood just now, it appears to mean principally what house-speculators call "modern improvements," mechanical appliances of physical science (telephones, phonographs, electric lights) and—light opera, and to have nothing whatever to do with *culture* or the highest capacity for culture. The Khedive of Egypt, Ismaïl Pasha, returned home an enthusiastic convert to "European civilization," announcing his intention to introduce it in his dominions, and, on his arrival at Cairo, straightway established a *café-concert* with the "stars" and all belongings imported from France.

[9] Scarcely an *empire* or even a state. These names cannot be given to a loose agglomeration of principalities, held together merely by the bond of race and, as regards their respective rulers, the all but fictitious one of family "seniorship" and precedence. The *Empire* does not trace its existence beyond the close of the fifteenth century, when Ivan III. assumed

the key to her national character as well as to her political situation. It is a country at once new and old, an ancient, half
Asiatic monarchy, and a young European colony ; a double-faced
Janus, turned westward and eastward, one face old and decrepit,
the other youthful, nay almost boyish.¹⁰

This sort of duality is the principle which underlies the contrasts that strike us in Russian life everywhere—contrasts so
frequent as to have become the rule and to justify us in saying
that, in Russia, contradiction might be erected into a law. Everything has worked towards that result : the geographical situation
between Europe and Asia astride on the Ural ; the mixture of
ill-amalgamated races ; an historical past claimed by two worlds,
and made of violently opposed phases. This law of contrasts
rules everything. Hence the variety of judgments pronounced
on Russia, and generally so false only because showing up one
side alone. This law of contrasts turns up everywhere—in
society, owing to the deep chasm that divides the higher
from the lower classes ; in politics and the administration ;
because of slight leanings towards liberalism in the laws,
and the stationary inertness of habit ; it shows even in the
individual,—in his ideas, his feelings, his manner. Contrast
lies in both substance and form, in the man as in the nation ;
you discover it in time in all things ; it strikes you at the first
glance in the clothes, in the houses, in those wooden cities with
wide parallel streets, so similar to the new cities of America and
not unlike the stopping-places along the steamer route in the East.

This duality, which sways all the conditions of Russian life,
also directly influences Russia's material and political growth as

the double-headed eagle of Byzance, the extinct Empire of the East and the
title of " Cæsar,"—*Tsesar*, according to the pronunciation still in use in the
Russian schools, whence—*Tsar*.

¹⁰ *Old*, Russia never can be called on any account. Whatever of "old"
and even "decrepit" there may be about her, is what came to her from
Byzance, whose effete and doting age made her but an indifferent associate
and mentor to a hardy, doughty young nation in her teens.

well as her moral development. At once a military monarchy and a young colony, she has the weakness peculiar to both without the full strength of either. Belonging to a new world, having deserts to people, Russia, owing to her contact with Europe, is subject to the same burdens, military and financial, that the old crowded and civilized states have borne for ages. When, under President Lincoln, the United States were threatened with secession, what they had reason to dread most was not a curtailing of their territory, it was a radical change in their whole economical and political existence, which would have been caused by the creation of two rival powers on the same continent.

Geography has placed Russia in the very position into which the secession of the South or the West would have forced the United States. Isolated from Europe by an ocean, as America is, she would have had a far readier and safer development ; she need not then have divided her efforts between two contradictory tasks. The discomforts of such a material situation are singularly increased for Russia by moral disadvantages : she has before her the tasks of both Europe and America at once, and in her inhabitants she possesses tools inferior in quality to those of both. She is like an actor who was compelled to appear on the stage before he could learn his part, or to a man whose education had been neglected in his childhood and who is forced to complete it in the midst of the labor and strife of manhood."

The Russians are a people in the act of getting itself into shape, and that from the moral as well as the material stand-

---

[11] Russia is behindhand not from lack of gifts, but from the simple fact that she is *the youngest of the European family*—a fact of which not even our best friends seem willing to give us the benefit. She can answer most accusations bearing on such shortcomings in the words of Pitt when, to attacks from the ministerial bench on account of his youth, he serenely replied : " I plead guilty to the accusation, but it is a fault that will mend itself." And it is not only unjust but cruel to assert like that, as a matter of course, that the Russian people, as tools of civilization, are " of inferior quality." The way in which they are every day coming to the front in all branches of culture, science and art both, is more eloquent than any words in defence.

point. In no respect can they, without injustice, be compared with the nations of Western Europe. Towards the latter, Russia stands in the position of an army just forming and still scattered, who should have to face an army with full numbers and concentrated corps. She may be weak to-day before nations who, in a hundred years from now, will be unable to cope with her. In this respect, the Bulgarian war has not erased the impressions left by the Crimean war. To this day, Russia's power is not in proportion to her bulk, nor to her population. The Russians know this; but they also know that time will raise their power to the level of the size of their territory.*

* See *France, Russia, and Europe.* Calmann Lévy, 1888.

BOOK II.

RACES AND NATIONALITY.

CHAPTER I.

Are the Russian People a European People?—Is there in Russia a Homogeneous Nationality?—Interest Attaching to these Questions—The Ethnographical Museum at Moscow—Causes of the Multiplicity of Races on this Uniform Land—Reasons why their Fusion is not yet Completed—How it is that Ethnographical Maps can Furnish only Insufficient Data.

WERE Russia a lately discovered virgin land, devoid of population, or roamed over only by a few nomadic tribes, she would soon offer to the world the same spectacle as the United States or Australia. She would rank with those countries where civilization, having left behind her the old institutions which protected her infancy, opens out for herself, on a new soil, a wider and more independent career. Left entirely to European civilization, Russia would quickly have rivalled America, for—according to a remark made by Adam Smith as early as the eighteenth century—nothing, once the foundations are solidly laid, can equal the rapidly increasing prosperity of a colony which, in a free land, is at liberty to construct an entirely new building. What makes Russia's inferiority is her elderly population, with its antiquated customs and old traditions; it is this indigenous population which, by shutting out immigration from the West, robs her of the advantages of the usual marvellous growth of colonies.[1]

[1] Once for all, we must protest against this off-hand acceptance of "Russia's inferiority" as a thing understood, not even needing proof or

54

Crudely contrasting with Western Europe, the Russian land was unfit to be the cradle of European culture, but is perfectly fit to receive it. Can the same be said of the different peoples that occupy those vast plains? Physical conditions cannot alone determine a country's fate; in fact they can do nothing without man, without the race that dwells there. Nature has marked Russia for the seat of a great empire; but has history placed there a people capable of making a great nation? We must ask the same question about the people as about the country. Does it belong to Europe or Asia? Has it a kinship with us, giving it an inborn aptitude for our civilization? or is it an alien in the European family, in blood as well as education, and condemned from its birth to remain an Asiatic people under the clothes borrowed from Europe?

This question which the Russians, as well as their antagonists, have turned in and out and from all sides with equal passion, amounts to nothing more nor less than the question whether or no the Russian people are capable of civilization at all. In our times, ethnography and the study of races has been made in certain countries to play a most untoward and equivocal part, even to being deferred to in the highest instance for judgment in questions of nationality, which, in any case, ethnography never could settle by itself. These exaggerations, prompted by self-interest, must not induce us to lose out of sight the real bearing of such studies. In order to know a people, a young people too,

---

discussion. Once for all let it be understood at last,—what is so plain as to "put out one's eyes," in the graphic French phrase, *cela crève les yeux,*— that Russia is inferior in the way that the youngest of a family, who is not yet out of college, is to his elderly brothers who have had the time and opportunity to make their mark in the world. And it is notorious how often the youngest is the most gifted; then, adding to his own attainments his elders' experience, the future is his when he survives them, as, in the course of nature, he must. There is nowadays but one opinion on the superior intellectual endowments of the individual Russians; how then can their country be inferior? As to the blessings of immigration, see preceding chapter, note 7.

which has had no chance as yet to manifest its own genius,[2] a knowledge of the elements of which it is composed, of the races from which it has issued, is imperative. To propound such a problem with regard to Russia amounts to asking whether Peter the Great could succeed in grafting Western civilization on the Moscovite wilding or whether, for lack of European sap, it cannot "take" on the alien trunk.[3]

Side by side with this question of the filiation and intrinsic value of the Russian people, another arises, quite as important to the philosopher as to the politician : that of the degree of cohesion possible to so vast an empire. The physical unity of the land is not sufficient to ensure political unity, there goes to that also the material and moral union of the populations, a certain kinship of blood or brain, without which national unity is impossible. Is there in Russia, as in France or Italy, a compact nationality, strongly cemented by history,—or is it, like Turkey till very lately and Austria to this day, a patchwork of heterogeneous peoples, each with traditions and interests of its own ?

[2] Here the fact of its being "a *young* people," laboring under the difficulties peculiar to youth alone, is admitted unconditionally. Is there not a slight inconsistency in speaking almost in the same breath (see the first paragraph) of Russia's "elderly population" as a drawback and a source of "inferiority" too ? This unconscious fluctuation occurs repeatedly in the present volume.

[3] Why should the Western type of civilization—"our civilization"—be the only type to be aimed at ? and indeed—see a few lines higher—the only possible one at all, so that, as the question is plainly put, if the Russian people turn out incapable or unwilling to be exactly like the French, the Germans, the English, they are to be set down "incapable of civilization" generally? Why—to keep up a simile which always fits—Why should the growing young giant's proudest ambition be to wear out his elders' old clothes or buy, at a high price, ready-made ones of precisely the same cut and material, though they are a manifest misfit and so much too tight that at each movement of his vigorous limbs they will crack at all the seams? Let him profit by their taste and experience so far as to take from their apparel whatever suits his figure and conditions of life and carefully modify the cut better to adapt it to both and secure freedom of movements, moreover leaving ample margin for growth and final development.

The Russian soil is made for unity. Nowhere do we find so vast an area so thoroughly homogeneous ; at the same time, nowhere do we find so many different races. The contrast which appears everywhere in Russia is most striking in this respect. The most uniform of geographical areas is occupied by the most motley human families. Races, peoples, tribes, are all tangled together *ad infinitum*, and their diversities are brought out and made conspicuous by the diversity of their modes of life, their languages, their religions. Among them are found all the Christian confessions : Greek Orthodox, Armenians, Catholics, Protestants, sundry sects unknown to the West ; all the beliefs of Asia face to face with those of Europe ; Jews—Talmudists, and Karaites ; Mahometans—Sunnites and Shiites ; Buddhists, Shamanites, and heathens of all descriptions. The bare enumeration of the various races encountered in European Russia is something frightful—no less than twenty ; and if no group, no smallest tribe is to be overlooked, this figure would have to be doubled, nay, trebled.

We possess several ethnographical maps of Russia. One of these, by Mr. Rittich, is both recent and excellent. But the Russians have done more : in the Dashkoff Museum, founded in Moscow on occasion of the Slavic Congress in 1867, they have attempted to give a presentation at once scientific and picturesque, something like an animated map, of the various peoples of the Empire. By means of mannikins of life-size and of waxen figures moulded after the exactest casts from nature, the peoples and tribes of Russia have been assembled there, in all the variety of their several types and garbs. On the north side of the vast hall, which is laid out after the fashion of a map, next to the Tungùz, the Yakùt, the Buriàt of Siberia, we see, in his garments of reindeer hide, the Samoyèd, who recalls the Esquimau, and the Lapp, who puts one in mind of the Mongol. Lower down, to the west, come the Finn peasant of Finland, and the Ehst of the Baltic provinces, both of them betraying, by their flattened faces, a distant kinship with the Lapp and the Samoyèd. On the eastern side we behold representatives of other groups of the Finnic race scattered over the basin of the Volga, and showing features less and less European, less and less noble : Permians, Votiàks, Tcheremìss, Mordvìns and Tchuvàsh, in the midst of whom a young Tatar woman from Kazàn, disrobed of her veil, is noticeable for her Oriental beauty. Facing this group, on the western side, are the Lett, Samogitian, and Lithuanian peasants, and at last the Bielorùss,—*i. e.*, the denizen of Western or White Russia, square-faced, in striking contrast to a Jewish tradesman and a Jewish mechanic, with their long faces and sharp, thin noses.

In the middle of the hall, on a wide platform, is enthroned the master of the empire, the "Velikorùss" (Great-Russian), in all the variety of his different crafts and provincial costumes ; the men in high top-boots, or low, slipper-like *lapti*, plaited of tree-bast, in the red shirt or long-skirted *kaftàn;* the women in rich *sarafàns*, with their diadem-shaped *kokòshniks*. Below the "Velikorùss" comes the "Maloròss" (Little-Russian), with more refined features, garments of more elegant cut and material ; the men wear high sheepskin caps, the girls flowers interlaced with ribbons. Behind the Little-Russians appear the Poles, then, from west to east, all the numerous tribes of the south of the empire : a Moldavian couple from Bessarabia, a *murzà* or Tatar prince from the Crimea, with his neighbor, a *Tsigàn* (gypsy) beggar, a *Karaïte* bride, a daughter of one of those Jews, enemies of the others, who pretend to be descended from the ten tribes transported by Nebuchadnezzar,—lastly two German colonists from New Russia or the Lower Volga, as different from the Russians to this day, in type and garb, as on the day of their immigration.

In the southwestern portion of the hall we are met by the Mussulman and Buddhist tribes of the oriental steppes, with their Asiatic features and resplendent costumes : the Kirghiz with his tall, pointed cap, Kalmỳks from the governments of Stavròpol and Astrakhan, with narrow-slit eyes, yellow-skinned, wearing the *beshmet* of silk or velvet in the tenderest colors. Next to these a Bashkir woman from Orenburg or Ufa, in her red cloth robe—*khalàt*—and head-dress fringed with coins. In the extreme south we greet the tribes of the Caucasus, the handsomest in the world as to features, the most elegant as to dress. Here an Armenian merchant in plain black *kaftàn;* further a Tcherkess (Circassian) in crimson morocco shoes, his *kaftàn* bristling with cartridge pockets on the breast, and the camel's-hair *bashlik* slung round his neck ; next, a Gruzin (Georgian) with *lapti* woven of leather straps, the *arkhalouk*,[4] and the *tchokka* or surcoat with the long embroidered sleeves, open in front ; a Mingrelian woman in a gown of light-blue silk and the long veil of transparent muslin, and a Kurd woman from the banks of the Araxus, in her silken tunic and wide crimson satin trousers, a ring passed through her nose ; the Armenian woman in a green robe—*khalàt*,—wrapt up in one of those immense veils which the women of the Caucasus enshroud themselves in to walk abroad ; the Gruzinka (Georgian woman) in a black satin petticoat with lavender bodice, and a band of brocade round her head, dances as she brandishes a tambourine. At the farthest end of the great hall, in a dark niche, a group of half-naked Ghebers from Bakù, the last survivors of the sect, worship the sacred fire.

The impression produced by this museum, where one single state exhibits so many human types, a plain ethnographical map would not produce in the same degree. The colors hardly have shadings enough to spare one to each tribe ; by their motley coloring, as by the puzzling intricacy of their lines they recall the geological maps of countries of the most complicated formations. It seems, at the first glance, as though in this country, where land and inanimate nature show such unity, all is confusion in the races of men.

[4] A sort of close-fitting doublet, with short but rather ample, gathered skirts. A becoming and comfortable garment, often worn, of soft quilted silk, by gentlemen as home costume.

The configuration of the Russian soil accounts for this quantity and diversity of races, apparently so little in harmony with it. Having no well-defined boundary line either to the east or west, Russia has always stood wide open to all invasions ; she was the highway of all the migrations from Asia into Europe. Nowhere have the strata of human alluvions been more numerous, nowhere more mixed, more broken and disjointed, than on this smooth, flat bed where each wave, as it was pressed upon and pushed on from the rear by the following one, met no obstacle ahead, save in the wave that had preceded it. Even as recently as in historical times, it were hard to enumerate the people that have settled on Russian land and established there more or less lasting empires —Scyth, Sarmatian, Goth, Avar, Bulgar, Ongre or Hungarian, Khazàr, Petchenèg, Lithuanian, Mongol, Tatar,—to say nothing of the migrations of the Celts and Teutons of old, and others, whose very name has perished, but who, obscure as they were, *may* have left in the population a trace, undiscoverable at this day.

If the configuration of the country left Russia open to invasion, the structure of the soil made it impossible to the invaders to settle down on it in organized nations, independent of one another. The multiplicity of races and tribes is not the consequence of a slow working of physical causes, but an historical heirloom. Setting aside the icy fields of the north, where none but hunting tribes can exist,—also the sandy and salt steppes of the southeast, impracticable to any but pastoral nomads, this complexity of races and tribes, far from being a result of their adaptation to the soil, far from being in harmony with their physical surroundings, is in direct opposition to it. The natural tendency of the land was not to diversify and break up races, but to bring them together to unity. To all these different peoples the country refused the comfort of boundaries within which they might have intrenched themselves, formed groups, led an isolated existence.

In the immense quadrilateral comprised between the Glacial Ocean and the Black Sea, the Baltic and the Ural, there is not a mountain, not one of the things that divide, that apportion. On this even surface the various races have been left to scatter apparently at random, not unlike the waters, which find no ridge or shed to separate from, no banks to contain them. Even when diversity of customs, religion, language, precluded their mixing, they were compelled to live side by side, to cross, to interpenetrate one another in every possible way, just as rivers empty themselves into one and the same bed and, at their confluent, roll their waters in the same current without ever confounding them. Thus it is, that, being scattered yet contiguous, frequently wedged into one another, the peoples and tribes of Russia have not been able to attain full national individuality. Exhausted in the act of spreading over too great expanses, or thinned down to the merest fragments, broken up into bits, one might say, all these races have easily allowed themselves to be gathered under one rule, and once so gathered, were more rapidly unified and merged into one another. From this fusion, begun centuries ago, under the sway of Christianity and Moscovite sovereignty, sprang the Russian people, this mass of sixty-five to seventy millions of men, which, compared to the other populations, assumes the appearance of a sea eating away its own shores, a sea strewed with islets that crumble away in its midst.

This people that calls itself Russian,—what is its filiation? Occupying, as it does, the centre of the empire, environed by the various races which it has pushed towards the extremities, it still contains numerous Finn and Tatar patches, persistent witnesses to the extent of the area once upon a time covered by similar tribes. In their ethnographic maps, the Russians represent the various populations in conformity to their local distribution at the present day. An external sign—language—is taken for a standard, and all are accounted Russian or Slav who speak the Russian tongue. No classifying method can be simpler; only it should not be forgotten that such a classification proves nothing as to the origin of a people, and that, in the matter of race, language is of all signs the most deceptive.   In order to adopt the Russian speech, Finn or Tatar tribes, in the act of "russification," do not infuse into their veins Slavic blood, any more than the Celts or the Gauls or the Iberians of Spain borrowed Latin blood along with Latin speech.   From the point of view of ethnographic gene-alogy, these maps, based exclusively on language, bring data, not results.   For a research of this sort, it is necessary to collect far more complex elements ; before we turn to philology, we should consult anthropology, *i. e.,* the physical constitution, the features, nay, the structure of the skeleton of each given type of the inhabi-tants, all that they have inherited directly from their remotest ancestors ; and, unfortunately, types are not to be numbered and classified with the same precision as languages and religions.

However, what matters most in an attempt to determine the place belonging to the Russians amidst the human family, is not so much the actual distribution of the various races, as the com-position of the Russian nationality, which tends to swallow up all the others.   What part in the formation of this people had the various elements of which, in and around it, we still behold the scattered traces?   And—to propound the main question, as it is so often propounded by Russia's foes—is the Russian people at bottom European or Asiatic?   Is it Slav, brother and neighbor of the Latin and the Teuton, and, by force of the same blood, called to analogous civilization? or—is it Turanian (Tatar or Mongol), fated by its constitution never to take more than the forms of a culture alien to its race?   If this problem has received the most contradictory solutions, the reason lies in the fact that it has been debated by passion, by grudge, by national pride, more than by study and observation.

BOOK II.   CHAPTER II.

The Three Chief Ethnic Elements of Russia—The Finns—Are they an
Element that Has no Parallel in Western Europe?—Diversity and
Isolation of such Finn Groups as Still Survive—Their Part in the
Formation of the Russian People—The Russian Type and the Finn
Stamp—Is this Relationship a Cause of Inferiority for Russia?—
Capacity of the Finns for Civilization.

OUT of the apparent chaos of Russian ethnology three main
elements—Finn, Tatar, Slav—clearly emerge, the last having
by this time in a great measure absorbed the other two. Setting
aside the three or four millions of Jews in the West, the eight or
nine hundred thousand Rumanians in Bessarabia, and one million
at least of Germans, scattered from north to south,—setting aside
also the Kalmy̆ks of the steppe of the Lower Volga ; the Tchet-
chens, the Lezghians, the Armenians, and the entire Babel of
the Caucasus,—all the peoples or tribes that have invaded Russia
in the past, all those that inhabit her to-day, can be traced to one
of these three races. As far back as we may pursue history,
representatives of each of these three groups are found, under one
name or another, on Russian soil, and their fusion is not even yet
so complete as to conceal from sight the distinctive traits of each,
or the area on which they respectively held their sway.

The Finn or Tchud race * seems to have in olden times occupied the greater part of the territory we nowadays call Russia.

* *Tchud*, following the Slav etymology, would mean "monsters, wonders," or "strangers." The name may possibly contain an allusion to the
"wonders" done by sorcerers, who enjoyed great renown everywhere
among the Finns.

It is manifestly not of Aryan or Indo-European stock, from which,
jointly with the Celts and the Latins, the Germans and the Slavs,
most peoples of Europe have sprung.   Ethnological classifications
generally place the Finns in a more or less extensive group,
labelled "Turanian, Allophyl, Mongolian, Mongoloïd,"—all more
or less correct designations of a frame with wavering outline,
which at times recalls a sort of "what-not" into which philologists and anthropologists cast any people of Europe or Asia they
did not succeed in classing with either the Aryans or the Semites.
Within the too extensive group which, from the Pacific to Hungary, comprises so many human families, the Finns mostly are
connected with a branch known under the name of Uralo-Altaïc,
because the space between the mountain chains of the Ural and
the Altaï seems to have been the starting-point of the peoples
belonging to this family.   The Mongols proper, together with
the Tatars, are usually placed side by side in this Uralo-Altaïc
group, which, on the contrary, rejects the Chinese and the nations
of Eastern Asia.   This classification appears best to fit the facts ;
only it is to be noted that, regarding the two sciences on which
are based all ethnographic studies,—philology and anthropology,
this group is far from offering the same homogeneousness as
the Aryan and Semitic groups.   The relationship between its
different branches is far less obvious, less intimate, than that
between Latin and German, and appears far more remote than
that between the Brahman or the Gheber of India, and the Celt
of Scotland or Bretagne ; at bottom it is hardly closer than between the Indo-European and the Semite.

From the philological point of view, the Uralo-Altaïc or Turanian race is distinguished by agglutinative languages, *i. e.*, such
as form their declensions and conjugations by mere juxtaposi-
tion instead of combining and merging into one another the root
and the desinences until they are unrecognizable, as in our
flexional languages.   These agglutinative languages which, Max
Müller tells us, characterize nomadic peoples, always compelled

by their roaming life to guard against any alteration of the words, do not show such intimate mutual relations as do the Aryan or Semitic idioms, a fact the more remarkable, that, owing to the absence of flexion, they would seem to be less susceptible of corruptions and variations. Their relationship, instead of showing at once in the unity of roots and in the concordance of grammatical forms, is limited to similarities in structure and syntactical proceedings, so that the filiation between them is more doubtful, more difficult to trace.

From the anthropological point of view, the unity of this vast group is possibly still less firmly established, the affinity still looser. The external, superficial characteristics by which other races are easily known—the color of the skin, the eyes, the hair, are unreliable guides on this ground, and separate many Finn tribes. The anatomical characteristics are the only ones that can apply to all the branches of the Uralo-Altaïc trunk ; and even those, essential ones too, vary greatly in some Finn tribes. The most important ones are supplied by the shape of the head, and of these the most general and persistent one is the flattening of the face and the high cheek-bones. And yet, within the Finn family alone, these Mongolian survivals are found in very different degrees—striking and well-defined in some tribes,—the Lapps, for instance,—very much weakened and modified in others, especially the Finns of Finland.

It is to be noted that these craniological characteristics as well as others, even less favorable, as a certain prognatism or prominence of the jaws, have been encountered in many of the old populations of Europe, whose traces have lately been discovered by prehistoric archæology. Most human tribes of the unpolished stone age and especially of the quaternary epoch, the remnants of which have been unearthed in the caves of Western Europe, appear to have belonged to these Mongolian races among which the Finns are classed, or to neighboring races. These primitive tribes appear to have occupied all of the north and centre of

5

Europe, previous to the coming of the first Aryan immigrants. It is not in subterranean caves alone, amidst the remains of the mammals belonging to the geological period immediately preceding our own, that these extinct races have left vestiges of their passage; they can be traced even in the features of those European populations who have taken their place. Covered over by later invasions, and buried under successive strata of Aryan alluvions, these old inhabitants of Europe are no longer visible to the vulgar; the anthropologist alone at times fancies he can detect survivals of those primeval Europeans on contemporary faces, in the midst of the most civilized countries.*

Instead of being exclusively Asiatic, the Turanian element and some other, analogous ones, may possibly have played in Western Europe a part at once ethnological and historical; they may have furnished the bottom layer, the *substratum*, vanished long ago, of the peoples of Central Europe. A few scientists have gone so far as to consider the Finns of the northwest of Russia as a survival of those quaternary tribes who, driven from the centre of Europe by Indo-European invaders, would naturally have sought shelter on the shore of the Baltic, in the lowlands but recently emerged out of its waters. It is more probable that the Russian Finns, instead of having sprung directly from those prehistoric peoples, to whom they appear, on the whole, to be vastly superior, are but very remotely related to them, and have themselves descended from the Ural at a comparatively late period. Whatever the date of their migration, they may be considered as established in Europe at least as far back as the oldest Aryan populations. Settled in Europe at a time as remote as any one of our European families, with as much claim as any to the name of "autochthons" or "aborigines," the Finns, later on, took a considerable part in

---

* On this subject we can refer the reader to *La Race Prussienne*, by M. de Quatrefages, although this scientist appears to have greatly exaggerated the inferiority of the Finn race, and to have, in dealing with Prussia, magnified beyond measure the part belonging to the Finn element, at the expense of the Slav and Teutonic elements.

the invasions that brought on the end of the Roman Empire. The most terrible of the Barbarians, the Huns, appear to have been of Finn extraction, as likewise the Avars, the Bulgars, and the Hungars—the latter being the only contemporary nation sprung directly from this stock.

How much should be credited to the Finn family in the formation of the Russian people, and what physical and moral aptitudes has it bequeathed to them? Slowly repulsed or swallowed up by rival races, the Finns, in their submersion, have left here and there, scattered over Russia, islets which bear witness to their former widespread presence, such as mounds of ancient make in a plain whence the waters have washed away the primeval soil, and covered everything with their alluvions. The Finn groups dispersed in the empire differ singularly in degree of culture, in religion as well as in languages and dialects. They number but a few millions of souls, yet, as regards all the elements of civilization, they exhibit more diversity than the great Latin or Teutonic families. Their relationship has been established by anthropologists and philologists ; it has long escaped the ken of those interested in the question, who never achieved a common national consciousness and have remained towards one another in a moral isolation as complete as their geographical isolation.

The Finn race, outside of Hungary, is almost entirely comprised within European Russia, where it numbers five or six millions, divided into a dozen different tribes, classed into three or four families.* There is first, in the north, the Ugrian family, the only one that still has representatives in Asia. It comprises only two small tribes, of a few thousand souls each, leading very nearly the same life as the Samoyèds, like them Christians in name and Shamanites in fact ; the Ostiàks, in Western Siberia ;

* All these tribes have, since the Finn scholar Castren, been the subject of numerous studies : ethnological, statistical, philological, even juridical, on the part of both Russian and Finn students,—Ahlquist, Maïnof, Rittich, Kuznetsòf, Làptef, Florinsky, Popòf, Maxìmof, Yefimènko, etc., to whose number should be added Ujfalvy, adopted by France for her own.

the Voguls in the northern part of the Ural.   But to this family, which includes the most miserable Finn tribes, is allied the only Finn people that ever played a part in Europe and attained a high degree of civilization—the Magyars of Hungary.   In the northeast comes the Biarmian branch, numbering from three to four hundred thousand souls, decreasing with every year, however, as they are rapidly getting russified, and unevenly distributed among the tribes of the Permians in the basin of the Kàma, that of the Votiaks on the Viatka, of the Zyrians on the Dvina and Petchóra, all three orthodox, the two former addicted to agriculture, the third to hunting and trade.   Lower down comes the family of the Volga, with the Finns of the south, more or less crossed with Tatar elements.   To this group belong the three most important Finn tribes of Russia proper : the Tcheremìss who, about two hundred and fifty thousand in number, dwell along the left bank of the Volga, around the government of Kazàn ; the Mordvìns, who, subdivided into several branches, number near on a million souls, in the very heart of Russia, between the Volga and the Okà, in the governments of Nijni-Nòvgorod, Penza, Simbirsk, Tambòf, Saràtof ; the Tchuvash, rather numerous, scattered along the banks of the Volga, the ancient territory of the Tatars of Kazàn, whose language they have adopted.*   Lastly, in the northwest, we have the Finn family proper, whose principal representatives are the Finns of Finland, subdivided into two or three tribes—the Suomi, as they call themselves, about the only ones that have a national feeling, the love of their mother-land, a history, a literature ; also the only ones who are tolerably sure to escape the slow absorption that is making an end of all their kindred races.   They make up five sixths of the population in the Grand Duchy of Finland, but a population almost entirely rural, as the Swedish element, much mixed with German and Russian,

---

* All these Finn tribes have long been mistaken by foreigners for Tatars.   The travellers of olden times thus helped to strengthen the fiction about the Russians being of Tatar origin.

is invariably predominant in the towns. Over and above the 1,800,000 odd they number in Finland, the Suomi come in for about 250,000 more in the population of the adjacent Russian governments.

St. Petersburgh, sooth to say, is built in the midst of a Finn land; the immediate surroundings only are russified, and quite recently too. Scarcely half a century ago, Russian was not understood in the villages at the very gates of the capital, even nowadays the latter is surrounded with fragments of Finn tribes. In the northwest, the Suomi of Finland stretch down nearly to its suburbs; in the west, where the great lakes are, the Karels and the Veses, who appear to have for a long time occupied a vast territory; in the southwest, nine hundred thousand Ehsts (Esthonians), who, having been, through four or five hundred years, subject to the rule of German lords, have resisted germanization in Esthonia and Northern Livonia.* To the same Finn branch belong the Livs, a tribe very nearly extinct, which has bequeathed its name to Livonia, and which, being pressed upon by both Letts and Germans, holds only a narrow strip of land along the sea, at the northern point of Curland. To the same branch belongs lastly the Lapp tribe—the very ugliest, morally the least developed, of all its kindred, the only one, perhaps, that has preserved the original, primeval features and mode of life of the parent stock. It appears that the Lapps at one time owned the whole of Finland, before they were cornered by the Suomi into the hyperborean regions to which they are to this day confined. On the other side of the White Sea, a small tribe which also once covered a far more extensive area, the Samoyèds, get shoved about a good deal, being numbered now among the Finns, now among the Mongols. At another extremity of the vast area covered by the

*According to Mr. Rittich, the Germans in the population of the three Baltic provinces (Esthonia, Livonia, and Curland) would count only for something less than $\frac{7}{100}$, the Finns for $\frac{89}{100}$, the Letto-Lithuanians for $\frac{47}{100}$, the balance consisting of Russians, Poles, Swedes, and Jews.

Tchuds, another tribe, much more considerable by its numbers, is also placed on the confine of two ethnic groups : the Bashkirs, one million strong, dwell on the slopes of the Ural ; they have been pronounced alternately to be Finns and Tatars ; in reality they are Mussulmans and speak a Tatar language.

Thus minutely is this race subdivided,—a race whose members profess every religion, from Shamanism to Islam, from the Greek Orthodox faith to Lutheranism ;—who are nomads, like the Lapp and Ostiàk ; pastoral, like the Bashkir ; farmers, like the Ehst or Finn ;—a race that has assumed the worship and at times the language of one and the other, everywhere ruled by people of different extraction, russified after having been partly tatarized,[1] so that every influence has contributed to break it up

[1] Why not mention the germanization, systematic and aggressive, to which the Ehsts and Letts are subjected in the Baltic provinces, where they make out fully three quarters of the population? Russification is nowhere intentional, much less compulsory, beyond demanding a reasonable comprehension of the language of the empire, and the passing of a very easy-grade examination from persons filling or desiring to fill official positions. The rest accomplishes itself naturally, by inevitable influences, community of interests, of social and political conditions, intercourse, and, in a *very* moderate proportion, mixing of blood. The German aristocracy and *bourgeoisie*, notwithstanding their extremely small numbers ($\frac{7}{100}$; see author's note on p. 69), have undertaken to germanize the provinces, and not only did they admit no language but German in private schools, refusing to send their children to the "gymnasiums" (public schools), colleges, special schools, etc., provided by the government, or to speak to the "natives" their own language, or even learn to understand it ; not only was the same proceeding applied to the Lutheran churches, attendance in which was made virtually compulsory by the wealthy and powerful noble German landlords ; but when the government, for reasons of statesmanship too obvious to need defence, decreed that business in the public government offices and courts of justice, police, etc., should be transacted in Russian and that the Russian language should be taught in schools, not to the exclusion of, but side by side with, German, also that the railway conductors and other public servants should, not necessarily be Russians, but understand and speak Russian, the discontent of the $\frac{7}{100}$ Germans was not only loudly voiced but vented in open, active opposition, while the foreign press was played off to such good purpose that philanthropic Europe soon raised the usual hue and cry of "tyranny," "oppression," "barbarism," with which she greeted the simplest measures of national unity and safety in Russian Poland, though she had never seen anything amiss in Prussia's well-known

into insignificant fragments. Although equal in numbers to their Hungarian brethren, the Finns of the Russian Empire are far from laying claim to an equal political weight.

If we but consider the distribution of the Finn tribes from the Ural and the great elbow formed by the Volga to the Neva, we shall find that the principality of Moscow and the surrounding appanages were comprised within the former territory of the Tchuds. Their diffusion will appear greater still if we note the geographical names; for, in many a region now thoroughly Russian, the names of places, villages, rivers, have remained Finnic. Moscow, as Petersburgh after and Nòvgorod before her, was built on land that was Tchud to the core. The same can be said of Sùzdal, Vladìmir, Tver, Riazán—of all the capitals where resided the *kniazes* (princes) of the Great-Russians. In the face of such facts, is it not allowable, in all the centre and north, to look on the old Finn blood as one of the elements that enter into the constitution of the young Russian nation?[2]

It is not only on history and ethnographic maps that this induction is based; it is also justified by the features of the people. But for this indelible stamp, it might remain an open question whether the colonists who brought the Slavic language into Russia, mingled with the natives, or, like the Anglo-Saxons in America, simply pushed them aside to take their place. An attentive investigation shows that both phenomena took place and that, too, simultaneously. The actual distribution of their tribes leads to the conclusion that the Finns really were pressed upon on two sides by the Slavs—pushed in the west towards the Baltic, in the east towards the Ural and the middle course of the Volga. Anthropology nevertheless proves that there has been a mingling

iron methods of "germanizing" her own "Polish provinces," as also, later on, Alsace-Lorraine.

[2] This is not the case quite to the extent supposed by Mr. Beaulieu, owing to the extreme scarcity of marriages, or even love passages, between members of different races among the lower classes, the only ones that, making the bulk of the population, count in such matters. This note should be borne in mind through the following pages.

of races, of which many a Russian face still bears the imprint. The way in which the Slavic element at the present day absorbs the Finn groups under our very eyes helps us understand the past. The russification of the contemporary Finns, their geographical distribution, the imprint left by them on the Russian features,—these are the three proofs in favor of this secular crossing ; the two former appeal to the mind, the latter is patent to the eye.

The Finn tribes of Russia differ considerably among themselves in physical characteristics as well as in their respective degrees of culture. A few, such as the Lapps and the Tchuvash, show a strongly marked Mongolian type. Others—the more important ones, such as the Suomi of Finland and the Ehsts, owing to the influence of their surroundings or of alliances the trace of which is lost, show nobler features, more nearly akin to the Caucasian type than to the Mongolian. Still, all these groups retain certain characteristics which have not entirely disappeared even among the Magyars, the people which, having mingled most with Europe, has undergone the greatest modification. The structure of the skeleton is less robust than that of the Aryans and Semites, the legs are shorter and leaner. The head is mostly round, short, little developed in the back, in a word—brachycephalous, like the heads of one of the chief geological races of Europe, now extinct. The face is generally flat, with high cheek-bones ; the eyes are small ; the nose wide ; the mouth large, thick-lipped. These peculiarities are frequently encountered among Russians of all classes, but most among the peasants and especially among women, who everywhere retain more tenaciously the ethnical stamp.

When confronted by such marks of kindred between this semi-prehistoric race and the most mighty in numbers of European nations, the observer inquires what genius, capacities, aptitude for civilization, we can credit the Finns with. Is it true that kinship with them must be to the Russians an irremediable cause of inferiority ? That may be doubted. Hampered by their isolation and their disruption into infinitesimal fractions, also by the thankless quality of the lands to which they are confined, the Finns never had a chance of achieving original development. As though in compensation for this disadvantage, they have everywhere shown a singular facility to assimilate with the more advanced races whenever they have come in contact with them. It is with them as with the country which contains most of their remains, as with the Russian soil : they readily yield to a civilization which could not have originated with them ; if they do not, by blood, belong to Europe, they are quite willing to be annexed by her. The greater part have long been Christians, at least in name, and it is Christianity which, more than anything else, has prepared their fusion with the Slavs, their incorporation into European civilization. From Hungary to the Baltic and to the Volga, the Finns have embraced with equal facility the three principal historical forms of Christianity ; the latest, Protestantism, thrives better in their tribes in Finland and Esthonia than among the Celtic, Iberian, and Latin peoples.

If we would look to language for the clearest test of a race's intelligence, we must admit that certain Finns—the Suomi of Finland and the Magyars of Hungary—have carried their agglutinative languages to such perfection as enables them, for power, richness, and harmony, to bear comparison with the most complete of our flexional languages. They have an innate taste for music and poetry, a taste the embryonic beginnings of which are perceptible among the most barbarous of their nomadic tribes, and which has endowed Finland with a treasury of popular literature, an entire cycle of indigenous poetry,—an epos which the most advanced nations of the West would feel honored to own.* To

---

* The *Kalevala*, a collection of popular rhapsodies, connected and put into shape by the Finn scholar Lönnrot, and translated into French by Mr. Léouzon Leduc, with the assistance of Lönnrot himself (editions of 1845, 1867, 1879).[3]

[3] While mentioning the French translator of the *Kalevala*, the name of Anton Schiefner should not be ignored, a prominent member of the Russian Imperial Academy of Sciences at St. Petersburg, a scholar of colossal Turanian erudition, who edited most of Castren's works and left a most scholarly German translation of the Finns' national epic.

these qualities of heart and mind they add others that do credit to their intellect and character.   If so be that the Finns are akin to the Mongols and other peoples of the extreme East, they can lay claim to the virtues of those Asiatic races, which, wherever they are engaged in strife with ours, stand the competition so well ; they have the same fortitude, patience, perseverance.   That may be the reason why, in all countries where their influence can be traced, they seem to have left behind them a leaven compounded of singular power of resistance and singular vitality.

These qualities have most brilliantly manifested themselves in the Magyars, who, in spite of their scant numbers, have held their own against Germans, Slavs, and Turks ; the same qualities are thought to belong to the Bulgars, the most industrious, the most patient, among the Christian peoples of ancient Turkey. And if (as M. de Quatrefages asserts and Virchow denies)—if the Finn element has really played an important part in Old Prussia, Modern Prussia possibly is indebted to them for some of the vigor and tenacity of purpose which have made her fortune.*   In Russia itself the Finns, far from being inferior to the Russians, at times show a real superiority over them.   If nothing can be meaner than a Tchuvash hut on the Volga, with its roof of bark and its single window, the wooden houses of the peasants in Finland are more roomy, more commodious, than the *izbas* of many Russian *mujiks*.⁴   Settled on a more thankless land, on a granitic soil which seldom insures their daily food, they work harder and are more saving.   They have earned a reputation for honesty and uprightness.   Only, it is rather difficult to make out whether this

* As regards the Bulgars, there is hardly room for doubt, although a Russian scholar, carried away by a retrospective Slavophil patriotism,—Mr. Ilovaÿski—undertook to demonstrate that the Bulgars are Slavs, pure of all Uralo-Finn admixture.

⁴ Constructed, however, on precisely the same plan, with identical interior disposition and furnishings : the immense brick stove, faced with tiles in the better class of houses, containing the deep, wide-mouthed, vaulted oven ; the massive wooden benches running round the sides of the room, and the ponderous family table built into the floor.

moral superiority of the Western Finns should be attributed to the difference of race, or to the difference of religion, or merely to a more ancient and wider use of liberty. The fact remains, anyhow, that an European traveller, finding himself in the midst of Finn peasants, with smooth-shaved chins and short coats, generally feels more at home with them than with Russian peasants, nearer to him in blood though the latter may be.

The Finns of Finland have been favored of history. The long and mild rule of Sweden initiated them to the civilization of the West and civil liberty.* From a political point of view the Finlander, to whom, under Alexander II. of Russia, was restored his archaïc constitution and his Diet composed of four orders,† is the most advanced of the peoples subject to the empire. Their neighbors and brethren, in religion as well as race, the Ehsts, having, until the beginning of this century, held the position of serfs to German lords, were less fortunate. Nevertheless they too have, at Revel and Dorpat, their own press and a national literature ; they too show themselves, in certain respects, superior to the Russian peasants. They are more patient and hardworking, and have been invited to settle on the estates of several Russian landlords, very profitably for the latter. Such Ehst colonies can be met with in the governments of St. Petersburgh and Pskof and even as far as Crimea. And lastly, should we wish to realize what contact with Aryans, and more especially Slavs, can make of peoples of Finnic extraction, as regards beauty of body and

---

* The Grand Duchy of Finland is less a Russian province than an annexed state, and the tsars have wisely respected its autonomy. Finland has preserved her own laws and institutions. In certain respects the transfer under Russian rule has been all gain to the Finns of Finland. The Russian monarchs ennobled the Finnish language, which before was spoken only by country people, by raising it to the rank of official language on a par with the Swedish language, which still is that of a portion of the littoral, the principal cities, and the higher classes of society. See further on, p. 134.

† Nobility, clergy, town-burghers, peasants, after the old Swedish constitution.

vigor of mind,[5] we have only to look at the Magyars, one of the handsomest, as well as most energetic races of Europe.   If there is any inferiority, it is certainly not from a political, nor from a military standpoint, for the Magyars have, at all times, been one of the most warlike nations of Europe, and through all their revolutions, have been truer to free institutions than most Aryan nations, be they Slav, Latin, or German.

[5] Here at last Mr. Beaulieu gives us the real gist of the matter, which he had somehow missed through the preceding pages : the influence is not from Finn to Slav, but the other way.   Such is ever the relation between Turanian and Indo-European.   To be entirely just, however, the very real superiority of the Finns of Finland, while certainly not an intrinsic racial one, as is more than hinted above, p. 75, is not so much due to Slavic influences as to Swedish ones.   As to the Magyars, they owe their aryanization to vicinity and actual cohabitation with Slavs in the same wide lands. The *Kalevala* is full of descriptions of simple rural life, and it is astonishing how many, even to minute details, might just as well apply to Russian or Swedish peasant life.   The same may be said of many of the customs therein pictured.   This goes far to corroborate the latest theories on the original unity or extremely close affinity of the " primeval Teutonic " (*Ur-deutsch*) and " primeval Slavic " (*Ur-slavisch*) stocks, since it is undoubtedly from these two elements that the Turanian Finn, from the first, absorbed those of his own social and national organization.

BOOK II. CHAPTER III.

The Tatar or Turk Element—Tatars and Mongols—The Kalmỳks—What is the Proportion of Tatar Blood in the Russians?—The Tatars in Russia and the Arabs in Spain—Slow Elimination of the Tatar Element—Ethnical Influence of the Turk Tribes Previous to the Mongol Invasion—Varieties of Type amidst the Modern Tatars—Their Customs and Character.

THE second of the great fountain-heads from which the Russian people might be said to have flowed—the one most peculiar to Russia, more decidedly Asiatic, has received from habit the name of " Tatar."   Never did more misleading designation steal into history, philology, ethnography.   At its first appearance in Russia this name was borne by one of the Mongol tribes who helped found the empire of Djinghiz-Khan.   In her terror of these new barbarians, who seemed to her the outcome of hell, Europe (it was in the thirteenth century) dubbed them " Tartars," and this name, suggested by a classical reminiscence, was extended to all the heterogeneous crowd of peoples dragged along after the savage conquerors.   As to the old name, " Mongols," the tribes to which it belonged by right were robbed of it, and it came to designate that branch of the Uralo-Altaïc stock, of which Turkestan was the starting-point, and of which the Turks are the chief representatives.   The Tatars who stayed on the banks of the Volga are nearly related to the Turks, or rather they *are* Turks, just as the Ottomans, both risen from the same cradle, both speaking dialects of the same language ; all the difference between them being that the Ottomans invaded Europe later and were converted to Islam only *after* that invasion.   To this day the

scions of the tribes from Turkestan who, coerced and led by the
Mongols, settled in Russia, have not lost the memory of their
origin : the Tatars of Kazàn and Astrakhan call themselves Turks,
a name endeared to them by the ancient glory of the Osmanlis and
a common religion.

The Turkish branch is, at present, nearer to the Finnic than to
the Mongolian branches.* Turks and Finns have often met and
mixed to such extent, that there are tribes—the Bashkirs and Tchu-
vashes for instance—in whom it is difficult to make out the share of
one and the other. The difficulty is still greater when dealing with
extinct peoples, such as the Huns, the Avars, and the old Bulgars
of the Volga, in whom the Finn blood seems to have predomi-
nated,—the Alans and Roxolans,† who appear to have been
mostly Turks or Tatars. The union of Turk and Mongol, especially in Asia, has taken place quite as frequently, and it is hard
at times to distinguish between them. One instance of such
fusion still survives in Europe : it is the tribe of the Tatar-Nogaÿ,
who dwelt in the steppes of the Kubàn and of the Crimean peninsula before they were driven out into those of the Kuma. The
features of these nomads seem to bear out the notion of an alliance with the Mongols. They have the same square, squat figure,
the eyes raised obliquely towards the external angle, the broad,
flat nose, the beardless chin. This case stands alone amidst the
Russian Turks. As a rule, whenever their countenance betrays a
cross, it is rather with the Finns or the peoples of the Caucasus.[1]

* In their primitive and unalloyed stage, the Turks may have been nearer
to the Mongols. (See *Revue d'Anthropologie*, vol. iii., 1874, Nos. 1 and 3.)
  † Some Russian scholars make out these Roxolans to be Russian Slavs.
  [1] There certainly is nothing in the features of the Tatars of the Volga,
familiar to all dwellers in large cities, where they ply their traditional trades
of peddlers, restaurant-waiters, and cab-drivers, to recall the no less familiar
type of the Ottoman Turk. The broad face, with slightly salient cheek-bones,
not too oblique eyes, and thickish lips, yellowish skin, and scant beard, is an
attenuated copy of the rampant Mongolian type. The same characteristics
are observable in the Finns of Finland, further modified by the considerable
strain of Scandinavian blood, to which they owe their lustreless dun or
sandy locks and almost imperceptible eyebrows over dull, fishlike eyes of

There still exists in European Russia a people of Mongol origin—the Kalmy̆ks—who dwell in the Caspian depression, this side of the Volga. There are about 130,000 of them, and they carry around their *kibitkas*, or felt tents, and drive their camels and their flocks along in the arid steppes of the governments of Astrakhan and Stavròpol. It is these twenty-five or thirty thousand families, roaming about at one extremity of the empire, whose name has been so frequently applied, as a kind of nickname, to the Russian people. At first sight their Chinese type distinguishes them nearly as markedly from the Tatars as from the Russians. It is to be noted that these Mongols of the Volga did not enter Europe in the rear of Batù and the successors of Jinghiz-khan, but settled down in that forgotten corner of Russia at a relatively recent period. It was as late as the seventeenth century that, after a long migration from the confines of China to the Ural River, these spiritual subjects of the Dalaï Lama of Thibet set foot in the steppes by the Volga. Taking advantage of the hereditary rivalry between the Mongol and Tatar tribes, Russia successfully employed these new-comers in her wars against the Turks and the Khans of Crimea; but any attempts to get them into more direct subjection caused numbers of them to return to their original fatherland. They went *en masse*, giving the eighteenth century the spectacle of a wholesale migration, like those of olden times. During the winter of 1770 from two to three hundred thousand Kalmy̆ks, with their flocks, crossed the Volga and Ural upon the ice. Then thaw came on and detained the rest, who decided to stay in Russia, while their brethren, notwithstanding repeated attacks from the Kirghiz, plodded on to their old homesteads on the confines of the Chinese Empire.

washed-out blue. If the long contact with their whilom masters has undoubtedly ennobled them morally and intellectually, it has not done the same service to their personal appearance, for they are the most appallingly homely people one can meet. It is related of the Emperor Nicholas that, stopping at a Finn village a hundred miles or so from the capital, he was so disagreeably struck by the *physique* of the villagers, that he ordered one of his handsomest guard-regiments to be forthwith stationed there.

The Kalmÿks who stayed in the cis-Caspian steppes, owning the Russian sovereignty, were, until very lately, all Buddhists. They had a chief to whom they gave the title of Grand-Lama, who, since Alexander I., was nominated by the Tsar, and whose residence lay somewhere near Astrakhan. There is one fact which has exercised vital influence on their respective destinies, it is that the three chief branches of the Uralo-Altaïc race have apportioned to themselves the three chief religions of the old continent. The Finn has become Christian ; the Turk or Tatar, Moslem ; the Mongol, Buddhist. To this ethnological distribution of worships there are few exceptions. It is in this diversity of faiths, above all, that we must seek for the causes of the widely diverging destinies of the three groups, especially the Finn and the Tatar. Religion has prepared the one to European ways of life ; religion has removed the other from the same influences. Islam gave the Tatar a more precocious national civilization, and helped him to build such thriving cities as ancient Saraÿ and Kazàn, and to found, in Europe and in Asia, powerful states. Islam gave him a more brilliant past, but, on the other hand, prepares for him more difficulties in the future.

It is to the Tatars that the Russians have long been indebted for the misnomer of " Mongols "; yet the Tatars themselves have but a questionable claim to the name. In any case, it ought to be dropped when dealing with the Russians, not because in itself offensive, but because resulting from a misapprehension.

The Russians have scarcely a few drops of Mongol blood ; have they much more Tatar blood ? Perhaps even less than the Spanish people have Moorish or Arab blood. In Spain the Arabs stayed much longer, occupied a far larger portion of the territory, settled down in far greater numbers, and held the peninsula under their own immediate rule. In Russia, the Tatars having entered the country in the thirteenth century, were, already in the sixteenth, driven back to the extremities. They ruled hardly more than one half of European Russia, and the greater part of even that they did not hold under their direct sway, but merely under their suzerainty. They did not destroy the Russian principalities, but were content to make them pay tribute. The Arabs colonized the fairest regions of Spain, those which, to this day, are the most fertile and most populous. The Tatars spread over the parts of Russia which are even now the most thinly peopled, —over the steppes of the south and east. Towards the centre they advanced only up the rivers, along the Volga and its tributaries, as shown even still by their actual distribution. It was not even into the midst of the Russians that these colonizers from Asia broke their way. The Russians at that time had barely reached the central basin of the Volga and the junction of this river with the Okà at Nijni Nòvgorod. So it was the Finnish peoples, discussed in the preceding chapter, in whose midst they appeared ; the peoples whose remains we see in the Mordvins, the Tcheremiss, the Tchuvash, and of whom several suffered themselves to be tatarized. The Russian Turks have not, like the Arabs in Spain, created a rich and industrious civilization ; far from devoting themselves to a sedentary agricultural life, they in part remained nomads. Their cities were not numerous, and the largest were small in comparison with the Moorish capitals in Andalusia. With a territory three or four times as extensive, it is doubtful whether the Golden-Horde ever came up in numbers to the Khalifat of Cordova. An analysis of the two languages suggests similar conclusions. The mark left by Arabic on the Spanish language is incomparably deeper than that imprinted by the Turkish or Tatar language on Russian.

Have the Moslem Tatars contributed more towards the formation of the Russian people because, instead of expelling the Mahometans, as did Catholic Castile, Orthodox Moscovia left them their religion and their newly adopted country? The contrary appears more probable. In Russia as in Spain the reasons for separation between victors and vanquished remained the same during the rule of the Cross as during its subjection, and they all centred in one thing—religion, which raised between the two races an insuperable barrier.   From the one to the other, before as well as after the national deliverance, there was but one road —apostasy.   If preaching and self-interest made many converts amidst the Mussulmans in Russia, especially amidst the Murzas or Tatar chieftains, a great many more must have taken place amidst the Mussulmans in Spain, subjected as they had been through many long years to the most unscrupulous proselytism, till the day came when they could keep their faith only at the cost of wealth and country.   In Russia no such alternative was ever placed before the Mussulmans.   The Tsars never had need to resort to such barbarities in order to decrease in their states the power of the Tatar element.   What was done violently in Spain, to her eternal damage, did itself, slowly, gradually, in Russia. All that she had to do was to leave things to take pretty well theii own natural course.

Simultaneously with the process of absorption, assimilation of the Finnic elements, another, inverse process has been going on in Russia,—that of secretion, elimination of the Tatar and Moslem elements which she could not assimilate.   After their submission numbers of Tatars left Russia, not wishing to remain as subjects of the infidels, whose masters they had been.   Before the advance of the Christian arms, they spontaneously recoiled back to the lands where the law of the Prophet still held sway.   After the destruction of the khanates of Kazàn and Astrakhan, they inclined to concentrate in Crimea and the neighboring steppes which, as late as the eighteenth century, went by the name of Little Tartary.   After the conquest of Crimea by Catherine II. they resumed their exodus towards the empire of their Turkish brethren, and even in our days, after the war of Sebastòpol and the submission of the Caucasus, the emigration of Tatars and Nogaÿ has begun again on an immense scale, at the same time as that of the Tcherkess (Circassians), so that they do not at the present day amount to one fifth of their numbers at the time of the annexation to Russia. From 1860 to 1863, nigh on 200,000 Tatars have gone forth from the government of Tauris (Crimea), leaving behind 784 *aouls* or villages, of which three quarters remained desert like the *despoblados* left by the expulsion of the Moors on the map of Spain. Since the introduction of obligatory military service, in 1874, this sort of exodus has begun again. Thus it is that defeat and self-banishment, apart from absorption and commingling, have reduced the Tatars to small groups—harmless islets in the countries where they have been rulers for centuries, in such even, like Crimea, of which, some hundred years ago, they were the sole inhabitants.

Recent examples show us the natural and spontaneous decrease of the Tatar and Mahometan elements in Russia ; that of European Turkey, where, up to the emancipation of the Danubian principalities, the Mussulmans made up only one third or one fourth of the population, from which we see that even at the time of their sovereignty the Tatars were numerically a minority in their own empire. The route followed by these invaders and the actual position of the Tatars along the rivers, in lands occupied by Finns, lead us to think that they formed a majority only just around their capitals, on the Volga and in such other countries like Crimea and the steppes of the southeast as seem mean by nature for pastoral life. The figures to which the armies of the khans mounted up must not mislead us as to the number of their subjects. In these armies, every healthy man hastened to enlist ; lacking fanaticism or patriotism, the bait of booty was sufficient to keep men from deserting in the course of these expeditions, of which the main object was plunder. A Crimean khan could call together 100,000 warriors without having a million of subjects. The Tatars scarcely ever got to the centre of Russia except with armed hand, and never settled there. Thus Moscovia was and remained towards them, from the point of view of population, in a condition similar to that in which Serbia, Hungary, Rumania, and Greece stood towards the Turks, who in all these countries had but few colonies.   Rarely have there been two situations so identical as that of the Russians under the Tatar yoke and that of the South Slavs under the Turkish yoke. In both cases the same races face each other, in both the same religions, so that we have before us the same actors in the same parts though under different names, with nothing changed but the stage.   With all these analogies the Russian has had a great advantage over the Bulgar or the Serb.   He was vassal and tributary, but never direct subject.   Therefore it may well be doubted whether there was any mixture of the two races on the banks of the Volga any more than on those of the Danube.   If there was some, through intermarriage, through slavery, rapes, and polygamy, a few perhaps through conversions, sincere or forced, it was perhaps rather at the cost of the Slavs, for through all these channels Christian blood was introduced into the Moslem's veins far more easily than Moslem blood into the veins of the Christian.

It has frequently been remarked how rare, how abnormal conversions of Mahometans to Christianity have at all times been ; the opposite phenomenon has attracted less attention : how much more frequent has been the passage from the doctrine of Christ to that of Mahomet.   All Western Asia, all Northern Africa, Egypt, and Barbary but too loudly bear witness to the fact.   Even in Europe, the extremities of which have alone been touched by Islamism, the Begs of Bosnia, the " true believers " of Albania, the Pomaks of Mahometan Bulgars, the Mussulmans of Candia and Crimea, of Greek or Goth origin, are descended from apostate Christians, while it would be difficult to quote a Mahometan people, nay a single tribe, ever having embraced the Christian faith. The reason does not lie merely in the fact that Islam seems adapted to certain races and certain modes of life, but also in the reciprocal position, in the dogma, and, it may be said, in the respective ages of the two religions.   Islam is a more recent doctrine than Christianity, and, in a great measure, aimed directly against the latter. It is, from the standpoint of dogma, a simpler faith, at least apparently,—more strictly monotheistic freer from any kind of anthropomorphism.

The Mussulman emigrates or dies out where the Christian rules, but does not become a convert, so that the mixing of the two races hardly can take place in any way but exchange of one faith for the other. It is certain that, in Russia, the force of example and self-interest,—proselytism, private or official, have, in the last three or four hundred years, effected many a conquest amidst the Tatars in favor of Christianity.* Several of the greatest Russian families come from this source, and, when baptized, the neophytes exchanged the title of a Tatar *Murza* for that of a Russian *Kniaz*[2]; but such apostasies, even when accom-

---

* About one-eleventh part (40,000 out of 450,000) of the Tatars residing in the government of Kazàn were baptized by the Russian authorities in the eighteenth century. They still are Christian in name ; but, their baptism notwithstanding, they are not yet russified : they retain their language, their own peculiar customs, generally even their faith in the Koran. (See vol. iii., book iii., ch. iii.)

[2] The thoroughly national title *kniaz* (the *k* to be well sounded), is that which is uniformly rendered in all other European languages by "prince." Nothing could be more misleading, for the word "prince" represents something that does not exist in Russia, at least not in the form familiar to other nations, those that have passed through the feudal system, which we have been spared. The title ought to be retained in its Russian form. A slightly parallel case is that of the Anglo-Saxon "*jarl*," now "earl," which is inadequately rendered in other languages by the Latin "count" (*comes*) and the German "Graf." But more of this in its proper place.—As to the families of Tatar origin, they are quite numerous in the higher nobility, and the women especially show it in their hair, which is dark, very long and silky, without a wave or ripple, and sometimes in the color of their skin, which is of a warm creamy tinge, not unfrequently leaning markedly to yellow and, unlike the dead olive complexions of so many Spanish women, capable of vivid bloom and quick blush. The names of such families often betray their origin. Thus "Bahmetief" (aspirate the *h* strongly) is corrupted from "Mehmet." The coats-of-arms improvised for the new Russian nobles also show transparent devices,—none prettier than that of a kinsman of the last Khan of Kazàn, who, having adopted Christianity, was given a wife from among the noblest maidens, with large landed possessions : the family 'scutcheon bears across the lower field a gold crescent on argent ground—symbol of the ancestral faith,—while the upper

plished wholesale, have been relatively rare occurrences. They took place amidst populations in great part already mixed with new Christian masters or old Finn subjects. Outside of Russia, nay, in their very cradles, the Tatars must have undergone a certain amount of crossing with Caucasian races,—first in Turkestan, where from times immemorial Eranians have dwelt in great numbers; then along the highroads of invasion, especially in the Caucasus, where the community of religion facilitated alliances which the beauty of the Tcherkess women made desirable in the eyes of the Turks of the Volga as well as those of the Turks of the Bosporus.

If then a noticeable strain of Tatar blood has very gradually filtered into the veins of the Russian people, it possibly came less from the hordes of Batù and the invaders of the thirteenth century than from the kindred tribes who, for thousands of years, have dwelt or roamed in the south of Russia, from the Scythians of old to the Khazars, the Petchenèg, the Pòlovtsi of the Middle Ages. Under the vague designations of "Scythians," the ancients used to mix up populations between whom there was no ethnical relationship whatever. It appears that amongst these Scythians there were some Aryan ones; but the majority of them seem to have been derived from a Finno-Turkish stock. That such was the case is more certain still concerning the Khazars, the Kumans, and other nomads who, up to the great invasion, wrangled for the possession of the south of Russia. These now extinct peoples were for a long time the only denizens of this immense territory, of which the Greeks and Italicans knew only

field is divided in two compartments, one of which has a crooked scimitar on gules ground—a reminder of the founder's bravery in battle,—and the other a star on azure ground, in poetical allusion to the lady. It may be mentioned here that, however correct our author's remarks are concerning the frequency of Christian apostasy, they do not apply to the Russian Slavs, who have never been known to forsake orthodox Christianity for any other religion. The only exception is the adoption of the Jewish religion by a very few ignorant fanatics, under very peculiar circumstances,—an exceedingly curious phenomenon, of which more hereafter.

the coastland. Must we infer from this that they were the ancestors of the thinly scattered population of these even yet half desert plains? The territory of all these barbarians, was the "woodless zone," the steppe-zone, where the population is still either very much scattered or very recent. In order to open these plains to culture, the nomads had first to be driven off. The Scythians and all their Turko-Finn kindred were pastoral nomads, who, with their wagons and flocks, led in the steppes, this side of the Volga and the Don, the life that their brethren, the Kirghiz, even now lead on the other side of these rivers. All these peoples, so much dreaded by the West, and so soon vanished from the ken of history, were as insignificant in numbers as the Asiatic tribes of the same race, who maintain, to this day, the same kind of existence. One famine, one epidemic, one battle, sufficed for their annihilation. They destroyed one another, leaving of themselves no other vestiges but their names. It is in the southern half of Russia that we must seek for traces of the Scythian or Tatar element, and it is from the west and north, from the wooded regions, that the present inhabitants of Southern Russia have emerged gradually, we might almost say under our eyes.

Great has been the influence of the Tatars, but more historically than ethnologically; it had to do with the conquest more than with the fusion of the races. However, while confuting a popular prejudice, we should not rush into the opposite excess; the Tatar's share in the formation of the Russian people has been the smallest possible, but cannot be *quite* explained away. On more than one point there has been some mingling of blood between the Turk and Slav tribes whence Russians have sprung, —on the banks of the Dniepr, when the rulers of Kief were collecting the remnants of the Pòlovtsi and the Petchenèg,—on the same river, on the Don, on the Volga, amidst the Cosacks, who, both in peace and war, frequently entertained close relations with their Moslem neighbors and foes. However that may be, the ethnical influence of the Tatars, even in the south, always remained far behind that of the Finns in the north, all the more that the Tatars themselves were frequently crossed with Finns.

Crimea and the region which, as late as the last century, went by the name of Little Tartary, is, after all, perhaps the country where it is easiest to study the manners and character of the Tatars. Scarcely a hundred years ago they were the masters and almost the only occupants of this region. In consequence of repeated emigrations, they are, this day, two or three times inferior in numbers to the Russian or foreign colonists who have taken their place ; in certain portions of the peninsula, however, you still feel that they are at home. On the steppe-land which occupies the centre and north, rebellious against culture, they continue to lead their nomadic life. In the fertile regions, they still own towns, of which they are themselves the chief and almost only population, as for instance Karasù-Bazar, or Bakhtchi-Saraÿ, the old capital of the Crimean khans. There, in a cool and narrow valley, around the verdant gardens and the marble fountain-basins of the palace of the Ghiréÿ, lives a Moslem community more purely oriental than those of the cities of European Turkey or of the littoral of Asia Minor. There the Mahometan law holds its sway in all its rigor, and were it not for the loneliness of the palace halls, with hangings and furniture all untouched, as they were under the last of the khans, nothing would recall the fall of the Tatar's might.

The Turks of Bakhtchi-Saraÿ and Karasù-Bazar are traders and farmers. So are those of the Volga. Having come to a land of bountiful soil, they abandoned their nomadic mode of life and became craftsmen or traders in the cities, tillers of the soil in the country. At Kazàn, once the capital of the most powerful of the three khanates which sprang from the dismemberment of the Golden Horde, the Tatars inhabit a suburb (*slobodà*)[3] of their own,

---

[3] The word *slobodà* means "a free place," probably because suburban life may have been free from much of the restraint imposed on those that dwelt in the city proper; also the suburb may have enjoyed some local franchises.

situated at the foot of their former capital, far removed from the Kremlin, taken from them by the Orthodox Tsars. Their suburb looks clean, quiet, and prosperous. They have their mosques and schools,* with their *mollahs* elected by the community and acting as arbiters and judges, according to Moslem custom.

At Kazàn, as well as in Crimea, the Tatars have preserved the specialty of certain oriental industries, such as the manufacturing of articles in leather and morocco : boots, slippers (*babushes*), saddles, sheaths for swords and daggers, etc. Many of them still boast the muscular strength which is proverbially attributed to the Turks, and the porters at the great Nijni fair are almost all Tatars. The high walks of commerce are not closed against them, and at Kazàn more than one of their merchants have achieved a considerable fortune. And although there are many differences among them, as well physical as moral, they are, on the whole, saving and painstaking, and noted for domestic morality and the harmony prevailing in their families. In all these qualities, the Turks of Russia are in no wise inferior to those of the Ottoman Empire, whose virtues in private life are unanimously extolled by travellers. For certain pursuits the Tatars are often preferred by the Russians themselves. Being noted for cleanliness, probity, sobriety, they are sought for in several crafts, and have made a sort of monopoly of certain employments, especially such as require most honesty and trustworthiness. The great Russian families, who own villas on the south coast of Crimea, are not afraid of taking into their homes Tatar servants, and in the restaurants of Petersburgh it is quite "the thing" for the waiters to be Tatars from the government of Riazàn, so that the unsuspecting

---

* In these, as in all moslem schools, the ground work of instruction is Arabic, the language of the Koran, which is frequently recited without being understood. This barbarous method is a great obstacle to the intellectual growth of the Tatars. Therefore the government is making praiseworthy efforts to introduce among them instruction in the Tatar language, in expectation of the time when it will be possible to get them to use the Russian language.

foreigner who orders his dinner from a French menu, is waited
on, in perfect ignorance of the fact, by descendants of Djinghiz or
Batù's rider-warriors.

The qualities of the Tatars come in part from their religion,
which enjoins temperance as an absolute duty ; their faults, the
causes that hamper their progress, come from the same source.
The race's only apparent inferiority consists in a lack of originality. Their ancient cities have perished. In order to find
monuments of their domination, we must go as far as Turkestan,
Samarkand, and there we find buildings entirely in Persian style
and taste. In Russia nothing is so rare as constructions from the
time of the khans. In Crimea, besides the palace of Bakhtchi-Saraÿ,
of late date and poor merit, nothing is left but a few mosques, of
which the handsomest do not amount to much. Kazan boasts a
grotesque brick pyramid in four tiers, held in great veneration
by the Tatars, but probably built after the Russian conquest.
It is in a city destroyed by the Tatars themselves at the time of
Tamerlan's invasion, in Bolgáry, near the left bank of the Volga,
that the most interesting Oriental ruins of all Russia are to be
seen—two constructions with cupolas, which will soon have
crumbled to pieces, and whose graceful Arabic architecture, seen
from afar, recalls the beautiful tombs around Cairo. The Turks
of the Volga, like those of Central Asia, and the Ottomans of the
Bosporus, show in everything they do, in architecture as well as
in poetry, imitation of the Arabic or Persian genius. Such a
lack of originality makes their entire culture dependent on foreign
contact, and the civilization which they have received from their
Mussulman neighbors, their religion forbids them to improve on,
except with the loss of their independence.

On due reflection, it will appear that the main vice of Islam,
the main cause of its political inferiority, lies neither in its dogma,
nor even in its morals ; it lies in the confusion of things spiritual
and temporal, of the religious and civil law. The Koran being
both Bible and Code, the Prophet's word standing for law, the

laws and customs are once for all consecrated by religion.⁴ This one fact is sufficient to keep the entire Moslem civilization at a standstill. Indefinite progress, which constitutes the very essence of Christian civilization, is to them an impossibility ; whatever the seeming rapidity of its development, society, as a whole, is, with them, in reality and of necessity, immovable. This inferiority of Islam, however, is more felt in public than in private life ; it affects nations rather than individuals, for, when subjected to foreign influences, Mussulmans can accept ideas and customs which could not have originated in their midst. The Mahometans may experience the same thing that happened to the Jews, no less handicapped by their religious law, in the midst of Christian society : had the Jews ever ceased to form a compact nation, they could not, without great effort, have risen to a civilization more complete than that of the Moslem nations. For these, as for the Jews, Christian domination may prove beneficial in the end, since from political subjection can spring moral emancipation. Thus it is that, wherever the Russian Tatars form a minority, and have been most affected by alien influences, they have done away with the external sign of Islam : the veil and seclusion of women. While yet in strictest use at Bakhtchi-Saraÿ, in the centre of Crimea, the veil has been doffed by the Moslem women of the south coast. The same influences are driving out polygamy, as they put an end to slavery. The Tatars, broken up into small groups scattered over Russia, are inclined to pass through the same phases as the Jews, who, while retaining their worship, gradually fall into our modes of life. Islam would probably not oppose a greater obstacle to their entrance into our civilization, than Judaïsm to that of the Israelites, hampered by

⁴ Yet, must not those who do not dissever religion from practical life, but try to think and act up to the teachings of what they have accepted as the "Sacred Word," possess a real moral superiority over those who would laugh to scorn the notion of introducing what they themselves proclaim as the standard of absolute goodness and uprightness into, say, their business dealings?

far narrower ritualistic prescriptions. Without amalgamating with the bulk of the population, the Mussulmans who stayed in Russia will for a longer or lesser space of time, preserve their language and customs and form a peaceable, industrious class, who will play a part very much like that now filled by the Jews and Armenians, with this difference—that, dwelling in the country as well as in the cities, practising agriculture as well as trade, their agglomeration in the eastern provinces can never give rise to the same economical disasters which are caused, in the west, by the agglomeration of the Jews, who are almost exclusively devoted to city life and trade.* '

From the political point of view, the Tatars of European Russia even now are scarcely more troublesome to the government than its Russian or Finn subjects. This was seen during the Crimean war : although they made at the time a full half of the population, they rendered hardly any service at all to the invaders,

* The polonized Tatars, who, residing in Lithuania, lost their language centuries ago, yet preserved their religion, and who are mostly tanners and traders, afford a glimpse of what their brethren of the Volga may become one day, when they are russified.

' It is a fact which cannot be sufficiently emphasized, in view of the senseless accusations of *religious* animosity continually thrown in our faces, that there is not and never was the slightest ill-feeling on the part of the Russian people towards any of the numerous aliens who live side by side with them as fellow-subjects—with the single exception of the Jews, meaning of course not the educated Jews, the "gentlemen," who practise various liberal professions, who have crafts, commercial and industrial positions, or those who, in Russia as everywhere else, rule the financial and high business world, but those wretched, squalid millions which, granting it is their misfortune and not their fault, still certainly are a terrible evil ; and the animosity of the lower classes—exasperated because of the close companionship forced on them, from which they have no possible escape— has nothing whatever to do with either religion or race. Naturally benignant and tolerant, the Russians know not of such feelings. Beyond good-natured banter, expressed in some long-standing nicknames, proverbial saws, their race feeling does not go ; only they do not intermarry, a few may not like to eat at the same board with their alien fellow-subjects. This latter, however, is the case with many religious sects composed of none but thorough-going Russians.

in whose ranks were their brethren of the Bosporus. The Bulgarian war, the fall of Khiva, and the submission of the other khanates of Turkestan robbed them of their last illusions. Divided, even more than the Finns, into minute scattered groups, locked in on all sides by Russians, the Russian Turks are no longer a people ; religion has, for them, necessarily stepped into the place of nationality, and repeated emigrations rid them of their fanatics. Everywhere in Europe, in the very places where they ruled longest, the Tatars incline to become a minority and this disproportion will go on increasing as the colonization of the Russian East progresses. In Europe, including the inhabitants of Northern Caucasus, Russia numbers only 3,200,000 Mahometan subjects. Setting aside the Caucasus, both slopes of which are comprised in the same political circumscription, the number of the Mussulmans sinks to 2,500,000 and from this figure we must, if we wish to deal with genuine Tatars, descendants of the invaders of the Golden Horde, deduct the Bashkirs and the tatarized tribes in which Finnic blood is predominant. Not quite 1,200,000 is all that remains of that Turk or Tatar race which so long ruled Russia and terrified Europe. In Russian Asia, their kindred by blood and brethren in religion are, in the first place, the Kirghiz, the most extensive of all the Turkish branches ; in Turkestan, the Turkmen or Turcomans, and the Uzbegs ; in the Caucasus, the Tatars (Sunnites or Shiites) from the banks of the Kura and the Araxus, the Kumuks and a few other small tribes ; lastly, in Siberia, some few Mahometans with more or less claim to the name of Tatars, with sundry tribes, now Christian and three quarters russified.* In Europe the Mussulmans exceed a half of the population only in one government, that of Ufa, and that only, thanks to the Bashkirs, in a half Asiatic region which is

---

* We do not count here the Tunguz, nor the Mandshu, nor even the Yakut, who are ranked amongst the peoples of Turkish stock, but who are separated from the Tatar group proper by distance and religion.

just being colonized.   In those of the other provinces where they are most numerous—in the Governments of Kazàn, Orenburg, Astrakhan, the Mahometans do not number even one third of the entire population.   Even along the Lower Volga, the majority has passed over to the Christians.

BOOK II. CHAPTER IV.

The Slavic Element and Russian Nationality—Slavs and Panslavism—Slavs and Letto-Lithuanians—Formation of the Russian People : Its Different Tribes—Differences between them, of Origin and Character—Great-Russians (*Velikorùss*)—White-Russians (*Bielorùss*)—Little-Russians (*Maloròss*)—Ukraïnophilism.

ABOVE the Finns and Tatars, whose ethnological part in the making of Russia has been very unequal, comes the race which has subjugated or absorbed all the others, the race whose name sounds proudly to every Russian ear—the Slav race. On the place belonging to the Slavs and their kith and kin there is no possible doubt. Like the Celts, the Latins, the Teutons, they are part of the great Aryan race to which the sovereignty over the world seems to have fallen. To this common origin their physical type bears witness ; so do their language and primeval traditions. Like Greek, Latin, and German, the Slavic languages are, sooth to say, but dialects of that Indo-European speech, of which Sanskrit is the oldest known form. The Slavic legends and tales, like the German ones, complete the data from which sprang the myths of India and Greece.* The Slavs are no more Asiatic than we are, or, if they are, it is only in the manner and degree that we are ourselves. Their establishment in Europe dates back beyond all historic times. It is not known whether the Teutons or they were the first to leave Asia ; at all events there can have been but a short interval between the two migrations. Between the great

* We have at present a great number of collections of Slavic tales from all the Slav countries. For Russia, must be quoted first of all Afanássief's Collection : *Naròdnyia Rùsskiya Skàzki* (Popular Russian Tales); then come those of Khudiakòf, Erlenwein, Tchudinsky, etc. For Little-Russia, those of Rudchènko and Kùlish.

Aryan tribes who have divided Europe amongst themselves, it is difficult to decide the question as to degree of consanguinity. The philologists insist on a closer tie between the Slavs and the Teutons ; but if the Slavs, as to language, seem to stand somewhat nearer to their Teutonic neighbors, they lean more, in character, towards the Europeans of the West and South.   From the remotest times we find them settled in Europe, on the Visla and the Dniepr.

Through the obscurities of primeval history it is difficult to make out the original type of these Slav tribes.   Classical antiquity confounds all alien peoples, whether Celts, Teutons, or Slavs, under the sweeping designation of "barbarians," painting them with the same colors, attributing to them the same customs, from which it would appear that these tribes did not then differ as much as they have done subsequently, and showed more traces of their common origin.   From these descriptions (often just as applicable to the barbarians of neighboring races), the ancient Slavs, whom we recognize under the names of the Antes, Vends, Slovens, appear to have been of large, robust build, with blue or gray eyes, hair yellow, chestnut, or auburn,— all features frequently met with in the Russians.*   Prehistoric

---

* It is perhaps at Petersburgh, in the Museum at the Hermitage, that we are to look for the portraits of the first Russian Slavs, on the admirable jewels found in the tumuli of Crimea, at the gates of Panticapæon (modern Kertch), the ancient capital of the Cimmerian Bosporus.   There, on golden belt-buckles or silver cups and dishes, we have before us, after a lapse of over twenty centuries, the live presentation of the Scythian horseman and archer, in high boots, tight-fitting trousers, short tunic, recalling the Russian shirt or blouse.   Besides the Greek jewels from Kertch, as superior to those from Pompeii, as Athenian art was to Roman art, similar figures ornament less handsome jewels which were discovered in the tombs of the southern steppes, and appear to be the handiwork of the Scythians themselves, already sufficiently in love with Greek art to try and imitate it.   On all these jewels occur types belonging to other races, some of them manifestly Aryan, others showing a mixture of Finno-Turkish blood.[1]

[1] This, then would be the first historical instance of one of our race's chief characteristics : its rare aptitude in appropriating every kind of learning, art, or craft, every trick of brain, or tongue, or hand, and its facile imitativeness.   Most precious qualities these for a young race, the latest come among the makers of human culture, who had to master all that had been done before it could produce original work of its own.

archæology seldom yields information more precise. As the Germans, so the Aryans of the East appear to have greatly changed in the course of the ages. Thus, for instance, the oldest tombs of the Slavic countries, in the neighborhood of Cracow, to name one place, have supplied skulls of elongated shape or dolichocephalous—of the purest Aryan type. Many Slav peoples of our day have lost this feature, so long regarded as characteristic of the Indo-European race, or have it in a degree inferior to most Latin or Teutonic peoples. Therefore, in the ethnological classifications founded solely on the shape of the skull, they have sometimes been placed side by side with the Finns amongst the brachycephalians or shortheads, while their Aryan brethren were, together with the Semites, classed with the longheads. However imperfect such a classification may be, it has the advantage of showing that, even if crossed with Finns, the Russians are not removed as far from the other Slavs as is often fancied.*

It is no easy task to depict the intellectual qualities of this race, which strives for the sovereignty of the world with the Latins and Teutons. It needs a long career of civilization to bring out the genius of races and nations in literature, in art, in political institutions. Most Slavs are too young, too new to independent life and to European culture, for their national individuality to have come out in as strong relief as that of their rivals. They were long despised by the nations of the West, who, out of their name (as *they* pronounced it), *Schiavoni, Esclavons*, made the word *schiavo, esclave*,—slave ; scorned to this day by their German neighbors, who persist in seeing in them mere "ethnological material" (*ethnologischer Stoff*) ; yet they owed

---

* It is notorious that, in our modern races, all produced by mixture, too much importance has been given this trait, and that, on the showing of the latest researches, many Germans, especially of South Germany, are, as well as numbers of French, shortheads. It would be of greater importance, should it turn out, as some scientists assert, that the Slavs had a smaller head and a brain less voluminous than the Western Europeans. But even should the fact be proved, it would be sufficiently accounted for by the relative antiquity of culture in Western Europe.

7

their inferiority probably only to their geographical position. Standing, as they did, in the East, so to speak at the entrance of Europe, in the most massive part of the continent and the most exposed to invasions from Asia, they were naturally the last to become civilized and the least deeply affected by civilization. Feeling themselves unqualified to lay claim to the culture of modern Europe, some Slavs have claimed that of the ancient world. Certain Serb and Bulgar writers have taken it into their heads to demand as their rightful patrimony the greater part of Greek civilization, from Thracian Orpheus to Macedonian Alexander. Such vindications, based on popular Bulgarian songs of doubtful authenticity, unfortunately rest more on patriotism than on science.*

Having been and remained almost total strangers to the discipline of Rome and Greece, the Slavs, by their situation, by their language and religion, have stood more or less aloof from the chief intellectual centres of modern Europe, nor could they have taken the same share in her work as did the two other great European families. It is no use denying it ; as the ancient civilization, so the modern, which they are enjoying themselves and of which, in the East, they have made themselves the apostles, was accomplished nearly without their help. Neither the Russians nor the Southern Slavs have contributed one stone to the building, and it could easily have dispensed with the assistance of the Western Slavs likewise—those of Poland and Bohemia. Had there been no Slavs at all,—had Europe ended at the foot of the Carinthian Alps and the Boehmerwald, her civilization would not have been less complete, while it could not have been robbed, without mutilation, of the share borne in the work by either of the great Latin or Teuton nations. Relegated to the uttermost

---

* This system has been more particularly formulated by Mr. Verkovitch in a collection entitled *The Slavic Veda* (*Veda Slavena*, Belgrad, 1874), a work which the more competent Slavists regard as a mystification. See on this subject L. Léger, *Nouvelles Études Slaves* (*New Slavic Studies*), Paris, 1880.

end of Christendom, the Slavs hardly could serve it in any way but with their arms, guarding its boundaries, from the Save and Danube to the Dniepr and Volga, against invasion from Asia.[2]

Is the race deficient in genius? Assuredly not. It is a noteworthy fact that it was Slavs who opened the way to the West in the two great movements which inaugurated the modern era—in the Renaissance and the Reformation, in the discovery of the laws that rule the universe, and in the vindication of freedom for human thought. The Pole Kopernik was the forerunner of Galileo, the Tchekh John Huss that of Luther. These are great titles to glory for the Slavs,—so great that they are contested by the Germans. For, as ill luck would have it, a rival race, after settling down in the land of their great men, managed to deny them even their names. If we take into consideration the secular encroachments of Germany, and the fact that the bulk of the population is Slav in Saxony and Eastern Prussia, the Slavs, very likely, would have more right to claim as theirs many of the great names of which Germany brags. In the wake of Kopernik and Huss, the two Slav peoples most closely connected with the West through religion and vicinity, Poland and Bohemia (*Tchekhia*) could read off a long roll of men distinguished in letters, sciences, politics, and war. And among the Southern Slavs (*Yugoslavs*) a small republic like Ragusa could, alone, furnish an entire gallery of men gifted in all lines.* Where remoteness from the West and foreign oppression made study impossible and prevented individual proper names from coming up, the people has mani-

---

[2] This is not, after all, such a very trifling service—to guard the door of the chamber of knowledge and with one's life blood secure to the workers within the necessary leisure and safety,—and in this sense at least it is probable that European civilization could *not* have dispensed with the assistance of the Slavs.

* On these various Slav tribes, *The Slavic World (Le Monde Slave)* and the *Slavic Studies (Études Slaves)* by Mr. Louis Léger may be profitably consulted. Mr. Léger has done most of all Frenchmen since Cyprien Robert, to give us a knowledge of peoples who, by their struggle against Germanism, are of particular interest to France.

fested its genius in such minstrelsy as has nothing to envy in the finest poetry of the West. In that kind of popular, impersonal poetry which we so greatly admire in the *romanceros* of Spain, the ballads of Scotland or the songs (*chansons*) of France, the Slav, far from yielding the prize to the Latins or Teutons, possibly surpasses both. There is nothing more truly poetical than the *pièsme* ("lays") of Serbia, and the *dùmy* ("reveries") of Little-Russia ; for, by way of natural compensation, it is among the Slavs least initiated into Western culture that popular poetry has blossomed out most freely.[3]

What will these new-comers bring to West-European culture? In poetry, in the novel, they already have struck some new notes ; what will they contribute to scientific research, philosophical conceptions, religious and political? This, for Western civilization, is a momentous question. May be the Slavs have come in too late to create for themselves a Pantheon or Walhalla as gloriously filled as those of the Latins and Teutons. May be, in literature and art generally, the heroic age, the age of the sublime, has passed away ; may be even in science, the great laws easily accessible to the human mind have all been discovered, and mankind is reduced, for a long period, to their application and to inventions of details. The Slavs, especially the Russians, are endowed with ambition, intellectual no less than material. With the recklessness of the youth who, ere he has learned all his masters can teach him, already dreams of distancing them in the race, they look on the old peoples of the West with a scorn that should be forgiven their youthful presumption. They flatter themselves they will solve the problems which the West bootlessly agitates ; they think they own the secret of the social and political regeneration of Europe and the Christian world.[4]

[3] Is not this a sign that "Western culture" had better be dispensed with, or rather—not to be sweeping and misleading—that it should not be forced in its entirety on a race which, as a whole, it does not fit and whose individuality it smothers whenever it is given its own way.

[4] Naturally, the future being theirs. It is easy to see that the predomi-

The future will judge. Meantime, let them widen and renew morally the Western civilization, which they are appropriating and extending territorially. After having been so long merely the warders of its frontier, they carry it forward. From being the rear-guard of Europe, they have become her vanguard in the conquest of Asia and the East.

By temperament and character the Slavs present an assortment of defects and qualities which places them nearer to the Latins and Celts than to their neighbors, the Germans. In the place of the Teutonic phlegm, they frequently exhibit, even under the northernmost skies, a liveliness, quickness, warmth, at times a mobility, petulance, exuberance, not to be found in the same degree even among southern nations.[5] In the political life of

nating bent of their mind—especially that of their main tribe, the Russians —lies towards the practical, the positive, that they will make the field of scientific research pre-eminently their own. In chemistry and medicine they are already avowedly in the van. In the arts, especially in music, it is no longer a question of what they *will* do. But in philosophy and political science they undoubtedly will have, in good time, some weighty words to say, and such as will probably astonish their older sister nations not a little. That they have no part or share in the great Latino-Teutonic civilization, which has never till lately had anything for them but ignorant contempt and utter lack of comprehension—is most true, just what Mr. Danilefsky so ably sets forth. (See p. 13.) Their mission will be to correct its faults, to fill its gaps, to rejuvenate it by bringing plain-speaking and genuineness to bear against the shams, catchwords, and cant phrases which are the rotten props of many an empty shell,—the stage of decadence to which every great civilization in the world has arrived after a long and glorious course, when the exhaustion of age puts an end to self-renewal and renewal has to come from outside. This renewal, in the sequence of ages and the logic of history, it is the Slavs' turn to bring, and when the Slavic spirit stands revealed and unfettered before the world in its solemn simplicity, its earnestness, sincerity, and broad tolerance, such glaring fallacies as those of the "*Contrat Social*" in politics, and the elucubrations of Voltaire and the Encyclopedists on religion and history, left to stand on their own merits, will fall to pieces of themselves, and their practical applications with all their dire train of consequences of course become impossible.

[5] There is, perhaps, no national character with so many sides to it as the Slavic. By this—the emotional and mercurial—side it is nearly akin to the Irish, especially the Southern or Little-Russians, with their love of melody, beauty, and—idling. There is an intellectual counterpart to this

those Slavs whose blood is least mixed, this natural disposition
has produced a mercurial, mutable, anarchical spirit, a spirit of
incoherence, division, separatism, which has thrown great difficulties in the way of their national existence, and which, together with their geographical position, has been the main
obstacle to the progress of their civilization. The distinctive
quality which pervades the entire race independently of the
various crosses of its several peoples, is a flexibility, an elasticity
of temperament and character, of the organs and the intellect,
which enable it to receive and reproduce any and all ideas or
forms. The gift of imitativeness characteristic of the Slavs has
often been spoken of. This gift extends to everything, to words
and thoughts alike ; it belongs to all ages, and both sexes. This
peculiar malleability, the property of both Russian and Pole, is at
bottom, possibly, only a result of the race's history, and, consequently, of their geographical situation. Being the latest comers,
and for a long while inferior to the neighboring races, they have
always been going to school to somebody or other. Instead of
living on their own capital, they have lived on loans, until
imitativeness became their leading faculty, because the most useful as well as the most constantly called into play.

too. Quick to seize, tenacious in retaining, and exceedingly prompt, in
common parlance, in "putting two and two together," our children guess
fully as much as they learn, and do not take kindly to the slow and ponder-
ously thorough educational methods so dear—and necessary—to the Germans. Thus Kindergarten instruction has to be considerably modified to
please and therefore benefit them, as a tot of five resents as an insult, for
instance, to be gravely shown "at school" an article in *papier mâché* and
be told to learn that it represents the familiar rye-bread which he lustily
munches *in natura* three times a day with his milk. Our youth have brains
active to restlessness and vastly prefer to exercise them by "making things
out" themselves, rather than learn things as they are set down in books,
by a mere effort of memory. It is very possible that this trait lies at the
root of the almost universal predilection for experimental and inductive
science, and the very general disfavor into which historical branches have
fallen. This peculiar quickness and intellectual bent, with its advantages
and drawbacks, we have in common with the Americans,—nor is it, by far,
the only point of similarity and, therefore, mutual sympathy and comprehension, between the two nations.

This in no wise means that the Slavs differ too little from the others to form distinct nationalities, each having its own separate language, literature, traditions, a character or genius proper to each. Far from it. History, geography, religion, the rule or contact of aliens, have separated them but too well, making a complete fusion impossible ; impossible, also, for consanguinity of race and language to effect forgetfulness of their different nationalities. Panslavism would prove as impracticable as Panlatinism. At bottom it really is nothing but a scarecrow invented by the Germans to arouse the mistrust of the West against the small nationalities engaged in a life-struggle against Germanism. The " Slavic rivulets " have no inclination whatever to lose themselves in " the Russian ocean." Catholic or Orthodox, neither Tchekh nor Croat, neither Serb nor Bulgar ever envied the fate of the Poles on the Visla. What these little " younger brothers " expect from Russia is not absorption into the domain of the Tsar, but the shielding of their independence. That is known in St. Petersburgh. It is also known that the empire incloses within its boundaries peoples and nationalities enough as it is, — enough not to want to increase their numbers any more. Even in Moscow, the dreamers of Panslavism, with the exception of a very few utopists, do not let their dreams carry them farther than a sort of " patronate " to be extended to the southern Slavs, a sort of Slavic hegemony ; and even this suzerainty may encounter opposition from the most devoted of the kindred peoples.

As far back as we can trace the past, we find the Slavs divided into two principal groups, which historical influences were to impel to fatal antagonism. In the east, towards the Dniepr, were the eastern Slavs, from whom, along with the Russians, the southern Slavs appear to have sprung : Bulgars, Serbs, Croats, Slovens.⁶ In the west, on the Visla and the Elb, are the west-

---

⁶ The Bulgars were originally a Turanian tribe that lived on the Volga, towards its lower course, and it is very likely that the river Ra took its

ern Slavs : the Liakhs, Poles, Tchekhs, Slovacks, with others, since destroyed or absorbed by the Germans ; a survival of these still confronts us in the Vends of Saxon and Prussian Lausitz. The geographical situation of each of these tribes determined their history and made enemies out of the two chief ones.   In the west the western Slavs were met by the influence of Rome ; in the east the eastern Slavs encountered that of Byzance ; hence the antagonism which, for centuries, has kept the two greatest Slavic nations in strife with each other.   The bond of a common origin and affinity of language was severed by that which most binds men—religion, writing, calendar,—by the very elements of civilization.   Hence, between Russian and Pole, a firmly rooted hostility, moral as well as material,—a struggle which, after all but annihilating the one, cost the other its life, as though, from the Karpathians to the Ural, on that immense, smooth and even area, there were no room for two distinct states.

Between these two main branches of Slavs, south of the Baltic Finns, there appears in the northwest, on the Niémen and the Dvina, a strange group, of incontestably Indo-European origin, yet quite isolated amidst the peoples of Europe, linked on to the Slavs, yet forming rather a parallel branch than a twig of the Slavic branch :—this group is the Letto-Lithuanian.

Relegated in the north, shut in by marshy forests, pressed upon closely by powerful neighbors, the Lithuanian group was closed to any outer influences, be it from the East or West.   Of all the peoples of Europe, this was the last to accept Christianity,

modern name from them.   They became considerably aryanized in the course of time, and migrated southwards, and turned up in the Balkan Peninsula—in Ancient Thracia—as a Slavic tribe.   But after the Turkish conquest, contact with their Turanian masters restored them in a great measure to their original race-affinities, and now the most cursory glance at a group of Bulgarian peasants shows that they have far more Turkish than Slavic blood.   Heavy and stolid in looks and mind, they are strikingly unlike the other members of the family, of which, however, they are admitted to be a branch.   And the race bond alone would hardly be very strong but for their common Orthodox Christianity.

and to this day its languages are, of all European tongues, the nearest to Sanskrit. No human family had so few migrations ; none ever occupied so compact a territory, and none ever was so cut and slashed into bits by conquests and by religions. Wedged tight between more races stronger in numbers which gradually drove them back, the Letto-Lithuanians, at the present time, are reduced to scarcely three million souls, speaking three languages : Lithuanian, Samogit, and Lett. They are divided between two states, Russia and Germany, not to mention the whilom kingdom of Poland, of which they occupy the northeast. Wrangled over by three nations—the Germans, the Poles, the Russians,—who by turns obtained a footing in their country, they accepted the religions of all three, some becoming Protestants, some Catholics, and some Orthodox. Their two principal groups, the Letts and Lithuanians, have gone through experiences sufficiently opposed to answer to all these contrasts.

The Lithuanian element, as the strongest in numbers, has for a long time played a considerable part between Russia and Poland ; indeed at one time, under the Yagellons, it was on the point of seizing on the leadership of the entire Slavic world. After four centuries of union with Poland, never, however, culminating in fusion,—after being aggrandized at the expense of old Russian principalities, the country that had its name from the Lithuanians was annexed to Russia at the time of the dismemberment of Poland, and became, between these two countries, the permanent object of an historical contest which was the chief obstacle to a reconciliation. Mixed with the Poles and Russians, who both threaten them with absorption, the Lithuanians and the Samogits, their brethren by race and language, still number in old Lithuania nigh on two million souls, mostly Catholics ; they constitute a majority of the population in the Governments of Vilna and Kovno. Hard by, in Prussia, a group of 200,000 Lithuanians still subsists. They are the representatives of the ancient population of East Prussia,—a country that has its name from a peo-

ple of the same race (Bo-russians, Po-russians),[1] and preserved its
language up to the seventeenth century. The second now living
group of this family, the Letts, possibly crossed with Finns,
amounts to quite a million souls. They form the majority in
Curland, and the southern half of Livonia. They were subjugated, made serfs of, and converted by the German Knights-
Sword-bearers, and became Protestants along with their German
lords. Like the Finn tribes who dwell out of Finland, the Letts
and Lithuanians, from their scant numbers and division into small
fragments, are incapable, by themselves, of forming a nation, a
state.

It is from the upper course of the Dniepr and the Dvina, near
the watershed which divides the waters between the Baltic, the
Caspian, and the Black Seas, that those Slavs went forth who were
to become the cement of the great race fated to rule within the
area bordered by the three seas. Slowly they advanced along the
rivers from west to east, radiating northward and southward ;
they pushed on into the very hearts of forests, driving before
them the Finn tribes, or cutting them asunder into isolated patches
to be absorbed at leisure by and by. Out of the mingling of the
two races, the ruder one being assimilated by the more cultivated
one, under the twofold action of a common religion and common
surroundings, tending to lead both to unity, sprang new people,
an homogeneous nation. For, contrary to certain prejudices,
there are in Russia not merely races more or less amalgamated,—
there is a nation, or what, in our days, goes by the designation
of "a nationality," as compact, as united, as self-conscious as
any in the world. With all her various races, her "*allogens*" or
aliens, Russia is by no means an incoherent mass, a sort of
political conglomerate or patchwork of peoples. It is not Turkey
or Austria, it is rather France she resembles as regards national
unity. If Russia is to be compared to a mosaic, it should be to

---

[1] *Bo-russi*, probably a corruption of *Po-russi*, which would mean "(the
people) *alongside* of the Russians," *i. e.* their nearest neighbors.

one of those antique pavements the ground of which is made out of a single substance and a single color, the border alone showing different pieces and colours. Most of these populations of alien origin are relegated to the extremities, and form around Russia, especially towards the east and west, a sort of belt, of uneven width and density. The centre is entirely filled with a nationality endowed with the twofold property of absorbing and expanding, in the midst of which vanish a few meagre German colonies or insignificant Finn or Tatar patches, devoid of cohesion or national bond.

In the interior of *this* Russia, instead of dissimilarities and contrasts, what strikes the traveller, is the uniformity of the population and the monotony of their lives. This uniformity, which civilization tends to spread everywhere, is found in Russia in a higher degree than in any people of Europe. Language, from end to end of the empire, has fewer dialects and *patois*, fewer fluctuations and gradings off of shadings, than most Western languages have on a far smaller area. The cities are all alike ; so are the peasants, in looks, in habits, in mode of life. In no country do people resemble one another more ; no other country is so free from that provincial complexity, those oppositions in type and character, which even yet we encounter in Italy and Spain, in France and Germany. The nation is made in the likeness of the country : it shows the same unity, we might say the same monotony, as the plains on which it dwells.

Yet there are in the nation, as in the soil, two principal types, almost two peoples, speaking two dialects, different and most clearly separate even in their mutual resemblance : they are the " Great-Russians " and the " Little-Russians.'' By their qualities as by their defects they represent, in Russia, the everlasting contrast of North and South. History has done no less than nature in this direction. The Great-Russians have their principal centre in Moscow, the Little-Russians in Kief. Stretching away, the one to the northeast, the other to the southwest, these two uneven

halves of the Russian nation do not exactly correspond to the
great physical zones of Russia.   The fault lies partly with nature
herself, partly with history, which hampered the development of
the one and favored that of the other.   The steppes of the south,
open ever to invasion, have for a long time hindered the expansion
of the Little-Russian, or Maloross, who was, through centuries,
kept shut up in the basins of the Dniepr, the Bug, and the Dniestr;
while the Great-Russian, or Velikoruss, freely spreading to the
north and east, went on settling in the immense basin of the
Volga, and, after taking possession of nearly the whole of the
forest land, from west to east, from the great lakes to the Ural,
slowly turned southward, to the Black-Mould belt and the steppes,
along the Volga and the Don.

Between these two principal elements there is a third, less important one, to which history, as well as nature, has left a more
thankless part to play.   It is the Bieloruss or White-Russian,
who dwells in the governments of Mohilef, Vitebsk, Grodno,
Minsk, a region owning some of the finest forests in Russia, but
the soil of which, all cut up by marshes, is meagre and unwholesome.   More nearly connected with the Great-Russian by his
dialect, the Bieloruss has been brought nearer to the Little-
Russian by the vicissitudes of politics.   The two tribes have often
been classed together under the name of Western-Russians.
Early subjected to the rule of Lithuania, whose dialect became
her official language, White-Russia, like the greater part of Little-
Russia, was joined to Poland, and remained, through centuries,
the stakes for which the Polish Commonwealth and the Moscovite
Tsars played a game from the effects of which she still bleeds.
Of the three Russian tribes, this is certainly the one whose blood
is purest ; nevertheless it has always been the poorest and least
advanced in civilization.

The White-Russians number about four million souls, the
Little-Russians seventeen to eighteen, the Great-Russians forty-
seven to forty-eight millions, which means that these alone, by

themselves, amount to about half the entire population of the European portion of the empire.

The Great-Russians constitute the most vigorous and expansive element of the Russian nation ; but it is the most mixed. The Finnic blood shows most in their features, the Tatar rule in their character. Before the Románofs were raised to the throne, this element, all alone, formed the empire of the Moscovite Tsars ; also, they assumed the title of sovereigns "of all the Russias" long before Alexis, the father of Peter the Great, began, by annexing Ukraïna, to have some claim to the title. Hence the Great-Russian has, under the name of Moscovite, been held by sundry foreigners to be the true, the only Russian. The name is a misnomer. The Great-Russian, the product of the colonization of Central Russia by the Western - Russians prior to the Tatar invasion, is anterior to the state and even the city of Moscow. If out of it did emerge the Moscovite autocracy, still it is impossible to sever the bonds which unite to it the great Slavic Commonwealth of the West, the name of which has remained a symbol of activity and liberty, Nòvgorod the Great.

The least Slavic of all the peoples who claim the name, the Great-Russian * has been the great colonizer of the Slavic race. His enemies call him Turanian, Mongol, Asiatic ; but, in point of fact, he, like the other Russians, had his starting-point in the West,— *i. e.* in Little-Russia, White-Russia, and Nòvgorod. He marched from Europe towards Asia. It is from the banks of the Dvina and the Dniepr that he started on that gigantic Odyssey which was, in the course of five or six centuries, to take him beyond the Ural, beyond the Caspian and the Caucasus. We have a good

---

* Yet the peasantry of the central governments, born tradesmen and industrials, are considered to present an Indo-European type of a handsome and noble order, with eyes blue, gray, or hazel, hair dark blond or light chestnut, and beard always a shade or two lighter, and uncommonly white skins. The children are absolutely ·rosy wherever their bodies are exposed to the air.

presentment of the Great-Russian's destiny and route in the river whose downward course he followed, from source to mouth. The Volga has traced out his itinerary for him ; like the Volga, he flowed from Europe to Asia. When with Ivan III. and Ivan IV., and, later, with Peter the Great, he turned his face aggressively towards the Baltic and the West, he merely went back to his source, seeking for his European basis of yore.[9] His entire history has been one long struggle against Asia ; his conquests enlarged Europe, every one. Though so long the vassal of the Tatar khans, the Asiatic sway never made him forgetful of his European origin, and in the farthest corner of Moscovia the very name "Asiatic," "Asiat," is even still an insult in the ear of the peasant.

Having won the victory over Asia, the Great-Russian could not traverse the space of six centuries, nor the distance from the Dniepr to the Ural without adopting by the way more than one trait, both moral and physical, of the populations assimilated or subjugated by him. These influences have left him a something harsher, but also more robust, than the gifts the other Slavs are endowed with. He has less spirit of independence, less pride, less individuality ; but these qualities are made up to him by greater patience, unity of views, consistency. According to a remark made by Herzen, the Great-Russian, if, in getting crossed with more ponderous races, he has lost some of the lightness peculiar to pure Slavic blood, has also lost some of the mercurial mobility which has become fatal to other Slavic tribes. The extreme Slavic ductility has been corrected by foreign alloy. In its fusion with the Tatar copper or the Finnic lead, the Russian metal has gained more in

[9] It should be remembered that Nòvgorod was a member of the Hansa, and that Anne, a daughter of Yaroslav the Great and granddaughter of Vladímir of Kief, of Christian and epic memory, was wife of Henri I. King of France, one of the first Capetians. These two facts imply a good deal of mutual knowledge and congeniality, as well as pretty regular and frequent intercourse.

solidity than it has lost in purity. It is perhaps owing to this cross that the Great-Russian has distanced all his rivals and become the nucleus of the greatest empire in the world. The triumph of such mixed blood in certain tribes over competitors more free from mis-alliances, far from being an anomaly, is on the contrary a phenomenon frequently recurring in history. These peoples, sprung from various races, make up in vigor for what they lack in delicacy. Thus Prussia in Germany, Piedmont in Italy, have given to the two countries the unity they could not derive from less mixed national elements and, in ancient times, Macedon and Rome herself have yielded analogous examples.

For being crossed with Finn or Tatar blood, the Great-Russians have not themselves become either Finns or Tatars ; for not being of pure Indo-European race, they are not Turanians. Language and bringing up do not constitute their only claim to the name of Slavs. The Russian of Great-Russia is not a Slav merely in the way that the French and Spaniards are Latins—by traditions and civilization, by adoption so to speak ; he is Slav by direct filiation. A notable portion of the blood in his veins is Slavic. The proportion is difficult, or rather impossible, to specify ; it varies according to the regions, to the classes, which have long ago formed themselves into more or less closed castes. It is larger in the regions more anciently colonized, such as the banks of rivers along which the Slavs formerly advanced. At times, when journeying from the banks of rivers into the interior, we pass from a type almost entirely Slavic to one almost entirely Finnic until we come to barely russified Finns who, while losing their language, have preserved their garb and customs. The portion of Slavic blood in the mass of the nation is nevertheless very considerable, if not predominant. The same arguments which demonstrate a Finnic alloy in the Great-Russian also show us that he is Slav at bottom.

Great-Russia was not subdued by the Slavs of Nòvgorod and Kief in a few brief military expeditions. It was not a conquest, a mere armed occupation, with no more important revulsion than a change of dynasty or landlords ; it was a long, slow immigration, a sort of scarcely perceptible infiltration of the Slavic element, that went on for centuries, almost escaping the notice of contemporary annalists, and only guessed at by history, and that not with sufficient precision to mark off the stages. There is nothing to compare with this in the West. The colonization of Great-Russia by the western Russians must have been something very like what is going on even now in the half-desert provinces of the east and south. We cannot picture to ourselves the forests of the north, in the Finnic period, being as densely peopled as those of Gaul or even Germany, before the Roman wars. The climate, soil, mode of life of these frequently still half-nomadic populations are opposed to such an idea. The little resistance met by the Russian invasion also bears witness to the small numbers of the natives. It is the same with the physical and moral differences which we can note among the few Finns still scattered on Russian soil. So great a diversity among manifestly kindred tribes must have been anterior to the Slavic colonization and proves the dispersion and extreme parcelling of the native tribes. It was easy for the Slavs to settle in the midst of these scattered tribes, more than one of which probably owed them its concentration into a comparatively compact group. Possibly even, the russification of the Finns did not proceed on a large scale until these tribes, packed close by pressure from the new arrivals, were closely encompassed on all sides by them.

It should not be forgotten, moreover, that mingling of blood is not the only way in which two hostile races react upon one another. Their mere coming into contact on the same soil, even without armed strife, is frequently sufficient to cause the decrease of one to the advantage of the other. This phenomenon so strikingly illustrated in our time in America and Australia by what followed on the coming of the Europeans, appears to have taken place in Europe itself, in prehistoric times, when the primeval populations began to vanish before the Indo-European race. Is it not probable that in Russia the Slavic, *i. e.* the Indo-European blood, may have had the same advantage over Turanian blood that it had in the other parts of Europe? Although we have, unfortunately, no statistical data on the subject, some observers assert that, at this very day, the Finn population tends to diminish in numbers wherever it is placed in direct contact with a Russian population, and that too, independently of intermarriages, very rare between Finns and Russians, independently of all mixture, from the mere fact of vicinity. Could not the mysterious laws of the "*struggle for life*" have acted in a more perceptible manner when, instead of Russians already crossed with them, the Finns found themselves face to face with Slavs of purer blood?

Tradition equally bears out the Great-Russian's claim to the name of Slav. Indeed, language is not the only link that connects him with the Slav family, and, through that, with the other nations of Europe; the chief link consists in his folk-lore; popular stories and songs, chips of mythology and still living beliefs and superstitions,—all documents that cannot be ignored when the genealogy of a people is inquired into. A noticeable fact is that it is in the north, in regions incontestably Finnic, on the shores of Lake Onèga for instance, that modern scholars have collected the largest numbers of tales and ballads in prose or verse—*skàzkas* and *bylínas*,[10]—although the farther the Russian Slav penetrated into the northern forests, the more careful he was to take along with him his family titles.*

---

[10] The *y* in this word, as in *Kalmỳk*(Kalmùk)is an attempt to approximate an untranscribable Slavic sound which comes nearest to *we;* so that *bylina*, *Kalmyk*, would read something like *bwelina*, *Kalmweek*, with the *w* much weakened. *Bylina* literally means "something that has been," while *skàzka*, from *skazàti*, "to tell," answers exactly to "tale" or the Latin equivalent, "legend."

* On this subject, which has given rise to so many controversies, see, apart from Russian writers: Mr. Ralston, *Russian Folk Tales*, and *Songs of the Russian People;* M. A. Rambaud, *La Russie Épique;* and M. A. De Gubernatis, in his *Zoölogical Mythology.*

The upshot of all this is that, on the plains of the Upper Volga and the Okà, heterogeneous, scattered, and loosely constituted tribes somehow congregated, and, out of all these bits and patches, a compact whole was formed, the various elements of which, associated before fusion, are still recognizable ; just as in granite, quartz, feldspath, and mica, mixed without being assimilated, together form one of the hardest substances in existence. Thus it is that in the Russian people, especially the Great-Russian, various national elements often are discernible to the eye : they are as yet in the aggregate stage ; the physiological fusion, begun centuries ago, is not completed yet ; the moral and political fusion, the only one that matters to a nation's constitution, has been beforehand with it. In certain senses the national type is still being elaborated and in what may be called the "sketchy stage" ; but the same cannot be said of the Russian nationality, even if at times it seems less finished than that of one or other Western people : there would be no gain for it in the obliteration of traces of an origin which the people do not perceive and the causes of which are to them unknown or matter of indifference. In their greatest divergence, the populations of Russia do not show oppositions in types and colors so violent as not to yield even to centuries of race mixing,—such oppositions as entail on the American States strife and race rivalries capable of endangering their liberty and safety. In all that concerns ethnological unity as well as the physical unity of soil and clime, Russia has the advantage of the United States and still more of Brazil.

In spite of the traces of crosses which he often bears on his face, the Great-Russian maintains unbroken his community with the Caucasian race, by the external signs which most clearly characterize it : stature, color of skin, hair and eyes. His stature is more often high than low, his skin is white, his eyes are frequently blue ; his hair is mostly blond, light chestnut or auburn,— all shades which almost exclusively belong to the Caucasian or Mediterranean stock. The long, thick beard which is the pride of the peasant's heart, and which all the persecutions of Peter the Great could not induce him to cut off,[11] is in itself a sign of race, as nothing can be barer than the chin of a Mongol or a Chinese.[*]

Thus then, with regard to race as well as soil, Russia, if she does differ from the West, differs still more from old Asia ; from both points of view, she embodies the conquest of the latter by the former. The Russian people, both by blood and tradition, is directly linked to the noblest, most progressive, most intellectual family in the world, but to the branch thereof the least illustrious so far. Of the two chief ethnical elements that enter into the making of Russia, the most European—the Slavic element—is, as regards its genius, nearly as unknown to the West as the other ; what surprises the singular people issued from their fusion reserves to the future, cannot even be conjectured.

The Little-Russians (Maloross) are Russia's Southerners. It is calculated that two thirds of them have brown or dark-chestnut hair. Of purer race than their brethren of Great-Russia, located nearer to the West, they glory in their comparatively unmixed blood, their milder climate, their cheerier land. They are handsomer of countenance and taller in stature, have finer limbs and are of slighter make ; they are livelier and more alert in mind, but at the same time more changeable and more indolent, more meditative and less determined, consequently more apathetic and less enterprising. Their climate having been less of a trial to them, and Oriental despotism having sat lighter on them, the Little-Russian and White-Russian have more personal

[11] Peter never meddled with the peasants in any way. His high-handed reforms in dress and mode of life did not go beyond the nobility and the urban classes. If he could have taken in hand all classes equally, there might not be now such a chasm between "the million " and the social "upper ten thousand."

[*] If these traits, unfamiliar to the races of Upper Asia, are more or less frequently encountered in certain Finn or Tatar tribes, that presupposes alliances, in remote antiquity, between these and peoples of Caucasian stock, and this very fact brings the Russians into closer relationship with the Western Europeans.

dignity, more independence, more individuality than the Great-Russian ; their mind is less positive, more open to sentiment and fancy, more dreamy and more poetical.* All these shades of character are reproduced in the melodies and songs of both groups, in their holidays and customs, although provincial diversities are gradually dying out under the influence of the Great-Russian branch, which bids fair to assimilate the western Russians as the other populations of the empire. The contrast is still visible in family and commune, in the house and the villages of both tribes. Amidst the Little-Russians the individual is more independent, woman is freer,[12] the family is less compactly agglomerated ; the cottages have more room between them and are frequently surrounded with gardens and flowers.

These people, who were subjected to western influences under the rule of Poland, were, towards the seventeenth century, the first intermediate agents between Europe and Moscovia, to which, besides vicinity, they were attached by mutual affinities of language and religion.   Prior to Peter the Great, and partly even in

* For a knowledge of the Little-Russian songs (*piêsni*), which vie with those of Serbia for the palm of Slavic popular poetry, consult Bodenstedt, *Die Poetische Ukrain* (1845), and Rambaud, *La Russie Épique* (1876).

[12] In what way? No peasant housewife could have a position more honored, independent, masterful than the mate of the Great-Russian and northern husbandman. As among the Spartans and early Romans, she is subject and responsible only to her "man," but even he does not interfere with her house-rule and her own specially feminine branches of farming. The produce of dairy and poultry left over from home use, the surplus of her spinning and weaving, are hers to sell, and the money, by immemorial unwritten, but all the more compelling law, is awarded her as her property to hold or spend, and many a husband has received a flogging by decree of the *mir* (village assembly), for having robbed the housewife of her private hoard. And many a heifer or colt finds its way to a peasant's stable that would never have come there but for her savings—and many a log house has been roofed, and repaired, and made snug against the winter with money from the same source. The southern woman may dance and sing more in the young folk's chorus on moonlight nights on the broad village street, and sport more many-colored ribbons and gay silk kerchiefs, and be freer of talk and manner with the village swells, but hardly to the increase of her dignity and moral worth.

his reign, it was chiefly through their instrumentality that Europe exerted her influence over Moscow and Russia.

To Little-Russia belonged the Zaporògs, the most famous of those Cosack tribes which played so prominent a part between Poland, the Tatars, and the Turks, in the Ukraïna or southern steppes, and whose name will ever be to Russians the symbol of free and independent life. *Kazàtchestvo*—Cosackdom—with its liberal or democratical traditions, is to this day the more or less conscious, more or less avowed ideal of a great many Little-Russians. Another thing, also connected with the history of Ukraïna, the foreign descent or denationalization of a great portion of the upper classes, half Polish and half Great-Russian, equally favors democratic instincts in the Little-Russian people. For this twofold reason, the Little-Russian is perhaps less impervious to political aspirations, and consequently more open to revolutionary blandishments than his brother of Great-Russia.*

Of the Cosacks of our day, those of the Black Sea, transferred to the Kuban between the Azof Sea and the Caucasus, are alone Little-Russians ; those of the Don and Ural are Great-Russians. To the seventeen or eighteen millions of Little-Russians residing in Russia, should be added, on ethnological grounds, about three millions more, dwelling in Austria, on both sides of the Karpathian Mountains, in Eastern Galicia, formerly " Red-Russia," in Bukovine, and in the " comitats " of Northern Hungary.

The claim of the Little-Russians to the name and quality of Russians has been contested, as well as that of the White-Russians,—virtually one third of the Russian people. In order to separate them from the Great-Russians, different national designations have been sought out for them. At one time the name of " Russian " would be reserved for the Great-Russian, and the others would be given the Latin name of " Ruthenes," or the

---

* This seems to be borne out by several political trials that took place between 1879 and 1888, and in which several Ukraïna peasants were implicated.

Hungarian one of "Russniàk," both of which are merely a transcription and synonym of the name they were to supplant. At another time the title of "Russian" would be reserved for the Slavs of Little-Russia and White-Russia, the first centres of the empire ruled by the descendants of Rurik, while it would be denied to Great-Russia, on which was inflicted the name of "Moscovia." These bickerings on words, gotten up not by Little-Russians, but by Poles, in no wise alter the facts. Their only effect was to keep up between luckless Poland and Russia irreconcilable pretensions, which have brought the stronger nation to ignore the nationality of the weaker, as Poland once had ignored that of her Russian subjects. Suffice it here to establish the fact that these designations : "Ruthene," "Russniàk," "Russin," like those of "Russ" and "Russian," used indifferently and interchangeably by old writers and old travellers, are at bottom merely forms of the same name, designating the same nationality at least within the limits of the empire.*

Separated from Great-Russia at the time of the Tatar invasion Little-Russia was through five centuries subject to Poland and Lithuania, not to much purpose. Only the polished surface,— the nobility of Kief, Volhynia, Podolia, became polonized.† It is

* Nowadays these different terms, particularly that of "Ruthene," ordinarily applied to Uniats, have assumed a more definite sense. Besides, the Little-Russians are divided into three distinct types with as many principal dialects : that of the plain of Ukraïne, that of the "Poliéssiye" or "forest region" of Kief, and that of Galicia and Podólia.

† Russian statisticians have long ago called attention to the fact that in the provinces of the southwest—Podolia, Volhynia, Kief—usually considered as Polish by the Poles, these latter are in reality numerically inferior to the Jews. The same observation applies to Lithuania and White-Russia, *i. e.* to all the provinces annexed in one of the three divisions of Poland. According to Mr. Tchubinsky, who has published some very detailed statistical tables on this very subject, the Poles could not muster 100,000 strong in the above three governments put together. Even allowing for some exaggeration in the Russian documents, still so much remains—that the figure of the genuinely Polish population is extremely low. In those three governments, the number of the Catholics, among whom there certainly are non-polonized Little-Russians, amounted to scarcely 400,000,—or less

owing pre-eminently to the Greek Orthodox rite that the bulk of the people, the immense majority of the inhabitants of Kief and Ukraïna have turned out quite as Russian as the people of Moscow. It matters little that the Little-Russian idiom deserves the title of language rather than that of dialect; such was the case with the Provençal in France;—it matters little even that the people of Little-Russia and Ukraïna are entitled to be considered as a nation or a distinct nationality. This question, ardently discussed by scholars as well as by Ukraïnophil patriots, is one of those which should not be settled with the assistance of ethnological or linguistical arguments, for nationality does not really reside in race any more than in language, but in a people's consciousness. What admits of no doubt whatever is that, in the eyes of Western Europe, the Little-Russian is as much a Russian as the Great-Russian.

If a few thinkers, such as the poet Shevtchènko * and the Ukraïnophils, have been suspected of a wish to erect Little-Russia into a nation, independent of both Russia and Poland, to resume the projects of Khmelnitsky and Mazeppa, such dreams found not much more echo among the Little-Russians than, in 1870–71, the projects of a southern league met with in the south of France. The contemporary writers, natives of Little-Russia, are almost unanimous in discountenancing any leaning towards secession, and the most renowned of them, Kostomárof, severely condemns Mazeppa, the last statesman who seriously undertook to separate Ukraïna from Russia. Ukraïnophilism and the Little-Russian poets are scarcely more dangerous to Russia than are to France's

than a seventh of the entire population (16.94 per cent.). In these same three governments, on the contrary, the number of the Israelites rose to over 750,000, nearly double that of the Catholics. See *Labors of the Ethnographico-Statistical Expedition; Materials and Investigations,* by P. Tchubinsky, vol. vii., pp. 272–290.

* On Shevtchènko, orginally a serf, then by turns footman and soldier, painter and poet, the reader might look up an interesting study by M. Durand, in the *Revue des Deux Mondes,* of June 15, 1876.

unity the revival of a Provençal literature, and those "*félibres*" of the south in whose language an over-fastidious police might easily detect more than one imprudent expression.   Even among their partisans the tendencies accused of separatism are mostly limited to wishes for decentralization and provincial autonomy, to regrets about the suppression, by Peter the Great and Catherine II., of ancient franchises, to a feeling of repulsion towards the bureaucracy imported from Moscow and Petersburgh.   The most determined of Ukraïnophils do not go beyond federalistic dreams, and the assertion that federalism can alone give satisfaction to the numerous peoples of alien origin scattered over the vast empire.*   At all events, the obstacles blunderingly thrown by the authorities in the way of the diffusion of Little-Russian literature and press, even of the use of a dialect which alone is understood by the people, are not exactly calculated to stifle in the Little-Russian's heart the hankering after autonomy which it is expected to destroy in the germ by such means.

It is a notable portion of the national genius that Russian censure dooms to silence and obscurity by the proscription of an idiom spoken by more mouths than Serb and Bulgar put together ; a notable portion of the Russian people, perhaps the best gifted for art and poetry, that Petersburgh bureaucracy deprives of all means of expression, all means of instruction.   In Russia less than anywhere else, spirits scornful of languages restricted within narrow bounds and provincial dialects should indulge in any illusions ; popular speech, doomed to perish in the course of time, does not suffer itself to be evicted in a few years ; it is easier to forbid the use of it by ordinances and decrees than to substitute for it in daily practice the official literary language.   In the interval, the hand which, under pretence of opening to them a wider window on the world, closes the humble transom through which

---

' * See especially *Hromáda* of Mr. Dragománof and, by the same author, *Historical Poland and Great-Russian Democracy*, Geneva, 1882.

light could reach them, consigns to ignorance millions of human creatures.

The differences in race, dialect, character, which distinguish the two chief Russian tribes, are not greater than those which exist between the north and south of the Western states whose unity, whether ancient or recent, is best assured. As to the race itself in the name of which certain ethnologists pretend to separate them, there is far less distance between the Russian tribes than is commonly imagined. If the Great-Russian has been mixed more with Finns, the Little-Russian perhaps mixed more with Tatars, of whom his princes at Kief received and sheltered whole tribes, while his Cosacks of the steppes recruited from among them numbers of fugitives and comrades for their life of adventure. Far from being naturally antagonistic to each other, the Little-Russian and the Great-Russian have much in common : geography, which would hardly allow of the weaker party having a separate existence ; historical traditions and antipathies, common to both ; religion, still regarded by both as the foremost power of all ; and lastly, the twofold kinship of language and origin. They mutually complete each other, and lend their common country that complex character and genius, which, when enfolded in unity, has made the greatness of all the great nations in history.

BOOK II. CHAPTER V.

THE Russian nation, including even the Little-Russians and White-Russians, occupies the interior of the empire, but does not begin to fill out the frame.   On no side, unless it be the Black and White Seas, and unless we take the Ukraïnians skirting Eastern Galicia, does the Russian people reach the limits of Russia.   On nearly all its frontiers, it is encompassed by populations of alien origin, divided into two principal bands : one in the east, towards Asia, composed of Finns, Bashkirs, Tatars, Kirghiz, Kalmyks ; the other, more considerable but not more homogeneous, in the west, facing Europe, along the most vulnerable flank line of Russia, the only one on which she confines with powerful neighbors.   At certain times the government at St. Petersburgh may well find there material for weighty and apprehensive thought.

It is to be noted that the main element of the nation—the nucleus of it—the Great-Russian—comes into actual contact with these western populations on one point only, and that the least exposed, the shore of the Gulf of Finland, by a region, moreover, that counts among the poorest and least peopled.   In the centre and south, between ancient Moscovia and the conquests of Peter the Great and Catherine II., between Great-Russia on one side and Livonia, Lithuania, Poland, on the other, lie White-Russia and Little-Russia, which being, as one might say, Russian only in the second degree are far less proper to russify others. This inconvenience is increased by the scantiness of the population in White-Russia and the swamps of Pinsk in the region bordering on Little-Russia. These two districts have dug, between the best-peopled regions of old Moscovia and her conquests of the last two centuries, a sort of half-desert gulf, which, in spite of the fine draining works going on in the marshes of the Prípet,* cannot possibly fill rapidly. The Poles, Lithuanians, Letts, and Germans of the west thus find themselves protected against russification by a double barrier ; and this accounts for the trifling progress it makes. The same phenomenon can be explained by still another consideration. Population, like water, naturally inclines towards a vacuum and finds its own level. So it is towards the east and Asia, not towards the west and Europe—towards the oriental regions, insufficiently peopled as yet, and not towards provinces peopled frequently more densely than the interior of the empire, that the surplus of Russian population naturally flows.

With sixty-eight or seventy millions of Russians, it is no very great thing to have some fourteen or fifteen millions non-russified, which is all that European Russia has to show, outside of Finland, Poland, and the Caucasus,—those being, moreover, divided into over ten peoples and nearly as many languages and religions. If we take in the kingdom of Poland and Finland, the figure will mount up to twenty-four or twenty-five millions, and to three or four more if we add thereto that Babel—the Caucasus, which should rather be considered as a colony, and which, alone, numbers about as many peoples and tribes as all the rest of the empire.† All these populations are for the most part too weak,

---

* The works carried out in this region constitute one of the finest undertakings of the kind in Europe. In 1889 a good deal over two million acres had been already drained.

† According to Mr. Rittich, the population of the Caucasus, even prior to the annexations sanctioned by the treaty of Berlin, was divided into twelve principal groups, speaking sixty-eight different dialects.

too fragmentary, to have any claim to independence ; they will let themselves be assimilated by the mere force of progressing civilization, everywhere unfavorable to small tribes and shut-in languages. Many of these *allogens* (aliens), as the Finns of the interior or the Gruzins (commonly called Georgians) of Transcaucasia, are nearly as devoted to the Tsar as his natural-born Russian subjects. Others, such as the two million Ehsts and Letts of the Baltic provinces, find in the Russian government a protection against the aristocratical oligarchy and the burgher arrogance of 160,000 Germans. These latter and their kindred of the interior are urged by self-interest, in spite of enticements from abroad, to remain subjects of a state in which, notwithstanding their scant numbers, they occupy so ample a place ; where, thanks to the antiquity of their civilization, thanks to certain Teutonic qualities—a taste for work, the spirit of order and exactness,—thanks also to comradeship, worldly connections, and influences at court, they have for a long time filled the high posts of the military and civil careers, so that, in the vast Slavic Empire, the Germans, until very lately, appeared to be the privileged race.*

* The proportion of Germans goes on increasing progressively from the lower to the highest charges, both civil and military. It is notorious how Alexander III., then heir to the crown, at a reception of the highest staff officers, after several generals with German names had been presented to him, exclaimed, " At last !" at the first Russian name he heard. Yet there have been stories current about the antipathy of the future Alexander III. and his wife against the Germans, which got some Frenchmen, who took them literally, into sad trouble. Thus once, at an official dinner, the then French ambassador having thanked the Cesarévitch for the sympathy he had shown France in the war of 1870–71, the latter turned his back on him without vouchsafing a word in reply.[1]

[1] There is a very popular story, illustrative of this galling state of things, about General Yermolof, one of the heroes of the now epic war against Shamil and his fanatical robber tribes of the Caucasus,—a blunt old warrior, as notorious for plain speaking as for bravery and military genius. It is said that the Emperor Alexander II. received him at a private audience, to congratulate him on a victory which prepared the final one by which Prince Bariàtinsky, another Theseus, freed Russia from the annual blood tribute which she had been paying for half a century to the murderous

This sort of supremacy, which the Germans exert both in private and public life, cannot but excite in the Russians feelings of distrust and jealousy which, at times, break out into loud protest. The national feeling rebels against the sway of the Germans, accused as they are of forming in the administration as well as in business a sort of corporation, the members of which support one another at the cost of the state and of private persons.' In Petersburgh, and especially in Moscow, the periodical press continuously

---

' There are sundry trades and professions of which the Germans have appropriated the monopoly, which they guard as fiercely as though it had been legally bestowed on them. Twenty years ago the bakers and the apothecaries (druggists and pharmacists) were all German, and that all over the country. It was impossible for a Russian to get into a bakery as apprentice or even errand boy. At last an enterprising Moscow man started in Petersburgh, in a fashionable quarter, a "Moscow bakery." The venture was a success, the number of "Russian bakeries" and "Moscow bakeries" increased rapidly—at first in the two capitals—till it rivalled that of the German ones. This was partly, of course, a "demonstration," but what made the success a permanent one, is the fact that there are some special kinds of plain and fancy breads, thoroughly national in quality and shape, which the Germans never could produce, and which, until this popular movement was started, could be got only from itinerant sellers or at open-air stands in the more populous commercial quarters. The pharmacists' "ring" was more difficult to break. On no consideration whatever could a Russian obtain access to a prescription counter or laboratory. I have personally known young men of good family, university graduates, having brilliantly passed all the examinations required by the law of pharmacists' assistants ("provisors") whose continuous efforts were met with as continuous defeats, till they were forced into some other work than that for which they had spent their youth preparing themselves. When I left, eighteen years ago, one Russian drug store had just been started, and the success was still uncertain.

Minotaurs of the mountain labyrinth. Alexander was a kind man and a generous master, and the thanks and praise he bestowed on his faithful old servant were meted out unstintingly, winding up with the command to select any favour within the power of the imperial hand to bestow. Whereupon the General is reported to have replied that his gracious sovereign's bounty had left him nothing to wish for—"Unless," bethinking himself of a crowning boon—"Unless it might be your Majesty's pleasure to promote me into a German!" The point of the story is greatly sharpened by the fact that the first half of the General's career had been one long struggle against German *esprit de corps* and nepotism. Whether the thing occurred just so or not—who shall tell? At all events it is eminently a case of "*se non è vero, è ben trovato.*"

stimulates Russia to throw off the political and economical yoke of the *niémets**—a yoke the weight of which certain patriots very greatly exaggerate, and which they seem as unable to shake off entirely as to bear it patiently. To the twofold jarring produced by individual self-love and by national pride, is added the antipathy in both mind and character which of yore exists between the Slav and the Teuton. This secular antipathy has repeatedly manifested itself in Russian society, especially since the treaty of Berlin, in rather curious ways : by more or less malicious jeers at the Teutonic accent and manners, in petty, often puerile, taunts, by affecting a more or less sincere contempt for the arts, literature, and products of Germany—affecting indeed to be ignorant of the German language or purposely disfiguring it, so that it came to pass that I, a Frenchman, more than once took up the cudgels in defence of the conquerors of Alsace-Lorraine against their neighbors, the Russians.

This repulsion against the Germans, which breaks out in periodical spells, might appear excessive and ridiculous, were it not justified by the political apprehensions aroused by the resurrection of the German Empire and the invasive propensities of the Germanic race. Had Alexander II. followed the national instinct and shared the preferences of his subjects, he should not have congratulated his uncle, Wilhelm, on the battle of Sedan, nor should he have connived at the mutilation of France. In unprejudiced eyes, Germany is assuredly more dangerous to Russia than to France. In France's case, indeed, the empire of the Hohenzollerns encounters a compact nationality, difficult to break into, offering no handle to Teutonic assimilation. The same cannot be said of the east of Europe, where Germany, jointly with Prussia, has been steadily aggrandizing itself, century after century. Now, the Russians don't care to see their Western neighbor carry on at their expense on the Visla, the Niémen. or the

---

* *Niémets* originally means "dumb," one who cannot speak ; therefore "a foreigner," a German.

Dvina, his secular encroachments on territory belonging to the Slavs or to the Letto-Lithuanians.

There are no German provinces in the Russian Empire. This designation, often used by the Germans and even by the French, as applied to the three Baltic provinces, is absolutely incorrect, and it is easy to understand why the Russians will decidedly not tolerate the misnomer. Statistics have long ago established the fact that, in these pretended "German" provinces—Livonia or Liefland, Esthonia or Esthland, and Curland,—the Germans do not, in reality, make out one tenth of the population, the immense majority of which consists of Letts in the south and Finns in the north. The modern principle of nationality, which, by the way, when not grounded in national consciousness, merely furnishes a novel instrument of oppression, supplies, from this side, no pretence for the clamoring for restitution kept up by the Germans. But neither numbers, nor race, nor language are everything in a country. It matters little that the Germans, on the lower course of the Dvina, constitute a minority amounting to a minimum; they have ruled the land too long by force of arms, by trade, by religion, by all that goes to make up civilization, not to have impressed their stamp on it.

The mark of the Hansa is discernible everywhere in the cities, and that of feudal Germany everywhere in the country, owned by the heirs of the "Sword-bearers." Take it all in all—manners, history, traditions—the Baltic country is far more German than was Alsace-Lorraine in 1870. It might even be said without paradox, that these Russian provinces, peopled by Letts and Finns, were the most German country on the continent, so largely had mediæval Germany survived there.

It is but natural that the Russian government, who has ruled them for the last two centuries, should seek to de-germanize and to modernize its Baltic provinces, in spite of charters or privileges granted to the Lieflanders by Peter the Great on the occasion of their annexation. It is but natural that, in order to diminish the

German preponderance, Petersburgh and Moscow should call in the aid of the former Finn or Lett serf; but such an undertaking everywhere requires more than average prudence, patience, moderation.

The German spirit and moral influence are too deeply rooted in the soil to allow of easy eradication, nor can a country's attachment be obtained without taking into account its customs and traditions.   Were it to follow all the inspirations of ultra-zealous russifiers, the Russian government, on the plea of assimilating the Baltic country, would run the risk of alienating it, nay, of creating in it a separatist party, by irritating the ruling classes, and those German-Russians whose allegiance to the Tsars has always been untainted and who, from Barclay-de-Tolly down to Totleben, and from Ostermann to Nesselrode, have furnished more than one illustrious general or distinguished statesman.[1]   On the Dvina, just as on the Visla and on the Dniepr, the best way of securing the Russian rule is, after all, to make it mild, not to do violence to the local manners and traditions, at least in so far as they are compatible with the spirit of the age and the preservation of the empire's integrity.[*]

The Baltic provinces are not the only ones where the Russians have to keep an eye on germanism.   In reality, it is not even

---

[1] It were a great mistake to imagine that a German name is a sure index of anti-Russian feeling, or a Russian one is a sure pledge of patriotism. Men with uncompromising German names, like Hilferding, historian-archæologist; Orestes Miller, philologist and folk-lorist; Dahl, the compiler of the great national dictionary, collector of the popular proverbs and saws, are found foremost in the front ranks of Russian nationalist workers, with a moderate leaning towards slavophilism, while a Count Shuválof was a notorious contemner of all things national, and did his best to scare Alexander II. out of his fixed purpose of freeing the serfs, by conjuring up insurrections, wholesale massacres of landlords, and other like bugbears.

[*] Perhaps no question in Europe has given rise to so large a quantity of writings of all sorts as this question about the Baltic provinces, which it is impossible to enter into here with any details.   A whole library might be made up of nothing but the Russian and especially German books and pamphlets called forth by George Samarin's *Borderland of Russia.*

the *niémets* who is most to be dreaded. Curland, Liefland, and Esthland are, by their geographical position, bound to the great empire of which they occupy the coastland, and whose traffic is carried on by their seaports. Severed from Russia, the three provinces would be as good as cut off from the continent and would fall into a situation analogous to that of Austrian Dalmatia before the occupation of Bosnia and Herzegovina gave her a "background." And it is not even in the Baltic provinces that there are most Germans.

Apart from their trading colonies in the cities and from their rural agricultural colonies, also scattered from end to end of the empire, the Germans gradually filtered into the provinces confining with Prussia and Austria—into Poland, Lithuania and Little-Russia.* On many points they slowly gained possession of the soil and capital, notwithstanding the competition of the indigenous Jews, who, moreover, might, under certain circumstances, as it happened in Poznania (Posen), become their auxiliaries and smooth the way for germanization.† In the Kingdom of Poland more particularly, the Germans are already more numerous in proportion than they are in the Baltic provinces, which are regarded as their main centre.

The Polish question, so many times settled in so many contradictory ways in the course of the last century, is, in reality, lined with a German question also. The fault is, partly, the Russian policy's, which, in its dread of polonism, favored germanism, permitting Germans, until 1884, to purchase land, while denying the same privilege to Poles and Jews. "I dread the Germans less than the Poles," wrote Nicolas Miliùtin immediately after

---

* The statistics of travellers crossing the frontiers show that 30, 40, and sometimes 50,000 more Germans enter Russia every year than leave it, not counting 30 or 40,000 Austrians, part of whom are Germans.

† To prevent rural real estate passing into the hands of Germans, Alexander III. has proceeded to radical measures. By an imperial *ukàz* or decree dated 1884, foreigners are forbidden from acquiring land in the western provinces, either by purchase or even by inheritance.

the insurrection of 1863.* Miliùtin would hardly speak so to-day. The most clear-sighted patriots admit that Russia could not solve this much-vexed Polish question against both Poles and Germans, any more than the Poles can flatter themselves that it could be settled against both Russians and Germans. The Russian who insists on denationalizing the provinces on the Visla, and the Pole who declines any terms whatever with Russia, are equally in danger of working for the Prussians, who have not forgotten that they ruled in Warsaw before Russia did.

There are indeed Russians who, to see the end of this ever-lasting Polish question, would like to make over to Germany the whole of Poland proper,† or at least the half of the kingdom situated west of the Visla, reserving the right to look for a compensation from Austria or from Turkey. This would be *Finis Poloniæ* indeed ; yet, though the combination was at one time much extolled, it would not find many advocates nowadays.

Not to mention a natural repugnance to sacrificing an old Slavic land to germanism, or the difficulty of drawing a boundary line at the gates of Warsaw, or else give up this capital itself to Prussia, the Russians understand that, once the Germans are suffered to take firm footing in the heart of Poland, they must fatally yield to the temptation of gradually absorbing the whole. Warsaw would be to the Prussians merely a stopping-place. Once installed on the Visla, they could extend their greed to the rest of the kingdom, and as far as Lithuania, Esthonia, and Livonia. They could, alone or jointly with Austria, devour the whole of ancient Poland, province by province.

* Unpublished letter from N. Miliùtin to Tcherkassky, 8/20 February, 1865.

† The kingdom of Poland or " Congress Poland " (*Kongresôwka*) was, as is well known, constructed out of such portions of the ancient " Grand Duchy of Warsaw " as were awarded to Alexander I. in 1815, and by him endowed with a constitution. In the eyes of the Russians this "Congress-kingdom " alone constitutes the whole of Russian Poland. They take their stand on history and ethnography when they refuse to recognize as Polish the provinces annexed by Catherine II. at the time of the three divisions of the eighteenth century.

The Poles should dread no less than the Russians any cession to the heirs of Frederic the Great. Poland's curse is that the Poles, with all their brilliant qualities, with their noble chivalrous spirit, their generous patriotism, have always, both before and after the divisions of the eighteenth century, shown poor political spirit. Still, in this respect, their long misfortunes do not appear to have been entirely lost upon them. They have become more practical, more positive, less inclined to indulge in the vast dreams and chimerical fancies of old. Many of them have found out that, for their nationality, the Russian rule is infinitely less to be dreaded than the German, and that Warsaw cannot nurse the hope of wholly escaping both. The reunion of Russian Poland with Austrian Galicia, the day-dream of certain patriots, is a mere Utopia, which geography alone would effectually dispose of. There exists a project, put forward at times in Germany, proposing the erection of the "Congress-kingdom" into a vassal state or confederate of Germany, but it is only a piece of delusive *mirage* behind which lurks German absorption. A fifth or sixth division would be the saddest thing that could befall Poland, and her patriots surely must regret that, in 1815, France caused the propositions of Alexander I. to be rejected, and suffered Poznania (Posen) to be made over to Prussia and germanization.

When we consider what history has done with Schlesien (Silesia), Poznania, and Old Prussia, we can assert that the Russian rule is, for the Poland of the Visla, for Warsaw and Mazovia, the best, perhaps the only, possible guarantee against germanization. The Poles, in declaring themselves irreconcilable toward Russia, appear to an impartial outsider to be committing a sort of national suicide.

This is felt more and more on the banks of the Visla, and anxiety for the future prevails over old grudges. Fear of Germany balances hatred of Russia. Economic considerations too work in the same direction. From a material point of view, Poland has everything to gain from union with the great Slavic Empire, which offers immense openings to her industry. Russian Poland has greatly changed since the insurrection of 1863. She is beyond comparison wealthier than Galicia and Poznania. Agriculture has prospered. The peasant, now a landholder, has enjoyed comforts hitherto unknown to him. The cities have become crowded with factories ; Warsaw's population has been doubled, that of Lodzi and other cities quadrupled, and more, all within twenty years. The rise of tariffs, the exaggeration of which is, in our belief, one of the obstacles to the development of Russia, has been of considerable advantage to Poland, placed as that country is in better conditions for production. A great portion of the empire pays tribute to Poland's industry—itself, it is true, frequently placed in German hands. Any custom-house barrier raised between the two countries would kill the industry of the kingdom, which then would find it hard to hold out against the competition of Schlesien and Westphalia. In our day material interests are a strong chain ; and Russia, by suppressing the custom-house system between the kingdom and the empire, has, perhaps unconsciously, bound the Poles by the only tie which Polish hands would be loth to sever.

Thus the two main and often hostile springs which govern men and nations—material interests and abstract considerations—are at one in this case, to bring about the reunion to Russia of the most unmanageable among the peoples subject to her imperial sceptre. In spite of irritating memories, of the blundering attempts at russification pursued since 1864, stubbornness is no longer so deeply rooted in Polish hearts. The conciliating policy of Viélopòlsky—a policy which, unfortunately for both nations, numbered so few partisans about 1860—would now command an immense majority.*

* According to Russian statistics, the number of the Poles subject to the empire scarcely reaches six million souls. They form a large majority in the kingdom created by the Vienna Congress, where they amount to about seventy per cent. of the total population, but in the other parts of ancient Poland they constitute a feeble minority. To these genuine Poles of Polish descent must be added, in order to calculate the efficient force of "Polonism," a certain number of Lithuanians, Little-Russians, White-Russians, and even of Germans, and more or less polonized Jews.

The trouble is that in the Russian "borderlands" (*okràïny*), as in Austria, as in Turkey, these questions of nationalities are far from being as plain as they appear in theory. With the best will in the world it is frequently impossible to solve them to everybody's satisfaction. Side by side with regions held by a clearly defined nationality, possessed of continuous historical traditions, there are countries inhabited by mixed races, often openly hostile to one another. The Baltic provinces are a case in point—but by no means the only one. The greatest portion of ancient Poland, the provinces annexed to Russia at the time of the three first partitions, are more or less in a like predicament. That indeed was one of the things which made the dismemberment of the Commonwealth easy, and reconciliation between the former and the new masters of the soil very difficult to achieve.

The chief obstacle to an agreement between Russians and Poles has always been the part of Ukraïna situated on the right bank of the Dniepr, and especially Lithuania, these provinces being looked upon by the former as Russian and by the latter as Polish, the Poles taking preferably the standpoint of the wealthy and cultivated classes, the landlords or the city burghers; the Russians, instead, taking thought of the rural classes, the peasant, the manumitted serf freed by Alexander II.

In the greater portion of ancient Poland—*not* the "Congresskingdom"—as well as in the three Baltic provinces, national rivalries often are made more complicated by strife between the classes. Nationalities, and at times religions, are, in a way, disposed in layers. While the upper classes—the nobility and landlords—are Germans or Poles, by race or by tradition, the bulk of the people is Lithuanian, White-Russian (*Bieloruss*), Little-Russian (*Maloross*), not to mention the Jews who, generally addicted to trade, form an additional class and nationality too. It is easy to perceive the difficulties of such a state of things and the temptations into which it can lead those in power.

In order to check the historical nationalities, with.their old-established nobility and burgherdom, which still hold the power by virtue of wealth and education, the Russian government has been induced to seek the support of the petty rural and, so to speak, "plebeian" nationalities,* until quite lately unknown to foreigners and scarcely self-conscious. To the Swede of Finland, to the German of Liefland or Curland, to the Pole of Lithuania or Ukraïna, it opposed the Finn, the Ehst, the Lett, the Samogèt, the White- and Little-Russian, thus making use for its own ends of ethnology and the principle of nationality and turning them against its adversaries, re-kindling national feeling in populations in whose breasts it had lain extinct for ages, with the mental reservation that it might be smothered again the moment it showed inclination to encroach. This is one of the reasons for "peasant policy," called by some democratic, by others socialistic, being adopted more than once by the tsars towards subject provinces, more especially those that constituted ancient Poland. Along her western frontiers Russia had two or three Irelands, which she felt all the more tempted to deal with on the principle of agrarian law, as the landlords, through their origin or tradition, were more obnoxious to her. What Alexander II. did in Lithuania, Podolia, even in Poland, sundry patriots should like to see done again in the Baltic provinces, at the cost of the German barons, for the benefit of the Lett and Ehst peasantry.†

At a time when conflicts of nationalities and class jealousies breed so much animosity, it is easy to see how greatly the social status would be endangered by a policy that would take pleasure

* The expression belongs, unless I am mistaken, to Mr. Dragománof, in his *Historical Poland.*

† In order to appreciate the conduct of the Russian government, it must not be forgotten that, at the time of the emancipation, the whole empire was placed under agrarian laws more or less favorable to the quondam serfs. The Baltic provinces alone were exempted, because emancipation had taken place there under Alexander I., on different principles. See farther on, Book VI., Chapter. II.

in envenoming and doubling, the one by the other, two of the weightiest incentives to antagonism that can divide those that dwell on one soil. The internal difficulties under which Russia labors, and the geographical situation of the provinces exposed to such divisions, would render such a game very dangerous for the empire. Far from having any interest in nursing the passions of the various races subject to its rule, the Russian government would find it to its advantage to get them to live peaceably together. Having once taken on himself the character of protector to the lowly and weak, of patron to long-enslaved majorities, the tsar might find himself called upon to take a turn at defending, against them, powerful minorities. Nothing could be less profitable to Russia than a renewal, directed against the Germans, of the popular riots against the Jews, or the perpetration of rural wholesale risings against the Baltic barons of Liefland or the Polish *pans* (squires, lords) of Lithuania and Podolia. It matters greatly to the empire not to allow racial rivalries to degenerate into class strife, so as to offer a handle to revolutionary agitation or foreign interference. The safest course for a government as well as for a dynasty, is to arbitrate between the different nationalities and the different classes without sacrificing the ones to the others. If the task is often difficult for Russia in those of her provinces that adjoin Europe as well as on the confines of Asia, this difficulty is but the price she has to pay for her greatness.

To escape paying it, Russia would have to give up the annexations of the last two centuries, the conquests of Alexander I., Catherine II., nay, of Peter the Great himself. If, on the contrary, she wishes to strengthen her authority over the various peoples of her immense domain, her best course is, after all, to show respect of their nationality, their language, their religion, so as to take from them all incentives to discontent, leaving it to time, to reason, to their self-interest, to the natural attraction of a great country, to bind them more and more firmly to the empire.' Unfortunately for herself, Russia lacks the most potent charm of all in the eyes of modern nations—lacks the magnet most powerful to attract them—lacks liberty. And one may, without claiming a prophet's gift, venture the prediction, that only on that day she can be certain of keeping all her European borderlands— Ukraïnes—when she will have contrived to raise them to the same political level as the rest of Europe.

The Emperor Alexander III. appears to have set himself the task of russifying Poland, Lithuania, and, above all, the Baltic provinces. He has successively introduced in the Baltic country Russian administration and courts of justice,* substituting every- where—in the university, the schools, the municipalities, the courts, Russian to German.† *Hofgericht, Manngericht, Land-*

---

⁴ That is what Russia has always done and is doing all the time, following in the footsteps of Rome's wise statesmanship. Not many chapters back, our author praised the Russian government for having respected the autonomy and self-government, customs and laws, of the annexed Grand Duchy of Finland. In the same way it leaves to all its own Russian rural populations their communal self-government, based on custom-laws of immemorial eld, easily traceable, many of them, to a primeval Aryan social status, such as is revealed to us by the Veda and later, but still very ancient, Sanskrit litera- ture. As to the alien subjects, their manners, their religions are not less scrupulously respected. Thus religious teaching is an integral and obliga- tory part of the course of instruction in all public schools of every grade. But this instruction is imparted to the children and youths in their respec- tive religions, by teachers engaged and paid by the State. Should there be in a school one Hebrew boy, or one Mussulman, there will be a Rabbi or a Mollah to teach him the Thora or the Koran, and he will not be required to assist at the Greek-Orthodox catechism. In the army all allowances are made for Jewish and Moslem soldiers, that are compatible with service and discipline, in the matter of food, religious observances, and the like. In return for this more than tolerance the state surely has a right to decree that the state language shall be used in public schools, courts of justice, and government offices, understood and partly spoken by the officials of railway companies and other public servants, and that the state institutions shall be accepted by all its subjects. Otherwise where would be the state?

* The judicial organization of the empire was not enforced until 1890.

† There are exceptions, especially in favor of the rural courts where it would have been impossible to enforce the use of the Russian language ; but the exception is made in favor of the local languages, Ehst and Lett.

gericht, all these are now memories—no more.⁵ It is to be feared that, along with these Gothic institutions, may perish the self-government which was the pride and prosperity of the three provinces. Russification is everywhere carried on to the benefit of centralization. There lies the evil. Possibly, it might have been to the imperial government's advantage to proceed with greater gentleness. In its religious policy at least, it would have shown greater wisdom by acting in a more liberal spirit. It is not by wounding the consciences of her Catholic or Protestant subjects, that Russia will win their hearts.*

⁵ Perfectly right and proper. Why should mediæval survivals, denounced and swept away through all Europe, be treasured only just here where they do infinite harm by fostering a rebellious and aggressive spirit, and perpetuating oligarchical oppression under the guise of a self-government which may have been the pride and prosperity, not of the three provinces but of the small minority of aliens that rules them, much against the feeling prevailing among the native population, which gravitates steadily towards the Russian element, especially as represented by the mild, unobtrusive, uninterfering Orthodox Church. Centralization? Well, no social or political life is possible without some—without much—of it, especially where heterogeneous elements have to be welded together, and where decided centrifugal tendencies have to be counteracted. Even in a republican confederacy, what is a federal government with its one executive head but centralization? And as to gentle and gradual means, Germany in like cases shows herself neither so lenient nor so long-suffering ; she makes repression unnecessary by at once, and on principle, laying on her iron hand, *without* the velvet glove, and leaving no room for unruliness. And Germany succeeds and is approved by the world.

* See Vol. III., Book IV., Chap. III.

BOOK III.

THE NATIONAL TEMPERAMENT AND CHARACTER.

CHAPTER I.

Utility and Difficulty of Studying the National Character—Russia One of the Countries Where Material Surroundings Act Most on Man—Some Effects of the Climate—The North, and Sluggishness Brought on by Cold—Winter and the Intermittence of Labor—Lack of Liking for Physical Exertion—Habitual Insufficiency of Food; Drunkenness; Hygiene and Mortality—Cold and Uncleanliness at Home in the North —Are Northern Countries More Favorable to Morality?

IT is something to know the origin of a people and the land they inhabit. It is not much if one cannot account for the influence of nature on man. From this action of the outer world and from the people's historical or religious training results the national character. Now nations do their politics as private people transact their business, temperament being a factor as well as self-interest.

For the character of a nation, like that of a man, depends on the temperament or blood, on the physical surroundings and on the moral training, not to mention what, in an individual is contributed by age, and, in a nation, by a long course of civilization. Between these three orders of influences—race, nature, history— now one, now another, has been awarded pre-eminence in the study of nations. All three have their importance; but, nations being, even more than individuals, of mixed blood, what is most difficult to determine is the share to be allotted to race and heredity. In Russia itself discussion is rife about the character of the Great-Russian : what distinguishes him from the western Russian tribes, what must be credited to his mixing with Finns and Tatars, what to his own settling on a new land. Both causes must have acted concurrently ; but the latter, being the more persistent, must have been the more powerful. Two circumstances combined to lend it a peculiar stress. It is one of the effects of civilization to neutralize the influences of clime and soil by lifting man beyond their action. In Russia, culture being of more recent date and therefore going less deep, the bulk of the people have remained nearer to nature, more submissive to her sway. Moreover, under northern skies, the domination of climate is more absolute, its yoke more difficult to shake off. The Russian soil is no pleasant habitation, fashioned and furnished for man by nature's kindly hand ; it must be conquered with armed hand and so maintained. How, then, in such a country, with a civilization not as yet very advanced, should not nature have imprinted on both the temperament and character an indelible stamp? Thus it is that, in dealing with Russian character, a goodly proportion of defects and qualities for which race, history, religion, are usually held responsible, should be credited to physical nature.

In order to appreciate how much, we must transfer ourselves into the northern half of modern Russia, the region which has been the cradle of the Great-Russian, and formed the nucleus of ancient Moscovia. Owing to the Tatar raids, this region lies entirely north of the 50th degree of northern latitude. There, besides Nòvgorod and Pskof, the two semi-republican cities, which on all accounts deserve to be set apart, we find Tver, Yaroslàvl, Kostromà, Vladímir, Sùzdal, Riazàn—all the ancient capitals of the Russian *kniazes*,[1]—describing a sort of circle around Moscow. That part of the country is essentially continental, colder than Petersburgh, with greater extremes of climate, where the average winter temperature is from thirteen

[1] See Appendix to this Chapter, No. 1.

to fourteen degrees below that of Paris. Setting aside Scandinavia and Scotland, both warmed by the nearness of two seas, this is the only region of both hemispheres that has a sedentary, agricultural population in such close proximity to the Polar Circle. At so great a distance from any sea and from the equator, it is only thanks to its want of elevation that it is inhabitable at all.

The action of such a climate on the life and body of man must be enormous. One feels that, but it is hard to demonstrate. Within a century or two, there has been in Europe much discoursing on the political effects of climate; there are few subjects that recur more often and on which we know less. In the actual state of our knowledge we cannot even determine scientifically the direct effects of external nature on organism and temperament. Montesquieu was the first to attempt a political theory of climates; but this experiment, being based on unreliable narratives of travellers and on incomplete observations, was premature. Since the last century, science, which has shed light on so many questions, has had scarcely a ray to spare for this one.

The most general effect of cold on vegetal or animal life is to produce numbness, sometimes even suspension of the vital energies. The sap stops coursing in plants; the blood coagulates in the veins of animals. Many of the latter hibernate in a state of somnolence, and, during the very coldest months, lie down in temporary graves. Man escapes this deathlike lethargy by force of his industry and civilization as much as by his constitution, but cannot entirely withstand the sluggishness which is so general a phenomenon throughout nature.

Montesquieu made out the North to be the home of activity, courage, liberty. This theory may be correct as far as moderately cold countries are meant; but extreme cold in the North produces effects analogous to those of extreme heat in the South, so that in tropical countries the sleep of summer siestas during the hottest hours or seasons corresponds to that of hibernation in polar ones. Bracing and stimulating for lungs and general activity, as long as it keeps within certain limits, cold becomes depressing as soon as it reaches too low a degree, or lasts too long. It then disposes to a certain indolence, physical and moral, to a sort of passiveness of mind and soul. To the excitement of the first frosts succeeds the torpor brought on by intense cold. Winter like summer, the North like the South, have each its own kind of sloth ; fire in cold weather exerts the same influence as shade in hot weather, both equally invite to dawdling and idleness. The mere weight of the garments is oppressive, their length is in the way.

With all this the North has a great, an immense advantage over the South. If cold counsels rest, it by no means makes it imperative ; action is one of the remedies against it. Instead of reducing man's needs, it increases them and thereby incites to work. Moreover, the cold is rarely unendurable out-doors in the centre of Russia, in the latitude of Moscow, and even Petersburgh, or severe enough to compel Russians to burrow, like the Lapps and Esquimaux, in their huts. When the air is calm—and in very severe cold it generally is—a temperature of from 20° to 25° below freezing point is quite endurable, 10° or 12°, the average temperature of the coldest months, gives very fine, even pleasant weather, very favorable to out-door exercise. In those latitudes it is the motion of the air, the wind, and not the degrees of temperature, which produces the sensation of cold and makes it painful.

Winter has its own peculiar tasks as it has its pleasures. In Russia as everywhere else, it is the season of city life, society, festivities. In the country it is the time of freight carrying—a most important item in a country where distances are such a drawback. In summer the peasant has roads which are insufficient both in quality and quantity. In winter frost and snow construct splendid roads for him, and traffic is at once enlivened. The opening of sleighing is sometimes delayed by scarcity of snow, and that is a calamity. It is during the transition weeks between frost and thaw in spring and autumn, that the peasant is condemned to in-door life. The long winter leisure created in the North all the handicrafts on which so many villages subsist, and which in their turn gave rise to peddling and to the numerous fairs where the products of rustic industries are bartered. It is in winter that the girls and women work those drawn-work laces which are being imitated in France, and those red and blue embroidered towels—*polotèntsa*—the designs of which seem in great part borrowed from the symmetrical flower patterns traced by frost on the window panes.[2]

There is in the North, over and above the direct action of cold on the organs, one thing which places labor under conditions less favorable than in tempered countries, and that is the violent alternation and opposition between the seasons. If we find it difficult to determine the physiological effects of climate, we perceive rather more clearly some of its economic influences. An English historian, Buckle, has noticed that nations living under high latitudes did not show the same taste for labor, the same energy, as those living under gentler skies. He attributes this defect to the interruption enforced by winter, which, by the rigor of its weather and the shortness of its days, breaks every year, for months, the sequence of agricultural pursuits. "Why

[2] The patterns are rather architectural— *i. e.,* they reproduce the national architectural ornament-motives in sawed woodwork. Besides that, they conventionalize every possible natural object—trees, flowers, animals, birds—in a very original and consistent manner, which gives a perfectly well defined and individual art type. The standing combination of such designs is: two birds, sometimes, but very rarely, quadrupeds,—facing each other, with a tree or plant of some sort between them—precisely after the manner of the Assyro-Babylonian ornamental art and its derived branches. The women have of course no patterns to work from. The designs are "stitched" and handed down through generations, from mother to daughter, and may be, nay probably are, many hundred years old. These towel-embroideries—which are used as well, only much wider, for borders of table-cloths and bed-sheets, for aprons, petticoats, men's shirts, etc.—are the most venerable and authentic documents we have for a history of national art. All Slavic nations and tribes have this cunning, but the characters of the designs, the stitches and the combinations of color vary according to country or even province.

sleepest thou, *mujik?*" says a popular song, in which the peasant is reproved for sleeping all day on top of the stove while Want comes and sits down at his door. If he sleeps, it is because his crops have been taken in, the autumn sowing has been attended to, and the snow has come, so there is no more work for him in the fields.[3] This intermittence of labor causes a certain desultoriness and instability which interfere with consistency and regular habits. The North throws peculiar obstacles in the way of agriculture and industry, by making them dependent on a climate at once rugged and whimsical, and it is not impossible that these failings may extend to the character. Here again, should not nature by rights be held responsible for some of the propensities or defects usually imputed to the Slavic temperament?

Foreigners who have had work done in Russia have generally noticed that Russians, like southerners, are better capable of a vigorous spurt of energy than of continuous steady effort. With more vivacity, probably an inheritance of his Slavic blood, the Russian frequently displays less activity than the northerners of Teutonic race ; he even often shows, in the lower as well as in the

[3] Accordingly the poet does not rebuke the peasant for sleeping, but for sleeping too long, for being caught napping by Spring who is at the door, as the second line explains. The author of this pretty poem and many more short pieces, all in lyrical-idyllic strain, remarkable for the sadly pensive, pathetic vein, sometimes deepening to passion, which runs through them like a rich minor harmony, is Koltsòf, often called the "Russian Burns." He was born in 1809, and died at thirty-three—at an age when achievement, even the best, is still promise. He belonged by birth to a lowly class, though not to the peasantry, as has often been averred ; his father traded in cattle, and he worked under him. In the midst of uncongenial surroundings and disapproving relatives, who did not spare him their jeers, and taunts, and wise saws, he faithfully plied the humble duties to which he was called, and only two or three times, business trips in his father's interests gave him the golden opportunity of snatching glimpses of the world of intellect, of literature and art, the world to which he was born, yet where he never could be but a passing guest, to join hands with men whose peer he was, yet whose society was not for him. He was patient, dutiful, profoundly unhappy—and died.

higher classes, less taste for bodily exercise. He appears to like it only in the shape of fast sleighing and driving, and that to an extent at which foreigners are amazed, and which may probably be accounted for by the long distances and the cold, which make it desirable to get to one's destination as quickly as possible, and thus a certain hastiness becomes a habit. Bodily exercise, violent games, sport and athletics in all their forms, do not seem more attractive to these sons of the North than to the modern nations of the South. Even skating is less in favor than in countries where it is not so easily to be had. In this respect as in so many others, the Russian may be said to be the very antipodes of the Englishman. Travellers have often been struck by the disinclination of Russian peasants to physical exertion ; at their numerous festivals their chief delight appears to be rest and immobility. Their favorite pastime is swinging ; nor do they boldly launch into space as Western children do, but are content with a soft, swaying motion.⁴ Their habitual dances, such as the *khorovód*, a sort of chaunted dance in a circle, apparently originating in old heathen rites, are slow and monotonously indolent. Climate and race may have something to do with this impassive laziness of mind and body ; the people's diet is also in great part responsible for it.

The principal physiological effect of cold is to activate respiration, to determine in lungs and blood a more rapid combustion and, as a consequence, to demand more substantial nourishment.

⁴ I cannot imagine what could give Mr. Beaulieu this entirely mistaken impression. The passion for swinging with dizzy recklessness is characteristic of Russians of all classes, and not of children and very young people alone, for swinging is the national amusement *par excellence*. The slow "chorus-dance" mentioned in the next line (a gentle swaying of a circle of maidens and women, holding hands, performed to their own singing) and the beautiful national attitude-dance too have their counterpart in the wildly delirious *solo* steps executed by men alone. One invariably follows and completes the other. This character of our national dancing was appropriated and intensified in their world-renowned *csárdás* by the Hungarians, whose culture-life, with much of their vocabulary, came to them from the Slavs, with whom they mixed for centuries before German influences began to make themselves felt.

The nearer we are to the pole, the more man needs food rich in carbon and azote, animal food. Now in the extreme north, as an effect of the cold itself, the fertility of the soil is rarely in proportion with the demands of the climate. This is nowhere more obvious than in the northern half of Russia, unfavorable to the growth of wheat, and beset by such obstacles to cattle raising as are unknown to temperate climes. Throughout this region the earth is niggardly in granting to man the food indicated by heaven itself : such a lack of balance between needs and supplies has very disastrously reacted on the temperament of the people ; they have through many centuries been condemned to meagre, almost entirely vegetable fare. Under a Northern sky they have lived as people do in the South. The use of meat, bacon, of salt pork even, is only now beginning to gain ground amongst them. Although great progress has been made in this direction since the emancipation, the majority of peasants even yet taste meat only on holidays. Their staple food consists of rye bread, broken into the *shtshi*, a sort of soup made of fermented sour cabbage —this latter dish being the national one *par excellence*.[5] To these edibles are added dried mushrooms and frozen or salted fish—two articles of food that are nowhere consumed in such quantities as in Russia. A religion imported from the South, with *four lents* and several oriental fasts, the strictness of which has been proof against centuries, increased the evil inflicted by nature.[6] However, the demands of the climate could not be entirely eluded, and— drink had to supply the lack of food.

The Russians have two national beverages : *kvass*, a sort of rye water, slightly fermented ; and tea, the use of which is well-nigh as universal as in China.* The tea-kettle—the brass *samovar,*

[5] See Appendix to this Chapter, No. 2.
[6] See Appendix to this Chapter, No. 3.
* To judge by the Russian name, *tchaÿ* (which is a Chinese word, *tcha*, as is, at the other end of Europe the Portuguese *cha*), the Russians had tea directly from China. There are in Russia two more beverages in use among the people ; one, called *miod* (honey), is mead or the hydromel

10

is always the first and chief utensil of a household ; no hut, be it ever so poor, is without it. Tea, especially in a country where the water is frequently of poor quality, is a great help, but, under such a sky, it is insufficient as a tonic. It is supplemented by grain whiskey, the pale, white *vodka.*[7] It has long been noticed that drunkenness increases along with the degrees of latitude. The taste for alcohol is as natural to the Russian peasant as temperance is to the Sicilian or Andalusian : it is not so much the man's vice as the climate's fault. As long as the fare is not better, whiskey will be to the peasant a tonic and stimulant, unwholesome, but difficult to find a substitute for. What is most to be deplored is, not that it cannot be proscribed entirely, but that it is impossible to regulate the use of it, so that on a "spree day" one inevitably beholds the absorption (for they do not *drink* liquor, they gulp it down)—of such quantities of *vodka* as, wisely dealt out, would further the peasant's health instead of helping to degrade him into a brute.

In point of fact, the intemperance of the Tsar's subjects has been greatly exaggerated. The Russian drinks less than the Dane, perhaps less than the Englishman, the German, the Frenchman.[8] Many peasants who get drunk on every holiday,

so much in favor with barbarians ; the other is beer—which, judging from the etymology of the name it bears both in Russian and Polish—(*pivo*, from *piti*, "to drink,") must have been known to the Slavs in remote antiquity. Beer is also called, only by the people, when they prepare it themselves, *Bràga*,—the identical name of the Scandinavian, or rather Northern and Teutonic, god of feast-drinking with its exalted exhilaration and the obligatory post-prandial *bragging* which is a distinctive feature of all archaic Aryan mythical and epical hero life.

[7] *Vodka* is the diminutive of *vodà*, "water"—a contemptuous diminutive.

[8] What a relief to find one man—of those who *know* and whose words have weight—find out and proclaim this fact, and lift from the Russian peasant this unthinking, cruel charge, doubly cruel because there seems to lurk in it a mockery ! Of course he drinks less than his neighbors, because, poor thing, he is so much poorer. Only *when* he drinks, which he cannot afford very often, he is very drunk, and the worst is they usually get drunk all together, which makes it conspicuous. The evil is much greater in the towns, among the artisans and especially among the factory people, where there is

go for weeks without a drop of spirits. Moreover, the consumption had noticeably diminished during the second half of Alexander II.'s reign, doubtless owing to the rise in the taxes, and also perhaps to the moral upraising of the former serfs.* Notwithstanding this progress, drunkenness, with all its attendant vices and evils, remains one of the plague-spots of rural life.

As a rule, the villages thrive in opposite ratio to the number of *kabàks, i. e.,* taverns or tap-rooms; therefore both public functionaries and private persons strive to reduce that number. The peasants are not always deaf to the preachings of the apostles of temperance. Certain communes forbid the opening of any tavern whatever on their territory, and when Alexander II. was murdered, several villages are known to have closed their *kabàks,* in token of mourning for the "Liberator." In former times such doings would not have been viewed favorably by the administration, from the fear of letting the most bountiful source of revenue run dry. Indeed the tax on the national vice brings in every year over two hundred and fifty million roubles, in other words, nigh on one quarter of the entire income of the exchequer, so that the wag who said that Russia paid her debts by getting drunk was

always a little money on hand. But where the effects are most deadly is in the upper classes, where the spirit fiend so frequently gets holds of the choicest, most gifted individuals, especially among writers and artists, who can afford to satisfy its insatiable demands in the present, even though at the cost of financial ruin in the end. To explain why this should be so, why the most fatally doomed should be preferably among the noblest and best, the salt of the land, would take us into such hidden and dark depths of national life and misery, both material and psychical, as would require a book by itself to explore. The deadly flatness and *ennui* of provincial life, and, for the army, of garrison life in the interior and on the far outskirts of the empire, suck into perdition thousands more of a race among whose qualities self-discipline and firmness of character are not the most prominent.

* From 1863 to 1879 the consumption had decreased 7 per cent. notwithstanding the increase of the population. The number of tap-rooms had gone down still more rapidly; from 257,000 (1863) to 139,000 (1875); true, it rose again to 146,000 (1881). For so vast an empire, even this is a very low figure. (See Mme. O. Novikof's paper, *The Temperance Movement in Russia,* in the *Nineteenth Century* for September, 1882.)

not so very far wrong. It was calculated, in 1882, that the nation spent *half a milliard* roubles yearly on whiskey, the real value of which amounted to not over *fifty millions*, the margin being divided between the liquor sellers and the government. Yet in these latter days the government, even while it is the party most interested in the sale of *vodka*, has spared no efforts to free the peasant from the bondage of drunkenness. One of the first acts of Alexander III. was the convocation of a sort of temperance parliament, the sessions of which kept Russia and the peasantry much interested up to the autumn of 1881.

The sorry hygienic conditions react on the economical conditions. The poorness of the fare lowers the peasant's capacity for work, and destroys, together with the necessary vitality, the taste and need for labor. Accustomed to his meagre pittance, he ends by being content with it. Like the Southerners, he often allows his indolence to benefit by his frugal habit of life.

Such a diet, in such a climate, cannot fail to exert a deplorable influence on health and even on the duration of life. The effects are apparent in the statistics of the country. We here meet with two extremes,—another of those anomalies which have led us to set up contrast as the law of Russia. This is one of the countries where mortality is highest, the average of life shortest ; it is also one of those where we find the most numerous cases of longevity, where human life attains its uttermost limits. This opposition is especially striking in the northern regions. Thus, in the government of Nòvgorod, out of a population of one million souls, there died in one year (1871), thirty-nine persons a hundred years old or more, a fact which presupposes the existence of others of the same age.* Side by side with this phenomenon, the number of persons who have passed their thirty-fifth year is, in all Russia, proportionately lower than in France, while those having passed their sixtieth

* In 1878 the Procurator of the Holy Synod, in his report for 1875, gave 262 as the number of all the centenarians deceased in that year in the Orthodox population.

year are only half as numerous—not fifty in a thousand, to a hundred and over, in France.*

It is especially the children on whom mortality descends. Under such a sky, the apprenticeship to life is harder, the child needs more care, and the care is not so easy to give. It suffers from the difficulty of breathing the air, from that of artificial nursing ; it suffers even from the distances which, during the working season, compel the mother to leave it untended for many long hours. Delicate infants are doomed ; only the stronger ones survive, to be subjected to an ordeal which, every year, is fatal to many. They undergo, at the hand of death, a series of siftings which successively eliminates the weaklings, until only the robust are left, for life and reproduction.

It would seem as though, in a population subjected to this kind of continuous selection, a vigorous temperament should be a common thing. Unfortunately it is far from always being the case. In this country of high statures and frequent longevity, where men six feet high live to a hundred, strength is more frequently apparent than real. The climate, which in a few years corrodes granite, is, in the long run, exceedingly depressing, debilitating. The lymphatic temperament prevails in Russia. Scrofula is habitual, contagious diseases are common, easy to take and difficult to cure. What is most to be dreaded is not severe frost, nor even the great contrast between the rigor of winter and the blazing heat of summer ; it is the intermediary seasons, with their long alternatives of frost and thaw, lasting sometimes for months, with abrupt variations of temperature, the difference amounting to as many as 20°. In these oppositions, in this instability of the climate, all diseases, all epidemics find favorable conditions, intensified, too, by insufficient nourishment. Owing to greater dryness of the atmosphere, at least in the centre and east, lung

---

* In the northern governments, the proportion is greater, reaching sixty-three to the thousand, while in some of the southern ones, as in that of Kief, it descends under thirty.

diseases are less prevalent than they are in England. In compensation, however, smallpox, typhoid fevers, puerperal fevers, diphtheria, and many more, break out periodically amidst the ill-fed, ill-sheltered populations, and their ravages are terrible.*

If the higher classes have a diet more in accordance with the latitude, their mode of life frequently robs them of the benefit they should derive from it. Nowhere else is the natural order of waking and sleep inverted to such an extent; nowhere else is night so universally turned into day. That also may be an indirect effect of the climate, which, in the North, suppresses by turns both day and night, or exaggerates beyond measure the one at the expense of the other.

To the debilitating influence of the climate are added habits tending to intensify the nervous sensibilities. The very precautions to which the cold compels are unhealthy. To resist the winter, people must live in a heavy, thick atmosphere of vitiated air, rarely renewed : to protect themselves against excessive cold, they must accumulate beforehand a reserve fund of warmth, and fabricate in the house, with the help of fires and stoves, an artificial climate almost as hot as summer in the south of Europe.

* For the greater part of the population who include meat into their habitual diet, this article of food may have lost some of it properties in consequence of the proceeding used in preserving it. The meat and fish needed through the season are allowed to freeze hard in the beginning of the winter. This singularly facilitates transport and provisioning ; but it is just possible that such meat, thawed before cooking, may be less wholesome than fresh meat. [9]

[9] This evil is really not as great as it would seem. When properly treated just before cooking, the meats and certain large fish, fresh and salt, do not perceptibly lose in flavor and nutritiveness, and as to game and venison, we almost never get it any other way in large cities in winter. For long winter journeys in the north, where travellers would go hungry but for the provisions they carry, certain articles of food containing minced meat are cooked, then frozen, and packed into boxes. As much as is required for a meal is thawed, seasoned, and warmed at the stopping-places. The plan works admirably. The greatest inconvenience of the frozen-meat system is that it gives facilities to unprincipled dealers for disposing of wholesale quantities of tainted meat, and the fraud is discovered only in the purchaser's kitchen. The police have much to do to watch the winter markets on account of this abuse.

The lower the temperature out-doors, the higher it must rise in-doors. Behind their double windows, calked with oakum and putty for the entire season, city folks convert their apartments into hothouses, where they breathe the same air as the tropical plants with which they love to decorate their dwellings. In his log cabin—*izbà*,—frequently surrounded with a rampart of manure, the peasant and his whole family crowd around the huge oven, on top of which they all sleep at night. Out of this enervating atmosphere people must, every day, emerge into the icy out-door air; after laying up a supply of warmth for the blood and limbs, a supply of air must be taken into the lungs. And so they go continually, during several months, back and forth, from house to street, the difference between the two temperatures oscillating between 40° and 50°,—which is the same as though one were to pass several times in the same day from a southern summer to a northern winter, from the shores of the Red to those of the White Sea.

The climate is hardly more favorable to cleanliness than to health. The houses, every chink of which is hermetically stuffed up against the winter, are difficult to keep clean. The stoves, the only agents of heating, cannot purify the air of the rooms into which they do not open. Wealthy or well-to-do families remedy this inconvenience by the size of the apartments, which open into one another and are kept in constant free communication, with frequent burning of perfumes. The peasant is condemned to live in a stifling atmosphere redolent with miasms. The warm and infected air of his cabin hatches out myriads of insects; it teems with all kinds of vermin. Out-doors, the filth thrown out all around the house vanishes in the snow to reappear with unimpaired fetidity in spring. Even in the cities the refuse is not always carried away by the sewers, as these are often shut off by ice; rendered harmless by frost, it keeps, and on the first warm days, fills the streets with pernicious exhalations. Nothing can equal the stench of a Russian thaw in the cities. The snow which under the sleighs' runners, was like sand or pounded glass, is transformed into a thick, nauseous slush, which pedestrians bring into the houses on their feet.[10] Under such sanitary conditions, is it to be wondered at that the people fall an easy prey to every epidemic, and that even the plague itself still occasionally puts in an appearance in European Russia?*

The necessity of keeping the body well covered is in itself, for the people, an obstacle to cleanliness as well as to hygiene. The peasant sleeps in his clothes, and lives night and day in the same sheepskin—*tulŭp*. True, he takes a vapor bath once a week, on Saturdays, the Sabbath eve, as an act of ritualistic purification. Unfortunately, he is compelled to get into the same clothes, teeming as they are with vermin. In winter he rarely takes them off on any other day, the only one, too, on which he changes his underwear, when he has some; ofttimes, when he owns no change, he washes his shirt after his bath, before putting it on again. Every village has its vapor bathhouse,—wretched wooden hovels, where vapor is generated by pouring water on a hot stone hearth ; a few inclined boards are used as couches by the bathers ; handfuls of shredded bark or linden rods take the place of sponges and washing-gloves. Whether it came down from the Greeks, the ancient Slavs, or the Finns,† this custom is perhaps more conducive to health than even to cleanliness. The vapor bath, often followed by an immersion into snow or ice-water, is a violent stimulant under a debilitating climate ; the only one, besides alcohol, within the *mujik's* means ; they are to him an

---

[10] See Appendix to this Chapter, No. 4.

* The contact with Asia is, in this respect, a great danger; that is why the plague is so often reported in the Russian annals. That which raged in the government of Astrakhan, in 1879, was probably imported from Turkish Asia in consequence of the Armenian campaign. It performed one good office anyhow, by drawing the attention of the government and the local authorities to the badness of popular hygiene.

† Vapor baths are still in general use among the Finns of Finland, where they appear to have been handed down from remote antiquity. They are frequently mentioned in the *Kalevala*. See, f. ex., Runo iv. and l.

equivalent of the mineral waters to which, and for the same reasons, the Russians of the higher classes are so partial.[1]

Public opinion, which credits northern countries with a higher degree of morality, is not always more correct in this than when it ascribes to them greater cleanliness. In Russia the climate does not favor, if not morality, at least refinement. True, the great number and precocity of marriages diminish the number of natural children; this however, is an unreliable gauge to measure popular virtue by. It is to be noted that in Russia, from various causes, the illegitimate births are much more numerous in the north than in the south, although the former counts fewer cities.* The winter reclusion, the long nights, the crowding of the family within one room, around one hearth, the sleep in common on top of the broad stove that serves as bed to the entire household—all these conditions are not exactly conducive to the sanctity of domestic life. Dreadful abuses frequently resulted therefrom in the times, quite recent still, when several families dwelt together under the roof of the family-chief. The custom of bathing in common, even though the sexes are kept strictly separate, so that none of those scenes come to pass for which travellers formerly used to reprove them,†— this most wholesome custom may have tended to entertain in the peasant a certain coarseness. With both sexes decency seems less strict than in the West, modesty is less easily alarmed, both men and women appear to take less thought of their nudity. In summer,

---

[11] See Appendix to this Chapter, No. 5.

* One cause of the greater proportion of natural children in the north is the absence of so many of the men, who go towards the centre in search of work, leaving the female population greatly in excess of the male. The average rate of illegitimate births in Russia is about three per cent., one of the lowest figures in Europe, outside of Greece.[12]

† For instance the Abbé Chappe d'Auteroche, to whom Catherine II. took the trouble of replying herself in her *Antidote*.

[12] Matters of course were a great deal worse in the times of Emperor Nicolas, when a man could be taken from his family to be sent away as soldier, for a term of service never under twenty years. The young wife's utter helplessness under these unnatural conditions could not but produce great leniency in the local public opinion.

the traveller is often shocked in this respect. Along the rivers, in the towns and villages on the Don and the Volga more particularly, it is not unusual, especially on Saturdays, the day set apart for ablutions by custom and religion, to see girls and women, with no garment of any kind, disport themselves in troops in scarcely sheltered spots, sometimes even under the most frequented bridges. If, as people say, temperaments are colder and the senses blunter in the North, there is, as a set-off, less delicacy in feelings and sensations.

APPENDIX TO BOOK III., CHAPTER I.—NO. 1. (See p. 139, note 1.)

The title *kniaz* (sound the *k* strongly) is usually rendered "Prince," which is terribly misleading, but probably not to be helped.   The only proper way would be to use original national titles without translating them. But all nations object to that, and so the Anglo-Saxon "Earl" has become "Graf" in the Teutonic languages, and "Count" in the Latin ones. Historically the *kniaz* was the sovereign of a given domain, or principality. The first known *kniazes* were Rurik and his immediate descendants.   At first they were few, and the domains, continually enlarged by conquest, extensive, so there was great power and real royalty attached to the title.   But the families multiplied, and as no privilege belonged to primogeniture in the matter of landholding, the domains, which were treated as private possessions, — the state-idea being embodied only in the various *kniazes'* allegiance to the head of the family, the "Grand-Kniaz" (commonly translated "Grand-Duke), who resided in Kief, — were parcelled and re-parcelled out to provide for all the young *kniazes* born into Rurik's house, just as communal lands in our day are re-distributed to meet the needs of a village community.   So there came to be a very multitude of *kniazes*, with ever decreasing power and territories ; moreover, habitually and hereditarily at daggers drawn with one another.   These two hundred years — eleventh to thirteenth centuries — are the "dark ages" of our history, and it is impossible to say to what depth of degradation and even penury the House of Rurik might have sunk, had not the Tatars come, and, in a certain sense, wiped out the past and made of the future a *tabula rasa*, on which the *kniazes* of Moscow, risen from obscurity, in obscurity and even meanness grown and strengthened, with a grand polar purpose ever before them, to redeem and ennoble their apparently abject policy, were to write a new and very different tale. The *kniazes* of the old and degenerated line still remained, a title being an unalienable birthright common to all the members of a family down to all times and posterity, but gradually settled into the condition of mere landlords, owners of estates — in a word, country gentlemen, with a claim, by courtesy, on court favours, state charges, honorable missions, and the like. Then came a time when the title—the only national one—began to be conferred at pleasure as a reward for state services, usually with lands attached. After this all vestiges of lingering royalty departed from the *kniazes*, who merely form a higher layer of nobility, whose position in life — eminent or obscure, wealthy or penniless — has nothing to do with their title, but is subject to the usual conditions and vicissitudes. There still are a number of families who can trace themselves back to Rurik, but several have lost or dropped the title by the way.

As for the word itself, it has come down a long way and tells the story of its mighty past: it is the Slavic equivalent of the Teutonic *chuning*, *konung*, *könig*, *king*, and equally derived with the Sanskrit *jánaka*, which originally meant both "king" and "father."

APPENDIX TO BOOK III., CHAPTER I.—NO. 2. (See p. 145, note 5.)

The cabbage soup referred to is made out of sour cabbage (almost identical with the German *Sauerkraut*) and water, without meat, and has received from the people the grimly humorous designation of "empty *shtshi.*" Cooked with fresh fat beef, which is served in it cut up into good-sized pieces, and enriched with a teacupful of thick sour (or clotted) cream— *smietána*—it is *the* national soup and—a dish for kings. Mr. Beaulieu forgets the *obligato* accompaniment—buckwheat baked porridge. It is much like oatmeal, only that, after having been steamed for a while, it is finished in the oven,—invariably in an earthenware pot of a peculiar shape, probably as old as the race. This is the renowned *kàsha*, the fragrance of which, when the thick, hard crust has been removed and the rich golden butter mixed in, haunts an exile's hours of gloom and gives homesickness a tangible form. For this porridge and the cabbage pottage—*shtshi da kàsha*— are the staple standby of every Russian table without exception, beginning with the Emperor's own, and the very name is replete with associations, national and personal, since there is not one of us but has grown up on it and the wholesome, toothsome, literally "*black* bread," made of honest, unmixed, unbolted rye meal ; and the same triad, so national as to have be come almost symbolical, has greeted us on every board we have been invited to, both where it was merely an accessory, ushering in an elaborate French banquet in graceful acknowledgment of the common bond of nationality—and where hospitality had nothing else, besides a hearty welcome and "with God's blessing" (*s Bógom !*) to bestow. Yes ! *Shtshi da kàsha,* and black ryebread (*tchórnoy hlièb,* the latter word, by the way, identical with the Anglo-Saxon *hlaib,* "bread," and German *laib,* "a loaf"), and the ubiquitously steaming, friendly *samovàr,* whether of silver or brass, with its glittering tea-equipage, whether of egg-shell china or homely stoneware—these embody Russian family life, from tsar to peasant, from cradle to grave.

APPENDIX TO BOOK III., CHAPTER I.—NO. 3.   (See p. 145, note 6.)

The name "Lent" properly belongs only to the forty days of fasting, meagre fare, and mortification of the flesh generally, preceding the Easter festival in the Catholic and Greek Orthodox Churches and their branches. But what other name can be found for the three analogous periods in the Greek Church year ? Six weeks before Christmas, a fortnight before the feast of Peter and Paul (29th of June), and another fortnight before the Assumption of the Virgin (15th of August). The fare prescribed is the same for all and makes us smile at what the Catholics call Lent : it means simply abstention from *all* animal food, under which head come not only the various meats of fowl and quadruped, but milk, butter, and eggs. The almost universal use of fish is in reality a concession to the degeneracy of modern constitutions and religious zeal, not extended to the clergy, especially the Black Clergy (monks and nuns). The moderately pious among laymen abstain from fish during the first week of Lent, the fourth and the last (Holy Week). It is astonishing how far mushrooms will go as substitute for meat. We have a dozen edible varieties, all of them wholesome, nourishing food, and some ranking with the choicest delicacies. The woods are as full of them as of berries, and the children of each family spend half the long summer days gathering them. Indeed, that and "berrying" are the chief national summer amusements in which young and old share with almost equal zest in the better classes, affording endless fun in the way of family and social picnicking, hay rides in springless farm wagons, etc. For the poor it is not a question of amusement and housewives' rival display of skill in preserving, pickling, drying, but actually a vital matter ; and dire indeed would be the winter prospects but for the chaplets of little shrivelled, leather-like black-ish morsels strung up along the rafters of the living-room in the *izbà*, eked out by a few strings of onions and, down in the cellar, a heap of those huge black-skinned, terribly strong radishes,—half-way between the pink-and-white table radish and the violent tear-compelling horseradish,—which, seasoned with various kinds of oil, yield a wholesome though coarse relish to relieve the monotony of the everlasting dry black bread. Green hemp seed oil is the staple article of the poor, though, as an acquired taste, with that same black radish, it is cultivated by many a *blasé* aristocratic palate. Not, however, with *kàsha*, in lieu of butter, as the common people use it in Lent time. Other oils, as rape seed and especially sunflower-seed oil, are very acceptable substitutes in cooking, and even pastry. The Lenten fare of the average well-to-do-family table, by long practice and ingenuity, reaches a highly respectable standard of excellence. It is a special branch of the art, and the skill and inventiveness displayed by high-toned club and restaurant cooks are crucial tests, so that many a church magnate—bishop or archbishop —takes pride in his Lenten fare as the crowning perfection of his establish-ment. Indeed the variety that can be attained in this seemingly poor and limited field—of course with fish included—is a constant source of amaze-ment to foreigners. The fish soups are renowned, and the king of them all, the sterlet soup, can compare, for richness of flavor and costliness of material, only with the turtle soup of aldermanic fame. The daintiness of the des-serts is unsurpassed—and no wonder, when there is the whole range of dried and candied fruits, jellies and syrups, and the place of milk and cream is taken by a substitute which every Russian woman knows how to prepare out of almonds pounded in a mortar with water measured according to the thickness and strength desired. That tea and coffee whitened and flavored with "almond milk" or "almond cream" are uniquely delicious beverages, is known to few outside of Russia. To sum up: the wealthy and fairly prosperous are not as much to be pitied as would seem at first sight if they are rigid observers of the Church canons in matters of food, although the prolonged deprivation of meat, milk, and eggs tells on most modern consti-tutions, for the palate is as frequently the gainer as the loser. How far *such* Lenten fare, requiring far more thought, care, and elaborateness in the prep-aration than ordinary meat fare, answers the original religious object of the institution, is a question which does not belong here. For the poor, the Lent periods are times of increased hardship and most debilitating want of nour-ishment. The specially appointed fast-days are equally severe for all. The two principal are the eve of Christmas and that of Twelfth Night. On these days neither food nor water must pass the lips from midnight until the rising of the evening star. This is the reason why a Christmas tree on Christmas Eve is an impossibility. The tree may be lit on Christmas night or any night of the ensuing week (the school holidays lasting from Christmas Eve to Twelfth Night—6th of January), but the usual time is New Year's Eve. It is a comfort to know that children, up to seven years, are exempted both from fasting and Lent fare ; from seven to fourteen the severity of the observances is considerably alleviated for them. A far larger proportion of the higher classes than is usually supposed are church goers and strict observers of Lents, fasts, etc. Then there are those who do in this line as much as they think fit or absolutely necessary for their souls' welfare, or— for respectability. The entirely emancipated, to which number the bodies of literature, science, and art belong almost without exception, form the class best known to foreigners. In this respect again Petersburgh is far ahead of Moscow, where it is not impossible to find old-time piety combined with distinction in these careers.

APPENDIX TO BOOK III., CHAPTER I.—NO. 4. (See p. 152, note 10.)

All that our author says about the out-door effects of the spring thaw and about the atmosphere in the rural *izbà* is unfortunately true in every detail. But his strictures on the city dwellings in this respect are unfounded. Our heating system, which we have in common with all the extreme north of Europe—Sweden, Norway, Denmark and some of the northernmost parts of Germany—is the only perfect one, combining the power of regulating the heat within half a degree, evenness of temperature throughout the dwelling, active ventilation, and great economy of fuel. The valves in the flues, by which we can let in the outer air, are six or eight inches in diameter ; there are two by the side of each stove, accessible by a little door opening into the room, and can be opened just as much or as little as desired. They are of course wide open during the hour or so which it takes the stove to consume its daily armful of wood, or—in the south—pail of coal. Such is the allowance for twenty-four hours, and only on extremest cold days, not thirty in the winter, is it doubled and the firing operation repeated after twelve hours. The perfect protection afforded by the putting up for winter of duplicate window frames calked all round the edges, with sometimes a strip of felt nailed over the putty for greater security, is scarcely to be counted a defect, and is surely preferable to the expensive and only half-efficient weatherstrips of this and other countries. In one at least of the windows of each room there is a pane made with hinges, to open and close. It is kept open in the morning while the chamberwork is being done, and is opened for as long as the cold allows several times in the day, though to do so is not always easy, as the edge often freezes hard and the ice must be broken to get the pane to work. On the sill the interval between the two window frames is filled, to the height of some three inches, with sand, in which are stuck a few small paper cornucopias filled with coarse salt, a great absorber of moisture. Owing to all these precautions the atmosphere of the dwellings is singularly free from dampness, consequently cannot be called "a hothouse atmosphere"; and it is further corrected by the universally popular window-gardens, and the tall, large-leaved foliage plants which are such favorites for both decorative and sanitary reasons.

APPENDIX TO BOOK III., CHAPTER I.—NO. 5. (See p. 153, note 11.)

A man who takes an obligatory thorough washing once a week, cannot be personally very dirty. For a Russian of the lower classes it is, besides, a matter of religious duty to wash his hands before "touching bread." For the same reason the table is kept scrupulously scoured, and is washed down every time a meal is to be spread on it, and the dishes, bowls, and platters are treated likewise. If the family can afford it, the table is covered with a snow-white linen cloth, homespun and homewoven. "Bread," the symbol of food, of life, has still much of the veneration of primeval ages clinging to it; it is not to be played with or frittered away by the children or wasted in any way, and no crumbs must be suffered to fall to the ground; they may be collected and served as food for the chickens, or scattered about for "God's little birds,"—a pretty custom which we can trace to one of the daily offerings prescribed to the Brahmans by ancient Hindu law. What Mr. Beaulieu says about the condition of the peasants' clothing neutralizing the effects of the daily bath, cannot be disputed, but it applies only to the very poor. A well-to-do peasant family often has a bathroom of its own and always sufficient change of raiment. In this as in so many respects, things stand worst in towns, in factory quarters, and others crowded with the poorer laboring class. But in the capitals, and in due time in the larger cities, great and thoughtful improvements have been made in the public baths. The most to the point is the arrangement providing for the bather's shirt and trousers being laundried and dried ready for him when he returns to the dressing-room if he has no change, and a certain iron press closet in which his *tulùp* (sheepskin) is subjected to a degree of dry heat which entirely frees it from vermin. They say that the floor of that closet seems strewn with a black powder and must be swept out every couple of hours. These two items, incalculably beneficial as they are, are included in the charge for the use of the bathrooms—from two to five cents, according to accommodation, of which there are three grades for the common people, apart from the really luxurious public bathrooms, with carpets, marble swimming basins, attendants, etc. (from fifteen to twenty-five cents a person), and the private *suites* of three rooms—dressing-room, washing-room with wooden benches all around, bath tub, and a sufficiency of wooden buckets and brass basins, and the small vapor room with its shelves along one wall. These *suites*, which occupy a separate part of the building, opening on both sides of a long corridor, cost from fifty cents to two dollars, according as they are fitted up, and you are not limited as to time—within reasonable bounds, say an hour and a half, or two hours.

BOOK III.   CHAPTER II.

The Russian Character and the Struggle against the Climate—The North far from Being the Natural Cradle of Liberty—Resignation, Passiveness, and Hardening in Evil—Practical Spirit and Realistic Instincts—Impressions Received from Nature ; her Sadness—Her Grandeur and Poverty—Effects of these Contrasts—On the So-Called Nomadic Tendencies of the Russians—The Monotony of Great-Russia and the Lack of Originality.

THE direct influence of climate on the human organism and habits, on the physical and economical conditions of existence, is neither the only nor perhaps the deepest one. Nature indirectly exerts a considerable influence over the thoughts, the feelings, the entire character by the passions she provokes and the faculties she calls into play. The first remark suggested by the physical formation of Great-Russia is that life there, more than anywhere else, is a strife against nature, a hand to hand combat against an ever-present and unvanquished foe. Under that sky man cannot, as in more temperate climes, forget his adversary ; nor can he ever completely triumph over that foe, and even while struggling for the land foot for foot, he is often made to yield before a superior force. Hence several apparently incompatible traits of the Russian national character. This warfare is first of all a school of patience, resignation, submissiveness. Unable to slip his neck from under the yoke of nature, he has borne that of man more patiently ; the one has bent and fashioned him for the other. The tyranny of climate prepared him for man's absolute power. The object of all his striving being bare existence, despotism weighed on him less. We should not indiscriminately acquiesce in the ancient theory which set down the peoples of the North as apt for freedom and those of the South as doomed to bondage. At a certain latitude, in a given environment of physical conditions, the North can bow the souls as well as the bodies, and culture alone can raise and straighten them. The grand advantage the North possesses, is that there the liberating efficiency of culture is always possible, while in tropical countries the final success remains still doubtful.

One of the qualities that have been most developed by the climate and the strife against nature, is passive courage, endurance, negative energy, the power of inertia. Hardening endurance has long been the Great-Russian's popular ideal. This feeling is very apparent in an old national game, a sort of rustic boxing match, in which the combatants vied not in strength and skill, but in endurance, the victor being not he who floored his antagonist, but he who could take most hard knocks without crying out for mercy. Life, at one with history, has fashioned the Great-Russian to a stoicism, the heroism of which he himself is not conscious of. Nobody can suffer like a Russian ; no one can die like him. In the quiet courage with which he faces suffering and death, there is something of the stolid resignation of the captive Indian, ennobled, however, by serene religious conviction.[1]

The first time I met a Russian peasant was is 1868, in Palestine, in March, at the beginning of Lent. I was camping out, under a

---

[1] Nowhere does the Russian's genuineness, earnestness, simplicity shine forth with a steadier and clearer light than on the deathbed, the battlefield, the scaffold. His inveterate hatred of cant, his contempt of "phrase," "attitude," catchwords (which, by the way, makes him out of sympathy with hero-worship or what is commonly called so) never leaves him, least of all at critical points and tragic climaxes. This is why the effective "last words," the deliberate "posings" and self-drapings with which men of other nations, even the great ones, generally think it necessary to emphasize their public acts and especially the last one of all—death under the public eye with a view to producing a certain impression, not only does not warm the Russian's heart or appeal to his admiration, but either jars on him and puts him out of patience, or leaves him coldly critical, with a curl of the lip not unlike a sneer.

tent, on the margin of Solomon's Ponds, not far from Bethlehem. The night had been disturbed by one of those tempests, bearers of wind and rain, which are of frequent occurrence in Syria at that time of the year. We had been joined by one of those groups of Russian pilgrims that walk over the Holy Land in small gangs, staff in hand, with no other luggage than a canvas bag and a wooden bowl. They were all peasants ; there were among them both men and women ; most of them were aged.* Tired out with the hardships of a distant journey and a long march, they were seeking around our tents, or at the foot of ruinous walls, for shelter against the driving rain. At dawn they wanted to return to the Greek Convent at Bethlehem ; but, although the distance was not over a few miles, cold and fatigue prevented several from reaching it. When their strength gave out, they would drop down on the ground, and the others would silently pass on, giving them up as they gave up themselves. We followed them very closely, on horseback, numb with cold too, and worn out, making for the Latin Convent at Bethlehem. I thus came on two of these peasants, lying on the rocky ground in the pathway, which the rain had transformed into a rivulet. It was in vain I tried to raise them, to revive them with rum, to haul them up on a horse ; they seemed bent on letting themselves die.[1] When we reached Bethlehem, we could send out assistance to them. That very morning one man and two women, Russians, had been found dead on roads and buried.

It was with the same feeling, the same calm and gentle fatalism that, during the Crimean war, Russian soldiers followed their leaders across the steppes of the south, marching until totally

---

* Household cares and the communal authorities rarely allow young people to embark on these long pilgrimages, whether within the empire or abroad, of which the lower classes are so fond.

[1] They probably were. Death such as this, at the goal of the long, weary pilgrimage on the sacred earth of the Holy Land, is a beatific vision to these simple, loving souls, as sure and short a cut to Paradise as death in battle to the Moslem.

exhausted, when they would die along the roads, by the hundred thousand, with not a cry of revolt, almost without a moan or murmur. It was with the same patience, the same resigned energy that, in the Balkan wars, they stood the extremes of cold, of heat, of fatigue, of hunger. The Russian soldier is the most enduring in Europe ; in this respect no other can be compared to him but his secular adversary, the Turkish soldier. Both have a capacity for suffering unknown to the nations of the West. And yet the Russian people are naturally the least pugnacious, the least warlike in the world. They never were, at any time. Whatever conquests they have achieved, they are devoid of conquering instincts. Essentially peace-loving, the Russian sees in war only a scourge to which he submits out of obedience to God and the Tsar.

From this strife against the climate, which has fashioned him so well for resignation, the Great-Russian derives two opposite qualities. Together with a singular mixture of strength and weakness, of tenacity and elasticity, it has given him a curious mixture of roughness and good nature, of insensibility and kindness. The ruggedness of the world around him, while hardening him for himself, teaches him compassion for others. He knows what it is to suffer, so can sympathize with his neighbor, and succors him as much as lies within his power. Family feelings, beneficence towards the poor, pity for the unfortunate of all sorts, —these are some among the most marked features of the national character. Contrary to a vulgar prejudice, the Russian, under his rugged shell, is generally affectionate, gentle, even tender ; but let him encounter an obstacle, let him engage in a struggle with an adversary, the latent ruggedness and harshness at once take the upper hand. In the unceasing struggle against a ruthless nature, he has learned to respect the laws of war, which he applies as he endures them—with inflexibility.[3]

---

[3] The Russian's mind is intensely theoretical, his conscience rigid in the extreme, holding all compromises with existing things as dishonest or, at

It is in those struggles in which Russia's very existence seems at stake that all these contrasts appear. Otherwise—as was shown in the French campaign of 1814, as well as in the Crimean war—the Russian is the most generous of enemies. Gentle and compassionate in his private capacity, he can, in his national and civil struggles, become pitiless as soldier or public servant ; but, the victory won, he often shows himself again as simply kind as he just was ingenuously stern. In the country whose sad privilege it was to draw on itself his worst severities, in Poland, I have sometimes heard pathetic stories told of this contrast in the Russian character. Here is one, told us by Poles : In one of those terrible insurrections, the consequences of which still weigh so heavily on this hapless land, a Russian non-commissioned officer, quartered on a Polish family, took the liberty of kissing the child of the house. In the eyes of the mother, who, like all the Polish women, was an exalted patriot, this Russian kiss was pollution. She was pregnant at the time, and committed the imprudence of giving the offender a box on the ears. Instead of getting angry or complaining to his chiefs, the Russian sergeant offered his other cheek and allowed himself to be turned out of the room. Soon after, he left the town, and, having requested a comrade to inform him of the birth of the expected child, sent it little christening gifts.

The Russian has not much comprehension for resistance unencouraged by the hope of success. Himself accustomed to bow before fatality, he thinks it but just that other people should do

the best, cowardly. Therefore, once possessed of an idea, they go all lengths, and therefore, too, should there ever be a Russian revolution,—which Heaven in its mercy forefend,—the horrors of French '93 will pale before it. How otherwise could we find among the most ruthless of "terrorists," ready at any moment for wholesale massacre, gentle, soft-eyed creatures that would take to their bosoms a hurt cur of the streets and go out of their way not to tread upon an insect? Remember the youth placed in charge of the mine under "Mikhaÿlofsky Street" in Petersburgh, who, when he left his basement chamber, flying from the police, did not forget to leave on the table the money due to his cat's butcher.

so too. If he does not worship force, he certainly respects it. Something like this medley of contrasting feelings is found amongst the Germans, especially the Prussians[4] ; but with the latter the affectionate side is more .exclusive, more turned inward, more selfishly domestic, while the rugged, brutal side is turned more outward to the world, with a superadded supercilious arrogance to which the Russian, as a rule, is a stranger.

The faculty which has been aroused most thoroughly in the Great-Russian by this struggle against a cold and implacable nature is a practical, positive spirit ; this is the feature by which chiefly he differs from the Little-Russian and from the western and southern Slavs.[5] This predominant quality of his shows in everything, and everything tends to account for it. As one of his writers remarks,[*] it was in the secular labors of colonization that he contracted this disposition to see in everything the immediate aim and the realities of life. Hence that presence of mind, that facility in devising ways and means, that wealth of resources, that tact in dealing with men and things, which characterize the Great-Russian. Very perceptible in the people's manners, politics, literature, this tendency is not less apparent in things where it

---

[4] The Prussian people are much mixed with Slavs, and a great part of them are Prussian only politically and from long habit, not in blood. This is especially noticeable in the Pomeranians, who, along with their purely Slavic name—*Pomoriànië,* "the people by the sea "—have retained a very pure and handsome Slavic type of features. Morally they are almost entirely germanized, with a superadded stolid obstinacy of their own, much like that of the Bretons of old Armorica. Does association with the rugged northern sea produce it in the course of time ?

[5] This is a feature of our national character very patent to us Russians, but until now scarcely even suspected by foreigners, who thus lost an important clue to the Russian nature and its practical workings. The first to point it out with a precision and surety due to intelligent observation, and to bring it out in the living form of an artistic creation, was Henri Gréville, in her admirable novel, *Un Violon Russe.* In this book, by far the best of her Russian series, everything is caught warm from life—even to the servant girl who appears just once, to open the door to visitors and go on with her scrubbing.

[*] Mr. Kavélin : *Thoughts and Notes on Russian History.*

would seem most out of place, such as poetry and religion. The Great-Russian popular songs show little taste for abstractions or personifications of any sort. No nation has a less metaphysical turn of mind, or takes less thought of the essence of things. His favorite sciences, those that most attract him, are the physical sciences, the natural sciences, the social sciences. The whole nation, the educated classes as well as the ignorant masses, is pervaded by a more or less conscious positivism. The quality most esteemed by the peasant is common-sense; he says his worst about the Pole when he calls him "brainless." Few nations are more devoid of sentiment, even while pluming themselves on it.

Indeed, the pretension to practical sense, with the Great-Russian, at times verges on brutality. Was it not a Russian who said that a piece of cheese was worth more than a Pushkin?⁶ These realistic instincts make themselves felt in literature and in all the lines of art, notably in painting, in criticism, in history, in philosophy, or, more correctly, in the absence of philosophy and metaphysics. The romanticism of the first half of the nineteenth century, like the classicism of the preceding century, and notwithstanding the genius of Pushkin and Lermontof, was little else than an importation from abroad. Nowadays the national literature belongs, and has belonged for quite a while already, almost entirely to realism or naturalism. Of all foreign writers, the one

⁶ This piece of criticism was beaten by one of the would-be prophets of "the last word of science," (how sick Russian ears have grown of the sound of that phrase—and a few others!) magazine reviewers, who retailed at third hand the materialistic theories of Feuerbach, Moleschott, etc. On one occasion he went into a rage against poetry in general, and became especially rampant against Shakespeare. Shakespeare? Faugh! What was the good of *him?* What was the *sense* of him? Why, there was more sense in "soft-boiled boots." The expression has become a by-word and a classic. It was the same wiseacre—or another of that ilk—who, in reviewing Victor Hugo's *Toilers of the Sea*, fell foul of one of the poet's sweetest creations, his "Bird-Girl," and triumphantly demonstrated in a lengthy anatomical dissertation that only an ignorant fool could liken a human being to a bird. Pretty work he would make of Austin Dobson's gem, charming *Avice!*

most read and relished is Zola, whom one of their novelists * calls "The Hercules of Naturalism,"—Zola, who has long numbered more admirers among the Russians than among his own countrymen.

Nothing is as complex as the character of a man, how much more that of a nation. After having portrayed one side of it, one is bound to present the opposite side, under penalty of producing a deceptive likeness. In Russia, as elsewhere, nature, which influences man in so many divers and roundabout ways, does not always impel him in the same direction. She not only acts on the temperament through the climate, the diet, and the habits, on the character through the needs which she imposes, or the faculties which she stimulates ; she acts, with no less force, on the imagination and the entire soul through her aspects, through the pictures she presents, the impressions she arouses. Now, as nature is nowhere simpler, these impressions are nowhere clearer. One of the first to be perceived by the traveller is a feeling of sadness. This sadness emanates from the sky and the climate ; Northern nations are all more or less touched with it ; in Russia the very earth, flat and monotonous, exhales it. The Russian of the south —the Little-Russian—is not less subject to it than is he of the north.

The Russian soul is melancholy. If incurable boredom, if hypochondria or British "spleen" are nevertheless of rarer occurrence than in England, it is because the climate, being more rugged, is far less moist and misty ; possibly also because the Russian's sadness is tempered or dispelled by his sociability, one of the qualities most generally common to all the Slavs, one which, in Russia, the enforced seclusion of winter with its long nights has done most to foster and develop. The Russian's relish for pleasure and emotions, his love of travelling, his passion for gambling, even his propensity to drink, frequently are with him, as with many other nations of the North, only an effort to forget, or to fill an inner void.

* Boborykin.

It is in the poetry and music of the people, in the songs or "*piêsni*" of Great-Russia, — those songs which Herzen used to call "sounding tears," — in those "airs" of slow rhythm and in minor keys, that the native melancholy, bred of soil and clime, finds its fullest expression. Between the Russian songs and the *canzoni* of Naples and Sicily, all sun-imbued, there is a distance as between the antipodes. In these popular songs, a cloud of soft sadness casts elegiac shades over the realistic background of the national character. In literature and cultured poetry, this sadness assumes a bitterer, intenser flavor. From Lermontof and Pushkin to Nekrássof and Tiùtchef, the poetry of all the schools is impregnated with it; it makes itself felt in the life as well as in the works of all these poets, most of whom died young, and some tragically. "Sadness, scepticism, irony—these are the three chords of Russian poetry" wrote Herzen, who might have quoted himself as an example. "Our laugh," he further remarked, "is but an unwholesome grin." * The fact is that Gògol's sarcastic mirth is at times more heartrending than that of the sombrest English humorists.

This sort of melancholy, inspired by the climate and entertained by the political *régime*, at times inclines the Russian soul to a mysticism which prevails over its realistic instincts, or combines with them in strange ways — witness more than one popular religious sect, and many a national writer, such as Jukòvsky, Gògol, Dostoyèfsky, Tolstoy. Between this spontaneous sadness, at times streaked with spells of joviality, and the kind of pessimism so prominent in several ignorant sects as well as in the nihilism of literary youths, it is equally easy to find a link.

In the lower classes, this unconscious melancholy frequently appears wedded to a resigned fatalism, and the outcome is a tranquillity, a sort of placidity which fills one with wonder. In crowds, in games, in his cups even, the Great-Russian is, as a rule, peaceable and not noisy. Very little quarrelling or riotousness, among men as well as among children. A crowd, silent

* *The Russian People and Socialism.*

as nature herself,—as the snow, which, in the streets of cities, muffles the sound of footsteps.

In order better to enter into the feelings of such a crowd, let us figure to ourselves the impressions gathered through centuries by the colonists from the West, during their slow settling on the soil of Great-Russia. Face to face with these expanses as boundless as the sea, man felt small. The consciousness of his power dwindled before the vastness of the land which encompassed him, and which, down even to our own times, he felt incapable of filling. These lakes and swamps, unnumbered and unbounded, these rivers which no bridge could span, these forests without end, these steppes with no horizon but the sky-line, — all these things brought home to him his inferiority.

If we would analyze the chief outer features, we shall see that all the impressions produced by Russian nature can be summed up in the word "contrast": the pictures presented to man by Great-Russia show him his own smallness without making him realize the energies of nature. It is not only by its extent that this land dwarfs man : it attunes the imagination to dreams and vague musings, without supplying, as in the South, materials for food and warmth, *i. e.*, that which trains it to the gorgeous poetry which we admire in the poems of India or Greece. Flat and bare, dull and inert, this nature has not much to stimulate the mind with, little nourishment for poetry and art. It is not very apt to suggest powerful conceptions or brilliant imagery. Even by its meagre fertility, the Russian soil is often inferior to the desert in its nudity, where, at least, nothing dwarfs the impression of immensity.[1]

---

[1] It is natural for a foreigner to think so, whose necessarily transient stay could not attune his soul to the tranquillity and inner silence, — *recueillement*—which would open it to the subtle charm, the mystery of local influences, repugnant, moreover, with their northern and oriental *melancholia* to his Latin temperament. But we are passionately fond of our steppe, our plains, our woods, and even a cursory acquaintance with our poets, novelists, and painters would suffice to show that art and poetry find therein ample and substantial food.

The land formerly called Moscovia is devoid of all those grand, spectacular attractions by which nature amazes and uplifts the spirit. It has neither mountains nor sea, and lacks the impulse which life by the sea or in the mountains gives to individuality. Its forests, sparse and stunted in size, lack majesty ; most of its numerous lakes have flat margins, like big pools. Russia has been denied the grand scenery of the North. She has no surf-beaten coasts ; no steep, beetling islands ; no gulfs or sinuous *fjörds;* no granite rocks or glaciers ; no torrents or waterfalls. She has no share in the mighty nature which has begotten the rugged myths of the North ; she has little of anything that stirs and stimulates the personality.

Russian nature has two opposite characteristics : amplitude and vacuity—wealth of space and scarcity of contents to fill it. Huge areas show no variety, either of forms or colors. In live and inanimate nature alike, there is an absolute want of grandeur and power. Picturesqueness is either totally absent or appears on such a minimum scale as leaves it imperceptible to a foreigner's eye. Travelling over these undulating plains, where towns and villages are sparsely scattered, produces almost the same feeling of satiety as a sea-voyage. When embarked on a long railway trip, one can, just as on board a steamer, close one's eyes at night and reopen them the next morning without being made aware of a change of locality. Only some few cities, rising in tiers on the margin of rivers or lakes, with their old walls and colored cupolas, such as Kief, the two Nòvgorods, Pskof, Kazàn, present from a distance an imposing front. The very size of the rivers impairs their beauty ; it is in vain that one bank rises into high acclivity, sometimes overgrown with handsome trees ; no matter how fine in themselves, they are always too low for the width of the stream and look crushed. This disproportion mars the most beautiful portions of the Dniepr, the Don, the Volga. For instance, in the great bend the latter describes between Stavròpol and Syzràn, where " Mother Volga " opens a road for herself through a range of steep hills, perhaps equal in height to those on the Rhine, the Danube, or the Nile, the width of the river exceeds the height of the hills, so they look dwarfed and the effect is lost. Everything in Russia suffers from this want of proportion between the vertical section and the horizontal plan of the landscapes. Perhaps the most truly picturesque scenery is presented by the calm ponds that lie in the desert forests, the ravines dug in the steppe by the melting snows, the wooded glens through which a slow river winds its silent course.

This reliefless soil is overspread by a vegetation lacking **both** vigor and variety. Nature repeats herself everywhere,—same species, same plants, same trees. The similarity that pervades the conditions of life brings about the sameness of live creatures, while the rigor of the climate weakens them. Free nature in Great-Russia shows the monotony that, in other parts of the world, man inflicts on nature enslaved. In this respect, the wooded zone, which comprises the vastest and oldest portion of Great-Russia, has not much the advantage of the zone denuded of trees. The forests are, if anything, of poorer aspect than the steppe, since the latter, in spring, dons its luxuriant grass robe. Fine trees are rare and scarcely to be met with outside of certain favored regions of the centre or west. The species are the same as in Sweden and Norway, but without their vigor. Instead of giving vent to the exuberance, the energy of an ever-youthful nature, these forests give you an impression of powerlessness, of indigence, lassitude. The trees now are poorly, stunted, small, and old-looking, now again they are slim and lanky, without being tall, and cast but scant shade on the bare ground beneath them. What most strikes the eye is the everlasting contrast of pine and birch, with their respectively reddish and white-bark trunks ; the pine straight and bare with its meagre head, the birch with its slender limbs, with its minute foliage.

The fields offer still less variety than the woods. The soil does not receive at man's hands the animation and variety which they impart to it in other countries. The cultivated crops are stricken with the same monotony as the spontaneous vegetation. You seldom see those different and adjoining crops which lend such life to the fields in the West. You might take it all for one and the same field, stretching away into the infinite, were it not broken now and then by a strip of fallow land. No hamlet, no homestead, not even isolated farmhouses. In the steppe as well as in the forest, the Russian husbandman seems afraid of finding himself alone in the midst of the immensity which encloses him on every side. Community of landed property, in general use among the peasants, increases the defect of nature; it deprives Russian rural scenery of those enclosures, those fancifully shaped fences which go for much in the charm of the villages in England and Normandy. Thence partly come the sad flatness, the dull wearisomeness of this impersonal, collective country, where the fields are undivided or cut up into long, even, and symmetrical strips.

This liking for common property, for association and the kind of organization known in Russia under the name of *artèl*, has frequently been ascribed to Slavic blood. It is more likely that it has its chief sources not so much in race as in nature on one hand, and in a given stage of civilization on the other. The persistency of agricultural communities in Great-Russia, this desire to crowd together, to live in close vicinity, is certainly not unconnected with the cold immensity of space wherein man, if isolated, feels lost and powerless.[8]

[8] Isolation in the midst of hostile populations has the same effect, and produced among the Balkan Slavs—Serbs, Bosnians, Bulgars—those famous family communes or "brotherhoods"—the *Zadrugas*—to which those persecuted branches of our race owe the preservation of their national consciousness, their inspiriting traditions, and — more prosaically — their safety. Each is an embryo state, a survival of primeval patriarchism ; a fossil, but instinct with life and with beating heart. When the necessity for them ceases, they cease to exist, naturally, of themselves — as the bodies in the old Etruscan tombs, seemingly unaffected by ages of sepulchral gloom, crumble to dust when touched by a ray of the sun of the living.

From the same roots springs another inclination tending in an opposite direction: the love of adventure, of travelling, of vagrancy — what foreigners designate by the high-sounding word "nomadic tastes." The little love the peasant bears to the sorry, thankless soil of old Moscovia is easily accounted for; besides, if the peasant at times really deserves this stricture, it should be set down for a good part to the institutions, serfdom, and the current form of property-holding.

There is, to this phenomenon, another reason still, which also, though indirectly, is bred of local conditions, and weakens the attachment to house and home : it is the materials of which the dwellings are built, more particularly the peasant's cabin — the *izbà*, — and the consequent frequency of conflagrations.

In Russia, especially Northern Russia, poor in stone and abounding in forests, in that region which the historian Soloviof calls "Wooden Europe" in opposition to Western or "Stone Europe," all villages, from the peasants cabin to the church and the old manor house, are built of fir-wood. So were most towns until quite lately, even the capitals. In such a country, fire— "the Red Rooster," such being the homely name for it among the people — is a terrible foe, both for the individual and for society. It is in vain that, to lessen the danger, a certain distance is left between the houses in the villages; they are about certain to burn down some time or other, every one of them. The chances of duration of a dwelling can, according to the region, be calculated with as much accuracy as those of human lives, only that the dwelling's term is frequently considerably the shorter. One feels how discouraging must be the prospect of destruction by fire, which overshadows a family's whole life, how hampering to any thought of embellishment, consequently to any added comfort or improvement. What is the use of getting attached to the frail construction of wood which is liable to be consumed by a spark and a breath ? So the peasants often listlessly allow their *izbà* to lean off its basis, as though ready to tumble down, and appear to wait for the flames to consume it, before they set it straight.

Independently of the chances of fire, the facility with which the peasant of the north-country constructs his house is not apt to inspire him with sedentary tastes. A peasant, up to very lately, was able to build a house in a few weeks, and all he wanted in the way of tools was an axe. In the times when the land had not been so denuded of woods, the *izbà*, though otherwise roomy and comfortable, could be replaced almost as easily as the Arab's hut, or *gurbi*. That may have been another of the causes of those "nomadic tastes," much too freely ascribed to the nation. At all events, the frequency of fires, which have not been stopped by the recently created insurance offices, still remains an obstacle to steadiness of habits, to the feeling of stability and permanency, to care for the morrow. This calamity, ever hanging over the villages, diminishes the love of home, a feeling which has everywhere been one of the greatest factors of morality, order, and economy, and which comes more naturally to the Russian than to any other people, as, since the emancipation, every peasant owns the house in which he lives.

As a rule, the people of the North are less attached to the land than those of the South. Emigration is less hard to them ; we see that in Germany and England, and in the Scandinavian countries, which, from a not very dense population, send off each year to Canada a considerable contingent of emigrants. The Russian—at least the peasant — does not easily leave his country ; he is held there by the institutions, by his prejudices, by his religion ; but Russia is vast enough to open a field to him when the wandering humor comes over him. The plain lures on the pedestrian ; nothing on his monotonous way invites him to loiter, to settle down. Hence, in the Cosack of old and the modern peasant, the ease with which they go from place to place, an instinct which manifests itself in so many ways — fairs, pilgrimages, seeking new land, — and which, historians tell us, was one of the reasons for establishing serfdom.[9]

This readiness to go ahead, at random, corresponds to a moral tendency perhaps more worthy of note, though less generally taken notice of. This is the adventurous inclination of the Russian nature, often longing to rush blindly into the most reckless speculations, impatient of obstacles, not shrinking before any extreme of boldness, be it in philosophy, religion, or social science, with a general tolerance or indulgence for all such flights at which other nations stand aghast. Russian thought is frequently not more conscious of limitations than are Russian plains and horizons ; it revels in the boundless, goes straight the

---

[9] From earliest times land used to be given as a reward for public services. This was only just, since public servants would have considered the offer of pay or salary as an insult. They defrayed all the expenses entailed by their respective posts out of their personal means, and some charges were so onerous as to leave them well-nigh penniless—for instance, embassies to foreign lands, or even only to other Russian princes' courts, with the numerous suite and the representation such a post necessitated. The people on the estates were not slaves to the landlord, though owing them certain service and dues, and in a great measure dependent on their pleasure and protection, much as Roman clients of the early times on their patrons. When they were or thought themselves ill-used, they would migrate *en masse* to the estates of some other landlord, of more popular fame, till some lands would become overcrowded and some remain almost deserted, to the destruction not only of the owners' interests, but of the country's economic balance. It was attempted to stem the current by an ordinance, forbidding change of land throughout the year, and permitting the peasants to leave their homesteads on one single day, the feast of St. George, 26th of November, when their work for the year was done and they had several months before them in which to effect their emigration and get settled on the new land. When even this restriction did not sufficiently reduce the peasant migrations, the decree "attaching them to the glebe" was issued by Borìss Godunòf (contemporary of the last years of Elizabeth and the first of James I.), an usurper and a murderer, yet a wise and careful sovereign, somewhat after the manner of Richard III. Thus serfdom came into being, and thence the dread of leaving free play to the supposed "migratory instincts" of the peasant, a dread which has become a sort of obsession, so that, even now that he is nominally freed, in another age and under entirely altered conditions, the main feature of his bondage—bondage to the soil—is still maintained.

whole length of ideas at the risk of encountering the absurd. By
this logical consistency, this longing for the absolute, the Russian
mind betrays a certain affinity to the French mind, only the latter
submits to correction by positive practical sense, which will not
suffer it to stray beyond the domain of speculation. Hence the
striking contrast, in so many Russians, of great audacity in
intellectual spheres joined to as great timidity in real life, of
excessive temerity in the one and the most cautious reserve in
the other.

The levelness of the soil and the debility of the Russian
nature ought to be held responsible for one of the accusations
most frequently, and possibly with least justice, brought up
against the Russian people : lack of individuality, of originality,
want of creative faculties. The history of the nation and the
tardiness of its civilization are certainly not blameless in this ; but
if—a thing we may be permitted to doubt—if this defect should
prove universal and incurable, the blame should first of all be laid
on the country's physical nature. If he is lacking in personality,
the Russian, in this particular again, reflects the characteristics
of the land of his birth. To its poverty, to its sameness, he is
indebted for the comparative barrenness of his mind. This land,
indeed, offers but few images to the poet, or colors to the painter ;
it does not lend itself to a renewal of impressions and ideas.* If
this unproductiveness is to be corrected in the future by the
enlarged horizons which are opening out on all sides into the

---

* On this occasion I shall make bold to remark on the great and prolific influence brought to bear on Russian literature by the mountainous
regions remote from the empire's centre and more or less lately annexed to
it,—Crimea and Caucasus more particularly. Owing in a great measure to
the mistrust of a suspicious police, always ready to banish writers to the
extremities of the empire, national poetry, as represented by Pushkin and
Lermontof, has found there a source of inspiration by which romanticism
has largely profited. In this respect the influence of the Caucasus on Russian poetry, in the first half of the nineteenth century, might be likened to
that which the Alps exercised on French and German literature in the
eighteenth century, after Rousseau.

world of science and culture, is it not the land itself which should, in a great measure, be charged with the long inferiority of the Russian—nay, the Slav genius, such as, for instance, the lack of vitality and vigor in the ancient mythology of the Russian Slavs, when compared to the fables of the Greeks or the Scandinavians? *

* On the religious and mystical proclivities of the Russian soul, see Vol. III., Book I.

BOOK III. CHAPTER III.

The Variety of Russian Nature Lies in the Alternations of Seasons—In what Way the Contraries of Winter, Spring, and Summer have Reacted on the National Temperament—Russian Character is all in Extremes, as the Climate—Its Contradictions—Its Flexibility—Its Adaptability—An Historical Embodiment of the National Character.

WE have perhaps dwelt too persistently on the uniformity of Russian rural scenery ; it has, after all, a variety of its own, which powerfully reacts on man, and helps to account for the seeming contradictions of the national character. This principle lies not so much in the soil as in the climate.

Variety in Russia, and the beauty and picturesqueness it brings with it, come more from weather than space, from the succession of seasons more than from that of scenery. It is the opposite of what we see in southern countries, especially tropical ones, where vegetation and the outward appearance of earth and sky change little, where the seasons are known only by shadings, and life flows on amidst these conditions, even and monotonous in tenor. In the North, especially in a continental region like Great-Russia, the seasons forcibly contrast with one another ; they clothe the earth alternately in garments violently differing in coloring. They lend nature the variety of aspect which enables the Russian to imbibe from them the variety of impressions and feelings he never could draw from the soil. Without leaving his village, he passes, at intervals of six months, through climates and pictures as different as though he were oscillating between pole and equator, scaling back and forwards a ladder of from twenty-five to thirty degrees of latitude. Such changes tell no less on the character than on the temperament, on the imagination than on the mind.   In Russia each season has its own labors, festivities, and pleasures ; each has its own songs, and even sometimes its own dances.   In fact, the seasons hold so great a place in the popular life and poetry, that they might very well serve as frames to classify many of the *piêsni* sung by the peasant.   When we wish to describe Russia, it is not enough to depict the soil ; it is, above all, the seasons which must be portrayed.   Nothing in the climate of Western Europe, marked as the contrast is there between winter and summer, can give an accurate idea of what that contrast is by the Volga or the Neva : who has seen Russia under one only of these two aspects does not know the country.

Of Russian seasons, winter is the longest and most original ; in its very monotony partly lies its picturesqueness and beauty. It casts over that lustreless nature the most gorgeous of bridal robes.   Snow is the most brilliant of ornaments, and its cold whiteness, by turns sparkling and dull, is enhanced by the pearly iridescence supplied by ice and frost.   Everything vanishes under the snow,—land, sea and rivers, roads and fields ; but in this viewless uniformity nature assumes a majesty with which the meagre variety of spring or summer never could invest her. Under this thick mantle the eye detects nothing but hollows and swellings, depressions and unevenness ; but this monochrome ground-tone receives from the sun the most dazzling splendor, from night and the moon the tenderest, the daintiest tints.   In the glare of fine sunny winter days the eye can scarcely bear the even and continuous blaze ; so that in the north, where the snow lies on the ground five or six months at a stretch, there are nearly as many eye-diseases, as many blind people, as in the lands of the south.

It is in the forests that the beauties of winter should be preferably sought.   There rime decks the birch and the aspen with crystal flowers more brilliant and delicate than their leaves would be, while, on the background of white snow, shot with bluish streaks, the sombre masses of the pines and firs take on warm, velvety tones, which make them appear almost black. At night these landscapes loom in solemn grandeur. By moonlight the cold plains, in their spectral pallor, recall to the mind the limbos of Catholic poets. On trees or monuments the snow assumes fantastical light effects, and crowns the cupolas of the churches with a mystic halo. On moonless nights the stars scintillate with the vibrating intensity which is theirs in severe frost. The gloom of the darkest nights is lightened by the reverberation of the snow ; it is then as though the light, instead of coming down from the sky, were rising from the earth. In winter, night is the favorite time for sleigh-rides and country picnicking. Coming out of theatre or ball, young women, wrapped in furs, get into open sleighs, and, carried along by swift *tròykas* (the Russian teams of three abreast), are driven "to the Islands," or to some "resort" just outside St. Petersburgh, to enjoy the threefold sensation of fleetness, cold air, and night. In the streets of cities, or on the high-roads, the sleighs give you a peculiar impression, due to the combination of motion and silence. On the most frequented "perspectives" the horses, stimulated by cold, are started at a gallop, or at the high-stepping trot known only in Russia. Sleighs and vehicles of all kinds crowd, press, pass one another on the white carpet which kills sound, giving to the eye the spectacle of life at its wildest, while the ear receives the impression of absolute repose.

The long winter nights, so highly prized in the capitals, are not devoid of pleasure for the peasants. They too are impelled to assemble together, for work or recreation. Quite lately, in the northernmost provinces, the women and girls used to flock into the most spacious *izbà* of the village, sometimes clubbing together to rent it for the purpose. In the wavering light of the *lutchinas* (a kind of torches made out of resinous chips) [1] they held their

---

[1] These *lutchinas* are long chips of pine or fir, carefully cut from the portions of the logs most saturated with resin. They are stuck into some

possidiêlki, the rustic "sociables" of a people whom winter disposes to good fellowship. After spinning flax or wool, talking all the while, the young maidens, now joined by their lovers or betrothed, begin to sing some of those *piêsni* with choral burdens so dear to the Russian people, or to dance one of their slow dances with *balalàÿka* accompaniment, but too often superseded nowadays by the vulgar accordeon.'

Spring puts an end to these village parties, by restoring to the peasant the grass and sward and fetching the *khorovòd* out into the open air. The end of winter or the first dawn of spring is, of all times of the year, the dullest and most disagreeable. Instead of the green grass, a sea of mud ; in place of rural scents, the stench of the thaw. It is something like a decomposition, a general corruption, of nature, coming just before her yearly resurrection ; but how thrilling this resurrection, how longed for and joyfully hailed after the long winter mourning ! Nothing in moderate climes can give an idea of such a rejuvenation. The spring recalls to life both earth and water. After a hundred and fifty or two hundred

fissure in the wall, those interstices between the natural logs which are stopped up—most effectively too, so closely do the logs fit—with oakum and moss. The other end of the *lutchína* is lit and a tin or sheet-iron dripping pan placed under it on the floor, for droppings of hot resin, sparks, and bits of burnt off tinder. The name of this primitive torch, which begins to grow rare, is an ambitious one, being derived from *lutch*, "a beam, a ray " which reproduces exactly the Greek *lykê*, the Latin *lux*, Italian *luce*, and the Teutonic *licht*, English *light.—Possidiêlki* literally means "sittings," from *sidiêti = sedere*, "to sit."

' The *balalàÿka* is the national strumming-instrument, a genuine antique, the body nearly triangular in shape. The strings are not pinched, only strummed by a very rapid wrist motion, up and down, with the ends of the fingers (the nail side) ; the range of harmony and melody is limited to the tonic and fifth or dominant chords, and the effect produced is as rakishly merry and " devil-may-carish " as ever drove "blues " away. When it is used as an accompaniment to chorus singing and round-chain dancing *(khorovòd)* in the silent moonlight in the middle of the broad village street, the girls swaying gracefully from side to side, scarcely stirring their long beribboned braids, and one *solo* voice launching into space on a high end-note held out *ad infinitum*, then broken clean off without grading,--the whole scene has a weird, penetrating, poetic beauty that leaves an indelible impression.

days of snow, it brings back to light the green earth which had totally vanished ; it reopens the rivers, lakes, and gulfs, converted by winter into sullen, dead surfaces ; breaks up the ice that fettered them ; restores their color, murmuring, the mobility of dancing waves; makes them over new, so to speak. It is a whole element—the entire liquid world, which April or March thus reawakens to life. When nothing has fallen from the sky but snow, even the first rains bring something of surprise and almost joy, not unlike the pleasure experienced in Southern countries at the first drops of rain after long weeks of heat and drought. And indeed the children greet the rain and welcome it by traditional songs. Together with the rivers and all the watery realm, leaves and flowers come to life once more in forests and meadows, preceded by the birds who had fled to softer climes and whose return is kept daily track of in a *naïve* popular calendar : to-day the lark, to-morrow the swallow, of which a Russian legend will have that it comes down from Paradise and brings warmth from thence. Nature, in all her forms, appears alive and young in proportion to her previous deep and death-like trance.

Man accepts this renewal of all things with a gladness that would be inconceivable elsewhere. The peasants of the north, in their popular songs, celebrate the departure of winter and return of spring in simple poetic strain. From hill-top or house-roof they greet his coming in the far distance, and sing to him as early as March : " Come, O Spring, beautiful Spring, come with joy, bring flax tall-grown and plenty of grain ! " In many parts of the country they call on spring some time ahead, bidding it hasten, with rites and incantations of heathen origin. In others the festivities that celebrate the resurrection of nature mingle with those held for the resurrection of Christ, as though the one were the type or symbol of the other. The first day of May is a people's holiday almost everywhere : they wander about the woods. whence, like the dove of the Ark, they take home young tree-sprouts as testifying to the return of verdure and the disappearance of winter. The sun and the tepid vernal breezes give a delicious sensation, perfect in itself. The body, freed from its heavy wrappings, feels lighter as well as younger.'

The Russian spring is brief. From the nastiness of the thaw it quickly passes into midsummer heat ; but this very shortness enhances its effectiveness. There is something wonderful in the sudden outbreak of vegetation which bursts into life all on a sudden. The eye all but follows its unfolding day by day, and the laborer's gladness is more intense as he watches the grain, which he has just laid in the ground, sprout, rise, color, and ripen all in six weeks. In the north the rapid growth of the days rivals that of the plants. In proportion as the interval is greater from the long winter nights to the long summer days, the days lengthen by a more notable piece in each twenty-four hours. Thus everything combines—earth and water, plants and light— to make more intense the impression of universal renovation.

' The glad feeling of deliverance, of revival, forcibly strikes the poetic vein which is never far away from the people's heart, and sometimes finds a vent in the quaintest bits of word-painting. One morning in early spring I asked my maid who had just been out on an errand what kind of weather it was. "Beautiful," she answered, her eyes still dancing with the exhilaration of exercise in mild unaggressive air ; "there is a wind, but it is so warm when it blows against you, *it wraps you round as with a fur robe.*" I knew a grand, venerable old man, of mighty build and majestic simplicity of mind and manner. There was something heroic, epic about him. He had been born a serf, but manumitted by a wise master in time to make something of his life, and was now consciously enjoying the last years of it in wealth and comfort, the father of many sons who all had made their mark in science, art, or the service of the State. He was so near the end that even Solon might, after some demurring, have pronounced him a happy man. There never was a spring, since he began to consider each added year as one of grace, that he missed walking to the mighty granite embankment of the Neva,—and as he gazed on the great floes of Làdoga ice drifting and dancing down the current, jostling and crunching one another with the cool slushy sound of melting cracked ice in motion, under the turquoise blue of the cloud-flecked sky and on the deeper blue of the boisterous river, he bared his head and, crossing himself with the broad gesture of the Russian peasant at prayer, spoke aloud : " I thank Thee, Lord, that Thou hast vouchsafed to let Thy servant behold Thy spring once more ! "

The old-time Russians did not count this fleeting spring as a season ; they acknowledged only three : autumn, winter, and summer. Summer, with some of the inconveniences it entails on southern countries, such as heat—at times oppressive—dust, and often drought, brings also some of the southern loveliness : the beauty of sky and atmosphere, the mildness of the air, the trans-lucent haziness of the horizon, the coolness of shade and waters, the delicious freshness of earliest morning and of the last hours of eve. In the northern half of the empire, summer has pictures exclusively its own, which fancy could not conjure without having enjoyed them in reality. The nights of the southern summer, with their soft temperature and their diaphanous sky, are beauti-ful ; but those of the north are no less so, and surprise you more. No brush could render the delicacy of their tints, the fineness of their gradations. On those nights on which the sun scarce dips below the horizon, the lively colors of a spring sunset are suc-ceeded by opalescent and pearly tints which might belong to another planet. The light, in paling, assumes a semblance almost ethereal. It is neither night nor day, neither dawn nor twilight—or rather it is both. As we near the Polar Circle, sun-set and dawn follow each other more nearly, in both space and time. Towards midnight, the pallor of the one and the blush of the other are very close together at both ends of the north, light-ing up the heavens simultaneously, as though mutually reflecting each other.

Under the 60th degree—the latitude of St. Petersburgh—there is already no night at the end of June, although not until we reach the 66th degree, just above Arkhangelsk, do we actually see the sun on the horizon at midnight. These weird nights, so soothing to the eye and imagination, have in them something exciting to the nerves ; they seem to repudiate sleep. Therefore, in order to better enjoy the long evenings, many Russians take a *siesta* in the daytime, as do all southern peoples. There is in this continuous daylight a subtle stimulant which renders it quickly wearisome to foreigners and makes them wish for the return of normal nights. They do return soon, and begin to increase just as fast as they had decreased. Already in the numerous and wholly pagan rites that celebrate the summer solstice on St. John's Eve, through the joyful songs in praise of the sun, arrived at the zenith of his ascent, some sad strains are heard, mourning beforehand his rapid descent towards winter.

With the lengthening nights autumn returns, the least conspicuous and least original of Russian seasons, but not the least beautiful. The forests don those hues, warm and varied, whose richness summer cannot match. The frequent atmospheric changes lend to the sky tones of a sombre and fitful beauty, and, on the boughs in the woods, or on the grass of the steppes, the first morning frosts descend, shedding over the scenery charms scarcely familiar to any eye but that of the early huntsman. Moreover, there is in this decadence of light and vegetation a feeling of sadness, a poetic vein of mild melancholy, which suits well with this northern nature. Autumn always lasts a long time ; the days shorten ; the leaves fall ; the birds depart on their migration, species by species,—the cuckoo, the most sensitive to cold, sometimes starts as early as the end of July ;—the rains come, then snow ; but winter, the genuine Russian winter, does not arrive until the earth lies enfolded in the heavy shroud which spring alone will lift.

All these vicissitudes of the seasons are strongly felt by the Russians, and nobody has rendered them more beautifully by word and brush. Not a shading of that pallid nature, not a gleam of light or color in the sky, not a deepening shadow on the face of the earth, has escaped their eye, not a murmur their ear. " By nothing but the motion of the leaves, I could, with closed eyes, tell the season or the month of the year," says one of their writers, somewhere.* They have lovingly depicted this land of theirs,

---

* Ivan Turguénief, the greatest word-painter amidst the great Russian novelists.

which, in the long run, does assume a penetrating charm ror anybody that has once felt it, like a face the beauty of which lies in
the expression.   Their painters have portrayed it in those alternations of the seasons which, at few months' interval, offer to their
brush different worlds.   Hence the twofold talent which often
strikes one in their pictures, the feeling of color and that of
shading,—the comprehension of great lines and large masses, and
that of detail and accessories.   It is because in these vast plains,
usually devoid of successive plans, there is not much of a medium
between the general effects and the isolated ones,—between the
long-stretched forest and a clump of trees,—between the boundless
steppe and a bunch of shrub.   As immensity draws the eye till it
loses itself in the horizon, so every slightly conspicuous detail irre-
sistibly attracts attention in the end.   Nothing could render the
grandeur of a sunset in the southern steppes, say between the
Azof and Caspian Seas.   At the same time, on these level plains,
as on an empty stage, every human figure, every object, stands out
with singular vigor on the uniform immensity ; a tree, a hut, a
man, a horse, assume an unusual importance, and almost appear
larger than nature in size.   It is thus, to make use of a homely
simile, that the Russians have a rare facility to contemplate nature
through both ends of their spy-glass, to see it by turns as a near-
sighted person sees it or a far-sighted one.   With this faculty
they possess the gift of accuracy, of hitting the right expression.
Things appear to them precise and lifelike—a gift which they
derive from that same nature whose forms and colors impress
themselves by perpetual iteration or are brought into relief by
their isolation.

The influence of these vicissitudes of seasons makes itself felt
especially in the temperament and the character of the nation.
To them the Russian owes the flexibility, the elasticity of organs
which have been fashioned by the alternations of winter and
summer, so as to adapt themselves to any climate ; to them
he is indebted for his intellectual plasticity, the ease with which

he passes from one idea to another, a faculty which matches the former, and makes moral as easy as physical acclimatization wherever he may be.

To these oppositions of climate I am tempted to ascribe also whatever at times appears in the Russians ill-regulated, exaggerated, disorderly, unbalanced. They are frequently accused of want of originality. Now we should arrive at an understanding as to what is meant by that word, that rebuke. If they lack originality in intellect, in ideas, on the other hand they have a great deal of it in character, mind, and expression. Russian poetry, novels, music, often show remarkable originality. What, perhaps, the Russians are wanting in—or, more correctly, what time and education have prevented their showing, as yet, as much as some other nations—is the genius of invention. Far from being generally deficient in individuality, the Russian often abounds in it—in feelings, taste, and habits. He is frequently original, in the new and commonly accepted sense of the word,— in tastes and manners. This originality, indeed, often degenerates into peculiarities, eccentricities, nay, into insanity. Ivan the Terrible, Peter the Great, Paul I., are appalling instances in point. If, among sovereigns, this defect should be laid to the account of personal temperament or of that unwholesome effect of absolute power which, among the Roman Cæsars has produced so many monstrosities, signs of the same disposition can be traced far below the level of the throne. It would be an easy task to report many a trait of Russian originality, and in the course of over two centuries more than one nobleman in Petersburgh or Moscow, besides Suvòrof or Rostoptchin, has made for himself a European reputation in this line. Eccentricity and singularity, in fact, are, on the whole, less rare in northern countries than in southern ones,—in England and the United States than in Italy or Spain. In the Russia of the times of serfdom, moreover, eccentricity could also be bred of the accumulation of riches in few hands, of the inordinate license affected by the owners of vast wealth, to whom the habit of indulging every whim and wish was like another kind of absolute royalty, who became as quickly satiated and *blasé*, and, to force some new sensation, exhausted the round of fancies.

In Russia the absence of political life, the frequently enforced idleness of talent, have for a long time done their work of warping the most active faculties. Even in the low classes the weight of want and bondage has not always suppressed eccentricity ; only it assumes a religious disguise. It were a vain attempt to try and catalogue all the singular sects with which the dregs of Russian society teem, for there is no extravagance too great to attract adepts. In spite of appearances, such abnormal or inordinate propensities, in religion or daily life, are not irreconcilable with a practical turn of mind or realistic common-sense in a nation any more than in an individual. The most positive, most matter-of-fact people—the American nation—are a proof in point.

If the affinities between man and climate easily turn to fancifulness, there is, between the Russian temperament and Russian nature, as manifested in the opposition of the seasons, a likeness not easily to be denied. Both are immoderate, both easily rush from one extreme to another. Alternations of all kinds, changes of moods, ideas, feelings, are always strongly marked ; a wide margin is open to the oscillations of mind and heart ; the various stages of life differ perhaps more than anywhere else. The Russian soul easily passes from torpor to buoyancy, from meekness to wrath, from submission to revolt ; in all things it appears to naturally incline to extremes. By turns submissive and irritable, apathetic and impetuous, jovial and morose, indifferent and passionate, the Russian, perhaps more than any other people, runs all the gamut of cold and heat, of calm and tempest. The Russian is prone to sudden infatuation, to unbridled whims, to impulses and transports of passion for things either serious or futile—an opinion, a writer, a singer, a dancer, a fad of fashion. This disposition makes itself felt as well in public as in private, in national

as in individual life, all the more that it is indirectly favored
by the political *régime*, which, forbidding one day a thing
it tolerates the next, seems to encourage to-day what it will
proscribe to-morrow.

The individual, society, the government, seem equally inclined
to think, to will, to act by fits and starts, so that periods of fever,
energy, and confidence are closely followed by spells of flat calm,
of inertia, of languor, during which a feeling of despair, a lack of
interest in things in general, overcasts the soul. This accounts for
many of the contradictions and alternations of Russian life. In the
same persons or in the same sphere there is the strangest inter-
weaving and intertangling of doubt and conviction, of indifference
and enthusiasm, and initiative in ideas is often seen attended by
routine in action.

Being made like that, the Russian at times yields to infatuation, to impulses at which he is the first to wonder. The Eastern
war of 1877–78 is a striking instance of this. Owing to the lack
of liberty and the want of interest in the political life at home ;
owing also to the urging of a press which enjoys getting excited
about something with impunity, and, lastly, to the need of emotion
vaguely felt by a public disgusted with the emptiness of daily life
and made hungry by a system of dieting and fasting, a sceptical
and chaffing society, lately almost indifferent to the sufferings of
the Balkan Slavs, becomes in the course of a few months fired with
an ardent and irresistible enthusiasm for the Serbs and Bulgars.
In the face of the reluctance manifested by the sovereign and
ministers, in spite of the bantering incredulity expressed in the
drawing-rooms of Petersburgh, Russia, stirred up from high to
low, starts on a sort of crusade, and wages a great national war in
which no one would have believed two or three years before,—a
war which, the suspicious attitude of the West notwithstanding,
was decided on not so much out of political calculations as from
a sudden explosion of feelings long suppressed and eager to
find a vent.

This mobility, this impressionability, so often pointed out in Slavs, especially Russians and Poles, this lack of balance, of measure, so repeatedly deplored by the Russian writers themselves, show too great an affinity with a climate persistently given to excesses not to be derived therefrom, at least in part. The successive oppositions of nature in her various phases seem to have stamped their impress on man. We should not wonder therefore at the Russians exposing to view so many contrasts, or our being continually forced into contradiction when we speak of them.

In the Great-Russian, moreover, this changefulness is usually moderated by practical sense, and, like a child, being but young as a nation, he can correct it by training, age, and experience. To look at it more closely, this defect may, after all, turn out to be the obverse side of a quality, itself ascribable to climate no less than to the Slavic trait of malleability. I mean that facility of adaptation, that faculty of comprehension, which so eminently distinguish the Russian, and for which Herzen coined the word "receptivity." This imitative instinct, this innate talent of assimilation, so striking in the cultivated Russian, has sometimes been doubted when discussing the common people. Yet we surely can trace it even in the latter in the technical sphere, the only one ordinarily open to the peasant, in that versatility which renders all work easy to him, and frequently enables him to ply ten crafts at once; lastly, in that suppleness of the Russian soldier and the Cosack, so promptly ready to meet all demands of either war or peace. Half hidden and as though paralyzed in the lower classes by the monotony of their existence, by habitual routine, attachment to ancient customs or half-oriental prejudices, this quality takes its free development in the higher classes, among the Russians who have shaken themselves free of popular prejudice; there it unfolds itself in all spheres at once— in ideas, manners, customs, literature, even language. In this respect, as in a great many others, the Russian is the exact opposite of the Englishman. The suppleness of his intellect appears to be unlimited, and the ease with which he appropriates may have been an obstacle to the spontaneous development of national originality.

With its inconveniences and its advantages, this flexibility remains one of the most marked features of the Russian nature. Were it not that it always is a somewhat arbitrary proceeding to establish a hierarchy among simultaneous faculties and interconnected moral leanings, one might say that this is the Russian's pre-eminent faculty. It shows in every part of him, in his intellect as much as in his body and organs, all of which are tempered and tested by those trying alternations of the seasons as by a sort of gymnastics, to which nature, stern mother, subjects him every year. Hence the success of the Great-Russian in colonizing the vast plains of his continent, spreading northward and southward with an almost equal facility of acclimatization under every or any sky ; hence, in the course of the last two centuries, the surprises given to aged and scornful Dame Europe by a people so long considered as an alien in the European world, and rebellious to its civilization ; hence, lastly, the difficulty for the observer of discerning what is possible in Russia from what is not. For this faculty of adaptation, confined until now to private life, to external politeness, to arts and sciences, can any day extend into novel spheres, such as government, institutions, public liberties.

Should an historical type be asked for, a living type of this Russian nature, which the weight of events has so long hindered from blossoming out into great men,—there is the Tsar Peter the Great. All through his semi-barbarism, in his very excesses and contradictions, with his foibles and infatuations, with his innovating recklessness and his practical good-sense, his scorn of obstacles and his positive instinct, his wide open mind and his marvellously cunning hand, his universal aptitude for all crafts and callings, Piotr Alexéÿevitch remains *the* national type *par excellence.* Few of the national defects are lacking in the great reformer, and many have reached in him the limits of the possible ; few of the national qualities but come to light in him, and several have, in him, risen to genius. The imperial carpenter of Zaandam may seem to us of a harder and stronger temper than most of his countrymen, but he is unmistakably wrought out of the same metal.[4] In the great reformer, the two extremes of the nation, the two Russians, so different even yet, that the one does not always appear to be evolved from the other,—the *mujik* and the cultured nobleman, the former with his stolid, massive stubbornness, the latter with his alert and mobile suppleness, seem combined and merged together, as though to correct and complete one another. Peter has shown that Russian flexibility need take nothing from energy, that Slavic ductility can abide together with solidity.

If one is astonished at finding, in one *people*, so many traits of character different or even opposite, one can, in the person of Peter the Great, behold them all united and centred in one *man*. This converging, in one individual, of so many qualities and defects, so many features scattered through a nation, has shaped a queer and well-nigh monstrous man, but, at the same time, one of the most mighty, most enterprising, the best endowed for life and action, whom the world has seen. No other nation can boast of owning a great man in whom it can embody all itself, who, in his very vices, stands out, a colossal incarnation of its genius. Peter, the pupil and imitator of foreigners,—Peter, who seemed to have set himself the task of violently breaking his people's nature, and who has been regarded by the old-time Moscovites as a sort of Ante-Christ,—Peter is *the* Russian, the Great-Russian *par excellence*. Standing before his face, one may say that sovereign and nation explain each other. A nation that resembles such a man is sure of a great future. If it is apparently wanting in some of

[4] Or he could not have succeeded, even with *his* force of will and summary methods.

13

those highest or most refined qualities on which mankind prides itself, it owns those which give power and political greatness.* [5]

* For personality, energy, consistency,—qualities too often denied the Russians, three men, vastly different, might be mentioned from among our own contemporaries : N. Miliùtin, G. Samárin, and Prince V. Tcherkassky. See *Un Homme d'État Russe, d'après sa Correspondance Inédite* ("A Russian Statesman, from his Unpublished Correspondence ").

[5] This chapter is one of great beauty — of an order of beauty one would least have looked for from an historian and political writer. And the comprehension of the Russian nature, both human and physical, the insight into the connection, the interdependence of both, must be a revelation to foreign readers. Mr. Beaulieu has here said things that no one said before him, because he has seen things that must remain a sealed book to any but a poet's eye, sharpened by science and scholarship.

BOOK III. CHAPTER IV.

The Russian Character and Nihilism—Origin and Nature of Nihilism—Its Three Successive Phases—By What Sides it Belongs to the National Temperament—Combination of Realism and Mysticism—In What Sense Nihilism is a Sect—Manner of Nihilistic Propaganda—Radical Instincts of the Russian Mind—The Slav Woman and the "Woman Question" in Russia.

By its rigor and demands the Russian climate inclines man to realism ; by the vastness and sameness of her plains, by her immensity and poverty, nature predisposes him to mysticism and melancholy. Therein lies the key to many of the contrasts with which the Russian nature abounds. Of this conflict or this union of tendencies often opposed to one another or apparently irreconcilable, several illustrations might be found in the bulk of the people themselves, in the ignorant sects of Great-Russia. We will take instead as a specimen a phenomenon not less curious, although less spontaneous, less thoroughly native. This is the development called "nihilism," or, as the Russians pronounce it : *nighilìsm*.[1]

Like nearly all the theoretical conceptions of the Russians, "nihilism," in its principle, is simply an importation from the West. It was from Europe and especially from German philosophy that, under Nicolas, the first intellectual seeds came into Russia of that spirit of negation and revolt which, in the land of autocracy,

---

[1] The letter *h* is lacking in the Russian alphabet, and the letter *g* does duty for it in words of foreign extraction. The Little-Russians sound it with a strong guttural aspiration, which makes a sort of compromise between the two. Concerning the pronunciation of the *i*, see note 3, on p. 18.

under the shades of a secular absolutism, found a soil more apt than their own original native sod.   It was from the latest sons of Kant and the revolutionary children of the peaceable and conservative Hegel, from the most extreme representatives of the Hegelian Left, that the first ancestors or first apostles of Russian nihilism drew their inspirations, if not their theories.   In all that regards ideas and views, negations and dreams, nihilism is nothing but a corrupted extract from French philosophy, criticism, and socialistic schools.   The interest and originality of Russian radicalism are not there to be found, not in speculations and abstractions unfamiliar to most young adepts of contemporary nihilism.   What the latter holds of truly original, it owes to Russia's political and to her economic situation, to social and religious status, and above all to the national temperament.

At bottom, nihilism is simply the Russian form of the negative and revolutionary spirit of the age.   Far from being an affection peculiar to Russia, it is a moral epidemic of which the germ has been imported, and with which all Europe, nay, the whole civilized world is more or less affected ; only the symptoms and the consequences of the disease vary with each people, according to the patient's age, constitution, and habits.   If, in the low plains of the Neva or the Volga, the attacks of this revolutionary fever, nowadays, become endemic, offer peculiar symptoms, that is due to the people's idiosyncrasies and also to their diet.

Nihilism, which has made so much noise from 1878 to 1883, is not exactly a novelty.   It can register, even under this uncouth name, a long existence, for it is not necessarily associated with revolutionary conspiracies or with political crimes.   It is anterior to all such attempts, and may survive them or again become, as formerly, a stranger to them.*

---

* Among the conspirators, many and not unfrequently the most enterprising are of Jewish extraction.   This gave occasion to certain Russian papers, happy to find an alien scapegoat, to assert that all the trouble came from abroad and from the Jews.   This should not be taken seriously.

Few designations have lent themselves to more misunderstandings than this term "nihilism," which, in reality, is only a witty nickname, disowned by the greater part of those to whom it is applied.* As often happens with such misnomers, the word has changed meaning three or four times, —or rather, this contemptuous surname has been successively applied to different doctrines or tendencies, naturally, however, connected with one another by a more or less direct filiation. Three phases are distinguishable, or, so to speak, three stages and metamorphoses. In its first acception, "nihilism" was untinged with politics; it was little more than a certain way of bearing oneself, thinking, talking,—a mannerism, a fashion, one might say a pretence and attitude, that came into favor among the young people of 1860 to 1870, among the students at the universities, and the girl-students with cropped hair residing abroad or in the provinces. This designation was pointed at a spirit of revolt against received ideas and social conventionalities, against all traditional authorities and antiquated religious or political dogmas, a spirit of negation, stamped with an intolerant materialism and *naïve* radicalism; nothing more, at bottom, than a violent reaction of the Russian soul against the system of government and the intellectual yoke under which it had long been bent. This was the first and, properly speaking, the true nihilism, the nihilism which has been depicted in immortal strokes by the most famous Russian novelists, the nihilism of which Tur-

Nihilism is a genuinely Russian thing, although there are numbers of nihilists outside of Russia. As to the Israelites, it might be said that there exists a kind of Jewish nihilism which naturally amalgamates with the Slavic nihilism. The inferior situation, created for the numerous Jews of Russia by laws or custom, has, moreover, much to do with their readiness to take part in plots.—See Vol. III., Book IV., Ch. III.

* The name is taken from a novel by Ivan Turguénief, *Fathers and Sons*, where, about 1860, the first generation of "nihilists" was taken off. The Russian revolutionists usually style themselves "socialist-democrats," or simply "propagandists." Their various factions are mostly named after the clandestine periodicals which they issue as their organs. (See Vol. II., Book V., Ch. III.)

guénief's Bazárof and Pìssemsky's Helen will remain undying presentations.*

After this theoretical and abstract nihilism, frequently dabbled in by amateurs, at times all made up of posing and outward show, and which did not attempt to carry out its maxims except in individual life and private relations, came, about 1871, under the twofold influence of the Paris Commune and the International, a nihilism all action and agitation, transformed into a militant socialism, which strove to spread its ideas among the people, a nihilism already given to politics and revolution, having recourse to association and secret propaganda, though not to plots and murder. It is only after several years of disappointment and bitterness, towards 1877–78, that this peaceably preaching nihilism, transformed into a violent party seeking redress from conspiracies and assassinations, takes for its weapon dynamite and for its watchword — terror.† Under the threefold aspect of speculative radicalism, socialistic apostolate, revolutionary terrorism, "nihilism" has shed on the Russian temperament a totally novel light. It has laid bare before the world a power of logic as to intellect, a force of will as to character, a capacity for passion, for fanaticism, stubbornness, and self-devotion, which might be matched among popular sects, but which, as found in civilized Russians, have been to Europe a veritable revelation.

However nihilism may reach out from afar towards Western metaphysics, it never was a system after the manner of Schopenhauer's pessimism or Auguste Comte's positivism ; it is not a new form of old scepticism or old naturalism. In its philosophy it is little more than a coarse and boisterous materialism, almost devoid

---

* Bazárof, the medical student, the hero of *Fathers and Sons ;* Helen Jiglinsky, the heroine of Pìssemsky's novel, which has been translated into French, under the title of *Dans le Tourbillon (In the Whirlpool),* Charpentier, 1882.

† What caused this abrupt evolution of socialism into terrorism will be made clear in Vol. II., Book VI., Ch. II., where we shall study the formation and organization of the revolutionary party.

of any scientific apparatus. In its politics it is a socialistic radicalism, fomented by bureaucratic despotism and exasperated by the capricious severities of an irresponsible power. It is not a party, for under its banner march revolutionists of all kinds—authoritarians, terrorists, federalists, anarchists, mutualists, communists—who keep on terms of mutual understanding only by putting off till the day of their triumph all discussion on future organization.*

In the midst of all its exaggerations, through its successive phases, nihilism has been little else than the pupil of the revolutionists of the west, a pupil, indeed, who flatters himself that he will outdo his masters, and who magnifies at will their boldest teachings. Russian radicalism can, it is true, claim one national theoretician, who, for talent, character, or influence, does not remain behind any one of his rivals and co-religionists of the west. This legislator of Utopia-land is neither Herzen nor Bakùnin,—neither of those exiles, agitators, so long friends and associates, yet so profoundly different in genius and sentiment that, in spite of their common aspirations, they could fitly represent each one of the faces of the national radicalism, or, more correctly, of the Russian spirit itself.† It is not Herzen, the paradoxical and fascinating writer, the great railer and great dreamer, whose eloquence is so warm and highly colored that his true home might be the land of the sun ; Herzen the poet and minstrel of negation, ever

---

* Under the influence of Bakùnin and the *Internationale* the greater part of Russian revolutionists appear to have adopted for their formula the federation of productive independent communes, suggested to them by their own communal organization. (See further in Book VIII.) In 1874, after the foundation of the paper *Vperiòd (Go Ahead)*, by Lavròf, discussions having arisen within the "emigration" on the manner of preparing the revolution, the most ardent ones declared with Tkatchòf that, instead of taking thought for future organization, "the action party" should keep in view only the work of destruction. This advice became a rule with the immense majority of nihilists.

† I had better recall to the reader's mind that Herzen died at Nice in 1869, and Bakùnin at Bern in 1878.

romantic and idealist in spite of himself, sceptical and sad at bottom, driven into revolutionism by his sympathies, by the craving for hope and faith ; a heart open to all the passions as to every noble feeling ; a mind accessible until the end to all ideas and even to the rough teachings of experience. Nor is it Bakùnin, the narrow, incorrigible sectarian, the logician, colder and harder than the ice of his native land, systematic as a geometrician, declamatory as a rhetorician, the fanatic of negation, the maniac with mind shut tight against all that is foreign to his craze, impervious to doubt, to discouragement, to all the teachings and deceptions of life.

Herzen, by the amplitude of his intellect, which, undisciplined, was ever in search of new things, by the breadth and winged flight of his imagination, which *would* carry him beyond his own system, strangely overlapped the scant frame of doctrinal nihilism ; he was less its lawgiver than its involuntary, free harbinger. With all his weaknesses and generous rushes, with his spells of unrealizable hopes and his numerous lapses into hopelessness, with his disappointment in revolution as well as in civilization, with all the inconsistencies and contradictions of his mind and of his life, Herzen, a sort of revolutionary Faust, remains one of the most living types of the modern Russian, thrown off his bearings by a civilization from which he demands more than it has to give.

Bakùnin, on the other hand, "the apostle of destruction," the prophet of anarchy and *amorphism*, or social formlessness, the involuntary disintegrator of the *Internationale*, and the founder of the bootless *Alliance Universelle*,—Bakùnin, the cosmopolitan conspirator, the man of deeds, more mighty by his word and personal magnetism than by the pen and written exhortation, has, notwithstanding his relations with Nietcháyef and the conspirators of the north, had more influence, perhaps, abroad, over the working-men of Switzerland, Spain, Italy, than in his own country, more power over professional conspirators than over the young people at school.* All through his long career, animated by a single idea, and that a barren one, he was not so much the theoretician or codifier of the national nihilism, of which he had appointed himself the peddler in the west, as its living impersonation, and, we might say, its blind and sterile incarnation.

The chief master and inspirer of nihilism was not, like Herzen and Bakùnin, an aristocrat brought up in the drawing-rooms of Petersburgh and Moscow, and whose existence was passed in great part abroad. He was a child of the people, the son of a country priest, who never stepped off the Russian soil and never spoke in favor of the West; who, instead of preaching "from the other side," *i. e.* from London or from Paris, wrote in Petersburgh, under the censors' eyes. This man, who during his brief apostolic career, from 1855 to 1864, had over young people an influence which his sufferings served to increase,—this man was Tcherny-shèfsky. This Russian Proudhon or Lassalle, sentenced to hard labor for revolutionary propaganda, lived twenty years in Siberia, of which seven in the mines. Then he aged in solitude and in-action, having been sent to reside at one of the uttermost stations nearest the polar circle, far removed from all intercourse with Europe and the outer world.† Well informed as a writer and unwearying as a worker, his weapon at one time a redoubtable logic, at another a biting irony, gifted with an intellect both vig-orous and supple, an energetic and all-of-one-piece character,—in so far like the rest that he too mixed the intoxicating fumes of sentimental idealism with the crudities of realism, Tchernyshèf-sky, by his faults not less than by his qualities, is and remains a

* Nietcháyef was a man of intrigue, who, under Bakùnin's inspiration, but in view of personal advantages, had organized in Russia a revolutionary society. He was arrested in Switzerland and tried in Petersburgh in 1871, for the assassination of one or his accomplices, from whom he dreaded betrayal, and sentenced to imprisonment with hard labor.

† In 1889 the papers announced his death at Sarátof, in the southeast of Russia, whither he had been transferred at his urgent request. He had resided in Siberia until 1883, then had been confined within the city of Astrakhan.

representative Russian. Philosopher, economist, critic, novelist, and everywhere the propagator of the cheerless doctrines of which he was the first victim, Tchernyshèfsky, in his scientific treatises, has given the theory or *summing up* of Russian radicalism. In a queer and indigestible novel, written in the gloom of a prison, he has given its poetry and its gospel.*

We shall hardly be wronging Tchernyshèfsky if we ascribe to his long and tedious novel more ascendancy over youthful Russian heads than his didactical treatises ever achieved. This man, whose influence had dethroned that of Herzen, and whom Siberia and long sufferings had circled with the martyr's halo, was regarded by many of his countrymen as one of the giants of modern thought, one of the great pioneers of the future, as a Russian Fourrier, or, better still, Karl Marx.† In spite of all the admiring homage of which he was the object, notwithstanding the sterling originality of his mind, his ideas have nothing very original about them, either in political economy or philosophy. The form and the details may be novel and marked with individuality, but the substance of his theories takes us to Germany, England, France.¹ What gives to

---

* Tchernyshèfsky opened fire, about 1855, by a treatise on naturalistic esthetics, his subject being *The Relations between Art and Reality.* A little later, in an essay entitled *The Anthropological Principle in Philosophy,* he expounded a system of transformistic materialism, defended the unity of principle in nature and in man, and reduced ethics to pleasure or utility. In 1860 he published in the *Sovremiénnik (Contemporary),* conducted by the poet Niekrássof, a review of the *Political Economy* of Stuart Mill, on wholly socialistic lines. This review was translated into French under the title, *Économie Politique Jugée par la Science ; Critique des Principes de Stuart Mill* (Bruxelles, 1874).—*(Political Economy Judged by Science ; a Criticism on the Principles of Stuart Mill.)* Lastly, in 1863, the *Sovremiénnik,* which was soon after suppressed, published anonymously his novel, *What is to be Done?* It was written in prison, in Petersburgh.

† See, for instance, the introduction to a pamphlet entitled *Unaddressed Letters,* a little book that was never finished, but was published in French, 1874, and also in Russian, in the same year, in the revolutionary review *Vperiòd.*

¹ Farther away and back too, as far as ancient India. Our theoreticians fall into plagiarism continually, but most innocently, from simple ignorance, since they deliberately throw the past overboard, under the name of "use-

Tchernyshèfsky's works, leastwise to this novel, the most native soil-flavor, is possibly that kind of mystic and visionary realism which we find in so many nihilists. Moreover, however great may have been the ascendant of Tchernyshèfsky and a few other writers of that ilk, nihilism is far from having followed in servile fashion the masters it glorifies, it is more indebted to their romantic fictions than to their scientific deductions.

From the psychological point of view, one might say that the nihilism of Turguénief's and Pìssemsky's heroes is the outcome of the union between the two opposite inclinations of the Russian character—that to the absolute and that to realism. From this unnatural connubium was born that repulsive monster, one of the sorriest births of modern thought. There again we encounter an instance of that impatience under restraint of any sort, that reckless boldness in speculation, which are frequently found among the Russians, but which, with them, lay less claim to science and method than among the Germans. From the moral and political stand-points, nihilism was first of all a sort of pessimism, half instinctive and half thought out, a form of pessimism not uninfluenced by nature and climate, fostered and intensified by history and the political order of things.* Seeing nothing around but evil, it longed to demolish everything—government, religion, society, family— in order to reconstruct, all in one block, a better world. Doc trinary nihilism, the oldest and most ordinary form, has never had anything in common with the critical scepticism which compares and analyzes, reserving its judgment and liberty. Being in sub-

---

less ballast" (not a felicitous simile, as no ship can go straight and steady without ballast). So they keep every now and then stating what they fancy to be novelties, in beautiful unconsciousness that they propound theories that have been tried and exploded hundreds of years ago; they are all the time, in the pregnant Russian phrase, "discovering Americas."

* Herzen (*The Russian People and Socialism*) wrote already about 1848, long before nihilism had a name : " The real character of Russian thought was developed in all its force under Nicolas. The distinctive feature of that movement is a tragical emancipation of conscience, an implacable negation, a bitter irony."

stance a negation which affirms itself and admits of no inquiry, it was from the very first a sort of dogmatism the wrong way, as narrow, as blind as, and no less imperious, no less intolerant, than the traditional creeds the yoke of which it throws off.

In the intemperateness and coarseness of their negation, flung in the face of all that humanity holds it an honor to respect, something could be felt in Bazárof's imitators of the boyishness of incredulity when it is as yet a novelty, something of the ill-regulated excesses of minds but recently set free. In these pretensions to maturity, advanced by a youthful generation disillusioned before having lived, something like depraved childishness peeps through. For many adepts the nihilistic theories were only a sort of protest against the old-time superstitions which still sway the masses, against the political servility, the intellectual hypocrisy, or conventional belief in dogmas which still prevail too generally among the higher classes.

A nihilist of the first manner was asked in what his doctrine consisted. "Take earth and heaven," he replied; "take State and Church, kings and God, and spit on it all—*that* is our symbol." Were it the raillery of an adversary, this definition still would be exact. The word, however, is less shocking to the ears of Russians, for spitting plays a great part in their life and superstitions. You spit to turn aside an evil omen; you spit to express wonder or contempt; you spit everywhere and all the time.† The nihilist took pleasure in spitting on everything; he delighted in challenging and defying the spirit of veneration and humility so tenaciously rooted in the Russian " of the people," who

---

† Turguénief somewhere tells that at Heidelberg, frequented at the time by many Russian students who had been expelled from their own national universities, there appeared, about 1865, a nihilist paper entitled *On All Comers I Spit*. When a Russian means "I don't care a snap," he says "I spit on it." [3]

[3] Spitting, in the Greek Church, is a form of exorcism. Thus at baptisms, at the point of the service where the godfather and godmother, in the infant's name, renounce Satan and his pomps, they emphasize the renunciation by thrice spitting at the Enemy—over their shoulder.

even yet bends in twain before his superiors, as before the holy *eïkons* or images. Herein lies an indication of the profound discordance in thoughts and feelings under which the nation labours. Morally and physically, in man and nature alike, the two extremes meet : to the most *naïve* veneration, political as well as religious, corresponds the most barefaced cynicism, intellectual and moral.

The coarse and repulsive realism, so obtrusively apparent in nihilism, so perceptible in the Russian schools, among the majority of students, could not fail to attract the attention of enlightened minds and the government. Against this unwholesome bent of the young and of the national mind a remedy had to be sought for, a counterpoise, primarily in the education of the young. Religion could not be relied on overmuch, for in Russia it has but little hold on the cultured classes, and orthodoxy is weakened rather than strengthened by the compromising support of the government and the imperfection of religious liberty. Lacking better means, recourse was had to classical studies, but in vain. Literature and the dead languages being the studies most disinterested, most removed from actual preoccupations, were thought to be the best corrective to the exaggerated naturalism of embryo Bazárofs. Under the influence of Katkòf and his *Moscow Gazette*, the ministry of public instruction, directed by Count Tolstoy, has been long at work, striving to subject the entire young generation to this classical discipline, and, through that, to a sort of idealistic gymnastics or drilling. The most singular thing about the business is that the languages and literatures, now suddenly called in to the rescue of society, had long been held "suspicious." Under the Emperor Nicolas the Greek and Latin classics had been denounced as fostering the spirit of revolt. Demosthenes and Cicero, all the republicans of Athens and Rome, were supposed to kindle revolutionary sentiments. In point of fact, they have been undesirable teachers of children destined to live and die under an autocratic rule. If not exactly proscribed, instruction in ancient history and literature had certainly been curtailed and lowered. In the schools tolerated by Nicolas, precedence had been given to the sciences, especially the natural sciences ; that meant pushing the Russian mind down the very incline to which it was naturally drawn.

By one of those abrupt changes so frequent in Russia, and quite compatible with the nature of the government, there was, under Alexander II., a sudden return to the classics and antiquity. It was announced as a discovery that the exclusive study of physical and natural sciences must lead to positivism. To counterbalance their realistic influence, the ancient literatures, treated but lately with distrust, were summoned in. After having been accounted the accomplices of revolution, Greek and Latin became the supporters of moral order. This restoration of classical studies in a country which pretended to have no use for Greeks and Romans, butted straight against the national inclinations which it was expected to correct. Accordingly it was violently kicked against by all the instincts, practical and positive, of the Great-Russian, the more outraged at such a treatment, as the awkwardness and harshness of the hand that inflicted it made it more painful and irritating. Notwithstanding the efforts made by Count Tolstoy, through fifteen years,* the study of antiquity could not restrain the realistic and radical tendencies of the contemporary young generation. As a protest against classicism, materialism and, along with it, revolutionary nihilism have never stopped increasing in the schools, irritated by petty restrictions and puerile vexations, which hit the teachers almost as hard as the learners. For, to prevail against such inclinations, indirectly encouraged by the social and political order of things, it is not enough to change

---

* Count Tolstoy became the most unpopular of ministers, and had to give up the portfolio of Public Instruction in 1880. In 1883 he was appointed Minister of the Interior, and died in 1889. Under Alexander III. another abrupt change. After having done everything to attract students to the classical universities and gymnasiums, regulations were issued in 1887, calculated to keep away from them young people not possessed of large means or influential family connections.

the school curriculum and make over the programmes of lessons and lectures.

Coarse negative materialism is not the whole of nihilism. This Janus has another face still, very different, yet equally Russian—mysticism. These men, so scornful of all creeds, all dreams, metaphysical or religious, themselves have speculations and dreams of their own ; and not the most timid or best regulated either. At the bottom of this naturalistic realism lurks a kind of idealism, anxious to take its flight through all the unexplored fields of possibilities. From out this pessimism, which curses the actual social order, issues an unbridled optimism, which ingenuously draws on the marvels of a utopian future. In Russia, a number of young people of both sexes, who would consider it the most cutting of insults to be called idealists, and the depth of humiliation to be held for such, do not hesitate, in matters the least apt, it would seem, for such treatment, to give themselves up to the most foolhardy dreams. It is in the domain of social and economical theories, in the field of positive realities, that the Russian, whether nihilist or not, loves best to indulge in the fumes of utopia and the search for the absolute. By entangling himself too deeply in realism and utilitarianism, he falls back into theories and chimeric vagaries, as though wandering in a circle ; it is when he has apparently strayed farthest that he returns to abstract speculation, as a traveller, after getting to the antipodes, might land on another part of the shore of the country he had quitted. The sphere which demands most moderation and intellectual sobriety is precisely that in which the Russian— and in that he does not stand alone—leaves the widest scope to his imagination. With a great difference in knowledge and method, have we not seen something of the same wrong-headed speculativeness among the most declared opponents of metaphysics —for instance, among certain positivists who, in economical and political questions, have at times arrived at conclusions so little in unison with their method and in reality so anything but positive? This contradiction, which is quite habitual with the majority of socialists or radicals, this sort of wheeling-round, which, in the most negative schools is so easily accounted for by an unconquerable craving for an ideal and for faith in a better world, is nowhere less rare or more striking than among the Russians. On this ground their natural turn of mind shows off, with all its contrasts, its distrust and contempt for generally received creeds, with its *naïve* trust in doubtful positions and its love of paradox.

Tocqueville has remarked that in our days the revolutionary spirit acts after the manner of the religious spirit. This is more true in contemporary Russia than anywhere else. For many young people revolution has become a religion, of which the dogmas are as little to be discussed as a revealed "creed," which has its confessors and martyrs as well as its gods and idols. With them negation has taken the aspect and character of a faith—the same enthusiastic fervor, the same sombre and contagious exaltation. From this point of view, the opinion of the ignorant abroad, who used to take nihilism for a sect, is not as false as it seemed at first sight. With its absolute spirit, intolerant of any criticism, with its blind faith and passionate self-devotions, it is indeed a sort of cult of which the god, deaf and unfeeling, is "the people," worshipped in its abasement,—a sort of church, kept together by the bond of love to that misjudged deity, and whose law is hatred to its persecutors.

These nihilists, detractors of all hope in the supernatural and contemners of every kind of spiritualism, are themselves, after a fashion of their own, believers and mystics. This can often be perceived in their manner of speech, in their writings, although most of them profess to despise poetry as babyish stuff. These foes to all superstition and veneration, who, in the noblest self-sacrifice pretend to see nothing but a reflex action or a refined form of egotism, honor the heroes and heroines of their struggle against might with a sort of poetical canonization. They celebrate the martyrs of their cause with a lyrism and a sort of piety which seems addressed rather to saints enthroned in their shrines than to modern conspirators.*

Read Tchernyshèfsky's famous novel, *What is to be Done?* † *(Shtò Diêlat?)*, and you will be surprised at the singular medley of mysticism and realism, of practical, wholly prosaic observations, and vague, visionary aspirations, all huddled together in this strange work of the radical doctrinarian. In this long, slow story, which claims to depict for us the reformers of society and the sages of the future, it is through symbols, in dreams, that to the heroine are revealed her own destinies, together with those of woman generally, and the human race. True, these sufficiently transparent allegories may have been suggested to the author, then already imprisoned, by the necessity of not arousing too much the distrust of the censors' office. In the prisoner's novel, side by side with this humanitarian mysticism, a sort of naturalistic asceticism shows itself, which to foreigners appears more peculiar still. His ideal revolutionist, the finished type of the "new men," Rakhmiètof, not only owns all the moral perfections of the brotherhood and universal solidarity, but, like a Christian anchorite, or a Hindoo *yogee*, takes delight in renouncing the joys of life and the pleasures of the senses ; inflicts privations on himself, hardships ; loves to mortify his flesh, so as to make himself like his suffering deity—the oppressed "people." When fruit was

---

* Take, for instance, the following translation of verses addressed to one of the heroines of one of the great political trials, Lydia Figner, who had studied medicine at Zurich and Paris : "Mighty, O maiden, is the impression produced by thy witching beauty ; but mightier than the witchery of thy countenance is the charm of thy soul's purity. . . . Full of pity is the image of the Saviour, full of sadness are his divine features ; but in thy eye of fathomless depth there is even more love, more pain still."—*Infanticide Perpetrated by the Russian Government*, Geneva, 1877. Compare the portraits of revolutionists given under the *nom de plume* Stepniàk in *Russia Sotterranea (Underground Russia)*, a small volume published in Italian, in Milan, 1882, with a preface by Lavròf.

† This novel has been translated, or rather epitomized, in bad French, in an edition published in Milan in 1878.

placed before him, he ate none but apples, because in Russia apples are the only fruit "the people" can partake of. If he did not wear a horse-hair shirt, this vindicator of the rights of the flesh used, instead of sleeping in a bed, to lie on a felt rug all studded with short nails, points upwards.⁴

Men like Rakhmiètof, doubtless, are rare outside of fictions. Of Tchernyshèfsky's admirers, only too many give themselves up to the unbridled license authorized by their wretched doctrines. This stoicism, this contempt of material delights, imperatively demanded for others, does, however, show up sometimes in real life. Among the innovators of either sex who profess and frequently practise free love, I have known such as considered it incumbent on their honor not to use for their own benefit the rights which they claimed.* This naturally is the case more often with women, as they are always more given to inconsistencies, more anxious to ennoble all sorts of aberrations. It is there, among some of these votaresses of nihilism, these young girls who are its most ardent proselytes and most courageous missionaries, that one can best see how much generous feeling and unconscious idealism can thrive under the mantle of this repulsive materialism.

---

⁴ This feat of asceticism, from its impossibility, has become proverbial, an equivalent of the *reductio ad absurdum* of classical rhetoric. So that a translator familiar only with the dictionary, in tackling very modern stories, sketches, comedies, etc., might at any time be nonplussed by phrases like the following, and not to be rendered in any other way :—"Oh, come now, you are talking yourself to nails" ; or :—" We talked and talked for hours ; but when they got to nails, I got up and left " ; or yet :—"At this rate we shall soon get to nails."

* Here is one of Rakhmiètof's maxims : "Seeing we demand that all men should be free to enjoy life in its entirety, we must prove, by our example, that our object in making the demand is not the satisfaction of our own personal passions, but the happiness of all." ⁵

⁵ This identical plea was put forward against the Neo-Christian reformer, Père Hyacinthe, when he took to himself a wife,—by his opponents and even by not a few of his followers. While he claimed that it was his duty to marry in order to enforce by his example his denunciations of clerical celibacy with its inevitable consequence — gross immorality,— he was accused of having made the point solely in order to justify in the world's sight his own self-indulgence.

Among these women who preach the suppression of family life and the free union of the sexes,—among these maidens with the close-cropped hair, who delight in mimicking the ways and tricks of speech of the young men, it is by no means rare to discover such, whose conduct, far from harmonizing with their cynical principles, remains pure and blameless, in spite of all the appearances of a life of adventure and lawlessness, in spite of a sort of moral promiscuity in which the best behaved appear to find pleasure.*

Nihilism has its virgins. Many girl-conspirators of twenty, exiled within the last few years, have carried into Siberia an immaculate virtue, the more meritorious that their doctrines do not inculcate it. Stranger still, nihilism has had its mystical or platonical unions, its married couples that were not such in reality, *i. e.* ostensibly married in the eyes of the world, but preferring to live as though they were not. These unions went in the sect by the name of "fictitious marriages." Since the trial of Nietcháyef, in 1871, few political trials failed to reveal some of these singular unions. For many—especially young girls—it was a welcome means of emancipation, which made it easy to carry on political propaganda. The young girl, won over to the sacred cause, was offered a husband, so she might enjoy the freedom of a married woman. Sometimes it was the man who had catechised and converted her, oftener an old friend, sometimes a stranger, enlisted for the purpose. Soloviòf, one of those who attempted

---

* In the university cities, students of both sexes were often known to dwell side by side. Their several rooms were divided only by a thin partition, or a door, barricaded merely by a bed or wardrobe. "Young men," says a man who has been established in Russia a long time, "look out for furnished rooms where some are occupied by women-students, who do them a hundred little services. It is not superfluous to mention that the greatest morality reigns in these mixed colonies."—Edm. de Molinari, *Journal of the Economists,* 1st of May, 1880. This frequent cohabitation, however, even though unprejudicial to the morals, helped to increase the exaltation of young people of both sexes, who mutually excited and, so to speak, wound one another up.

the Emperor Alexander II.'s life, had contracted a marriage of this sort. In reality the bride had espoused only the sect, her slender dowry went into the common till, and the couple separated frequently on the very day of their wedding, to go their different ways, " to make propaganda " at some distant spot. That is what Soloviòf had done, and when he and his wife left the province for Petersburgh, they took separate lodgings. To some this "fictitious marriage" was an association, a sort of co-operation between two comrades. Others regarded it as a fine chance to show their contempt for an institution blessed by the Church and sanctioned by the State, a way of placing themselves above society while pretending to obey its laws. The husband took no advantage of the rights awarded him by religion and law ; the wife preserved her liberty while legally bound. After thus practically sneering at regular unions and denying herself to her husband, she could, with his consent, go and practise free love. For some few, again, " fictitious marriage " became a sort of novitiate or test stage, which, after a few months' or years' trial, made room for a more natural union. Thus it is that, in Tchernyshèfsky's novel, Véra and Lapukhòf live together at first as brother and sister ; they occupy under the same roof two separate apartments, divided by a neutral ground, until one day they move into a common chamber, when the husband finds out that a mutual attachment has sprung up between his wife and one of his friends, and discreetly disappears, in order not to place them in an awkward position, or cause them to feel any scruple, meaning to return under another name, at the end of a few years, and witness in good comradeship the happiness of the new couple.

It was in the manner of carrying on the nihilistic propaganda, during its period of secret socialistic preaching, that the faith, enthusiasm, and religious devotion of the adepts shone forth most brightly, and that not only in the recklessness of their attempts, or in the doggedness with which they braved deportation and death. Such pathetic courage before judge and hangman other sectarians, revolutionists of other countries, have often shown as well ; there is no folly however perverse but has had its believers and martyrs. The power of exaltation characteristic of the Slavic soul only manifests itself here in a more singular manner. What is peculiar to contemporary Russian nihilism is its way of appealing to the masses ; "going forth among the people "—*(itti v-naròd)* —is the consecrated phrase. In order better to understand the people whom they wish to indoctrinate, to make themselves better understood by them, they go forth and mix with them, strive to assimilate with them, to live their own life of privation and manual labor, discarding the prejudices and habits of their bringing up. In this the missionaries of nihilism apparently propose to imitate the first apostles of Christianity. What other country has seen young men of good family, university students, cast off the garb and habits of their class, put away books and pen, to labor like workmen in factories, so as to be in a position enabling them better to understand " the people " and initiate them to their own doctrines ?* In what other country do we see young ladies, well-bred and well-informed, on their return from foreign countries, rejoice at having obtained the position of cook in the family of a superintendent, so as to get nearer to " the people " and personally study the labor question ? †

In Russia, where manners, ideas, even clothes, place a greater distance between the different classes, this sort of disfranchisement must assuredly be more painfully felt than anywhere else. In this manner of "making propaganda," getting into direct contact with the people, do we not recognize, through all its attractions, the practical sense, the realistic turn of mind of the

* That is what, to quote one instance, Prince Titsiànof and his accomplices did (trial of 1875) ; also Soloviòf till 1878. Others learned trades and opened workshops in various cities : a locksmith's shop at Tula, a carpenter's at Moscow, a shoemaker's at Saràtof, etc.

† Testimony of a young lady in the trial of Prince Titsiànof (1877). The trials of 1878–1882 have brought to light other facts of the same kind. From such models Turguénief drew the heroine in his novel, *Virgin Soil.*

Russian? Instead of holding aloof and hovering in the misty regions of theory, he descends to the laborer's level and the peasant's, associates with him in the factory or the workshop, in the school or the common dwelling.* With him practical sense combines in quaintest guise with his speculative eccentricities ; thus a sort of idealism is grafted on the most uncompromising naturalism.'

Scarcely anything can be more heartrending to the observer than this combination, among the young of both sexes, of qualities and defects opposed to one another and almost equally extreme, than this pledging to nefarious doctrines of the loftiest, most generous capabilities of the human heart. However that may be, however repulsive in its principles and odious in its practical attacks on life and property nihilism may show itself, it cannot be denied that it reveals several of the finest qualities of the Russian mind and character, and precisely those which foreigners are most apt to deny. If it brings out into the glare of daylight some of the most unlucky traits of the Russian temperament, its sinister blaze illumines one of that temperament's noblest and least showy phases. This people, so often accused of passiveness and intellectual torpor, is shown to us capable of energy and initiative, of sincere and active enthusiasm, capable of devotion to ideas. From this point of view I will venture to say that this terrible phenomenon does credit to the nation which suffers under it. In Russia it is not, as elsewhere, want and ignorance, cupidity and ambition, that are the most active leavens of the revolutionary spirit; frequently they are noble and lofty passions, feelings generous in their very errors. The men who claim to be the apostles of human

---

* One of the means of propaganda revealed by the political trials is for the adept to procure an appointment as village schoolmaster or communal scribe. Soloviòf had served in both capacities. Many agitators of both sexes embraced, for the same reasons, the medical profession.

' All this forcibly recalls the ground taken by Walter Besant in that wonderful book of his, *All Sorts and Conditions of Men,* which is as much a clarion-note and call to arms, though only spiritual, as *Uncle Tom's Cabin.*

solidarity can, when called upon, share in the labors of the lowly and in the sufferings of the poor. They are not unaware that, in their country, a revolution is not as yet a career nor a game at which ambition has all to win and nothing to risk.

The greater part of the nihilists, of those at least who figure in the trials, are very young—mere boys and girls. It is among such that the revolutionary faith enrolls almost all its neophytes. Among sentenced or arrested conspirators, men of thirty are rare, few are over twenty-five, many are not of age. On the other hand, nothing can be more common than to see young people, inclined to every kind of visionary chimeras, become, at the end of ten or fifteen years, practical men of the earth earthy, of the world worldly, who deem it a good bargain to get rid of principles in order to further their interests. Russia is not the only country where such transformations are habitual, but in Russia this contrast between the seasons of life—youth and maturity—appear prompter and more marked than elsewhere. Maybe, in matters concerning politics, the Russian, with his practical sense, sooner becomes undeceived regarding revolutionary vagaries, is more quickly struck with the disproportion between the aim and the means of the agitators. Maybe, again, we have here another trait of the national character, a new indication of its propensity to fall from one extreme into the other. Anyhow, there are few countries where parents and children have so much difficulty in understanding one another. In this respect the pictures drawn by Turguénief in his *Fathers and Sons* are in great part true even now. At the contact of real life, the practical and positive instincts, as well as the egotistical, usually resume the upper hand over revolutionary romance and utilitarian idealism, until the latter are completely choked up or waved away into the quietude of dreamland, where the most reckless theories do not interfere with the most matter-of-fact prudence. Hence so many young utopists swearing to demolish everything, and so many mature men resignedly bearing everything; hence, in one word, so many Russians with whom ideas do not interfere with material interests, with whom the most daring radicalism jogs along comfortably with the care of a fortune and the vulgar anxieties about a career. True, such a moral collapse after the sure excitation of several years is only too natural, no matter where : has not France herself, after each of her revolutions, had her hours of exhaustion and prostration. The phenomenon is, nevertheless, to be noted in Russia. In the Russian soul discouragement seems to follow ever close at the heels of enthusiasm, dejection on exaltation. With whom lies the fault?—with the political *régime* or with the people's temperament ? Perchance with both !

With the Russians nihilism and radicalism are mostly a matter of age ; it might be called a disease of childhood,—and that would be true, not only of individuals, but of the nation at large.* It is owing to his intellectual and political youth, to his country's political inexperience, that the Russian is so eager on so many questions, in the pursuit of daring speculations, so scornful of other people's experience, so confiding in the easy achievement of a social regeneration. To this propensity is added a secret feeling of conceit. Even while accepting the ideas of the West, the Russian likes to magnify them, he takes pleasure in overdoing things, and pride in overleaping the West, in revolutionary as well as other matters. Being engaged in growing when the other nations had long been grown up, compelled to be their pupil, and

---

* A humoristic writer with tendencies at once national and aristocratic, Prince Mesh-tchérsky, has given in a pamphlet, *Exposing the Times*, 1879, a pathological explanation of nihilism, which, paradoxical though it be, is not wholly devoid of truth. According to him it is a sort of neurosis, produced by anæmia caused by the lack of muscular exercise in the schools. It were easy to generalize the observation, and to say that, aside from the lack of equilibrium between the bodily exercises and those of the intellect, bad hygienic conditions, the students' poor fare, and their being for the most part badly lodged, and even poorly clad,—all these things have much to do with the morbid cerebral exaltation of so many young people of both sexes. (See Vol. II., Book VI., Ch. II.)

mortified at the necessity, he longs to get ahead of his masters in all things. The new-comer is apt to think his elders timid and backward. The Russian of whatever persuasion frequently feels towards the West as young people do towards mature or elderly men ; even while enjoying the West's ideas or lessons, he is inclined to think of it as lagging behind, vows to go the whole length of the roads and ideas that same West has opened before him. " Between ourselves, to what amount your European nations ? " said to me, fully twenty years ago, one of the first Russians I have known. " Old fogies who have given all they had to give. It would be unreasonable to expect anything more from them. When our turn comes, we shall not have much difficulty in beating them hollow." But when *will* their turn come ? Many get tired waiting. Unfortunately this piece of national bragging is far from always implying effort. Too many Russians await their country's grand future as a thing that *must* come on its appointed day, as a fruit ripening on the tree. Too many others, scorning the possible, rail at the liberties of which the West offers them the models, as insufficient, adopting the attitude of sceptics and *blasés ;* while the most impatient, fancying that they can revolutionize the country with one wave of their magic wand, do not scruple to have recourse to the maddest, most odious machinations.

The radical instincts of the Russian mind, or, if preferred, its propensity to novelties and bold strokes of theory, frequently manifest themselves in other things besides nihilism as practised in schools, or the ignorant sects of the lowest classes. I will mention one instance only, taken from the last fifteen or twenty years. I mean the movement in favor of the emancipation, or, more correctly, the independence of women. * Very different

* The Russians do not like to use the word "emancipation " in this case. They will tell you that, with them, woman *is* emancipated, since the law allows her to manage her own property in wedlock. Therefore this subject is referred to, in Russia, as " *The Woman Question.*"

from nihilism, although in its vagaries it associated with it too closely not to get compromised by it, this remarkable movement of public opinion has its principle partly in that same side of the Russian character—the contempt for prejudices, the taste for daring propositions and social reforms. In the beginning of the last century the Russian woman was, like the Turkish woman of to-day, kept under lock and veil. Nowadays she, like man, more than man, perhaps, aspires to enfranchisement and liberty. Through all the exaggerations which expose them to ridicule, these feminine pretensions are less out of place and less surprising than they would be elsewhere. The sex, emancipated by the rough hand of Peter the Great, profited most, it may be, by a civilization which, in giving it freedom, singularly flattered its natural tastes. If in the empire, so many times and so gloriously governed by women, the woman of the people is still kept in a sort of servitude,' it is very different in the cultivated classes. In intelligence and power of will, as well as in knowledge and in the rank she holds in the family, the Russian woman is already the equal of the man ; in some ways she even seems superior to him, perhaps through the fact of this very equality which, by exalting one sex, seems to lower the other.

This remark on the Russian woman might be extended to the Slav woman in general. Polish society, for instance, would lend itself to similar observations. It would appear as though, in this race, the psychological differences between the sexes are at times less marked, the moral or intellectual chasm less wide. Between the Slav man and woman there is not unfrequently a sort of exchange and indeed of inversion of faculties and qualities. If the men may sometimes be accused of a certain femininity, *i. e.*, of something mobile, flexible, ductile, or impressionable to excess, the women, as though in compensation, have, in their minds and characters, something strong, energical, in one word, virile, which,

---

' Not as much as it seems. See note on p. 116.

far from robbing them of any portion of their grace and charm, often adds to them a strange and irresistible attractiveness.

Feeling herself the equal of man in character and intellect, the Russian woman is inclined to claim the recognition of this equality, with its advantages and drawbacks : equality in labor and instruction, equality in rights, equality in duties. Girls and married women—and that in well-to-do families too—have been known to take pride in providing for themselves, making it a point to earn their livelihood without the assistance of their husbands or fathers. Women, and especially young girls, have rushed into all the careers open to their sex, loudly clamoring for new openings.* The passion for knowledge, even for science, has been one of the consequences of this desire for moral and material independence. Young girls crowded the courses of lectures, gymnasiums, universities. A few took hold of the classic languages—a much greater number went in for natural science and medicine.†

The revolutionary spirit could not fail to turn to its own profit these pretensions and aspirations of a sex always more prone than the other to give way to impulse and infatuation. Among these

* It should be mentioned that this feminine movement is partly due to economic causes which should be taken into account : perturbations in many a family budget in consequence of the emancipation of the serfs, growing difficulties in family life in consequence of the increase in prices ; difficulty for the young girls of a certain class to settle in their own circles, especially in cities, where the number of marriages has greatly diminished ; lastly, certain legal restrictions, which allow to the women of a family only a very small share of the paternal inheritance.

† Under the pressure of similar moral or economical causes, the same longing for independence, the same striving to provide for themselves, have grown up among the young girls of Hebrew parentage. In the number of the female medical students registered in 1878, the Jewesses represented $\frac{3}{100}$. This steadily increasing percentage reached $\frac{34}{100}$ in 1879, *i. e.*, a full third of the total. This figure is accounted for by the fact that, owing to legal obstructions or to custom, the medical career is about the only one open to Jewish women. [See *Razsviét (The Dawn)*, an Israelitic organ, Sept. 11, 1880.] Since 1887 the Jews have been systematically excluded from the higher lines of instruction. See Vol. III., Book IV., Ch. III.

women, hungering for knowledge and liberty, among these strong-minded young girls, sometimes too careless of the proprieties, who combined a sort of instinctive idealism with an affected realism, and substituted humanitarian dreams for the religion of their childhood, the coarse seductions of nihilistic radicalism have made all the more victims that many of these *coursistes* or students could find no way of putting their studies to practical uses and making a livelihood out of the acquired knowledge. The evil was often made worse by the remedies which distrust inopportunely suggested to the authorities, who, instead of widening the field of feminine activity, in some cases half shut in its face even those careers which they had but lately opened before it.*

Thus it was that, in the large cities, sprang up a sort of feminine proletariate—if the word may be applied to young girls, well informed, enthusiastic, more diligent and usually not less revolutionary than their school brethren. The West, especially Zürich in Switzerland, has lately seen numerous specimens of these girl-students, who strove to eradicate in themselves all the qualities natural to their sex, in order better to establish their right to the pursuits of the other sex,—of these, as Shakespeare says, *unsexed* girls, who, the better to rise to the level of men, worked hard to cease being women. Many noble and generous natures were hopelessly warped and worn out in the effort. The most ardent and energetic, arrested in the front ranks of the conspirators, in the flower of their youth, got themselves sent off to Siberia. Others, less lofty or upright of soul, fell into excesses, which must have been to them a severer punishment still.

---

* That is what happened about medicine, under Alexander III., as well as under his father. The government, dreading the propaganda which women doctors would carry on in the rural districts, more than once opposed the appointment of a great number of them by the provincial assemblies *(Zemstvo);* at other times, and notably in 1882, it suppressed the special courses of medicine for women, allowing, however, others to be opened by private subscription.

All this cannot hinder the movement in favor of feminine emancipation from being one of the most interesting and most characteristic phenomena of contemporary Russia. Of all continental states, Russia, by this side, comes up nearest to the Anglo-Saxon countries, though in the two cases claims in reality analogous present themselves under very different aspects. If a revolution of this kind is ever to take place, Russia will doubtless be one of the first countries on the old continent to give the new order of things a trial.[8] In the meantime she has already made, in the matter of higher female education, experiments of which some might serve as models to states that think themselves much more advanced.* The Russian mind does not shrink from daring initiatives, even risky ones. From that side, to which we do not much look for examples, we shall some day receive more than one lesson.

In no other nation have the traditions of the past at one and the same time wielded more power and less authority, or been venerated more superstitiously below, cast off more scornfully above. At the two extremities of the same people the opposite

[8] There will be no need of a revolution. There would be no " woman question " but for the mania of aping the West. The law lays no restriction on our women ; whatever opposition they encounter comes from public habit and prejudice, and these are by no means stubborn in Russia ; the educated Slav is not conservative. It is not only that our women have full control of their property, married or single, from the age of eighteen ; they also vote in local elections—for instance, when the so-called " marshal of the nobility " is appointed, a functionary whose duty it is to represent the nobility of each government (province) on gala occasions, to look after their interests as a class, to be their spokesman and entertainer. The right to vote on these and other public local occasions is conferred by a property census, from which women are not excluded, only it is customary for them to send in their vote in writing or by power of attorney, as their presence would be undesirable at these usually pretty festive celebrations.

* The "Bestùjef Courses" (pronounce the *j* as in the French *joli*) in Petersburgh, the courses of Mr. Guerrier in Moscow, both founded by private endowment, gave young girls a genuine "higher education." To these free institutions the state substituted, in 1888–9, higher courses for boarders and day scholars, the access to which is much less easy.

exaggerations meet.   Of all men the Russian, once rid of his traditional ideas, of his national prejudices, is the most completely
freed.   In this respect no other can be compared to him but the
Jew, the modern Israelite.   He, too, at the contact with aliens,
passes from the extreme of the spirit of veneration to the extreme
of free-thinking, from the oriental traditionalism, to which the
bulk of his brethren stubbornly cling, to the most daring feats of
the spirit of innovation.   By one of those contrasts perpetually
recurring in Russia, while the peasant, like the humble oriental
Jew, remains obstinately conservative, guardian of rites and
forms, the man of the cultured classes glories in having cast
behind him all the old traditions together with the old creeds.
Some people liken the Russian intellect to those virgin steppes,
where the ages have left no imprint and which have treasured up
for the future all their fertility.   We shall see in the following
chapters in what sense such beliefs are justifiable.   At all events,
we can say even now that the feeble hold of national tradition, the
poorness of the inheritance bequeathed to Russia by ten centuries,
have something to do with the radical propensities of the Russian
mind and "nihilism,"—or rather, to borrow a barbaric but
graphic word from Joseph de Maistre, the *nothingism (rienisme)*,
more or less thought out, of the contemporary generations.

BOOK IV.

HISTORY AND THE ELEMENTS OF CIVILIZATION.

CHAPTER I.

Has Russia an Historical Inheritance ?—Is it True that she Differs from the West by the Principles of her Civilization ?—Various Theories on this Subject—Slavophils and Occidentals—Origin and Tendencies of the Slavophils—In what Way the Apologists of Russian Civilization Meet the Detractors of Russia—Secret Affinities between Slavophilism and Nihilism — The Three Conceptions of the National History and Destinies.

AFTER wandering over the Russian soil and successively examining into the genealogical titles and the national temperament of the Russian Slav, we should like to find out what elements have been brought to him by history, how the ages in their course have confirmed or corrected the influences of clime and race, what features they have added to the character of the people, what bases given to its culture and institutions. "We know enough of the history of barbarous times when we know that they *were* barbarous," says one of the eighteenth-century philosophers, referring to Russia before Peter the Great.* This saying bears the stamp of the ignorant and *naïve* presumption which, in the matter of historical and political sciences, has led that century into so many mistakes and deceptions.

The Russians themselves will say at times they have no history. Some, like Tchaadáyef of old, deplore the fact in

* Condillac, *Modern History*, vol. vi.

melancholy strain, passionate and eloquent,* nor can anything console them for having missed the most brilliant epochs of European life, or allay their fears that, for lack of the same trials and upbringing, their country never can achieve the same civilization, for that a nation without a past is also without a future. Others, more numerous, boldly congratulate themselves on the same fact, boasting of their freedom from the trammels of all tradition and all prejudice, from the fetters of a past in which, in spite of her revolutions, old Europe remains entangled.† Looking on all the bequests of past ages as on so many burdens and hindrances for the present generations, they make light of the inheritance left them by their forbears, and rejoice that they have received from them nothing worth handing down to their children. They delight in considering their country as free land, as a *tabula rasa*, on which science and reason are free to construct, with materials all new, the building of the future. This point of view, dear to radicalism, is the one which most revolutionists hold. In that, it must be confessed, they really do little else than appropriate the views or imitate the examples of the authorities, who, ever since Peter the Great, have been the first to teach the subjects to make stable litter of the national past and history.

In a state which, in 1869, celebrated its tenth centennial, such views cannot be accepted literally. Many of those Russians who express them would be justly indignant if they were taken at their word. If a past of a thousand years has merely littered the national soil with useless rubbish or brittle structures lacking base and cement, it is that past itself which should tell us the reason.

* " We belong to none of the great families of nations, either Oriental or Occidental ; we have the traditions of neither. We live, so to speak, outside of time, untouched by the culture of mankind," etc.—*Letters of Tchaadáyef*, 1836. For these letters, written in French, the author was officially declared insane. (See Herzen, *Revolutionary Ideas*, and Pypin, *Characteristics of Literary Views*, Petersburgh, 1869).

† In his *Apology of a Madman*, subsequently written, Tchaadáyef himself, changing his mind about the gloomy pessimism of his letters, partly adheres to this opinion.

The taste for historical studies, the crown of honor of the nine-teenth century, made itself felt in Russia as well as in the West. For the last fifty years, especially the last twenty-five years, a band of historians who in nothing—number, intelligence, or con-scientiousness—are behind those of England, France, or Germany, study with passionate zeal the annals of their country, and seek in its past the key to its destinies.*

Russia has a long history, but the chain of her national exist-ence has once or twice been so rudely snapped that it is an arduous task even yet to reunite the severed links, and there remains in the popular consciousness a sort of blank. This history the Russian people have suffered rather than made ; it was not, as in the countries of the West, the people's own personal work, sprung from the free development of their national genius ; it was passive rather than active. In this respect the history of Russia resem-bles not so much the histories of European nations as the annals of Asiatic ones. Whether it came from abroad or from above, from aliens or from its own rulers, it often remained all external or superficial ; it has, so to speak, passed over the people's head, and, having at times bowed it low, still weighs heavily on its shoulders.

It is neither in the climate nor in the race, it is in history and geography that we should seek the causes of the inferiority of Russian civilization. Many foreigners, the Catholics especially, account for it by the adoption of a barren form of Christianity ; others, chiefly Germans, by the absence of Teutonic influence, a double defect sometimes lumped under the designation of *byzantin-ism.* Some see the cause of it in the lack of the classical heritage,

* In the foremost rank of contemporary historians are especially dis-tinguished : Soloviôf (died in 1879), Kostomárof (died in 1885), Bestújef-Riùmin, Zabiélin, Ilovàisky, etc. Contrary to what is usual in other coun-tries, most Russian historians bravely undertake a general history of their country since Rurik's times, and each usually has an historical, more or less original, theory of his own. As very few reach the end of their task, it follows that the initial periods of Russian history have perhaps be_n more studied than the epochs nearer our own.

15

the greater number in the Mongolian domination. The Russian historians everlastingly face the same problem ; placed between Europe and Asia, Russia is, so to speak, the offspring of both. But of which is she morally or politically the daughter ? We have to ask the same question in its bearing on social development, only as regards soil and race : In what is Russia European, in what Asiatic, in what merely Slav and Russian? Have the centuries of her long infancy disposed her, by an appropriate education, to European life, or have they fashioned her for a culture of her own —original, substantially distinct from that of the West ? To borrow the expression used by a native writer, does the difference between Russia and Europe lie in the degree or in the principle itself of civilization ? *

That is the point round which revolve most of the serious questions that have come up in Russia. The question under discussion is no less a thing than the vocation of a country, of a people. To acclimate a civilization, it is not sufficient that the soil should be apt, it is imperative that the nation into which it is transplanted should be prepared by the elements of culture. When it is the Russian people we have to deal with, so long buffeted between opposing influences, the question is far from being a merely theoretical one ; it is a live one, the solution of which awaits a practical application, and must decide the way the country shall go.

What we must find out is this : what attitude is Russia to assume towards Europe ? Is she to consider herself Europe's pupil ? as such to submit to Western schooling and persist in imitating and adapting Western things ? Or, on the contrary, is she to proclaim herself a stranger to the West ? give up borrowing things which suit neither her genius nor her temperament, and stand up unfettered, once more her own self? [1] On the way that this fundamental conception of her national destiny is decided depend

---

* Youri Samàrin : *The Jesuits and their Relations to Russia*, p. 364.
[1] See appendix to this chapter.

all the views the Russians shall hold on their civil and political life. Accordingly it is on the view they take of their history that their diversity of opinions is mostly based. Historical parties take the place of political parties, or, rather, the tendencies which are in the stead of parties have for their point of departure a different conception of their national history. Such is the substance of the battle which, under various names, has been raging, ever since Peter the Great, between the Old-Russians and their adversaries, between Moscow and St. Petersburgh, between the *Slavophils* and the *Occidentals.**

In the eyes of the *Západniki*, or partisans of the West, there is, in Russia's past and her traditions, nothing that need radically separate her from Europe. She has no culture of her own, really original, national, indigenous ; she is only behindhand with her Western neighbors. She still is a mediæval state, an *ancien régime* state ; but there is no reason why she should not appropriate all the culture of more advanced nations, why she should not do for Teutono-Latin civilization what the Teutonic peoples once did for Roman civilization.

In the eyes of the Slavophils, on the contrary, and of many patriots instinct with the same spirit, Russia is substantially different from Europe. Having received from the past peculiar institutions, she is, by her origin, her beginnings, and bringing up, by the elements of her culture, called to entirely different fortunes. In the manner in which her land has been peopled, in which her state has been founded, her territories have been occupied,—in her conception of family, property, authority, Russia possesses the principle of a novel civilization, and, naturally, if local patriotism is to be believed, of a better balanced civilization, more stable and harmonious, more really capable of progress *ad infinitum* than the senile and effete Occidental civilization, threat-

---

* " Occidentals " (*Západniki*) : partisans of European imitation. As to the name of " Slavophils " (*Slavianophíly*), it is frequently mistaken in the West for a synonym of " Panslavists."

ened, as the latter already is, with decomposition, as a result of its internal conflicts.

One of the most curious phenomena of Russian life in the nineteenth century is undoubtedly "Slavophilism." The ascendancy it has gained over the contemporary thinking heads is entirely out of proportion with the number of its adepts. The little Slavophil Church, with its exclusive beliefs, its stiff dogmas, numbers as yet few declared followers, few faithful orthodox believers ; but the sort of national apotheosis which lies at the bottom of it draws to it many more or less unconscious proselytes, among men apparently strangers to Slavic fetishism of any kind. Then, too, one not unfrequently stumbles on some Slavophil dogma or superstition, among people of the world, or writers who make it a point to have nothing to do with such idolatry. As sometimes happens in the domain of thought, the Slavophil formulas and positions were shattered in the shock of discussion, but the contents, the spiritual essence, escaped out of the broken vessels and spread far away into the air.

A remarkable and characteristic thing is that this Russian school, which claims that it is to shake off the intellectual domination of Europe, was itself formed under Occidental impulses, under the influence of European thought. Not in the direct study of national history or popular life, but in the study and pondering of foreign writers, have the founders of Slavophilism taken their method, their dialects, and, indirectly, their ideas.

This vindication of the Russian spirit, this rebelling against foreign sway, was itself, at its origin, a loan or imitation, an adaptation of foreign things. The period between 1830 and 1840 was one of debating, of theoretical speculations and hypotheses of all kinds, a time when everywhere, but more especially in Germany, systems sprang up full-fledged, philosophical, historical, political. And it was from German metaphysics, from Hegel's logic and philosophy of history, that the Slavophils of Moscow took the first elements of their ideas, the shape and mould of their doctrines.

To Russia and the Slavs they applied Hegel's proceedings, claiming for their race and country the overlordship which the Prussian philosopher, in the history of mankind, ascribed to the Teutonic races. Slavophilism was entirely a birth of the speculative spirit, originally merely a combination of the abstractions of German metaphysics with literary romanticism, and with the religious mysticism, this latter representing the contribution of the national element. The originality and virtual superiority of the Russian or Græco-Slavic over the Occidental civilization were proclaimed *a priori*, by deduction. Later on, in order to adapt the facts to their theory, these philosophers of the national idea began to turn their attention towards history and the people.

Putting away metaphysics, the Slavophils began to search in the religion and the character of the people, in the regulation of property, and in the constitution of authority, for the principles on which rests Russian life. In their quest after all the original features of the national civilization, they solemnly condemned the moral subjection of the Petersburgian period ; they declared the foreign intellectual yoke all the more intolerable that Europe, whose pupil Russia avowed herself, was going full tilt the way of decadence.

Russian history, at that time but little studied, lent itself better than any other to the vagaries of systematizing. To this day, many fine works notwithstanding, it is for many writers a field open to any and all hypotheses. In this career, the Slavophils were, by their point of departure, exposed to commit remarkable blunders. They were more than once to mistake for essential traits of the social and political life of the Slavs things which, in the eyes of their adversaries, were only survivals of an obsolete past crumbled to ruins long ago. They were to proclaim as signs of race or nationality what ofttimes was but a token of infancy or childhood. They brought out into relief all the real or imaginary differences which, in the past, had distinguished Russia from the West, and of all these distinctive traits, more or less well-sorted, they made up the elements of a Russian civilization. With the help of a little generalizing they discovered and endowed their native land with a civilization of its own ; indigenous, complete in its principle, though abruptly arrested in its growth by the hapless "Petersburgh period." This culture is, after a fashion, European, but not after the manner of Western Europe—of Italy, France, England, Germany. To Teutono-Latin culture, a Græco-Slavic culture was opposed, of which the broad and solid basis had been preserved intact in the lower layers of the people below the surface, where nationality had been undone by imitation of foreign things. Once they had entered on this way, the Slavophils were not content with bringing into relief the features by which Russia differs from the West ; not content with pointing out differences too great to stand in need of exaggeration. They delight in transforming this diversity into opposition ; they undertake to prove that the national traditions are incompatible with the principles that rule Occidental life.*

The long and arduous campaign of Bulgaria, the "attempts" of the nihilists, ascribed to European contagion, the advent of Alexander III., loudly greeted in Moscow as that of the old-Russian spirit incarnate, had restored to the but lately obsolete inheritors of Slavophilism a fleeting ascendancy. In the life of nations there come hours of patriotic fever and public anguish, when all that bears a national semblance easily commands applause. The battles fought on behalf of the Bulgars temporarily raised to high honor on the other bank of the Pruth all that, in name or appearance, is Slavic, just as in Germany the struggle against Napoleon brought into vogue once more all that was or seemed Teutonic. In Russia this tendency is, at certain epochs, all the more urgent for the many reasons which patriotism

---

* That is what Aksàkof did in his paper, *Rus*, up to his death (1886), what more than one writer did even outside the circle of " neo-Slavophils "— Prince Vassìltchikof for instance. (*Landholding and Farming*, St. Petersburgh, 1878, pp. 24, 30, and ff.)

has at others to feel discouraged and apprehensive. National feeling gets wound up the more willingly for the self-delusion it has to practise in order to work itself up to sticking point. That is what excuses the ranting of certain Russians anent the superiority of their Slavic culture, the intellectual decadence of Western Europe, its political decomposition and rottenness.

Slavophilism was born, under Nicolas, of a violent and legitimate recoil against the long intellectual enslavement of the eighteenth century. By re-awakening in the country's breast reverence for its history and traditions and a liking for its national antiquities, by winning the attention and affection of the higher classes back to the *mujik* and the rural population, by serving as counterweight to the systematic copyists of the West and the innovators of the bureaucracy at St. Petersburgh, the Slavophils have rendered their country a most undoubted service. Thanks to them, Russia has recovered her national consciousness, which threatened to become obliterated under a vain and sterile cosmopolitism. At one time it was a wholesome reaction of "home" against "abroad." With nations even more than with individuals, the feeling of personality is a great power, but on the understanding that the over-excited national feeling do not degenerate into a sort of intellectual "Chauvinism," or moral protectionism. When it goes the length of depreciating and contemning all that is foreign, it becomes the worst adviser a nation, no matter how great, can have; but in no country could this exclusive self-admiration, self-deification, be so baneful as in Russia.[2] In his most exaggerated aberrations, the least moderate of Slavophils is not more laughable than the Teutonic patriot,

---

[2] Is it not rather the only safeguard when a nation's righteous self-consciousness is in danger of being sneered away from abroad, stamped out by self-abasement within? It is only a wholesome reaction. The qualities demanded of nations are different from those that become individuals. Amiable qualities are not necessary—only such as secure the existence,—and self-assertion is the most directly to the point. We all admire England for "not knowing when she is beaten."

who, in the wide modern world, perceives nothing but German culture, German science, Teutonic influence. But of the two the Slavophil is certainly the worst inspired as regards the good of his country, for in preaching the contempt of the West and of the nations out of which have come art, science, and the whole of modern civilization, he runs the risk of teaching Russia the contempt of all these things themselves, and of liberty and progress to boot. Thus it is that Slavophilism and all analogous doctrines involuntarily join hands on one side with revolutionary nihilism, and on the other with the Western detractors of Russia.

When, under pretence of bringing out the originality of their country, Russians are not content with accentuating the really existing features of their national individuality, but insist on placing Russian history and culture, Slavic genius and society, in complete opposition, in radical incompatibility, with European civilization, they unawares arrive at the same position, the same conclusions, as their foreign opponents and contemners. The Slavophil of Moscow echoes the Russophobes of London or Pesth, who represent the "Muscovite" as substantially foreign to European civilization, as incapable of appropriating it as the Ottoman of Stamboul. The extremes of eulogizing and depreciating meet, as other extremes do. There is nothing in that to flatter the reasonable patriotism of the Russians, for Western civilization has traversed crises enough, has taken strength enough from its various revolutions, to have little cause to dread the scorn of those who take pride in remaining strangers to it, let such pretensions come from Stamboul, Pekin, or elsewhere.

Another no less remarkable thing: Moscovite Slavophilism, by its point of departure as well as by its attitude towards Occidental civilization, is not without some analogy with the revolutionary nihilism which would appear to be the opposite pole of Russian thought. This name, "nihilism," which it repudiates, Russian radicalism has earned chiefly perhaps by its disrespect to that civilization on which it has more than once passed condemnation, and to which it also loves to oppose an ideal Russia, if not of the past, then of the future. It was the classico-Christian culture, as it came out of the Teutono-Latin peoples, that the fathers of nihilism chiefly denounced. What they aimed at, what they denied, was not so much Russia as the West. Russia, her customs and traditions, most modern Russians had long ceased to believe in, in this respect all but the Slavophils had long been nihilists. They had pinned their faith on Western culture, with which they strove to become impregnated. In the beginning of Nicolas' reign, as in the eighteenth century, the civilization of which Peter the Great and Catherine had been able to import only the outer shell and formulas, still was to the literary world a religion which, outside of a few belated conservatives, counted in Russia neither incredulous nor indifferent spirits. The young generation were more fervent believers than the Occidentals themselves in the lights and the liberties that came from the West; they believed, with the ardor of a neophyte's faith, in the efficiency and sacredness of "the principles of '89," in the infallibility of the human revelation brought by the great Revolution.

Towards the middle of the century, a sudden and violent revulsion occurred, as we have already seen, in the Russian intellect; but this evolution was not always to turn out favorably to the Slavophils and the admirers of the national past. On a closer view of this civilization, to which he looked for salvation, when he touched its failings and heard it cursed and denied by many of those who had been nurtured by it, the Russian began to doubt it. He saw that, against ills and suffering, it had only uncertain remedies or idle palliatives, and its liberty, its science, its wealth, appeared to him but as a lie, a cheat. All the institutions and formulas he had learned to reverence, became to him a hypocritical and sacrilegious profanation of the truths half perceived in the days of simple, youthful fervor. The modern Scythian fancied he had found out the emptiness of that Græco-Latin culture whose splendor had dazzled him, and, with his race's versatility and proneness to rush from one to the other extreme, with the bitter wrath of a believer undeceived and ashamed of his long credulity, he blasphemed what he had worshipped but yesterday. The Russian of the nineteenth century renounced his childhood's faith as a puerile superstition ; he made it his study and pleasure to insult, the while he could not yet shatter them, the false gods to whom he had lovingly burned his incense ; he hurled from the pedestal his own hands had raised, all those brilliant but worthless idols whose seductive beauty had fascinated his youth ; he swore to tear down the proud temples erected for these deceitful modern deities who, under the ill-gotten names of liberty, equality, fraternity, keep up amidst men error, discord, and the sordid bondage of poverty. Such was, for its most illustrious founders, the starting-point of nihilism.

Looked at in this light, nihilism, instead of being a produce of the West and European contagion, becomes a sort of protest of Russia against Europe, a "tragic emancipation of the Russian consciousness." If we consider, not the logical sequence and the historical filiation of ideas, but the feelings it nourishes, often unknowingly, nihilism turns out to be, like Slavophilism, a sort of violent reaction against the long intellectual domination of Europe, against her society, her science, against the whole modern world. It is the rebellion of a child indignant at having been deceived by his master ; and the more confiding, the more respectful his docility has been, the more bitter, the more passionate will the rebellion be.

The spectacle of Western Europe's incessant and barren revolutions was not calculated to lead Russian radicalism back to admiration and imitation of the Occident. After having, like Herzen, eulogized with ingenious enthusiasm its various revolutionary experiences, they proclaimed, like Herzen still, that it was as narrow as inconsistent, as incapable of progress in revolution as in conservatism. This Europe towards which he kept turning his eyes and his heart's desires, as the Mussulman towards Mecca, he despaired of it ; he proclaimed it decrepit and " played out " ; he turned his back on it, and sought elsewhere, on a younger soil, the site for his New Jerusalem, for the humanitarian earthly paradise, to be opened by revolutions. By an abrupt revulsion quite in accord with the national character, always prone to sudden changes of front, Russian radicalism overthrew its own position and turned its own theory inside out. The part of initiator and rescuer, lately held to be the undoubted privilege of the West, it suddenly transferred to its own ignorant and belated native land. The light it had looked for from abroad and from Europe's enlightenment, it took to expecting from out of the darkness at home. In losing faith in the West, the radical, like the Slavophil, went back to his faith in Russia, but for reasons the opposite of the Slavophil's. In this native land of his, so severely scorned by him, he all at once discovered a secret superiority, born of its very inferiority.

And this recoil was logical. Modern civilization, modern society once condemned, the country most apt for future creations is that where the past leaves the most widely open field to the present, where the land is easiest to clear. Now in this respect Russia manifestly heads the list. Of all civilized states, it is that where the institutions and the arts which are the pride and joy of the modern world have struck their roots least deeply and bear the least luscious fruits ; where it is easiest to destroy, and where destruction would be effected at a minimum cost to imagination, heart, reason, prejudices. The Russians are the veritable chosen people of revolution, because they are the people that has least to lose by it. By this sort of rehabilitation and glorification of the land, lauded up by its children not for its wealth, real or fancied, but for its barrenness and poverty, the revolutionary spirit has assumed in Russia a singular vigor and confidence ; it has, so to speak, taken a national and patriotic character, through its very negation of nationality and love of country.

Thus, even apart from their common origin from German philosophy and Hegel, Slavophilism and nihilism, as doctrines, have had the same points to depart from and to arrive at.   Both these "hostile brothers" departed from the insufficiency of the *bourgeois* civilization and the disappointment it entailed ; then, after keeping their backs turned on each other a while, they unexpectedly met on the ground of the glorification and apotheosis of Russia, to whom they both promise a sort of primacy, leadership in the future, though they all find to praise at present but one thing —the *mir*, or the collective property scheme of the peasant class.

One of the causes of the waverings, the inconsistencies, the worries which the tsars undergo in their home politics in this nineteenth century is the violence with which they, no less than their subjects, are tugged at and pulled different ways by the two chief tendencies that strive together for the direction of the public spirit.   Under Alexander I. the influence of Western Europe and her admirers was almost constantly predominant.   Under Nicolas public sympathy veered round to the so-called national spirit. Under Alexander II. the government yielded to each current by turns, to successive but opposite impulses.

Since Alexander III. came to the throne, greeted by a portion of the nation as a sort of Messiah, destined to restore Russia to her own real self, the neo-Slavophil or national tendencies once more came to the fore, both at court and in the government.   It can be predicted without much risk of going wrong, that Russia will pass through many more such oscillations, driven this way to-day and that to-morrow by the contrary winds which fight for the control of her.   That alone accounts for many of the difficulties among which she flounders, for her uncertainties, her reluctance to enter on the road of political transformations.   As long as she cannot make up her mind and choose between the neo-Slavophils and their opponents, Russia will drift along rudderless.

Against the Slavophils who claim for their country a culture all its own, original, capable of indefinite development as soon as it will be rid of the false gods of the foreigner, the "Occidentals" (*Západniki*) will long struggle,—they who will not allow the Slavs to possess the elements of a new civilization, and are bent on carrying on the tradition inaugurated by Peter the Great. Between the two hostile camps nihilism stands up, grown tall in their shade, under cover of their wrangles,—nihilism which sports the armor of both, and, taking its cue from the negative portions of both their doctrines, denies Russia with one breath and the West with the next.

Such are the three extreme directions between which, under various names, with more or less determined opinions, the Russian mind oscillates. Some assert that Russia has enough stuff in her traditions to provide for herself; others derive from imitation of the foreigner all the ills of society and the government. Others again, not allowing their country any social or political principle of its own, look on it as on a belated member of the great European family and see no chance of progress for it except along the lines opened to it by the West. Still others will have it that, in the shapeless survivals of the past, there is nothing worth preserving, and call for the destruction of all that now exists, so as to clear the ground for putting up a building constructed after no known model whatever, either native or foreign. A glance down Russian history will show us how these three seemingly incompatible conceptions can all emerge out of the same past, and in what measure each may consider itself justified by facts.

APPENDIX TO BOOK IV., CHAPTER I. (See p. 226, note I.)

ONCE FOR ALL—WHAT IS RUSSIA'S RELATION TO EUROPE?

This question, which continually turns up in any earnest discussion of Russia's historical position and the future that must spring therefrom, being as difficult to settle as impossible to dismiss, was already touched upon by Mr. Leroy-Beaulieu in the initial chapter of this, his great work. We there supplemented his remarks with some pithy lines from Mr. Danilefsky's thoughtful book, *Russia and Europe*. In the present chapter our author is brought back to this master-question, on which he rests with greater insistence. It may not be out of place to follow his lead and here present our readers, as briefly as possible, with the sequel of Mr. Danilef-sky's argument—or, more correctly, review of facts, and the conclusions, they force on him.

Russia is *not* Europe, either geographically or historically, is his verdict (see pp. 13, 14), supported by a breadth and wealth of illustration at which limited space does not allow of our even hinting here, and concludes: "Having no part either in the European good or the European evil, how can she belong to Europe? Neither true modesty nor true pride allow her to assume that she does. Only low-bred upstarts push their way among their betters. . . . But, it will be said, if Russia does not belong to Europe by right of birth, she does by right of adoption. She has appro-priated to herself (or should strive to do so) all that Europe has worked out ; she takes (or at least should take) her share of Europe's labors, Europe's triumphs. But who has done the adopting? We don't, somehow, perceive much of Europe's parental feeling in her relations with Russia. But there lies not the point. It lies in this : is such adoption a possible thing any-how? Can an organism, so long nourished on its own saps, drawn by its own roots out of its own soil, fasten itself by suction on to another organ-ism, let its own roots dry off, and, out of a self-dependent plant, become a parasitical one? . . . But, for the sake of argument, let us have it so : Russia, though not by birth European, has become so by adoption. Why then, of course, our motto should be : *Europæus sum et nihil europæi a me alienum esse puto.* All Europe's interests must also be Russia's interests, her wishes must be our wishes, her aspirations—ours ; *il faut les épouser*—we must become wedded to them—in the expressive French phrase. We may differ in details with France or Italy, England or Germany, but with Europe as a whole, *i. e.*, with ourselves, we cannot possibly differ or disagree : we must be conscientious, consistent.

"What *rôle* on the universal stage does Europe assign us, her adopted children? To be the bearers and propagators of her civilization in the East —that is the lofty mission allotted to us, the task in which Europe will sym-pathize, which she will advance with her blessings, her best wishes, her ap-plause, to the edification and delight of our humanitarian progressists. Very well. Eastward-ho! then. But stop—*what* East? We had thought to begin with Turkey. What could be better? There live our brethren, in blood and spirit,—live in agonies and yearn for deliverance. 'Whither away? You have no business there,' thunders Europe ; 'that is not the East for *you ;* there 's more Slavic trash there than I like, and *I* 'm going to manage them. My Germans have done such work before. Clear out of there.'—We tackled the Caucasus—that 's a sort of East too. Mamma got very mad : 'Don't dare to touch the noble paladins of freedom ! much it becomes you to meddle with them. Hands off ! '—For once, thank goodness, we did not obey, and forgot our Europeanism. There is Persia now ; something might be done there in the way of sowing the seeds of European civilization. The Germans would not have minded ; their *Drang nach Osten* ('Eastward Push '), scarcely would reach so far ; but out of respect to England we had to be checked : 'Too near India. Move on ! '—To China, perhaps?—'Well, no. Is it tea you need ? We 'll bring you all you want from Canton. China is a wealthy country—we can teach her without your help. She is smoking our Indian opium like a charm—let her alone.'—But, for mercy's sake, where is *our* East, the East which it is our sacred mission to civilize?— 'Central Asia, that 's the place for you, do not forget it. We could not get there anyhow, besides it would not pay. There lies your sacred historical mission. . . .'—So then we shall have gone through a thousand years of labor, streaming with sweat and blood ; we shall have built up an empire of a hundred million souls (of which sixty millions of one race and blood, a thing unequalled in the world, except in China),—all to tender the blessings of European civilization to five or six millions of tatterdemalions, the denizens of Kokan, Khiva, and Bokhara, with two or three millions of Mongolian nomads thrown in—for that is what the high-sounding phrase about bearing European civilization into the heart of the Asiatic continent really amounts to,—an enviable lot indeed, and a mission to be proud of. In sooth, *Parturiunt montes, nascitur ridiculus mus.* . . ." Then the author depicts in glowing colors what a glorious thing it would have been for Europe had Russia existed only as an empty space, with no tiresome Russian and other Slavs to exercise there a sort of right of pre-emption, and only savages of the Red-Indian type to be summarily dealt with—what a fine set of United States, with all European improvements, would have grown up there, opening out to Europe a gorgeous " Far-East," in an unending golden perspective ! Curious enough, the identical thought came, in a somewhat different spirit, to Mr. Leroy-Beaulieu, and, our sincere friend and earnest well-wisher as he is, much of the regret which the Russian writer banteringly supposes and expatiates upon, shows, seriously, between his lines. Even he cannot help grudging us Slavs, the Europeans not of Europe, a little, and, perhaps unconsciously, our broad place in the sun (see p. 54).

What wonder then if Mr. Danilefsky, dropping banter for the graver tone becoming the subject, announces this result :

"Thus, then, after conceding that Russia is European by adoption if not by birth, we are led to the conclusion that she is not merely a colossal superfluity, a huge historical pleonasm, but a very positive, hard-to-be-over-come hindrance to the evolution and propagation of the alleged only uni-versal—in reality European, *i. e.*, local Teutono-Latin—civilization. *In this light—and in this light only—Europe regards Russia.*"

BOOK IV. CHAPTER II.

The First Russia and Europe—Traits of Kinship—Similarities and Dissimilarities—The Varangians—Christianity and Byzantine Training—The Principalities and Frequent Shiftings of the National Centre—The Great Unhingement of Russian History.

EUROPEAN civilization grew upon a triple foundation : the Christian element, the Græco-Roman or classical element, the Teutonic or barbaric element.*   All the Western states were erected, so to speak, with identical materials, in the same style, on a more or less similar plan.   The three great bases on which reposes the culture of the West, are they found in the foundations of Russia ?   If we dig deep enough, we do come upon them, but they have neither the same proportions nor the same importance as in the other countries.

The ancients knew of Russia only the shores of the Euxine. The Greeks dropped colonies only on those shores ; the Romans scarcely held a nominal sway over them.   With the former those wide plains passed for the home of the Cimmerians' eternal night ; to the latter the regions north of the Danube and the Black Sea were a sort of Siberia, whither they sent state criminals.   Russia was too compact, too continental for antique civilization, which, wending its way along shorelands, could gain a hold only on essentially maritime countries.   Germany already had proved too solid a mass and too severe a clime for it ; Russia was just touched by it along her southern beaches.   The Greeks had had some preco-

* It should be mentioned that the following pages were mostly written before Mr. Alfr. Rambaud's admirable *History of Russia* came out.   See *Revue des Deux Mondes*, January 15, 1874.

cious intercourse with the natives. They have themselves preserved for us the memory of the Scythian—*alias* the Russian—
Anacharsis,[1] and the jewelry discovered in the graves of the steppes
shows that these remote wildernesses were not closed to Hellenic
art. As has been the case with all great states of Europe, some
portions of Russia's territory have been under Greek or Roman
rule. It was not, however, till the Middle Ages that the Russians, through Constantinople, came, though remotely, under the
influence of Greece and Rome ; and the channel was a roundabout and corrupt one. Byzance, at the time of her decadence,
was the only Rome they knew, the Lower-Empire was the only
model supplied them by Greek and Latin civilization.

Very different were the part and importance of the barbaric
element. Like the states of Western Europe, the Russian state
appears to have been founded by Teutons amidst a people that
was soon after to be won to Christianity. This, to begin with, is
a patent similarity to all those European histories which all seem
to be the repetition of one and the same occurrence. Yet, under
the similarity, the difference already shows. Russia was a different
material, though of kindred substance—Slavic material, instead
of Celtic or Teutonic. What is the Slavs' original contribution
to civilization? The Russians would fain base on them their culture as well as their nationality. History unfortunately knows
little about them at the time of their separate existence. There

---

[1] This young prince is the first-known prototype of the much-travelled,
brilliant, cosmopolite Russian of our day. He, too, fell down and worshipped "civilization," "progress," "liberalism," which the Athens of the
Pisistratidæ and of Solon, no doubt, embodied in a form no less entrancing
than the Paris of to-day. And when recalled by duty to his "barbaric"
realms, the poor fellow sweetened his exile by initiating his companions
into the delights of Hellenic culture and easy social manners. But there
was a stern elder brother—the Slavophil of the time—who made it his mission to guard his people from the pollution and dangers of foreign innovations, and, in the name of nationality, put an end to all attempts at reforms
by taking the would-be reformer's life. Things were simple in those days,
and if the end was admitted to be desirable, the surest and shortest means
to it were naturally the best.—See Herodotus, iv., 76, and Lucian, *Scytha.*

was no Tacitus to leave us a *Slavia* to match the *Germania* of Agricola's son-in-law. In old-time Sarmatia we find the Slavs at their earliest known stage in contact with Teutonic or Finnic "allogens." Since some time before Rurik, the Slavs of the Dniepr and the Vòlkof were settlers and farmers ; already they lived in solid wooden houses ; already they had cities or "enclosures" that served for shelter, the so-called *gorodísh-tshê*,[1] thence *gràd* or *górod*,[2] like Kief and Nòvgorod ("new enclosure," or "new city "), the very names of which presuppose other older ones. The different tribes lived in isolated clans, which do not seem to have had much cohesion, since, to shape them into a state or nation, foreign alloy was needed. Compared to the Teutons, the Russian Slavs appear to have had a preference for association and community as forms of social life, to have possessed a more peaceable and less hierarchical spirit, a more outspoken or more persistent leaning towards patriarchal life, or, more correctly, towards family life on a large scale. The *rod*, or "family," in the sense of the Latin *gens*, seems to have been the only basis of their entire social organization. These tendencies, so blurred and indistinct at this distance of time, perhaps contained the first germ of Russian institutions.

The Teutonic element, which in all Europe has played a part, rather too promptly contested just at present, was not entirely

[1] The peculiar and rather vigorous Slavic double sibilant compounded of the sounds *sh* and *tch* is so puzzling to foreigners that the only way to make the pronunciation clear to them is to separate the two component sounds by a hyphen, which at once shows how really simple and easy it is. This is the sound which the Latin alphabet of the Poles and the Tchekhs, inadequate for Slavic phonetics, renders by the bewilderingly bristling combination, *szcz*, the conventional sign for *sh* (as in *shy*) being *sz* and that for *tch* or *ch* (as in *church*) *cz*. The old Slavic alphabet (adopted by the Orthodox Slavs), compiled half of Latin, half of Greek characters, has signs specially invented for this and a few other peculiarly Slavic sounds. But when the Western Slavs accepted Latin Christianity, they had to accept also the Latin alphabet of the Latin prayer-books, and to twist and force it into phonetic uses for which it was insufficient.

[2] Identical with Lithuanian *grod*, English *garden* and *yard*, German *garten*, Latin *hortus*, Greek *khortos*.

missing in Russia. It was most probably Norman adventurers, like the Vikings that were at the same period ravaging the Western countries and founding there their various dynasties, who, in the ninth century, laid the grounding of the state out of which was evolved the Russian Empire. The Kief chronicler, Nestor, shows us Rurik and his brothers called by the Slavs of Nòvgorod, tired of their intestine squabbles.* The chronicler of the eleventh century may already have, out of national conceit, disguised a Norman conquest or invasion under the veil of a voluntary call from the Nòvgorod Slavs. In our days a new-fangled historical criticism and retrospective patriotism have attempted to wrest from the Scandinavians Rurik and his companions, the Varangians. The Russians have looked about for a more national genealogy to endow the founders of their empire with. No historical question has called forth more passionate discussions among the scholars of Moscow and Petersburgh. They have applied Niebuhr's proceedings with Roman history to their own country rather late in the day. One scholar holds Rurik and the Varangians to be exiled Nòvgorodians, another—Slavs from the southern coast of the Baltic, or from the Isle of Rügen ; another takes them for Lithuanians ; others still for bands of adventurers of mixed races, Slavs and Scandinavians. In these latter days some have gone so far as to make of this most essential incident a myth invented by the self-conceit of the monks of the twelfth or thirteenth century, anxious to discover an illustrious origin for their nation or their princes, after the fashion of the French chroniclers who brought down the Merovingians from Priam of Troy.† In spite of the latest researches, the Varangians will have to be left to

---

* On this legendary call the Slavophils lately constructed a whole historical system, which placed the Russian state, based on the people's voluntary submission, on a different footing from the Western states, all based upon conquest. This position, now abandoned in history, can still be found in the economical or political theories of many a Russian writer.

† This position, very ably upheld by Ilovaïsky, has been refuted by Soloviòf, one of Russia's most eminent historians.

Scandinavia. This filiation accords better with the Byzantine annalists and with Nestor as well.[4] The names of Rurik and his comrades betray their Teutonic stock ; the character of the leaders' authority, their method of parcelling out occupied lands, and even to their manner of warfare confirm this origin. They were Normans, seeking for a road to Constantinople, and who, having gained possession of Nòvgorod and Kief, founded a military and trading state between the Baltic and the Black Sea, along the Dniepr, then one of the great commercial thoroughfares of the East. Like their brethren in the West, these Russian Northmen were, as Gibbon observes, more formidable by water than by land ; on their small barges they went down and attacked Constantinople, and imposed on it tributes or commercial treaties, of which the chronicles have preserved the very practical clauses.*

The first Russian law-book, *Rùsskaya Právda*—the *Russian Right*—still bears the Teutonic impress. In this code, put into shape by Yaroslàv, over a century and a half after Rurik, some have fancied they could trace more than one custom of Normandy. Like the Western nations, the Russians then had the ordeal and the judicial duel ; like them, they admitted, for murder and other crimes, compounding in a sum of money ; the very name of this fine, *vira*, answers to the German *Wehrgeld*. Between this first Russian and the European states founded by Teutonic tribes, numerous similarities can be adduced. The difficulty lies in discriminating what belongs to the Varangians and to the Scandinavian influence and what should be credited to the Slavs. In

---

[4] See appendix to this chapter.

* The Western scholars, especially those of Scandinavia, stand up for the old tradition which, to use a Russian writer's expression, stands firmly based on two hitherto unshaken pillars : the names of the first Russian princes, and the names of the falls of the Dniepr. (See, for example the learned researches of the Rev. Fath. Martỳnof, in the *Revue des Questions Historiques*, July, 1875, and the *Polybiblion*, May, 1875.) W. Thomson, Professor at Copenhagen, has given three lectures on this subject. They were translated into German under the title, *Ursprung des Russischen States (Origin of the Russian State)*, 1879.

Russia even more than in the West, we run the risk of ascribing to the Teutons what the Barbarians can lay claim to, of attributing to race the effects of culture. Slavs or Teutons, no matter which, all these tribes had similarities of customs and character which render it no easy task to make out in the institutions the part of each.

The Teutonic impress, having gone less deep, was also less enduring in Russia than in the West. The absorption of the Scandinavian top-layer by the Slavic subsoil was rapid and complete. No matter how many recruits from Scandinavia the Varangian princes kept calling in during more than a century, their settling in Russia is rather to be compared to that of the Normans in Neustria than that of the Merovingians and the Carlovingians in Gaul. Rurik's grandson, Sviatoslàv, already bears a Slavic name and worships Slavic gods.*

In Russia, as everywhere else, it was a woman who opened the way to Christianity. Olga, the Russian Clotilda, was baptized in Constantinople. Her example, scorned by her son Sviatoslàv, was followed by her grandson Vladímir, who was Russia's Clovis and Charlemagne in one. No nation ever accepted Christianity more easily; it had been prepared for it all through the last century by its relations with Byzance, and Christianity itself had been prepared for the Russian people by the translation of the Gospels and of the liturgy into Slavic. By ushering his subjects into Christianity, Vladímir at the same time introduced them amongst the European nations. Although Christ's creed has been to our civilization much more a nurse than a mother, still this civilization never could become naturalized in any nation but such of which the majority were Christian. Even at this present day, when it seems most free of its infancy's swaddling-clothes, it is doubtful whether it could become entirely acclimated among people professing alien religions. No country

---

* On the *drujína* of the *kniazes*, as on the *boyàrs* of the next following epoch, see, further on, Book VI., Chap. II, *The Nobility.*

yet has entered into civilization by another gate than that of Christianity.* In Vladímir's time more particularly the Christian faith drew the moral boundary line of Europe. This boundary was crossed by Russia as early as the tenth century ; but the Gospel was not to clear a place for her in the family into which it had just introduced her. Here, again, through the resemblance of Russia to the West, shows an essential dissimilarity. The Cross comes to her by another road—from Byzance, not from Rome, and thus the very bond which appeared to link her to Europe, in reality, was to hold them apart.

To gain a knowledge of the elements of Russian civilization, it were needful to appraise this oriental form of Christianity, to determine its value as a civilizing agent. Unfortunately this is too lofty a question to be lightly touched upon in passing ; it will have to be reserved for our study of the Russian Church.† Let it suffice here to remark that, if less favorable to the progress of its proselytes, the Greek creed need not, therefore, be inferior to the Latin. By sequestering Russia from the West, the Eastern Church took from her one of the principal advantages of her conversion ; she robbed her of the benefit conferred by membership in that vast intellectual community of which Rome was the centre, and which, for the West, was one of the most favorable conditions of civilization. Russia remained, as though excommunicated, outside the pale of the Christian republic ; morally as well as physically, she was banished to the frontiers of Europe.

Christianity, through Constantinople, brought Russia into some sort of connection with antiquity. Under the " Grand-Kniazes " of Kief, she became a sort of colony of Byzance. That is what one of her writers calls by the name of "the first of her intellectual bondages." The Russian Metropolitans were Greeks, the

* This precisely is one of the things that lend so fascinating an interest to the grand experiment that is being tried in Japan.

† The third volume of the present work will be devoted to the Russian Church and sects. It will there appear in what measure heathen ideas and practices have at times persisted under Christian rites.

"grand princes" took pleasure in marrying Greek princesses and visiting the Bosporus. The numerous schools endowed by Vladímir and Yaroslàv were founded by Greeks, after Byzantine models. For over two centuries, Constantinople and her daughter entertained a close intercourse, by means of commerce, religion, arts, etc. Byzance impressed on the Russians' manners, character, taste, a stamp which was not quite obliterated by the Tatar impression which came on top of it.

The first social type which civilization held out to the young Russian Empire was the autocracy of the Lower Empire, a state without political rights, ruled by Imperial Omnipotence, aided by a close hierarchy of functionaries and employés.

This Byzantine training was corrected by Kief's relations with the other European states. The isolation to which geography, religion, and, later on, the Mongol yoke condemned Russia, was not as severe then as it soon became. The schism between the two churches, undecided as yet, had not brought about the hostility in which the crusades resulted. It had not yet vetoed unions between worshippers of the two rites. The Russia of the eleventh century was part of the political system of Europe. Yaroslàv, Vladímir's son and continuator, was connected, through his children, with the King of France, Henry I., as well as with the Eastern emperors, the rulers of Poland, Norway, Hungary, with German princes and with the Saxon Harold, the hapless rival of William the Conqueror. At the time of Kief's supremacy Russia was more European than at any other time before the eighteenth century. Her relations with Constantinople, the last refuge of the arts and sciences of antiquity, gave her an easily gotten advantage over the West. Kief, beautified by Greek builders and limners, came to be, as one would say, a reduced copy of Byzance, a Ravenna of the north. The superb mosaics of her grand Cathedral of St. Sophia, the magnificent insignia now to be seen in the treasury at Moscow, bear witness even yet to the wealth of this capital, the wonder of chroniclers—German,

Greek, and Arab. The Russian state was already then the vastest of Europe, one of the most active in trade and by no means the least cultivated. In the eleventh or twelfth century it could seem more favored than Northern Germany, which at that time still was in great part under Slavic or Lithuanian rule, sunk in heathenism and barbarism. It was an empire firmly seated on European foundations, yet possessed of elements of originality already clearly marked ; a country which in the midst of Christendom appeared called to some special mission, that of serving as a link between the Greek Orient and the Latin Occident. But history denied to it the simple boon of a normal development. On the threshold of youth its growth was stopped by one of the greatest perturbations recorded in human annals. The Mongol invasion was not merely to put back the hand of Russia's timepiece three hundred years, it was to turn her from the European road on which she was travelling, bend her to alien manners, and, in a measure, twist her out of shape. It was in the early years of the thirteenth century, at the very dawn of Western civilization, when mediæval Europe was on the point of blossoming out on all sides—in poetry, in architecture, in scholasticism,—that the hordes of Djinghiz-Khan cut away from Europe Russia's co-operation.[4]

Long before the Mongol invasion the development of the first Russian Empire had been hampered by an internal evil, the division of sovereignty. All the descendants of Rurik were entitled to

[4] But what a compensating boon to have escaped such influences as those of Innocent III. and the Albigensian wars ! Terrorizing Christianity is uncongenial to Russian nature, and would have warped it, ruined it irretrievably. Not even the divine trio, Dante, Giotto, and sweet Francis of Assisi, could have made up for the moral havoc that would have been wrought by these two things alone—the blasphemous Albigensian " crusade " and the Inquisition. Catholicism, being hostile to the Slavic nature, must have destroyed, defaced, perverted—(*dénaturé*)—what is best in it. See what became of Poland in the hands of Rome ! Thus the Mongolian visitation was really an escape. How, in other ways it brought out and strengthened the best in the nation, we shall see farther on. Another escape—no scholasticism. Better a thousand times the *naïve* poetry of popular beliefs.

some share in the common inheritance, or rather the common property. The eldest, the head of the house, the "Grand-Kniaz," residing in Kief, had over the others a merely nominal supremacy. In the course of two or three generations this system of absolute equality of rights had brought about a parcelling out of the country nearly amounting to trituration. This Russian system of appanages was not the feudal system of the West ; it differed from that in many particulars, and instead of favoring the introduction thereof, rather hindered it. Notwithstanding all these successive divisions and subdivisions, the sovereignty, like the nation, remained one and indivisible, or, at least, was regarded as such. The *kniazes*, who divided it among themselves, held only a life interest in it, very much as to this day in the rural communes each member of the *mir* has only the temporary use of his lot, the land itself remaining the property of the community.*

As though to make this resemblance more complete, the appanaged princes frequently passed from one appanage to another. The national unity was maintained by, or, more correctly, was vested in, the unity of the reigning family, the claims of the *kniazes* to one another's inheritance and to the title of "Grand-Kniaz." Russia formed a sort of patriarchal federation composed of princes of one and the same blood, having at their head their "senior," or, rather, the oldest of the line. From such a constitution or custom naturally sprang civil wars, which mutually enfeebled the princes. This and their frequent transfer from one appanage to another enabled a few cities, as, for instance, Nòvgorod, to preserve their liberty and to rise to a high pinnacle of power.†

* See, further on, the chapters on collective property and the village communities. The Russian word for the princely appanages, *udièl*, signifies "portion," "share," "lot" ; it has the same radical and nearly the same meaning as the word *nadièl*, designating the lot of each peasant in the communal land.

† The appanage system has given rise to many discussions and various hypotheses, an epitome of which will be found in Mr. Ralston's excellent volume, *Early Russian History*, pp. 192, 193.

The period which these competitions made one of misery
was still not barren of good. In the midst of these dissensions,
possibly thanks to them, Russia was accomplishing the great
work set her by destiny : the colonization of the vast regions
now known under the name of " Great-Russia,"—a colonization
entirely continental and, as a rule, peaceable, which lasted
through centuries, and is going on still, and which, with regard
to results, is no whit behind the maritime colonization of the
Western nations. The Slavs of the Dniepr or Vòlkof, turning their
backs on Europe, marched eastward into the wilderness, looking
out for new lands. Ambition or religious zeal urged each *kniaz*
to extend his dominions and to found new cities to endow his
children with. The peoples of Turkish race, who called the
steppes of the south their own, headed the new-comers off towards
the centre and the north, the wooded region, which, owing to the
nomads, was for a long time the only one fit for settled life.
Between the Slav immigrants and the Finn aborigines Christianity served as link ; it became the cement of a new people.

To judge by the very vague memory which the Great-Russian
retains of the old Slavic gods, compared to his brethren of Little-
Russia and White-Russia, this colonization proceeded on a large
scale only after the conversion of the Russians to Christianity,—a
conversion so rapid, so easy, that in a short hundred years these
central colonies rivalled the cities of the West, and tended to
become the centre of the empire. In the middle of the twelfth
century, a *kniaz* of Vladímir on the Kliàzma took, without
changing his capital, the title of " Grand-Kniaz," exclusively
reserved, so far, to the prince ruling at Kief. A little later the
holy city on the Dniepr was captured and sacked by Russian
hands. In these strifes between prince and prince there was,
however, no strife of race, no national scission between the new
Russians of Súzdal and the original *Russ*, as those have since pretended who would fain make two different nations of the Great-
and the Little-Russians. If this war between Súzdal and Kief

had any historical sense, it was as the first collision between the patrimonial *régime* of the north and the patriarchal anarchy of the south, as the first triumph of the autocracy just sprouting amidst the forests of the east over the family traditions of the *kniazes* and the traditions of independence boasted by the cities or tribes of the west.

On the banks of the Volga, the Kliàzma, the Moskvà, the mutual relations between Rurik's heirs had been but little modified. In the feeble cities founded by the *kniazes* in the midst of countries either desert or inhabited by heathen natives, there were few or no popular assemblies or *viêtchês*,* to limit the authority of the *kniaz*. In these remote regions the prince clings to the soil conquered or colonized by him ; he settles down in a fixed residence, instead of passing from one appanage to another. To the undivided sovereignty vested in Rurik's house is substituted the patrimonial hereditary *régime*, which, by inheritance or conquest, is one day to unite the entire nation under one single rule.

From the fertile banks of the semi-classical Borysthenes, the centre of Russia had been shifted to a land farther removed from Europe, and differing more widely from it, to a poorer soil and a severer clime, to a people more mixed, more foreign to all Teutonic or Byzantine influence. The Western customs, which in the Russia on the Dniepr had but feeble roots, were not given time to strike any at all in this ungracious soil. There we find still fewer European elements, fewer political rights for the individual, for corporations or cities. A country almost entirely rural, where the base and type of social order is the "house and yard," the *dvor*, with the head of the family at the top. Already so distant from Europe, this nation was to be removed still farther away by two centuries of the domination of tribes the most impermeable to the manners, religion, civilization of Europe.

* Viêtchê (from *viêsh-tchâti*, "to speak, to discourse—" *cfr* "parliament" from *parler*)—the public popular assembly, long retained in Nòvgorod and Pskof, while in Rostòf and the cities of the province of Súzdal, Moscovia that was to be, the *viêtchê* was early suppressed or shorn of all power.

APPENDIX TO BOOK IV., CHAPTER II. (See p. 245, note 4.)

Mr. Beaulieu dismisses this question far too summarily and with less of his habitual conscientious deliberation than might be expected when treating a subject of such vast import and capital bearing on a host of Russian issues, one moreover that so nearly touches the very core of the nation's patriotic sensitiveness. He passes sentence on it from evidence taken for granted at second hand ; there is no trace of personal investigation in these pages, and they are, accordingly, not up to date. Mr. Zabiélin, in the second chapter of his sterling work, *A History of Russian Life* (1876), gives an exhaustive history of the momentous question of the racial identity of the Varangians, as presented by both sides. It is most instructive and, if not absolutely conclusive, leaves the *onus probandi* very much to the German party—abroad and at home,—who had settled the matter for us after the most ponderous scientific methods, never dreaming of an appeal to a later tribunal, with added materials and new lights for the revision of the old. The merest epitome of these most interesting two hundred pages is far beyond the limits of even the most liberal appendix, though it would yield the substance of a fascinating magazine article, and we must be content with emphasizing the following facts : that the entire southern littoral of the Baltic, as well as several islands of the same, are irrefragably proved to have been thickly peopled with Slavs and, in some parts, wholly occupied by them ; that the Isle of Rügen was one of their chief centres, emporiums, gathering-points, for, like their Scandinavian brethren and neighbors, the Northmen of various tribes, they were professional pirates, as indicated by the designation of *Variàgy, Vàgre, Vargy* —all more or less incorrect phonetic approximations of, not a proper, but a common Scandinavian noun, *vargr,* meaning "wolf, fugitive, robber," etc., and still surviving in the modern *vagrant*—which they by no means exclusively owned, but shared with the other Northmen ; that the particularly warlike and powerful tribe of Slavic Varangians or Vagrians with which we are concerned, sailors as fearless, robbers as fierce as their southern brethren of the Adriatic, were next-door neighbors to the Anglo-Saxons from before their wholesale invasion of Britain, occupied the sheltered and convenient cornerland by the sea and the mouth of the Elbe, which to this day teems with Slavic names of places, some only slightly germanized, like Lübeck = *Liùbitch,* Wismar = *Vsemir,* or translated, like Oldenburg or Aldenburg from the Slavic *Stargràd.* That these things and many others to the point were really so is amply established by the

testimony of mediæval North German chroniclers, naturally hostile to the
Slavs, but simple and honest in their work. Helmold (twelfth century)
writes expressly : " The city of Aldenburg, the same which in Slavic bears
the name of *Starygràd, i. e.,* 'the Old City,' lies in the land of the Vagrians, on the western shore of the Baltic Sea, and on the furthest confines
of Slavia. This city and all the Vagrian land were, from of old, inhabited
by very brave men, because, standing in the front of all the Slavic peoples
and bordering on the Danes and Saxons, they always were first and leaders
in the warlike expeditions against their neighbors and bore the brunt of
their blows." Helmold mentions having been told that the Varangians
"at one time ruled many very distant Slavic peoples." These Slavic
Northmen differed from their Scandinavian rivals chiefly in this : that,
famous as they were for their "excessive prowess by land and sea," they
were not content with the precarious gains of a piratical existence, but early
turned their attention to the arts of peace, especially agriculture and commerce, until, in the words of eye-witnesses, this northern part of modern
Germany became "like unto a promised land, full to overflowing with all
good things, unless it were grapes, figs, and dates." Adam, the venerable
canon of Bremen, who wrote a most valuable geographical work in the
eleventh century, waxes enthusiastic as he describes the glories of the Slavic
cities of Pomerania (*Pombriyé*), while Jornandes, the Gothic monk-chronicler and secretary of the Gothic kings in Italy, as early as the sixth
century mentions the brisk trade in furs between the Baltic Slavs and the
"Roman South," and remarks that their name was made famous by the
extraordinàry beauty and natural black color of the sables which they
brought to the Italian markets.

As for Nestor, the Russian monk-chronicler of the twelfth century, the
first and only native authority concerning the beginnings of Russian state
life, and who might be less misleading were he not unfortunately rather
deeply versed in the confused and misty erudition of the age,—his hand, in
an evil hour, while telling the famous story of the delegation sent from
Nòvgorod to invite the Varangian princes over to rule a "vast and rich,
but ill-ordered land," penned the following luckless sentence : "They went
beyond the sea, to the land of the Varangian *Russ.* These Varangians
called themselves *Russ ;* just as some were named Swedes, others Northmen, Angles, others again Goths, so these ones are named *Russ.*" This
sentence of Nestor's is brought forth as the strongest possible proof that
they were undoubtedly Scandinavian. Why? "On the strength," says
Mr. Zabiélin, " of the following logical argument : If in a room there are

five inmates, of whom four are Germans, the fifth must of necessity be a German also; indeed the word 'inmate' itself must mean 'a German.' Swedes, Norwegians, Danes, Englishmen, are called Europeans. It is well known that these peoples are German. Consequently, the Russians, who also call themselves Europeans, must be Germans too."

Strange that such a fallacy should have been accepted by numbers of respectable scientists for sound, conclusive reasoning! Sad effects of partisanship in science!

It is hard to have to abstain from developing in its principal phases and following out to its conclusions this most interesting theme. But it would seem as though a little reflection must show which way lie the probabilities, the natural and easy solution of many problems of national history and life which, under the other hypothesis, have always remained puzzles that vainly exercised the ingenuity of its own propounders.

(Besides Mr. Zabiélin's *History of Russian Life*, consult Alexander Hilferding's classical *History of the Baltic Slavs*, a very valuable work bearing the same title by Kotliarefsky, and the works of the Tchekh historian Schafárik.)

BOOK IV. CHAPTER III.

The Tatar Domination, its Effects on the National Manners and Character
—On the Reigning Family and Political Status—Causes and Character
of the Moscovite Autocracy—In what the Russia of the Seventeenth
Century Differed from the West of the same Period—Gaps in Russian
History.

THE invasion of the Mongols, in the beginning of the thirteenth
century, snapped the thread of Russia's destinies. The consequences of this terrible event were peculiar to Russia ; the causes
were not. This catastrophe, seemingly isolated, was only an
incident in the great struggle between Europe and Asia, of which
the crusades were the chief incident. In this collision of two
worlds the same causes were at work from the Russian steppes to
the Spanish *sierras.* Russia defended the left wing of Christendom against the immense converging host which advanced from
Asia and Africa, in the shape of a gigantic crescent, ready to
extend its extremities so as to coil itself round Europe, while
Spain defended the right wing, and France and England, Italy
and Germany, boldly taking the offensive, attacked the enemy's
centre by means of the crusades. Russia had done that sort of
fighting, in her own southern deserts, against the Petchenègs, the
Pòlovtsy, and other nomads of Turkish race, bearing the brunt of
the strife against Asia, long before the great invasion of the thirteenth century. Being placed at the most perilous outpost, in the
neighborhood of the most extensive gathering-place of the Barbarians, her fall was a foregone conclusion. The Russian princes,
united against the hosts of Djinghiz-Khan, had valiantly held out
against the first shock on the Kalka (1224). A second invasion

encountered resistance only behind the walls of cities. The two capitals, Vladímir and Kief, were taken at the first onslaught. It seemed as though the Russian nation was to vanish, and those immense plains, a prolongation of Asia, were to become, definitely, Asiatic.

Nature, after preparing the invasion, herself marked its bounds. The Tatars, now masters of the steppes in the southeast, which felt to them very much like home, grew ill at ease as soon as they began to lose themselves in the forests of the north. They did not settle there. These regions were too European to suit their half-nomadic habits, and they cared more for tribute-payers than for subjects. So the *kniazes* received their principalities back from the hands of the Mongols—as fiefs. They had to submit to the presence near their person of a sort of Tatar "residents,"— the *baskàks*, whose duty it was to take the census and to collect the taxes. They were compelled to take the long, long journey to the "Horde," often encamped in the heart of Asia, in order to receive their investiture from the successors of Djinghiz, and ended by becoming the vassals of a vassal of the "Great-Khan." At this price Russia retained her religion, her dynasties, and—thanks to her clergy and her princes—her nationality.

Never yet was nation put through such a school of patience and abject submission. St. Alexander Nevsky—the Russian St. Louis—is the type of the princes of that epoch, when heroism was taught to cringe. Alexander, the victor over the Swedes and the German knights of the Baltic, who, instead of assisting Russia, strove to wrest from her a few wretched roods of land, was forced, if he would protect his people, to make himself very small indeed before the Tatars. The Russian princes, in their dealings with them, had no weapons but supplication, presents, and—intriguing. Of these they made use largely for the preservation, or even aggrandizement, of their power, freely denouncing and slandering one another to the foreign masters. Under this humiliating and impoverishing domination the germs of culture laid in the old

17

principalities withered up. The meagre and marshy region of the northwest alone, the land of Nòvgorod and Pskof, secure against invasion, could, under cover of a merely nominal subjection, lead a free and European life.

Of the manifold effects resulting from the yoke imposed on the country, the moral ones are perhaps the least obscure. For nations, as for individuals, slavery is unwholesome ; it bows their souls so low that, even after deliverance has come, centuries are needed to straighten them again. The oppressed are all alike ; bondage breeds servility ; abasement breeds baseness. Craft takes the place of strength, which has become useless ; finessing, being most called for, becomes the universal quality. The Tatar domination developed in the Russians faults and faculties of which their intercourse with Byzance had already brought them the germs, and which, tempered by time, have since contributed to develop their diplomatic gifts.

Spain and Russia, standing isolated, one at each end of Europe, both fell under the Mussulman rule, and, as a consequence of this similarity in their position, the destinies of both also are comparable. Between the political and religious development of these two countries, different as they are, this double analogy created peculiar resemblances ; but on the character of the two nations, a yoke, apparently identical, has had the most opposite effects. The Spaniard, conquered, but never cowed into submission, the Castilian, who, to drive out the infidel, had recourse to the sword alone, retains, to this day, as an effect of the invasion, an overweening haughtiness, an excessive national pride, a scornful stiffness in his demeanor to strangers. The Russian, forced to give up his arms, compelled to look for help exclusively to his own patience and suppleness, has brought down from the time of his bondage a character perhaps less dignified, but of which the very faults are less of a danger to the progress of his country than are the Spaniard's qualities. The oppression by man, added to the oppression by the climate, deepened certain traits already sketched in by nature in the Great-Russian's soul. Nature inclined him to submission, to endurance, to resignation ; history confirmed these inclinations. Hardened by nature, he was steeled by history.[1]

One of the chief effects of the Tatar domination and all that makes up Russian history, is the importance given to the national worship. That again reminds one of Spain. Suffering opens to faith the hearts of a people as well as those of individuals ; religion draws new vigor from public calamities as well as from private misfortunes. Such an impulse must have been deep and enduring in the thirteenth century and in such a country as Russia. On all sides sprang up prophecies and apparitions, every city had its wonder-working *eïkon* that could stay the hand of the foe. In the midst of universal penury, wealth flowed freely into the churches. The black Byzantine paintings were cased in massive gold and silver, and set with those gorgeous jewels which even yet astound the traveller. The men crowded into the monasteries whose battlemented walls afforded the only retreat within which peace of mind and security of life and limb could be found. The policy of the Tatars was wholly favorable to religion and the clergy. The khans, desirous to conciliate the conquered through their religion, almost became its protectors. Church property was by them exempted from taxes, and the Metropolitans received from the Horde the confirmation of their dignity, like the "Grand-Kniazes."

The domination of an enemy who was a stranger to Christianity fortified the sufferers' attachment to their worship. Religion and native land were merged into one faith, took the place of

---

[1] The Spaniards had mountains, where a few can hold their own, where independence can always be bought at the price of hardships and watchfulness,—mountains, which demand and fashion a character and qualities the exact opposite of those which alone can ensure the preservation of the races that dwell on plains, open to all attacks, for whom danger and disaster are one, from the lack of fastnesses to fall back upon. Where successful resistance is physically impossible, unbending stubbornness would be suicidal,—and nature forbids wholesale self-destruction.

nationality and kept it alive. It was then that the conception sprang up which still links the quality of Russian to the profession of Greek orthodoxy, and makes of the latter the chief pledge of patriotism. Such facts occur in other nations, but it is Russia's peculiarity that all her wars have had the same effect. Owing to the differences in worship, her wars with Pole, Swede, or German have assumed a religious character, just as her long crusade against Tatar or Turk. Every war has been to this people a religious war, and patriotism was reinforced by piety and fanaticism. In his battles against infidel, heretic, or Latin, the Russian learned to consider his native land, the only one exempt from both the Mussulman and the Popish spiritual yoke, as a blessed land, as sacred soil, and came at last to regard himself, after the fashion of the Jew, as the chosen of God, until, filled with religious reverence for his own country, he named it " Holy Russia."

Upon Russia's political sovereignty the Tatar domination had two parallel effects : it hastened national unity and it strengthened autocracy. The country which, under the appanage system, was falling to pieces, was bound together by foreign oppression as by a chain of iron. Having constituted himself suzerain of the " Grand-Kniazes," whom he appointed and dethroned at will, the Khan conferred on them his authority. The Asiatic tyranny of which they were the delegates empowered them to govern tyrannically. Their despotism over the Russians was derived from their servitude under the Tatars. Thus, thanks to the Horde, there ensued a territorial concentration of the different principalities in the hands of the *Veliki-Kniaz* of Moscow, transformed into the general agent of the conquerors, as well as a political concentration of authority. All liberties, all rights and privileges disappeared. The bell of the *viétche* ceased to call the citizens to the popular assemblies. The *boyàrs* and the princes who used to hold appanages in their own right no longer had any dignities but those which the Tatar suzerain conferred on them. Every germ of free government, whether aristocratic or democratic, was stifled. Nothing remained but one power, the *Veliki-Kniaz*, the autocrat,—and such now, after more than five hundred years, still is the basis of the state.

To the Mongols, said Karamzìn in the beginning of the present century, Moscow owes her greatness, and Russia owes autocracy. This opinion nowadays is contested by Russian patriots: they prefer to seek for the foundations of Moscovite autocracy in the physical and economical conditions of Great-Russia, in the character of the people themselves, in the primitive or patriarchal form of their institutions, in their conception of the family and of domestic sovereignty.

Formerly it was the fashion to account for everything in Russia and for Russia herself, for the character of the nation as for the nature of its government, by the Mongol domination. Nowadays this view is almost entirely exploded. Of the contemporary historians, the greater number regard the long rule of the Tatars merely as the superposition of an alien element, which by its weight, it is true, lay heavily on the conquered people, but without the manners or mind of the Asiatic invaders having at all penetrated as far as the hearth or the soul of their Russian vassals. This contact of three centuries is admitted to have had scarcely more than indirect effects, through the isolation into which it threw Russia, and the abrupt stoppage to which it brought her moral growth.[2] Indeed Soloviòf, the great Moscovite historian, has gone so far as to say that the three centuries of subjection left hardly more traces in Russia than the raids of the Petchenègs and Pòlovtsy of yore.

There is nothing astonishing in this reaction against the old historians and their antiquated views. All nations just now are rehandling their histories in the same sense, trying hard to reduce to a minimum or to eliminate altogether out of their national life

[2] Not a very close contact either, since the conquerors did not **live** among the conquered, but only sent their agents and collectors.

all that comes from abroad, and especially from conquest. So the English often do with regard to the Norman conquest ; so do the French with regard to German invasions. The reason is twofold. On one side, the modern historian treats the evolution of nations much as the geologist does that of our globe, and both reduce more and more the importance of revolutions and sudden catastrophes in favor of slow, continuous action and permanent causes. On the other side, under the influence of frequently unconscious patriotism, historians set aside impulses received from abroad, smooth over the violent shocks of invasions, that their peoples may appear to owe nothing but to themselves, and give all their attention to the spontaneous and internal development of the national genius. The new scientific methods, the tendencies, —one might call them naturalistic and biological,—of modern criticism and history, strengthen this bias. One takes pleasure in considering nations as living organisms, each of which has in itself the principle and the law of its own growth. In accordance with this conception, each nation loves to vindicate the spontaneity of its genius and of its historical development.

What the Russians do with regard to the Tatars, the Spaniards do with regard to the Arabs. The peninsula which, more unfortunate than Russia, has for centuries, almost the whole of it, been under the direct rule of Semites or Berbers, denies having undergone any moral fashioning at the hands of its Mussulman masters.

In such vindications there is much truth : it is neither the Tatar who has made Russia, nor the Moor who has made Spain. If, by a natural reaction against antiquated and exaggerated views, we now fall at times into the opposite extreme, forgetting that, after all, a people could not, without retaining some mark of it, be for several centuries in a state of subjection, it appears beyond doubt that the Mussulman influence on Russia formerly used to be greatly overestimated, even to forgetting that, besides their religion, the Russians have always preserved their own form of government and their own laws, and that all these things protected them against too servile an imitation of their foreign masters.

The nomads from the steppes of Asia are far from having been the only historical teacher of Moscovia. Side by side with the Asiatic influence of the Mongol or Turk conquerors, Russia, as has already been said, was early subjected to a more discreet but not less powerful influence which both preceded and survived that of the Tatars,—an influence which, instead of being combated by the beliefs and prejudices of the people, was strengthened by their sympathies and superstitions. From Vladímir down to Peter the Great, Russia never quite got clear of the Byzantine ascendancy which was exercised through the clergy, the schools, the laws, and literature. Is not Moscovite aristocracy, for instance, as much indebted to the Orthodox court of the emperors on the Bosporus as to the half nomadic *seraglio* of the Mongol khans? If the *régime* of the Horde, which might also be decorated with the epithet of "patriarchal," could give so Asiatic a coloring to Tsarism, grown up beneath its shade, was it not of Byzance and the Greeks of the Lower Empire that the Russian princes borrowed the type and the model, together with the forms, the etiquette, and the very name of their autocracy, when, after the fall of Constantinople, Ivan III. assumed the imperial eagle, as an inheritance from the Paleologues.[*]

What applies to autocracy and government, applies to a good many other things. A great part of what, in the manners, the fashions, arts, laws of the Moscovite state, we are tempted to ascribe to the Tatars, might with equal justice be traced to the Byzantines. The veiling and sequestration of women, shut up in the *térem*,[†] were customs quite as much at home at Byzance as

[*] The Russian title, *Samodièrjets*, is nothing but the literal translation of the Greek *autocrator* ("self-ruler").

[†] *Térem*, the Russian for "gynæceum," comes from the Greek *téremnon*, signifying "chamber, house." [3]

[3] Compare the German *thurm* and the curtailed English *tower*, from the French *tour*—with this again Italian *torre*, from the Latin *turris*, which brings us back to the Greek word.

with the Tatars ; to Byzance also very likely belong the prostrations, "with brow beating the ground " (*tchelobítiyé*), and other humiliating formalities observed at the court of the "Grand-Kniaz " ; to Byzance, lastly, the long garments, the *kaftàn* and *armiàk*,* to this day worn by the Old-Russians. And Byzance too may be credited, through the codes of her emperors, with the scourging with rods, if not with the *knùt* itself, with corporal punishments and elaborate tortures. The same question may be asked concerning art and poetry, in which Asiatic inspiration used to be too hastily taken for granted. We may venture to doubt the opinion of those scholars who, in the historical popular songs, the *Bylínas*, insist on recognizing imitation of Tatar lays,† or of those archæologists who, in the Russian bulb-shaped cupolas, flatter themselves they have found a Mongolian type, in vogue from the Ganges to the Dniepr, wherever the successors of Djinghiz and Timur ruled. ‡

Generally speaking it is no easy task to apportion their several parts to the Mussulman oppressor and the Orthodox instructor, either in private or in public life, as the peaceable teachings of the one generally confirmed the rough examples set by the other. Between the lessons taken at the schools of two such different

* Still *kaftàn* comes from a Turkish or Tatar word, and *armiàk* is an Armenian one.[4]

† On the Aryan *vs.* Turanian origin of these songs, see Mr. A. Rambaud's *Russie Épique.*

‡ Viollet-le-Duc, in his book on *Russian Art*, claims that he can trace everywhere—in architecture, in ornamentation, in calligraphy even—an influence decidedly Tatar or Indian. Russian scholars, such as Count S. Strògonof and Buslàyef, have shown how fanciful and erroneous this theory is, when thus generalized. They have proved, with the help of the monuments, that most of the strokes and ornaments, which the French architect wanted to force on the Mongols and on India, came in reality from the Southern Slavs and from the Byzantines. (See especially Buslàyef, in the *Critical Review*, published in Moscow—January and March, 1879 ; also the pamphlet of the learned Father Martỳnof, in *L'Art Russe*, Arras, 1878.)

[4] Probably indicating an originally Armenian garment, a lighter, sleeveless *kaftàn*, which leaves the arms, in their wide, long colored shirt-sleeves, pleasantly cool and free for work or exercise.

masters, it is the more difficult to discriminate that, through all the oppositions of the two races and the two civilizations, both, on the whole, taught young Russia very much the same things. From Byzance and from Saraï,—from the effete court of the super-annuated empire in its second infancy and from the half nomadic camp of uncouth shepherds,—from the pale heirs of classical traditions and from the sturdy hordes who had become, through their conversion to Islam, the disciples of the Arabs and Persians,— what most regularly came to Russia were models of despotism and examples of servitude. Therefore, in the coarse web of popular Russian life, it is often difficult to separate these two threads, both equally Oriental, so similar do their colors appear to us. Unfortunately for the Russians, the threadbare civilization of their Christian instructors, the stationary barbarism of their Moslem conquerors, instead of mutually acting as correctives, or neutralizing each other, only confirmed them in the same faults. Far from each counteracting the other, the double impulse drove them along in the same direction, and almost equally isolated them from Europe. Either as the Tatar's vassal, or as the Byzantine's pupil, the Moscovite breathed an air, Oriental if not Asiatic, for the Byzance of the Lower Empire was as much related to Asia as to Greece or Rome.

A terrible and wonderful story is that of Moscow's autocracy, growing up under the protecting shade of the Horde. Never did such lowly beginnings leap up so rapidly to greatness ; never was there more striking instance of the power of tradition in a sovereign house, whose members, along with blood and inheritance, transmit, from child to grandchild, a sacred goal and task, whose views, at first narrow, go widening from generation to generation, the faculties themselves seeming to grow by a kind of natural selection.[1]

[1] The beginnings and destinies of the House of Savoy—its struggles, self-imposed patriotic mission, and ultimate glorious success—are no unapt counterpart of those of the House of Moscow. And the personally not very

As men they were crafty, grasping, anything but chivalrous, of few scruples, patiently building up greatness on self-abasement ; as princes they were mostly of mediocre parts, far from shining with the brilliant qualities that distinguished the *kniazes* of the preceding epoch ; dull-faced, with countenances devoid of relief, of individuality, with features that from afar seem to run into one another.* All these Ivans and Vassílis of the fourteenth century kept on hoarding wealth in their treasury and aggrandizing their patrimony after the fashion of a private inheritance, and, as it appears from treaties and wills, without any very well-defined political idea, more after the manner of landholders anxious to "round up " their estates, than of sovereigns ambitious of extending their territories.† This character—private, domanial—the vast Moscovite Empire was to preserve in its government and administration, through all its achievements and conquests, down to the reforms of Peter the Great.

The establishment of heredity in the direct line gave Moscow the advantage which enabled her to triumph over all her rivals, Asiatic or European.⁶ A *kniaz* of Moscow, Ivan Kalità, obtained amiable but politically invaluable qualities of the early princes of the Italian house—their craft, stinginess, stubbornness, queerly combined with a suppleness often verging on unscrupulousness,—all these forcibly recall the unsympathetic yet venerable figures of the *kniazes* and tsars of the Russian house. Before the magnitude and righteousness of the results achieved in both cases, history forgets to moralize, and is compelled to own that here, if ever, the end justified the means.

* "All these Moscow *kniazes*," says Soloviòf, " look like one another. In this passionless mask it is difficult for the historian to make out the characteristic features of each. They are all imbued with the same idea ; they all tread the same path, slowly, cautiously, by fits and starts, yet inflexibly."

† The word *gossudàr*, which now signifies " sovereign," and is used only in speaking of the Emperor, had then the meaning of *khoziàïn*, "thrifty landlord and farmer " (a sort of domestic economist much in the spirit and after the pattern of Cato the Elder).

⁶ Among the sources of discontent and dissensions with which the old appanage system abounded, one of the most unfailing was the law regulating succession—or rather inheritances, since it has already been observed that the House of Rurik treated the land it was their lot to rule after the manner

from the Horde, about 1330, the title of " Grand-Kniaz " ; he also constituted himself general collector of taxes for the Tatars, and thus rapidly increased his wealth as well as his power. His grandson, Dimítri Donskòy, the only hero of the family, already felt strong enough to put his differences with the Horde to the test of arms. Crowned with victory on the field of Kulìkovo, on the Don (1380), he paid the price of heavy reverses for his premature success. Sometimes in open rebellion, more often the Tatar khans' humble tributaries, Dimítri's successors restored, by finessing, the Moscovite power momentarily endangered by his bravery.⁷ While Russia, under their rule, was working out her unity, the Golden Horde was dismembered into three Khanates. At the end of the fifteenth century appears Ivan III., a really great monarch, after the manner of the greatest among his contemporaries, Louis XI.

of a private patrimony. By this law—an immemorially old Slavic one, which, if duly pursued, might very probably be traced back to nearly primeval Aryan antiquity—it was not the eldest son who succeeded or inherited, but the next brother, or cousin—in short, the oldest of the race, the " Senior." This institution, which may be designated as " lateral heredity," was never cordially accepted by those who, from a very natural feeling, law or no law, felt disinherited and aggrieved. Thus there was a standing feud between uncles and nephews, brimming with incidents of violence, treachery, and cold-blooded cruelty, such as would have enlivened the chronicles of rival tyrant houses in mediæval Italy. It was Dimítri, the victor of the Don, who, with far-sighted political wisdom, realized the absolute necessity of a change in the order of succession. But it was like cutting off an entail : he could do nothing without the consent of the person immediately concerned. This, fortunately for Russia, was Vladímir the Brave, his heroic cousin and life-long friend. For the good of the country for whose deliverance they had fought side by side at Kulìkovo, Vladímir renounced his right and claim forever, and pledged himself to hold his young nephew, Dimítri's eldest son Vassíli, " in the place of elder brother." Thus the ancient unnatural custom was broken at last and a rational order of succession established, cutting off for all future times one mainspring of civil strife.

⁷ Yet the " Mamaÿ Massacre "—as the battle on the Don is often called, from the name of the defeated Tatar general—is universally acknowledged to have " broken the back " of the Tatar domination, to borrow the picturesque expression with which Southerners describe the effect of the first cool showers, which are said to have " broken the summer's back," though they may be followed by many more warm days, or even weeks.

of France and Ferdinand the Catholic. Ivan III. reduces the Khanate of Kazàn to vassalage. His grandson, Ivan the IV., brings Kazàn and Astrakhan into subjection. Ivan III. despoils the appanage-holding princes ; Ivan IV. abases the *boyàrs* and ancient families. The former compels Nòvgorod's submission, the latter completes the proud republic's ruin by executions and transportation. The last principalities, the last free cities disappear, and with them all traces of individual rights, alike for princes, nobles, and people. Russia is one, from the White to the Caspian Sea, and in this empire, already the most extensive of Europe, there is only one master—the Tsar. Under Ivan IV.—the Terrible— autocracy, arrived at its zenith, became a sort of methodical Reign of Terror. A strange compound of craft, mysticism, inhuman in his piety, sarcastic in his atrocities, bloodthirsty in his reforms, bred in the midst of plots and suspicion, possessed of a mind singularly free and inquiring for his time and country,* combining the Russian's practical sense with the ravings of a maniac, the assassin of his own son and husband of as many wives as Henry VIII., Ivan IV., the enemy of the *boyàrs*, has, like Nero, remained popular. Too much reviled at one time, possibly overrated at the present day, this royal leveller is the fierce forerunner of Peter the Great, with whom the ballads sometimes confound him, and who also might aptly have been surnamed "The Terrible." ⁸

Scarcely delivered from the Tatar domination, the Russians spread themselves in all directions across their vast plains. Then

* See the curious correspondence between Ivan IV. and the rebel, Prince Kùrbsky, also with Queen Elizabeth.

⁸ It might help the imagination to form some adequate presentment of this unique and wellnigh monstrous historical figure, were we to try to mix together, then cast into one mould, Tiberius, Louis XI., and Richelieu, not only with their horrible individual instincts and qualities, but also with their very real greatness of political genius, statesmanship, and patriotism. The objects of the French king's and minister's life-long endeavors—their country's aggrandizement and unity and the abasement of an ambitious nobility— were also those of the Moscovite tsar. Even the means used were of much the same nature.

they descended the Volga and came out into the Caspian Sea, entered the Caucasus and Central Asia, ascended the Kama, crossed the Ural, and a Cosack outlaw conquered Siberia.[9]

Under the Tatars, "the Plain" (*pòlie*), *i. e.*, the southern steppe region, had temporarily domineered over the northern forest lands, although unable to assimilate them. Under the Moscovite tsars, the forest region, now the seat of an agricultural state, stable and centralized, such as never could have developed on the " dry sea " of the steppes,[*] in its turn subjects the woodless region, and, by the defeat of the nomads, by colonization and farming, incorporates it into Europe.

At the same time, the Russians quickly turn towards the West, towards the Baltic and the Dniepr, their European starting-points. The Mongol invasion had separated Moscovite Great-Russia from the cradle of Rurik's empire, from White-Russia and Little-Russia, which, in the meanwhile, had fallen into the hands of the Lithuanians and the Poles. In the north, the Swedes and the Teutonic Knights, after the Sword-Bearers, were holding the shores of the Baltic. So that Moscovia was compressed between two rows of hostile states which seemed ready to choke out her breath : in the east the Tatars, in the west the Lithuanians and the Teutonic Order. And after Russia was free from the Tatars, there still remained, between her and the West, a broad Christian barrier, a hostile wall, built up out of her own ruins. She had to cut her way through, to Europe and to the sea ; hence her strife with Sweden, the inheritor of the German Knights on the Baltic,— against Poland, the inheritor of Lithuania,—a strife which, after all but making an end of Moscovia, did end by costing Poland her life.

The death of Ivan the Terrible's sons ushered in a crisis in which Russia nearly fell to pieces ; the great work of the Moscovite princes, barely achieved, seemed on the point of perishing along with their family. In this country, where sovereignty was

---

[9] See appendix at the end of this chapter.
[*] A word of Soloviòf, the historian.

everything, it suddenly failed. The condition of Russia at that period recalls that of France at the death of Charles VI., when an English king lorded it in Paris. The Tsarian house was extinct; the Kremlin was wrangled for by a series of usurpers and pretenders, supported by foreign arms. At one moment, the Poles were encamped in Moscow, and Ladislas, a son of the King of Poland, was proclaimed Tsar. Russian nationality and Greek Orthodoxy, equally endangered, found salvation in their union. It was from the lower ranks of this people, to all appearance inert, that the movement was started which put an end to internal anarchy and foreign rule. A butcher of Nijni-Nòvgorod, Mínin by name, provoked the popular rising, the direction of which was entrusted to Prince (*kniaz*) Pojàrsky. The Poles having been repulsed, a new family, that of the Románofs, was called to the throne by the *zémsky sobòr, i. e.*, "popular assembly," a sort of States-General. In this people who had just rescued themselves by their own act, the fact of the throne being vacant awakened neither the sense of, nor the wish for, liberty. In the words of the Slavophil Khomiakòf, " the people, having restored order and made another tsar, retired from political life." The new Tsarian House was to have the same power as the old, only it invested that power with a more religious, more paternal character. In vain the example of the Polish nobility and the Swedish aristocracy aroused the emulation of the *boyàrs;* in spite of a few empty formulas,* in spite of the "*zémsky sobòr*," autocracy remains the law of Russia. The serfdom of the peasant, tied to the glebe by Borìss Godunòf, the usurper, was the only advantage won by the nobles. Neither minorities, nor interregnums, nor invasions could give to any class of the nation any rights or liberties before the face of the sovereign.

A Russian was saying to a foreigner that autocracy raised Russia from the ground, where she lay prostrate at the Tatars' feet; to which the foreigner remarked that it had raised her to

* The formula, " The *boyàrs* have deliberated, the tsar has ordained," is well'known.

her knees. The habitual formulas used by the Moscovites in addressing their sovereigns leave far behind all that was ever invented in the way of servility by the courts of the West. In the public petitions or declarations high and low entitled themselves the tsar's serfs, his varlets or *kholòpy.* Catherine II. was the first to show a repugnance against these abject designations ; they were so deeply seated in the nation's habits that they were fre-quently employed as synonyms for "subjects." In his famous letters to Prince Kùrbsky, Ivan IV. calls the King of Poland a "slave of slaves," meaning that he was the subject of his own subjects. Peter the Great himself, in reporting about the siege of Azof, which he was conducting, to Rodomànovsky whom he had appointed, in play, to act the part of tsar, took to himself, in addressing this sham sovereign, the qualification of *kholòp.**

---

* Ustriálof, *History of Peter the Great.* Russian scholars, indeed, main-tain that these designations were in no way abject originally ; *kholòp* meaning simply "servant." [10]

[10] These and other similar conventional forms, waifs and strays of the Tatar domination and of Byzantine influence since Ivan III., certainly *have* come to be as meaningless as the letter endings of European episto-lary etiquette, especially in countries of the so-called Latin race. One might as well exclaim at the "servility" of the Spanish national character because the Castilian winds up the long rigmarole of "service" and "devotion" and "humbleness" which precedes his signature with the initials *Q. S. P. B.,* which stand for "*Qué Sus Piés Besa*"—"who kisses your feet." The Rus-sian of the lower classes never loses personal dignity in his demeanor to superiors, even while using the traditional forms of speech, and one of his chief objections to the Pole of the same and indeed a far higher class—even to the lower nobility—is the cringing manner of the latter, not merely in words, but in acts, such as kissing the hand, the hem of the garment, or—if the difference of rank be not quite so great—the shoulder. Such things should not be taken too literally. And as an offset to a few offensively humble forms, we have the fact that the peasant to this day addresses his landlord and lady and his superiors generally as "father" and "mother" (*bàtiushka, màtushka*), while they respond with the affectionate "brother," "little brother" (*bràt, bràtiets*), both using the familiar "thou," the only form of address known in Russian, as in Latin, Greek, and all ancient or root-languages, until Peter's wholesale innovations, extending to language itself, introduced the absurd use of the second person plural. The "Occidentals" strenuously advocate, in word and practice, the use of the European forms of politeness in the intercourse with the lower class—and it is notorious that since they have in great part succeeded, the two classes are further from mutual under-standing than they were before. The old cordial familiarity is being frozen out, and it will be long before there is between them the common level of average culture which might take its place.

Nor was this an empty form under Peter any more than under Ivan : the sovereign did dispose at will of the property as well as the lives of his subjects.   Being in the habit of prostrating themselves before their masters until their brows struck the ground, the Russians gave the name of "brow-beating" (*tchelobítiyé*), to the written petitions placed in the tsar's hands.   In token of self-abasement before the sovereign, even when not personally admitted to his presence, the Moscovite *boyàrs*, instead of signing their full names in their petitions, used servile diminutives. These degrading formulas descending from class to class, every one making himself small before his superiors, baseness, hand in hand with arrogance, permvated the entire nation down to its lowest depths.

It is but just to note that these formulas, so repugnant to Westerners, were ennobled by religious sentiment and simple earnestness ; there also lingered in the custom some of that patriarchal feeling which we encounter everywhere in Russia even to this day.   The tsar, as the landlord, was called "father," and these names, taken from the dearest family ties, which even yet lend the forms of popular politeness a character so primitive and affectionate, were not, to the people, empty titles.   The last of the peasants in speaking to the tsar, could say "thou" to him ; he saw in him a natural protector against the oppression of the *boyàrs*, and all tsars have regarded themselves as such.   The sovereign was at the same time the father, wielding absolute authority over his children, and the master, the supreme landlord, disposing of the land and of all things therein as of his property.

An incident from the history of the sixteenth century places in bold relief, together with the rigorous severities of tsarism, the submissiveness of the subjects, dignified and touching even in its self-abasement.   The occasion was the reduction of Pskof, Nòvgorod's sister city, by Vassíli, son of Ivan III., and father of Ivan IV., both decorated by their contemporaries with that surname of "dread" or "terrible" (*grózny*), which appears to suit the entire dynasty or *régime.* "Thy patrimony, the city of Pskof, throws itself at thy feet," said the delegates of one of the two or three Russian cities which have known liberty, to Vassíli, come to take from them their last franchises. "Deal mercifully by thy old patrimony. We, thy orphaned children, are attached to thee and thine unto the end of time. To God and thee all is lawful in your patrimony." * Vassíli sent them word that it was his will to suppress the *viêtché* and all the privileges which his ancestors had, under oath, awarded to Pskof." "It is written in our annals," said a citizen at the last popular assembly called together in the city, "that the men of Pskof swore allegiance to the 'Grand-Kniaz,' who thereupon permitted them to live freely according to their customs. It is said that the Divine Wrath shall smite him who shall not keep his oath. By the grace of God, our lord this day disposes after his pleasure of Pskof, his patrimony, of us all and the bell that was wont to call us together. We have not perjured ourselves, we will not raise our hand against our sovereign ; we are rejoiced at his presence, and only beseech him not to annihilate us quite." The Pskovites, with tears, took down the bell which, for centuries, had been wont to call them to the *viêtché.* Vassíli, having entered the city, assured them of his good graces, and having bidden together the chief inhabitants, ordered the announcement to be made to them, that they should, with their wives and children, depart from their native city, to settle down in the centre of Russia, and "live there happily by the grace of the tsar." That same night, three hundred families were started on their way to Moscow, and soon after, Moscovites from the basin of the Volga came, by Vassíli's order, to occupy on the shores of Lake Peïpus the place of the transported Pskovites. Similar proceedings, renewed from the usages of ancient Nineveh and Baby-

---

* *Chronicle of Pskof,* quoted by Karamzìn. This parallel between God and the Tsar often recurs in the *Russian Chronicles,* and still survives in popular adages. "It has pleased God and the Tsar "—"God and the Tsar will see to it "—are proverbial expressions.

18

lon, had been employed towards Nòvgorod. By such means did the tsars work out the unification and levelling of their empire. Such examples help us to comprehend the autocracy of Peter and Nicolas.

This concentration of all branches of authority and of the whole of national life in one hand—was it entirely a produce of history, of Tatar oppression, and Byzantine teachings? By no means, and the Russian historians are justified in denying it. The cause lies in the country's nature and the soil itself, in the physical and economic conditions of Russia, in the extent and poverty of the meagre forest regions in which the Moscovite state grew up; it lies in the disproportion between the immensity of the territory and the sparseness of the population; and these things, from Rurik to Peter the Great, account for the mould into which the Russian government has been cast, for the slowness of the country's political and civil development. By these, too, the long period of formation, and, so to speak, of the country's embryonic historical life, is accounted for; these explain what Soloviòf calls "the long duration of the fluid state period." What, indeed, can be more difficult than to base something solid and lasting on those boundless plains, over which freely rolled the swell of invasion, where the population forever seemed about to sink and be lost, like streamlets in the sands of the desert, so that, to keep it in place and fix it to the soil, recourse had to be had to serfdom!

In such a country, the frailer the bonds between the various regions and the various tribes, the stronger the authority had to be, that was to be capable of creating and keeping alive a state. Thus Soloviòf could say that the excessive energy, the boundless strain of the government organism, was a natural consequence of the feebleness and incomplete development of the body politic. The weakness of internal and spontaneous ties was compensated by external centralization, by the mechanical concentration of all the national forces in the hands of autocracy.

In what way did the Russia of the first Románofs, the Moscovia of the seventeenth century, belong to Europe? Constructed on Slavic foundations by Teutonic leaders, cemented by Christianity under the influence of the "New Rome," the Russia which the Tatars laid low did have European bases. The Russia which Moscow raised on her own ruins was patched out of heterogeneous materials, partly borrowed from Asia : it was a building of mongrel architecture, made up of Byzantine and Mongol, of Gothic and Renaissance, a building resembling the church of Vassíli Blajènnoy, quaint wellnigh to monstrosity, which was built in Moscow under Ivan the Terrible.

One thing strikes the student of Russian history : its barrenness, its comparative lack of interest. Through all its vicissitudes, it is wanting in those large movements, religious or intellectual, those broad epochs, social or political, which are the landmarks of the stormy and active lives of the Western nations. In fact, the history of Russia differs from that of other nations more by what it lacks than by what it possesses of its own, and to each gap in her past answers a gap in the present, which time could not fill,— a gap in her culture, her society, at times in the Russian mind itself. This blank in the country's history, this absence of certain traditions and institutions in a people who has not yet learned how to appropriate those of others, seems to me one of the secret causes of the negative bent characteristic of the Russian intellect, one of the remote sources of nihilism, or "nothingism," in morals and in politics.

In this state, over which ten centuries have already passed, nothing is consecrated by time. The country is old, yet all therein is new. "In your country," one of the men who have known Russia best wrote to a Russian, "nothing is reverenced, because nothing is old." *

* Joseph de Maistre, letter to Prince Kozlòfsky, dated October 24, 1815. Twenty years later Tchaadàyef expressed an idea the same in substance, when he said : "The civilization of mankind has not touched us.

Russian history, compared to that of the Western nations, appears entirely negative.   Moscovia never had a. feudal system which, along with the conception of reciprocity in service and duty, fostered the feeling of right ; nor chivalry, from which the West received the feeling of honor,—according to Montesquieu, the foundation of the monarchy,—and which, where liberty became extinct, still maintained alive human dignity.   Russia never had any class of men answering to the French *gentilhomme*, and her only apology for a chivalry was the Cosacks—bands of deserters and runaway serfs, republics of adventurers, half crusaders, half pirates, whose savage freedom was guaranteed them by the steppe.

Russia never had communes, nor charters, nor a real burgher-dom, nor a third estate.   Nòvgorod, Pskof, Viàtka, stationed at the uttermost ends of the country, were exceptions, creditable to the genius of the nation, but which did not perceptibly influence its development.   Besides, the cities were too few.   Moscovia, but just freed from the Tatar yoke and forthwith levelled by autocracy, could scarcely be said to have in reality more than one city, the monarch's residence, and this capital itself was nothing but a huge village.   Moscovia was a commonwealth of peasants, a rural empire.   Now, without cities there can be no wealth, nor art, nor science, nor political life ; in short, etymology tells the story : without cities—*civitates*—no civilization.

As in the countries of the West, so in Russia, centralization meant monarchy ; but Russia had had none of the instruments or institutions of European monarchies ; neither parliaments nor universities, men of the robe, nor the pen.   She had sovereigns ; she never had a court.   Shut up in the *térem*,—the gynæceum bequeathed by the Tatars or Byzance,—the *tsarítsas* and *tsarévnas*

What with other nations has long since passed into their life, with us is to this day speculation and theory." Herzen himself said much the same thing, when he wrote (*On the Development of Revolutionary Ideas in Russia*) : "We are untrammelled by the past, because our past is empty, poor, narrow."

left the tsars to the coarseness of their sex. Moscow had neither castles nor palaces. The Kremlin was nothing but a combination of fortress and convent, where low pleasures fit for common soldiers alternated with a tiresome ecclesiastical pomp.*

The Russian Church had a national clergy, patriotic and respected. She also had her monasteries, and, later on, her synods or national councils. But she had no religious orders, no scholastic training, no great heresies, nor the grand councils of the Latin Church. Russia had ignorant sects—has them still—rustic, with no knowledge of the ancient tongues. She remained outside of the Reformation, of the learned and literary polemics, which, through the liberty of thought, led to political liberty. A stranger to the Reformation, she was one also to the Renaissance. Classical antiquity, which once upon a time had just brushed her, did not become naturalized in Russia, as it did in Germany, as by a second education.

Bound to Byzance by the ties of religion and neighborliness, Russia probably sheltered a greater number of Greek emigrants than Italy and the West. After the fall of Constantinople and the marriage of Ivan III. to the heiress of the last emperors, the Greeks began to flock to Moscow. Thither they brought Byzantine etiquette and devotional tracts. They did not find there, as in the West, the classical letters and genius smouldering under the ashes of antiquity, waiting to be revived. Though Russia did, besides the Greeks, import a few Italian artists and a few German artificers, she harbored neither the arts nor the literature of Europe, nor printing, the propagator of thought, nor the geographical discoveries which, together with the conception of the world, widened the modern mind.*

In emerging from under the Tatar domination, Moscovia

* See the two works of Zabiélin, on the *Domestic Life of the Russian Tsars and Tsaritsas.*

* Ivan the Terrible patronized the introduction of printing in Moscow, but the first presses, looked on suspiciously by the people, produced only books of devotion.

awoke in the midst of the Middle Ages—minus crusades and knighthood ; minus troubadours and *trouvères*, scholastics and legists—the Middle Ages shorn of romance. No Reform, no Renaissance, no Revolution—Russia's later history must needs be more incomplete still. Of the great facts and great epochs of European life, from the twelfth to the eighteenth century, she felt only a feeble shock. What would a Western nation be that had missed all that ? And with what could such gaps be filled ?

In the seventeenth century, Russia was as yet but a rudimentary embryonic organism ; outside of the Church, she possessed only two institutions, one at the basis, the other at the summit, of the state, and both not particularly favorable to the development of individuality : the commune with mutual solidarity of the members, and autocracy ; the bond between them—serfdom. The Tatar oppression and the struggle for life against Poland had absorbed all the country's vitality. Sieyès, to those who asked him what he had been doing during the Terror, used to reply : "I lived." To a similar question concerning her long inertness Russia might have given a similar answer. In order not to get crushed quite out of existence by the Mongols, she was compelled to sham death for centuries. The whole task of Moscovia consisted in making, materially, a nation of herself. Similar to a child of a robust temperament, she came strengthened and steeled out of trials that should have killed her ; but the assaults which gave her bodily vigor hindered her intellectual development. Compared to the other nations of Europe, she had but a coarse, rustic bringing up ; the masters, and even the time for cultivating the mind, were wanting.

APPENDIX TO BOOK IV.   CHAPTER III.   (See note 9, p. 269.)

THE FIRST CONQUEST OF SIBERIA.

Unlike so many important names of peoples and places that of Siberia gives no occasion for learned disputes as to its origin. There is no obscurity about it—of course up to a certain point, beyond which our interest does not extend. We know that, as early as the beginning of the sixteenth century, Sibir was the name of a Tatar kingdom on the Asiatic side of the Ural, along the rivers Tobòl, Irtỳsh, and Túra. After the conquest, by Ivan the Terrible, of Kazàn and Astrakhan the Siberian Khan Yediger tendered his voluntary submission, in the hope of finding protection against the rebels and pretenders who beset his life and throne. In vain ; he soon after lost both at the hands of the neighboring Kirghiz Khan Kutchùm, who immediately proceeded to make trouble for the Russian pioneer-borderers on this side the mountain chain, which, from its peculiar tameness and want of altitude, never was a serious obstacle to raids and invasions. The greatest sufferers from this state of things were the Strògonofs, a wealthy, enterprising family who owned untold thousands of acres—to be had for the taking—in the wild borderland which now is the government of Perm. The founder of this famous family's greatness had gone out into the wilderness early in the fifteenth century, and towards the end of the sixteenth they were the centre and soul of a large Russian colony, and had opened the industries—especially salt-boiling, and fur trade—which have always been this region's main source of wealth. In 1581, finding themselves unable to cope with the many nomadic tribes— Ostiàk, Vogùl, Tcheremiss, etc.,—who harassed the Russian settlements on all sides, with more united and unremitting efforts since they were sure of support from the Siberian khan beyond the mountains, the Strògonofs obtained from the Tsar an order to the *Voyevòd* or military commander of the Permian region enjoining him to lend them armed assistance and authorize them to enlist men from the colony and supply them with arms. They stretched this rather elastic decree to its widest reach and, in 1582, sent across the Ural a regular expedition, under command of *atamàn* Yermàk Timoféyevitch, a Cosack officer in the government's service stationed at Perm, thus taking a decidedly aggressive attitude instead of limiting their measures to self-defence. When Ivan IV. heard of this undoubtedly arbitrary proceeding, he was very angry and sent off post-haste special messengers to inform the Strògonofs of the fact and order them to recall their forces and send Yermàk back to Perm, to his post of service, and, furthermore, to beware how they attacked or provoked any quarrel with the Siberian " Sultan." The message came too late ; the Cosacks had already half achieved their wonderful venture.

It will be seen from this that Yermàk can in no wise be described as a brigand or "outlaw,"—an error, however, which has crept into popular history and has only recently been rectified. What gave rise to it may have been the fact that the men under his command were picked for bravery but certainly not for law-abiding morality. It was a handful of daredevil adventurers, of the same mettle as those of Cortez and Pizzaro, of the kind that do great things and shrink from few. His own chosen lieutenant, Ivan Koltsò, *was* an outlaw, under sentence of death, for capturing and sacking a small town of the Nogaÿ. They had a few cannon and muskets, and were well supplied with all things needful, including guides and interpreters. Beyond that, no resources nor real knowledge of the country. They started in boats up a not very considerable river, from which they soon had to strike inland. The boats had to be left. But whenever possible, they still kept to the rivers, a mode of transit familiar to them from their experience in navigation on the Volga, and each time had to build new boats, an operation fraught with delay and danger in the midst of a hostile country, notwithstanding the abundance of material. At times, where the distance was short and the soil even from one river to another, they carried or dragged them across. Thus they came to a town ruled by a third-class khan tributary to Kutchùm. The natives were taken utterly by surprise ; besides, they had never seen firearms, so fled at the first discharge. Some never stopped till they had reached the presence of Kutchùm, who heard from them the first tidings of the Russian invasion : " Warriors have come into our land," the fugitives reported, "with bows which give forth flashing fire, and strike like to the lightning from heaven. No arrows are to be seen, yet they wound and kill, and no armor avails for protection. They pierce clean through our plate and mail armor."

Now that Kutchùm was aroused, the crisis came quickly. The Cosacks were pursuing quite a triumphant course down the river Tobòl, when they were arrested by a large and comparatively regular army, gathered from all the tribes subject to Kutchùm, and led by a son or nephew of his own. There were thirty Siberians to one Russian. The Cosacks held a council of war. Several advised retreat. The greater part applauded Yermàk when he said : " Retreat ? Whither ? It is autumn. The rivers are beginning to freeze. Do not let us lay up an evil name for ourselves. Let us be mindful of the promise we made to honorable men (the Strògonofs), before God. If we turn back, shame will be ours and the name of word-breakers. Whereas, if God Almighty help us, our memories shall not die out among men, and glory will be ours forever." One would almost think that Shakespeare had inspired himself from the old Russian chronicler, when he penned the famous harangue of Henry V.

The Tatars fought desperately, but the Cosacks routed them completely, though with the loss of 107 men—a large one for their small force. Kutchùm himself snatched together all he could of his treasure and disappeared into the woods. When Yermàk entered the capital, Sibir, or Isker, it was empty, and yielded a mighty booty in furs, precious tissues, and all sorts of valuables. Soon the surrounding princelings began to drop in and make their submission ; Yermàk, suddenly developing remarkable statesmanship, treated them with great kindness and courtesy, and, after receiving their oath of allegiance in the name of the Tsar, forbade his men, under the severest penalties, to offer the slightest violence to the natives. At the same time he made good use of the enforced idleness of the long winter, by sending his lieutenant, Ivan Koltsò, with a small retinue, to the Tsar, to inform him that God had given into his hand the land of Sibir, and beg for reinforcements, also request that a *Voyevòd* might be sent, to take official possession of the country. Ivan the Terrible received Koltsò most graciously, granted him a free pardon, and sent him back with presents to Yermàk,—the fur robe he was wearing in the number, than which no greater mark of sovereign favor could be given. The *Voyevòd* Yermàk had asked for accompanied Koltsò, also a considerable detachment of soldiers.

After this things went wrong for a time. Most of the first conquerors perished in one way or another, when spring of 1584 had reopened hostilities, and Yermàk himself fell into an ambush on the banks of the river Irtỳsh, and was drowned while trying to swim in his heavy armor, out to his barge, which was stationed in the middle of the river. But he had done his work, and it was never abandoned. Slowly but steadily, one Siberian country after another was subdued and thrown open to colonization from home ; forests were cleared, towns grew up and, later on, large cities ; trade, mostly in the form of barter, was established with the natives, who learned to prize Russian cloths, linens, hides, etc.—and, to their destruction, Russian whiskey. For a long time furs were the staple and almost only article of Siberian export ; then came walrus tusks, (that go by the name of " fish-ivory ") ; it was in the time of Peter the Great that Siberia's inexhaustible wealth in metals, precious stones, and other minerals was discovered—wherein lies the chief value of the immense dependency for the possession of which Russia is indebted to the simple heroism of the Cosack *atamàn* Yermàk Timoféyevitch.

BOOK IV.   CHAPTER IV.

Russia's Return to European Civilization—Antecedents of the Work of Peter the Great—The Reformer's Character and Way of Proceeding—Consequences and Defects of the Reform—Moral and Social Dualism—In what Manner Autocracy Seems to have Fulfilled its Historical Task.

In this belated and isolated country there arises one day a man who undertakes to bring it to Europe and make it jump at one leap all the interval that divides the two. Was it possible for Russia to snatch at one stroke all that ages had given to her rivals? to get at one pull to the term of a long road, the historical stations of which she had not travelled? Was this the conception of a genius or a chimerical dream, an individual fancy doomed to failure? or was it, in spite of its daring, a plan suggested by nature, facts, and men? For a long time Peter the Great was regarded as one of those lawgivers after the antique pattern, who fashioned states at their will, as a sort of Deucalion, the maker of peoples. History in Russia has not, any more than elsewhere, proceeded by leaps and bounds. The Russians have been the first to feel this; one of their historians' favorite tasks is to fill the apparent chasm between ancient and new Russia.

The work of Peter the Great did not lack historical antecedents. In principle, if not in form, it lay in the logical destinies of the Russian people. Russia was too near Europe, had too much affinity with her, by blood and by religion, not to feel one day the contagion of her civilization. The two parts of Peter's work—bringing his people nearer Europe materially, territorially; and morally, socially, by imitation of foreign customs—had been almost equally indicated, attempted, or prepared by the two preceding centuries.

Ever since Ivan III., the Russian sovereigns strove to force their way to the north through the rampart formed by the Swedes, the Teutonic Order, and Lithuania ; to the south, through the Tatars, the Turks, and Poland, in order to reach Europe and the sea.

In his attempts on Azof and the Black Sea, as in his conquests over the Baltic, Peter did no more than continue what his predecessors had begun : his father Alexis, who had accepted the submission of the Ukraïna Cosacks ; his sister Sophia, who had directed two expeditions against Crimea.

Since Ivan III., also, most tsars had called in foreigners, with a view to introduce in their states the arts and inventions of the West. The influence of European manners naturally made itself felt first from the nearest countries—Poland, Little Russia, Lithuania ; then it came from Germany, Holland, England, Italy, from France at last, and so from the whole West. As early as the fifteenth century, Ivan III., who was in this respect, as in so many others, the precursor of Peter I., entered into relations with the sovereigns of Europe and asked them to send him physicians, artists, and mechanics. From Italy, at that time the teacher of Christendom, Moscow received through Byzance and Germany architects and engineers. It was artists from Bologna and Venice who, under Ivan III. and his successors, built the handsomest towers of the Kremlin. A noteworthy thing is that, instead of bringing along their Renaissance style, which, in Western Europe, they masterfully imposed everywhere, these Italians took Russian models and constructed the most distinctively Moscovite edifices of Moscow. This anomaly has an instructive side. The queer, bulb-shaped cupolas of the Vassíli church bear witness to the condition of foreigners in Russia at that time : instead of imposing on the Russians their own tastes and customs, they were compelled to adopt theirs.

Along with artists, Ivan III. called in craftsmen of all sorts—founders, goldsmiths, miners, masons, pyrotechnists. Thus, from the first, the road was traced for Peter the Great ; it was from the material, technical, industrial side that Russia first came in touch with Europe. As Peter the Great, so Ivan III. and Ivan IV. before him are more anxious to train their people to mechanical arts than to sciences or fine arts. After Ivan III., Vassíli IV., married to a Lithuanian, not content with calling in foreigners, goes the length, to please his wife, of adopting their customs and cutting off his beard. Under Ivan IV., the Terrible, Moscovia, through Arkhangelsk, enters into relations with England ; he it is who, despite the monks, introduces printing in Russia. He sends out emissaries to Europe, to collect skilled workmen for him ; but the greater part are detained on the way by the military jealousy of the Teutonic Order, and the commercial jealousy of the Hansa Cities, which, in the interest of German arms and trade, attempt to place Russia under an interdict.

The period of usurpers endangered European influence by giving it too wide a scope. On the point of lording it over Russia with the false Dimitri or the Polish *voyevòds*, the foreigners narrowly escaped being driven out with them. The Románofs seemed little likely to favor Western civilization. They were carried to the throne by a national reaction. The first sovereign of their house had been brought up in a convent by a mother who had taken the veil, and it was his father Philaret, raised to the rank of Patriarch, who governed in his name. This dynasty, of Russian blood and all but sacerdotal origin, made it their task to restore the old-fashioned manners. It nevertheless contributed to throw the seeds of European culture, and with the assistance of certain Little-Russians, trained in the sciences of the West under the Polish sovereignty, founded in Moscow, long before the majority of Peter the Great, a "Slavo-Græco-Latin Academy," the náme of which sufficiently indicated new aspirations. Michael Románof already sends abroad for merchants, craftsmen, even soldiers, and concludes commercial treaties with the West. Alexis, a genuine Moscovite tsar, clad in long Byzantine garments, which lend him a likeness to the saints on the *eikons*, acts as his son Peter's forerunner. Under his reign the foreigners increase in numbers, as though the father had collected for the son teachers and materials of instruction. These Occidentals occupy in Moscow a separate quarter, the *"Slobodà* of the *Nièmtsy"* (Germans). They are men of all crafts—skippers, carpenters, mostly Dutchmen ; a bark of theirs, left for useless on a pond, was to arouse in Peter the liking for marine things. Some are officers and instructors, as was the future tsar's counsellor Lefort, from Geneva. Along with mechanical arts, Alexis introduced a few accomplishments ; he had an opera in Moscow, in a real theatre ; his daughter Sophia wrote a tragedy, and had a play of Molière, translated by herself, represented in the Kremlin.

Peter grew up among these foreigners. From them he took lessons in civilization, and also in vice, for the German *Slobodà* teemed with drinking dens and places of debauchery. A Hollander was his tutor, a German girl his mistress ; Europeans of all nations formed his social circle. Most of them, even Lefort himself, appear to have been men of middling information, more capable of exciting the young tsar's curiosity than of imparting to him vast or profound knowledge. Under his brother Theodor and the regency of their sister Sophia, the foreigners already were numerous and played an important part, but they did not rise above subaltern positions. Under Peter, their pupil, they were to become the instructors of the nation [1] ; under his niece Anne they were to be, for a short while, its tyrants. The old tsars had prepared their rule a long while ahead. Peter did not violently alter the course already steered by Russia, did not turn her head forcibly away from Asia and towards Europe ; he only hastened

---

[1] Had there been any geniuses among them, Peter would have been more wary how he trusted them : he was not the man to endanger or share his authority, or to let the helm slip out of his own hand.

her progress on a road on which she had entered of her own accord.   He did not throw her off the track ; he only made her take a short cut, to catch up with Europe.

Tsar at the age of ten,[2] sole master of the empire at seventeen, Peter undertakes to transform the manners of a nation, of all the most devoted to its ancient customs.   Surrounded with foreigners—the Dutchman Timmermann, the Genevese Lefort, the Scotchman Gordon, the Frenchman Villebois—he falls deeper and deeper in love with foreign civilization, and, in Leibnitz's graphic phrase, " sets to *deb irbarizing* his native land."   Before he attempts to remodel his subjects after the pattern of European ideas, he makes himself fully familiar with them.   He travels in the West, and, the better to become naturalized there, he lives the life of the people.   He gives his mind less to institutions than to manners : it is these he is chiefly bent on importing into his own country.   His genius is marred by the faults of his race and his own education, by his temperament and by the possession of autocratic power.   He may play the European ever so much, he is unable to " debarbarize " himself; he continually offends that same Western culture of which he makes himself the missionary. Like a child or a savage, he at times appears infatuated with only the exterior of civilization.   In order to polish the Moscovite, he shaves his beard and makes him change his clothes.   He does not always distinguish between essentials and accessories.   He at the same time creates a navy and introduces smoking ;   he pursues with bitterest hatred beards and long-skirted *kaftàns*.   To certain things, as for instance to the navy, he gives undue importance. His reformer's zeal at times trenches on mania, his regulations descend to pettiness.   He frequently is content with appearances,

[2] Jointly with his half-brother, Ivan, a frail and sickly youth.   The brothers were on affectionate terms, and for his elder's sake, Peter bore with the arrogance of the self-appointed regent, his half-sister Sophia, who had incited a mutiny of the archers of the guard, and attempted his life before he was ten years old.

altering the garb rather than the man, the names rather than the things; he more than once appears satisfied with a mere Western disguise. No matter. In his exaggerations, the indefatigable reformer is more perspicacious than he seems; measures, puerile at first sight, concealed a deep-laid scheme. It is by the outside of things, fashions, and exterior usages, that the Russians could most easily be turned back into Europeans. The remainder—the substance, the essentials—would follow: after adopting the garb of Europe, his subjects would want to adopt also her manners and learning.

What in his travels particularly fascinates Peter, what he strives most earnestly to introduce at home, is every kind of mechanical inventions, crafts, technical proceedings. In that again there may have been much of the child or the barbarian, who is less impressed by theoretical knowledge than by its practical applications; still, this certainly is the most accessible side of a civilization, and in a country like Russia, it was not only the easiest but the most useful to appropriate. To master the technical part, Peter at Zaandam becomes a journeyman: he wishes to be not only the foreigner's pupil but his apprentice. He gives himself what we would call to-day a professional education. In his first trip to the West, his initiation trip, it is not to the universities, the academies, that he goes for lessons, but to the shipyard. In his second trip, even if he does give more attention to arts and sciences, still he is always guided by the Great-Russian's bent towards the positive, and by the reformer's practical sense. The *natural sciences* are those that most exite his interest: anatomy, surgery, mechanics, nautical sciences, civil and military engineering. He brings home with him few scientists and fewer artists, but is followed by an army of mechanics and overseers.

On his return he follows out the same method; no detail is too mean for him, and he is bent on teaching everything himself. In the army, in the navy, he takes pleasure in passing through all the grades, acting drummer one day, pilot the next. First of all he teaches his people discipline,—shows them how to submit to the foreigners whom he has placed as instructors over them as well as over himself. In true reformer-guise the first lesson Peter gives is by example ; of that lesson he is lavish. He puts his shoulder to everything ; handles the laborer's pick-axe, nay, the headsman's axe. Never was man seen to practise so many different crafts at once. He is the true jack-of-all-trades ; there is nothing he cannot manufacture with his own hand : boats, ship-models, pulleys, all that has anything to do with marine things, these latter being his hobby. He produces masterpieces of work-manship ; he also is an artist, he can engrave, carve. The supple and versatile genius of the Great-Russians no less than their realistic tendencies assert themselves in their emperor on a magni-fied scale. Contrary to the ways of closet-reformers, execution is what he has most at heart. He takes hold of all things with equal ardor, reforming the primer and the calendar at the same time as the administration of church and state and the manners of society, asking Leibnitz for projects just as he demands models from his craftsmen, gathering objects of art and scientific collections, even while he is creating a navy and remodelling the army, endowing industry with new fabrications, agriculture with foreign breeds of cattle, and, as though he had had time to accomplish nothing, leaving to the future numberless plans on each and every subject and for all the portions of his vast empire.[1]

This manifold task was in reality one. Peter's conquests and public labors were the outcome of his social reforms, of which the

[1] It is said that Catherine II., whose reverence for her great predecessor amounted almost to superstition, never took up any project of reform or of a new creation, before she had ordered a search in the state archives or those of the respective departments, to ascertain whether Peter had not left some memorandum, note, or directions, jotted down in his usual hasty but clear and comprehensive manner on the particular matter in hand. The search was scarcely ever in vain, and Catherine found support, encourage-ment, and luminous guidance every time she sought for them, leaving to the world a most touching and majestic instance of the communion, for the good of the living and of those to be born, of two great spirits across the dividing gulf of death.

transfer of his capital was both symbol and means. When he built St. Petersburgh and connected the Neva and the Volga by canals, he gave the longest of Russian rivers one European mouth, and by reversing the current of this great central artery he made Russia recoil on the West. Morally and physically, it was the same task still : the emperor suddenly brought back to Europe a country whose head had for centuries been turned towards Asia.

Unfortunately, man is less easily bullied than nature, and Peter treated both alike. In his passion for civilization, he inflicts it ; he goes about it as much after the fashion of a barbarian as of a great man, of a tyrant as of a reformer. His method at times defeats his end. In the words of a modern historian (Kostomárof), he employs Asiatic proceedings to europeanize his country. His most familiar tools are the *knut* and the axe, to say nothing of the cudgel which he did not spare to his favorites. He civilizes by means of the rod.

Peter's great motor, great lever, is despotism, autocracy. He neither corrects nor limits, but regulates and renovates it. He does for autocracy what he has done for himself and for his people: puts it into European clothes, shorter and lighter, so as to give it greater liberty of movements. To the scandal of the Old-Russians, the semi-sacerdotal robes of the ancient sovereigns are exchanged for a military uniform ; the biblical and patriarchal designation of *Tsar* makes room for the foreign and heathen title of Emperor * "Public Weal" is Peter's deity ; to this idol he offers up everything in sacrifice—his health, his family, his people ; for its sake he does not shrink from any measure, not from a renewal of the sacrifice of Abraham. As a true revolutionist, he takes no more account of historical obstacles than of moral or material ones. Sentiment, tradition, facts—all are equally powerless to arrest him ; he thinks himself strong enough to break through everything.

* Whatever its etymology, Oriental or Roman, the title of *Tsar* is the one usually employed in the Slavic Bible: " Tsar Solomon," " Tsar Herod," etc.

19

And he was. But how ? Could the energy of one human will, with impunity, do violence to nature, history, time? By no means. The fact is, all those barriers which Peter broke down with so daring a hand were in reality frail and stood not high from the ground ; those traditions which he shook so rudely were not solidly rooted, either in the soil or in history; the people which he undertook to turn up as with a plough, having no institutions of its own, grown out of its own soil, could, without too much presumption, be treated as a fallow field, or a *tabula rasa.* With any other European nation, a reform so radical and so sudden would have been insensate ; in Russia, it struck less against history and nature than against preventions and prejudices partly come from without ; opinions and habits which, although inveterate, had not been of necessity imposed by either climate or race, or by religion. The outer side, the manners, the domestic fashions and usages— these were the things in which Peter encountered the most for- bidding obstacles, and that alone accounts for the fact that he waged war most passionately against external things : the long garments and beards of the men, the veils of the women.

Peter the Great's undertaking was carried out by the most de- termined genius, assisted by the most formidable array of power ; that, however, was not what made its success. If his work did not die with him, it was because it lay in the natural order of his people's destinies ; it was because, in the words of Montesquieu, "Peter I. was giving European manners and customs to a nation which was of Europe." *

"Scratch the Russian and you will find the Tatar " is a sort of proverb. It were rather more historically correct to reverse the saying. In shaking off the Mongol domination, in washing off the stain of bondage, in doffing the garb and habits taken under alien masters or instructors, the Russian, the Christian Slav, could not but gradually feel himself European once more. In its vital portions, Peter's reform was merely a moral throwing off of

*Esprit des Lois, livre xix., ch. xiv.

the Tatar or Byzantine yoke, a reclaiming of soil and climate from the habits of another race and sky, brought by Asiatic conquerors and Oriental influences. There happened to live in the nineteenth century a sultan nearly as determined as Peter the Great, armed with power as absolute, who used nearly the same means in pursuance of a similar design. The people he ruled also belonged, geographically, to Europe ; but what a difference between a Turk and a Russian, after both have passed through the reforming process ! The reason is that Mahmud was handicapped in his task by all those very factors which had prepared the solution of *his* task for Peter : the national spirit, religion, the very elements of civilization.

Peter left no heirs. Nevertheless what he had begun was continued. Never was undertaking seemingly so bound to one man's life—yet, contrary to all calculations, it survived him. Never was order of succession more disturbed ; never consistency more impossible :—four women, partly or wholly foreigners, two boys, two maniacs—such were, in the course of a century, Peter's successors. At each accession—a barrack or bed-chamber revolution, an overthrowing of ministers and policy. Each new reign takes its stand in opposition to the preceding one, and the mighty of yesterday are sent off to Siberia or the scaffold. The history of Russia through the eighteenth century is one series of alternations and reactions. It is through a haphazard succession of conspiracies and regencies sprinkled with attempts at aristocratic oligarchy, in the hands of governments at once weak and violent, that Russia is called upon to pursue the road opened out to her by Peter the Great. The reform accomplishes itself in the midst of intrigues, crimes, and debauchery, by the hands of adversaries almost as much as of partisans. The capital, transferred to Moscow, is brought back to Petersburgh ; the foreigners, by turns expelled and recalled, ascend the throne with Peter III. and Catherine II. In the midst of their bickerings, Peter's successors complete his task, now correcting it, now overdoing it, but always, willingly or not, carrying it onward.

To get itself done by such hands, the reform must needs have been part and parcel of Russia's vocation. What singular guides to civilization, what mortifying instructors for a great people! First—a Livonian peasant, who can neither read nor write, assisted by a former pastry vender, now prince and regent.[4] Then comes a boy of twelve, who dies at fourteen, succeeded by a coarse woman, who is ruled by the son of a Courland groom,[5] and for the space of ten years, yields up the empire to the tyranny of Germans, who despise the Russians as an inferior race, yet do credit to Russia by their arms, even while they oppress her and suck the life-blood out of her, as the Spaniards or the Dutchmen did with both the Indies. Emerging from this foreign domination, the memory of which has remained as vivid and hateful among the people as that of the Tatars, comes another child, an infant in arms this time, then again an ignorant and sensuous woman, who has no policy but the whims of her passions, or the spiteful promptings of her vanity.[6] When at length the crown comes to a man once more, Peter III., he proves an idiotic brute and has to be deposed. The land of autocracy must wait half a century for a sovereign capable of ruling it, and when that sovereign appears, it is a woman, a German, a disciple of the French philosophers.

[4] Catherine I. and Alexander Ménshikof. The origin and earliest life of Catherine are and always will be wrapped in uncertainty. There is no doubt, however, that Peter raised her from a low estate when he made her his companion. She gave him what he most needed : rest and cheerful unceremonious comradeship, comprehension and sympathy. In marrying her, he not only discharged a debt of gratitude, but did the best possible thing for himself. She was to the end a good wife to him, and—what he most prized with his peculiar tastes—a good, thrifty *house*-wife. As to Ménshikof, he was one of Peter's most trusty, zealous, and intelligent helpers. The reformer had need of such and took them where he found them ; his marvellous, instantaneous insight into character never stood him in better stead.

[5] Anne, a niece of Peter the Great, and Biron—a disgrace to humanity, a foul blot on even the pernicious race of court favorites.

[6] Elizabeth, youngest daughter of Peter the Great.

At home and abroad, Catherine II. was Peter I.'s true successor. Like him unburdened with scruples and moral sense, wholly devoid of virtue, and gifted with the highest faculties of statesmanship, Catherine had over Peter the advantage of belonging by birth to the civilization which she strove to propagate among her subjects. With her woman's hand the Tsaritsa, who remains European even in her faults, corrects and softens the reform initiated by the Moscovite Tsar, invests authority with more humaneness, lends more decency to the court, to the government more polish and dignity, as well as greater regularity to the working of the institutions. Catherine herself, however, in her mode of governing, is lacking in one of the chief qualities of her great model : unity of views, logical sequence in action. With her it is the reverse, especially during the second half of her reign, when she is too much inclined to neglect the internal development of the nation in favor of its material aggrandizement.

The work done by Peter the Great triumphed over the incapacity or the vices of his successors as well as over the reluctance of his people. History has witnessed few such successes. Has this success been as complete as has long seemed to the West? In the material order of things, it has, marvellously so : army or navy, administration or industry—the whole of modern Russia was started by the son of Alexis. Some few of his innovations, such as his "administrative colleges," may have been mistakes ; others, such as his "Table of Ranks" and his bureaucratic nobility, good perhaps for a period of transition, have in time become nuisances. Such an undertaking was doomed to imperfection, to error even. What it were desirable to know is, whether, while materially successful in his reform, Piòtr Alexéyevitch morally accomplished his design. Has the steep path up which he forced his country taken it to Europe and civilization more rapidly than it would have arrived there by a more circuitous and easier road?

However hard on the man's genius and the power of his will such a verdict may be, the fact may be doubted. It may be that Russia, left to the sole allurements of contact with Europe, might have, by degrees, become more deeply imbued with her influence, opening out wider, because spontaneously, to the breath from the West, taking from it more discerningly what best suited her temperament. If he did spare his country a long period of transition and took it at a leap over one or two centuries of uncertain gropings, Peter could not achieve this miracle without making his people pay for it dearly. The abruptness of the proceeding entailed on Russia a fourfold failing : a moral evil, an intellectual evil, a social evil, a political evil, came of it. Considered from any one of these four points, the reform imposed by Peter the Great produced sad results which still have much to do with the woes and uncertainties of contemporary Russia.

In his passion for progress Peter neglected one thing without which all others are fragile. He left out morals, which may not be one of the principles of civilization, but which no civilization can with impunity dispense with. Material culture was what he envied Europe, what he was chiefly bent on borrowing from her. There was in that something of the Great-Russian's realistic spirit, the age was also partly to blame. The moral corruptedness and intellectual anarchy of the eighteenth century gave pernicious examples to a semi-barbarous people, more disposed, after such peoples' wont, to appropriate the vices than the qualities of their foreign instructors. Peter himself, being no longer a Moscovite and not yet a European, having the bringing up of neither, owned absolutely no moral restraint. The brutality of his pleasures, the ferocity of his vengeances, made of him a singular apostle of progress. The Moscovite coarseness combined with the sceptical license of the West found their climax, around him and his first successors, in a cynicism as repulsive to the Old-Russians as to Europe.

The means and the men employed by Peter in his work frequently drew on it, instead of sympathy and admiration, the peo-

ple's horror and contempt. How could the latter love and honor
a learning and civilization which, in Herzen's words, were tendered to them at the *knut's* end, and that by hands frequently
impure ? By the rigor of his laws, the indiscretion of his regulations, the cruelty of his punishments, the reformer, busy principally over external discipline, himself taught hypocrisy and baseness. By unscrupulously doing violence to the public conscience,
he weakened it ; while trying to polish, he demoralized. The
men he used as instruments of reform made the evil worse. Peter
often took the boon companions of his drinking bouts for associates
in his work of reformation. Germans and Europeans from every
land,—the foreigners who, during a century, kept swarming into
Russia,—generally brought sad moral teachings to the people they
pretended to renovate. Among these missionaries of Western
culture an honest man was perhaps as rare a bird as a great man.
The majority were adventurers, anxious to make a fortune, with no
other civilizing qualification than an immoderate appetite for
power and wealth. The best and most skilled still offended the
popular conscience. Being strangers to the people's customs and
beliefs, they ran their heads straight against prejudices and scruples deserving of respect even in their ignorance.*

The eighteenth century was for Russia a school of demoraliza-
tion. The court of St. Petersburgh is a repulsive spectacle even
in the time of Louis XV. One feels that, in that young colony of
old Europe, two ages of corruption mix together. Debauchery,
venality, and bloody repression—such are the three stages or the
three acts, of public life. A French philosopher who had been the
guest of Catherine II. said of Russia as it was then, that it was a

---

* Haxthausen (*Studien*, vol. i., p. 48) expresses the singular opinion
that the whole evil came from having forsaken German culture, introduced
by Peter the Great, for French culture, which prevailed from Elizabeth on.
This is one of those claims familiar to German arrogance, too *naïve* to merit
discussion. There is only one remark to be made in reply : that in the middle of the eighteenth century French culture prevailed everywhere, not to
mention that it was, of the two, the more congenial to the Russian nature.

fruit rotten before it was ripe.[1] If the censure was merited, Europe was in great part responsible. The Russians claim a high standard for the manners of Old-Russia. Without disputing the West's primacy in matters intellectual and scientific, they are fain to vindicate for their country and its patriarchal usages a moral superiority.* They flatter themselves that, by remaining outside of the West's great historical epochs, it has escaped the threefold corruption of Middle Ages, Renaissance, and modern times. Paying tit for tat, they take pleasure in alluding to the rottenness of the West ; they say that in the ancient empire of the tsars civilization had a basis more moral and religious than in the brilliant Western societies reared on heathenism ; they are prone to ascribe the vices of new Russia to European contagion. The pictures drawn by old travellers do not always endorse these claims.† In the North, as everywhere, despotism and serfdom were a sorry school for virtue. Still the traditional foundations of Moscovite morality certainly were shaken by the imperial reform and the teachings from the West. In a large proportion of the nation the old-time manners and beliefs were destroyed before anything was ready to take their place. Here, perhaps, lies another of those remote springs of nihilism even in the classes converted to civilization. By his way of casting to the winds national traditions, institutions, prejudices, by his unceremoniousness in dealing with the past of his people and his scant respect for his subject's customs, Peter, the most masterful of crowned revolutionists, might be looked upon as the true progenitor of modern nihilism or *"nothingism."*

[1] With the usual amiable candor of honored and petted guests, of which this noble country, like our own, has had some edifying experience.

* This opinion of the Slavophils will be found developed at length in the *Histoire de la Civilisation en Russia*, from the Russian of Jerebtsòff. It crops up at every step in the writings of many of Russia's most popular writers. See, for example, *A Writer's Diary*, by Dostoyéfsky, 1880.

† Olearius, Mergeret, Fletcher, draw a black picture of the morality of both laymen and clergy. Others, it is true, such as Herberstein, give accounts more favorable to Russian manners.

To the moral evil in Peter the Great's work was added an intellectual evil, and, by a fatal concatenation, this latter brought in its train social and political evil. The mind, like the heart, was forced off the track. The reformer pressed too hard on certain Russian qualities almost unknown before his time and soon to be, thanks to him, carried to excess: the ease with which the Russians comprehend and assimilate any and every thing. Or, what comes to the same, the reform emphasized certain faults which they held from nature or history, such as the want of originality, insufficient personality. Peter unconsciously made echoes and reflections of his subjects. Urging them violently along the road of imitation, he smothered in them the spirit of initiative and thus deprived them of the most active leaven of progress. By getting them into the habit of thinking with other people's brains, he prolonged their intellectual nonage under the foreigner's tutelage. This tendency to imitation delayed by a century the birth of an original national literature. The Russian of St. Petersburgh was subjected to every influence from the West, obediently reproducing the most contradictory ones, going to school by turns to the Encyclopedists and the French emigrants, to Voltaire and Joseph de Maistre, and, be it from weariness or supineness, too often inclining to a hollow scepticism, too often carried away by externals and appearances.*

To these intellectual vices corresponds the social vice,—the denationalization of one half of the nation, the severing of the classes. By dint of copying the foreigners, the reformed Russian ceased to be a Russian. All that was national went the way of the *kaftàn* and the beard, the way of the language too, reduced to the condition of a dialect left to the "common people." Peter, so thoroughly Russian in character, seemed to have set himself the task of germanizing his subjects. To the cities which he founded,

---

* "Everything is always changing in your country, Prince, the laws like the ribbons, the opinions like the waistcoats, the systems of all kinds like the fashions ; a man sells his house as he sells his horse. Nothing is constant but inconstancy." (Letter from Jos. de Maistre to Prince Kozlòfsky, 1815.)

to the institutions which he created or renovated, he gave German names, often fabricating useless barbarisms, incomprehensible to the people. At one time, he is said to have been on the point of making German the official language. Under his daughter Elizabeth it was the French language's turn, and that stayed over a century as undisputed sovereign.

The surface layer, the upper classes alone, became impregnated with the manners and ideas of the West. The substratum, the bulk of the people, remained impermeable. As the latter remained Russians while the former were transmuted into make-believe Germans and Frenchmen, Russia split herself into two peoples, severed by language and habits, unable to understand each other. The great cities and lordly mansions arose in the midst of the rural population like foreign colonies. As for the masses, the precipitancy with which the leading classes rushed westward rather delayed their progress. Having been left too far behind ever to join their masters, the common people were abandoned to barbarism.

This social evil crops up in politics. Unconnected, unharmonized, the institutions were out of tune with the country. Imported wholesale and with no roots in the soil, they often were transplanted before it was made ready for them. While in the West the modern era rests on the Middle Ages and each century on the preceding one, in Russia the entire political building, as the entire civilization, had neither a national basis nor historical foundations. The whole government organization was an appendage, to which the people remained strangers. Most of the laws were growths of other climes : they resembled borrowed clothes, suiting neither the figure nor the habits of the wearer.

A contemporary thinker * makes the remark that one of the characteristics of the modern era, and one of the evils the peoples of the continent have most suffered from since the eighteenth century, is too much law-making, too great a confidence in the

* Mr. Le Play, *Social Reform.*

written letter, regarded as the supreme and irresistible vehicle of progress. ·Well, nowhere has this fault been carried to the extent it has reached in the Russia of Peter the Great and his successors. No other state perhaps has seen such abundant and intrepid legis-- lating, because the legislator nowhere else disposed of such means of action. The whole history of Russia, the whole long Mosco- vite period in particular, apparently served only to fashion in the person of the imperial autocrat an omnipotent lawgiver, free to do and dare all things. The heirs of Peter and Catherine outdo one another in raining *ukàzes*, believing all things lawful to them, never appearing to doubt the success or efficiency of these decrees so hastily issued and annulled, innovating and modifying without rest or pause, commanding and forbidding, and frequently—by dint of variations, inconsistencies, contradictions—warping and discrediting in the public mind the very notion of law itself, which, in Russia, appears as the expression of an individual will, power- ful and dread, but fleeting and changeful. The people at last are reduced to a state like that of an inert patient, if not of an unfeel- ing corpse, over which the masters of the empire bend in the guise of physicians performing dire experiments *in anima vili*. More than that, the sovereigns themselves, not of their own will but by the force of their everlasting altering, remodelling, upsetting all that seemed settled and done with, have taught their people to look on the country as on a *tabula rasa*, or on the stage of a theatre the scenes of which are shifted at the whistle of the machinist.

The Russia of Peter the Great, that of Catherine II. and of Alexander II., afford the best illustration of what written law can and what it cannot accomplish. In no other state has law-making so often shown at once the extent and limit of its power. In the hands of autocracy, modern Russia seems, once or twice in a cen- tury, on the point of being entirely transformed in the course of a few years, but the most long-suffering of peoples are not to be thus kneaded by their masters' knuckles. To look at the laws, Russia has been more than once upturned from the very bottom ;

but laws do not reach a people's soul. To be efficient, the changes accomplished in the legislation should have a parallel in the minds and customs. Otherwise, no harmony existing between law and custom, nothing comes of it but disturbance and a general ill-at-ease feeling, and this is what, in the course of the last two centuries, the Russians have too frequently experienced.

Moral or intellectual, social or political, all the ills under which Russia suffers ever since Peter the Great may be summed up in one: dualism, contradiction. The nation's life and consciousness have been cleft in twain; the country, stirred to its core, has not yet been able to recover its balance. That is, possibly on a larger scale, the uncomfortable feeling familiar to France since the Revolution. Whether they are started from above or from below, these violent transformations, which become for a people the starting-point of a new life, always leave behind them a painful trail. There remain in society and in the public mind discords which sway aside the soundest judgments. France had this advantage, that her Revolution was made by herself, in accordance with her own genius, and that, in its errors as in its successes, it was wholly French. In Russia the revolution was made by the authorities, under foreign influence, the schism between the past and present was deeper, the jar and wrench in the nation's life more painful. To Peter's reforms are traceable many of the oppositions, or rather anomalies, which, in Russia, caused contrast to become law. Institutions and customs, ideas and facts find it hard work to get attuned together. In the nation as in the individual, dissonances of all kinds abound. The Russian is divided against himself, he feels double; at times he does not know what he believes, what he thinks, what he is.*

Being no longer herself, and not feeling herself European yet, Russia is as though suspended between two shores. In order to

---

* "Peter," wrote Joseph de Maistre in another letter to his Russian friend,—"Peter has placed you in a false position towards the other countries: *nec tecum possum vivere, nec sine te* ["I can live neither with nor without you,"]—that is your motto." (Letter to Prince Kozlòfsky, October, 1815.)

get out of this duality from which her sufferings come, is she to lean wholly to one side and rush forward on the West, or to recoil and resolutely return to old-time Moscovia? What is best—to wade knee-deep into imitation, or, casting aside all foreign importations, practise rigorous self-sequestration, and return to all that is national? But in the scantiness of the inheritance left by the past, in the midst of the ruins and rubbish accumulated by Peter and his successors, where is "all that is national" to be found most of the time? Russia is physically and morally too near to Europe, to which in these last two centuries she has drawn nearer still, to be able to snap the bond. She is European, but her historical bringing up has given her with regard to the peoples of the West certain dissimilarities which one or two centuries did not suffice to obliterate. The solution of the problem of her future lay in the conciliation of these two terms : Russia and Europe, civilization and nationality.

It is with Peter's reform as with the French Revolution: we may deplore their violences, we may point out their fallacies ; not the less for that will both remain, each for the nation it has renovated, the steadfast basis of all future moral development. Russia's task with regard to her European reform is the same as France's with regard to her Revolution : it is no use lamenting and regretting. All there is to do is to carry on the work, correcting it as we go, but also strengthening and completing it, giving way to neither discouragement nor precipitancy.

What reason counsels Russia, her own impulse leads her to carry out through inevitable delays. The three last reigns bear witness to this, even though two of them were as barren, seemingly, as the third was fertile. Open to all generous illusions, in love by turns with a vague liberalism and a sort of authoritative mysticism, Alexander I. was conscious of his people's discomfort, and during many years his dream was to heal it. In him the final reformer appeared to have arisen, the Messiah expected through centuries ; but he proved only a precursor. He had it not in him to go beyond feeble flutterings of will, timid attempts.

All the aspirations and contradictions of his time appeared to be centred in him, and his time was one of the most troubled in history, and the most fitted to trouble well-meaning souls.

In him also came out most clearly all the faculties and all the contrasts characteristic of the modern Russian, the civilized Russian, frequently at strife and at odds with himself, such as he came out of the reforms of the eighteenth century. Like Peter the Great, although in a very different way, Alexander I., with his nature so weirdly made up of strength and softness, "of manly qualities and feminine weaknesses"; with his noble infatuations and his facility to become enamoured by turns of the most divers ideas; with his alternations of illusion and discouragement, of action and apathy,—this monarch of enigmatic character, so variously and sometimes so unjustly appraised, might be given as one of the historical types of the national temperament.*
The brilliant, versatile son of Paul I.—the liberal pupil of the republican Laharpe—the mystic confidant of Madame de Krüdener—appears to embody not merely an epoch and a generation, but an entire race, with its collective intellect, a race that to this day is alive on the banks of the Neva.

As man and as sovereign, Nicolas was the direct opposite of his brother and predecessor. In him the old Moscovite tsars appeared to revive, rejuvenated and polished up after the modern fashion. Tall, well-built, stern, indefatigable, never doubting himself or his system, Nicolas was the true, typical autocrat. Distrustful of all change, stability was his ideal. The revolutions in the West scared him, and he cut himself adrift from Europe. For nigh on a third of a century Russia seemed to be going backwards; but this very reaction served as corrective to the main blemish of Peter's reform—denationalization. The tyranny of imitation relaxed, nationality began to crop up everywhere, and first of all it revived in its proper place—in art and literature.

* See the portrait of Alexander I. by Metternich (*Mémoires*, etc., vol. i., pp. 316, 317).

Slavophil theories notwithstanding, the European influence did not suffer. Between the West and his subjects Nicolas had raised a Chinese Wall, or rather, after the manner of Russian house-keepers at the approach of winter, he had hermetically closed and caulked up the windows—carefully going over every chink through which the outer air might thread its way into the house. But even if the breath from Europe and the pression of external air could not have defied the custom-house and the imperial censure, the Russian atmosphere was already too impregnated with European ideas to be capable of disinfection. The reign of Nicolas has shown that, with all its omnipotence, autocracy was not strong enough to keep Russia long from rolling down the incline on which Peter the Great had started her. The Crimean War made patent to all eyes, together with the feebleness of the stationary system, the necessity for Russia of placing herself, socially, if not as yet politically, on one level with the West, if only to be in a condition to stand her own against it.

Under Alexander II. the gates were thrown open and the reform came at last that was to reconcile Russia with herself as well as with Europe. This time it was not a whitewashing or a patching up of the façade-stucco, or a mere outer casing ; it was an upheaving and a remodelling of the very foundations of society ; it was the whole people, not one class, that was called to liberty and civilization. Until the emancipation of the serfs, the work of Peter I., having left out the bulk of the nation, lacked a basis ; the emancipation gave it one.

Like Peter's, Alexander's reforms were worked from above, by the hand of autocracy, but not again were they enacted before a passive, inert people, through the agency of foreigners called in from abroad, with the help of rods and *knut ;* they were accomplished with the co-operation and at the demand of a power entirely new in Russia—public opinion. Already the chief motor of Russian history, its main or indeed only spring, autocracy, does not appear to be the only factor of progress. It is that, indeed, which, as in past times, sets in motion the vast machinery, but the impulse which formerly had no other spring often now comes from below. This change is but the prelude to another which must gradually modify the habits and traditions of the state. Russian civilization has, so far, been fashioned by *ukàzes ;* it cannot be completed without the participation of the nation. The proceedings of Peter the Great and Catherine II. have served their time ; Russia is sufficiently European now to be associated to the work. After having compelled her to taste of the arts and sciences of the West, it becomes awkward to hinder her taking a bite at its liberties too. The reign of Alexander II., therefore, may be considered as the closing of a long historical cycle—the cycle of autocratic reforms.

By persisting in maintaining the absolute *régime* in its integrity, autocracy attempts to survive itself. By refusing to lend itself to transformations that have become unavoidable, it only risks to make them more difficult and perilous without rendering them less necessary. From Ivan III. and Ivan IV. to Peter, from Catherine to the three Alexanders, autocratic power appears to have fulfilled its historical mission. It has been said that states are preserved by the same means that made them. This seems to apply particularly to Russia. By her traditions, by her size, by her social and ethnical composition, colossal Russia manifestly needs a strong governing power ; but it can be strong without being absolute—Prussia and the German Empire are a proof of that. After the great economical, social, administrative reforms of the eighteenth and nineteenth centuries, the political reforms must come sooner or later. However complicated, however arduous they may be, Russia scarcely can put them off much longer. That task will be the inheritance of the twentieth century. May it be achieved peaceably, gradually, by the hand of the tsars themselves, for the happiness of the people of the great empire ! *

* See, on this weighty matter, Vol. II., Book IV., Chaps. III. and IV.

BOOK V.

THE SOCIAL HIERARCHY: THE TOWNS AND URBAN CLASSES.

CHAPTER I.

Class Distinctions in Russia: In what Respects they are Superficial and External, in what Deep and Persistent—Blow Struck at the Old-Time Social Hierarchy by the Emancipation—All Subsequent Reforms Tending to the Lowering of Class Barriers—How, in this Respect, the Work Done by Alexander II. Resembles that Done by the French Revolution, and how it Differs Therefrom—Character and Origin of all these Social Distinctions—Privileged and Non-Privileged Classes—Lack of Solidarity between the Former; Lack of Homogeneousness in Each— Accessory Classes.

THE most salient fact presented to the French observer by Russia's social constitution is the division of the population into distinct groups, into classes neatly defined,—for a long time one might almost have said into castes. History and law have divided the Russian people into compartments, superposed like tiers which, from base to summit, would go tapering off abruptly. Russian society thus looks from a distance much like a pyramid in stages— that of Saqqarah on the Nile, or the pseudo-Tatar four-tiers tower in Kazàn, each tier further subdivided into secondary steps. To look on the outside of it only, this society, elaborately partitioned, appears made for people who, in the classification of the various social layers, see the first condition of a nation's greatness. From afar, with all her denominations and official rubrics, Russia would seem to realize the dreams of the utopists of hierarchy ; one seems to see a vast Salentum, where every man, at his birth finds his place and pursuits marked out for him by the law.

On a nearer view it turns out something quite different. At the very time when all the demarcations were most precise, those official frameworks, in which the different classes are arranged according to a pre-determined order, might possibly have misled the theoreticians enamoured of social distinctions. How much more is it so now, when such manifold reforms have rehandled, overhauled, altered in a thousand ways the old hierarchical order ! Were Russia's strength *there*, as foreigners so generally fancy, Russia would have already lost the inner power long attributed to her by the prejudiced West.

Russia's social constitution, such as it was, fashioned by the two or three last centuries, was based on the servitude of the peasantry ; the emancipation could not fail to shake it. In this regularly stratified society, it was difficult for the lower tier suddenly to straighten itself up without disturbing the balance of the tiers it was supporting. The old-time classification into orders still subsists before the law—nominally, externally, of course ; in reality it is considerably honeycombed. This progressive decrease of class distinctions and social privileges, indeed, proves on a closer inspection to be one of the main characteristics of contemporary Russia.

If we attempt to sum up into one all the alterations that have taken place in our own days in the immense Empire of the North, it will be found that they all culminate in this one essential fact : the progressive abrogation of the differences existing between the classes or castes, or, what amounts to the same thing—in the successive reduction of both prerogatives and burdens peculiar to each of the various classes. This is the central point towards which converge the numerous reforms of the last reign, the climax from which the observer can best appreciate their order and bearing.

Administrative or judicial, ecclesiastical, financial, or military —all these alterations, which strike at all the branches of public life, tend at bottom, more or less directly, more or less consciously, towards one and the same end—the lowering of caste barriers, the obliteration of old boundary lines, the widening of social compartments,—in one word, the equal distribution of state favors and state burdens among all the parts of the nation. Whether or no the goal were distinctly perceived by the promoters of the reforms, whether they pursued it of their own free and clearly defined will, or unknowingly yielded to a secret and involuntary impulse—the final terminus stands out afterwards with extraordinary distinctness. Whatever branch of administration one may take up to study, courts of justice, army, taxation, municipal or provincial institutions—the same tendency will invariably assert itself. Therein, we repeat, lies the bond which links all the late reforms together, and which, notwithstanding serious breaks and gaps, and singular inconsistencies, lends them that which is the stamp of great things—unity.

There certainly are incoherences, restrictions, contradictions, shortcomings of all sorts; within the last few years especially there have been many waverings, side-starts in the direction of reaction, attempts at backing out; the fact is not the less there. In the Russia of Peter the Great and his successors, all the rights, all the immunities—administrative, judicial, military—were bestowed on each class separately; it is the other way now; the democratic proceeding prevails, which deals with a people and wots not of classes. In the midst of the nineteenth century Russia still clung, in this respect, to mediæval views and ways; under Alexander II. she became a modern country. In this respect the work, as yet incomplete, of the Liberator, bears a striking resemblance to that of the French Revolution; its final terminus is civil equality, without distinction of classes, races, religions.

There are, however, important differences between the two, in the manner in which each was prepared, and in the manner in which each was carried out. In the France of the *ancien régime* the moral barriers between the different classes, especially between the nobility and the middle class (*noblesse* and *tiers-état*), had been overthrown and obliterated by custom before they were abolished by law. The distance between noble and burgher, still so impassable in the seventeenth century, had been bridged over in the eighteenth. *Salons* and *belles-lettres*—the drawing-room and the study—had brought the two together, frequently even merged them into one. The only distinction now lay in the outer man, the costume, and on the day on which the noble laid aside sword and embroideries the last difference vanished. Uniformity of garb and manner betokened spiritual similarity. As a living historian remarks, equality *de facto* had preceded equality *de jure; noblesse* and *tiers-état* were placed on a par by education and mental capacity, even while still separated by privileges.* Not so in Russia, even on the eve of the latest reforms. The noble, the priest, the townsman, the peasant, were severed not merely by legal privileges, but by habits, bringing up, even natural inclination ; they were so many different men, and in order to make them alike it was not enough that the law should place them on an equal footing. The classes not having been brought together by manners before they were so by law, the taking down of the legal fences which kept them apart did not suffice to bring about a fusion ; it is only with time and indirectly that the great results of the social reforms will unfold themselves.

Between the French Revolution and the imperial reforms there is another difference, an opposition in the midst of resemblances. For reforms made by monarchs and those made by popular revolutions cannot, even when tending the same way, be accomplished in the same manner ; the former do not proceed after the violent, abrupt, uncompromising fashion natural to the latter. While the revolutions started from below aim first of all at the outer shell of things and bear a grudge against names as much as against substance, reforms from above are often inclined

* Taine : *Les Origines de la France Contemporaine : l'Ancien Régime.*

to respect the shell, content in proportion as the innovations are less apparent. The class distinctions have not been abolished in Russia, the forms and moulds are still untouched. Instead of dropping them as empty shells and taking them down as useless scaffoldings, the lawgiver has kept them all. The lovers of the past are thus left free to dream of some day forcing back into them the various classes of the nation, of reconstructing the social order on the old lines with some slight modifications.

These distinctions, it should be remembered, have, in history and manners, roots too deep to be eradicated in a few years. There are still reasons for their existing in Russia which in Western Europe have vanished long ago, or never existed at all. One is the exotic manner of the introduction of modern civilization and, as a consequence, the enormous, the incalculable difference in manners and culture ; another is the double system of land tenure, inalienable and held in common by the recently emancipated peasants, individual and hereditary for the former serf-owner.

Legislation and society itself are, with regard to this matter, in a state of transition ; a study of the different classes is all the more arduous and complicated. It is often difficult for a foreigner to find out what has been abrogated by the recent reforms, and what has not, to distinguish nominal rights and privileges from real ones. Yet nothing is of greater importance for the discrimination of facts from appearances. Outwardly, this society, the best framed, most neatly partitioned and pigeonholed, seems to be one of the most aristocratic in Europe. Virtually there is none more democratic. Here again, there is, between show and reality, one of those contrasts so familiar to Russia and so bewildering to strangers.

" In our country," one of the principal compilers of the Emancipation Act, Prince (*kniaz*) V. Tcherkassky, once said to me " the distinctions of classes have never existed but on the surface. From the Varangians of Rurik to Peter the Great and Catherine II., the nobility has been only a thin and superficial alluvion. On scratching the soil you find the old Slavic hard-pan, smooth and even."

A foreigner, therefore, must not be beyond measure astonished if, contrary to the evidence of his own eyes, he hears Russians assert that there are no class-distinctions in Russia, that every kind of hierarchy has always been repugnant to the Russian nature. This assertion, first made by the Slavophil school, is joined in by all the Slavic nations, with the exception of the Poles, who, in this respect, as in many others, are different from their race-brethren. Fundamental unity of the people, social homogeneousness, is given out as the distinctive feature of the Slavic genius, as the characteristic of their civilization and the main condition of their future development.

In Russia the individual does not, as in France, stand isolated before the state. Each man is classed in the administrative nomenclature under some rubric ; each belongs, by birth or profession, to a given group, of which he shares the rights and obligations. The law distinguishes between the noble, the priest, the peasant, the townsman. Until the last few years, every one held a different position as regards taxation, the administration of justice, and military service. Each order had its own organization, its co-operation forms, its assemblies and elective officers, sometimes its own judges and courts ; each assumed guardianship over those of its members who were under age, and at times was held responsible for its grown-up members. These charges or immunities, as well as this internal self-government, in many cases still subsist ; but the various classes are no longer kept apart.

The government of the Emperor Alexander II., in endowing Russia with provincial assemblies, has for the first time called on the different orders of the nation to deliberate in common ; but such is still the distance between them that, in the common sittings of these assemblies, pointedly entitled "of all classes," each class usually has its separate representatives, elected in private partial gatherings. While introducing self-government into local administration, Russia appears to be wavering between the system which gives to each group of the population special representatives, and that of mixing all the inhabitants up together in one common representation. The former method, but lately in general use, prevails in the provincial councils, in the *zémstvo*, the most important of deliberative assemblies in contemporary Russia ; the latter has recently been applied to the municipal town-councils as well as the jury. Which of the two systems will finally triumph ? Which will be preferred on the day on which the empire will receive a political constitution? Will the nobility, the towns, and the peasants have separate representatives, separately elected, and deliberating in common ? Or will one of the orders—the nobility, for instance, with or without the clergy—have a separate house, as in England? There lies, concerning the future of Russia, a question not unlike that which had to be met at the outset of the French Revolution, at the time of the convocation of the States-General— a ticklish question, which no one could solve without first becoming familiar with the social organization of former times, and without having gauged the value and real force of each of the great groups which, together, constitute the nation.

A whole volume of the bulky Russian Code is devoted to "classes, orders, or conditions." The Code contains no less than sixteen hundred articles on this difficult matter, and numerous amendments and appendices continually increase its complexity. The law recognizes in Russia four principal classes : the nobility, the clergy, the inhabitants of the towns and cities, the rural population. This division is the natural outcome of the country's history—indeed of the social state of all primitive peoples. From India to Scandinavia, everywhere almost, at a certain stage of civilization, these four fundamental orders are found, the two latter either separated, as in Sweden, or united under one name as in France, without being really one in fact ; the warriors or nobles at the top, together with the priests or clergy ; lower down the men of trade and crafts, the burghers (*bourgeoisie*) ; quite below, the peasant or rustic, the husbandman, tiller of the earth. This similarity in classification and hierarchy does not imply perfect identity everywhere. Though the social groups in Russia may bear in French and German the same names as the classes of feudal Europe—in Sweden's old constitution, for instance,—they do not differ the less deeply from their foreign homonyms, and it would be rushing into serious blunders to judge them one by the others.

In Western Europe, whatever may be the actual social condition of the different nations—in Spain or in Germany, in Italy or Belgium,—the words "nobility," "burgherdom," "peasantry," have at bottom the same meanings; they convey to the mind analogous notions, because the classes designated by these terms were born in the same age, under the same influences, at an epoch when all Europe, Latin or Teutonic, had institutions nearly identical. Russia, in common with most Slavic peoples, was not then a part of the European community, and therefore the same names cannot possibly have there the same meanings. These terms, "nobles," "burghers," we use in speaking of Russia only from the lack of more fitting ones, and in order not always to utter sounds unfamiliar to the European ear. This Russian hierarchy, with all its class denominations, was indeed also born in the Middle Ages—but in Middle Ages of her own, different from the same period in Western Europe. By their origin, by the spirit of their kind and their historical *rôle*, the Russian noble (*dvorianin*) and burgher (*miêsh-tchanin*) are probably still further removed from their European equivalents than the Greek clergy from the Latin, the Orthodox married priest (*pop*) from the Catholic priest vowed to celibacy. Between the two, there is scarcely as much as a family likeness.

As all things in Russia, the constitution of the four principal classes of society in their modern form dates from Peter the Great, and, after him, from the great Catherine. It was Peter who, in establishing the official hierarchy of ranks according to the degree or pursuit of each person, definitely gave its national character to the Russian *dvoriànstvo*, the class entitled "nobility" in the other languages. It was Catherine who, under the influence of Western models, erected this nobility, as well as the class of townspeople (so-called *bourgeoisie*), into corporations, endowed with certain privileges. In the society regulated by Peter each citizen seemed to have his place marked by the law, each class its well-defined sphere of action, its specialty, so to speak. For all classes or social categories, the nobility, as well as the rest, corresponded at bottom to a determined occupation, and answered to common charges and obligations, not to exemptions and privileges. To the peasant fell the working of the land ; to the townsman, trade and crafts ; to the noble, public service ; to the priest, the altar. Each wheel, each attachment had its work marked out in the service of the state, and none might shirk it. These classes, so precisely outlined, between whom custom and training even yet draw a harsher line than does the law, were, nevertheless, no closed castes. The very nature of the governing power, whose handiwork they were, could not allow them to shut themselves up within themselves. Superior as well as inferior classes existed only for the convenience of Throne and State, not in or for themselves, and the sovereign was always free to raise or lower his subjects, in accordance with his needs or views, from one category to another.

In such a society, where no class held any rights or prerogatives on their own merits or their ancestors', or in virtue of a national tradition, none could have any rights that the governing power need consider. All remained alike dependent on the pleasure of him from whom they had received their prerogatives. There was in these classes, especially in the nobility and burgherdom, no living organism instinct with a principle of spontaneous action ; nothing but an inert mechanism, obedient to the directing hand. Russia's example shows that hierarchy and class limitations are not always safe pledges for a people's freedom. It is easy to lament the crumbling of social forces in countries where the individuals, in their theoretical equality before the state, are at once merged together and isolated, like the grains of sand in a beach. This evil, however great, is difficult to remedy artificially. To give social groups cohesion and unity it needs something more than taking individuals and agglomerating them into corporations, orders, classes. From a political point of view, nothing has real consistency except the spontaneous products of nature and history, the bodies which have formed and become cemented organically, that have within and not outside of themselves the principle of their life and power.

In Russia no class possesses political rights of any sort; each insures to its members personal rights and privileges which it holds from the law and the sovereign's pleasure. In this respect Russian society is divided—or rather was, for the late reforms have gradually wellnigh obliterated the distinction—into two main groups, the privileged classes and the non-privileged. The former were exempt from military service, from the heaviest of direct taxes—the poll tax—and from corporal punishment—the *knut* and the rods. As everywhere, these privileged ones were the nobility and clergy, to whom were added the selectest of the townsmen and tradespeople, what would be called in French, "*la grosse bourgeoisie*," the big-wigs of the middle class. The rest of the townsmen—the small fry among tradespeople and mechanics —were, like the serfs, subject to conscription, capitation, and the rods. Thus the rural and urban *plebs* formed one great rightless mass, which from times immemorial went under the graphic appellations of *smerd* ("the stinking") and *tchern* ("the dirty").

But even amidst the privileged classes there was not by any means the unity of spirit, the uniformity of culture—in a word, the moral homogeneousness, which was found in other countries under similar conditions. Between the nobility and clergy there was nothing like the union or solidarity, there were none of the manifold ties, of family and interests, which, in old-time France, made one of the two first orders of the state. Even before Peter the Great the high church dignitaries had fallen into disfavor with the nobility. Already the clergy, condemned to recruit itself out of its own ranks, had become a sort of hereditary caste; not that it was closed by law against outsiders, but because the sons of priests were almost the only candidates. Since Peter the Great, the clergy, confined to its church duties, and long suspected of ill-will towards the innovations,[1] had remained, like the bulk of the people, true to the old customs, usages, ways—to Old-Russia. The nobility, on the contrary, recruited from among foreigners of many lands, favorites of the sovereign and adventurers of all sorts, had, after a short resistance, opened its door to the breath from Europe ; it was the only class that adopted the garb, the mode of life, the ideas of the West. This nobility, composed of serf-owners, mostly state functionaries, and the privileged portion of the urban population, had not much more in common in the way of interests or sentiment, for the tradespeople and "townsmen" generally are less far removed from the people in tastes or bringing up in Russia than in any other country.

One of the peculiarities of this social constitution is that each of the four classes is divided into sub-classes, generally strangers, frequently quite hostile towards one another. The dualism which pervades the clergy, divided into priesthood and monkhood—white and black clergy,—shows up to a certain degree in all the classes of society. In the nobility there are the personal and the hereditary nobles ; among the townsmen there are the "notables" on one side, the mechanics and "small people" on the other ; even the peasantry is divided into peasants attached to private landlords and peasants of the Crown demesnes.

[1] Not "suspected"—*convicted*. At the head and at the root of all opposition, the inspirers and instigators of rebellious discontent, the hidden soul of ever reviving conspiracy, in the van of open resistance, lurking in the gloom of church and convent cell, ear to lip with fair penitents and callow youths, inciting to riot, treason—and murder.

The complexity of this social order does not stop there. Outside of these four great frames, further cut up by inner partitions, there are smaller compartments, accessory or secondary, some being remnants of an earlier organization, others destined for the use of the inhabitants of countries more or less recently annexed, and fitting but awkwardly into the older frames. Up to the time of the reforms of Alexander II., the army, no less than the clergy, could be regarded as a class by itself. In Russian statistics the soldiers, their wives and children, figured in the midst of the social nomenclature under a special rubric.*   This was a consequence of the long term of military service ; when a man knew that he was to remain in his regiment twenty or twenty-five years he entered the army very much as one enters the church—for life.†   Once enrolled, the peasant ceased to belong to his native commune ; once shaved, he never again donned the garb of his younger days.   As a rule, when age shelved him as to active service, he would continue, in the humble functions that were generally awarded him, or in the places where he appealed to public charity, to wear the military tunic.   It is only since 1872 and 1874, *i. e.*, since the reduction of the term of service, that the recruit is no longer severed from his class and commune by the call under the flag.

In the first half of the present century, under Alexander I., there was a moment when, owing to the military colonies invented by Count Araktchéyef, the profession of arms seemed on the point of becoming a livelong and hereditary one.   In certain districts, the inhabitants of which were dubbed " soldier-husbandmen," the girls were, equally with the boys, devoted to the army, destined

---

* These statistics, blundered over by the West, have sometimes led to singular mistakes.   Thus the figure of the *class* would be given as that of the *army*, regardless of the fact that this figure, in the case of the Cosacks, represented for over half its value women and children.

† The long-term service was partly a consequence of the social organization ; frequent levies and large contingents would have ruined the landlords by robbing them of their serfs, who, once entered on the army rolls, were *ipso facto* manumitted.

at their birth to marry and bear soldiers. It was a novel sort of serfdom, the promoters of which flattered themselves that they would draw great profit therefrom, both for the forces and finances of the empire. The resistance of the peasants, which sometimes reached actual revolt, compelled Nicolas to give up this attempt. Alexander II., in this respect, followed tendencies directly opposed to those which prevailed under Alexander I. The law which abridged the term of military service at the same time that it rendered it obligatory to all, struck another hard blow at class distinctions. Instead of being an isolated body, a recipient of privileges, or a bond slave, the army will become a levelling agent, one of the principal factors in the fusion of classes and ranks.*

There is in the Russian army, or rather military forces, an important element which continues to form, to a certain extent, a distinct class, a warrior caste ; it is the Cosacks. Along the southern frontier of the empire, along the lower course of the Don, the Volga, the Ural, the Kubàn, the Térek, there are still found populations of mixed origin, all equally subject to a military organization. This is the only resemblance the Cosacks bear to Alexander I.'s soldier colonies or the old-time Granitchàrs ("Military Confines") of Austria. In compensation for the special burdens imposed on them, they have from the oldest times enjoyed immunities which they always valued very highly ; hence they were regarded as privileged bodies, although their individual and corporative privileges were greatly curtailed in the course of the centuries. Abroad the name of "Cosack," associated with memories of invasion, awakens the ideas of barbarity and plunder; at home, the same name, associated with memories of the unfettered life of the steppe, recalls the ideas of liberty and equality. "Free as a Cosack" is to the Russian a deeply significant saying, for it designates the man who has never borne

* Obligatory military service, mitigated by certain provisions, was instituted in 1874. The term of service is, since 1888, five years in the active army and thirteen in the reserve. A man belongs to the "territorial army" (*landwehr*) till he is forty-three.

either a foreign yoke or the bondage of the " glebe." Among the chief Cosack groups, those of the Dniepr and the Don, equality reigned as well as liberty. Both of them—the former under Polish sovereignty, the latter under the Moscovite sceptre—formed a sort of democratic republic. They elected their own *atamàns*,² and, among themselves, knew of neither nobles nor serfs.*

In this respect the extreme south of Russia used to resemble certain regions of the extreme north, where serfdom and nobility never quite struck root. Like the peasants of Arkhangelsk and Viàtka, the Cosacks long preserved the forms of an ancient Russian commonwealth foreign to class distinctions. These free colonists of the steppe, for long years partly recruited from among runaway serfs, had cast behind them, in flying from their old homes, all traces of social hierarchy. The class distinctions gradually regained ground among them, together with the administration of modern Russia. Their officers were ennobled, and of the old-time equality, as of old-time liberty, little more is left than a memory.†

² *Hetman* is the genuine Little-Russian title. *Atamàn* is a Great-Russian corruption, and has somewhat deviated from the original meaning, inasmuch as it has come to be used especially for "*robber*-chief." Thus the renowned Stiénka Ràzin, and, under Catherine II., Pugatchòf, were the *atamàns* of their dreaded bands, but could never, by any possibility, be entitled *hetmans*, while even Great-Russian historians never would designate Hetmans Mazeppa or Khmelnìtsky as *atamàns*.

* The Cosacks of later times, forming the vanguards of Russian power, have contributed wonderfully to the conquest and colonization of the steppes of the southeast and certain regions of Asia. Of all modern states, Russia perhaps has best known how to utilize military colonization. On the old-time Cosacks of Little- and Great-Russia, the reader might do well to peruse the book of Prosper Mérimée, *Les Cosaques d'Autrefois*, in reality an epitome of the researches of Mr. Kostomàrof, one of the most eminent of Russian historians.

† Even serfdom itself stole in amidst the Cosacks at the last, and, at the moment of emancipation, there were nowhere so few free peasants as on the territory of the "Army of the Don." As to the administrative and financial immunities and privileges, they got gradually curtailed and almost annihilated by the constant encroachments of centralization, as well as by the progress of commerce and means of communication. Thus it is that the

Among the accessory classes placed outside or, it might be said, in the gaps between the normal classes, one only deserves special mention; it is the class the members of which bear the quaint name of *odnodvòrtsy* (meaning literally "one-yarders"). They are men who own only one house and yard, and one lot of land. They are freemen who, unlike the peasants, owned the land they worked, in full property, individual and hereditary. In this respect they stand nearer to the nobles, while, by their bringing up and pecuniary circumstances, and by the fact that they were subject to poll-tax and conscription equally with the lowest classes of the nation, they might rather be counted with the peasantry. This class, intermediate between the two main orders of the state, numbered somewhere between two or three million souls of both sexes. Some of them have achieved a degree of prosperity unusual with the peasant, while others have sunk to the level of the poorest *mujik*. Like the Cosacks, these people might be regarded as representatives of another age of Russian society. Their origin is somewhat obscure ; their ranks appear to have been filled from several different classes. They themselves consider themselves, sometimes rightly no doubt, as nobles fallen into penury and stripped of their privileges. The greater part appear to be descended from soldiers, formerly settled along Moscovia's southern border, and, in acknowledgment of their services, provided for by gifts of land exempt from taxes for a long time ahead. These warlike husbandmen formed, in front of the Tatars, a line of observation and defence which, shifting slowly southward, gradually strayed down into the steppes. To this day it is in the Governments of Vorònej, Kursk, Oriòl, in the provinces confining on Moscovia of old, that these "one-yarders" are met with in greatest numbers. Whatever their origin, they are, outside the nobility, almost the only representatives of free land interest, as known in Europe ; by right of this, they form an in-

individuality, as well as the self-government, of the Cosacks is steadily disappearing.

termediate link between the former serf and landlord, and may, some day, contribute to endow Russia with one of the things she is most lacking in—a rural middle class.

Most of the classes into which the Russian population was divided were of their nature so peculiar to Russia, to her social state, that one hardly sees where alien populations were to come in, without increasing the number of special subdivisions. Accordingly, in order to do no violence to local customs, not to infringe the recognized rights of the conquered countries, the Russian government, at each new annexion, be it in Europe or Asia, found itself compelled to create for its new subjects new rolls, new rubrics. Each region, each race, each form of worship even, in the act of being embodied in the empire, gave rise to special divisions, social categories, each with its own rights and obligations. The diversity of the nationalities that inhabit Russia is one of those things which, even in Europe, delay the fusion and legal unification of all the peoples scattered over Russian land. The nomadic tribes, like the Samoyèds and Kalmỳks, are naturally not included in the four main classes. The Tatars, the Bashkir and all the Mahometan population, still occupy in the cities or rural districts a special position. The same applies in some ways to the free agriculturists of Bessarabia, the burghers of what was once Poland and of the Baltic provinces, to the German and Greek colonists in the interior, lastly to the Jews of the western provinces. If they do not form, as they did in the Polish Commonwealth, a fifth order in the state, and a veritable caste, the Israelites, even after the last reforms, are still subject, as to place of residence, property, and elective functions, to certain restrictions which keep them in the condition of a special category in the midst of the very classes of which they are members. This inferior position in which they are held has probably much to do with the part taken by many Jews in the political crimes of the last years. The supineness with which the government acts in the matter of protecting them against popular outbreaks, and the severe measures against them urged from time to time by the patriots of Moscow and Kief, are not the things to inspire them with love or respect for the laws of the empire.

Such is, in its archaic complexity, the social structure of Russia. Under the law, or from custom, it is still, in a great measure, a country of classes, though not of castes. This character some contend she must preserve, under penalty of becoming another China, sacred to the "mandarinate." The reforms of Alexander II. tended to a change in this respect, but some laws of Alexander III. seem rather to favor a retrograde tendency. The barriers which the father had lowered the son seems inclined to build up again.

21

BOOK V. CHAPTER II.

Disproportion between the Urban and Rural Populations—Relatively Small
Number of Towns and Cities in Russia and all Slavic Countries—
Explanation of this Phenomenon—Reasons which Hinder the Agglom-
eration of the Population—The Towns and their Inhabitants before
Peter the Great—Efforts of Peter and Catherine to Create a Middle Class.

THE first thing that strikes one about the distribution of the
classes of the Russian population is the proportion—or rather
the disproportion—in their numerical force, and especially between
the population of cities and that of the country. This latter
rubric alone comprises the vast majority of Russian subjects. In
European Russia, not including the Kingdom of Poland, the
Grand Duchy of Finland, and the Caucasus, the latest census
(1867) gave for the " rural class," comprising the Cosacks, the
figure of about 55,000,000; for the "urban classes " proper—
tradesmen, merchants, mechanics, townspeople,—less than
6,000,000. The nobility and clergy are omitted in this valuation,
the former numbering from 800,000 to 900,000 souls, the latter
about 600,000. The clergy mostly live in the country, while the
nobility are divided about evenly between town and country.
Notwithstanding the fact that the urban population has been
increasing rapidly for the last twenty years, the peasantry —"the
rurals "—still represent an immense majority. This is a notable
fact, of vital importance to the social, economic, and political
status of Russia.

The disproportion between the two chief elements of the population becomes more conspicuous if we realize what goes by the
name of town in Russian statistics. It is not only by their
scarcity, their dispersion over a vast territory, that Russian towns

differ from those of Western Europe. With their wooden houses, low and far between, with their preposterously wide streets, for which only the fear of fire accounts, streets usually unpaved, where, as on country roads, snow, mud, and dirt alternate, these towns are lacking in what constitutes the first characteristics of cities in Western eyes. Instead of standing their houses closely side by side, instead of heaping tier on tier up to the sky, like the old cities of France, Italy, and Germany, and thus forming a little world entirely distinct from the country, brimming with only men and men's works, the Russian towns stretch and sprawl out into the fields into which they merge, leaving between the houses and the public buildings acres of waste land that can never be filled or enlivened. To the traveller arriving from Europe they appear as something huge, desert, unfinished ; they often seem to be their own suburbs, and the foreigner expects to enter the city when he is just leaving it behind him. To him they are so many overgrown villages, and, in fact, there is less difference here than anywhere else, between village and town, as regards the manner of building and of living. All Russia was, for centuries, nothing but one village of a great many square miles. During the whole Moscovite period of her existence, there was in reality only one city—the capital, the "throne city" or residence of the sovereign, and even that was nothing but a huge borough built in wood, scattered around a stone stronghold. It is only since the fire of 1812 and the subsequent reconstruction, since stone, or—more correctly—brick caused wooden buildings to be reserved for the suburbs and allowed the houses to rise higher and draw closer together, that Moscow has really assumed the appearance of a great city. The capitals of governments, gradually reconstructed on the model of the rejuvenated old empire capital, are, as a rule, the only cities deserving of the name in a foreigner's eyes.*

* Ten years ago Russia, apart from Warsaw and the Kingdom of Poland, owned only four cities having 100,000 inhabitants : St. Petersburgh, Moscow,

In comparing the areas, we find that in European Russia the cities — even if we award the title to a crowd of boroughs three quarters rural—are ten, fifteen, twenty times farther apart than in Western Europe. This is a most striking contrast, and not without influence on all the relations of life. In Russia, the cities are like islets scattered at great intervals over a rural ocean, while in the West they press against one another like the islands of a group : the difference between the Pacific and the Ægean Seas.

The contrast is not less great as regards population. In France, in Germany, in Belgium, in England, the towns and cities contain one third, even one half or more, of the entire population ; in Russia, scarcely more than a ninth, and even of that number a good many hardly come under the head of townspeople. It is kept fluctuating by the peasants, who are only temporary residents, on business, or in pursuit of winter earnings, their great and only resource during the months of forced inaction in the country. The little importance, the insignificancy of the towns in Russia, for which even building materials seem to be wanting, is one of the historical characteristics of old Moscovia, of what Soloviòf calls "Wooden Europe" ; and so it is, in due proportion, of modern Russia, especially Great-Russia. The two main elements of the population stand towards each other in a very different proportion from what we see in most countries of Europe and America. What contrasts in manners and customs, ideas, aspirations, what differences in the whole drift of the two civilizations are implied by this one fact ! By the light of its statistics, the vast Empire of the North, in spite of its rapid and unceasing progress, looms before us as a rural state, an empire of peasants ! [1] Russia and the United

Odessa, and Riga, the latter, however, far more German than Russian. Even at the present time there are scarcely ten cities that reach this figure : the four just mentioned, Kief, Khàrkof, Saràtof, Kazàn, Vilna, perhaps Lodzy, the Polish Manchester, perhaps Berditchòf, the great Jewish mart in the West, and possibly Kishiniòf, the huge, half Rumanian village-capital of Bessarabia.

[1] What a magnificent vista this opens in the future, when freedom will have become habit, and the normal increase of population will have raised the

States of America, which, as regards extent of territory and distribution of the population, offer so many points of comparison, stand in this respect in the most perfect opposition, represent the two poles of modern civilization. It is to be observed, however, that even in Russia, amidst the regions which can show the relatively largest urban population, figure Ukraïna, New Russia, and most of the lately peopled tracts. Which goes to show that modern colonization, there as everywhere, proceeds first of all to create cities.

The same phenomenon, the same disproportion between town and country, is observable, in various degrees, in most Slavic peoples—the Slavs of the West as well as of the East and South. This is, one may say, one of the principal signs, at the same time as one of the principal causes, of the historical inferiority of the Slavic nations.[2] At the first glance the Slavs of the West—the Tchekhs and Poles—appear to differ in this respect as in so many others, from their Slav brethren, and to lean more towards the Western Europeans. The Kingdom of Poland especially is, in this respect, singularly unlike the empire to which it is annexed. The urban and the rural population there stand to each other in much the same relation as they do in the wealthiest countries of Teutono-Latin Europe, *i. e.*, as one to three ; about two millions in the cities, nigh on six in the country. Unfortunately this resemblance is delusive. The population of these Polish towns is made up in great part of Jews and Germans, and but too frequently remains a stranger to the Slav people in the midst of which it lives, in spirit and interests as well as in origin. Founded mostly by German colonists, and all more or less peopled with Jews talking a German jargon, these towns, as a rule, were governed according to the

average of education to that of American farmerdom : a cultured, land-owning, self-governing peasantry ! Why, it 's the ideal, and another affinity between Russia and America, far rather than polar opposition. (See a few lines lower.)

[2] The Western mind never can quite divest itself of the feudal point of view. Centralization is the universal bane bred and bequeathed by feudalism. There was no need of hiding behind city walls from a brigand nobility, where no such nobility, born of alien conquest, existed, where all the classes, high and low, were of one race and blood.

old Magdeburg code, and remained isolated in the midst of a commonwealth composed of nobles, confined within their narrow enclosures, hedged in by their privileges, with no place in the constitution, no part to play in the state, without influence on the civilization and politics of the country, for which this lack of a national middle class was not one of the least causes of ruin. In ancient Poland the towns were like so many half foreign colonies in the midst of the people, or, in the picturesque words of a German journalist, "like drops of oil on a pond." In the whole of Western Russia, in Lithuania, White Russia, and those parts of Little Russia which once were annexed to Poland, the situation is still about the same as in Poland proper. The Jews, crowded in the towns and boroughs, are there also one of the main elements of the urban population, and no fusion between them and the other inhabitants has ever taken place.

In Russia proper, on the contrary, the towns were genuine growths of the national soil; but they were few, scattered, shabby; with no institutions or life of their own, they hardly emerged out of the immense rural ocean. Under another form the evil was the same; the spirit of progress, of investigation, and liberty was wanting. There were no towns or boroughs in old-time Russia, hence no burghers, no town-class. Nòvgorod and Pskof, both not distant from the Baltic, both in contact with the merchant association of the Hansa, were a glorious but barren exception. Moscovia, which swallowed them up, was an essentially rural country; hence in great part, among the Russians as among other Slavs, the persistence, so often remarked on, of the patriarchal or family spirit. In this state of peasants and landlords, the manners, institutions, all the social relations, have long preserved something simple, primitive, and as though rudimentary.*

* As the historian, Mr. Zabiélin, observes (*History of Russian Life from the Oldest Times*), these patriarchal forms, the persistence of which amidst the Slavs has so often been pointed out, really spring from the predominance of home life in the absence of public life. As this fact can be traced mainly to the scarcity and insignificance of urban centres, it is not

The want of towns had another serious consequence ; it implied the want of the first economic element of modern civilization, liquid wealth—personal effects, circulating capital,—an essential principle of all great material development, of all fruitful social activity.

Is the character of the Russian people, are the supposed nomadic tastes of the Slavic race, responsible for this long absence and persistent scarcity of towns ? By no means. We must look for the reason elsewhere. It lies in the economic habits, in serfdom, partly also in the soil, the climate, the very formation of the land. The Russian market has, so far, no demands capable of keeping at par the productions of a numerous urban population. The trades or professions, the crafts of all sorts, which generally have their seat in towns and cities, are as yet but little developed, or still remain scattered in the villages. The serf-owners of old found it convenient to have everything they needed manufactured on their own estates, articles of luxury alone excepted, and those they imported from abroad. The severe climate, the huge distances, have a similar action. In the north especially, the poverty of the soil, the long, enforced idleness of the winter time, with its endless nights, compel the peasant to seek means of existence in other things than the tilling of the ground. Hence it is that this immense rural population is far from being occupied exclusively with agriculture. Rural and industrial life are less separated, less specialized than in the West. Articles which, in other countries, were manufactured in workshops or city factories, by essentially urban operatives, were most of the time turned out in villages in the *mujik's* cabin.[3]

to be wondered at that the same historian should admit cities to be the first nucleus of civil society and the first agent for organizing the Russian state. Owing to the lack of vigor and the small number of these hearths of civil life, the private relations between men must necessarily, for a long time to come, retain a greater importance in Russia than in the Western states.

[3] This in part accounts for the greater intelligence of the Russian "common people." Nothing is so deadening to mind as excessive division of labor.

Thus the towns had against them the social status, which formerly bound the peasant to the glebe, and to this day binds him to his commune ; they had against them the few wants and scant wealth of the masses, and even the rigor of the climate, even the people's own best qualities. The easy imitativeness, the skill and deftness of hand, natural to the Russian, discouraged urban agglomerations by doing away with the need of permanent professions, of sedentary trades, of specialties. The peasant, being amply capable of manufacturing for himself all that his humble needs require, has rarely occasion for the services of townspeople or the products of town life. The town is thus reduced to being little more than an administrative centre and a place of barter—a mart, lively enough and even crowded at fair times, empty and dreary during the greater part of the year. Many of these towns are only artificial creations, born at the beck of the sovereign hand, and, were it withdrawn from them, would fall back into rural nothingness.*

This mode of formation of urban centres accounts for the fact that, in Russia, town and country differ generally so little, while sometimes they differ very greatly. While most district towns look to us like pretentious villages, the large cities, especially the two capitals, seem colonies of another nation or another civilization. There you find all the luxury, all the pleasures, all the arts of the West ; life seems altogether European, while in the provinces it seems Moscovite, half Oriental still. The contrast is thrilling ; yet it is all external, on the surface : appearances differ, man is the same. Setting aside a highest class, trained to foreign discipline, the bulk of the city people, by tastes and bringing up, by intellect and custom, is very near still to the rural population. In these cities, frequently built all in a lump and already populous,

* The introduction of machinery, of steam, and the improvement of means of communication, tend to change this state of things by encouraging factory industry on a large scale to the detriment of the lowly village industries. This revolution, which is going on in Russia as everywhere else, must naturally benefit the urban centres.

the peasants reside in great numbers, and manners are half rural still. There is no *bourgeoisie*, in the French acception of the word, nor an urban *plebs* comparable to the working population of large French cities and their suburbs.

Old-time Moscovia made little difference between town and country,—townsman and husbandman,—of which modern Russia has made two separate classes. To foreign travellers the condition of the one appeared to differ very little from that of the other. The Englishman Fletcher, Queen Elizabeth's envoy at the court of the son of Ivan the Terrible, looked on the tradesman and craftsman as part of the lowest class, to which he gives the humiliating designation of *mujiks*.* Not until the seventeenth century are the towns habitually treated by the administration as something separate from the country. Only at this epoch, when serfdom was established, did the urban populations begin to be regarded as a separate class and the towns as separate communities, based on a special scheme.† Until then the towns and boroughs and the peasantry were, on the whole, subject to one and the same law (*jus*) and authority. The condition of the lower classes in the towns was little more to be envied than that of the rural classes. The townsman was "attached" to his native town as the husbandman to his native glebe, for similar reasons too—that the exchequer

---

* Ivan the Terrible himself, in his letters to Queen Elizabeth, contemptuously refers to the English merchants, come to Russia for trading purposes, as trading *mujiks*.[4]

† All this and what follows naturally does not apply to either Nòvgorod or Pskof, who had maintained their right of self-government, and where, as in the Republics of Mediæval Italy, we find the strife between rich and poor, between "*popolo grasso*" and "*popolo minuto*."

[4] This fact alone proves that the designation which so shocks Western delicacy is, to the Russian ear, neither "humiliating" nor "contemptuous." It was continually used simply in the sense of "man," and is so still by the people. When a man is admiringly spoken of as "a handsome, portly, robust *mujik*," or as "an honest, quiet *mujik*," those who so describe him certainly do not mean to disparage him, but use the word *mujik* exactly in the way that Englishmen, in like case, would use "fellow" and Germans *Kerl*. The peasant woman who speaks of her *mujik* does not mean any more disrespect to him than the English laborer's wife in speaking of her "man."

might not be defrauded by the departure of the tax-payer, and
that the community, being taxed in a lump and mutually responsible, might not have to pay for the absentees. The prohibition
of going from one town or borough to another was enforced by
measures that recall the laws invented for the *curiales* in the latter
times of the Roman Empire. For such flight or desertion the
Románofs, in 1658, established the penalty of death.

Yet there was in the Russian towns a sort of privileged class :
the wealthy merchants, wholesale dealers, especially those who
traded with foreign lands. They were called "guests" (*gòsti*),
probably because originally the greater number of them were foreigners. There are mentions of these "guests" in the times of the
Varangians. In primitive Russia, where the vast distances and
the internecine wars made commerce at once more precarious and
more profitable, the men who were sufficiently enterprising to
devote themselves to it were surrounded with a respectful consideration, which remained their due even in the midst of the abasement into which the quarrels of the princes and the Tatar domination plunged the national trade. This name of *gòsti*, probably of Teutonic origin,[5] was awarded by the princes as a title
of honor, and many of them served the *kniazes* in the capacity of
advisers or ambassadors.[*] After the *gòsti* came the merchants
of lower standing and the mere townsmen—*possàdskiyé*,[†]—both of
which classes were divided into sundry categories, each of which

---

[5] It must be traced much farther back. It is part of the word-treasure
which primitive Sanskrit bequeathed to all her daughters, among whom Old
Slavic and Old Gothic claim equal rank. The original word meant "cow-
killer," in appropriate, if slightly realistic, allusion to the ponderous
hospitalities of primitive ages.

[*] It is from these *gòsti*, in the sense of merchants, that the Russian
equivalent for the Oriental *bazar* is called *gostìnoy-dvor*.

[†] From *possàd*, a "borough" ; the chief magistrate of Nòvgorod was
called *Possàdnik*.[6]

[6] The title corresponds to "mayor," but with more power ; rather to the
podestà of the Italian Republics. The word *possàd* is derived from *sidiéti*,
"to sit, settle " = *sedere*.

had its own council or *Dúma*,' invested with the right of deciding questions arising between its own members.

It was difficult for these merchants and townsmen to develop into an influential class, in a country cut off from Europe and the sea, and from all the commercial highroads by Lithuania, the Teutonic Order, and the Tatars. Ivan IV. the Terrible, the foe of the old princely and *boyàr* races, strove to raise the people of towns, especially those of Moscow. But the hand of the tsars could not implant in Moscovia the liberties it was rooting out in Nòvgorod and Pskof, where they had long flourished. The absence of feudalism or aristocracy, which at first sight would seem to favor the development of a town-class, rather proved an obstacle. The sovereigns had not so much interest in leaning on the cities for support, and the cities did not find in the dissensions between the great vassals and the central power opportunities for rising and obtaining franchises.

Thus, then, when Peter the Great came to the throne, there was, in spite of some attempts made by his father Alexis, nothing at all answering to what Europe knows under the name of *bourgeoisie* in all these towns, devoid of industry, unprovided with means of communication, with scarcely any permanent population.

Such a gap could not but strike the practical Tsar, whose favorite model was Holland, the most *bourgeois* country in Europe. A middle class, unfortunately, could not be improvised as quickly as a fleet or army. Peter's special regulations, the administrative self-government with which he endowed the cities, probably did not help to create an urban class as much as the reformer's general activity, the introduction of new industries and new means of communication, and especially the opening up of Russia to Europe.

' *Dúma*, from *dúmati*, "to think." It is the name given to all the town-councils and extended to the buildings in which they are held. The Paris Hôtel-de-Ville and the New York City-Hall would both be translated *Dúma* in Russian.

Yet the progress was slow. The maladministration of Peter's successors, the restrictions imposed on the franchises of the towns and merchants, and, lastly, under Elizabeth, the erection of the chief branches of commerce into monopolies, to be granted to court favorites, delayed the birth of a middle class over half a century. Catherine II., in this as in everything, took up and carried on Peter's work. She wished to constitute at the same time a nobility and a *bourgeoisie*, both which things Russia equally lacked.* It was Catherine who divided the inhabitants of towns and cities into the different groups which still exist. Merchants, tradesmen, small burghers, mechanics, received from her a corporative organization. Each of these groups had elective "heads," and all were united into municipal corporations, to which was restored the right of doing justice and of internal administration or self-government.

In organizing the urban class, both Peter and Catherine naturally imitated the contemporary institutions of Western Europe, especially those of Teutonic countries—England and Germany, Holland and Sweden. Hence, partly, the faultiness and failure of a work, mistakenly copied from foreign models already in the stage of decay. Just when they were on the point of disappearing from the more enlightened Western states, the craft corporations and the merchant guilds were introduced into Russia. Whatever its merits and demerits, this corporative organization, which sits so easy on the German, does not fit the Russian at all. He has, according to a very just remark of Haxthausen, the spirit of association, not that of corporation, and they are two very different things. He has a national form of association, the *artèl*, of which

---

* In this respect, as in several others, some of Catherine's advisers sometimes commended singular devices or gave way to strange delusions. Nicolas Turguénief (*La Russie et les Russes*, v. ii., p. 221) tells how one of the most prominent men of this grand reign took a great and active part in the foundation, in both capitals, of gigantic foundling houses, because he flattered himself that he was thereby preparing the creation of a third estate !

all the members have equal rights and work for the common good, under chiefs freely elected by their peers. He does not care for closed corporations, bristling with privileges and monopolies, hierarchically subdivided into unequal ranks or grades, like the craft-corporations of old in Western Europe, with their "masters," "companions," and "apprentices." The corporative spirit was only a form of the feudal spirit, which had introduced into the world of labor the same principle of privilege and vassalage that prevailed in the nobility and the tenure of property, and therefore is nowhere to be found in old-time Moscovia, nor could it obtain in modern Russia. Vainly Catherine II. strove to combine the mechanics into crafts or *tsekhs*—the word being taken bodily from the German *Zeche*—they remained lifeless registers, to serve little else than the uses of police registering, and wherever the unwieldy things with their superannuated pomp and circumstance still survive, we cannot see that either the mechanic or national industry has derived much profit from them.*

* On this point, as on so many others, there is, in the laws and administration, a lack of unity and precision, which too often breeds confusion and arbitrariness. The law does not define the crafts that must be made into corporations; accordingly such or such a trade is free in certain cities, while in others it is bound by licenses, which are delivered by a board of experts on the applicant's passing an examination.

BOOK V.   CHAPTER III.

Classification of the Urban Population since Catherine II.—The Mechanic and the *Miêsh-tchanìn* or "Small Burgher"—Urban Proletariate—How this Class has, as a Rule, Preserved the same Spirit as the Rural Population—The Merchant Guilds and their Privileges—How Emancipation has Made it Possible for them to Own Real Estate—The "Honorary Citizens" or "Notables" among the Townspeople—Russia, till very Lately, Had none of the Professions out of which the Western *Bourgeoisie* Used to be Recruited—In how far the Reforms Help Create a Middle Class in the European Sense.

THE town population, ever since Peter I. and Catherine II., has been classed under five or six rubrics, themselves divided into two main categories: the wholesale traders, forming a superior class, which was long a privileged one ; and the retail traders, the mechanics of all sorts, subdivided into several categories, differing only in name.   There are the poorer townspeople,—the mechanics,—the members of trade corporations, and lastly the "miscellany," a sort of town-rabble, containing all those who do not fit into any particular class.   Of these categories, the first is the most important, and can be regarded as the type of the entire lower class of the urban population.   Its name, *miêsh-tchanìn*, is usually translated in French *bourgeois*, yet the man thus designated answers little enough to the French term.   The *miêsh-tchanìn* * is a person who dwells in towns and who, being neither noble nor priest, is not rich enough to inscribe his name on the roll of the merchants, yet does not belong to a trade corporation. He usually gets his livelihood from some small business or some

* *Miêsh-tchanìn*, plural *miêsh-tchánié*, from *miêsto*, "a place," which gives the diminutive *miês-tiêtch-ko*, "a borough, a small town."

manual trade. Many have no assured means of existence. Their business or real property is, or was until lately, subject to limitations : they could not do business beyond a certain figure, or own real estate worth more than five or six thousand roubles. If they passed that line, they had to register as merchants. Although legally a townsman, indeed, the typical townsman, the *miêsh-tchanïn* is frequently compelled to migrate to the country to seek a living. In some governments there is quite a number of them settled in villages, while the peasant, to whom the working of the soil does not always yield permanent occupation or sufficient returns, often crowds the cities, where he has appropriated the monopoly of sundry crafts. In St. Petersburgh alone there live over two hundred thousand peasants.* The two classes frequently exchange residences, now opening a competition in manual labor and retail trade on the smallest scale, in the factories or at the fairs ; now again keeping each to its own favorite pursuits, the townsman carrying into the country city ways and crafts, the peasant bringing to town his pair of arms, his axe, his horse, both taking many risks, often more to the prejudice of the townsman than the countryman.

This class of *miêsh-tchánié* and the kindred groups of mechanics form the large majority of the town populations. It is perhaps the portion of the Russian people least favored by fortune. The peasant is given his cabin and small enclosed house-lot by the Emancipation Act ; he also has his share of the commons—the communal land. Very different is the condition of the *miêsh-tchanïn*. He lives, like the working population of Western Europe, from hand to mouth. The law has no guarantee for him, the commune is usually unable to supply him with any certain share of land or work. If a few do achieve a competence, or even wealth, the greater part lead a precarious existence. Perhaps one tenth of them own houses in the towns. The rest hire lodgings.

---

* According to some statistical reports, the peasants would average 20 per cent. of the urban population.

Those who go to seek a living in villages are not entitled to a share in the communal good things. Some, now and then, elect to become peasants : they have to obtain admittance into the rural commune, and pay cash down for a right to the land to which the peasant is entitled by birth.

Until very lately it was these two alone—the poor townsman and the mechanic—who, along with the peasant, bore the two heaviest burdens of the state : the poll-tax or capitation, and the blood-tax or military conscription. Alexander II. lightened the latter burden, by imposing it equally on all classes. Alexander III. freed them from capitation in 1883. The law has given to the townspeople equality in burdens and rights ; it cannot go further and give them real property, as to the husbandman. The Russians, disposing of vast communal lands, boast that they have no proletarians, and bend a scornful gaze on the dangers with which this social plague threatens the West. In reality, however, Russia already has an urban proletariate, always the most trouble-some, in some nations—in France at any rate—the most riotous, the only one to be dreaded. There are certain social troubles which no country, be it never so new and bold, so vast and rich in land, seems fated to be exempted from ; of this number are urban proletariate and the wages question in cities. If the Rus-sian proletariate is not more numerous, the reason is that the cities themselves are relatively neither many nor populous. The progress of industry and civilization, the very increase of the population will necessarily have their usual effect—of increasing the proletariate by enlarging the towns. This class has already received from the emancipation an important reinforcement : it has become the refuge of several categories of former serfs, especially the so-called "court-people," *i. e.* the house-serfs. These people, who, by virtue of their attendance on their masters' persons, had been estranged from the village commune through generations, were not in a condition, on finding them-selves free, to vindicate their share of the communal land. Freed from the control of their masters, they must live by their labor, owning no right to the land they tread or the house they live in, with no other inheritance to hand down to their children than the light hoard of their slender savings. No ; Russia has not yet found, any more than any other country, the secret of securing to each man a permanent dwelling, to each family an hereditary homestead, to place the ever increasing swarms of human units above the reach of vice or improvidence.

As to their mode of life, these *miêsh-tchánié* and mechanics come very near to the least favored classes of the western cities of Europe. They differ from them, however, in an important point : the absence of class spirit, of " city feeling," so to speak. They have not, like the corresponding classes in the rest of Europe, the spirit of opposition against both the upper *bourgeoisie* and the rural population. In ideas, beliefs, and feeling, as well as in garb and manners, they differ very little as yet from the latter. Religion, which, in Russia, still is one of the great social forces, still holds under control those urban masses which, in the rest of Europe, it appears to have irretrievably lost, be its name Catholicism or Protestantism. Thus it is that the Russian people are pervaded at bottom by a unity, a harmony of feeling which deserves the more to be noticed that it is getting so rare elsewhere, and that, even where it still prevails, time will inevitably weaken it. This moral condition of the urban working classes accounts for the failure of the nihilistic propaganda to influence it. Sundry tokens, however, warrant the fear that the Russian workingmen may not always remain deaf to revolutionary incitements. Wage questions and strikes may yet do their wonted evil work.

In this state of things Russia has, for a more or less prolonged period, a principle of strength and stability which all the other nations of the European continent lack. She is less exposed to those struggles for influence between town and country from which the West has suffered so much and which, by causing perpetual disturbances and reactions, hinder any kind of progress,

22

and is exempt for a while longer from those intermittent collisions between the sceptical and at the same time utopistic spirit of the city workingman and the coarsely conservative and blindly positive spirit of the peasant.

Russian legislation separates the inhabitants of cities into two accurately defined groups : the mechanics or townspeople who have not risen above the foot of the social ladder, and those townsmen who have swung themselves up to the higher rungs. The latter are usually designated as "merchants" (*kuptsý*). This title is legally awarded only to such as own a certain capital and pay certain license-dues. The merchants, long in possession of important privileges, never could constitute themselves into a closed class : the poor townsman, the peasant, the nobleman even who devotes himself to commerce, can have his name inscribed on their roll ; it is a question of means. These "merchants" again are subdivided into several categories, known under the foreign name of "guilds," introduced by Peter the Great. There are three of them, which for a long time enjoyed very different prerogatives, but at the present day have identical civil rights. The distinction between the guilds is based only on the figure of the capital declared and the proportionate dues they pay the State for their license. The members of the first guild have the freedom of trading through the entire extent of the empire, as well as abroad ; they pay five hundred roubles a year. The members of the second are limited to home trade. The guilds have in every city their boards and elective "heads" or syndics. The merchants, however, rise or descend from one to another, as their fortune grows or decreases, and if business is very bad they are always in danger of falling down into the lowest urban class, the *miêsh-tchánié.*

The merchants of the two first guilds belong, or rather belonged, to the privileged classes. The emperors had granted them all the personal rights which the nobility enjoyed : exemption from the poll-tax, from military conscription, from corporal punishment. In a country like Russia, nothing more could be done for the encouragement of trade and *bourgeoisie*. The merchants were free to acquire wealth, free to enjoy it. One thing only was refused them, and this restriction itself well could pass, in the lawgiver's eyes, for a stimulus to trade. Merchants, as all persons not belonging to the nobility, were forbidden to own "inhabited lands," which means that they could not hold serfs. This virtually excluded them from owning rural property and limited them to houses in the towns and cities, and country houses in the suburbs or environs. This lessened the temptation to withdraw from commerce the capital that had been launched into it

This prohibition had a surer and less beneficial effect : it kept apart commerce and agriculture, by maintaining a chasm between the merchant or manufacturer and both the noble landowner and the husbandman. While serfdom made the formation of a middle class in the country almost impossible, the monopoly held by the nobility prevented the middle class slowly forming in the cities from spreading over the country. The merchants were as good as prisoners in the towns, tied down to business. Now that the abolition of serfdom has, *ipso facto*, done away with the distinction between "inhabited" and "non-inhabited" real estate, rural property has become free to all classes. By this indirect consequence emancipation closely touches the middle class, and this fact alone amounts to a social revolution of deep bearing on the future of Russia.

The merchants of the first guild were possessed of nearly all the nobility's personal privileges ; the wealthier ones nevertheless strove to get out of their condition. They coveted, for themselves or their children, the shadow of which the substance was theirs, and many took a road which led to it rapidly : state service. This was another cause of enfeeblement to the middle class, which seemed to grow and thrive only to benefit another class, which, in its turn, felt this accession as rather an encumbrance. Yet it would be unfair to see mere puerile vanity in this chase after such functions and decorations as conferred nobility. For if the merchant enjoyed all the substantially useful privileges of the nobility, his tenure of them was entirely dependent on his name being inscribed in the guild roll. One stroke of ill luck could take them from him and lower him to the level of the *miêsh-tchanîn*, subject to capitation, conscription, and corporal punishment. Hereditary nobility and state service could alone protect a family from such a fall.

To remedy the precarious position so galling to the merchants, the Emperor Nicolas created a new category for them, which, while straitening the road to nobility, secured to them the advantages they were striving for. This new rung of the Russian social ladder has name, " honorary citizen," nearly answering the "town-notable " of old. These "notables " enjoy the same privileges as the merchants of the first guild without being bound to be inscribed on the guild rolls. It was in reality a new variety of nobility, a sort of burgher-nobility conferred by the sovereign or by letters-patent from the Senate as a reward for certain services and the performance of certain functions. As the nobility proper, this one was divided into two categories. There was the " personal " and the " hereditary " " honorary citizen," the latter transmitting to his posterity his qualities and exemptions. This rubric still exists, but has become a merely nominal distinction, the main exemptions attached to it having been extended to all the inhabitants of cities. The abrogation of capitation and corporal punishment on one side and the institution of universal obligatory military service on the other have left but little value to all these distinctions. Town notables and merchants can scarcely retain many privileges when so few are left to the nobility.

Nowadays it is education, manners, the degree of culture,which keep the different classes of society separate. The habits of life raise between them barriers which the law is powerless to pull down. In this respect, the distinctions are more marked than even in Western Europe. From the uneven manner in which civilization entered the various layers of society, it could not be otherwise. The nobility, which has long had the monopoly of European instruction, continues to live apart from the merchants and a middle class whom wealth has not yet lifted over the threshold of culture. Thus, in large cities, there always are two clubs : one for the nobility, the other for the merchants. The two classes, socially, form two separate towns, which mix very little in private life, differing even in their mode of life. There are, however, signs of a change in the near future. The nobility and the *bourgeoisie* now meet not only in public assemblies to deliberate on the affairs of town or province, but begin to draw nearer together by manners, tastes, and culture, the one becoming more national, the other more European.

Some years back, a Russian merchant usually was a man with a long beard, in a long-skirted *kaftàn*, and high leather boots ; he remained as faithful as the peasant himself to Moscovite traditions and the national garb. Nowadays there is the old-time merchant, strict guardian of old customs ; sometimes owner of a large fortune, yet not the less attached to the old mode of life ; orthodox or dissenter (*raskòlnik*), like the common people, the peasant or small townsman, from whom he really differs only by his wealth ; a faithful observer of fasts and holidays, combining to a singular degree superstition and slyness, plain living and vastness of commercial operations. Then there is the modern merchant, often the son or grandson of the other, with clean-shaved chin, anxious to give up ancestral customs and to imitate the nobility and assume French fashions. The number of such naturally increases daily ; they have palatial houses, drawing-rooms furnished luxuriously if not always tastefully, and all the comforts of the West. Their sons learn French and travel abroad ; many already lead in Paris an existence as worldly, as dissipated as the young nobles, and many contrive, after coming home, to get themselves admitted into the drawing-rooms of the nobility.

Between these two types there is an intermediate one, which marks the transition from one to the other and frequently combines the pretensions and foibles of both ; it is the tradesman who has made money, in love with modern luxury, yet unable to get used to it, surrounding himself with furniture and bric-a-brac the use of which is a puzzle to him, always ill-at-ease in his own house, in his own clothes. Be it love of luxury or the tradesman's calculating instinct and the wish thus to strengthen his credit, the merchant of this kind often develops a taste for show and gorgeousness seldom to be met with in other classes, even though the whole country has a leaning that way. There are provincial merchant-nabobs who have splendid apartments where they do not live, sumptuous drawing-rooms which are opened only to strangers, plate and china which they don't use, richly appointed beds to which they prefer rugs and divans, after the old Russian fashion.

There is nothing in the Russian "guilds" that recalls the "third estate" of Western Europe, with its stirring spirit, its varied information, its pushing ambition. [1] There is scarcely yet the least stir of political or intellectual leaven to be felt. Until these latter years, science and literature owed nearly nothing to the middle class.[*] As the name itself (*kuptsỳ*) indicates, there has been in Russia until now only a counting-house middle class, representing trade and industry, swayed by an exclusively mercantile, conservative, and routine-ridden spirit. Most of the professions commonly called "liberal" were almost as much wanting in the Russia of Peter I. and Catherine II. as in the Moscovia of the Ivans and Vassílis. No lawyers, no physicians,

[1] Because Russian society is not based on feudalism. We never can have a "third estate" like that of Western Europe, because there it was the embodiment of a continuous protest and struggle against feudal arrogance and oppression. In Russia there is nothing for it to protest against.

[*] The only two exceptions are, in the first half of the present century, the provincial poets, Koltsòf and Nikìtin, twins in gifts, inspiration, and origin ; one a tradesman in a small way, the other a mere *miésh-tchanìn* of the poorest class. Some writers and scientists risen from that class might be quoted at the present time.

no engineers, no writers, no professors, not even notaries or attorneys;—nothing but clerks and scriveners, uneducated, and as unlike as possible, as to personal dignity and social standing, to their congeners of the West. There could not be many lawyers in a country where, until 1865, the procedure was secret and written, while legislation was a chaos, and justice an object of traffic, where functions of all orders were performed by the same class of functionaries, frequently by the same persons, unqualified by professional training or the choice of a specialty. The Russia of the first half of the nineteenth century was, in this respect, behind the France of the sixteenth.

The reforms of Emperor Alexander II., especially the judicial reform, will help fill this gap, by creating pursuits and professions requiring serious intellectual culture and providing for it manifold and honorable openings. The universities and the progress made in instruction, the railroads and greater rapidity of intercourse, the widening of commerce and industry work in the same direction. The result will be a new middle class, liberal, wideawake, with varied aptitudes. But this future, truly Russian middle class will have to be looked for outside of all official rolls. It is being recruited from all classes, among the sons of merchants and still more of the nobility. *This* middle class, which is, sooner or later, to be the directing class, will grow up outside of all class distinctions, and will have little trouble in overcoming birth-prejudices, because, contrary to appearances, they have never been very strong in Russia.

The chief outcome of the eighteenth century and the reforms of Peter and Catherine was the formation of a cultured upper class, a nobility brought up after the European manner ; one of the chief outcomes of the nineteenth century and the reforms of Alexander II. will be the creation of a truly European and modern middle class. The progress made in this direction during the last fifty years is easy to follow. "There is no third estate in Russia," wrote Madame de Staël in the reign of Alexander I. ; "it is

a great inconvenience as regards the progress of letters and arts,
. . . but the absence of an intermediate class between the high
and the low makes them love one another the more. The distance
between the two extremes appears greater because there are no
degrees between them, but in reality they are more closely
in touch with each other for not being separated by a middle
class." * These words give matter for much thought. It is true
that the two extreme classes, the noble and the *mujik*, the lord and
the serf, were in close contact, nothing coming between them ;
but it was only a material contact. There was between them
neither mutual sympathy, nor mutual comprehension, nor moral
bond.² Between the people, faithful to the old Moscovite manners, and the nobility, semi-French, the distance was the greater
that there was nothing to bring the ends together. This gap it
is that a new and cultured middle class is to fill, belonging to the
people by their sympathies and interests, to modern civilization
by their bringing up.

"Heaven guard us from such a thing ! " many Russians will
exclaim. For many, whether aristocrats or democrats, are inclined to resent the harmless word *burjoasía*, which they have
borrowed from us and which, in dealing with the West, they
misuse in the strangest manner. Many affect towards it about
the same feelings as the proletarians of our large cities. They
cannot show sufficient contempt for our *bourgeois* society and
civilization, for our *bourgeois* liberties and *régime*. They are
quite proud of having nothing of the sort, they don't care to resemble us in this respect.† In their pretensions to social unity

* *Dix Années d'Exil.*

² Madame de Staël was right. Her woman's intuition guided her more
surely and showed her the hidden truth of things more clearly than learned
abstractions can do where living souls are in question.

† This aversion against the *bourgeoisie* is found equally, and for similar reasons, among the small Slavic nations. True, with most of the latter,
it is accounted for by the fact that the *bourgeoisie* of their cities consists
mostly of Jews and Germans—a remark which applies in no small measure
to the greater part of wealthy Russian cities.

and homogeneousness, in their systematic antipathy against class distinctions, they look on the *bourgeoisie* as on some sort of a new caste, or an oligarchy hostile to the people, not perceiving that the fusion of classes must necessarily produce a new, intermediate class, independent of all caste prejudices and alone capable of realizing that moral unity of a nation which they have so much at heart ; that this alone can put an end to the social dualism, the moral schism which, ever since Peter the Great, has been one of Russia's principal diseases and which survives the abolition of privileges and the progress of equality. Then only this nation, once divided against itself and even now cut into two halves, both powerless through their separation, will be in a position to give Europe the measure of its genius.

BOOK VI.

NOBILITY AND TCHIN.

CHAPTER I.

The Nobles and the Peasants, Personifying the Two Russias, Appear Like Two Different Nations—By its Origin and Manner of Recruiting, the Russian *Dvoriànstvo* Differs from all Corresponding Institutions in Western Europe—Personal and Hereditary Nobility—Great Number of the Nobles—Russian Titles—The Descendants of Rurik and Guedimìn—Why this High-born Nobility does not Form an Aristocracy—Constitution of the Russian Family—Equal Division among the Males—Political Consequences of this System—Attempts to Introduce Entails and Primogeniture.

THE noble and the peasant ; the former landlord and the former serf. These two men, these two classes, even now embody two different Russias : one modern, the European Russia of Peter and the reforming emperors ; the other old-fashioned, the Moscovite, semi-Asiatic or semi-Oriental Russia of the old tsars.

Between the noble and the peasant serfdom was, up to Alexander II., a material bond ; a moral one it never was. This secular bond once broken, the former landlord and former serf found themselves almost as closely linked together as they were before by the soil and the demands of rural life, and nearly as widely separated by intellect, tendencies, and manners. For the difference between them lay not merely in the degree of culture ; it lay in the principle, in the very nature of the civilization. Therefore it is that now, as well as before emancipation, the distance betwixt them is so great that they appear to the foreign observer to form not so much two classes as two separate nations.

Of these two men, the *mujik* and his former master, one is almost an entire stranger to Europe, the other is almost at home with her. France, Germany, Italy, have often harbored the latter as guest ; he cultivates them, as traveller, man of the world, and pleasure-seeker. Western Europe knows the Russian noble, and is utterly ignorant of what Russian nobility is. In this respect the highest order of Russian society is scarcely better known, better understood of Europe than Russian peasantry ; we know neither what their functions have been in the past, nor what part they play in the present, and are therefore not qualified to augur their future. We do not know what place the nobility occupies in the nation and in the state, what prerogatives are conceded it by custom and law, what vista the evolution of Russia opens before it. There is much babbling in Europe of aristocracy and democracy ; even in France, aroused at last to some curiosity concerning foreign nations, the latter are often questioned on the point by parties and schools, which like to bring forward, in the form of instances more or less faithfully reported, arguments in favor of this or that thesis, usually settled beforehand. What lessons can Europe learn from Russia in this matter ? Towards which side leans that society, in so many ways dissimilar from the French ? Can it long hold its footing on the declivity down which all the West gradually slides ? Is there in Russia an aristocratic force capable of becoming one day a political lever, a support to the throne, and a restraint on the people ? Such questions may appear premature, but they *will* naturally occur to minds uneasy about the future of Europe and civilization.

The Russian nobility (*dvoriànstvo*) has neither the same origin nor the same traditions as what is called by that name in Western Europe. The *dvoriànstvo*—"the hereditary cultured class" a Russian writer with aristocratic tendencies defines it—is an institution special to Russia, unknown to Europe, unique of its kind.

Two things especially are distinctive of it : in the first place it never was anything but a tool of the ruling power, being literally nothing but the men in the service of the state united into a body ; in the second place it has always been open to all and, being continually renovated by influx from below, it has been preserved from any tendency towards exclusiveness, all caste spirit.

Thus the Russian nobility is admitted by its most serious panegyrists to have no counterpart in Western Europe ; some even would fain say no antecedent in history. It is only when they look at their country through foreign glasses and allow themselves to be taken in by an entirely external likeness, that certain Russians forget their national traditions over their European training and give themselves airs as English lords or German *Herren.* If we render the term *dvoriànstvo* by those of *noblesse, adel, nobility,* it is only from lack of equivalents in the languages as well as in the institutions of the West. The term which designates officially the highest class in the state at the same time tells the story of its origin. The Russian word *dvorianìn* means "a man of the court" and might be translated " courtier " had not this word taken an entirely different sense.*
It appears that originally the *dvorianìn* was an officer or dignitary of the Moscovite court, more or less analogous to the chamberlains of Western Europe. Later on, this term was extended to all who were in the personal service of the sovereign or, what amounted to the same, of the state. The *dvoriànstvo* has kept, through history, the stamp of its origin ; it is a court nobility, a serving nobility, which, in our days as of old, can be acquired by the *tchin, i. e.,* a given grade or rank in the army or administration.

---

* *Dvorianìn,* plural *dvoriàniè,* from *dvor,* "court," also "yard," with all the meanings attaching to these words and a few more besides. Thus it is that *dvòrnik,* "porter, janitor," and *dvoròvyiè,* the "household serfs," are words derived from the same radical as that designating the national nobility. May there not be some affinity between the ideas represented as well as between the words ?

Russian legislature distinguishes two sorts of nobility : transmissible or "hereditary," and "personal," *i. e.*, not descending from the father to his children. This exactly renders the peculiar character of the Russian hierarchy. The *dvoriànstvo* being only the servants of the state, it became necessary, when the complicated bureaucracy of the West was introduced in Russia, to draw a distinction between high offices and inferior ones. Hence the creation of two nobilities for the use of men in public service. To the subaltern this title of " personal *dvorianìn* " insured the rights of the freeman, in a country where only the noble or functionary had any recognized rights. In point of fact he has nothing that the privileged town classes do not have. His children enter the rubric of " honorary citizens," *i. e.*, hereditary town notables, and really enjoy the same rights as their father, whose nobility they have not inherited. The title therefore is an empty one and its suppression would make no change in the social hierarchy.

Only hereditary nobility deserves attention as possessing real value. Like personal nobility, it has for centuries been open to all. For over a hundred years, all through the eighteenth century and the first portion of the nineteenth, from Peter the Great to the close of the reign of Alexander I., hereditary nobility belonged by right to every army officer and every civilian of corresponding grade ; it was won with the first epaulet, with the grade of ensign, which is inferior to that of sub-lieutenant. It is easy to see what a nobility must have been to which the door was so wide and the threshold so low. In order to raise its level somewhat, Alexander I. in 1822, his brother Nicolas in 1845, and Alexander II. in 1854, successively heightened by several degrees the threshold of the entrance to hereditary nobility. Under Alexander II. it was open only to colonels or civilians bearing the title of "Actual State Councillor " (Fourth class). Under Alexander III. the nobility has at last succeeded in doing away with ennoblement by grade and service. Besides the great gate of the *tchin*, there were sundry side entrances into hereditary nobility ; certain imperial orders used to ennoble *ex officio.* The monarch still has the faculty, which he seldom uses, of conferring nobility by his sovereign pleasure.

The first result of such a system is naturally the great number of nobles, accompanied by generally straitened circumstances, lack of education, and the not very high standing of a great many among them. In European Russia alone, statistics give about 600,000 souls as the figure for hereditary, and not less than 350,000 for personal *dvoriànstvo.* There is enough to raise an army composed entirely of nobles. The consequence is, nobles are found everywhere, on all steps of the social ladder, the top of which should alone be reserved to them. It is there, rather than in official city burgherdom, that the equivalent of the European *bourgeoisie* might be looked for. " What is your nobility ? " once asked one of my fellow-travellers of a justice of the peace at whose table we sat, on the banks of the Volga. " Our nobility," replied the host, "why, they are my guests—we all that are here." This reply could often be given in Russia and abroad too, wherever many Russians come together. The nobles are all that are not peasant, priest, or merchant—tradesman or shopkeeper ; all the people you meet in society, all those of a certain culture, in town or country. In this respect one might even still almost say : " In Russia, the nobility is everybody."

From the obscure background formed by this nobiliary plebs, naturally stand out a certain number of families, of which some shine with a lustre that pierces through the gloom of ages, back to the days of old Moscovia, while others have been more recently brought into prominence by brilliant services. Such families, such " houses " there are in Russia as in most countries that have a past. The Russian language has, to designate them, a word peculiar to itself; it calls them collectively " the *znat* " (from the verb *znàti,* " to know "). These are, irrespective of titles or antiquity of race, the illustrious or renowned families who have held, down to our days, a high rank in the state or society. In this highest nobility, or, more correctly, in this topmost social layer, there are titled families of ancient pedigree or recent extraction, but there are also untitled families whose nobility and splendor can be traced to the times of the old tsars. This nobility will probably be the only one to survive the gradual fading out of the *dvoriànstvo*, as the latter has nothing, either in name or form, or in the country's memory, to keep it permanently distinct from the mass of the nation.* The bulk of nobles is not set apart by any external sign, there is nothing to proclaim their quality, they have no title to show but an inscription in the registers of their province.

There are in Russia several sorts of titles, and something like a nobiliary hierarchy, but this is an importation from the West, a recently borrowed thing. To the Moscovites as to the other Slavs, all these designations of dukes, counts, barons, were unknown, for the reason that they never had anything like feudalism, no duchies and counties, vassals of one another and of the central power. Old Russia knew nothing of all these gradations ; indeed she did not know much even of hereditary qualifications ; herein again the Russian *dvoriànstvo* differed entirely from the nobility of Western Europe. There was but one exception, and that confirmed the rule : it was in favor of the collateral branches of the reigning dynasty.

---

* Many Russians, when abroad, add to their names the French prefix *de* or the German *von*. There is nothing of the sort in their own language. Russian names often take the form of a genitive, or rather a nominal adjective : Davydof from David, Semiònof from Semiòn (Simon) ; but far from belonging specially to the nobility, such names are met with among the priests, the merchants, the peasantry. If there is any kind of distinction in this matter, it lies not in the family names, but in the desinence *vitch* (feminine, *vna*), which the Russians add to their father's given name, which they then use as a patronymic : Alexander Petròvitch, Alexandra Petròvna. In old-time Moscovia this now almost universal desinence was used only by persons of some standing. Only one merchant family, which formed in itself a sort of privileged class, the Strógonofs (now counts), were entitled to it. To this day the desinence *of* instead of *òvitch* is used in this way for the lower classes : you say Ivan Petròf, Alexis Ivánof. This is probably the origin of the many names in *of*.

The descendants of the *kniazes*, the appanage-princes, continued to bear the title after the incorporation of their principalities into that of Moscow.   All other dignities or distinctions, especially that of *boyàr*, were conferred directly by the sovereign and only for a lifetime.   It was only when brought into contact with Europe and on annexing provinces that had long been subject to Teutonic influences, that Russia appropriated some of the nobiliary denominations produced by feudalism.   So she made counts and later on barons, but had to borrow foreign names for these imitative creations.*   Peter the Great and his successors began to vie with Western monarchs in conferring hereditary titles. They were not as lavish, though, with these distinctions as other sovereigns, and the number of families bearing foreign titles is comparatively small.   A hundred or so of counts,† some fifteen princes, and a few more barons, the latter mostly financial men,— such is the approximate number of titles created by imperial diploma.   They all are naturally of more or less recent date, few going back a century, and these families do not enjoy any high degree of popularity and consideration.   There are, side by side with them, others, more ancient, whose names are sufficiently illustrious not to need the glamour of title.   The Narỳshkins, for instance, have none, and appear to deem it an honor to dispense with one.

One thing strikes you in the Russian *znat*, that of St. Petersburgh especially : it is the great number of families of foreign extraction.   Probably one half of this court aristocracy comes from abroad ; the blood in their veins is Tatar, Gruzìn (Georgian), Greek, Valachian, Lithuanian, Polish, Swedish, German, even

* *Graf* for " count," and *Baron.*   The old title *kniaz* is the only Slavic and rational one.   I cannot see why we translate " grand-duke," and not " grand-prince," the ancient title *veliki-kniaz*, formerly borne by the sovereigns of Kief, Vladímir, Moscow, and now by the members of the imperial family.

† There are said to have been, from Boriss Sheremétief in 1706 to General Totleben in 1879, 157 creations of counts ; but many left no posterity.   The Emperor Alexander II. alone created over twenty.

French and English. All the tribes subject to the imperial sceptre, all the adjoining nations, have contributed their contingent
to the *dvoriànstvo.* Thus the most exalted class is the least
national of all, in origin as in manners and breeding. Here lies
another source of weakness, another cause for its lack of influence
and authority.

In the midst of all these families of doubtful origin and date,
the *kniazes,* the lineal descendants of the ancient Russian rulers,
occupy a separate place. In the state, founded and so long
governed by their forefathers, these scions of the house of Rurik
represent a native aristocracy, which, in virtue of its secular glory,
claims high consideration. No aristocracy in Europe boasts a
loftier and longer pedigree. "In Russia," once said M. de Talley-
rand, "they are all princes." This opinion is still widely spread
in Western Europe. Yet nothing can be falser. Setting aside the
foreign intruders, and the families deriving their nobility from all
sorts of sources, the number of national princely families, in that
immense empire, scarcely exceeds sixty.* Nearly forty write themselves from Rurik, the founder, and from Vladímir, the apostle of
the empire; they are the representatives of the dynasty which
reigned from the ninth down to the end of the sixteenth century.
This house, probably the most prolific sovereign race known to
history, had as many as two hundred different branches a century
or two ago. Many have no living scions left; others, the Tatìsh-
tchefs for instance, have dropped or lost the title. Another group,
composed of four Russian and four Polish families, comes from a
no less illustrious stock and nearly as national in the eyes of the
Russians : they are the descendants of Guedimìn and the ancient
sovereign house of Lithuania, known in Europe under the name of
the Yagellons, and which, before it ascended the throne of Poland,
at one time ruled the whole of Western Russia. From Rurik and

* We mean here only the genuinely Russian families, not those who,
by their nationality, belong to the alien dependencies of the empire, especially the Caucasus, where Grùzia (Georgia) alone has contributed quite a
bevy of native princes.

the first Russian dynasty are descended the Dolgorúkis, the Bariátin-skys, the Obolénskys, the Gortchakòfs, the Mossàlskys ; from Gue-dimìn and the Lithuanian dynasty, the Khovánskys, the Galítsins, the Kurákins, the Trubetskòys in Russia, the Czartoryskis and the Sanguszkos in Poland. To this double line, issued from the oldest native rulers, should be added seven or eight families descended from Tatar, Tcherkess, and Gruzìn chieftains, formerly admitted into the ranks of Russian *kniazes*, and most of whom—the Tcherkàsskys, the Meshtchérskys, the Bagrations—bear historical names.

A mere roll-call shows that these Russian *kniazes* are not behind any nobility in Europe in antiquity and renown ; to this day there is none that can show more men of distinction. Nevertheless, in all of these houses of quasi-royal blood, by whose side rank many old *boyàr* families,—in all this brilliant national nobility, there are not the elements for a political aristocracy, there are not the materials to make, say a House of Lords, a house of hereditary *boyàrs*. There is a twofold reason for this disqualification : one lies in the historical constitution of Russian society ; the other and main reason lies in the constitution of the Russian family itself.

Equality among all the children—equal rights, title common to all—is the law of the Russian family, as well that of the plain *dvorianìn* as that of the *kniaz*, the merchant, and the *mujik*. This democratical principle, always staunchly maintained by the Russian nobility, stifled in the sprouting such germs of aristocracy as sank here and there into the soil. In these princely houses, the recipients of the blood of Rurik and Guedimìn, as in the poorest nobleman's house, there is no "eldest son," no "head of the family," as far as any special rights go. The father's possessions are divided equally among the sons ; the ancestral title is transmitted to all without distinction, and, as it is the only property that is not impaired by successive partitions, it frequently is the only inheritance that remains to them. Hence the frequent debasement of a title which, while belonging to but few families, can at the same time belong to many individuals. By dint of branching and ever more branching out, many of these princely families—and sometimes the most illustrious—end by forming a bushy shrub, the boughs of which are so intertwined that they hide and choke one another.

Some of these houses of *kniazes*, the unity and fortune of which are secured neither by primogeniture nor by the entrance of the younger sons into the Church, have become veritable tribes or clans, with no bond between them but the name and the title. Thus there are some four hundred princes and princesses Galítsin by right of birth. In these huge families grown out of the same trunk, there are naturally, by the side of limbs that spread in the sun, blossom-crowned and overflowing with sap, branches pining away for want of air and nourishment and bare of foliage. As early as in the sixteenth century, when Rurik's dynasty still ruled, Fletcher remarked that many *kniazes* owned no inheritance save their title, with nothing to support it. "There are so many of them in this position," wrote the envoy of aristocratic England,— "that these titles do not amount to much. Accordingly you see princes only too happy to serve a man of no account for a salary of five or six roubles a year." Matters have not much improved with time and the multiplying of more families. At this very moment one meets in Russia descendants of Rurik and Guedimìn following more than modest pursuits. In Petersburgh I have seen one conduct the orchestra of a *café-concert;* in Italy I have met, on second- and third-rate stages, princesses singing under assumed names, and I was told there had been princes who drove cabs and princesses who took positions as lady's-maids. Such things account for the fact that several families issued from Rurik dropped their title. With such division, such crumbling away of families and fortunes, it were vain to look for family feeling or *esprit de corps* in the high nobility.

Would you know whether a country inclines to aristocracy, first of all inquire into the laws or customs that regulate the distribution of wealth. According to a remark of Tocqueville's, it is the laws on succession which, by centring, grouping around a few heads first property, then power, force aristocracy, in a manner, to spring from the soil,—or, by dividing, frittering, and scattering property and power, pave the way for democracy. Now, in the Russian nobility, the custom of dividing the property equally among the sons has always prevailed,—that levelling law, which, "passing over the soil again and again, razes the walls of dwellings to the ground and pulls down the enclosures of fields." If in Russia the law of equal division has not yet reduced all the large estates into house lots, destroyed all possibilities of living broadly, the reason is that Russia, so far, has been placed in exceptional economic conditions. It was, at first, the immensity of the territory ; then the rapid rise in the value of land owing to the opening of new issues ; lastly, serfdom and the nobility's exclusive right to own " inhabited estates." In many a region the land revenue has increased so fast, in proportion to the population and means of communication, that the properties would double, treble their value, sometimes increase it tenfold, in the space of twenty or thirty years. At this rate, it was not impossible for two or three sons, after dividing among themselves the paternal inheritance, to find themselves each as rich as their father had been at their age.[1] There was another cause still, at least to all appearance, for large fortunes : that is the fact that property is divided only among the male children.

The sons, being those whom it behooves to perpetuate the family, share the estate. To the daughters who have living brothers, the law awards an almost nominal portion : one fourteenth of the paternal inheritance, at least of the real estate. Often

---

[1] In the present and for the future the true safeguard is that we Russian nobles have been led by the late economic revolution *to work*, and to like it ; so that a moderate inheritance becomes—what alone inheritances should be in an ideal state of society—an encouragement and aid to effort, a stepping-stone, a stirrup, a reserve fund, not a bed to lie down on and idle away the best forces of manhood and the few years given to use them in.

they get only their marriage outfit. In the spirit of ancient civilizations, a wedded and dowered daughter is put out of the family. A slice of bread once cut off, in the popular saying, does not belong to the loaf any longer. True, the dowry given to the daughters sometimes amounts to more than what would be their legal share ; there even are cases where the daughters had, in this way, received a portion as large or larger than that of their brothers. This law by no means proceeds from contempt of the female sex ; for Russian law, so niggardly in its provision for them, is in many ways more liberal towards women than the French Code, which, with regard to inheritance, places them on an equal footing with the men.* If the Russian Code awards to the daughter but a trifling portion of her father's property, it ensures to the wife the free enjoyment and independent management of her own property, even in her husband's lifetime. The married woman is never, as in France, a ward under her husband's guardianship, and, in a general way, it may be stated here that, with regard to the emancipation, or rather independence, of women, no society in Europe is more advanced or more liberal than the higher classes of this same Russia, whose laws, in other respects, treat them so meanly.[2]

The mode of succession which consecrates the inequality of man and women, even still numbers partisans in the countries ruled by the Napoleonic Code. Even in France it has the sympathies of those who dread the inroads of democracy, and is avowedly preferred by a whole school of contemporary publicists. Lacking

* It should be mentioned that the Emperor Alexander III., in 1882–83, appointed a commission to set up a project for a new civil code, better adapted to the conditions of modern life.

[2] One often hears expressions of blame and indignation against the carelessness, if not heartlessness, of Russian customs in the matter of marriage settlements—which are not used,—from which it is inferred that the Russian man is careless of the interests of his daughters and their children. Whereas the reason is that settlements are not much needed in a country where a husband has not the right of cutting down a tree on his wife's property against her will !

primogeniture, the privilege of one sex over the other appears to them as a social guaranty, a way of protecting the transmission of property and of perpetuating families. This opinion, however, is not always borne out by the example of the Russian nobility. Where the law recognizes all the children's equal right to the paternal inheritance, the curtailed portion of the sons is re-completed by marriage ; on the average, the wife restores to the husband what the sister took from the brother. If the division between the males alone cuts up lands and fortunes less, that between all the children offers greater facilities for reconstituting or rounding them up by means of alliances. Nowadays, when almost the only factors of wealth are industry, banking, and trade, there is no other bridge between the opulence of the new-made families and the neediness of the old ones but the girls' right of succession. With the opposite *régime*, power and wealth are in danger of passing wholesale to a ruling class of *parvenus.*

The exclusive division of property between the males has, from a conservative point of view, another disadvantage, which must make itself specially felt in Russia : it disturbs the balance of fortunes and the relative position of families more quickly, in a manner more subject to chance than the equal division between all the children. Two fathers, owning equal fortunes and having an equal number of children, leave their male descendants in very different plight according as they happen to have more sons or more daughters. On the whole, the Russian custom does not seem to foster aristocratic influences any more than the French, seemingly more democratic, custom. However, public opinion in Russia leans so much in favor of the independence of women, that legislation or custom may very possibly in the near future refuse to sanction any longer the curtailing of those children's birthright who are by nature less apt to make a fortune for themselves, and then the equality of the sexes would prevail in the North as it does in France.

From the day when they began to associate with the nobilities of Western Europe, the Russian *dvoriànstvo* understood that, with the succession laws as they stood, there could be no real aristocracy. Then some of the descendants of *kniazes* and *boyàrs* attempted to implant in their country the foreign custom of entail. Singularly enough it was one of the least aristocratically minded of sovereigns, Peter the Great, who was the first to start this innovation. Was it done merely to imitate the West and better to assimilate Moscovia to Europe? Was the object really to place between the people and the throne an exalted and influential nobility? Such views fit ill with the conduct of the monarch who made all rank in the state dependent on the grade in the state service. The most likely explanation is that he wished, by the help of this new loan from Europe, to secure to his own country, then just thrown open to civilization, a rich and well informed, consequently a European and civilized class. As instituted by Peter, nothing could be more manifestly overdone and so manifestly opposed to the national customs. In order to give the new institution some chance of life, the first thing to do was to abolish and then transform it. By an *ukàz* (decree) of 1714 all the landed estates belonging to the nobility were made subject to entail, or, more correctly, were to pass to one single heir. Personal property, at that time amounting to very little in Russia, alone remained at the free disposal of the *dvorianìn* during his lifetime, and alone was to be divided among his children at his death.

This system differed from that in force in Western Europe in one essential point. Instead of ensuring the paternal estate to the eldest son, Peter the Great gave the father the faculty to appoint his heir. This entail without primogeniture introduced into the family an autocratic element : the private succession law seemed copied from the law on succession to the throne, which Peter, in memory—or in defiance—of his son Alexis, left to the choice of the sovereign. Such a system could hardly produce better consequences in private than in public life. This sort of artificial primogeniture did not work well, as it made the succession to depend on the paternal arbitrary pleasure and not on the chance of birth. Peter's *ukâz* was revoked as early as 1730, having been, during its brief existence, an occasion of endless trouble in families. The old national custom of equal division was restored, and entails, when they were once more authorized, had to be made in favor of the eldest sons, all the way down the line, as in England and Germany.[2]

Under these new conditions, entails have not yet become popular with the Russian nobility. Notwithstanding the favor with which they are apparently regarded in some high social regions, their number as yet is very small. It was of little use that an *ukâz* of the Emperor Nicolas, dated 1845, granted to all nobles the right of establishing one or more entails : the nobility never availed themselves to any extent of the prerogative. The high value of such entailed estates demanded by the law only in part accounts for the abstention. According to the terms of the *ukâz* of 1845, the land thus set apart must be entirely free from mortgage, peopled with at least 2,000 peasants, and bring an unencumbered yearly income of not less than 12,000 roubles. Thus regulated, the institution was within the reach of only the very wealthy ; but then, to be of some political efficiency, an entail should always represent something big ; else it would be to society only a useless and cumbersome sort of mortmain. The chief obstacle lies in the national custom and tradition and in the democratic instincts of the nation. The Russian spirit shows itself in this respect very different from the Polish as well as the German spirit, which latter, in the Baltic provinces subject to Russia, has hitherto succeeded in affording predominance to its aristocratic propensities.

[2] In the succession law as it now stands there is a provision which, if not exactly equivalent to entail, nearly approximates it in spirit. A landholder cannot dispose by will of landed property that has come to him or her by inheritance, but only of such as he or she may have acquired by purchase. As, however, there is no law preventing landholders to dispose of their patrimony in their lifetime, they have the resource of selling them or alienating them by deed of gift in favor of any chosen heir.

There are, indeed, partisans of the right of primogeniture—in theory—who, from the fear of breeding discord between their sons, do not dare to choose an heir from amongst them. I am acquainted with a nobleman, the owner of vast estates, and infatuated with English institutions, yet who, having three sons, and being unwilling to rob any of them, divided his property between them, entailing each lot.

Notwithstanding such examples and the encouragements given by a certain world, the custom of entails has remained in Russia an exotic plant which does not seem inclined to spread very fast. Such as it exists to-day, in a limited number of families in whom the others acknowledge no superiority, this foreign importation cannot have the political effects which, in other countries, justify its existence.* In Russia it is simply inconvenient economically and morally—a piece of public wealth withdrawn from circulation and the wealth of a privileged few artificially insured against the punishment due to improvidence or vice. The Russian *dvoriànstvo*, deprived, in the case of the great majority of its members, of any legal protection against the competition of the other classes, cannot, by merely concentrating property and perpetuating it, insure to itself the hereditary authority and independence which go to the making of genuine aristocracies.†

* In Russia proper there were lately, I am assured, not forty entailed estates. In the old Polish provinces, the government has itself founded, by means of crown demesnes and confiscated estates, small entails, in lots bringing a yearly income of 2,000 or 3,000 roubles. In this there is, evidently, less an aristocratic intention than a political expedient. The object is to forestall the sale of lands granted to Russians, and thus to retain a Russian element in the country.

† Since Alexander III. came to the throne various systems have been mooted to prevent the increase of poverty amongst the nobility and the frittering away of its lands. Some have suggested that entails should be placed within the reach of all purses; others, that the law should hinder further steps in this direction, by instituting "normal indivisible lots"; Mr. Pobiedonòstsef advises to adopt the American homestead law, and allow landholders of all classes whatever to shield estates of a certain standard value, to be determined, from division and seizure by having them entered on a special register.

BOOK VI. CHAPTER II.

How the Monopoly of Territorial Proprietorship could not Confer on the Nobility any Political Power—Historical Reasons of this Anomaly—The *Drujína* of the *Kniazes* and the Free Service of the *Boyàrs*—Ancient Conception of Property : the *Vòt-tchina* and the *Pomiéstiyé*—The Service of the Tsar the Only Source of Fortune—The Disputes about Precedence at Table—Why no Real Aristocracy could Come out of all this—The Hierarchy of Families Succeeded by the Hierarchy of Individuals—The "Table of Ranks," and the Fourteen Classes of the *Tchin*—Results of this Classification.

THIS authority, this independence of political aristocracies, the Russian nobility never possessed, not even at the still recent time when it enjoyed the exclusive privilege of owning the soil, and when those who tilled its lands were its slaves. In order to account for this apparent anomaly : a nobility in exclusive possession of the soil, yet debarred from the power which such possession imparts everywhere else, we must work our way back into the past to the roots of the Russian nobility and the Russian system of property. An aristocracy is the work of centuries, the strength of it can be tested only by the depth to which its roots have reached. Those of the Russian nobility are easily laid bare. From a remote period history shows us the *dvoriànstvo* under the two aspects it has preserved ever since : as servant of the state and as holder of the soil. History shows us the bond between the landlord and the state functionary ; it shows us how the one has always kept the other dependent and subordinate.

Among the ancient Russian Slavs there does not appear to have been either a nobility or an aristocracy of any kind. The original progenitor of the Russian *dvoriànstvo* is the *drujína*, which makes its appearance among the Slavs of Nòvgorod and Kief with Rurik and the Varangians from the North. Originally of the same race and rank as the founders of the Russian Empire, the *drujìna* were the companions of the *kniaz*, his peers. Such associations are met with everywhere ; they surround the person of the Teutonic chieftains who were the founders of all the modern European states. The word *drujìna*, from *drug*, "friend," recalls the *trustes* of the Frank kings, so that the *drujìnniki* (members of the *drujìna*) answer to the *antrustions*. Only in Russia this body preserved its primitive features longer and more faithfully, although circumstances did not allow of a feudal class springing from it.[1] What did come of it was the *boyàr*, a title which confronts us at a very early time, with the meaning of "prince's councillors," and which at first seems to have merely indicated a high rank in the *drujìna*, as suggested by the word, derived as it is from the radical *bòliè*, "more, greater," thus literally corresponding to the familiar European form of speech : "the great of the land," "*les grands.*"

The essential quality of the *drujìnnik* was that of *free* companion, voluntary associate and follower. He served the *kniaz*, he left him, at his own will and pleasure ; he was free to exchange the service of one *kniaz* for that of another. That was his only right, his only prerogative,—one, however, which was to him the safeguard of all others, for, if the *kniaz* wished to keep his *drujìna*

[1] There is nothing but what is perfectly natural and logical in the fact of no feudal class or social system having sprung up out of the occupation of Russia by the Varangians, once we admit that they were Slavs ; whereas, if the German theory is accepted, this same fact becomes an anomaly and a puzzle. *Why* should a band of Scandinavian Northmen have abstained from treating this one country in the same way that their brethren had treated all the countries in which they had obtained a footing? Because they had been invited over? So were the Saxons by the Britons—and used the invitation only as a stepping-stone to conquest. No ; nothing but race-kindred explains the difference, but *that* explains it fully and satisfactorily, with all its sequels, such as the prompt adoption by the new-comers of the lateral order of succession, so distinctively Slavic. (See Appendix to Book IV., Ch. II., p. 253.)

and his *boyàrs*, he was fain, on occasion, to ask their advice, and take it, too. This right of free service the *boyàrs*, heirs to the *drujína*, treasured long. At Moscow itself, under the first "Grand Kniazes" of the new line, there was a formula to that effect: "the *boyàrs* and free servitors " . . . ("are free to come and go," completes the saying). This freedom and choice of service, however, could last only as long as the system of appanages and the division of sovereignty. The *drujína's* ancient privilege went with the last appanages, and in fact itself contributed to bring about the fall of the appanage-principalities, without which it could not subsist. The *boyàrs* naturally made use of their freedom by tendering their services to the wealthiest and most powerful, around them they crowded. The "Grand-Kniazes" of Moscow gradually drew them to their court, and, by forsaking and consequently weakening the other *kniazes*, the *boyàrs* undermined the appanage system and themselves prepared the incorporation of the smaller principalities. The reins of sovereignty once gathered into one hand, the *boyàrs*, from companions and voluntary associates of the "Grand-Kniaz," quickly became his servants or, as they entitled themselves, his "varlets"—*kholòpy*.

The *boyàrs*, then, to begin with, lacked the base on which rested the feudal aristocracies of the West : the territorial base, a hold on the soil of the country. The *drujínnik*, attached to the person of the *kniaz*, whom he followed in all his expeditions, was bound to the soil by no permanent tie ; he lived on his share of the booty and on his prince's bounty. The very right, so jealously guarded, of free service, hindered the *drujína*, ever on the move, from settling down anywhere and striking roots into the soil. Thus the prerogative, so precious a safeguard of the *boyàrs'* personal independence, became an obstacle to their political emancipation ; another lay in the constitution of the property tenure.

Two things above all others decide a country's social status : the mode of holding property, and the laws regulating inheritances. Now in Russia the legislation on landed property lingered long in stages which it traversed rapidly in the West ; it never had either the same fixity or the same precision, nor, consequently, could it have the same importance. These differences can be accounted for by various causes, by custom, by the grade of civilization and the training of the country, by the immensity of the territory coupled with the scantiness of the population.

Among the early Russians, the right of proprietorship seems as yet ill defined, not clearly distinct from the right of sovereignty. The soil, at that time so imperfectly and scantily settled, was long regarded as a public demesne. In those vast plains, unprovided with natural divisions, it seems less natural than elsewhere to fence up the land and award the ownership of it to individuals.[2] The Russian of Moscovia inclines to a twofold conception of land-tenure, closely akin at bottom and similar. In his eyes, the land belongs to the prince, the sovereign of the country, or else to the commune, to the body of men who till it. In both cases it is public property, inalienable in principle, a common good, of which the individuals, be they noble or simple, enjoy only the use, in exchange for certain services and dues.

The *kniaz* in appanaged Russia, the tsar in unified Moscovia, considered himself as the owner, the supreme landlord, whose will is law. His quality of landlord for a long time even took precedence of his quality as sovereign : it is as landlord that the " Grand-Kniaz " of Moscow rules and manages the territory of his state, as he would a private domain. These, his own lands, the *kniaz* distributes to his *drujína*, the tsar to his *boyàrs*, as guerdon for their services. In a country of sluggish trade and

---

[2] American readers will need no explanation of this seeming inconsistency. They have only to look to their own West and Southwest for a similar state of public feeling. In Texas, it is to this day a serious matter requiring some nerve, to fence in a property and limit the general right of way through it and over and across it. Such attempts are frequently met by systematic fence-cutting ; and as both the wooden stakes and the barbed wire are expensive affairs, many a ranch-owner has desisted, especially in the remoter and more lawless districts, where public irritation is apt to take even more direct and dangerous forms than fence-cutting.

little wealth, where coined money comes in late and remains scarce always, land is for the sovereign the most handy thing to use for compensations and rewards ; it is pay for the captain, salary for the functionary, pension for the retired servant,—and in these capacities it is received, not as a perpetual, hereditary homestead ; it is neither the centre of a family, nor a focus of influence.

For the *drujína*, and later on for the nobility, landed property became a bond of dependence, a fetter—anything but an agent of independence and power. Two modes of personal land-tenure confront us in ancient Russia, and, consequently, two categories of landed property : the *vòt-tchina* and the *pomiêstiyé*—the land inherited from ancestors, the patrimony, and the land awarded by the sovereign, a grant to be enjoyed by the servants of the state.* These grants somewhat recall the fiefs or benefices of the West. In Moscovia, as in Western Europe, the land grants, conferred as recompenses for services done, early superseded the patrimonial estates ; the *pomiêstiyé* absorbed the *vòt-tchina.* From the *pomiês-tiyé* proceeds the present nobleman's estate, so that the term *pomiêsh-tchik* has come to mean merely " landlord." There was an important class of *vòt-tchinnikí*, or men who held land in their own right, and as an inheritance from their ancestors : it was the *kniazes*, the appanage princes, with whom the ownership of land sur-vived sovereignty. The Moscovite princes undertook to remedy this state of things which, under their rule, was a sort of anomaly. The Grand-Kniaz took care not to leave to his kinsfolk of the collateral lines the proprietorship of demesnes annexed to the main principality. The mediatized princes were reduced to exchange their hereditary *vòt-tchinas* against *pomiêstiyés* situated far from the regions where their fathers had reigned and of which themselves sometimes bore the name. The Englishman, Fletcher, Queen Elizabeth's envoy, noticed, as late as the end of the sixteenth

* *Vòt-tchina* or *Ot-tchina*, "patrimony," from *otiêts*, "father" ; *pomiês-tiyé*, "rural estate," from *miêsto*, "place,"—a word which, like its French and English equivalents, designates both locations and employments or functions.

century, how persistently the Moscovite tsars strove to weaken, to
eradicate so to speak, the families descended from Rurik, by tearing
them from their native soil and transplanting them into a strange
one. The only Russian families who had a territorial footing, the
only ones that seemed destined to found an aristocracy as opposed
to the "Grand-Kniaz,"—the heirs of the appanaged princes, were
thus lowered to the level of mere *pomiêsh-tchiki*, men who held
their land and fortune from the master's pleasure.

[The Moscovite tsar remained the only supreme landlord as well
as the only sovereign. The most illustrious families were scattered here and there over the land, owning no traditional homestead, no centre of local influence, similar to that singular herb
of the steppes, which the autumn winds wildly chase across the
plain haphazard in dry bunches. Between the *dvoriànstvo* and the
soil there never has been the same bond, the same association as in
the West. The nobility is not identified with the soil as in the
rest of Europe, nor with the region in which it resides. The
nobles do not bear the name of their estate or their township, as
indicated by the French *de* and the German *von* prefixed to the
names.³] Now, every aristocracy resembles the giant of the
Greek myth, who derived his strength from contact with his
mother, Earth. [This lack of localization, of centre, of territorial
basis, sufficiently accounts for the incurable feebleness of the *boyàrs*
as a class, and the failure of all aristocratical attempts in ancient
Russia. Nothing there recalls the proud dwellings of the Western
aristocracies, the inheritors of feudalism ; nothing resembles those

[² This remark, though correct on the whole, is somewhat too sweeping.
Several old princely families bear the names of their former principalities,
as the author himself remarked just now ; so, for instance, the Mossàlskys,
some branches of whom have dropped the title, were named for a small
principality, the capital of which, Mossàlsk, is even yet a flourishing third-
class city. Many noble families were originally named after their oldest or
finest estate. The frequent name-ending *sky*, which takes gender and
number, is an adjective desinence, so that "the Mossàlskys" really means
"those of Mossàlsk," and might very well be rendered by *de* or *von*
Mossàlsk.]

mediæval castles, so solidly squatting on the soil, so haughtily pervaded with the might of the families whose strongholds they were.[4]   Russian nature herself seems to repudiate these domestic fortresses, by providing neither the sites nor the materials for them—the rocky steeps whose brow they should crown, the stone of which they should be built.   The wooden house, so often burned down, so quickly worm-eaten, so easy to transport or to reconstruct, is a meet emblem of Russian life ; the very dwellings aptly represent the precariousness of the aristocracy's destinies

Owing to the *pomiêstiyé*, the Russian noble appears before us, ever since the Middle Ages, in the twofold aspect in which we see him to this day : that of owner of the soil and servant of the state. These two qualities, sometimes separated in later times, at first hold closely together ; the latter is the condition, the cause, of the former.   It is as servant of the Grand-Kniaz that the noble receives his *pomiêstiyé*, it is as such that his children retain possession of it.   The *pomiêsh-tchik* remains dependent on the sovereign who gave him his land, and, later on, when serfdom is established, gives him, in the peasants attached to the glebe, the instruments of cultivation. For the Russian noble, landed property is a bread-giver, a means of subsistence, of maintenance ; he does not settle on it, does not become attached to it, for he knows that the river of his fortunes flows from another source.

Under the old tsars, as under the successors of Peter the Great, it was in the capital, at court, that government places were obtained, that wealth and influence were to be acquired.   The fascination which Versailles under Louis XIV. exerted on the high French nobility was wielded no less imperatively by the barbarous Kremlin over Moscovite *kniazes* and *boyàrs*.   The court spirit, so opposed to the true aristocratical spirit, already per-

<hr>

[4] Families, no matter how "mighty," needed no strongholds, since they were a growth of the same soil as the people, scions of one race, unlike feudal aristocracies, which, being based on an iniquitous thing—conquest—naturally were the objects of both race-hatred and class-hatred, and consequently iu constant danger.

vaded the entire *dvoriànstvo.* In France, even when most under
control, the *noblesse* maintained the gentleman's outward dignity ;
in Russia it was not supported by ancient traditions, nor by the
conventional code of " honor, " nor by the habitual politeness
which tempers the master's arrogance and gilds over the courtier's humility. At the semi-Byzantine court of Moscow, the
tsars did not take much thought of disguising under a becoming
garment the bondage of the *boyàrs*, or the *boyàrs* of throwing a
veil over their servility. Everybody knows the saying reported
of the Emperor Paul I. by J. De Maistre or Ségur. " Sir," he is
said to have remarked to a foreigner, " I know of no *grand seig-
neur* but the man to whom I am speaking, *while* I am speaking
to him." An Ivan or a Vassíli might already have spoken in the
same way. Outside of their sovereign favor, the tsars did not
like to concede to their subjects any personal advantage, any
superiority of birth. If a subject was allowed to derive any glory
or profit from his ancestor's titles, it was from the rank obtained by
them in the service of the *velíki-kniaz*. This gave rise to a novel
hierarchy, a peculiar order of precedence, which, under the name
of *miêst-ni-tchestvo*, was in force as late as in the sixteenth and
seventeenth centuries.

At the Moscovite court, precedence gradually ceased to depend
on birth and the rank of blood ; all the subjects of the *velíki-kniaz*
were measured by one common standard—state service. The
"place occupied "—*miêsto*—was the only gauge applied to every
one's claims and titles, and the rank it conferred extended not to
individuals alone, but to their families as well. In force of the
precedence thus obtained, a man could not serve under another
who had at any time been placed under the orders of his father.
Such a system must in time have led to heredity of office. The
dignity of *boyàr*, the highest in old-time Russia, although
nominally enjoyed only for life, was in reality fast getting to pass
from father to son. Sixteen families, the historian Soloviòf tells
us, had received the right of having their members enter at once

24

the ranks of the *boyàrs.* In some fifteen others the young men began in the rank of the *okòlnik,* the second Moscovite dignity. Of these privileged families, twenty bore the title of *kniaz* and were descended from Rurik or Guedimìn. In the other families a son entered service two grades below the grade attained by his father; if he did not advance, *his* son started two grades lower still, and, if this went on, the family of course dropped into obscurity. For the regulation of each individual's rights and each family's claims, special registers or service-lists were kept.

It is easy to see how great must have been, in the eyes of the *velìki-kniazes,* the advantages of this system, out of which a new aristocracy seemed sure to grow. In Moscow itself, the side branches of the reigning house naturally enjoyed, at first, a special consideration. In order to deprive them of it, the *velìki-kniazes* began to raise their *boyàrs* to the same level as that on which stood the descendants of Rurik, reserving the right of lowering by and by both *kniazes* and *boyàrs* at one stroke. The law of precedence obliged the heirs of the dispossessed princes to renounce all tradition of independent greatness. Not otherwise than all other subjects of the tsars, they were reduced to seek lustre and nobility only in the favor and service of the sovereign. The effect of the iron rule of precedence was to merge both the former appanage-princes and the Moscovite *boyàrs* into one court nobility, holding all dignities and prerogatives from the pleasure of the tsar. In less than a century the fusion was so complete that, when the reigning dynasty became extinct, it was not from its side branches that the new head of the state was taken.

This artificial hierarchy was, in the course of nature, to make things awkward for the monarch, who at first had made himself a tool out of it. The effects proved especially disastrous in war, by strictly limiting the choice of officers, and to this the frequent defeats endured by Russia in the sixteenth and seventeenth centuries are partly to be imputed. No aristocracy could have been more exclusive, more stationary, more rife with rivalries, owing to the difficulty of settling the rights of each man and putting a stop to the altercations which occurred even on the battle-field itself. Ivan the Terrible, indeed, had, in 1550, attempted to restrain these unseemly wranglings, not only by forbidding disputes on rank to any noble who was not the head of his family, but by prohibiting all nobles, while on active military duty, to raise in the army any question of the kind with *voyevòds* (generals) of families inferior to theirs, so long as they were not themselves *voyevòds*.*

To have held its ground so long in spite of such intrinsic faults, this institution must have had some moral hold on the nation. This the historians think to find in the strong family feeling, the sort of patriarchal tie that narrowly bound together men of one blood, and made these bonds of kindred the stronger that in Moscovia there were no others. The individual could not be conceived apart from the kin, the *rod* (Latin *gens*). The honors conferred on a man were in a measure bestowed on his people also; when one of its members was raised to a certain dignity, the whole family felt lifted in rank along with him. Thus, in our days, a general does not like to serve under another general whom he ranks in grade. Death was as nothing to a Russian when his ancestral rank was in question; to yield would have been to write himself a traitor. The *kniaz* who titled himself the tsar's slave, who almost cringed out of existence before him, refused to sit at his table below a man whom he ranked by the law of precedence. In vain, the chroniclers tell us, the tsar would command him to be seated by force in the place appointed him at the table; the offended guest would resist, rise from his seat opposing violence to violence, and leave the hall, shouting that he would lose his head before he would give up the place which he could claim by right. These disputes about precedence are perhaps the only indication of the feeling of *right* in the old Moscovite nobility, or of the feeling of *honor*, both so mighty in the feudal society of the West.

* See A. Rambaud, *Histoire de Russie*, p. 241.

In spite of appearances, this order of hereditary precedence, so unfavorable to personal merit, was incapable of producing a genuine aristocracy. What was consecrated by *miêstnitchestvo* was not the rights of a class, the prerogatives of a caste : it was a set of individual, private claims, the rights of such or such a person, of such or such a family. Even among these privileged ones the order of precedence created, instead of solid bonds, an everlasting antagonism. Even for the kind of oligarchy that was benefited by it, it was a source of rivalry and discord. It made impossible the first condition of an aristocracy—homogeneousness, solidarity ; it kept each noble in strife with his equals, each family at war with its rivals. The motto of the system might have been : " Each against all." There was nothing there out of which to build up an enduring force. Accordingly, when its inconveniences became too obvious, the rival claims and competitions too complicated, it collapsed, with the consent of the very families who were benefited by it. It was abolished without effort, under the reign of one of Old Russia's feeblest tsars, Feódor Alexéyevitch, the half-brother, and, in that as in sundry other things, the pale foreshadowing of Peter the Great. All he had to do was to order the public burning of the books, to which was substituted a plain genealogical register, which, under the name of *Velvet Book* exists to this day ; an interesting relic, as it gives a census of the high nobility previous to Peter. It shows that then already the greater part of noble families, about five hundred, were of foreign or half-foreign extraction : Lithuanian, Polish, Tatar, German, etc. About a hundred were of unknown extraction, and two hundred only pure Russian, among these one hundred and sixty-four families of *kniazes*, descended from Rurik.

The natural successor of a hierarchy classified after the functions exercised by families was a hierarchy classified after the posts filled by individuals. The standard of rank remained the same—state service still. But the services of ancestors ceased to be taken into account. It was not noble birth that gave a right to certain posts, but the posts which conferred and perpetuated the titles of nobility. Every *dvorianìn* was *bound* to enter service, military or civil. Thus the entire body once again became a class strictly of servants of the state, and, the hereditary titles of some families being overlooked, there was in its midst no other classification, no other order of precedence, but those instituted by service.

Peter the Great abolished the old title of *boyàr*, which recalled antiquated claims. To the barbarous and ponderous Moscovite hierarchy he substituted the "Table of Ranks," which, in its fourteen classes, encloses to this day the entire Russian official world. The civil functions, even the ecclesiastical dignities, are there assimilated to the grades in the army and, from the ensign and "college registrar" who stand on the lowest rung of the ladder (fourteenth class), to the field marshal and the chancellor who are alone enthroned on the top, all the servants of the state are distributed in tiers, each according to his *tchin* or grade, in a double parallel series, on fourteen numbered rungs or ranks. It is not in the darkness of the Middle-Ages, under the Tatar yoke —it is in the eighteenth century, by the hand of the greatest of modern reformers, that this institution of the *tchin* was established with its Chinese sounding name, and indeed recalling that of the mandarins with their classes symbolized by buttons of different colors.[5] It was from Europe, though mainly from Germany, that Peter borrowed most of these titles, obsolete and devoid of

---

[5] What is here incidentally and jestingly remarked has been seriously advanced as proof of the alleged Mongolian origin of the Russian people and its *national* institutions (a wholesale recast of the German, bureaucratic hierarchy, with even the titles either retained or translated). Now the word *tchin* is a good Slavic radical with the meaning of "action, work," the progenitor of a vast family of derived words, which, by the aid of desinences, prefixes, suffixes, and the like, express every shade and grade of the parent idea : *pri-tchin-a,* "cause" ; *tchin-iti,* "to do, operate, repair" ; *so-tchin-itel,* "composer" ; *u-tchin-iàti,* "to cause, to make" (trouble, good, evil), etc., etc. *Tchinòvnik,* therefore, which has become the typical word for "bureaucrat," "employé," "red-tape-man," originally meant simply "a worker" (but not a manual laborer). *Tchin-òvnitchestvo* (tchindom) is the entire system or *régime,* as well as the whole class as a body.

meaning nowadays: "college registrar," "college assessor,"
"State councillor" (*Staatsrath*), "actual State councillor"
(*wirklicher Staatsrath*), "privy councillor" (*Geheimerath*), etc. ;
all foreign designations which in Russia never designated any
real functions, and which now, as from the first, represent only
a sort of civil grade, often unconnected with any duties. If the
names were foreign, however, the spirit of the institution was
thoroughly Russian, well adapted to this autocratic soil where
neither a strong aristocracy nor a free democracy ever could
thrive. In establishing his "Table of Ranks," the great imitator
of Europe only took the old Moscovite traditions and tricked out
in modern garb the policy of the old tsars.

During a century and a half Peter's "Fourteen Classes"
have made of Russia a sort of army in which each man was
ranked according to his grade. Such a hierarchy could be good
for a period of transition, for a people still full of prejudices, poor
in trade and industry, at a time when the only road to greatness
was the service of the state, when public functions were the only
school of a higher culture. By tying down the nobles to service, Peter made of the nobility the instruments and support of
a reform which in itself did not inspire it with much sympathy.*
There was some sense in the thing when the men enrolled in the
fourteen classes were alone possessed of the rights of freemen,
when a diplomat laughingly proposed, as a means of freeing
Russia from corporal punishment, to raise the whole people to the
fourteenth (lowest) class. In a more advanced state of society,
with a civilization so varied and manifold, which opens so many
outlets to intellect and activity, such an artificial classification
according to services becomes an idle hindrance. It is, to say
the least, an anachronism. At a time in which private initiative
under all its forms, in which science and art, commerce and

---

* A great stroke of genius which more than counterbalances any drawbacks
or faults. Peter usually had a choice of evils, and his greatness showed in
choosing the evil from which good was likely to come in some form.

industry, hold so large a place, the men on public duty are not always the most useful or notable servants of their country. It is getting more and more awkward to class talents, impossible to stamp each man's rank and merits with an external sign, a figure. There is no longer an accepted weight to weigh minds, no longer a legal, official standard, one common measure suiting so many different capacities. The effort is vain to assimilate to military grades professions naturally independent and rebellious to every kind of hierarchy, or careers from their nature subject to all the hazards of competition.

In Russia, the habit of fitting all things into the fourteen pigeon holes of the "Table of Ranks" is such that not even the arts have escaped it. The actors and singers of the imperial theatres are officially divided into several categories, each having its own particular rank and rights. Hence the ridiculous Russian titles and designations, such as "candidate," "commerce councillor," "manufacture councillor," (German, *Kandidat*, *Kommerzienrath*, *Manufakturrath*),—appellations which raise a merchant with a fortune of several millions to the level of the seventh or eighth class, *i. e.*, to the rank of a major or lieutenant-colonel. With such a method it would have been but logical to create generals of commerce, and we ought to have marshals of science or poetry. There was a story current at the time I was travelling in the East, of the Sultan's having raised his physician to the rank of general of division to reward him for having cured him of an anthrax. Nominations, or rather promotions, of this kind are habitual in Russia ; the *Official Journal* is full of them. It would be difficult to count the physicians who have a *tchin ;* there are among them "actual state councillors " (fourth class), answering to the rank of major-general, "privy councillors" (third class), ranking with generals of division. The same with scientists, professors, writers ; tricked out in the same titles as administrators or magistrates, they may advance *pari passu* with them in the civil career.

All these promotions in the line of the *tchin* do not hinder others in that of imperial "orders." There are five or six of these orders of knighthood, some more, and some less sought after, mostly divided into two, three, even four classes. There are the orders of St. Andrew, of St. Alexander Nevsky, of Ste. Anna; of St. Vladímir, of St. George, not to mention those of St. Stanislaus and the White Eagle, originally Polish orders. Since the last war in Bulgaria, one more order has been invented, for services to the wounded, the order of the Red Cross, which the empress distributes to ladies. There was already a decoration specially reserved to women, the order of Ste. Catherine. There is besides, for the army in time of war, the sword of honor with eulogy; for civilians or for generals in time of peace, there are diamond rings with the imperial monogram, and at all times golden snuff-boxes set with diamonds and adorned with the emperor's portrait or monogram. Few are the high functionaries who cannot show on their bric-a-brac shelves one of these imperial snuff-boxes. The ladies of high rank also can receive analogous distinctions; no one has read memoirs on the court of St. Petersburgh but knows about the "maid of honor with portrait."

Over and above the *tchin* and the orders of knighthood, Russia possesses quite a number of social distinctions conferred somewhat indiscriminately and therefore comparatively little prized. These are the court charges, graduated after the manner of the "Table of Ranks," and, like the titles in the civil service, for the most part purely honorary and nominal. To the "state councillors" and "privy councillors," "actual" or not, who never assist at any council, correspond the "court masters" (*Hofmeister*), who have nothing to do with the palace ceremonial. In no other country are the means of classing men, of stamping merit and putting it, so to speak, at a premium, so numerous, so varied, and—so unproductive. If the fruits of this system of official encouragement are not more plentiful, the fault lies only with its natural barrenness.

In such a scale of classification, science and public instruction, which has always been one of the imperial government's chief cares, could not be ignored. University degrees accordingly confer a *tchin*, the graduating examination at the end of a gymnasium or college course entitles to the lowest class of the bureaucratic hierarchy. Thus, by the fact of entering the university, the student already has his foot on the ladder, and each diploma raises him one rung. As it is work which, with the assistance of the "Table of Ranks," gives access to places and opens the ranks of the nobility, it may be said that, rank depending on grade, and that again on success in study, the entire Russian hierarchy is but the hierarchy of labor and knowledge, and that the nobility which results therefrom is a nobility of knowledge and culture. Such, indeed, is the case, and this it is that justifies the *tchin*—or rather justified it in the past. Such a method, though good in a school or one particular career, is inadequate, as every artificial hierarchy must be, when applied to an entire society. Such attempts at numbering and pigeonholing men and merits have almost always missed their aim ; or if, exceptionally, they seemed to succeed, it was only by swathing society in uncomfortable bands.

We can match the hierarchy of the *tchin* with examples taken from Asia—for instance, China and Turkey. We can even find in modern Europe a few more or less analogous institutions, such as the first Napoleon's Legion of Honor and his nobility. The latter, in its fundamental conception, was much like Peter's "Table of Ranks." The founder of the "Légion d'Honneur" also claimed that he would enroll, dispose in a given order, all the social forces of the nation : but, having to do with a later and more advanced stage of society, he was even less successful than Peter the Great; his institution survived as a mere order of knighthood, with no greater social value than any other decoration. All goes to show that, in our state of civilization, it is not any easier to invent a rational way of classing individuals than to do so for families. Any such hierarchy can have no other type than the service of the state, no other standard than public functions ; therefore it can, in the end, only encourage place-hunting and correspondingly discourage free labor, whether intellectual or material, and weaken the great mainspring of our civilization —individual enterprise.

The *tchin*, which makes rank to depend on post and post on merit, appears at first sight to be an altogether democratic institution ; it is so, in certain ways ; in others it is, on the contrary, a brake to any kind of healthy, free democracy. The practical perfection of the *tchin* and the fourteen classes would be the triumph of *tchinòvnism*—the exclusive and absolute reign of bureaucracy, to the profit of despotism and the detriment of democracy and aristocracy both. And in the inner workings of this sovereign bureaucracy, this system, which from afar appears so favorable to personal merit, is so in reality to routine, sloth, and mediocrity. It can be asserted without injustice that the "Table of Ranks," in the end, has lowered the level of state service which it was instituted to raise.

In the transformation which Russia is undergoing, the *tchin* naturally forfeits much of its importance ; its sway is less tyrannical, and liberties are sometimes taken with it. The new provincial institutions, the electoral system founded on the free choice of persons, the representative system founded on the appointment of a representative by his peers—these things are not easy to conciliate with the "Table of Ranks," and will sooner or later make short work of it. The extension of public liberties will leave both the sovereign and the country free to choose the servants of the state outside of all categories, and will destroy the privileges of the *tchin*, which has been substituted for the privilege of birth.[1] The suppression of the "Table of Ranks" has been spoken of already, both under Alexander II. and Alexander III. If it has not been done yet, it is probably due to reluctance to change old

[1] See Appendix to this chapter.

habits and to the dread of having to pay higher salaries to functionaries whom it will no longer be so easy to satisfy with titles. There also is perhaps a lurking fear that such a measure may prove too profitable to favoritism and nepotism.

APPENDIX TO BOOK VI., CHAPTER II. (See note 6, p. 374.)

That the system, faithfully described in this chapter, could be so easily adopted and so promptly acclimated, is owing to the fact that, however clumsy in the application, it appeals in principle to the inborn, sturdy democratism of the Russian nature, which boasts that "it has no nonsense about it." "Be a worker, not a drone ; service and knowledge, not birth," is the demand made of each member of the community ; "what is he?" not "who is he?" the ever ready question. Both these feelings—respect for personal merit, contempt for claims based on the achievements of others— are embodied in the famous apologue, *The Geese*, of our great fabulist, Krylóf, as perfect a representative and exponent of the Russian spirit, as Lafontaine, with whom, both as writer and man, he has remarkable affinities, was of the national French spirit. We will give the apologue complete (in Mr. Ralston's translation) for our readers' delectation and to complete their comprehension of the complicated subject treated in the present chapter.

"A peasant, with a long rod in his hand, was driving some geese to a town where they were to be sold ; and, to tell the truth, he did not treat them over-politely. In hopes of making a good bargain, he was hastening on so as not to lose the market-day (and when gain is concerned, geese and men alike are apt to suffer). I do not blame the peasant; but the geese talked about him in a different spirit, and, whenever they met any passersby, abused him to them in such terms as these :

"'Is it possible to find any geese more unfortunate than we are? This mujik harasses us so terribly, and chases us about just as if we were common geese. The ignoramus does not know that he ought to pay us reverence, seeing that we are the noble descendants of those geese to whom Rome was once indebted for her salvation, and in whose honor even feast-days were specially appointed there.'

"'And do you want to have honor paid you on that account?' a passer-by asked them.

"'Why, our ancestors——'

" 'I know that—I have read all about it; but I want to know this—of what use have you been yourselves?'

" 'Why, our ancestors saved Rome!'

" 'Quite so; but what have you done?'

" 'We? Nothing.'

" 'Then what merit is there in you? Let your ancestors rest in peace —they justly received honourable reward; but you, my friends, are only fit to be roasted!'

"It would be easy to make this fable still more intelligible; but I am afraid of irritating the geese."

Krylôf (Ivan Andréyevitch), who flourished under Alexander I. and Nicolas (1768–1844), was much seen at court, where he was a greater favorite with the sovereigns than with the courtiers, and often read by imperial request his latest productions, of which the satire or pathos was brought out by the inimitable humor of his diction. There is a literary tradition that when he thus gave *The Geese* to a select and only too appreciative audience, he read or rather spoke the two last lines as a spontaneous afterthought, and, pausing after the first, to send a circular glance round the company, added the second with a malice of eye and lip which did not lessen the number of his enemies.

BOOK VI. CHAPTER III.

Effects of the " Table of Ranks " on the Nobility—The Functionary and the Landlord, Formerly Combined in the Person of the *Dvorianìn*, Frequently Dissevered in the Nobility of our Day—Hence Two Opposite Tendencies: Radicalism and *Tchinòvnism*—Revolutionary Dilettanteism —High Society and the Aristocratic Circles—The French Language as a Social Barrier—Cosmopolitism and Lack of Nationality.

ON the Russian nobility the more than secular rule of the "Table of Ranks " has laid an impress which not even the abolition of this official hierarchy would avail to remove. The strict dependence to which it reduced the entire nobility was by no means the only result of this institution, which estranged it from the other classes, and especially from the soil, the only natural basis of all lasting influence. The service of the state drove the nobility from their estates to launch them in the army or the administration, in the cities in every case, and detained the better part in the capitals, where alone rank and importance were attainable. The rich landowner, compelled to start out on the conquest of a *tchin*, left his property in the hands of stewards who frequently ruined him by their ill management or their dishonesty. The institution which bound the *dvoriànstvo* to the service of the state thus at the same time loosened his ties to soil and hearth, and did much to cast him adrift. The "Table of Ranks " robbed of all social influence the very nobility it had created. Hence the loathing of a portion of this same *tchin*-born nobility for the parent that kept them in a perpetual nonage and forbade all thoughts of emancipation.

According to the law, as established by Peter the Great, a family which, for two successive generations, abstained from public service, forfeited its nobiliary rights. Peter III. set the *dvoriànstvo* free from this obligation. Nowadays, if most nobles still enter service, they stay there but a short time. After a few years of youth spent in the Guards or in a civil career, such gentlemen as are endowed with an independent fortune devote themselves freely to study or pleasure, to work or rest. This is how we can at present make out two vocations, two different types of men in the nobility, and, consequently, two parallel currents of ideas. As not every noble landowner nowadays remains in "the service," as not every public servant obtains landed property, as well as nobility, the two qualities, the two social functions, formerly united and co-ordinate in the body of the *dvoriànstvo*, have now been severed and have entered a stage of more or less overt antagonism. Since they are no longer the two aspects of one and the same man, the landlord and the functionary, the *pomiêsh-tchik* and the *tchinòvnik* occasionally become rivals.

In the great landowner, free of his time and fortune, new aspirations are coming to light, aristocratic pretensions, more or less discreetly advanced in the name of the rights of culture and property, ostensibly based on conservative considerations, on the interests of social order and the throne. In the functionary, held in the dependence of service by lack of means, survives the old-time spirit of the *tchin*, occasionally surging up into instincts of equality, of levelling, more or less openly acknowledged, in the name of the rights of intellect and personal merit, and ostensibly based on the love of progress, on the interests of the state and the people. Of these two men, the former is naturally more of an aristocrat, and frequently more of a liberal ; the latter more of a democrat, but also more of a martinet.

The two rivals are both quite right : they represent and embody two tendencies which are at odds in every society. The one—the great landowner—has on his side and in his favor the apprehensions inspired by the instability of affairs and the revolutions of Western Europe ; also the conservative scares and secret influences at court. The other—the functionary—has the advantage that he represents more faithfully the national tradition and at the same time follows the most manifest drift of modern civilization. The *tchinòvnik* throws in the face of the landlord, with his aristocratical pretensions, a shortness of memory as to the fact that he himself, as a rule, holds his rights and lands only from state service. The Russian nobility, indeed, such as it was fashioned by history, is a sort of double-faced Janus : on one side the face of the noble and landowner ; on the other the face of the functionary or bureaucrat ; and when one face looks at itself in the glass, it is tempted to forget "the other" at the back.

In the eyes of certain Russian aristocrats the bureaucrat has grown into the natural adversary, the hereditary foe. It is him, it is *tchinòvnism*, as embodied in Nicolas Miliùtin, that a number of landholders hold responsible for the sacrifices imposed on the former lords by the liberation of the serfs. The *tchinòvnik*, especially of humble origin, frequently taken out of the rank of seminarists—the class which one of its noble adversaries scornfully refers to as the "crimped and curled proletariate,"—is the target at which are aimed all the sarcasms of a world which yet does not itself always keep out of the service. And yet, as a witty writer, Samárin remarks : "The noble is just a bureaucrat in a dressing-gown, while the bureaucrat is a noble in uniform." This historical truth does not always prevent mutual envy and ill-will between the two, although, even yet, they are often one man ; the distinction lies between the needy *tchinòvnik* and the wealthy *pomièsh-tchik*. In the higher nobility there is a marked tendency to restore the close union of landholder and functionary, but in a manner the reverse of the old Moscovite tradition, *i. e.*, by making authority and power dependent on property, not rank and property on state service.

The aristocracy numbers its most determined opponents amidst the legal gentry, which would seem to be naturally subservient to it. Too numerous, poor, and mixed to expect a share of aristocratical privileges, the bulk of the nobility does not forgive such of its members as dream of prerogatives in which all could not share. Out of the *tchin* and small land gentry issued a needy and envious nobility, a semi-cultured proletariate which civilization has endowed with more wants and covetous longings than means of enjoyment or instruction. In Russia, this class, the most restless and embittered all the world over, is the offspring of either the nobility or the clergy, and comes out of the government offices or the church seminaries. The students who are so fond of dazzling the eyes of the ignorant with the glitter of an approaching golden age unshackled by property or family, are mostly nobles ; so are nearly all the young men who go about distributing among the peasants and laboring-men revolutionary primers and catechisms. Nobles, too, are the emigrants or refugees who, in the clandestine press of the interior or in the Russian publications edited abroad, preach to their countrymen revolution and socialism ; and nobles are the greater number of those champions of demagogy of both sexes, at home or abroad, who set themselves up as apostles of nihilism.

It is not only on the lower rungs of the social ladder, on the threshold, so to speak, of official nobility, that these radical tendencies confront us, but frequently much higher, in families placed by rank or fortune above the jealousy and cupidity proper to the lower middle classes. Nor is this merely the result of a national propensity towards theorizing radicalism, or of the blind and reckless generosity natural to youth, which, all over the world, hankers after risky and advanced ideas, as those that appear to it the noblest and bravest. To look closely into the matter, this phenomenon is not as singular as it may seem at first sight. More than one Western country might, at certain given epochs, have supplied material for observations of the same kind. As long as revolutionary ideas still retain something speculative about them, as long as they have not passed the test of practice, they easily find partisans in the midst of the very classes that are marked for their victims. Much painful experience is needed to teach the young of the nobility and the *bourgeoisie* to resist its inclination towards all things new, towards overbold thought and humanitarian dreamings. Russia, until quite lately, had been almost entirely spared these costly lessons ; but then nations, like individuals, seldom benefit by any but their own experience. Men who have never felt the earth quake under their feet, gaily engage on a run amid the misty mazes of theory. On the thick ice of northern winters, which he never heard crack beneath his tread, the skater fearlessly indulges in the maddest flourishes. In this respect Russian society more than once presented the same spectacle as the French aristocracy just before the Revolution, so that many of the traits in the brilliantly life-like picture presented in Taine's *Ancien Régime* apply perfectly to the society of St. Petersburgh during the eighteenth century. There, too, the *beau monde* for quite a while loved to play with ideas : " good society " juggled the more freely with the most inflammable or explosive of them, that they were not likely to burst on the thickly carpeted drawing-room floors, and that the walls of the splendid private palaces held no hiding-places for combustibles.

There was another reason besides to all this boldness and recklessness. The nobility, the cultivated class, while trained to the customs and ways of thinking of Europe, could not freely practise them after the European manner, and therefore felt constrained and oppressed in the very country where it held so privileged a position. Superior education only made the moral inferiority of Russian life more keenly felt. In Russia as it was before the late reforms, a cultivated man felt the lack of air and elbow-room ; he easily passed from a state of morbid depression to one of no less morbid exaltation,—from the numbness of prostration to the high pressure of fever. True, the reforms have greatly lightened the social atmosphere ; yet civilized man cannot always fill his lungs to their full capacity ; he often experiences a vague and irritating feeling of discomfort. There as everywhere else it is reserved to

25

the growth and free practice of public liberties to weaken the revolutionary spirit.

It was impossible that, in the midst of so accessible, so motley an assemblage as this Russian *dvoriànstvo*, there should not be deposited and crystallize a narrower, more exclusive society, jealously keeping aloof from its surroundings, anxious to rise above the *plebs* of the *tchin*, which threatened a general levelling. In this sense, there does exist an aristocracy in Russia, based on manners, position, family—an aristocracy of the drawing-room, of which the members know one another not by titles and heraldic bearings, but by connections and bringing up.   For even in this exalted sphere, so full of the consciousness of its own superiority, caste-spirit and birth-prejudice are less controlling than in most other monarchies.   There are in it old families and families of recent date,—large fortunes and mere competences.   Birth, wealth, position, intellect—all these, to be sure, smooth the way into this social sanctum, but none of these things alone can open it with unfailing key.   This drawing-room aristocracy is the more exclusive, or rather the more guardedly reserved, that, having no legally determined boundaries, it is compelled to defend the line it has itself drawn.   Almost everywhere in Europe one of the results of victorious democracy, next to the overthrow of the old landmarks, is to raise around " society " gossamer barriers woven of threads so light and delicate as to be imperceptible to the vulgar eye, and these are of all the most indestructible.   Nowhere, perhaps, does this art of keeping up real distinctions in the midst of nominal equality, an art, which marks distances so effectively,—nowhere does this science of society manners and conventionalities reign supreme as in Russia.[1]

Could this not stand just as it is for a picture and explanation of American society,—the "upper ten thousand " of it? It is thus that, by piercing into the essence and core of things, one gradually discovers the innumerable subtle affinities that are at the root of the strange and, to the unphilosophical observer, puzzling sympathy which mutually draws two seemingly so different countries as Russia and America.

The Russian nobility prides itself on its culture and takes pleas-ure in referring to itself as "the cultivated class;" the "upper crust" improves on this claim and pushes culture to the verge of hyper-refinement. The very manner in which European civiliza-tion was introduced into Russia laid it open to a twofold danger : it could not but remain for a long time an alien and a surface thing. These two defects were historically unavoidable, and the national bent, the aristocratic instincts, the desire to operate a reaction against the *tchin*, intensified and confirmed them. The more imminently the dominant class was threatened with a flood of *parvenus*, the more it strove to keep them at a distance ; the easier official assimilation, the harder social assimilation was made to them. Thence the great importance attached to foreign languages, especially to French.

French in Russia was not so much an instrument of study, a means of instruction, as a sign of higher education. It was the polished language, that of society and the drawing-room, the standard and test of culture and "tone." For this, it was not sufficient to understand French and speak it like any foreign language ; purity of accent, ease of elocution, were accounted essentials ; for French was before and above everything else a *shibboleth*, a token of social free-masonry, a barrier to keep in-truders out. No society, no aristocracy legally open to all, could possibly barricade itself more efficiently. French became a sort of society passport, without which no naturalization papers could be obtained in the higher circles. There would have been no great harm in that, but for the fact that the habitual use of a foreign language became the sign and symbol of foreign habits, ideas, and affectations.

In the spheres naturally the most aristocratic, this anti-national craze, confirmed and transmitted by heredity, threatened to develop into a constitutional taint. The high-and middling nobility, the cultivated class, prompted by fashion, "tone," ("good form" it would be called now), by exclusivism, widened the chasm that separated it from the masses, not perceiving that it was aggravating the disease of modern Russia, not realizing that, for classes as well as individuals, isolation means weakness. With face forever turned toward the frontier, Russian society ended by not seeing Russia any more, or, at all events, not comprehending her. Open to every breath from the West, it grew cosmopolitan and lived as an alien in its own native land, somewhat after the fashion of an European colony in the midst of barbarians. By sheer contact with the West, by dint of dyeing and anointing itself with imported ideas, the man of the world lost all trace of national coloring ; his success in society was in proportion as the Russian was most completely obliterated in him. Brought up by French or German tutors, in ignorance or contempt of all that was indigenous, the heir of the Moscovite *boyàrs* came to look on his father's tongue as a boors' dialect, or rather *patois*. " I have been married twenty-five years," said a Russian gentleman to me, " and I am not sure that I have addressed my wife in Russian twice." The time is not so far behind us, when almost any well-bred man might have said as much. This contempt for the Russian people was extended to the Russian books, which was a great hindrance to the growth of the young national literature,—a drawback which, added to the craze of servile imitation, accounts for its prolonged, pallid infancy.[2]

[2] So far from being overdrawn, this sketch gives an inadequate idea of the state of things it depicts and of which even we of my generation were the victims in childhood, especially the girls. No fault was so severely punished as a word spoken in Russian to anybody but the servants. The discovery of a book of Zola in a convent cell could scarcely cause greater horror and commotion than that of an inoffensive Russian book in a schoolgirl's room. I myself learned Russian when I was about ten or eleven, fluently using French, German, Italian, and English, and spoke it at first with a purely French accent which was the delight of my elders, and which only my own common-sense made me feel ashamed and get rid of, to their great concern. I was just past twenty when I *discovered* my country, my people, their history, and literature. It was on returning from an almost life-long residence abroad, in the middle of the sixties, when I found our national Renaissance in full swing. The revelation was dazzling and my intense joy in it only comparable to my sorrow—remorse it could not be, not being my own doing —for the time and all I had lost.

The nobility at length felt how debilitating for Russian civilization, especially for the so-called, "cultivated class," was this unnatural denationalization and this superficial cosmopolitism. Already under Nicolas a marked reaction took place in literature, in public opinion, in private feeling, although not yet in the ideas and manners, and, like all reactions, it soon tipped over to the opposite extreme. Under the influence of the Slavophils, the Russian name, the Russian language, the Russian man were restored to honor. Some fanatics or eccentrics, like the poet Khomiakòf, went the length of parading the sleeveless *armiàk* and the *kaftàn*. Nationality, so long scorned and trodden down, became universally glorified. Fashion and the readiness of society to take up "crazes" had much to do with this sudden revulsion. But even where conversion is sincerest it is often unenlightened and inconsistent. After having so long held aloof and played at cosmopolitism, the higher classes could not all in a moment divest themselves of the second nature which they had so laboriously cultivated. After having kept themselves estranged from the people for a century and a half, they could not clear at one bound the chasm which they had so long and patiently dug with their own hands.

And now the two uneven halves of the nation are still morally estranged, to their mutual harm and that of the country and of civilization. There are only two ways out of such a situation. One is to recognize officially, to sanction legally the scission of the two classes, by placing the one under the other's guardianship. The other is to create an intermediate class for the purpose of bringing the other two together and serving as link between them. Of these two alternatives, the first has in its favor the aristocratical theories and artificial combinations which, in one or other form, tend to place the people under the exclusive control of the nobility and of the landlords ; the other has for it the facts, the drift of civilization, and the natural creation of a middle class, a *bourgeoisie*, of which the nucleus is already formed.

BOOK VI.   CHAPTER IV.

Personal Privileges of the Nobles, and Prerogatives of their Order—What
Emancipation has Taken from the Nobles besides Landed Property—
The *Dvoriànstvo* Threatened with Gradual Expropriation—How, though
not Despoiled, it Practically Lost all its Privileges—Importance of the
Prerogatives Conferred on the "Nobiliary Assemblies" by Catherine II.
—Why they did not Manage to Benefit by them—Has Russia the Ele-
ments of a Political Aristocracy?

A NOBILITY can have two kinds of privileges : personal, which
each noble enjoys individually ; collective, belonging to all the
nobles as a body.   The law awards the Russian *dvoriànstvo*
prerogatives of both kinds, both greatly reduced in our day by
the extension of public liberty.   The nobility, as a rule, has not
been despoiled of its rights ; but that which was the privilege of
one class has become the right of all.   Its prerogatives, collective
or personal, the *dvoriànstvo* held not from the will of the rest of
the nation, nor from its own achievements or ancestral conquests,
but wholly and entirely as a gift of sovereign bounty, and they
were all comparatively recent still when they were extended to
the rest of the nation.   Before Catherine II. the nobility had no
sort of corporative rights, and if the nobles did claim some individual rights, they were ill-defined and ill-observed.

The nobles were not only, like all the rest, subject to the
sovereign's will and pleasure ; there was no coarse freak of whim
or impertinent fancy which the sovereigns or their favorites
scrupled to indulge in at the expense of members of the most
illustrious families.   The reign of Anna Ivànovna and Biron is
full of instructive anecdotes to the point.   The inheritors of the
greatest names could be compelled to play clown for the delec-

tation of the court. One day, wishing to punish a Prince Galìtsyn for some trifling misdemeanor, the Empress Anna ordered him to personate a hen, and the descendant of the Yagellons actually had publicly to squat on a heap of straw and make believe to hatch eggs, imitating the clucking of a sitting hen. Another time her fit of pleasantry was not so harmless, when she forced the same Galìtsyn to wed an idiotic old woman. Such freaks show what respect, what authority the high nobility enjoyed in the middle of the eighteenth century, under the reign of the very princess whose power those same Galìtsyns and the Dolgorùkis had at one time attempted to limit in favor of a kind of oligarchy.

Up to the last reforms of the reign of Alexander II. the nobles were in the personal enjoyment of only three main privileges, and even these they had long shared with the so-called "privileged classes," *i. e.*, with the clergy and the merchants. They were exempt from military conscription, from direct or poll-taxes, and from corporal chastisement. Of these three immunities the first fell away in 1876, when universal military service was introduced ; the last has been extended to all classes ; the second also has already ceased to be a privilege, the abolition of the poll-tax having been decided on by Alexander III. For the *mujik* as well as for the noble landowner, a property tax is to be substituted to the tax on persons. The Russian nobility has no immunity from taxes. In the times of serfdom, the poll-tax indirectly fell on the nobility, who were responsible for their serfs, and now that their estates are curtailed by the emancipation, they are directly subject to taxation. The burdens that weigh on the noble land-owners are even now, it is true, less heavy than those borne by the peasant communes ; but this difference comes partly from the difference in the constitution of property, partly from a just consideration for the interests of the nobility, which has been sorely tried by the emancipation itself and the succeeding period of transition. As to the exemption from corporal punishments, now extended to all classes, two things astonish one : that it should so

long have been a privilege, and that the nobility should have ac·
quired it so late. Scarcely a century did it rejoice in it, and it
was put in possession of it only some twenty years sooner than the
town-merchants. It was Peter III., Catherine II's husband and
predecessor, who, in 1762, delivered it from the cudgel and the
knut. As long, however, as the rods were not suppressed for all,
even the noble was not wholly safe from them. To make him
liable to corporal chastisement, nothing more was needed than a
condemnation which degraded him from his nobiliary rights, or
an order to serve in the army as common soldier.

In the same way as the immunity from corporal punishment,
the greatest part of the rights and privileges ensured by the code
to the nobility are of a nature to be easily extended to all the
other classes of the nation, which shows that they were not, in
reality, nobiliary prerogatives, but only freemen's rights, such as
a civilized country recognizes as belonging to all its inhabitants.
The *dvorianìn,* says the law, cannot be, without a trial, deprived of
life, or of the rights belonging to his class, nor yet of his possessions. Such articles of the law help one to comprehend the
notions about nobility of such Slavs as have remained untouched
by the passion of imitating the aristocratic West. The Serbs, for
instance, since their deliverance from the Ottoman yoke, take
pride in saying that all Serbs are now noble, which means—freemen. In this sense, the Russians will soon all be nobles too.

The real, substantial privilege of the Russian nobility, that
which, belonging to that class alone, gave it a distinctive character, was the right of owning "inhabited lands," *i. e.,* lands peopled with serfs. The emancipation has carried away that privilege
along with serfdom, but could not quite obliterate the traces of
what had existed for nearly three centuries. To this prerogative
the nobility owed, down to our day, the almost exclusive monopoly
of landed property, individual and hereditary. The day after the
emancipation there were, outside of the lands it retained in its
hands, only those just made over to the emancipated peasants,

and the immense "state demesnes." In every-day language the term "landlord"—*pomiêsh-tchik*—is still synonymous with "noble,"—*dvorianìn*. It is from this quality of individual landlord that the *dvoriànstvo* derives one of its chief claims on the sympathies of Western countries, where the same mode of land tenure is customary. Compared to the *mujik*, who merely has the use of collective property, the *pomiêsh-tchik* may be looked on as the representative of personality, of modern individualism, as well as of European culture. It is also from the same source that, in renovated Russia, the nobility derives its importance as well as its claims. It has to-day what it lacked in the Middle Ages : a basis of influence in the soil ; and it is on this relatively recent basis that the theorizing partisans of hierarchy would like to rise, for the good of the richer nobility, a sort of landed aristocracy. What is needed to give such views as these a chance of success, to insure, in this rural and agricultural country, the rule of the great landlord, the noble *pomiêsh-tchik ?* In the first place, property should be more stable and the monopoly of it should be guaranteed to the nobility in the future as it was in the past. Now there is nothing of the kind. With serfdom and the designation "inhabited lands," fell the only barrier which defended the noble landlord against the encroachments of the other classes.

But for this protection, but for this sort of legal prohibition, the greater part of the land would have slipped from the *dvoriànstvo's* hold long ago,—as proved by the burdened condition of landed property on the very eve of the emancipation. In 1859, nigh on two thirds of it ($\frac{65}{100}$) were mortgaged in the *lombards*, as the state credit institutions are called, and the remaining third was in great part mortgaged to private persons. Had there been in Russia at the moment of the abolition of serfdom, a numerous and wealthy middle class, the first order of the state would have been despoiled of the greater portion of its estates. As it was, the absence of competition, the scarcity of available capital, the penury of the peasants —all these favorable conditions did not avail to maintain it in the possession of all the lands that were not taken from it legally. It has been calculated that the nobility lost one fourth of its estates since the emancipation,—in some provinces even more. The Emperor Alexander III., to help them out, instituted a special bank, which lends on land at reduced rates of interest. Unfortunately, such facilities often prove ruinous temptations : the easier to borrow, the deeper the nobility gets into debt.

There is then already a noticeable tendency in landed property to change hands, to the prejudice of the *dvoriànstvo*. To rescue its old land monopoly, there is really but one thing to do : to entail the lands and thus make them inalienable. The expedient would be unfailing, and there have been men bold enough to propose it. But such a proceeding applied to the totality or generality of private estates would only tend to propagate the inconveniences inseparable from entails and to paralyze property, capital, in fact the country. Individuals may yield to the temptation of placing their name and their descendants beyond the reach of ruin and above the chances of competition ; a modern government will never allow one class to insure to itself for all time the possession of the soil. And yet, in Russia as elsewhere, the legal and indissoluble bond of entail is the one thing that can insure to the nobility this exclusive possession. No longer protected against itself and others by the impossibility of selling to members of another class, nor by the system of succession, the Russian nobility is threatened with slow expropriation in favor of a middle class or of the peasantry, both of which lay hands on a larger share of the lands each year at its expense ; and, together with the monopoly of individual land-holding, it will lose its distinctive character, all social preponderance,—nay, all reason for existing at all. *

* Another thing contributes to lessen the influence of the nobility : it is the small number of wealthy landlords residing on their own estates. So that certain political writers with aristocratical tendencies—Prince Mieshtchersky for example,—while claiming the principal local functions for the landed nobility of each given district, propose, more or less seriously, that the nobles should be bound to reside on their lands during a certain portion of each year.

After the ancient prerogatives have fallen off one by one, or degenerated into fictions, what will remain to this nobility, shorn of privileges, to distinguish it from the rest of the nation? Very little. So little, that the question obtrudes itself: what would the nobles lose if the nobility were to be suppressed? Nobody intentionally raised a hand against it; nobody thought of despoiling it in any way; yet the *dvoriànstvo* saw nearly all its rights drop from it—by the mere fact of the changes that took place around it. The nobility practically found itself abrogated by the reforms of Alexander II., without being so much as mentioned by name. If it is still standing, it is as the tree stands, around whose foot the soil has been dug up, touching its roots by mistake, so that it finds no support in the loosened earth against the first gust of storm wind. Nobility will end, in Russia as in other countries, by being a mere honorary distinction, without social importance or political meaning, a bauble to flatter vanity, with value all the smaller for being more common and having fewer external signs to facilitate mutual recognition. In reality the *dvoriànìn* has only one personal privilege left, that of enjoying certain facilities for entering the service of the state and for making his way therein more rapidly.* To this latter advantage the nobility will perhaps cling the more tenaciously that the others are slipping from them. Despoiled of their prerogatives and threatened with expropriation, the impoverished *dvoriànstvo* will have no other refuge left but their original cradle—state service and *tchin*. And even on this ground, the privileges still accorded them by law and custom will gradually fall away before the levelling of culture or the demands of equality. Service, like other careers, will have no

* This privilege draws after it another analogous one—that of getting their children admitted into certain educational establishments, such as the Alexander Lyceum in St. Petersburgh, or the Smòlnoy Institute of Noble Damsels. In 1880 the Alexander Lyceum, until then reserved for the more ancient portion of the nobility, was thrown open to the entire *dvoriànstvo, i. e.,* to the children of all state functionaries of a certain rank.

rights left, only favors; no advantages save such as everywhere go with credit and position.*

Personal privileges, inherent to the individual and the family, may constitute a nobility; but it needs common prerogatives, exercised in a body by the entire class of nobles, to make an aristocracy. Of such prerogatives the *dvoriànstvo*, though weak, possessed several—important ones, too. True, they were no bequest of a remote past, nor a revered survival of ancient national customs, but only an imitation of foreign things, a tardy copy of already antiquated models. Nothing of the kind was known to old Russia, where the servants of the state had no rights save such as they derived from the service itself. As their personal privileges, so their corporative rights were a gracious, free concession from the crown. This, again, was Catherine's doing. Carried away by the liberal spirit of the end of the eighteenth century, in the interval between the American War of Independence and the French Revolution, she endowed the Russian nobility with novel rights and made over to that class, the only cultivated one at the time, the only one capable of exercising some political discretion, an important part in the administration of justice. Until this date there were nobles in Russia, but there was no corporate nobility. Catherine was the first to organize the *dvoriànstvo* into provincial corporations, with a view to furthering administrative self-government. That was not a solitary innovation. What she did for the nobility, she did at intervals for other classes also, notably for the cities and the town-classes. She aimed at uniting the various parts of the nation into compact groups, organized bodies, having common

---

* In the meantime, a thing that always strikes one in Russia is the great number of persons bearing the same name whom one encounters in all official positions. So that there are some fifty—perhaps hundred—families, forming a sort of bureaucratic oligarchy, whose names reappear these many years on almost every page of the military, diplomatic, administrative annuaries. This, however, is a natural consequence of absolute monarchy and court influences.

interests and animated with one spirit, intending to call on them to take part in local affairs, each in its sphere, in the only way in which a nation's participation in its own government was understood at the time—by class, order, corporation.

What caused the failure of this noble attempt? First and foremost, the incapacity of the various classes to make use of the rights conceded to them. In order to get any benefit out of these corporative privileges, one thing was absolutely necessary : the corporate spirit (*esprit de corps*), and in that all classes were equally lacking. The scant results of the nobiliary assemblies is accounted for in the same way as the failure of merchant guilds and corporations of laboring men. They none of them knew how to form a body, with an instinct of cohesion and a feeling of solidarity, exercising co-ordinate rights in view of common aims, and pursuing through generations a well defined political or social object. Nor did the nobility, any more than the other classes, know how to form a living organism, animated with a traditional spirit of its own, binding together its own members and at the same time distinct from that of the other classes. Such a thing might be found on Russian territory in the Polish nobility of the western provinces, or the German nobility of the Baltic provinces—never in Great-Russia, in the native, national nobility—never, at any time. The spirit of caste, of class, is so repugnant to the Russian nature, that it has remained closed hitherto against even the most elementary *esprit de corps*.

The patent or charter given by Catherine II. invested the *dvoriànstvo* with considerable rights : of calling together periodical assemblies ; of making itself heard of the Crown at any time by means of petitions ; of nominating most of the local functionaries and judges. In any other country such prerogatives would have resulted in a conflict with the Crown or served as starting-point for an aristocratic constitution. In Russia—nothing of the sort. For nigh on a century the nobility of each government has gone on assembling, electing its presidents or marshals, designating functionaries and magistrates, doing police duty, without giving any of Catherine's successors the slightest cause for uneasiness, without ever encroaching on the sovereign's absolute power.   The *dvoriànstvo* had neither tendencies of its own nor traditional views to put in practice ; the functionaries appointed by the nobles did not, in the exercise of their duties, act as representatives of their class.   All these *ispràvniks* (chiefs of police) and other local administrators did not embody the spirit of a class, nor consider themselves in any way responsible to their electors ; if they did show special zeal to please some, it was only such as were influential.   To the central authority they were tools as devoted and docile as the functionaries directly appointed by it.   So that any hopes that may have been cherished to counteract through this institution the excessive influence of the bureaucracy were deceived.   Russia in this case yielded a striking illustration of the inefficiency of institutions which are not rooted in a country's customs, of the inanity of political forms and public liberties unsupported by the public spirit.

The recent creation of assemblies in which all the classes of the nation are represented naturally robbed the special assemblies of the nobility of nearly all their prerogatives ; but in these new provincial estates, the *zèmstvo* of district or government, the nobility, as a rule, retains a decided preponderance.   It is, as we shall see, to their marshal that belongs the right of presiding at these gatherings of the different classes ; it is the landholders, the former serf holders, who by number and position, exert over them an overbalancing influence.   While reducing the nobility's direct privileges, the extension of public liberties has in reality enlarged its sphere of action.   No one disputes its claim to be entitled the controlling class ; its attributions have gone on multiplying along with the institutions ; a place has been reserved to it in all the new creations.   The government appeals to it both as the cultivated and as the conservative class.   Alexander II., as far back as 1874, solemnly invited it to constitute itself the guardian

of popular instruction. Alexander III. has done more : he
restored to it, in 1889, a direct influence over the rural administration and the peasant communes, by creating "rural canton
chiefs," invested with both administrative and judicial functions,
to be appointed by the governor, with the concurrence of the
marshals, out of the noble landowners of the district. Nihilism
has turned out profitable to the *dvoriànstvo.* In the war waged
against the conspirators, Alexander III., like his father, has
more than once called on the nobility for co-operation. What
will come of it all ? One thing is certain : no rights conceded to
the nobility can transform the time-honored character of the class.
No matter what they are and how broadened, such privileges are
not going to turn from its way the historical march of Russian
society. In this respect apprehension and hope are equally vain
and illusory.

An examination of the present and a study of the past lead to
the same conclusion. There is in Russia a nobility of a kind ;
there is no aristocracy, and it is not at this time of day that one can
be created. There is a nobility as ancient, as illustrious as any if
considered in its great families, and, considered as a whole, as
civilized, as enlightened as any in Europe, the most open-minded
of all, the freest from prejudice, the most exempt of arrogance or
caste-spirit, and at the same time the most mixed and motley, the
most devoid of tradition, of common life, and *esprit de corps.*
This *dvoriànstvo,* lacking in homogeneousness and coherence, is
totally wanting in the qualities as well as the defects of aristocracies. Is it for good ? Is it for evil ? That matters little ; it is a
fact : the rest has merely a speculative interest. There is no aristocracy in Russia ; there are individual aristocrats. There are
men who consider a hierarchical basis to be the only solid foundation for societies to rest on. You hear it said and asserted, in a
certain sphere, that an aristocracy is as essential to the social body
as bones are to the human body, and that the best support for an
hereditary monarchy is an hereditary privileged class. In all this

there may be some truth.   But, in order to be to a society a framework and skeleton, an aristocracy must have its strength in itself,
in its organism, its traditions.   How can a state or a throne lean on
supports which draw all their strength from favors bestowed by
that throne and the laws of the state?

And those men who, in Russia, represent the nobility as the
natural support of the monarchy, fall into another and peculiar
mistake : they misapprehend the nature of the sovereign power
as well as the character of the nobility in their own country.   Between *dvoriànstvo* and tsarism there never was any bond but that
of service,—never any intimacy, affinities, family ties, as have elsewhere existed between sovereign and nobility.   The theory or fiction of a king, first among peers, first gentleman of his kingdom,
is absolutely foreign to Russian manners and tradition both.
The Tsar properly belongs to no order in the state ; he is neither
noble nor burgher, neither urban nor rural.   Autocracy always
has kept outside and above all classes.   Therein lie some of the
historical motives of its force and popularity ; it never could
descend from this height without being untrue to its traditional
mission and weakening itself.

An aristocracy is not the sort of building to be constructed at
will, on a marked out spot, after a given plan ; nature herself
must have disposed the location and cut and trimmed the materials.
These materials the Russian aristocrats are compelled to seek
amongst the great landlords, the *dvoriànstvo*, as a whole, being
manifestly unavailable for such a construction.   Under Alexander
II. and now under Alexander III., in the very midst of all the
transformations of our times, the political builders have been busy
setting up all sorts of plans for social reconstruction.   Some of
these plans and devices are very ingenious and do very well on
paper ; we shall come across several as we study local institutions
and administration.   Unfortunately the social status is independent of library combinations, however skilful,—of governments,
however great their authority.   Political calculations and reason

itself have little hold on it ; it is altogether at the mercy of the national genius and the spirit of the age.

Now in Russia, manners, traditions, popular instinct, combine in loudly opposing the restoration of an hereditary privileged class. The entire Russian literature bears witness thereto, although it is almost wholly the work of nobles, written by and for nobles. The antiquity of race is a very feeble claim on the respect of the positive-minded realistic Russian. All class distinctions notwithstanding, he has remained free from caste-spirit, and has not the inborn awe of birth with which the German and Englishman are imbued.'

The promoters of hierarchical ideas in Russia fall in reality into the same blunder as the promoters of radical ideas. Aristocrats and demagogues merely, though unconsciously, ape the West. Both insist on applying to national problems borrowed solutions ; both undertake to trick out their own country after foreign fashions. The great difference between them lies in this : that the aristocratical conservatives have chosen the model which is least adaptable to the national ways and clashes most with the new tendencies. If it is easy to discover, in such or such old institutions of England or Prussia, such or such conservative guaranties, it is not so easy to take from foreign countries, to endow one's own with, what nature or history have withheld from it. It is with social forms as with the soil, as with a country's natural structure. While racing across his flat steppes of the south or jogging through his peaty woods of the north, a Russian may think how much variety high hills would add to the scenery and to agriculture, what capital bulwarks against the winds, what excellent reservoirs of moisture a few chains of snow-capped mountains would make,—but it will not enter into his head to go and raise hills and construct mountain chains. Yet such is the pretension of men who, in a society denuded of privileges and rolled level by centuries, flatter themselves with the idea that they can

' See the Appendix to the preceding chapter.

26

construct steep summits and dig impassable ravines and chasms, *i. e.*, revive a privileged class and put prerogatives on their feet again.

Between Russia and France there is greater similarity in this respect than would seem : in both, it is outside of class privileges and artificial combinations, it is down in the depths of the nation's consciousness, that a conservative basis must be sought for.   Only in Russia, where equality as yet is not so much in the customs and culture as in the national instinct and the logic of facts, where the old-time framework of society is still outwardly kept up, the delusion of aristocratic day-dreams is at once more excusable and not as harmless.

BOOK VII.

THE PEASANT AND THE EMANCIPATION.

CHAPTER I.

Russian Literature and the Apotheosis of the *Mujik*—Various Classes of Peasants—Origin and Causes of Serfdom—Labor Dues and the *Obròk*—Situation of the Peasants before Emancipation—Napoleon III., Liberator of the Serfs.

On one of the Paris stages a French piece has been played of late—a play of Russian manners and Russian authorship—original and incomplete, a play which was favorably received by the French public, although it is not likely to have been really comprehended : I mean *The Danishefs*.* This comedy, or, more truly, drama, which depicts Russian society prior to the emancipation, has a peasant for hero, and its subject may be said to be the moral pre-eminence of the *mujik*. The nobility, conceited and frivolous,— the clergy, dependent and cringing,—the merchant, newly enriched and servile,—cut a poor figure by the side of the man of the people, the quondam serf Òssip. " This man is great, this man is worth more than we are, mother," the young Count Danishef says of him. These words give the keynote to the piece. The conclusion to which we are led, perhaps unconsciously, by this rustic drama, is the apotheosis of the man of the people to the detriment of the classes privileged by birth, knowledge, or fortune. From

----

* This play, whose author signs himself " Nevsky," was rehandled for the stage, as everybody knows, by Alexandre Dumas.

this point of view, the comedy played at the Odéon, though written for the French and in their language, belongs by rights to
contemporary Russian literature. To use the word of a humorist,
Russian literature just now " reeks of the peasant " ; the *mujik* is
its hero, and has been for the last thirty years. At first sight, this
strikes us as a singular anomaly ; on closer inspection, the thing
explains itself.

In a state almost entirely rural, such as Russia still is, the
peasant forms the most important as well as the most numerous
class of the nation. There, more than elsewhere, the workers of
the soil embody the country's fund of nationalism. When brought
face to face with the comparative insignificance of the towns and
urban population, the peasantry still is the nation—or appears to
be by comparison. Yet the being who fills so large a place has
long been scorned and uncomprehended by a higher class trained
to foreign manners and ways of thinking. The reaction of the
national spirit against the superficial cosmopolitism of the last
century, the rehabilitation of nationality in art, literature, politics,
were bound to benefit, in the first place, the peasant, as being the
Russian man *par excellence*. This people of the fields and woods,
a people of serfs, so long a target for all that weened themselves
above it to spurn and hit at, all at once found itself studied in its
ways and customs, its songs and beliefs. Finding in the higher
classes only colorless reflections or commonplace copies of foreign
things, the Russians suddenly felt very happy on discovering, in
their own rural people, originality, character, individuality. Delighted at having at last found her own self again under all her
borrowed finery, Russia took to admiring herself in the most rugged of her children, her most legitimate representative—the peasant. For a large proportion of a hyper-refined society, the serf,
but just set free, the ignorant villager, unwashed, coarse, became
an object of infatuation and enthusiasm, of respect and veneration.
The *mujik*—the Russian Man,—but lately considered undeserving
of a glance, saw himself hoisted on to an altar, and the homage

rendered by his devotees of to-day—his contemners of yesterday
—has not always been free from superstition and fetishism.
Fashion naturally could not remain a stranger to the success of
this new worship, which, amidst its devotees, numbers some
hypocrites. In this, as a rule, realistic country, men habitually
unbelieving and sceptical turned up amidst the most zealous
sectators, the most intolerant priests of the new dispensation.
True, this religion, like so many others, often remains a thing
of the brain and the imagination, and the idol might not unfrequently complain of the irreverence with which its most fervent
worshippers, in theory, treat it in practice.

This apotheosis of the *mujik*—the boor, the clodhopper—can
be accounted for by reasons proper to Russia, and others, taken
from the social status of Europe. As people did in France before
the Revolution, a number of Russians profess the doctrine that it
is by returning to the people's simple life, by quaffing invigorat-
ing draughts at the fount of uprightness and all popular virtues,
that the higher classes of society will recover moral vigor and
health, will become purified of the corruption with which contact
with the West has infected them.* The mystical panegyrists of
the *mujik* do not perceive that they are unconsciously renewing,
for their country's benefit, one of the old, old themes of the French
eighteenth century, returning to the doctrines of Rousseau and the
guileless belief in the perfections of "the natural man." In Russia such tendencies come from a secret discouragement, an involuntary humility of the cultured classes, and a great national pride,
a blind faith in the native energies and the people's future. Men
who have grown sick and tired of aping the foreigners, and who
feel that they have incapacitated themselves, for a long time to

* Thus the great novelists, Tolstoy and Dostoyèfsky. The latter queries,
in *A Writer's Diary* (February, 1876) : "Which is better, the people or
we? Is it desirable that the people should take examples from us, or we
from the people? I must answer in all sincerity : it is for us to bow down
before the people, to take from it both idea and form, to acknowledge and
adore its genuineness."

come, from doing anything but assimilating what others have done, —men perforce resigned to their own impotence and all the more ambitious for their country, have come, through lassitude and irritation at their own inability to accomplish more, to glorify that element which has remained free from all outside contact, whose powers are as yet untried, which is new, intact, unpolluted,—in one word, the popular force. Hence this adoration of the uncultivated by the cultivated man, these kneelings and salutations of lettered and informed men before the *armiàk* and the *tulùp*—the peasant's sheepskin.

" We civilized men, we are nothing but old rags ; but the people—oh, the people is great ! " exclaims one of Turguénief's personages, in *Smoke*. Struck with the comparative sterility of the controlling classes, these disillusioned sons of Western civilization turn their backs on it and their faces to the *mujik*. With glad admiration they contemplate this Russian people, still dumb and uncouth in its swaddling-clothes,—this people which covers the widest habitable region of the world, which, in numbers, is already now ahead of every other Christian nation on the globe. With this compact mass of over fifty or sixty million peasants before them, the patriots take to dreaming of the future as a mother or nurse beside a cradle. For this people still in its infancy, still crude and unlettered, they dream of an intellectual greatness, a moral place in the world proportionate to its bulk and the immensity of its empire.* This people of peasants is like a gigantic egg as yet unopened. One does not know what will come out of it, but one naturally expects something huge, because, in spite of the fable, it seems as though the mountain ought to give birth to something more than the " ridiculous mouse." One understands the instinctive respect, the semi-religious reverence of the Russian before this

* " You have only to look on a world's map to be filled with awe before Russia's future destinies," wrote Nadièjdin as early as 1831. " Can such a colossus have been upreared for no purpose by the wisdom of the Creator ? " (Fragment from the *Telescope*, quoted by Pýpin in his *Studies of the Russian Nationality.—European Messenger (Viêstnik Evròpy)*, June, 1882.

incubation, proceeding in mystery and gloom, and on which hang all the destinies of his native land.

The Russians are fain to look to the *mujik* for a new departure, a political or social revelation, a renovation of Europe and mankind. The seers and prophets, who announce his greatness, can prophesy the more freely what this popular sphinx will say, will do, that he has not yet opened his mouth and is not yet awake. Certainly, such soaring hopes cannot prove free from illusion. Not the less, however, we have there a mystery, an occult riddle, which interests civilization very highly, and if patriotism, by dint of meditating over it, somewhat overleaps sober reason, it is to be excused.

Thus, for one portion of the lettered classes, the man of the people is an unconscious deity, similar to those infant gods, the embryonic gods of Egypt, whose divine force is all *in posse* still, whose latent energies are adored before they have had a chance of manifesting themselves. For another school, the man of the people, the peasant, is merely a sort of raw material, of human first matter, a potter's clay having no form but that given to it by the higher classes.* It is needless to demonstrate what those two points of view have in common, and wherein both overreach the mark. If literature in Russia has got very near to the people, it too often approached it with preconceived views, seeking in it only what it was determined to find. Some fancied that they could discover in the hidden depths of the popular mind latent forces which they opposed to the barrenness of the vaunted culture of the higher classes; others, more scornful or more superficial, could see in the people's soul nothing but darkness and barbar-

---

* This was the view of one of the most distinguished defenders of aristocratic tendencies, General Fadiéyef. In opposition to the higher classes, the nobility, which he habitually refers to as "the cultivated layer," he usually designates the people under the names of "elementary force," "plastic matter," "protoplasm." And this elementary force he considers as being one and the same in all countries, and everywhere devoid of any spirit of its own, everywhere incapable of spontaneous development.

ism, emptiness and nothingness.   In practical life views concerning the peasant clash quite as much and we encounter the same
differences as in the literary world.   " Why in the world should you
be interested in our *mujik ?* "   I was asked by a lady on the Lower
Volga.   " He is a brute of whom you never will make a man."
And the same day, on the same steamer, a gentleman-landholder
was saying to me with a conviction just as firm : " The most intelligent peasant in Europe is, to my mind, the *contadino* of
Northern Italy ; but our *mujik* could give him points."   Thus
extolled by some, contemned by others, the Russian peasant's
place really should be where Pascal would have placed man in
general : neither so high up, nor so low down.

The *mujik's* intelligence is not a matter of doubt, and his panegyrists are perhaps nearer the truth than his detractors ; but this
intelligence has been hampered and heavily handicapped by the
course of events.   There is in the Russian legends a giant of
prodigious strength, a sort of rustic Hercules or Samson, Iliyà of
Múrom by name, often regarded as an impersonation of the people,
the peasant.*   This popular colossus could not, for a long while,
show his power and genius.   Iliyà was in bondage.   For years
he was attached to the glebe and could neither walk nor otherwise act freely.   Now that the emancipation has knocked off his
fetters, the giant can move once more ; but, after being so long
weighed down with chains, he has not yet recovered the free use
of his limbs, and has lost the consciousness of his strength.   It is
only after years of freedom, possibly after several generations, that
this so lately enslaved people will learn to know itself and will
show what the future has to expect from it.   The peasant, with
back still bent under the servitude of years, could not straighten
himself all at once ; through the freeman of to-day the serf of
yesterday still shows.

The emancipation has been for Russia an event of capital im-

---

* See *The Songs of the Russian People*, by Mr. Ralston, and Alfred
Rambaud's *La Russie Épique.*

port, an event unmatched by anything in the history of nations ; for in all, serfdom has died out gradually. The emancipation has been the starting-point of numerous changes and reforms in the entire domain of the nation's life ; but this great revolution could not, in a few years, yield all its fruits. It was the less to be expected that, in reality, this vast operation is not altogether completed even yet ; it is being carried on still, and will not come to an end before the first years of the twentieth century. Until then a study of the free peasant is inseparably linked to that of serfdom and the conditions of his enfranchisement.

The emancipation, the work of Alexander II., has benefited only about one half of the peasants of the empire. The others, known as "Crown peasants," and settled on the demesnes of the State, were considered as free, although they, too, were attached to the soil and were virtually serfs of the emperor or the State. The great bulk of the peasants was thus divided into two classes, nearly equal in number, and which, even after the emancipation, have remained separate and distinct. On one side, the free or "Crown" peasants ; on the other, private peasants or serfs, free-men now. Between these two categories there was a third, to a certain extent intermediary one : the peasants of the appanages, or estates reserved for the endowment of the members of the imperial family.*

* The following were, prior to the emancipation, the relative proportions between these three categories of peasants, in European Russia, not including the Caucasus, Poland, and Finland. The entire number of serfs of both sexes was 22,500,000 ; that of the "Crown peasants" something over 22,000,000, comprising certain odd groups of free peasants, such as colonists of foreign extraction ; the appanage peasants amounted to about 2,000,000. A few years earlier the proportion was more unfavorable. In 1838 the serfs numbered 44 to every 100 of the population. The relative number of the serfs was evidently slowly decreasing, owing to individual manumissions,—to military service which set the soldiers free,—to the mortgaging of estates to the State, which foreclosed on them after the interest had remained unpaid a certain time, adding them to the Crown demesnes. In this way serfdom, left to itself, would have become extinct at the end of a few centuries, without the formality of emancipation.

These peasants, long distributed into groups, originally enjoyed the same liberty and the same rights. In Russia more than in any country of the West, freedom has ever been the normal condition of rural man. The bondage of the glebe came very late ; but it gradually became heavier and heavier, until it degenerated into a sort of slavery. Only at the end of the sixteenth century, at the moment when the bonds of serfdom fell off or were much loosened in the greater part of Europe, were they made fast in Russia.

In old-time Russia there were bondsmen (*kholòpy*, *rabỳ*). They usually were prisoners of war, insolvent debtors, or men who had sold themselves to escape penury. The number of such bondsmen was small, and the bulk of the peasants were considered as freemen. Yet the men of the country found themselves at an early period in an inferior and despised condition as regards the men of war and the *drujína*. They were called "little men"—*mujikì*—or else "half-men," in opposition to the warriors, the *drujìnniki*, who rejoiced in the appellations of "men"—*mùji*—and "full men," *i. e.*, complete men. Such is the original meaning of the diminutive ending of the word *mujik;* it corresponds to the Latin *homunculus*.* In Moscovia this name was given to rurals and urbans indifferently, to tradesmen and villagers.

Long before the establishment of serfdom the *mujiks'* or "little-men's" main task was to provide the "men's"—*mùji*—livelihood, to cultivate for them the lands which the sovereign granted his servants as salary or for their maintenance. The *mujiks*—also called "black [*i. e.*, dirty] men," *tchòrnyiè liúdi*—were not, however, attached either to the master they served, or to the soil they cultivated. Just as the *boyàrs* and the members of the *drujína* could pass at will from one *kniaz* to another, so the peasants could change masters, by passing from one land to

---

* This distinction answers that between the *leudi* and the *manni,—leute* and *männer*—in old-time Germany. The official name of the Russian peasants as a class is *krestiyàne*, singular *krestiyànin*—Christian—a name evidently dating from the days of the Tatar domination.

another. They also, like the *boyàrs* and *drujìnniki,* enjoyed the right of free service as well as of free passage, and likewise lost the first of these rights when they were deprived of the second, which was its guaranty.

Under the last of the Rùrikovitchs, the peasants usually exercised this right of theirs once a year, at the close of the agricultural year, nominally on the 26th of November, the feast of St. George, practically all through the week preceding and that following that feast. Prior to the establishment of serfdom when the demand for working hands was already great, the *pomiêsh-tchik* or landlord who wished to retain his peasants had recourse, it is said, to their innate love of liquor, and kept them in a drunken state all through the fateful fortnight. There came a time when the peasant, in the interest less of the landlords than of the state, was deprived of this right of taking short leave of his master, but he never lost the memory of the privilege that was taken from him. Even now, after three centuries of bondage, the *mujik* has not forgotten the feast day which once on a time restored him to freedom ; the feast of St. George is incorporated in many proverbial expressions of disappointment.

In order to attach the peasant to the glebe, all that was needed was to forbid his changing land at St. George's. This prohibition, temporary at first, then renewed and confirmed by successive sovereigns, at last became a fundamental law of the state. Thus the chief institution of the Russia of these latter centuries was evolved out of a simple police measure. The most important fact of the people's history passed wellnigh unperceived in the national annals. Serfdom was established, as everywhere else it vanished, almost insensibly, without a shock to the minds of the contemporaries.

It was the end of the sixteenth century, and the great wars against the Lithuanians and the Teutonic Order were at their height. The servants of the state, supplied with lands by their sovereign, complained that their means of support were inadequate. Labor was scarce and costly in this country where land abounded

while the population was scant and sparse.   The landowners—
pomiêsh-tchiks—wrangled for men.   The lesser accused the greater
of enticing and retaining all the laborers.   Such a state of affairs
imperilled Moscovia's military forces, at the most critical moment
of her history.   The financial system of the state, no less primitive
at the time, saw itself threatened equally with the military system
by the frequent flittings of the taxpayers and laborers, and the
liking for a vagabond life which resulted therefrom.   It was the
age when the Moscovite Empire, recently enlarged at the expense
of the Tatars, held out to the tillers of the thankless northern regions the allurement of the more fertile southern lands,—the age
when, to escape from taxes and share the free life of the Cosacks,
adventurous men fled to the Volga and the Don, to the Kama and
Siberia.   In stealing his own person from the landlords, a man
also robbed the exchequer of its dues.   In order to insure to the
country regular financial and military resources, the simplest thing
to do was to make man a fixture, to bind the peasant to the field
he tilled, the burgher to the town or city where he dwelt.   And
this is what Boris Godunôf did, and after him the tsars of the
seventeenth century.   From that time down to Alexander II., a
fixture the *mujik* remained, tied down, "made fast" to the soil,
for such is the meaning of the Russian word, *kriêpostnòy*, which
all European languages translate by *serf*. Russian serfdom had
just this origin and no other : it was evolved out of the prevalent
administrative system and the economic, indeed the physical, conditions of Moscovia, considerably aggrandized as the country was
by the last rulers of the house of Rurik, and threatened with the
dispersion of its thinly scattered population, which tended to ooze
away into the steppes, as a thread of water into the sands of the
desert.

In this Europe of the East, this land of log-cabins, almost as
easy to transport or reconstruct as the tent of the Arab, man felt
little attachment to the soil, little liking for agriculture.   Three
centuries of bondage have been unable wholly to eradicate in the

mujik his hankering after a wandering life,—a propensity encouraged by the long rivers and endless plains. Serfdom, which
bound man to the soil, may be regarded as a reaction of the state
against these adventurous instincts, which drew to the uttermost
ends of the empire, on the track of the Cosacks, the most vigorous,
the most enterprising portion of the Russian people. The less
Russia was bounded by nature, the vaster her horizon, the more
necessary it became to impose restrictions on her sons : serfdom
kept them in place, doomed them to immobility.

It was in 1593, under Theodor, a son of Ivan the Terrible, and
by the influence of Godunòf, his brother-in-law and eventually his
successor, that the right of free passage from one estate to another
was taken from the peasant. Out of this one, originally temporary,
fact resulted his bondage. Something analogous had occurred
twelve centuries before, in the Roman Empire, at the time of the
institution of the *colonate* under Christian emperors.[1] Once " made
fast " to the soil, the Moscovite peasant gradually lost all his civil
rights and fell into a state of dependency which the lawgiver had
not foreseen. He became the landlord's property, his chattel.
Godunòf's work was confirmed and completed by *ukàzes* of the
first Románofs. Peter the Great's reforms tightened the peasant's
fetters instead of loosening them ; his bondage became more irksome as it was better regulated. The first general census (" revision "), taken in 1722 and renewed since at uneven intervals,
provided serfdom with regular registers. With a view to a simpli-
fication of the administrative machinery, and also out of economy,
the State gave up to the landlords nearly the whole of the local
administration as well as the police duties within their domains.
Serfdom now became the more difficult to abolish that it had been
transformed into a tool of the government's, one of the chief
wheels in a political machinery as yet not very intricate.

[1] The colonist could not sell the land that had been allotted to him before
a certain, considerable number of years, twenty or more. This, of course,
amounted to compulsory residence, as only the poor applied for and received state lands and naturally they had to cultivate them themselves.

Until as late as 1861 the landlord—*pomiêsh-tchik*—might be considered as an agent of the State, commissioned to see to the enlistment of soldiers in rural districts and to the collection of taxes, in short as a sort of hereditary functionary, invested with administrative powers and the guardianship of the peasants on his lands.

Serfdom did not spread over Russia evenly.   Into the remoter and almost desert parts, where the landlords were few, into the region of the great lakes and of the White Sea, as well as into the portion of Siberia conquered by the Cosacks, the new ordinances had not made their way or had not been enforced.   These regions, treated so harshly by nature, have always almost entirely ignored both serfdom and nobility ; primitive liberty and equality kept their ground there down to our own days.   In the south the Cosacks also would not hear of the new institution, which swelled their ranks with runaways.   Ukraïna—the portion of Little-Russia situated on the left bank of the Dniepr—remained exempt from the bondage of the soil until the reign of Catherine II.   When the hour of freedom struck, the historical centre of Russia was also that of serfdom, which, from the lands around Moscow, radiated to the north and to the south, towards Europe and towards Asia. In the west Moscovite serfdom encountered—in Lithuania and White-Russia—Polish serfdom, to which the entire rural population, whether Russian or Lithuanian, had long been subject.   By a singular anomaly, it was the predominant race—the Slavic race, and especially the Russian—which, in the Russian Empire, was most generally bowed under the yoke of serfdom.   The Tatars in the east, the Rumanians in Bessarabia, the German colonists, even the Finn tribes, had, as a rule, maintained their liberty.

The condition of the peasants settled on lands belonging to private owners varied greatly according to localities, customs, and masters.   To adequately describe all forms of serfdom, it would be necessary to classify the serfs into some twenty different groups.*

* The reader might profitably consult M. X. Marmier's *Voyages*, or Mr. de Molinari's *Lettres sur la Russie*, and, for greater detail, see the works of Haxthausen and Schnitzler.

These various grades and forms of bondage can be reduced to two types, which were in general use to the last : the labor dues (the French *corvée*, *boyàrsh-tchìna*, for short *bàrsh-tchìna*), and the dues in money, the *obròk*.

The *bàrsh-tchìna*—the personal service rendered by the serf to his landlord in labor—was the primitive, the rudimentary form. The peasants worked three days for the landlord, the other half of the week they attended to the lands which he gave up to them, for their support.* The transformation of the labor dues into an annual payment in money was a great improvement, a very real relief. This system prevailed chiefly in the neighborhood of manufacturing centres, or in regions with poor soil. By the payment of the *obròk* the peasant temporarily ransomed his personal liberty, and could leave his landlord's estate, to ply a craft in the towns or other country places. This arrangement enabled many peasants to give up rural pursuits altogether. Only, they were liable to be called back to the plough at any moment by a word from the master. This was a way to "get round" the law, to defeat the original object of serfdom, that of attaching each man to the soil : the *obròk*-paying serf became virtually his own master. Ostensibly, he was free ; but an invisible link bound him to his landlord. The amount of the yearly payment varied considerably according to localities, the master's exactingness, the individual aptitude of the serfs. On an average the *obròk* oscillated between five and ten dollars a year. At this rate a landlord, clearly, could not be really wealthy unless he owned villages or rather, whole districts. The petty landlords were actually compelled by penury to draw from their serfs all they could possibly grind out of them. The peasant whose lot was cast with the owner of broad acres, whom wealth enabled to be liberal, was more fortunate ; he was habitually subjected to a fixed rate of pay-

* By a law issued in 1797, by Paul I., the *bàrsh-tchìna* was fixed at three days. In many communes or families one half of the members worked for the master all the week, while the others worked for the benefit of the household.

ment. Few masters took advantage of their people's capacity for and success in business to raise their *obròk*. Great landlords might be named—a Sheremétieff among others—who numbered among their serfs millionaire merchants, and who would have scorned to claim any of their wealth, but who indulged their vanity by refusing to let them ransom themselves.

The "Crown peasants" or "free peasants," settled on State lands, were all on the *obròk* system. Over and above the poll-tax and the local taxes, they paid the State a yearly due which might be regarded as a sort of land-rent, and which oscillated between two and three roubles for each male peasant. These peasants, with no landlord but the State, enjoyed two great advantages : the dues they paid were fixed and very moderate ; and they were not exposed to change of masters, variable in their humor and ways of doing business. They were allowed to enjoy some communal franchises, and, at the time of the emancipation, their institutions partly served as models for the administrative organization of the liberated serfs. In spite of the oppression and extortions to which they were occasionally subjected by corrupt functionaries, the "Crown peasants" were generally better off than those on private lands. To this day their villages have a look of greater prosperity, by which they are often known at first sight. These peasants of the State demesnes, attached to the glebe like the others, formerly constituted a living treasury or reserve fund, from which the sovereign took the grants which he distributed to his servants in the form of lands stocked with serfs. Catherine II. made use of this fund on a large scale, for the endowment and gratification of her ministers and favorites ; but she was the last to practise these liberties, which are one of the blots on her reign. To the Emperor Alexander I. is due the credit of having put a stop to these gifts of men, and created a class of free husbandmen.

Serfdom in Russia, like slavery in America, has had its defenders in the past and is not even yet without panegyrists.

There is no doubt that servitude was not, for the peasant, without some compensation. If the serf endured hardships from being subject to his landlord's guardianship, he also benefited thereby ; if he served the master, the master protected him. Not being based on conquest, as in the Baltic provinces, nor on difference of race, like American slavery, serfdom in Russia preserved to the end a certain benignity, something more paternal, more patriarchal. It is no less certain that, in spite of many attenuating traits due to custom and law, such a system worked harm in the end,—harm to the country, harm to the bondsman, harm to the master himself. The peasant who fell into the hands of a whimsical, corrupt, or dissolute man, was exposed to every kind of wretchedness, oppression, ignominy, the law being unable to shield him efficiently from the landlord's cupidity, brutality, or lawlessness. There was in serfdom one incurable evil : the violence done to the human conscience, the obliteration of moral responsibility.

Nor was the economic evil less great ; the institution yielded little profit to the class for whose benefit it existed. Although the right of owning "inhabited lands" extended to the entire hereditary nobility, there were, at the moment of the emancipation, not over one hundred odd thousand serf holders, and of these the greater part barely enjoyed a competency. Three or four thousand of them owned no land, for in the eighteenth century serfs had come to be sold without land.* To be at all well off, one had to own hundreds of "souls" ; to be wealthy, thousands,

* Owing to the imperfection of statistical proceedings, the figures given on the division of properties and serfs present notable discrepancies. A little over two million "souls," *i. e.*, male peasants, the only ones subject to capitation and set down in the "revisions" (census), were divided among less than 80,000 owners, who had from 1 to 100 "souls" each, and were accounted as "petty landlords." Five and a half millions were allotted to 22,000 owners, having from 100 to 1,000 "souls" each, and regarded as "medium landlords." Lastly there were 1,400 serf-holders, owning more than 1,000 male peasants each, with a total, between them, of three million souls, and they were accounted "great landlords." Of these, some few families—the Sheremétieffs for one—had on their lands as many as 100,000 serfs.

27

so little did serfdom produce, so terrible was the depreciation of labor caused by this confiscation of it through several centuries. The peasants' unpaid labor did not suffice for the support even of those who held the monopoly of it. Servile labor used to be discounted and consumed years ahead by numbers of landlords. At the moment of emancipation, two thirds of the "inhabited lands" peopled with serfs, or, in plainer words, two thirds of the serfs themselves (for it was at the rate of so much per head that the banks effected their loans), were found to be mortgaged in the *lombards* or credit establishments kept by the State. Frequently, therefore, the *pomiêsh-tchik* had only the semblance of proprietorship, and the sums loaned by the State on human capital, instead of being sunk into the ground and there bearing interest, were usually squandered in dissipation and hospitalities.

One is astonished at such a state of things having lasted so long. In a certain sense serfdom might be said never to have been thoroughly accepted by the people themselves. Several times, in the seventeenth and eighteenth centuries, the peasants rose to the cry of liberty, under such leaders as Stiénka Ràzin and Pugatchòf. The Crown which had imposed it, the nobility which was supposed to benefit by it, had long looked on serfdom as on an irretrievably doomed temporary institution. It is likely that the emancipation would not have been so long delayed, but for the apprehensions aroused by the revolutionary troubles in Europe, which appeared calculated to hasten the operation. The Emperor Alexander I. seemed created for just such work. He prepared the way for it by a partial experiment—that of ordering the manumission of the serfs of the three Baltic provinces : the Ehst and Lett peasants, the most oppressed of all, because they were of another race than their German conquerors and masters. The Emperor Nicolas, following his brother's example, lightened and loosened as much as possible the bonds he dared not break. Emancipation was his pet scheme. On the eve of 1848 he had already appointed, to study the question, a secret committee, which the February revolution caused to be dissolved. The disasters of the Crimean War had, in his latter days, led his thoughts back to the same projects. It is affirmed that, on his deathbed, Nicolas bequeathed to his son and successor the task which he himself had been prevented from undertaking. On the whole it may have been fortunate for the empire that the great work was not started sooner : the preparatory studies were more matured, the task itself was carried out more boldly.

One of the things that should on no account be lost sight of by any one desirous of fully understanding the transformation of contemporary Russia, is the part taken in it by public opinion and public spirit. Literature which, in modern nations, always opens and shows the way,—literature in all its forms : poetry, fiction, drama, history, criticism, had done its work ; it only had to direct the attention of the higher classes towards the people, its life and manners. As in America, the novelists became the apostles and prophets of emancipation. But Russia has something better than *Uncle Tom's Cabin* and the didactic novels of the American women. In Gógol's *Dead Souls*, and Ivan Turguénief's *Memoirs of a Huntsman*, she has pictures admirable for truth and earnestness, or, more correctly, mirrors, in which, as in polished glass, are reflected, unaltered in either outline or coloring, the countenances of both serfs and masters.* The press debated the conditions of the reform, an ardent desire for which was aroused by the novelists. On this one point the two currents which usually carry the Russian mind opposite ways, for once carried it in the same direction. All the schools, whether Slavophils or Occidentals, liberals, or democrats, were at one on *this* issue ; the cause numbered amidst its advocates Nicolas Turguénief, Samárin, and Herzen. It was neither a sovereign, solitary in his power, nor a few exceptional individuals, fashioned

---

* Russia may be said to have her counterpart of *Uncle Tom's Cabin* in the stories written by a woman, Mme. Markévitch (Màrko-Vovtchòk). These stories, written in the Little-Russian dialect, had the honor of being translated into Russian by Ivan Turguénief.

by foreign discipline, who led the nation, using bridle, spur, or whip, as the case might be,—it was public spirit, public opinion, which gave the impulse. This was a national movement, comparable in a way to that which, in the West, had culminated in the French Revolution. This phenomenon, so novel in the history of Russia, is in itself as worthy of attention as the emancipation and all its accompanying reforms. In this respect the work done by Alexander II. is totally different from that accomplished by Peter the Great, and shows the stride taken by the country in the interval : the first work was that of a man ; this latter one is that of a nation. Russia, on the eve of the emancipation, appears not as a sort of inert material, for governments to experiment on, or, to borrow the expression of a frenchified Russian, as a sociological laboratory ; it is a nation that is coming of age and, not content with blindly following the paternal guidance, works out its own development.

And yet, however carefully prepared, however desired of the nation and public opinion, the emancipation might have hung fire for years still, but for the bitter disappointment entailed by the Crimean War. There are, in the lives of all nations, reforms of such deep import, so complicated, touching on so many interests, that those at the helm make up their minds to tackle them only under the pressure of some mighty event, under the threat of some national peril or calamity. For nations as for individuals, adversity frequently is the best counsellor. A blow dealt from abroad, a military disaster, has more than once been the point of departure of the moral renovation of a great people. What Jena was to Prussia and Germany, what Novara was to Piedmont and Italy,—that the Crimean War was to Russia, though it scarcely altered her frontier. This campaign, so barren of results for the Porte, which, under shelter of the West, only grew more and more corrupt, has teemed with results for the vanquished empire. The fall of Sebastòpol was serfdom's death-blow.

I have been told that a quondam serf kept in his room a

portrait of Napoleon III. with this inscription : *To the Liberator of the Serfs.* After the Crimean War, it appears, the rumor spread among the peasantry of certain provinces, that the Emperor of the French demanded the abolition of serfdom, and had consented to sign a treaty of peace only on condition that a secret clause should be inserted insuring the liberation of the serfs.* May be there lurked in this rumor a vague remembrance of the hopes excited by Napoleon I. in 1812. At all events, this popular belief was nothing less than, under a childish form, an instinctive presentiment of the inevitable connection of events. It was indeed, although they knew it not, for the benefit of the *mujik*, of the Russian people, that France and England were fighting. In this respect Russia's defeat was a stroke of good-fortune for her ; never perhaps did a country buy its national regeneration so cheap. Of a war of which the issue cost her only some pangs of wounded vanity, of a peace the humiliating clauses of which were promptly obliterated, nothing was left to her but an enduring inner transformation.

* This rumor is mentioned by Tchernyshèfsky, in his *Letters without an Address*, published in the *Vperiòd* (1874).

BOOK VII.　CHAPTER II.

Questions Raised by the Emancipation—Expectations and Disappointments of the Nobility—Agrarian Laws—Was it Possible to Free the Serfs without Giving them Lands?—Reasons and Conditions of the Territorial Endowment of the Peasants.

It was, then, a national movement which, under the pressure of defeat, urged on emancipation from all sides. Should the nation take a direct part in it? Should the Tsar, like Catherine II., and with design better defined, call together the delegates of the different classes into a sort of States-General? Some thought he should. It was announced that, by way of compensation for the loss of their serfs, the nobility were to be given political rights, and that, out of the emancipation, would grow a constitution. This hope did much to enlist the landlords and the nobiliary assemblies in favor of the project. In spite of appearances, it is probably fortunate that things did not take this course; that the government did not invite the delegates of the nobility to deliberate and to pass laws, but only consulted them. On the question of the necessity of the emancipation, opinion was nearly unanimous throughout the empire; on that of ways and means, and that of the position to be given the peasants when free, there was in the public and in the government itself a very Babel of confused and discordant views. An elective assembly, numerous and tumultuous, would have had some trouble in sifting and clearing such a chaos. Then, to be equitable or impartial, an assembly should have included representatives of the opposed parties—of both serfs and landlords. The former could not be called upon to ordain their own future; yet it would have been unfair to leave the deliberation to the masters alone. Between peasant and *pomièsh-tchik* there was but one natural judge, one disinterested umpire : the Crown. The situation was one where autocracy, exalted above all classes and true to its mission—impartiality,— was the meetest tribunal for rendering an equitable sentence.

The nobiliary assemblies of the different provinces were invited to investigate the question and report their opinion ; but the inditing of the project was entrusted to commissions directly appointed by the sovereign. These commissions were composed partly of high functionaries, such as Nicolas Miliútin, the chief inspirer of the Statute, partly of landlords or "experts," mostly taken from the minorities of the provincial committees, such as Prince Tcherkàssky and Yúri (George) Samárin, allies and fol- lowers of Miliútin. In these "drafting commissions" (*Commissions de rédaction*) the interests of the landlords did not lack defenders ; nor was it without arduous struggles that the majority, directed by Miliútin and his friends, brought about the triumph of their ideas and their acceptance by the sovereign.*

The project, elaborated by the commissions, was incomparably more favorable to the people than the views adopted by most local assemblies. The bases of it, indeed, were considered so democratical, that sundry clauses were modified through court influences. To the end of the reign of Alexander II., a portion of the official world inclined more or less openly to retract several of the principles proclaimed on the 19th of February, 1861.

The landed nobility did not attempt to conceal their dis- approval as well of the democratic tendencies in favor in the "drafting commissions," as of the manner in which the govern- ment had set them aside from participation in a task in which it had, at first, invited their co-operation. Several of the

* I have told in another book, from the unpublished correspondence of Miliútin, Tcherkàssky, and Samárin, the struggles and vicissitudes through which the emancipation had to pass. See : *A Russian Statesman from his Unpublished Correspondence (Un Homme d'État Russe d'après sa Correspondance Inédite).*

great landlords gave loud expression to their disappointment at being denied a share in a reform which they had hoped to direct ; and that, too, in favor of a bureaucratic commission which appeared to have no other task than that of collecting and reducing into a code the views of the provincial committees of landlords.* This was the nobility's first disappointment, and a heavy one.

The passions and angry feelings aroused by these questions were so violent that the principal inditers of the Emancipation Act, while they were able to overcome opposition, could not quell the personal grudges which accumulated against them. Immediately after the proclamation of the Statute, of which they had been the most zealous instigators, N. Miliútin and his friends, loudly abused as "reds" and "radicals," both at court and in society, fell into a scarce disguised disgrace. The work was sanctioned, the makers were sacrificed. Nothing less than the Polish insurrection was needed to cause the government to call once more for the services of Miliútin and Tcherkàssky.† This inconsistency, apparently incomprehensible, was not due solely to the sovereign's hesitations to court intrigues. By dismissing Miliútin, at the very moment when it seemed but natural to entrust him with the practical application of the laws drawn up by his friends and by himself, Alexander intended to pacify public feeling. In order to put an end to the uneasiness and the grumblings of the nobility, half crazed by the phantom of impending ruin, he took the execution of his *ukàzes* out of the hands of a man reputed to be, systematically, opposed to the nobility, and entrusted it to persons who could not be suspected of hostility against it.

* See, for instance, the *Letter from a Committeeman* (Count Orlòf-Davýdof) *to the President of the Drafting Commission*, Paris, 1859.

† "I am given leave of absence for a whole year, or, more correctly, I am shelved by being made a senator . . ." wrote N. Miliútin to Tcherkàssky in May, 1861. "I had asked only for a four months' leave ; but the reaction helped me out. Lanskòy and myself [Lanskòy was the Minister of the Interior and Miliútin his assistant] had to clear out of the cabinet to please the nobility."

The excessive demands put forward by the peasants gradually reconciled the greater part of the nobility to the Emancipation Act. Once they found themselves face to face with the distrust and the rapacity of their former serfs, the landlords were brought to look on the Statute, so fiercely attacked by many of their number, as on their "anchor of salvation." Experience soon convinced most of them of the inanity of the illusions they had entertained concerning the *mujik's* supposed attachment and docility.*

The advantages provided for the peasants by men like Miliútin, Tcherkàssky, Samárin, account for the rancor which they aroused. For truly, nowhere did the lawmaker take such thought for the interests of the quondam serf. The task accomplished by Russia was not unexampled or unprecedented in Europe. To mention only neighboring states, Prussia and Austria had, in this very century, at different intervals, accomplished analogous ones, though on a more modest scale. The emancipation as conducted in Prussia after Jena, under the inspiration of Baron von Stein, was to the Russians a lesson by which they profited, without, however, copying anybody's proceedings.† Two things especially distinguished from others the method adopted at Petersburgh.

---

* "What did and still does most contribute to convince the nobility of the absolute necessity of doing as we have done, is the attitude of the peasants, into daily conflicts with whom the landlords are being forced ; it is, more especially, the demands of the peasants, and, above all, the radical distrust *of the entire bearded Orthodox population* towards the nobles. The latter had, much against the grain, to give up the idea that their former serfs placed in them an unlimited confidence ; the landlords' eyes have been opened in this respect as completely as possible. . . . Everybody, at the present hour, has been made to see how indispensable was a detailed and precise statute, and how unfounded were, for the most part, the malevolent outcries and uproar which have been kept up through two years against the ' drafting commissions ' and their supposed mania for subjecting everything to regulations." (Unpublished Letter from Prince Tcherkàssky to N. Miliútin, dated July the 23, 1861.)

† See, for the examples given to Russia by foreign countries, the *History of the Abolition of Slavery and Serfdom in Europe*, by Samuel Sugenheim (St. Petersburgh, 1861) ; and Samárin's study on the *Abolition of Serfdom in Prussia*, reprinted in 1879, in vol. ii. of his collected works.

Not content with giving the peasants their bare, personal liberty, Russia endowed them with lands. Instead of leaving the manumitted peasants, as Prussia did in 1809 and 1848, under the patronage and tutelage of their former lords, to linger on in a sort of administrative servitude, Russia at one stroke converted the former serfs into communes independent of their late masters. While the *Bauer* of Eastern Prussia remained, at least until the reforms of 1872, subject and vassal to the *Ritterschaft*, the Russian *mujik*, thanks to his ownership of land and to the autonomy of his commune, was fully emancipated, at once economically and administratively.

The main object of the system adopted in Russia was to provide the freedmen with lands, to convert the serfs into landholders. There, naturally, also lay the main difficulty. In the opinion of a part of the nobility, in that of many politicians, it was sufficient to give the peasants their personal liberty. That is what Alexander I. did for the serfs of the Baltic provinces. What is serfdom? asked the theoreticians of this system. It is the labor of one man, gratuitously conceded to another man. To abolish serfdom, it is enough to abolish unrequited labor.* How, they went on, was serfdom established? By a police regulation, forbidding the peasants to pass from one domain to another. How is this institution to be annulled? By restoring to the *mujik* the right of coming and going. Conceived in this way, emancipation would have been a very simple operation ; but what would have been the results? The peasant would have recovered his liberty only to fall into a condition often more miserable than that which he endured in the time of his bondage. He would have remained for years, maybe for centuries, totally debarred from the holding of land. All this host of freedmen would have been turned into a nation of proletarians. Thus argued the

---

* This opinion, which pretended to be based on the data of political economy, was upheld by numbers of foreign economists. (See, for example, Molinari's *Letters on Russia.*)

partisans of territorial endowment, and their opinion carried the day in the commission, with the public, and with the sovereign.*

Through these views, most justifiable in all that concerned the liberation of the serfs, showed a high ambition, not exempt from self-delusion. A worthy, tempting object surely : to create not merely a nation of freemen, but one of land-holders. Press and public kept repeating that the only escape from the evils of ancient societies lay in not falling into those of modern societies —pauperism and proletariate. By giving lands to the serfs, it was confidently hoped to avoid proletariate, and to avoid proletariate was to steer clear of the social and political commotions of the West.

The Russian government was thus led on to create, in favor of the peasants, a veritable agrarian law, a sort of territorial expropriation for reasons of public weal. It has frequently been blamed for this, so-called, revolutionary measure. This forced distribution of lands taken from the nobility has been compared to the confiscations and creations of national property perpetrated by the French Revolution. Such comparisons are strangely exaggerated. In order justly to appreciate these measures, political necessity must not alone be taken into account, but the ambiguous origin, the obscurity, the uncertainty of the Russian laws on property should also be remembered. Whose, in reality, was the soil—the landlord's or the peasant's ? Both had claims. If the

* Address delivered by the Emperor in the "Council of the Empire," on January 28, 1861. In it he openly deplored the manner in which the emancipation had been accomplished in the Baltic provinces and the kingdom of Poland. For Poland, the rising of 1863 was soon to supply the government with an occasion to apply, with the assistance of the same men, —Miliútin, Tcherkàssky, and their friends,—the same principles to the provinces of the Visla. As to the Baltic provinces, the land, according to a system in use in several parts of Germany, has been divided into two categories : the *Hofland*, which remains at the free disposal of the former lord, and the *Bauerland*, which can be sold or rented only to peasants. The agrarian question, repeatedly raised by Russian journalists, produced among the Lett and Ehst peasantry, in 1882 and 1883, an agitation not unlike that of the Irish Land League.

law decided officially in favor of the former, the latter could appeal to custom, at least as far as those lands were concerned, the use of which had been conceded to him by the masters, in obedience to traditional habit. If the *pomiêsh-tchik* had received his estate from the sovereign in exchange for his services, the *mujik* could be considered as having lived on and had the use of the land before the grant was made to his landlord.* Going back to the beginning of things, the position could be upheld, that the domains, with their serf population, which often alone gave them their value, never had constituted full property, that they stood less under the jurisdiction of the civil than of the political law, these lands having been granted to the nobility in exchange for services from which they had gradually exempted themselves.†

If we look at things in this way, the Russian government cannot be said to have taken from one side to give to the other. Rather, it has discriminated between rival claims, arbitrated between conflicting rights and interests, by holding both adverse parties to a compromise. The peasant received a portion of the land, but he was made to indemnify his former landlord. If, on both sides, there were complaints and disappointments, it was because, coming down from theories to practical ground, the

---

* There were, indeed, some kinds of lands to which this line of argument did not seem to apply, such as the recently colonized land on the Lower Volga and in New Russia, the domains on which the landlords had themselves settled peasants, inviting them to come. Unfortunately, it would have been very difficult to take this difference into account.

† We saw in a preceding chapter (Book VI., Ch. II.), that there were originally in Russia two classes of landed property : the *vòt-tchina* or " patrimony,"—land inherited from ancestors ; and the *pomiêstiyé*, or " grant-land," conceded to servants of the state for their support. The estates of the modern nobles generally belong to the latter class ; but, by exempting the nobility from the burdens and personal service which had long been obligatory for the *pomiêsh-tchik*, the sovereigns had virtually transformed the *pomiêstiyé* into a *vòt-tchina*. So that, in this respect, the Emperor Alexander II. may be said to have strained a point in favor of the peasants, by ignoring what his predecessors had done for the nobility. In strict historical equity, the emancipation ought to have taken place on the day on which the *pomiêsh-tchik* was freed from the obligation of serving the state.

umpire's sentence could not satisfy fully either of the two contestants.

The government's decision was the wiser, that an opposite resolve would have found the resistance of the peasants difficult to overcome. And under such a system, Russia would have been forthwith converted into an immense Ireland, rife with agrarian troubles. The peasant, serf as he was, never ceased to consider himself as the owner of the land he cultivated, that land at least which the landlords had for generations allowed him to use for his support. "We are yours," said the serfs to their masters, "but the land is ours." To give them their liberty and at the same time to take from them the lands of which they had the use, would have seemed to the *mujik* a hypocritical form of spolia-tion.* As it is, he finds it hard to understand why, in order to become full owner of this land which he looked on as his own, he should have to indemnify the former landlord, who, anyhow, left it to him.

When the manifesto of the 19th of February, 1861, was pub-lished, setting forth the conditions of the emancipation, the peasants could not conceal their disappointment. In the churches, where the imperial manifesto, announcing freedom, was read to them, they murmured aloud; more than one shook his head, exclaiming, "What sort of liberty is that?" † The discontent

* Here is a rather edifying story to the point : A landlord of the govern-ment of Smolensk had, under Alexander I., drawn up a plan of emancipa-tion which would have given to each peasant, besides his liberty, his house with the enclosed yard or "house-lot" thereto belonging. "And how about the arable lands?" asked the peasants, when he laid his scheme before them. "I shall keep those," answered the philanthropist. "Well, then, father" (*bátiushka*), replied the serfs, "suppose we leave things as they are. We are yours, but the land is ours."

† A word quoted in the memoirs of a country priest, published in 1880. "During the reading," says the priest, "the peasants bowed their heads ; it was easy to see that they expected nothing good from *that* sort of liberty. They listened as to a sentence of banishment." In several villages the parish priests had to endure all sorts of persecutions at the peasants' hands, who accused them of having suffered themselves to be bribed by the land-lords to conceal from their parishioners the orders of the Tsar.

was universal. In many localities the peasants suspected a mystification. They refused to believe in the genuineness of the manifesto. On many points there were troubles, and the police had to call in the aid of the military, who, in some villages, were compelled to fire. For this unlettered people, accustomed by oppression to incurable distrust, the balls of the soldiers were the only sufficient demonstration of the authenticity of the imperial ordinances.*

It was rumored in the villages that the manifesto read in the churches was a fabrication of the landlords, and that the genuine Emancipation Act would be forthcoming later on ; there may even yet be peasants who are looking for it to appear. There assuredly are many who in the long winter evenings dream of a new emancipation with a redistribution of lands, gratuitous this time.

It took the peasants several years thoroughly to understand the conditions on which liberty was given them and to become reconciled to them. Truth to say, these poor people were mostly quite unqualified to comprehend the clauses of the Statute. They lacked the knowledge of legal terms, a clear notion of the rights of property, indeed of liberty itself; they also were wanting in confidence towards their masters and the local authorities commissioned to explain to them the new order of things. Nothing could be more characteristic in this respect than the lines written from a remote province to N. Miliútin, by one of his most illustrious fellow-workers, one of the most earnest and devoted lovers of the people, the Slavophil Samárin, in September, 1861 : " The chief stumbling-block is the peasants' distrust of everything and everybody. Nothing is to them immutable or impracticable. . . . Between them and us there is no common point of view ; they have not a peg on which we could hang our arguments. They

* " This poor, uncultured mass, imbued with a profound distrust of all that surrounds it, seemed anxious to stimulate the action of the troops, and to challenge repression, because force has until now been to the people the only certain pledge of the sovereign will."—[Unpublished letter from Yúri Samárin to N. Miliútin, dated August 17, 1862.]

listen to us attentively, good-naturedly, even with pleasure. But, to anything you say to them, you hear the same answer : ' We are ignorant, *bátiushka* ' *;* we know nothing, but this is how we reason : what the Tsar commands, that should be done.' ' But *this* is the Tsar's will ; written down here, in this book.' ' Ah, but how should we know that ? we are ignorant ; what there is in that book, we know it not.' . . . And thereupon you despondently feel that all your talk glides off them as water down a slope. The peasants submit to the Statute ; they submit to the Regulation Contracts ; but in their own hearts they remain deeply attached to their own hopes, and it will be long before they give them up.''

This same spirit shows very plainly in sundry dissident sects, those especially that foretell the impending *millennium*, the "descent of the Kingdom of Heaven.'' Several years after the publication of the Emancipation Act, certain prophets from the people, one Pùshkin in the number, announced that, by the will of God, the land was soon to be made over to the peasants, with nothing to pay. A little earlier, in 1861, there appeared, in the region of Kazàn, a pretender or pseudo-tsar of the good old Russian type. A certain Antòn Petròf gave himself out among the peasants for the Emperor ; driven out of his capital, he told them, by the nobles and the *tchinòvniks* (bureaucrats), who, between them, had altered his manifesto to the people's detriment. The troops had to be brought out against this embryo Pugatchòf. Thus political vagaries combined with religious delusions, the frauds of impostors and tricksters with the hallucinations of the illumined. Here is a curious instance in point, that came to my knowledge in the government of Vorònej. A seminary student on his vacation trip was returning from the country with no money left and quite at a loss how to procure horses to finish his journey, when

---

[1] '' We are *dark people* '' is the standing expression which peasants use for their profession of ignorance. Could anything be more graphic—and more pathetic? There is great promise in a people who have, unaided, grasped the perception that ignorance is '' darkness,'' blindness.

he hit on the expedient of taking advantage of the *mujik's* credulity. "I am," he declared to the peasants, "a Grand Duke travelling incognito, in a plain *teliêga* (springless village cart) to judge for myself of your condition, and to see what, in your interests, should be altered in the Emancipation Act." The stratagem succeeded; the seminarist got taken several relays on his road, hospitably entertained and thanked by his dupes. Numerous political trials, from 1879 to 1883, have shown how willingly even yet the *mujik* lends himself to mystification on this point.

To comprehend the material position and the feelings of the liberated peasants, one must know how hard are the conditions of this difficult division of land, this sort of liquidation between the noble landlord and his former serf, which Russia is carrying on ever since 1861. The principle adopted by the government is that of a compromise. The peasants were to have the perennial use of their dwelling with its enclosed appurtenances, and, furthermore, lands equivalent to the fields which used to be reserved for their support; but these lands they had to redeem from the owners, who were made to give them up. Yet there is a large class of serfs who have been given no lands, consequently have no payments to make; they are the domestic serfs (*dvoròvyié liúdi*, or "court people"), *i. e.*, the serfs employed in domestic service and personal attendance on their masters. There was a good reason for passing them by—that they never had had any land, having generally entirely given up agricultural life. So they received their personal liberty and that was all. Emancipation, for them, was almost immediate; after two supplementary years of gratuitous service, they were free to leave their masters, or to stay with them for a salary. It is chiefly among this class, many of whom swelled the ranks of urban proletariate, especially among the old men, that numbers were found unwilling to avail themselves of their freedom.

At the moment of the emancipation there were about a million and a half of these domestic serfs,—an unnecessarily large number. As is the case in all slaveholding countries, the dwellings of the wealthy were cumbered with servants of both sexes, untidy, shiftless, lazy—cooks, valets, coachmen, grooms, maids, needle-women, waiting-women, etc. This crowd, half civilized and half corrupted by life in the cities and contact with the masters, frequently was the most objectionable and unwholesome portion of the serf population. The facility of always having at one's beck and call hosts of men and women, the consequent waste of human labor, were for the higher classes one of the great material conveniences, as well as a great moral evil, of serfdom. By this side of it, Russian life came nearer that of the planters in the colonies than the European mode of existence, and gave to the *pomiêsh-tchik* the indolent habits which masters of slaves contract everywhere.

The principle of territorial endowment once accepted, it remained to determine what quantity of land should be conceded to the peasants. In a country so vast, it was impossible to set up a fixed and uniform rule, to allot the same quantity of land to all the late serfs. The government's standard was that each lot should be sufficient to provide for one family, and should be as nearly as possible the equivalent of the lot it had the use of in the old time. This rule also being admitted, it had to be adapted to the differences of soil and climate, to all the inequalities of the population. In spite of the general homogeneousness and uniformity of the Russian soil, this operation alone required colossal labor. Then the relations established by custom between master and peasant had to be taken into consideration. It also became necessary to have recourse to several distinct regulations. Special regulations were made for Little-Russia, Lithuania, and the former Polish provinces. Great-Russia and New-Russia—thirty-four governments between them, over two thirds of the entire Russian territory in Europe—were divided into three wide parallel zones or belts, according to the nature of the soil or the density of the population :

28

the northern zone, comprising the poorest lands ; the Black-Mould zone, comprising the richest ; the Steppe zone, comprising the least populous. Each of these great zones was itself subdivided into ten regions, and for each region a maximum and a minimum were fixed. The average from all these regions gives from three to four *dessiatínas* per male head.* This average sometimes rises to seven *dessiatínas* in the north, to ten in the steppes of the south ; it sometimes goes down to two *dessiatínas* and less in the rich Black-Mould region. † A family numbering three " souls," *i. e.*, three male members, thus received on an average from twenty to twenty-five acres,—which, in most parts of the country, was about what they used to have in the times of serfdom. Although this equivalence was admitted in principle, the peasant's advocates— Miliútin, Samárin, and their friends—were not always able to obtain for him a lot equal to that of which he had the use before his liberation, and, when it came to practice, the manner after which the division was effected frequently still further increased the difference.‡ This was evidently a great disappointment to

* The *dessiatína* is equal to about 2¾ acres. The State performed a similar operation on its own demesnes, and as it had, as a rule, given up to its peasants all the cultivable lands, they have, on the whole, been more favored than the serfs on private estates.

† Here are the valuations of a Russian statistician, Mr. Ianson, concerning the distribution of land before and after the emancipation (1876).

BEFORE.		AFTER.	
Lands of the state......64.6 per cent.		Lands of the state.....45.6 per cent.	
" " " nobility...30.6 " "		" " " nobility...22.6 " "	
" " " appanages 3.3 " "		" " " appanages 1.8 " "	
" " " peasants		" " " peasants	
and colonists.. 1.7 " "		and colonists..30. " "	

The nobility, which before 1861, according to the same authority, owned 105,000,000 of *dessiatínas*, (about 280,000,000 acres) had not over 63,500,-000 left in 1876, while the former serfs owned over 64,000,000 (about 176,000,000 acres).

‡ Miliútin's adversaries contrived to get the territorial allotments cut down in the Drafting Commission itself. Thus Samárin, in one of his letters to Miliútin (September, 1861) complains with much earnestness that Count Pánin, president of the Commission after Rostòvtsef, succeeded in lowering the average for the peasants of Samára from 5½ to 5 *dessiatínas*.

begin with, a first cause of discontent for the peasant, all the more that the increase of the population naturally tends to curtail every year more the original allotment. That, however, was not the only source of disappointment. In some regions the territorial concession was manifestly insufficient ; in many others it was as manifestly too onerous for the peasant, owing to the rate at which the redemption was fixed. The extent of the allotted lands is, indeed, only one side of the question ; in order to appreciate the condition of the freedmen, it is necessary to know how much the land cost them, and in what way they were enabled to pay for it.

BOOK VII. CHAPTER III.

Manner and Conditions of Redeeming the Lands—Advances Made by the Exchequer—Actual State of the Operation—Slackening in the Last Years of Alexander II.—How there still Subsisted, in the Form of Labor Dues, a Sort of Half Servitude, which was Abolished only Under Alexander III.—Why Landed Property is often a Burden to the Freedmen—Unequal Treatment of the Peasants in the Different Regions —The Gratuitous "Quarter Lot"—The Peasant's Disappointment—In what Manner he Understood Liberty.

So vast a liquidation could not be accomplished in a day.   It was important to avoid too abrupt a transformation, which would have landed the country into the midst of a most dangerous crisis. During the two years which followed the Emancipation Act, all the landlords and their tenants had to draw up by mutual agreement an instrument, called "Regulation Charter," which exactly determined the lands to be ceded by the landlords, and the annual payment, in money or labor, to be effected by the peasants for the same.   These things were to be arranged, as much as possible, amicably; but as the clashing of interests, and, still more, the peasants' distrust, gave little hope of such a solution, the decision, in case of conflict, was left to certain magistrates created on purpose, under the title of Arbiters of Peace.   During the first years, men the most independent and superior, such as Prince Tcherkàssky, Yúri Samárin, and others, made it a point to take on themselves these wearisome and delicate duties.   These judges, elected by the nobility, were commissioned to approve the contracts for both sides, and, if need were, to settle the difficulties, subject to ratification by a provincial court.   One would think that these arbiters, appointed by the landlords out of their own ranks, would have been inclined to favor those of their own class. Nothing of the kind. By a phenomenon which does honor to the Russian nobility, and which can be, in part, accounted for by the generosity and sensitiveness of the national character, these men, the chosen of the landlords, of whom the majority were opposed to endowing the serfs with lands, took their mission so earnestly to heart, that they quite frequently laid themselves open to the accusation of taking the peasants' side.* Unfortunately for the latter, these first arbiters, who represented the more noble-minded portion of the nobility, were succeeded by men of a very different type, who felt no scruples in sacrificing the peasants' interests and in applying the local regulations in a spirit opposed to the legislator's intentions.

The Regulation Charters once drawn up (and nearly all— 110,000 to 112,000—were ready within the prescribed time), the peasants, now free and placed in possession of their lands, still owed the landlord perpetual rent in money or in labor. All the difference was that, since 1863, these dues were freely discussed by the contracting parties or legally fixed by the local regulations. Such a state of things too closely resembled serfdom itself to be regarded as anything more than temporary. The tenants subjected to it were designated as being "under temporary obligations." These peasants had only, as it were, traversed the first phase of emancipation; they were in an intermediate position between freedom and serfdom.

Then came a second operation, more complicated, more pro-

* "The 'arbiters of peace,' themselves nobles, even the members of the former 'provincial committees,' have become completely transformed by their new duties" (wrote Samárin to Miliútin in August, 1862); "in entering on them they have not only cast from them, but quickly forgotten, all the past. The desire to conquer popularity among the masses has so entirely triumphed over their former sentiments, that the 'peace assemblies' are flooded with complaints from landlords against the 'arbiters of peace,' on account of their partiality towards the peasants, whereas there is scarcely an instance of the peasants accusing them of partiality towards the land-lords."

tracted, which Alexander II. was to leave unfinished : the "redemption," which put an end to the obligatory territorial relations between the two classes. This question did not bear on the serfs' personal liberty—the nobility never claimed any indemnity for that—but on the lands allotted to them, or rather in the rents which, in force of the Statute and the local charters, burdened those lands. The Redemption Act made the peasants full owners of them ; it freed them from all dues and obligations towards their former masters.

But the law had regulated neither the mode nor the time of redemption ; it was left to the contracting parties to take up that question, to fix the conditions and the time of the operation. Exceptions were made only for the western—former Lithuano-Polish—provinces, where the government, immediately after the rising of 1863 and for political reasons, declared redemption obligatory.   In Russia proper, the State did not interfere in the matter until Alexander III. came to the throne, except by rendering financial aid.

This operation, if left to the peasants' unaided means, would have presented numerous difficulties, both for them and the masters.   It might have lasted centuries and not have been completed then.   The State, therefore, whenever requested by the freedmen, advanced to them the necessary sum, or rather four fifths of that sum, calculated at the capitalization rate of the dues with which each given piece of land was burdened.*

To the landlord, this system offered the immense advantage of converting a private debt on the peasant into a public debt on the State, and the freedman's annual dues into a sort of temporary

---

* The redemption price, as a rule, was calculated not after the marked value of the land, but after the sum-total of the *obròk* paid by the former serfs for the lands ceded to them by the "Regulation Charters." The legal redemption rate was established by capitalizing at 6 per cent. the dues paid in species—in other words, by multiplying the latter by 16⅔. Hence it is that the redemption rate is frequently quite independent of the real value of the soil,—sometimes higher, sometimes lower.

tax, the collection of which is ensured by the fiscal agents. As to the peasant, his gain was that he became without further delay full owner of the soil, and could break off at once the obligations which still bound him to his former master. The State, for their mutual interests, has, as it were, constituted itself banker for both parties.

In proffering its aid to the peasants, the State was naturally entitled to determine in what measure and on what conditions it would grant it. In order not to become engaged too deeply, it had, of course, to fix limits to the financial assistance it was willing to render. Such, according to Miliútin, is the true meaning of the official valuations inserted in the Regulation. By fixing before-hand, according to the regions and to circumstances, the figure of the capital which the State was willing to advance, the legislator intended to mark the limits within which the public credit might be pledged.

Some such precaution was imperative, and this necessity has too often been lost sight of by those who criticised the valuations, some as being inadequate to compensate the landlords, others as being too onerous for the peasants. Both sides were free to con-tract other agreements ; only in that case the peasant was not to count on assistance from the State.*

The advances made by the government to the freedmen are to be reimbursed in the course of forty-nine years at 6 per cent. ; the rate of 6 per cent. annual payment covers the interest and extinguishes the debt. Anticipatory payments are permitted, but of course rarely occur. Thus, in half a century, with the govern-ment's aid, the peasant will be finally liberated and the gigantic operation finally closed. † Only in the course of the twentieth

---

* Such free contracts have been very rare.

† These forty-nine years, moreover, are to be counted, not from the promulgation of the Emancipation Act, but from the moment when the contracting parties determine to avail themselves of the facilities for redemption offered by the State. Now not a few peasants had not yet decided on this step when Alexander III. came to the throne.

century, then, the peasant, freed from all temporary dues to his former master and the State, will have become full owner of the piece of land allotted to him, and will be able to realize all the benefits of emancipation.

This feature of the great reform — the redemption of the lands — turned it into a vast credit operation, which, being undertaken immediately after the Crimean war, might be styled daring. The government could not hand over in cash to the landlords the amount of the debt which it undertook to clear in the tenants' name. Two new titles or bonds, therefore, were created to meet this demand, both interest-bearing and guaranteed by the State : one "to bearer," bringing 5 per cent. interest and negotiable on 'Change; the other at 5½ per cent., bearing the holder's name and subject, with a view to prevent crowding the market, to complicated formalities in case of transfer ; these bonds were subsequently and successively converted, by means of lottery-drawing, into titles "to bearer," extinguishable within thirty-seven years.* It is impossible to enter here into all the details of this vast and complicated operation, materially assisted by the forced course imposed by the Russian government, with the assistance which such a course affords, but also liable to all the risks which it entails on financial enterprise. The most crying need of the noble landholders, deprived of their human capital, was for capital in money. To help them out, the redemption indemnity should have been immediately realizable, and the paper issued by the government was not, or only on onerous conditions. As the holders of the new bonds were pressed

---

* The reader will note that the bonds placed in the landlords' hands were to be extinguished in thirty-seven years, whereas the redemption annuities, paid by the peasants and meant to reimburse the government, are distributed over forty-nine years. The peasants were expected to fall behind with their payments, and that is why the two operations, though connected with each other, were timed differently. These arrears, as anticipated, have been considerable ; still, they remained below the expectations ; payments have even sometimes been anticipated, so that instead of involving the state in debt, the redemption operation brought in a bonus of several million roubles.

for money all at the same time, the money market was glutted with them, and a depreciation ensued which the government's precautionary measures could but imperfectly forestall. This was one of the chief causes of the pecuniary straits, sometimes amounting almost to want, which the emancipation brought on numbers of landlords. What is really wonderful is that such a transformation should not have determined a radical economic crisis ; that Russia, already laboring under financial perturbations, should have come out of this one as unscathed as she did. When Alexander III. came to the throne, the advances disbursed by the government amounted to something like 750,000,000 roubles, and it is remarkable that the State should have been able to open such a credit to the peasants without embarrassment or loss to the exchequer.* If the operation were ended, if all the peasants had taken advantage of the government's assistance and redeemed all the land they were entitled to by law, the advances made by the State would have risen to over one milliard roubles. As it is, they amounted to 862,000,000 on the 1st of June, 1886.

A few figures will make plain the state of the operation at the time of the death of Alexander II. On the first of January, 1881, there still remained, in the thirty-seven governments of the interior, 1,553,000 " revision souls, " † or more than three millions of peasants "under temporary obligations, " *i. e.* such as still owed their former masters, for a time, either labor or *obròk.* The number of serfs having proceeded to the redemption

---

* The metallic rouble is worth 4 francs or 80 cents. During the years that preceded the Bulgarian war, it was near on 3½ francs, and in 1889 it was quoted at about 2½. On the 1st of April, 1880, the total of loans made amounted to 739,000,000; the annuities collected under this head in 1879 reached 43,000,000, to which should be added arrears to the amount of 17,000,000. The Russian Bank had, on an average, advanced 31½ roubles on the *dessiatìna* (20 dollars on each 2¾ acres, approximately), and 107 roubles or thereabouts (about 60 dollars), per male peasant.

† As in the times of serfdom, the male peasant alone is understood under the term "soul" (*dushà*); he alone paid poll-tax, and the increase of population from one " revision " (census) to another was not taken into consideration.

of their lands was 5,750,000 "souls." Of these 5,100,000 had availed themselves of the government's aid ; about 645,000 had not. To these figures we must add 2,700,000 "souls" for the nine western provinces, where, as a consequence of the Polish insurrection, the bonds of serfdom had been abruptly snapped and immediate redemption made compulsory. This gives us, for these forty-nine governments, which comprised the immense majority of serfs, over eight millions of "revision souls," or about twenty millions of persons, finally delivered from bondage, and having in future only to serve the interest on the redemption loan. The operation was conducted on the same principles in the rest of the empire, even to the remotest provinces, such as, for instance, the Caucasus.

During the last years of Alexander II, there was a noticeable slackening in the redemption operations. The number of peasants who had recourse to them had steadily decreased since 1873 : there were not 20,000 in 1880. The final cessation of "temporary obligations" seemed, in consequence, about to be delayed some fifteen or twenty years more, and the forms of serfdom threatened to survive in places into the twentieth century.

Contrary to generally received ideas, there were, at the accession of Alexander III., numerous peasants who, by force of the Statute itself, still remained in a state of legal dependence from the nobility. In 1882 over three million peasants of both sexes still were under their former masters' tutelage and, in plain words, in a state of semi-servitude, since the prerogatives conceded to the landlords by the law were very extensive. The article 148 of the agrarian statute appointed the former master the natural trustee for such communes as still were " under temporary obligations " to him ; article 149 invested him with the police supervision on the domain and the duty of protecting public safety ; he could demand of the commune the arrest of guilty or suspected peasants. Article 160 went the length of awarding to the noble landlord the right of revising the communal resolutions and suspending their execution. More than that, the landlord had, in certain cases, the right of demanding the destitution of the "elder" (*starshinà*) or elective head of the commune, and the appointment of another, and even of authorizing or forbidding the temporary absence of any member of the commune. It is easy to see how abnormal such a state of things was twenty years after the emancipation. In order to become really free, these peasants, in the words of a St. Petersburgh journalist, needed another emancipation.

This second emancipation had been foreseen and prepared by the law ; it was being gradually accomplished by the redemption which freed the liberated serfs from all obligations towards their late masters. Unfortunately, this great measure was carried out unevenly in the various provinces. Landlords and peasants were far from showing everywhere the same zeal in settling accounts. In the government of Kursk, for instance, scarcely one half of the peasants, in those of Nijni, Túla, Oriòl, Àstrakhan, not over two thirds, had begun operations in 1880. In the eight governments which compose the agricultural zone of the centre, *i. e.*, in the richest region of the empire, over twenty-five per cent. of the emancipated serfs, *i. e.*, 1,500,000 peasants of both sexes, were still "under temporary obligations" at the same date. Whereas in other governments — those of Viàtka, Orenburg, Khàrkof, Khersòn—the operation was very nearly completed. The cause of these fluctuations lies in the diversity of the conditions laid down for the redemption in different regions.

In the more fertile regions of the Black Mould belt, where, owing to the outlets opened by the railroads, the value of land has rapidly increased, the landlords frequently found it to their advantage not to consent to its redemption, so as to retain the compulsory services of the peasants. Now the Statute did not give the peasant the right to demand the redemption ; this right belonged exclusively to the master, and all that the peasants could do in such a case was to reduce their lots to the legal minimum allowed for that particular locality. Such a law easily accounts for the slackening of the operation in the course of these last years. In order to put an end to this anomaly and to hasten the completion of this gigantic liquidation, Alexander III. issued an *ukàz* making redemption obligatory. Thus to the son belongs the honor of finishing the father's work.

Strange to say, scarcely two fifths of the redemption operations were undertaken by mutual consent. In over sixty cases out of each hundred, the demand came from the landlords or from the credit institutions where their estates were mortgaged. The peasant's distrust partly accounts for this, and his reluctance to pay for a field to which he considered himself entitled ; but this is not the only, nor even the chief reason. The law itself indirectly encouraged him in his passive resistance. For the Statute, indeed, authorized the landlord to demand the pecuniary settlement with his tenants ; but in this case he was bound to content himself with the sums advanced by the State, *i. e.*, with only four fifths of the price established by official valuation ; the law forbade him from claiming any more.

It was therefore manifestly in the peasants' interests to have the redemption forced upon them, since in this way they secured a reduction in the price. The official valuations being based on the capitalization of the dues, they found themselves pledged to the payment of less onerous annuities, even while they gained full ownership of the lands.* This was, in fact, what the sovereign and the members of the Drafting Commission aimed at. Everything in this operation seems intended to benefit the freedmen, yet these same peasants, apparently so favored, are frequently the

---

* One illustration will make the matter plainer. Certain peasants paid to their former lord, as laid down in the Regulation Charters, a yearly due of seven and a half roubles. The rate of redemption for this due, based on the capitalization at six per cent., was 125 roubles. But of this sum the peasants, being constrained by the landlord to redeem, had actually to pay only four fifths, or 100 roubles, that being the amount advanced by the State ; and for this advance they pay the State only six per cent. interest, which includes the extinguishment of the debt,—that is to say, six roubles a year instead of seven.

most dissatisfied. The reason is simple : the valuations of redemption rates being based on the figure of the annual dues, and not on the actual value of the soil, the land, thus ceded apparently at reduced prices, is frequently far from having in reality the value which the freedmen have to pay for it. That is why numbers of them, on being forced to redeem, availed themselves of their right of acquiring only the legal minimum.

Compulsory redemption is prevalent in the north : governments of Petersburgh, Nòvgorod, Pskof, Tver, Smolensk, Moscow,— and in the less fertile regions generally. Redemption by mutual agreement obtains chiefly in the south : governments of Poltáva, Tchernígof, Khàrkof, Khersòn, and in the rich Black Mould regions generally. In the north, the soil being unproductive and the redemption rates, based on the annual dues formerly paid, comparatively high, it was entirely in the master's interest to get out of his tenants whatever the law empowered him to demand. In the south, the soil generally being remarkably fertile and, owing to the railroads, steadily rising in value, the landlord was by no means anxious to give it up at the legal rate, which, as a rule, fell far short of its actual value.*

It is plain from this that the emancipation, even while conducted everywhere after identical rules, could not everywhere produce the same effects, but must have overburdened at times the landlord, at others the peasants. That, partly, explains the difference in the judgments pronounced in Russia itself on the great reform. Of the noble landholders, the least wealthy came off worst. The State was forced to come to the aid of such among them who, owning only a few serfs, whose labor they rented out,

* The reports of the agricultural inquest commissions show that the redemption rates, as fixed in 1861, were, in the northern portions of the Black Mould belt and in some western localities, ten, thirty, fifty, and sometimes a hundred per cent. below the actual market value of the land. In the northwest, the north, and the east, on the contrary, it was as much above the current prices. It appears that there were only nine governments in which the difference one way or the other did not amount to more than ten per cent.

found themselves on the verge of total ruin. Among the freed-men, no given class had any claim on indemnities or assistance ; but the State had to help out some indirectly by remitting them part of their tax arrears. This was done, among others, in the government of Smolensk, where the price charged for the land is out of all proportion with its producing capacities, and where the lot which the peasant has been compelled to redeem is notoriously insufficient to cover his taxes and dues.*

Where the conditions were most favorable to them, the peasants did not always know how to avail themselves of the advantages proffered them. They showed a repugnance for this operation, which could be accounted for only by their prejudices and their distrust. " Why," they objected, " should we redeem land that belongs to us ? " Many saw there a trap and got it into their heads that the land was to be made over to them some day unconditionally, wherefore redemption, they reasoned, was all profit to the master. In a certain village, situated in one of the richest Black Mould governments, a great landlord—an upright and liberal man, tried to make his peasants understand that it was in their interest to redeem the maximum allowed them by the local regulation. His insistence only increased their dis-trust, and his proposals were repulsed by the commune after long debates. For the decision in such cases must be passed by the commune as a body, that being an engagement which involves the solidarity of all the peasants. In the communal assembly of this particular village, then, those who were inclined to follow the landlord's advice, and opined for immediate redemption and the legal maximum, were accused of siding with the master. The others pulled their beards and abused them : " You are nothing but serfs ; you are the *bárin's* men ; you don't know what it means to be free." They meant that the land would be coming to them of itself by and by, along with their liberty.

---

* Some ten million roubles, taken from the treasury funds and in great part distributed through the provincial nobiliary assemblies, were devoted to this use.

Numbers of communes acted in the same manner under like circumstances. Such facts show that the law-makers had their good and sufficient reasons when they imposed on the peasants the obligation of redeeming a minimum of land. Had the landlords not been empowered to force them to it, they would have been waiting forever for gratuitous possession and never have come to any understanding at all. So in the village just mentioned, the peasants now have only two or three *dessiatínas* (six to eight acres) per " soul," whereas, by accepting the legal maximum, they would have had more than double as much. The lands which they refused to redeem, they now rent from the landlord, at a rate very little below that of the redemption annuities. By paying a few copecks more for the next forty-nine years, they would have become proprietors instead of remaining tenants. That is a point that many peasants never took in, or— their courage failed them, being filled with chimerical hopes, and more alive to the burdens of the present than to the fair promise of the future.

Into the statute which regulates all the details of this immense liquidation, somehow crept a certain " Article 123," which rose to great importance during the first years of the emancipation, owing to the peasants' improvidence. In virtue of this article, the landlord could, instead of selling to his tenants the quantity of land stipulated by the local regulation, and with their agreement, free himself from this obligation by giving up to them gratuitously one fourth of the legal maximum. This article 123, nicknamed from its inventor, " Gagárin article," appears not to have been much to the taste of Miliútin, Tcherkàssky, Samárin, and others of their stamp,—in other words, of the peasants' more ardent champions in the Drafting Commission. Owing to the ignorance of the former serfs, this clause was, at first, in great favor with them, but, of course, caused much disappointment later on. In the rich Black Mould regions, where the soil in most cases rapidly rose to a value far beyond the legal redemption rates, the tenants, who had everything to lose by this combination, ofttimes hailed it with joy, and even insisted on its being carried out, glad to be delivered from the burden of the dues and secretly cherishing a vague hope of a new and gratuitous distribution.

Another noteworthy trait : one of the things that confirmed the hankering of many peasants after this gratuitous " quarter lot," was the repugnance with which it was at first regarded by most landlords, too shortsighted to understand from the first that it could be to their advantage to sacrifice their indemnity in view of the probable rise of ground-rent. Experience soon opened the peasants' eyes ; most contracts of the kind are dated from the first two or three years. The people gave to this gratuitous " quarter lot " the designation of " orphan's " or " poor man's lot," and, as a matter of fact, the communes which have accepted it are now, as a rule, poorer than their neighbors. * In the rich Black Mould regions, where the increase in value has already taken place, the peasants who have elected this mode of settlement have before this become bitterly aware of their mistake. † They complain and try to make out that they have been cheated. In a village I am personally acquainted with the women now upbraid the men with their improvident decision : " You are wretches," they repeat to them ; " thanks to you, our children will always be beggars." And to crown all, the workers of disturbances are

* I just now came across a characteristic page in a letter of Yúri Samárin : " The great popularity, among the peasants, of ' Article 123,' which they have named ' the orphan's lot,' is accounted for principally by a blunder of the landlords themselves, who generally opened the discussion by declaring themselves ready to accede to anything, except ' the gratuitous quarter lot.' (Art. 123). That was sufficient for the peasant to imagine that in that provision lay perfect bliss for him. For myself, I announced that I was willing to agree to anything, without taking exception to any article whatever, so I had not a single demand for ' the orphan's lot.' "—Letter to N. Miliútin, August, 1862.

† It seems at first sight as though the 642,000 peasants who, on the 1st of January, 1882, had accomplished the redemption of their lands without assistance from the State, should be accounted the most fortunate ; that, however, is not the case in reality, since they are mostly those who had been content with the " quarter lot," so that, practically, there had been no redemption at all.

trying to make capital of this dissatisfaction and the inequality in the condition of the different communes, brought about by an act of their own free will, for the revolutionary propaganda.

All the peasants are far from having the same cause for regrets, yet nearly all have experienced the same feeling of disappointment. The best treated have failed to find in the longed-for liberty the wonder-working fairy whose wand was to operate a magical transformation in their *izbà*. The expectations aroused in the masses by the very word "emancipation" and overwrought by the longings of centuries, were too lofty, too visionary not to shrink and pale before reality. In the serf's dreams the image of liberty took tints the more glowing, a glamour the more radiant, that the form of it was so vague. The liberated peasant forgets the ills of serfdom, the unpaid, compulsory labor, the *obròk ;* he inclines to see only the present charges and the vanishing of his dream. "Father," said an old woman in my presence, speaking of her late husband, "father saw a field in a dream one night, at the time that the manifesto came out, and said to me in the morning : I know what that means—we shall never be free." To the old crone, this word had a profound meaning ; fifteen years after, she still saw in it a sort of prophecy or divination. How did she interpret the mysterious dream ? Was the field seen by her husband a symbol of servitude in her eyes, or perhaps an emblem of that prosperity which the peasant sees in his dreams but never can grasp ? No matter, the *mujik* and his *bába* * understood each other : they should never be free ! This guileless cry of the heart reveals vague and misty aspirations, not unlike some of the theories of Western socialism on the bondage of the people, and modern servitude generally. This is why a writer of subtle mind gave the advice—probably easier to give than to follow : to untie the bonds of serfdom quietly, to free the serfs "without ringing in their ears that terrible word *Liberty*, for the true meaning of which Western Europe has been seeking through centuries."

* *Bába*, woman, especially old woman ; *bàbka*, *bábushka*—grandmother.

29

BOOK VII. CHAPTER IV.

Results of the Emancipation—How the Manners and Social Status were less Affected by it than was Expected by either Adversaries or Partisans—Disappointments and their Causes—Economic Results—They Differ according to the Regions—How it is that the Conditions of the Master's Existence have been Modified by the Emancipation, on the Whole, more than the Peasant's—Moral and Social Consequences.

I⊤ was not only in the *izbà* that the emancipation left an undercurrent of dissatisfaction. This revolution, which struck at the very bases of society and property, which, in the opinion of statesmen, was likely to imperil the entire social order, was accomplished peaceably, with hardly any disturbance. It was a great success; yet, to many of those who took part in the work, it proved disappointing.

At the two extremes of the civilized world—in Russia and in the United States of America—two tasks of similar import were achieved at nearly the same moment, although by very different means. In America, the liberation of the slaves, bought at the price of a murderous war and carried out by force, without umpires or mediating power, has temporarily cast the white master at the feet of the colored freedman, and established on the shores of the Gulf of Mexico a state of things as saddening, as perilous, as slavery itself. In Russia, on the other hand, the same event has brought about no class strife; as for race strife, there could be none; it has bred neither animosity nor rivalry; the social peace was not disturbed. And yet, of the two countries, the best satisfied with its own work possibly is not the Empire of the North.

How is this seeming anomaly to be explained? First of all by the excessive hopes raised—a feeling which, with the Russian, beyond every other people, is apt to overleap reality; then by the passionate longing of desire, of which the joy of possession always falls short. Not less than the ignorant serf, the politician and the literary man, private speculation and public opinion, had built up illusions. The cultivated Russians had conjured up a vision of an Eden very nearly as fanciful as the Eldorado of the peasant's dreams : of a free Russia, all new, all different from the Russia of serfdom. In reality, the change neither was effected as rapidly, nor reached as deep as was expected; there was no sudden transformation scene. And so, many choice spirits gave way to disenchantment, depression, discouragement. This is a point that should never be lost sight of: the emancipation and all the great reforms which accompanied or followed it have not brought about, in manners, social relations, in the national life, all the changes which both its adversaries and partisans had augured from it. The consequences, for good or evil, have been less great, less visible, less striking than was hoped by the ones and feared by the others. After so much discussing, after such lofty flights of ambition and such sombre forebodings, it was a surprise to both progressists and conservatives to find themselves so nearly at the point whence they started, to have made so little way. In this respect Russia is not unlike a man who, after undergoing a dangerous operation, does not find himself as much benefited by it as he had hoped, and is at once glad to have come out of it alive and dissatisfied at not feeling more relieved.

Russia is not the only country that has passed through such painful and contrary impressions. France, too, on the eve and on the morrow of her revolutions, has known but too well these alternations of enthusiasm and despondency, that moral collapse which follows on mighty efforts, after the exaltation of the struggle has passed away. In Russia the reaction has been the greater, the disenchantment the bitterer, that the country, being younger, had the superb confidence of youth in its own powers. It is therefore not to be wondered at, if, long before the assassination of Alexander II., disappointment showed on all sides, in public opinion and in the press ; nor should too much credence be given to the laments of fashionable pessimism, which, since the nihilists' attempts, has become quite outspoken. In the same way that, in France, the failure of 1789 and the bankruptcy of the Revolution have been proclaimed, the bankruptcy of the emancipation and the failure of the reforms have been denounced in Russia. Public opinion, having declared itself disappointed, lost all interest—especially in the provinces—in the questions which had roused it to such a passionate pitch under Alexander II. Such hours of depression are inevitable in the lives of nations ; to throw all the blame on the alleged fickleness of the Russian character would be unfair. In all countries trees grow too slowly to please the hand that planted them, and the eyes that watch them are always astonished at the tardiness of the fruit.

Not content with complaining almost universally of the slow progress effected so far, many Russians proclaim, as a sort of axiom, that the condition of the rural population is worse than it was before the emancipation. This kind of paradox has almost become a commonplace, so quickly are the woes and the shame of serfdom forgotten over the sufferings and difficulties of the present day.

One would naturally look for such an opinion principally from those men who, from their education, their principles or their age, are all, the world over, prone to laud the past. But they are far from being alone of this mind ; their cue is taken up by progressists, the least apt to shy at innovations. Curiously enough, indeed, it is in this latter camp that pessimism often stalks most rampantly. Those who denounce most vociferously the failure of the 19th of February are not always men who dread and condemn the principles proclaimed on that day, but more often such as are inclined to regard the agrarian laws of 1861 as inadequate or incomplete.

One of the causes which account for this anomaly and also, in part, for the general feeling of disappointment left by the Emancipation Statute, is the fact that the great reform was not carried out by the same hands that had so laboriously prepared it. It should not be forgotten that, on the very morrow of the day on which their agrarian code was solemnly promulgated, its chief authors, together with their leader, Miliútin, were consigned to disgrace. Whatever one may think of their work and their doctrines, there is scarcely a doubt but that, in their hands, that work, in its practical application, would have been conducted more resolutely, logically, consistently, than in the hands of men antagonistic or indifferent to it.

One thing is certain, that the same spirit did not preside at the drawing up of the rural charter and at the carrying out of it. This initial reform, like most of those that were soon to follow, labored under incoherences and hesitations,—at least in the application,— also under lack of conviction and lack of method.

The most illustrious among the instigators of the Statute of the 19th of February would have wished, as did Miliútin, after observing how it worked, to go over again certain amendments which had been forced on the commission ; to base the new construction on administrative, economic, financial reforms, which were not, after all, undertaken in time or not in the same spirit. Their most earnest wish, it is asserted, was to alleviate the peasant's sufferings, to strive to lighten the burdens which crush him, to seek, among other things, for a way to facilitate the agrarian liquidation by means of a systematic process of colonization, instead of leaving the *mujik* to go forth at random to look for the promised land. It may be that, even had they been allowed to conduct the practical application of the reform in their own way, they would not have been able to fulfil all their hopes and avoid all disappointment. But it is manifestly unfair to cast all the blame for any mistakes or illusions from which the great work may not have been exempt, on men who were repeatedly compelled to introduce into it alterations opposed to their views, and who after laboriously drawing up and ordering into a code most complicated laws, were commanded to entrust the practical application of them to other hands.

Moreover, the work, though not having yielded all that was expected of it by the impatience of its promoters, is far from having proved as barren of results as certain people would have us believe. Politically, the effects of the emancipation have been almost *nil ;* but in all other respects its consequences are numerous and already apparent. It would be difficult to enumerate them in a few pages. Still they might be reduced under three main heads : economic progress, owing to the stimulant applied to production by free labor and free competition ; moral progress, owing to the removal from the public conscience of a long standing stain and to the new-born feeling of responsibility ; social transformation, owing to the slackening of patriarchal habits in favor of individualism.

The economic results are perhaps the most difficult to appraise, for two reasons : 1st, because property, agriculture, and the whole of rural economy have not yet been rescued from the confusion and uncertainty inseparable from any epoch of transition ; 2d, because the effects of the emancipation vary, for both classes concerned, according to the regions, the provinces, the communes, and indeed, as regards the former masters, they vary according to the character, the qualities, good or evil, of individuals. The traveller, therefore, should not wonder at the diversity or even contradictoriness of the views which he encounters on this subject, or at the complaints which he hears from both landlord and freedman, since both of necessity are temporarily uncomfortable and each considers himself aggrieved.

As a rule, the landlords have, at all events during the first years, lost a notable portion of their income—frequently as much as one third. In the Black Mould provinces, where the soil is generous and the population comparatively dense, the substitution of free for servile labor was not long a matter of regret. In such rich governments as Kursk, Oriòl, Tambòf, Voronej, the land-lord, if possessed of some capital and a well-ordered mind, fre-quently drew from his diminished acres, at the end of a few years, an income as large, if not larger, as an estate of double the extent yielded in the times of serfdom. In this favored region, where new railroads have opened wide facilities to agriculture, where the land has ofttimes doubled, trebled, quadrupled in value, both landlords and peasants have been enabled at once to reap benefit from the new dispensation.*

Not such the state of affairs in the steppes of the south ; still less in the meagre regions of the north and west. In the steppes, where land is plentiful and the population scarce, the suppression of forced labor inflicted on the landlords such losses as could not be made good by the redemption dues. In the thankless plains of the north and northwest,—Pskof, Nòvgorod, Smolensk, Tver,— where the soil is niggardly in bearing and hands are scarce, the lands left to the nobility are far from bringing in what they used to bring when labor was unpaid. So great is the difference, that many landlords, finding farming too burdensome and unremunera-tive a pursuit, have given it up, and gone into the cities, there to live on state service, industry, or commerce.

These northern *pomiêsh-tchiks*, the most heavily stricken by the expropriation of 1861, are often those who received the highest indemnities. For, if the lands left them have considerably gone down in value, the redemption rates for those which they ceded to

---

* The rapid rise in the prices of land, in the more fertile regions, is not due exclusively to the creation of railways ; it is one of the direct conse-quences of emancipation, which frees the soil itself and makes the owning of land accessible to all classes of the nation. It enabled tradesmen and other urban classes to invest capital in land. Accordingly, the reports of the agricultural inquest commission of 1873 show that the number of rural landholders had trebled in the ten first years after the emancipation. On the other hand, there is a proportionate decrease in the ranks of the noble landholders. Many *pomiêsh-tchiks*, already ill at ease in the time of serf-dom, had now been forced to liquidate.

the peasants were calculated on a basis much above their real worth. So here again the peasant is most to be pitied of the two. A large proportion of the serfs of these provinces had ceased to work on their masters' estates, and were plying various trades in the cities or villages, paying the usual annual due or *obròk*. To avert complete ruin from the landlords, it became imperative to compel these serfs to redeem, equally with the others, lots on which, half the time, they could not make a living, at rates which, being based on the figure of the annual dues they had paid from other sources, was usually much higher than the normal income from the land—sometimes than the net income of the best years. For this class of peasants—and it was a numerous one—the compulsory redemption of the land virtually meant the redemption of their personal liberty.

The Emperor Alexander II., in his address of the 27th of January, 1861, while commanding the project of emancipation to be laid before him, informed the Council of the Empire that "the fundamental object of the entire work was to be the amelioration of the peasants' condition, not merely in words, but in deed." In conformity with these generous instructions, those who were appointed to draw up the charter calculated the rate of the obligatory redemption in such a manner as to afford to the peasants immediate relief; but they had left out of their calculations the increase of taxes and contributions of every kind, to be levied on the state in general, on the provinces, the communes. Great is the number of peasants who, to-day, pay taxes and dues as heavy as in the time of serfdom,* while they have less land, less forest, often less live stock, and less credit than before the emancipation,

* All the local administrations complain of the disproportion between the direct taxes and the income from the land,—a disproportion in consequence of which the taxes really fall on the personal labor of the husbandman. Not to lay on too gloomy colors, however, it should be remembered that one half of the rural population—the peasants of the Crown demesnes, are, as a rule, much better off than the others. They have more land and pay less for it.

which, under such crushing conditions, could not rapidly augment the well-being of the people nor improve the culture of the soil. It has frequently enriched wealthy districts and sometimes appears to have still more impoverished poor ones. Official statistics have ascertained that in many localities the cattle had diminished in number ; hand in hand with the lack of cattle, goes that of agricultural implements and of manure, so that the peasant's already primitive mode of farming not only has not improved, but has, in places, actually deteriorated since he is free. The soil has become exhausted, the fields have even sometimes been abandoned, so that in many regions bad crops and dearth have come to be of almost regular occurrence.

In order to compensate all these inequalities, and to distribute all these burdens more evenly among the various regions, the State should have taken upon itself a portion, at least, of the redemption payments, instead of merely advancing the money to the peasants. That in fact, and everything considered, would have been but just, for the State itself and all the classes of society, especially the merchant class, to which the reform opened the access to landed property, were interested in its success. And indeed it was in this very manner, with the co-operation of the State, that the corresponding process took place in the Kingdom of Poland, a few years later, under the direction of Nicolas Miliútin, and that is probably one of the reasons why, notwithstanding the harshness of the conditions imposed on the Polish nobility, the agrarian laws have perhaps worked better there than in the centre of the empire.

The Emperor Alexander III. has alleviated the sufferings of the peasants in twofold guise : by revising the direct taxation, and by reducing the redemption dues. The State has made an effort to equalize the burdens of the former serfs and of the Crown peasants who have been endowed with land from the State demesnes ; it has striven to aid the portion of the rural population whose load was heaviest. The difficulty lay in the financial straits of the imperial exchequer. The Bulgarian war, which drew it into unexpected extra costs, to the amount of one milliard of roubles, would, it was feared, stand in the way, for a long time to come, of any such operation. This difficulty has not arrested the Emperor Alexander III. and his councillors.

In spite of the penury which afflicts the treasury, the imperial government contrived to lighten the burdens which crush the life out of the rural populations. The Emperor Alexander III., constantly preoccupied with the welfare of his faithful peasants, appears to have set this task before himself as his main object in life. Already towards the end of his father's reign, the suppression of the poll-tax had been spoken of, as well as the expediency of spreading the sixty million roubles supplied by this tax over all classes. One of the present emperor's first acts was to carry out his father's intentions by abolishing this tax, in use through many centuries, the last relic of serfdom. This was definitely accomplished in 1886, and a land tax substituted, also an income tax (on incomes derived from other sources than real estate), and a tax on inheritances. As long ago as 1880 the salt excise was suppressed, a tax which, though classed under the head of "indirect," in reality amounted to a sort of poll-tax, weighing most heavily on the poor.

As to the reduction of the redemption dues, the government of Alexander III. decided in favor of a compromise between two different systems. At first it had been planned to make use of all the resources that the State could dispose of to liberate the poorest and most overburdened localities. The difficulty of such an undertaking, and the wish to enable the entire rural class to share in the good things provided by the new reign, caused the project to be given up. Alexander III. accepted the opinion expressed by a "Commission of Experts" appointed on this occasion, and a general reduction for all the former serfs of Great- and Little-Russia was decided upon. The imperial *ukàz* which announced this boon, as a sort of gracious greeting from the new sovereign,, promised at the same time a further supplementary reduction to the more particularly overburdened villages. This meant twelve millions annually lifted from the *mujik's* shoulders.* It came to about one rouble per " revision soul," *i. e.* per male peasant, as carried on the old capitation rolls.†

Such an alleviation may seem less than trifling. Yet it generally amounts to about one seventh of the average rate of redemption payments up to 1882. However inconsiderable the reduction, it has nearly everywhere effaced the disproportion between the dues paid by the former serfs and by the Crown peasants. The four or five millions destined to succor the least favored regions, were unfortunately insufficient to ensure the well-being of the more overtaxed among the peasants. It might have been better to reserve for them alone whatever resources were to be got at, instead of scattering them over the whole of Great and Little-Russia. Notwithstanding the government's praiseworthy efforts and the real alleviation awarded them, numbers will, for a long time to come, be weighed down by want and taxes. It is to be feared that in many a region the burdens, of which Alexander III. has done his best to rid the peasant, may fall back upon his shoulders under some other shape. In many instances what the former serfs gained from the reduction of the redemption dues bids fair to be swallowed up by the continually increasing provincial and municipal taxes.

Paradoxical as it may appear at first sight, the emancipation has, on the whole, modified the manner of life of the liberated serfs far less than that of their masters. In truth, the advantages, the conveniences afforded by serfdom to these latter could never be

---

* Of this sum three millions were charged directly to the treasury ; two millions were covered by the surplus in the redemption fund ; seven millions by the profits of the State Bank and the liquidation of former credit institutions.

† This general reduction costs about seven or eight millions of roubles annually, for it does not apply to the peasants of the western provinces, where the dues were reduced as early as 1863, in consequence of the Polish insurrection.

appraised in money. Unpaid service, with a host of nameless petty privileges, made farming a far simpler and easier matter than it became under the free labor system. The loss of their hands compelled the landlords to rouse themselves out of their traditional indolence,—to take thought for their affairs themselves,—to adjust themselves to new demands and to struggle with hitherto unknown difficulties,—to transform all their methods and proceedings, their mode of administration at the very least,—to hire laborers and discuss wages,—to let their lands on leases or go halves with their former serfs,—a very complicated programme in a country where farmers and capitals are scarce, and where every peasant has his own bit of land to till.

There are many morose conservative landlords who do not think even an increase of income an adequate compensation for all these worries. And petty worries are frequently more galling than great difficulties. One, in particular, is often complained of : Formerly, the greater part of the manor houses were situated close to the villages, to enable the master always to keep an eye on his subjects. Now, that the peasants' dwellings, with their little enclosures and the communal lands, are their property, the noble landlord, who cannot afford to build himself a new residence on an isolated site, is next-door neighbor to people who are no longer subject to him, who have no kind even of official relations with him, and whose lands are wedged in with his own. This proximity is exasperating ; he does not feel at home any more, has no privacy, and is all the time fuming at the drunken, thievish vicinity he cannot escape from. More than a few, on this seemingly futile ground, declare the country to have become uninhabitable.

Of all the consequences of emancipation one of the most noteworthy assuredly is the decadence of the old patriarchal manners, not only in the relations between landlord and peasant, but in the *mujik's* own *izbà*. Along with the bond between master and serf, that between father and son—the family bond, has become slackened. They have tasted of freedom, and now, in the same way

that the serf is rid of the master's yoke, the son strives to rid himself of the yoke of paternal authority, almost absolute until now.
Young couples want to be independent of the old people. They
each want a house and lot of their own.

The awakening of the peasant to a liking for independence
and the restoration of his liberty of action must, in the end, benefit
the towns and the richer, more fertile regions, possibly to the
detriment of the poorer, where the population is no longer held
fast by the artificial barrier of serfdom.

Men, like capital, tend to where labor is most remunerative.
The colonization of the arable steppes of the south and the east, as
well as of the remoter dependences of the empire, must logically
follow on the breaking of the peasant's fetters. If it has not yet
taken an active start, it is because of the hindrance opposed to it
by the administrative conservatism which still binds the peasants
to their lands through the institution known as communal solidarity, which forbids a member to absent himself unless by the consent of all the others.

One of the chief, but naturally also slowest, benefits of emancipation will be the moral improvement of both serf and master. Both
have grown up to man's estate under the reign of serfdom ; both
bear the marks of the training they have received from this sorry
educator. Many of the faults imputed to the Russian nobility,
many of those thrown in the Russian peasant's face, come from that
demoralizing training. The vices, opposite, yet connected in their
very opposition, of the master and the serf—the fatuity, frivolity,
prodigality of the one ; the self-abasement, duplicity, thriftlessness
of the other ; the laziness and improvidence of both—flowed from
the same source. The landlord, who was supplied with a certain
income despite his incapacity or ignorance, is now compelled to
deal with men and things, to study characters, to regulate his
domestic as well as his rural expenditure ; he has no alternative
but either to bestir himself or to accept ruin.

As for the peasant, the stigmata left on him are too ancient and too deep to allow of the mark being obliterated in a few short years.   The *mujik* is lazy and devoted to routine, he is crafty and untruthful ; a proverb of his own says he would outwit the devil any day.   What else could be expected from this long personal bondage superadded to political servitude and which robbed him of his liberty at the very moment when his country had recovered her own ?   The liberated peasant is certainly far from showing him-self worthy of the half-idolatrous honors rendered, in his person, to the Russian people by its numerous admirers.   The *mujik* goes on getting drunk and beating his wife ; he has not yet learned to invariably respect the rights of property.   But all these evil propensities have long been fostered by servitude : drunkenness comes from a longing for oblivion ; domestic brutality is warranted by that of the master or his bailiff ; pilfering, by the old habit of regarding as in a manner belonging to him what belonged to his master.   These faults have not vanished ; some even, if we are to believe the croakers, may have become intensified through the sudden removal of restraint.   Drunkenness especially, they aver, has made frightful progress : for drink the peasant will sell even his tools.   The evil in this direction is great, undoubtedly : the surplus shown by the State budget is almost invariably supplied by the excise department.   Still, as this surplus is generally due to an increase in the taxation of spirits, as it is not accom-panied by a diminution in the revenue yielded by any other branch subject to taxation, it turns out, on the provincial statis-tics' own showing, that, in spite of his poverty, the *mujik* earns enough to enable him to add to all his compulsory payments the voluntary contribution of the tap-room, apart from the fact that the redemption dues which he annually pays are, in reality, a form of compulsory saving.*

---

* The alleged progress of drunkenness is, in fact, very questionable, especially for these latter years.   Recent statistical reports show a diminu-tion of 3 % in 1874 in the production of *vòdka* (rye whiskey), which in 1864 reached the figure of 27 millions of *vedrò*, a measure containing about twelve quarts, while there was in the population an increase of 10 % ; and

Another reproach often cast at the freedman is his improvidence. He now knows even less than he did how to protect himself, by liberal savings, against the instability of the climate and consequent bad crops, which, in Russia, always threaten even the very best lands. This attack, however, from the advocates of the past turns against themselves, for it is servitude which has accustomed the peasant to rely on the master for everything, as a child on his guardian.

It appears to be an established fact that since the peasants have no longer their *bárin* at their back, they, as a rule, stand accidents of all sorts, so frequent in Russian rural life, worse than they did before : epidemics, epizoötics, fires, destructive insects, insufficient crops find them more helpless. It is therefore quite usual to hear regrets about not having an institution which should, as did the landlord in bygone days, succor the *mujik* when he is the victim of calamities and disastrous visitations. But whatever way you turn—whether you appeal to the commune, to the provincial assemblies, or to the State, or simply have recourse to a credit bank, it is no easy matter to organize such a special providence, all the less that the peasant's own thriftlessness and ignorance prove obstacles in the way of every contrivance invented for his benefit.*

The upshot of it all is that the *mujik* of to-day is in a phase of transition, he has not yet been able to throw off the faults bequeathed to him by servitude, and now adds to those certain other faults, proper to liberty. After being so long bent double under the yoke, it is not astonishing that he should not yet have straightened himself to his full stature, that he should not always know how to conduct himself in a manner becoming a freeman, that personal dignity should as yet be as unfamiliar to him as the sense of responsibility. Nor is it to be wondered at that, from the stand-

since 1874 another diminution is said to have taken place in the home consumption. The number of taverns or tap-rooms (*kabàks*) is said to have gone down 40 %, more particularly in the villages. On the other hand the peasant consumes a greater quantity of tea and sugar—a sure token of prosperity.

* Several popular banks have recently been founded for this very purpose.

point of intellect and instruction, his progress should not have been more rapid ; that is not entirely due to the inadequacy of the schools and the resources of the State, the provinces, the rural communes ; it comes in great part from the huge thickness and density of the popular layers, and from the absence of an intermediate class which would help to reach the bottom of them.

The portraits—or caricatures—constantly drawn of the liberated *mujik*, abroad and at home, give no reason to augur badly for his future. Let us recall what sort of a being, under the old-time monarchy, was the French peasant, the animal with two feet and a human face depicted by La Bruyère, such as Fléchier shows him in his *Grands Jours d' Auvergne*, or the Englishman Young on the very eve of the Revolution. There is certainly nothing there to put the *mujik* to the blush or make Russia's friends despair of her civilization. There are countries—Egypt for one—where the rural man, the *fellah*, though nominally free, has been so lowered by sixty centuries of oppression, that one wonders whether he will *ever* have the strength to rise. The Russian peasant never suggests similar thoughts.

In spite of several centuries of servitude, the manumitted peasant has rapidly become conscious of his rights and is ready to defend them against any and everybody. That is easily accounted for : the former serf, accustomed to look on the tsar as on his natural protector, had never ceased to hope for liberty and, in his relations to his master of yesterday, is always inclined to count on the support of the government. Only a few months after the inauguration of the Statute, one of the principal members of the "drafting commission," himself a great landholder, Yuri Samárin, in his letters to his friend N. Miliútin, was exulting at what he called the "transfiguration of the people" and loudly rejoiced over the manner in which the peasants were getting educated by their conflict with the nobility.* For the peas-

---

* Samárin who, as a rule, and not without reason, was regarded as a pessimist, wrote the following lines, which may appear at this day sanguine

ants' most generous advocates as well as for the eloquent Slavophil journalist, there lay the main point; in their eyes the material advantages of the emancipation were a secondary consideration. The great object with them—we can see that from Miliútin's correspondence—was to raise the people, to awaken the peasant to a consciousness of his own personality and of his rights as a freeman, even should yesterday's masters be hurt at times from being "the grindstone on which the people's wits were getting whetted."

The *mujik*, as a rule, thoroughly grasped his novel rights; unfortunately he did not always show as clear a perception of his new duties and obligations. In this respect he promptly undeceived his best friends' hopes. One of the faults the famous Statute can most justly be charged with is an excess of faith in the *mujik's* honesty, or rather simplicity. Prince Tcherkàssky did not hesitate to acknowledge as much in private conversation. He confessed to it in the first years in a confidential letter to his friend and former colleague, Miliútin. While expressing much legitimate pride in the success of their common work, peaceably accomplished in spite of so many ill-natured prophecies, Tcherkàssky regretted only one thing: not having taken more precautions against the peasant's unprincipled propensities.

Among all the faults that can be, on the average, imputed to the liberated serf, there is one from which he seems to be absolutely free: it is acrimony or ill-feeling of any kind towards his former master. He is not exactly scrupulous where his interests

to an excess of optimism: "Without any exaggeration, the people are transfigured, from head to foot. The Statute has loosened their tongues, it has broken through the narrow circle of ideas within which, as though shut in there by a spell, the people vainly went round and round, finding no issue." (Letter to Miliútin, May, 1861.) A few months later, coming back to the same idea, Samárin again wrote: "The Statute has done its work. The people have straightened themselves and are transfigured: they look, walk, talk differently. That is acquired; it is impossible to suppress, and that is the point. In their conflict with the other class, the peasants are now getting their civic education." (November, 1861.)

are at stake ; but he commits his iniquities ingenuously, with a sort of good-natured slyness, without bitterness, without any feeling of envy or animosity, any systematic ill-will.   In spite of his incurable distrust and all that has been said about his ingratitude,[*] the mutual relations of the two classes, but lately linked together by so galling a bond, have retained, at least externally, a character of cordiality, both in public and private life.[1]   For the provincial assemblies, where the two orders are placed side by side ; the peasants, far from opposing their former lords, are more apt to be led by them.   Thus all the speculations on imminent class-strife and popular grudges have proved vain.   Provided the late master was not actually a tyrant, the *mujik* still calls him "his good bárin"; if he has no occasion any more to assume an humble demeanor to the *pomiêsh-tchik* of whom he implores a boon, prostrate at his feet and touching the ground with his forehead, he has not given up saluting him when they meet with one of those

[*] This was, for some years, a source of much heartache for those among the landlords whose rule had been mild and generous.   " I have already mentioned," wrote Prince Tcherkàssky, "and cannot help repeating, how feeble is the feeling of gratitude among the peasants towards even the kindest masters, even those whose conduct towards them has always been marked not only by conscientiousness but by magnanimity.   One reading of the proclamation has swept away all memory of benefits received, and unfortunately the nobility could not bear with resignation the thought that this fact, however painful, was, after all, rather natural."—Letter to Miliútin, June, 1861.

[1] It can be positively asserted that the character is not "external" merely, but very real.   What embitters the mutual relations between two classes is when the superiority of one over the other is due to conquest and difference of race.   Where, as in Russia, such is not the case, no bitterness exists, neither at the time nor retrospectively.   Certain family differences have been adjusted by umpire, that is all.   There is at first some soreness, some difficulty in getting into the new lines, but family feeling prevails through it all and helps over many a hard place.   And the distrust is only skin deep, in petty matters of pecuniary interests—the universal distrust of the peasant all over the world, who feels at a disadvantage before trained intellect and is always afraid it will be used against him.   In greater and vital things the *mujik* instinctively turns to his superior in knowledge and experience for guidance—as the author remarks a few lines lower,—and that his confidence is not abused, the astonishing experience with the " Arbiters of Peace " (see pp. 436–437) has abundantly proved.

profound inclinations of the body with which he does homage in church to the holy images (*eïkons*). I once happened to be present, in a southern government, at a business interview between a delegation of peasants and a landlord whose guest I was. There were a dozen of them, come to discuss with the *pomiêsh-tchik*, on behalf of their commune, the leasing of some land belonging to him. As they neared the manor house, they removed their caps and stood bareheaded at the door, patiently waiting for the master to finish his dinner. When he came out to them at last, accompanied by his bailiff, they stood before him in a circle, cap in hand, and launched out into a long dissertation. Sometimes they spoke by turns, sometimes all together, frequently lapsing into the old humble forms of speech : "*Bátiushka* (father), take pity ; kind *bárin*, you would not beggar us,"—yet never losing ground, holding their own, standing up for their interests, and trying to touch the landlord's heart.

As a set-off, however, to the profound deference which they invariably show their former masters, the peasants are very far from always keeping faith with them. They have not yet been able to fully realize that work voluntarily undertaken should be punctually carried out. Respect for agreements, the obligation imposed by a contract, are things that do not at all accord with the idea the *mujik* has made to himself of liberty ; he takes things easy—to such an extent that his unreliability has become one of the sores of rural life. By a contradiction not unfrequent in simple natures, the same man who would fain dispense with all obligations towards others on the ground that he is a free man, still thinks himself at times entitled to make use of the privileges pertaining to his former condition as serf. Does he need timber ? he serenely cuts some in the master's forest. Just as before the emancipation he is always ready to appeal to the landlord's purse. If a cow is taken sick or a horse is hurt, he quite innocently goes to his former master and asks him for another, forgetting that he has no longer any claim on him.

Yet, though neither landlords nor peasants, so far, bear malice, it is not impossible that the new state of things may contain a latent germ of disaffection and covetousness, for time to mature. We must not forget that the *mujik* is rarely satisfied with the piece of land allotted him. Instead of appeasing his craving for property the imperial proclamation of 1861 only aroused and sharpened it. The compromise imposed by autocracy on master and serf is not regarded by the latter and his children in the light of a final, irrevocable thing.* The land liquidation, so boldly undertaken by the sovereign, has stirred in numbers of peasant heads a dull, dim notion of a coming social liquidation, another agrarian operation, more extensive still and more to their advantage—a *mirage* which the people's self-instituted, doubtful friends skilfully play off before his eyes in the distance. The revolutionary propaganda and the radical spirit, both impatient of anything in the shape of compromise and restraint, have been steadily working for the last thirty years to represent the imperial reform as illogical in principle and inadequate in practice. They are at one in this with the *mujik's* secret instincts, and strive with might and main to second them still more by demonstrating to him that another expropriation of the noble landholders and a redistribution of the land will be the natural sequel and clinching of the task left incomplete at the first installment.

It cannot be denied that, in this respect, the entire social edifice has been shaken by this first and great reform, which claimed that it would merely broaden and strengthen the basis of it in a way that has given the moral ideas, the juridical notions, the political conceptions of the people, such a shock as the country, after more than twenty years, has not yet recovered from. All wise precautions, all ingenious temporizing and expedients notwithstanding, it may be said that, in this sense at least, the eman-

---

* In one of the districts that had been most favored in 1861, a functionary asked the peasants a few years later if they were satisfied. "Yes, *bátiushka*," they replied; "but we live in hopes that the tsar will not forget our children and will give them land, too, some day."

cipation, so skilfully calculated, so happily conducted, has not been foreign to the progress of the radical spirit ; that, by feeding agrarian cupidity, it has unwittingly supplied weapons, examples, pretences, to the enemies of order and property.

The ease, the harmlessness, with which this revolution was decreed and carried out, have enticed the people to dream of others, no less lawful and no less easy. For, in the peasant's eyes, the tsar both can and may do anything, and the marvel of a power so great as to transform in one day, by a single *ukàz*, all the conditions of property, breeds in the popular mind delusions which disappointment may possibly some day turn against that power itself. For the ignorant masses,—and this cannot be too much emphasized,—the Emancipation Act has effected no final settlement whatever : one *ukàz* can be modified by another ; what the tsar has done in 1861, the tsar is free to undo, twenty or thirty years later, for the greater advantage of his faithful peasants.

There is nothing surprising in this ; and the most generous promoters of the emancipation, the most stoutly convinced advocates of territorial endowment, were too clear-sighted not to perceive the truth very quickly. Nothing can be more characteristic in this respect, or go deeper to the root of the matter, than a letter of one of the most illustrious members of the Drafting Commission, Prince Tcherkàssky :

" This transformation," he wrote confidentially to his friend and former colleague, N. Miliútin, " has another and undesirable side to it, of which I do not speak in public, but which I mention here, so as not to leave the impression incomplete : it is (a thing inseparable from so colossal a piece of work, from so vast a transfer of rights and obligations) an unhinging of the popular moral consciousness as to right and wrong, possible or impossible, in regard to questions of 'mine and thine.' This feature, the inevitable accompaniment of every great social revolution, has perhaps never in all history manifested itself with such clearness as at this present moment. Just now, owing to the undying consciousness which always abides in our people, but is more than ever wide-awake in them in consequence of the transformation operated before their eyes by one imperial *ukàz*, the peasant has the profound conviction that there are *no* limits to the action of the sovereign authority, no end to the things that may be expected of it, and which it can give, no matter at whose cost, as a legitimate compensation for the long labor and hardships heroically endured by their class.   At the present hour this is the deep-seated thought in the breast of every peasant, and you will admit that it ill-accords with the teachings of the economists.   Hence, not to mention more weighty facts, the propensity to cut down our trees, impartially to use our pastures,—things that are really very unpleasant in daily life ; not that they are so very ruinous, but the perpetual worry is wearing.   This disrespect of the peasant's for the rights of property has nothing to do with any sort of revolutionary spirit ; on the contrary, from a certain point of view, it even is not devoid of method and a semi-juridical character.   It is evident that in the people, obscurely, but down to a great depth, a tradition has survived, a memory of a time when landed property was not yet, or not to any great extent, in the hands of the nobles, when nearly all the meadow lands and the forest lands in particular were used indiscriminately and in an undefined way by all.   For one brief instant the peasant has had a vision of the return of this good old time, and even now he firmly cherishes the conviction that the government, if it had the right and power to suppress serfdom, has the no less incontestable right and power to change all other conditions of landed property, at least such as are galling to the peasant.   I believe,'' added the Prince, with entire candor, ''that many former delegates of the ' government committees,'* and in particular of the Polish, would-be economists, should these lines come under their eyes, would rub their hands with glee, and would remind us that they had foretold it all.   And

---

* He means the delegates representing the provincial committees of the nobility before the Drafting Commission.

yet, I must say that, in spite of all these worries, inevitable consequence as they are of the great transformation, I do not see even now that there was the least possibility of doing the business in any other manner ; even now, taught as we are by experience, I would not hesitate to repeat the same advice that we gave then. To my mind, all these discomforts only prove that, in the best things, there is an alloy of evil.''

And that is the truth of it. Tcherkàssky was quite right in repeating that, outside of the road that had been taken, there was no other to take. In spite of their opponents' gloomy predictions and virulent upbraidings, he and his fellow-workers cannot possibly be held responsible for an evil inherent in the situation, due to the nature of autocracy as much as to the vagueness and obscurity of the property laws in old-time Russia. By liberating the serfs without giving them any share of the soil, the way would have been opened to far worse agrarian troubles, far more dangerous weapons would have been given to the revolutionary propaganda.*

Deceived in all his hopes, despoiled of the piece of land to which he believed himself entitled by inalienable right, the *mujik*, had he lost faith in the tsar's paternal power, might have fallen a prey to the anarchist emissaries. If the agrarian laws have stirred in the people a vague sense of covetousness, it is perhaps owing to those same laws that the insidious appeals repeatedly addressed, in the course of these last years, to the rural *plebs*, calling to them to " strike out for land and liberty,'' have not found more response in the peasant's smoke-blackened *izbà*, that, notwithstanding the ominous threats of a certain set of propagandists, the Russian fields and villages have not yet had their *Jacquerie* or their land-league on the Irish model.

* The revolutionary pamphlets destined to be read by the people, especially insist on the smallness and high price of the lands allotted to the peasants. One of them, analyzed by Mr. Ralston (*Nineteenth Century,* May, 1877) and entitled *From the Frying-pan into the Fire,* strives to demonstrate to the *mujik* that he is worse off than in the old times, and that he soon will fall into a miserable condition similar to that of the English people, "whom the rich have despoiled and enslaved."

The nihilists have taken care to keep alive in the people ideas and aspirations which time might already have disposed of had they not been adroitly nourished by interested hands. Ever since the last Oriental war, especially during the years of plotting, 1878–1882, the agitators never tired of spreading among the rural population a rumor of an impending redistribution of lands ; so that, on some estates, the peasants actually attempted to proceed to the division of the noble landlord's acres. To put an end to such rumors, the government repeatedly had to assert, solemnly and publicly, by means of official circulars, that the Emancipation Act had settled the conditions of landed property for the future once and forever. But, says the proverb, there is no deafer man than he who won't hear—and, on this question, the peasant is wonderfully hard of hearing,—and many good stories, true too, are told about it. Thus, in an out-of-the-way village, an educated peasant was reading aloud to the others one of those circulars which gave the lie direct to all rumors of new agrarian laws : "Pshaw !" exclaimed one of the rustic audience, with a sly smile, "that stuff is written by *tchinòvniks* (bureaucrats, government employés) ; the tsar is master all the same." What makes such protests wellnigh hopeless is that the lower police agents and other subaltern functionaries, as well as the village elders, frequently share the delusions which it is their duty to try and dispel. So they compromise with their conscience by announcing to the villagers that the new division of lands is adjourned until further orders, and in the meantime it is not to be talked about.

What he has long looked for in vain from the generosity of Alexander II., the *mujik* persists in expecting from Alexander III. With the rural masses, the agrarian question which the Liberator and his advisers flattered themselves they had solved in 1861, will long remain an open one. None of the measures taken by Alexander III. to settle it—neither the suppression of "temporary obligations," nor the abrogation of the poll-tax, nor the reduction of redemption dues—seem to have the desired effect as far as the people are concerned. The kindness and sympathy lavished by the Liberator's son on his faithful peasants rather tend to keep alive their chimerical hopes than to undeceive them. At the time of his coronation, the Emperor made it a point to declare with his own lips to the village-elders assembled in Moscow, that the property question was settled for good and all, that the peasants were not to look for any more allotments. Many subsequent facts show that even the Tsar's own loyal word did not set their minds at rest. The smallest spark will kindle the latent fuel. A local inquest, a rural statistical operation suffices to start the rumor afresh. This almost universal expectant state of mind opposes a serious obstacle to a general census, because the rural population is disposed to regard anything of the kind as a forerunner of a redistribution of lands, unless—such is the *mujik's* readiness to give credence to the most contradictory rumors—unless, as has happened in some villages, it is regarded as prefacing the restoration of serfdom !

To comprehend the whole bearing of these popular notions on land, and the rehandling of property, it is necessary to be familiar with the form of land tenure in use outside of the cities. The vague aspirations called forth by the emancipation are perhaps to be ascribed less to the sudden expropriation of the former lords, than to that immemorial institution—the *mir* and the peasant commune.

BOOK VIII.

MIR, FAMILY, AND VILLAGE COMMUNITIES.

CHAPTER I.

Land Tenure Unchanged by Emancipation—Is the Mir a Slavic Institution? Antiquity and Origin of Communal Property in Russia—Differing Views on the Subject—Difference between Moscovite Russia and Western Europe from the Standpoint of the Agrarian System.

WE have seen that the Emancipation Act, while endowing the *mujik* with land, practically left him very much where he was in the times of serfdom. He now owns the land of which his land-lord formerly let him have the use, but the mode of tenure is the same still. Now as formerly the land belongs to the peasants in common, not personally, not individually, by hereditary right. The lots purchased from the landlords were not distributed to the various members of a village community, but remain the collective, undivided property of the commune. The peasant, decorated by the law with the title of landholder, usually owns permanently and certainly only his cabin, his *izbà*—and the small adjoining en-closure, *usàdba ;* as to the rest he in reality only has the usufruct of the lot he is paying for.

Such, from times immemorial, has been the form of land tenure in use amidst the peasants of Moscovia or Great-Russia. The emancipation has not changed it. As the tenure of the lands was usually collective, so the redemption of them has also been operated, not individually, but, as a rule, by communes. It is

474

the entire village and not the individual or the family which, under the guaranty of mutual solidarity, is answerable to the State or to the landlord for the repayment of the advances made by the former, so that the emancipation has temporarily rather strengthened the old-Russian commune by giving the State an interest in its preservation until payment in full of the ransom from serfdom —this new solidarity being superadded to that for the old taxes.

The respect shown for the old form of land tenure has greatly simplified the transition from servitude to freedom, removing, together with the advantages, also the dangers which brand-new institutions would have brought on. From dependence on the noble landlord, the *mujik* has fallen into dependence on his commune. The bond that tied him to the soil has, then, not been really broken. He is still bound to it by a double chain : undivided property and tax-solidarity. The peasants' liberty is, in a way, like their property : undivided and collective. They still are bound, if not to a master, to one another, and cannot move freely outside of the community. It has been said that the peasant, liberated from the landlord's yoke, had become the serf of his commune. This is a manifest exaggeration. The domination of the commune, which, after all, is only a control exercised by the peasants over themselves, cannot be likened to the control over them of an individual belonging to another class, of different bringing up.

The Russian rural commune thus presents for study two main sides or faces : the system of land tenure, and the administrative or governing system. Intimately connected and interdependent, the economic and administrative communes are still sufficiently distinct to merit a separate study of each. We will begin with the rural commune, *i.e.* the commune in its capacity of collective landholder.

In the eyes of Europe, this sort of agrarian communism is perhaps the most noteworthy feature, and the strangest, of contemporary Russia. In an age of systems and theories such as ours, a study of this kind is fraught with interesting and priceless lessons to the nations, uneasy as they are about their social status and oppressed by a vague unrest. Unfortunately, our Western bringing up, our national habits and our school prejudices do not exactly predispose us to a calm and impartial comprehension of such a system. When brought face to face with community of property, under no matter how attenuated a form, the most sober-minded find it difficult to forbear from prejudging the question. And yet it is precisely those social phenomena that seem most novel and queerest to us which it is most important to consider in themselves, weighing the facts, unbiassed by any preconceived idea.*

Collective property as it is in use among the peasantry, while it now strikes us as Russia's most prominent feature, was one of the last things perceived there by Western Europe, one of the last to be noticed by the Russians themselves in their own country. It was a Westphalian gentleman, Baron Haxthausen, who made the discovery during his travels in 1842–43 ; he was, at least, the first to impart it to Europe, in his famous studies on the inner condition of Russia.† Scientific Europe, as was but natural, was immensely struck at encountering, in the autocratic Empire of the

---

* Through all the following study of the agrarian system, I shall take my facts from the numerous Russian writings on this subject, especially from the grand agricultural inquest held in 1873, the results of which were collected by the government under the title of : *Labors of the Imperial Commission for the Investigation of the Actual Condition of Rural Economy.* These documents have been supplemented by the answers to the lists of questions propounded by various learned societies, such as the *Collected Materials for the Study of the Rural Agrarian Commune,* and by divers publications issued by the Central Committee of Statistics, by the Ministry of State Demesnes or by various Provincial Assemblies *(Zemstvos),* such as *Materials for the Study of Contemporary Landed Property and Rural Economic Industries in Russia* (St. Pet., 1880), and *Statistics of Landed Property and the Inhabited Portions of European Russia* (1880–1881).

† *Studien über die innern Zustände, das Volksleben und insbesondere die ländlichen Einrichtungen Russlands* (1847, vol. i., ch. vi. ; vol. ii., ch. xvii.).

North, an institution which seemed in a measure to realize the dreams of Western utopists. The Russians, suddenly aroused to a knowledge or a consciousness of this national peculiarity, joyfully took hold of it. Naturally impelled to bring everywhere to the front the originality of the Slavs, as the Germans vindicate that of the Teutons and we ourselves at times that of the Celts, numerous Russian writers credited these agrarian communities to the Russian spirit, the Slavic genius. Slavophils, respectful admirers of the past and of Moscovite tradition,—democrats, disciples of the West, vied together in extolling the Great-Russian commune. All insisted on seeing in it the primordial institution of the nation and, at the same time, the formula of a new civilization, the future principle for the impending regeneration of Europe, actually a prey to class strife and imperilled by the excesses of individualism. In the eyes of a certain class of patriots, land-community, obscurely kept alive by the enslaved peasant, became a sort of secret revelation, confided to a chosen people, and of which the Russians, for the good of humanity at large, were bound to make themselves the apostles and the missionaries.

The recent studies in comparative history and law have dispelled these visions of national self-conceit. Within the empire, agrarian institutions similar to the Slavic communities were discovered to exist in most indigenous tribes of alien race, from the Lapps and the Samoyèds of the north to the Mordvin, the Tchuvash, the Tcheremiss of the centre. Abroad, agricultural communities more or less similar to those which still flourish in Russia, are met with among the most different peoples—in India, on the isle of Java, in Egypt. In the past they have turned up at the two extreme ends of the earth—in Mexico and Peru, as well as in China and in Europe. To the *mir* of Great-Russia was opposed the *ager publicus* of the Romans (which differed from it in every particular), the Teutonic *mark*, which appears to have come a little nearer to it, and which can be traced all through the Middle Ages—in Germany, in Switzerland, in Scandinavia, in England, even in France. On this point the labors of Sir Henry Maine, Maurer, Nasse, E. de Laveleye, leave no doubt.* It little matters that one or other of these scholars should have allowed himself to be carried too far by external analogies or the love of system ; it little matters that, where classical nations are concerned, and more notably the Spartans, our historians have been duped by mendacious legends and communistic romancing. The collective mode of tenure appears to have been, with a great many nations, the most ancient form of landholding. It is only after having been for centuries the undivided property of the tribe, the clan, or the commune, that land ended by becoming the permanent and hereditary property of individuals. Contrary to the conceptions of certain democrats of Russia or the West, individual property is a comparatively new, modern form of land tenure ; collective property is the old, the primitive, archaïc form. So that the Russian village community, far from being an innovation, an experiment or a prophecy, is really a block from a vanished world, a witness of a perished past, a sort of fossil, preserved in a country long shut off from the influences which shaped the course of things on the rest of the continent. With regard to this, as to many other things, the originality of Russia and the Slavs has nothing to do with either race or national genius ; it simply means that the Russians and the greater part of the Slavs have stopped

---

* Henry Sumner Maine, *Village Communities in the East and West ;* Maurer, *Einleitung zur Geschichte der Mark-Haf-Dorf und Stadt-Verfassung ;* E. de Laveleye, *De la Propriété et de ses Formes Primitives.* It should be noted that, according to one of the most perspicacious investigators of history, M. Fustel de Coulanges, there is nothing to prove the existence of collective property, with periodical divisions, either among the Greeks or the Romans, the Gauls or the Merovingian Franks, or, even Tacitus notwithstanding, among the Germans. The author of the *Cité Antique* is of opinion that property, with all these nations, was hereditary, mostly in families, in this sense—that originally the individual had not the right to alienate any of it. See Fustel de Coulanges, *Le Problème des Origines de la Propriété Foncière,* in the *Revue des Questions Historiques,* April, 1889 ; further, by the same author, *Recherches sur quelques Problèmes d'Histoire* (1886), and *Histoire des Institutions Politiques de l'Ancienne France ; L'Alleu et le Domaine Rural pendant la Période Mérovingienne* (1889).

at an economic and hence social status old enough to have sunk into oblivion in other countries. The difference between them and the West in this matter lies less in man and race than in the external conditions, less in the nation's character than in the age of its civilization.

It would be a study of the deepest interest if we could follow through the ages the transformations of the village communities in Russia. Unfortunately it is with them as with most institutions that are emphatically a people's own. For the philosopher and the historian these are the most important, and they are always those wrapped in the thickest, most impenetrable veils ; they rest in the darkness in which the disdain of the chroniclers leaves the popular masses and rural classes to the sleep of oblivion. The obscurity on this subject is such, that, even between Russian writers, there could arise violent discussions, not only on the origin but on the antiquity of the Russian village communities. Distinguished journalists, Mr. Tchítcherin in particular, have contested the antiquity or patriarchal filiation of the commune based on mutual solidarity. Long before the researches made in the West on this delicate matter, this writer, already preceded by Granòfsky, demonstrated in Russia itself, that far from being a national institution peculiar to the Slavs, village or family communities, such as the Russian *mir* or Serbian *zadruga*, had long existed in more than one people of alien race. In the face of the prejudices entertained by many of their countrymen, these writers reminded their readers that everywhere property had developed hand in hand with the feeling of individuality ; that the progress of the one is in direct ratio to the development of the other. With seeming inconsistence, the same journalists who brought out into such relief the primitive and cosmopolitan character of the agrarian communities, regarded them in Russia as being comparatively recent. To hear them, the Slavic race, out of which has come the Russian state, did indeed start from collective property, but there is nothing to prove that the *mir* based on mutual solidarity—the Russian commune in its actual form—should be directly descended from this primitive patriarchal communism. Mr. Tchítcherin claims, on the contrary, that communal land tenure, and especially periodical re-allotment, were foreign to Moscovia so long as the peasant remained free.

It is serfdom, says this school, it is the solidarity to which the peasants submit in order to ensure the payment of the taxes, and military conscription, which caused the introduction of this kind of equal division. To make their point, they quote ancient historical documents, authentic charters, wills, deeds of division ; they refer to Little-Russia, a radically Slavic and Russian country, where, prior to the Moscovite domination, only personal land-owners were known, noble or Cosack, and peasants attached to the soil by contracts freely entered into. Instead of being a patriarchal or family institution, the Russian commune, Mr. Tchítcherin contends, is merely ''a creation of the state.'' The Moscovite *mir*, he asserts, has neither the same origin, nor the same character as the *zadruga* of the Serbs and Bulgars, whose family communities retained, through all these peoples' history, the patriarchal impress. The Russian commune, on the contrary, is not the spontaneous outcome of primitive property or of the free union of husbandmen ; it is an outcome of the bondage to the soil and the imperative wants of political sovereignty, under the influence of certain proceedings of the government.

To this system, opposed by the greater number of Russian writers, be they historians or critics, may there not be a certain portion of truth? It is hardly to be admitted that the Russians, who, of all Slavs, have preserved this primitive mode of land tenure in its most unimpaired form, should have come back to it one fine day, after having completely abandoned it. One cannot, on the other hand, bring oneself to believe that, inversely to all known nations, the Moscovite peasants should have stolen a march on the modern utopists and quickly stepped, at the end of the sixteenth century, from personal to collective property.

What sounds admissible, nay probable, is that the establishment of serfdom and the solidarity in the matter of taxes, strengthened in the people's mind the attachment to a mode of land tenure out of which Russia might otherwise have worked her way as well as the other European nations. Serfs and masters, State and private individuals could very well have found it to their interest to uphold and restore, where it tended to disappear, a system which, owing to regular re-allotments, insured to the country a more equable distribution of taxes and dues. Serfdom, and the entire financial and administrative system of Moscovia based on it, thus could, keeping pace with the regular increase of the population, contribute to the general adoption, if not of the principle itself of village communities, at least of the custom of periodical re-allotments, which at the present day appear to be one of the essential features of the Russian *mir*.

In this debate, which we do not pretend to settle one way or the other, care should be taken to discriminate between collective property and the custom of re-allotments. The former can maintain itself a long time without the latter, and the absence of one is no proof against the existence of the other. So long as pastoral life prevails, or the still more primitive life of hunting and fishing,—so long as, even in the agricultural stage, the figure of the population remains very low in proportion to the area it occupies, there is very little reason to divide the land into regular lots. To this day, in many Siberian villages, even in some districts in the north of the empire, each head of a family is free to till as much land as he can manage. Some writers think they have proved that, up to the eighteenth century, allotment was unknown in the north of Russia, the land still being regarded all the time as common property. Similar remarks have been made about the southern steppes : Mr. Mackenzie Wallace tells us that among the Cosacks of the Don, where land is very plentiful, periodical re-allotments are of recent introduction. So long as the number of Cosacks was insufficient to occupy all the land, every one was welcome to as much of it as he could handle, provided he did not encroach on other people's cultivated lots.   The increase of population was, in the natural course of things, to put a stop to this unlegalized right of pre-occupancy.   In order that each Cosack should have his share of the soil enabling him to acquit himself of his obligations towards the state, regular allotment had to be recurred to.   Similar causes may have led to similar results in various regions.

Many and various causes combined to keep up in the eastern portion of the empire a state of things which had long ceased to exist in the west of it : the degree of civilization and the economic condition of Moscovia,—the political system and the patriarchal, or, more correctly, the patrimonial, domanial character of the government,—and lastly the very nature of land and soil.   In those vast plains, unbounded to the eye, man, living always at large, did not feel the necessity of securing a piece of land for his own use by fencing it in.   Where population was dense, crowded on a restricted space, as in Greece and Italy, the god Terminus early became a revered deity, one of the essential wardens of social life.   In Russia, where the land was vast and the population scant, it must have been long before men felt the occasion for such a deity.   The crisis that hastened the transition from collective to individual property has everywhere been increase of population.   Everywhere, the curtailment of each member's lot in consequence of the greater number of sharers was one of the things that put an end to the community, by putting a stop to the periodical re-allotments and leaving each family in full possession of the lot of which it had been hitherto usufructuary. "They change fields each year," says Tacitus of the Germans, "and there still remains untenanted land." To whom could these words apply better than to Moscovia? The eastern half of Europe, the richest in land and at all times the least populous, was of necessity to be the last to give up the primeval system. This result was helped by Moscovia's isolation, moral as well as geographical. Had Russia been more intimately connected with the West, through religion, politics, manners, Latin or Teutonic influences might have accomplished the change much sooner—resulting in Roman law or feudal customs.

In Great-Russia, *i. e.* in all Moscovia, collective property almost exclusively prevails to this day, both among the former serfs and the Crown peasants. In all that immense region extending from the Neva to the Ural, the number of peasants owning land on personal titles does not exceed 1 % or 2 % of the totality, and even these few individual possessions are nearly all of recent origin. Down to 1861, the only individual landholders, outside of the nobility and the foreign colonists, were the *odnodvòrtsy,* who formed a small class by itself.* In Western Russia, at one time subject to the domination of Poland or Sweden, and hence brought into closer contact with Europe, individual property is the rule. The limits of the two systems may almost be said to mark even yet the old boundaries of the Moscovite and the Lithuano-Polish States.† In some few governments, such as those of Kief and Poltáva, there is a mixture of both forms. In one or two, in that of Moghilèf for instance, the Russians have attempted, not very successfully, to naturalize the community system. It was introduced there after the emancipation and the Polish rising of 1863 ; but, if certain testimony of the agricultural inquest is to be believed, the peasants shirk it in the practice and look on it as another form of serfdom. In the adjoining government of Minsk

---

* See Book V., Chap I. And even with them the mode of land tenure was frequently a sort of family community. See following chapter, p. 491.

† In Lithuania proper, *i. e.* in the governments of Kòvno and Vilna, as well as in the three Baltic provinces, no other form of property than the individual is known. The latter has even been introduced in a few communes of the government of Pskof, by the Ehst or Lett colonists from Liefland. In White-Russia and Little-Russia, individual property takes the lead even yet, though its predominance is no longer as exclusive as it was. In Bessarabia, where the Russians show a mixture of Rumanians, both systems exist side by side. It is to be noted that several of the most prosperous German colonies, especially those on the Lower Volga, have adopted the Russian custom of periodical re-allotments.

they were not to be induced to exchange the Western, European mode of land tenure for the Great-Russian. The Little-Russians also are reputed to object to community. It is not always so, however : on the eastern bank of the Dniepr, in the government of Vorònej for instance, Little-Russians may be met with who are not less accustomed and devoted to the system of common land tenure than their Great-Russian neighbors.

Elsewhere, in Podolia and Volhynia, where individual tenure appeared rooted in the local manners, there have been cases of peasants, after the emancipation had provided them with lands, overthrowing their landmarks and effecting a new division on the communal basis. It is even said that some villages in these governments have taken to annual re-allotments. This fact, often quoted in arguments on the side of communal property, can be accounted for in two ways. The method of redemption adopted was so well adapted to the system of village communities that, solidarity being taken as the basis of the payments, it brought about the re-introduction of that system, even if not of periodical re-allotments, in districts where it had long been out of use. The exorbitant taxes, which frequently absorb the greater part of the income yielded by the land, may also have contributed towards the same result, as though to confirm, by modern instances, Mr. Tchítcherin's theory concerning the establishment of periodical allotment in old Moscovia. Lastly, as certain observations of the agricultural inquest would lead us to conclude, the vacillating uncertainty of the *mujik's* ideas on the rights of property, the confusion of his juridical notions on the subject, the little confidence he reposes in his title,—all these things may, in many localities, have swelled the tide in favor of the change. If one of the local " marshals of the nobility" is to be believed, the peasants have not sufficient faith in their permanent right to their property to venture opposing any resistance to the fiat of the commune when it is the majority's pleasure to submit to a new division. The well-to-do peasants this curious document represents as needing to be enlightened concerning the validity of their titles, and to have the ownership of the lands allotted to them in some way guaranteed. However it may stand with these details, it is a fact that the emancipation may have indirectly opened to communal property and re-allotment districts which until now were closed to these institutions.* Singular ! that the Statute of 1861 should have apparently, if only for a time, not merely confirmed in its former area, but extended to new villages, a form of land tenure which appears to have been strengthened, if not actually introduced, three hundred years before, by the establishment of serfdom !

* The question here is naturally not of isolated cases. In transferring to the peasants the ownership of the lands of which they had the usufruct, the agrarian laws of 1861 respected the form of land tenure current in every region. Though often accused, both at home and abroad, of partiality towards collective tenure, the compilers of the Emancipation Act were merely content to let it alone where it existed and very careful not to introduce it anywhere else by legislative authority. N. Miliútin remarked in Paris, in May, 1863, before the *Société des Économistes :* "The lawgiver does not impose on the rural class any one form of property preferably to others ; it may be individual or communal according to the custom prevailing in each given region, and it will be left to the purchasers' own pleasure whether they will transform the lands acquired by the commune into private and individual property."

This was strictly true ; the communes, even the individuals, were free to pass from communal to personal property. Article 165 of the Statute, it is true, did not empower the peasants freely to dispose of their lots until they had fully redeemed them. The article, even with this restriction, was regarded as a threat to the *mir.* There have been speculators who have got the peasants to sell them their lots by advancing the redemption money, thus allowing themselves to be despoiled of the property which the law was trying to secure to them. Accordingly, several Russians spoke up in favor of having Article 165 suppressed and making the peasant lots inalienable.

BOOK VIII.   CHAPTER II.

To the village communities of Great-Russia a prototype may be found, even simpler and more ancient, yet living still—the family. In the *mujik's izbà*, the family, in truth, has preserved to our day a patriarchal, archaïc character. Property remains undivided between the children or between brothers who dwell together under one roof ; each son, each male of the house, has an equal right to it. The agrarian community seems to be contained in embryo in the family, the former being constructed on the model of the latter. So that the Russian commune may be regarded as an enlarged family, in which the soil remains the collective property of the community, each man or each household receiving for his support an equal share thereof. The Moscovite *mir* is often considered simply as an extension of the family, grown too numerous to reside in the same enclosure or to go on cultivating the land in common. This view, held by many economists, both Russian and foreign, may in many cases be correct, though not invariably. It is not always easy to prove the members of a village community to be descended from one common ancestor, even when there is tradition to show for it. There may exist reasonable doubts concerning the historical conditions of the filiation from family to commune, even concerning the order of filiation. There may have been in a given generation a sort of alternation between these forms of property, the commune being originally born of the family, and the family communities, in their turn, of sections of the village community.*

Here is not the place to linger over these curious and obscure questions. By whatever process collective property may have been evolved in the Russian peasantry, the tie between family and commune, between domestic life and *mir* life, is too close to allow of understanding the latter without the former. A glance at the *mujik's* home life offers the greater interest that the old manners are fast disappearing. What, up to the emancipation, was the distinctive characteristic of the family in the lower classes, was its unity : joint habitation, undivided property, and paternal authority. These time-honored customs, as already remarked, have, in a few years, been shaken by the emancipation. The

---

* The family communities, at least in their actual form, do not always appear to be more ancient than the village communities—the Serbian *zadruga* than the Russian *mir*. In fact, the former, such as they still exist among certain Southern Slavs, presuppose an hereditary appropriation of the soil in favor of certain village residents ; in this sense we may see in them an advance towards individualization, a transition stage between clan or communal property and personal possession. Moreover, the domain of these family communities is usually far less extensive than that of the village communities, and the number of members far less considerable. The Serbian *zadruga* numbers, on an average, between ten and twenty-five members ; those with fifty or sixty are exceptions. When the *zadruga* grows too numerous, it usually splits itself in two. There are, in Serbian lands, villages that bear the name of one family, and the inhabitants of which do appear to be descended from one stock ; but such villages almost always consist of several communities. [See, for instance, *Custom-Law (Droit Coutumier) of the Southern Slavs, after Researches by Mr. Bògil-chitch*, by F. Demélitch, Paris, 1877.] In brief, then, a Serbian *zadruga* can, by successive separations, be evolved out of an original family community, whereas it could scarcely be the outcome of village communities,—while the Russian *mir*, by splitting itself into fractions, may very well have begot family communities, very similar to the *zadruga*. Such, indeed, appears sometimes to have been the case. (See further on, pp. 491–493.)

same peaceable revolution which has severed the bond between master and serf, has loosened that between father and children. Together with liberty, a taste of independence came to the domestic hearth. This was one of the chief and most natural results ; it is at the same time a fact which cannot but react on the commune, indeed on the entire material and moral existence of the *mujik*.

The father, according to the ancient Russian custom, is absolutely master in his house, like the tsar in the nation, or, as an old saying has it, like the khan in Crimea. To find anything at all analogous in the West, we must retrace our steps back beyond the Middle Ages, to classical antiquity and paternal authority among the Romans. The Russian peasant was not liberated by age from his father's authority ; the adult and married son was still subject to it, until he had himself children arrived to years of discretion, or had in his turn become the head of the family. This domestic sovereignty remained intact through all the revolutions, all the transformations of the country. Like the tsar, the father was thought to hold from Heaven a sort of right divine, to rebel against which would have been sacrilege. In the sixteenth century, in a manual on domestic economy, entitled *Domostròy* ("House-Order "), the priest Sylvester, the intimate adviser of Ivan IV., extols the authority of the head of the house and his right of repression not only over the children, but over the wife. In the nobility, this paternal power became worn and blunted through long friction against the West and modern individualism ; little is left of it beyond a few formalities, such as the graceful Slavic custom for children to kiss their parents' hand after meals. In the people, *i.e.*, the peasantry and the merchant class, the old traditions had survived. In these two classes, the most genuinely national ones, the framework of family was, until this last quarter of the nineteenth century, more solidly constructed than in any other European country. In this respect, as in many others, Russia may be said to have been, till very lately, the antipodes of the United States, so deep was the chasm dug by paternal authority between two families based on equality between the children.

In the Russian people, paternal power is supported by religious feeling and reverence for age. No nation has, in this respect, upheld more faithfully the simple and beautiful habits of another age. The Russian of the lower classes greets men superior to him in years by the names of "father" or "uncle"; at all times in public as in private, he treats them with a gentle deference. This feeling was until quite lately the foundation-stone of communal self-government. "Where white hairs are, there is good sense, there is right"—such is, with variations, the burden of many popular proverbs. From an old man—from his father especially —the Russian peasant used submissively to endure all things. Two *mujiks* were out on a Moscow street one day—a holiday,—one of them in the prime of maturity, the other already bent under the weight of years. The old man, who appeared somewhat the worse for drink, was showering abuse on his companion, and even blows. The younger and vigorous man opposed to his violence only expostulation and entreaties, and on some people's wanting to separate them, said : "Leave us ; he is my father." Such traits are by no means rare. The trouble is that, every virtue being apt to encourage to abuse those who profit by it, paternal anthority thus pampered frequently degenerated into downright tyranny. The father, coarse and unmannered, with the double model before him of state despotism and landlord's despotism, lorded it in his cabin as a veritable autocrat ; he continually transgressed the natural limits of his rights, and the son, fashioned to obedience by both custom and servitude, seldom knew how to assert his own or his wife's dignity as human beings. Paternal power but too often got hardened by contact with serfdom ; no wonder that the emancipation loosened the bond, and that young couples, liberated from a master's yoke, should wish to cast off that other and not less irksome yoke.

In the *mujik's* patriarchal domestic scheme, undivided property, *i.e.* community of possessions, was the logical sequence of paternal authority.* Thus the family can be regarded as an economic association, the members of which are united by the ties of blood, and have at their head, in the capacity of chief and manager, the father or "elder," bearing the title of "master of the house " (*domokhoziàin*) or "senior "(*bolshàk*).†

What is the basis, the principle, what the essential character of the undivided Great-Russian peasant family? These questions have been much discussed. It has been asked whether it was a sort of association—or, to use the genuine Russian term, of *artél*—founded before all on economic relations, on property and pecuniary interests; or whether, on the contrary, it rests in the peasantry as in other classes, principally on personal relations created by affection and sympathy, on blood and kinship.‡ To this question often settled too peremptorily, too exclusively, in one or the other sense, the best solution would seem to be that the Great-Russian family is founded, like almost every other, on both principles, and that one or the other becomes predominant according to what side you consider it from. If it is an association, it is a closed one into which there is no entrance except through birth or marriage.

Certain it is, that, in the peasant class, marriage and the creation of a new household, have at all times been regulated chiefly by utilitarian considerations. In no other country perhaps has personal inclination had as little to do with rural marriages. But is Russia the *only* country where such cares—which, after all, do not necessarily exclude relations born of sympathy and are far

---

* Mr. Le Play, in his *Ouvriers Européens* (first edition, pp. 58 and 59), gives a complete description of the economic system on which a Russian family was based previous to the emancipation. In the same work is found a similar and in many ways analogous description of a Bashkir family on the confines of Asia.

† *Domokhozàin*, from *dom*, " house," and *khoziaïn*, "master, husband-man, administrator." *Bolshàk* from *bolshòy, bòlshiy,* " big, senior."

‡ The former opinion is the more generally adopted ; still the latter has been repeatedly supported by eminent scholars.

from invariably banishing domestic affections—interfere with the foundation of the family? If economic considerations, always particularly powerful in the country, prevail with the *mujik* more than with other classes, that is a consequence, first of all, of the conditions of rural life, of the habits bequeathed by serfdom, of the *mir* system and collective property,—all things which impress on the union between man and woman a more than usually materialistic, practical stamp. Taken all in all, the distinctive feature of the Great-Russian family does not lie there. Elsewhere too—in the West and everywhere—the family, composed of father, mother, and children in their nonage, may be regarded as an association and a community. The distinctive characteristic of the Great-Russian family, up to these latter times, is that, instead of being habitually limited to father, mother, and unmarried children, it included several households and several generations, united at once by the bond of blood and that of common interests.*

It often happened that several married sons, several collateral households, would live together in the same house, or round the same enclosure or yard—*dvor*—working in common under the authority of the father or grandfather. The family thus became a sort of commune on a small scale, ruled by its natural chief, assisted by his wife for the indoor management.† The principle

* The Russian economists, who, of late years, have much agitated these questions, frequently draw a distinction between two types of peasant families : the "great" or patriarchal (*bolshàya or rodovàya*,—the latter from *rod*, "race"=Latin *gens*), and the "small" or "paternal" (*màlaya or otsòvskaya*, from *otsy*, "fathers")—the family in the narrower sense. And indeed, both types are to be found, sometimes side by side in the same regions ; only, contrary to what used to be in old times, the former tends to grow rarer. But between these two forms of family life and farming, the passage from one to the other is too easy and frequent to warrant their being erected into two opposite types.

† To the head of the household, the Russian *domokhoziàin*, may be compared the *domàtchin* or head of the Serbian *zadruga*. Indeed, there is between the Great-Russian undivided family and the Yugo-Slavic *zadruga* an analogy which it were vain to deny. It has been proved that in certain Russian governments, especially in those of Samára and Kursk, there recently still existed family communities very similar, as regards their

of election asserted itself only in default of the head of the family. When the father died, his place was taken, in the order of patriarchal succession, by one of the oldest members, the brother, or the oldest son, according to local custom. Sometimes it was the widow who took the management of the house, or else—as in the *mir* and in the Serbian *zadruga*, the elder was chosen from among the members of the family, not for absolute seniority of age but as being the most capable, the most respected.* The father or head of the house had full authority for the management of the property belonging to the community, and his wife for the direction of operations at home. Still, in large families, composed of several households, it was usual for the "elder" to take the advice of his relatives and associates. But he was by right the representative of the family in all business matters, private or public, when he and his peers formed the council of the commune ; but even there he took his seat not as an individual, but as the family representative.

In the times of serfdom, the rural family loved to keep close together.† Divisions of property were dreaded ; they took place

organization and juridical character, to the *zadruga*, which itself presents various types. The family communities in which certain Russian scholars see a special type of land tenure, which they call "landed property consisting of a yard or house-lot," are of frequent occurrence among the peculiar small class, called *odnodvòrtsy* more particularly in the government of Oriòl.

* Such was the case in a family of the government of Kursk of which a special study has been published. This community, known under the name of Sofrònitch, comprised, in 1872, forty-two persons, all descendants—at least the men—of one common ancestor, deceased sixty years before, whose sons having died in their turn, the grandchildren and great-grandchildren had agreed to live together and cultivate their lands in common, under the direction of one of their number. In 1872 the family consisted of eight married couples, two widows, and over twenty young people and children of both sexes. They all resided in four *izbàs* built round the same *dvor* or yard. About 1876, domestic disasters, especially the insanity, then death of the "elder" who had ruled them through forty years, caused them to separate into four groups, each of which still formed a small community.

† As in the Serbian *zadruga*, the house, live stock, tools, furniture, and crops belonged to the community. Nothing was left for individual possession except articles of personal use, such as clothes and trinkets.

only when the dwelling with its yard had become too small for the number of inhabitants. This necessity was regarded as an evil, and the division of the small patrimony or capital went by the name of "black division." The interest of the landlord, who was bound to furnish the timber and other materials for the construction of the new *izbàs*, was at one with the traditional prejudice against the separation of families. Owing to these customs, had the land, redeemed by the former serfs, been definitely allotted to the different households, the large village communities would probably have been succeeded by small family communities after the manner of the Serbian *zadruga*. Now that, in the footsteps of liberty, the spirit of individualism and independence has invaded the dwelling of the *mujik*, if the collective tenure of land comes to be abrogated, it will be for the benefit of the individual ; the Russian peasant will not pass through the intermediate stage at which other Slavic peoples have stopped.

In a house in which property remains undivided, it is not so much the decease of members of the family which opens successions, as the separation of the living which becomes the occasion for partitions. The rules for such partitions vary according to localities, but one general feature is that only men or widows with young children are considered. The married daughters have nothing of their own, being regarded as belonging to their husbands' families ; the unmarried daughters can claim only a portion of the furniture and money, sometimes of the cattle, cows, sheep, etc., according to local custom.

Among the Great-Russians as well as among the Little-Russians, in the wider as in the more restricted family, the women— especially the daughters—are not an integral part of the family or community as regards property. The daughter is only a temporary inmate of her father's house, which she is to leave some day, to follow a husband. The wife herself—the consort—claims no share in the common fund even while she has the internal management of the conjugal home. If sometimes a widow obtains a portion, if she even fills the place of the head of the house, it is as the representative of her unmarried children. The woman really has no claim on the property of either her father's or her husband's family. As a compensation, she is allowed the privilege, denied to the men, of saving up a little hoard of her own outside of the common property, on the flax or wool out of which she manufactures her husband's and children's clothing ; these savings, in some provinces, go by the name of her "box" or "casket" (*koròbka*). This casket, the keys to which the women alone hold, the girl takes away with her when she marries : it is her dowry.* When a woman dies childless, her *koròbka*, as a rule, returns to her own family,—not to her father or his community, but to her mother, or, if she be dead, to her unmarried sisters. Thus there is a sort of feminine line of succession. The mother's money and clothes usually go to the unmarried daughters, and if, in family partitions, custom admits the daughters' claim to a portion of the house-gear and even of the live-stock, the reason probably is that these things are regarded as belonging to and more particularly befitting their sex.

In speaking of family partitions, a difference should be made between the *bona-fide* partitions of the whole estate among all entitled to a share of it, and the dowering of a member on his departure out of the community. The latter is the case when a member of the family, a son for instance, leaves the house in his father's lifetime to go and live somewhere else by himself. The father, then, is free to give him nothing, to let him go " with nothing but his cross," as the popular phrase has it—in allusion

---

* Where custom allows young girls to save for themselves a *koròbka*, indirectly raised on the common property, it is usual for a bridegroom, who, indirectly also, is to benefit by this same *koròbka*, to pay to the bride's family a certain sum as compensation, either in cash or nature. This contribution usually defrays the wedding feast, an item which mounts up considerably, all the way from 20 to 80 roubles. This custom must not be confounded with the purchase-money given for the bride, a practice which still flourishes in some parts of Russia, among Finn or Tatar populations. (See for details on these curious customs a study of Mr. Matvéyef, in the *Memoirs of the Imperial Russian Geographical Society*, Ethnographical Section, vol. viii., part 1st, 1878.)

to the brass or silver cross worn round the neck. If, however, a married son leaves with his father's consent, he receives his share of the common patrimony ; but it lies with the father to determine what that share shall be. There even are different words, at least in the government of Samára, to express whether the departing son receives a full *pro-rata* share of the family property or not. If in a family governed by the eldest brother, one of the younger unmarried ones chooses to settle somewhere else, there is no general partition. But there necessarily is, if it is a married brother who goes, *i. e.* a man possessed of full rights according to the popular code. Genuine partitions therefore take place only in families bereaved of their natural head and composed of several collateral households, where there are several co-proprietors possessed of equal rights to the common patrimony, for instance married brothers who have lost their father. In this case, the property, real and personal, is divided into so many shares of equal value which are frequently adjudged by drawing lots, just as is done in the *mir* for communal lands. The married grandsons are entitled to a share only if their father is dead, because the rights of children lie in abeyance during the father's lifetime.

It is easy to see from all the above what predominance is conferred on the father and his authority, and also how great, in these rural customs, is the importance that attaches to marriage, which takes the place of age-majority. It is, in a way, the first condition under which is held the right to succession, or, more correctly, to property. In our study of the commune, we shall soon see that marriage is usually there also the first condition for using the communal lands. The reason of this singular custom is that neither in the home nor in the commune can a man be a complete workman unless he is married, and can place at the community's service, together with his own hands, those of his wife.

In a certain measure, it might be said that in the peasant family—at least in the large, patriarchal family—there is no succession or inheritance at all, but only dissolution or liquidation of an association, each member of which is invested with an equal right to a share in the common capital and stock-in-trade. Though relationship may be one of the conditions of heredity, blood alone does not confer a right to the inheritance : association with the head of the family and labor for the benefit of the community are required over and above that. The only sense in which the term "succession" is applicable under this form of family life, is this : that the father's death entitles the married sons to claim a share in the common patrimony.

It follows from all this, as Mr. Matvéyef remarks, that testamentary dispositions and bequests are possible in families in the stricter sense, where in lieu of several associates having equal rights on the family estate, there is only one representative of the family rights. In this case, the father or the mother—the latter if, being widowed, she is the recognized head of the house—may, in dying, bequeath legacies. These testamentary dispositions, whether made in writing or orally declared before witnesses, are usually admitted by the communes and peasant courts, the more readily that the common people pay a sort of religious reverence to last dying wishes and even regard opposition to them as sinful. The number of such wills naturally tends to increase in proportion to the dissolution of large families. By them the father, as a rule, merely distributes his possessions among his children, so as to forestall any disputes between them. If bequests are made beyond the line of direct heirs, they usually are in favor of the widow, sometimes of a married daughter or a son gone out of the house, or perhaps of some orphan nephews or some child taken in by the dying man. Custom, however, would scarcely permit, the father of a family to despoil his children of the house in which they were born and of their entire inheritance, in favor of strangers possessed of no moral title to his estate. How ever great his respect for paternal authority, the peasant does not admit of its being unlimited, under cover of what is elsewhere known by the name of testamentary liberty.

All that concerns the division of family possessions, as also all that bears on the allotment of lands by the commune, is left by law to custom, to tradition. The Statute says so in the following explicit words : " The peasants are authorized as regards the order of succession to inheritances, to follow the local customs." By this simple little clause, the rural commune is placed outside of the civil law, outside of all written law.*

Such liberty is in keeping with the nature and the conditions of self-government which distinguish the Russian *mir*. Yet these excessive private rights give rise to so much opposition that, in an epoch of transition and ethical transformation like the present, such latitude must needs lend itself to abuses and injustices. Accordingly, at the time of the agricultural inquest, enlightened men, of most dissimilar tendencies, such as the ex-Minister of the Interior and of the Crown Demesnes, Mr. Valùyef, and Prince Vassìltchikof, requested that the private law of the peasants, instead of being entirely left to custom, might be regulated by official legislation. The difficulty lay in avoiding to do violence to custom while regulating its exercise. Legal usages vary much, according to provinces and communes, according even to the origin of the population. In one village, for instance, it is the eldest son who, in case of division, retains the homestead ; in another again it is the youngest, as in some parts of Switzerland and Germany, because it is supposed that the oldest had opportunities of settling elsewhere during the father's lifetime. In treating of heredity questions among the peasants, it should not be forgotten that the communal lands, although they do not directly fall under it, are obliquely affected by these family partitions, which usually necessitate the allotment of separate lands to the members who depart out of the family community. And, though these are private concerns which do not affect the general distributions of land among all the members of a commune, there are

---

* A law of the present Emperor's, however, passed in 1886, regulates such family transactions without infringing these principles.

villages where a family cannot divide the land allotted to it collectively without the commune's consent.

Such divisions are no longer rare nowadays. Few *izbàs* shelter several married couples.* Young people, especially young wives, wish to be independent ; newly married couples take delight in feeling themselves the heads of a household, the only position which gives them complete liberty. This spirit, seemingly in opposition with the system of communal land tenure, sometimes finds in it an encouragement, for it is precisely under this system that each man or each couple can claim a lot. On the other hand, the construction of a wooden house costs comparatively little ; every Russian is a born carpenter, every peasant can, in a few days, build a dwelling for himself. So that the number of new *izbàs* has increased considerably since the emancipation ; to be sure they are generally smaller and poorer. This increase of *dvors* or separate homesteads is valued at 25 % or 30 % at least.† This breaking up of families, though merely an indirect consequence of the emancipation, seems to be one of the main causes of the apparently inconsiderable results it has produced, of the scant progress made by agriculture and prosperity in numbers of provinces. These divisions, now of frequent occurrence, bring about two complications almost equally hard on agriculture and popular prosperity. The first is the excessive parcelling of the land, caused by separating the small lots affected by the commune to the support of one family ; the second consists in disabling the peasant from working the soil to its full bearing capacity, owing to the indefinite division of capital, stock, and tools. If the *mir* furnishes the land, it does not advance the means of tilling it. In

---

* Statistics show that, to every 23,000,000 " souls " (male peasants subject to the poll-tax), there were, only a few years ago, 7,220,000 *dvors* or homesteads, *i.e.* on an average, taking into consideration the increase of the population since the last census, seven or eight persons to the *dvor*, which, Russian families being usually prolific, generally represents one household.

† In some governments, such as that of Tver, the number of the *dvors* or *izbàs* is said to have nearly doubled in ten years.

this manner the disadvantages inherent to the communal system are still more aggravated by family partitions. The peasants themselves admit that this new fashion usually does harm, but give in to it, *because* it is getting to be the fashion.

It is thus that the decadence of the old patriarchal ways may indirectly retard the progress of the peasants towards prosperity and even national production. Among these peasant-landlords, impoverished by successive divisions, a great many households are almost wholly destitute of cattle and laboring implements. The depositions of the great agricultural inquest almost unanimously deplore this tendency of the peasants towards isolation.*
It was to remedy these disadvantages by subjecting family partitions to legal restrictions that the inquest commission suggested that the possessions of a family, and especially their agricultural implements, should be shared with departing members only within limits determined by the law. The ministry more directly concerned with the peasant affairs, that of Crown Demesnes, more than once went into this question. Thus, for instance, it was proposed to authorize partitions only if there were no arrears of taxes, and if the separation left to each member a lot of an extent sufficient for remunerative cultivation. There was some talk of giving to the parents or to the head of the house the right of authorizing or forbidding the operation instead of leaving it, as

* This commission, convoked on the proposal and under the presidency of the ex-Minister of Crown Demesnes, Mr. Valùyef, was composed of high functionaries from the ministries of the Interior, of Demesnes, and of Finances. The principal object of their investigations, conducted and directed with the assistance of an extensive list of queries, was the study of collective land-tenure and its effects. The commission received and published about a thousand reports and written depositions, besides oral ones from over two hundred persons, mostly governors of provinces, marshals of the nobility, members of the provincial assemblies, etc. Unfortunately, but out of so many witnesses, few are peasants or rural functionaries, men directly concerned in that mode of property which is being investigated. In spite of the high intelligence and impartiality demanded of the compilers of reports, the absence of such naturally indicated representatives of the rural communities partly weakens the commission's conclusions.

done at present, to local custom.   However pressing the interests of agriculture and of the peasant himself, it were difficult to impose such restrictions without encroaching on the liberty but just restored to him, without again placing the individual under the yoke of the family, the commune, or the central administration.*

Not that this new tendency to individualism should be unconditionally deplored.   Disturbing as it is economically, it has some undoubtedly good sides : it compels young people to rely more on their own powers, and, by stimulating individual energy, may increase the sum of labor.   It affords advantages especially as regards health and morality.   Among coarse, poverty-stricken people, the patriarchal system is not all profit and virtue.   It is notorious how many evils of all description, in the great cities of the West, are derived from the closeness and overcrowding of tenements.   Things are no better in Russia when one small *izbà* shelters several generations and several households, when, through the long nights of an endless winter, fathers and their children, brothers and their wives, lie promiscuously huddled together around the huge stove.   Such a promiscuity is as unwholesome to the morals as to the body.   Even when the married children occupied several *izbàs* disposed around the one yard, the domestic autocracy was a danger to the family's union and chastity ; the head of the house, "the old man" who, owing to the custom of early marriages, might be scarcely forty, often arrogating to himself certain seignorial rights over the women of his family, in imitation of the noble landlord's ways with the serf girls and women on his domains.   Nowadays, young couples can more easily escape this paternal rule, and family life becomes purer through isolation.

* By the terms of the law of 1886, partitions can no longer take place except with the consent of the head of the family, and they must besides be approved by at least two thirds of the communal vote.   Moreover, the administrative reform of 1889 places them under the control of "rural chiefs"—functionaries elected from among the local landed nobility.

The old patriarchal manners also contributed as much as serfdom to the abasement of women, whose subordinate condition is the ugly side of popular life in Russia. In the higher classes the woman is, in culture, bringing up, and manners, the man's equal ; in fact she often is, or seems, superior to him. With the popular classes—peasants and tradesmen—the case is reversed. In nothing does the moral dualism still existing between Peter's Russia and old Moscovia manifest itself more clearly. The common people have retained the ideas and habits of old-time Russia, and it is this side of their life on which Asiatic, or rather Byzantine influences have left the deepest impress. The ill-treatment and contempt under which women lived were among the things that most shocked foreign travellers down to the eighteenth century, from the German Herberstein, who was the first to reveal to Europe the inner life of Moscovia, to the French academician Chappe d'Auteroche, whose assertions the Empress Catherine II. herself took the trouble to refute.* There are a great many popular sayings on the subject of wife-beating, some of them purporting to be spoken by women, such as : " A good husband's blows do not hurt long," and the popular songs are full of references to the same custom.† Peasant husbands have not relinquished this patriarchal prerogative, especially when tipsy, and the father-in-law, until quite lately, joined in with his stick. Justice now tries to protect the women, but has not always the power. With such customs it is out of the question to make of wife-beating a serious offence, entailing separation. The *mujik* still finds it difficult to grasp the idea that anybody should have any business to dispute his right of chastising the wife of his bosom. A peasant, cited before the justice of the peace for this offence, kept repeating in

* In *The Antidote, or an Examination of the Evil Book entitled " Travels in Siberia,"* a work ascribed to the Tsarítsa herself.

† "I went along with my true love dear—And to my love I said : 'O, darling dear !—Beat not thy wife without a cause,—But only for good cause, beat thou thy wife,—And for a great offence.—Far away is my father dear, —And farther still my mother dear ;—They cannot hear my voice,—they cannot see my burning tears.' "—Ralston, *Songs of the Russian People,* p. 11.

reply to all reproofs : " Why, she is my own."—" Whom, then, is one to beat?" inquired another after listening to a lecture on the respect due to women.   Acquitted or fined, it is on his wife, in the end, that the delinquent lets out his wrath at the interference of justice.

In Great-Russia, the wife has not yet quite got beyond being regarded as a domestic animal, Bielinsky tells us.   What the peasant seeks in his helpmate first of all, if not exclusively, is a good workwoman.   In some provinces at least among the " allogens," or aliens of Finn and Tatar origin, such as the Mordvins of the Volga, the peasant still buys his wife ; at times he carries her away —" steals " her is the word,—often, without consulting or even knowing her, as she is from another village.   In Little-Russia, family life has more of the humane element ; affection plays a greater part in wedlock, the woman's lot is a milder one, she enjoys more consideration and has more rights.   This difference may be partly due to the gentler Maloross character, to the milder climate, and purer Slavic blood ; but especially to the fact that serfdom not having lasted so long in Little-Russia, it has not hardened the people's manners to the same extent, and that the Maloross peasant woman, instead of being subject to the often heavy rule of a father- and mother-in-law in a large agglomerated family, usually keeps house by herself for her husband and children.

Still, even in Little-Russia, the women's lot is far from being an enviable one and only appears so by comparison.   On the Dniepr as well as on the Volga, the husband still looks on his wife as on an inferior being.   Hence the popular songs bear many a trace of the pain which the woman habitually smothers in her breast, and the so-called "wedding songs" of both North and South, those rhythmical poems with chorus, a rudimentary musical drama enacted by the bride and the various personages who take part in the event, invariably show us the bride full of sadness and fear. True, most of these songs date back to times when she had reason to tremble before "the alien robber," the Tatar or the

Lithuanian, who came to take or buy her from her people. But even in the latest of these popular poems, whether born in Great- or Little-Russia, or in the freer Cosack-land, the maiden in touching strains gives vent to her grief at leaving her father's house, even though life was not always made very easy to her there, at exchanging her girlish liberty for the matron's subjection. Always life before marriage is extolled as a woman's best time. Serfdom, of course, greatly embittered her lot, for on her head fell the weight of a double bondage. And so heavy is the yoke at times, that to this day many a peasant woman frees herself from it by killing her tyrant. This crime is by no means uncommon, and the woman is, more often than not, acquitted by a compassionate jury who knows what she has gone through.

But a better time is dawning. The emancipation is not for man alone. Already in the villages, the mother of adult children, especially the widow of the head of a family, enjoys very substantial respect ; such a widow is often entrusted with the management of the family affairs, and sometimes, in the communal assemblies, women represent their absent husbands. In this, as in everything, education will do much ; the progress of individualism will have a great share in elevating woman's condition, for it fosters, in both sexes, the feeling of personal dignity. Once alone with her husband and children, she will more easily become the companion and equal of the one, the guardian and teacher of the others.*

Will the spirit of independence and individualism, which is undermining the patriarchal family, end by reaching collective property ? Is the Russian commune of sufficiently solid grain to

---

* The popular songs depict in graphic terms the irksomeness, to young matrons, of life in larger agglomerated families. Here is a brief specimen : "They are making me marry a lout—With no small family.—Oh ! —oh—oh ! Oh, dear me !—With a father and a mother—And four brothers —And sisters three.—Oh—oh—oh ! Oh, dear me !—Says my father-in-law : ' Here comes a bear ! '—Says my mother-in-law : ' Here comes a slattern ! '— My sisters-in-law cry : ' Here comes a do-nothing ! '—My brothers-in-law exclaim : ' Here comes a mischief-maker ! '—Oh—oh—oh ! Oh, dear me ! "— Ralston, *Songs of the Russian People*, p. 289.

resist this active dissolvent, which, by attacking the old customs and paternal authority, cuts out the core of despotic communism in the family ? Family and commune, domestic life and public life,—the life of the *mir*,—had one and the same basis, principle, and spirit; it is impossible that the alterations which the one undergoes should not react on the other. Anything that weakens traditions and popular customs must also weaken the village communities, in which all rests on custom and tradition. The man who has freed himself from the paternal yoke, will soon want to slip that of the commune. He who is tired of remaining a boy forever in the house, will not like being always a minor before the *mir;* he who finds family solidarity irksome, will promptly grow tired of the solidarity imposed by the commune. The spirit of independence is, of its nature, a thing that, once it has entered a certain sphere, is not to be shut up within it : close the house as you will, it will find a way out to spread abroad.

If the commune is to survive the transformation it is undergoing at present, it must cease to oppress the individual, it must leave full liberty to persons. The ancient agrarian system's only chance lies in adapting itself to the demands of modern individualism. Now, is the Moscovite *mir* capable of this ? The communism of the patriarchal family necessarily implies the solidarity of the members ; there lies one of the reasons of the dying out of the Serbian *zadruga* and the family communities among the southern Slavs. Is this the case in the same measure with the village communities ? In our age of individual liberty and ardent competition, between nations as between men, an economic or political institution can, in truth, exist only on two conditions, narrowly connected : not to interfere with individual liberty, and not to hinder national production. A study of the manner in which land is divided and used under the control of the *mir* will show us what are, in both these respects, the effects and the defects of the Russian rural commune system.

BOOK VIII.   CHAPTER III.

Village Communities: Manner of Division and Allotments—Large Communities and Free Use of Vacant Lots—The *Mir* of the Present Day and Periodical Re-allotments—Division by "Souls" and by *Tiàglos*—Epochs of Division ; Disadvantages of Frequent Re-allotments—A Portion of the Defects Charged to the *Mir* Due to the Large Agglomerated Villages —Consequences of Excessive Parcelling.

AT the times when population was more sparsely distributed than it is now, the Russian communities, at present limited to mere villages, were able sometimes to cover much more extensive tracts of land.   Such instances are still to be encountered at both extremities of Russia—in the north, in the government of Olònets, on the confines of Finland, and in the south, amongst the Cosacks of the Ural, Great-Russians by descent, mostly *old-believers* by religion, and as much attached to the old customs as to the old rites.   There, by the river Ural, a vast commune has existed down to our own time, covering an entire extensive geographical region ; there a whole army, sole proprietor of the soil it occupied, formed one undivided community.   Here was to be found, nearly intact, in the nineteenth century, the form of property and usufruct of the tribe or clan of prehistoric ages.*

Immense steppes, but moderately fertile and almost desert, to say the truth,—a space of nearly 27,000,000 acres,—composed the collective property of the Cosacks of the Ural.   Along the entire

* Haxthausen (*Studien*, vol. iii., pp. 153–162) gives a description of the regulations under which these Cosacks lived prior to the recent reforms and the invasion of individual property, gradually introduced to favor the officers in consequence of the constitution of a military hierarchy, opposed both in origin and spirit to the local Cosack traditions.

course of the river Ural or Yaïk, which has been made the conventional boundary between Europe and Asia, there was not yet, in the middle of the present century, a single lot of land belonging to any individual man, nor even to a town or *statítsa*, as the villages are called, which are also administrative and military centres of Cosack districts. The system of usufruct was common as well as that of proprietorship. On a day fixed by the *atamàn*, at a signal given by the officers of each *statítsa*, haymaking began on the meadows along the rivers. All the men bearing the name of Cosacks went to work simultaneously. First, each one cut with his scythe, in the tall grass, a line enclosing the lot which was to be his to mow, and all the land that had in this manner been appropriated by a Cosack became his by right—he could then mow it at his ease, with his family. In this vast community, the land as the water, the meadows and arable fields as the fisheries on the sea or the rivers, were common property and worked after the same manner, all starting at the same moment, by order and under the supervision of the chiefs, but every one working for himself—for this common proprietorship and common usufruct had nothing to do with the system of equal remuneration preached by certain socialists. Notwithstanding this important restriction, such a system, from the moment that the inhabitants are numerous enough for the products of the soil to become the subject of dispute, leaves little liberty to individual action ; it leads to despotic democracy or to bureaucratic regulations. That it could survive to our days on the banks of the Ural, was only owing to the military organization of the Cosacks.

In the steppes of the south, as in the forests of the north, the existence of these vast communities, where periodical re-allotments were unknown, depended first of all on the productiveness of the soil and the scarcity of labor. As population increased, the rights of each member had to be defined more strictly, the lands had to be assigned to each village and distributed among the inhabitants. In the more recently colonized regions, the time is

still remembered by many when the use of the soil was not confined within such narrow limits. With the Cosacks of the Don as
well, the time is not so far removed when every Cosack was free
to take possession of any vacant piece of steppe-land. In the
government of Samára, on the eastern bank of the Volga, old
men recall the time when every man could cut as much hay as
would make a wagon-load.

Similar customs still survive in sundry of the thankless northern regions, the rough climate and meagre soil of which offer but
few attractions to colonists. This is seen especially in Siberia,
where it often happens that the meadow-lands alone are divided,
while of the arable lands each man works as much as he is able.
In the region north of the Làdoga and Onéga lakes, in the chill
wastes of the government of Olónets, the proportion of individual
usufruct depends entirely on the amount of efficient work accomplished by individuals or families. Each peasant is free to cultivate as much land as his strength permits him, or the number of
hands he disposes of ; all he has to do is to indicate by some sign,
generally a notch on the trees, the spot he has selected. This
form of land tenure is usually allied in the province of Olónets,
to the system of vast communities comprising ofttimes whole districts. The reason is simple. The dwellers in one and the same
valley form together a community whose domain extends, between
forests, along a river or a lake. The traditional boundaries of
these immense communal tracts have repeatedly been traced, less
in view of agricultural achievements, than for the sake of the
fisheries which represent the most unfailing resource of these
otherwise disinherited wastes.

In the district of Olónets, each community numbers, on an
average, a score of villages and hamlets, grouped in *volosts*—
cantons—around one large village which often gives its name
to the others, the latter regarding themselves as its colonies or
offspring. A single one of these rural syndicates comprises, it is
said, over one hundred villages and owns 550,000 acres with

about 40 miles of meadow-land on the river Svir.   We learn from recent researches that these associations of numerous villages into huge communities, or, to put it more correctly, this system of appropriation of the soil in vast tracts, with the right for the hamlets and families of freely helping themselves to the land, appears to have been formerly in almost universal use.   In this case an investigation of the facts and historical documents but confirms what theory would make us surmise.

The village federations of Olònets are the last remnants of those huge communities which can no longer subsist in any but half-desert countries, where agriculture itself still holds a very subordinate place.   The Russian communities of the present day are generally limited to one village, where the custom of working the land in common, for the good of all, or each for himself, has long become an anomaly.   In the remote regions, there still may exist a few commons where the products of the soil and of labor are divided among the co-proprietors.   Such a state of things may be met with in a few dissident (*raskólnik*) villages or out of the way settlements ; but even there it should be ascribed not so much to the persistency of ancient usages as to religious influences and the communistic spirit of monastic associations.*

With the Russian *mir*, as a rule, the pasture-lands and woods alone remain undivided.   Unfortunately these two kinds of lands represent but an insignificant proportion of the communal lands. In this country so rich in forests, where wood is used so freely, the villages best provided with lands, do not, most of the time, own either a patch of forest or a stick of timber.   The reason of this anomaly is very simple.   In the times of serfdom, the peasant was generally allowed for his regular use only cultivated lots, with the addition of a few lots of pasture and meadow.   The Emancipation Act merely aimed at vindicating for him, as his full

---

* Several of the more extreme dissident sects (*raskól*) have very pronounced socialistic tendencies ; one actually bears the name of " Communists " and orders that *all* property shall be in common. (See Vol.III. of this work, Book III., Chap. IX.)

property, the land of which he had had the usufruct ; and, in the application of the agrarian regulations, the peasants frequently were defrauded of part of those lands which they used for pasture. The woods, where they are not the property of the State, were left to the former landlord, a thing the more to be regretted that, originally, the peasant was to have the use of the forests and that, prior to the emancipation, he was generally allowed to get his timber from the master's woods.

This evidently is one of the weak sides of the new agrarian system and the liquidation of serfdom as it has been enacted. It would have been much to Russia's advantage had she, as has been done in other countries, secured to the rural communes the proprietorship of a portion of her vast forests, with the proviso that communal woods should be, as in France, subject to strict government control. Such a system is entirely favorable to the forests, and free from all the drawbacks it presents when applied to arable lands. That might have been an efficient way of preventing the too rapid denudation of the country with all the evils it entails. By leaving the forests to the former landlord, a double damage has been indirectly inflicted on the forest wealth of the empire, consequently on its entire rural economy, and even, in a measure, on the soil and the climate, which both deteriorate through deforestation. The *pomiêsh-tchik*, impoverished by the emancipation, had a double incentive to cut down the woods left in his possession ; it was for him the surest way of making money, and, at the same time, of opposing the depredations of the peasants, insufficiently repressed by the police and by the laws. It is not too much to say that, for having failed to protect the woods against the rapacity of the want-ridden landlord and the plunderous propensities of the *mujik*, the emancipation may be taxed with having helped to bring about the devastation of the forests, so manifold and unforeseen have been the consequences of the great reform.*

* In the kingdom of Poland, on the contrary, the right of usufruct enjoyed by the peasant over the forests has been maintained and even extended beyond measure, without any compensation to the landlords. This was the opposite extreme and, as such, did not benefit the forests.

The communal domain is generally composed of arable and pasture lands. These latter, too much restricted by the Statute, are nearly always used in common, each family sending out their cattle, usually marked, under the care of a herdsman hired by the commune. The arable lands are divided—and redivided at more or less regular intervals—between the members of the commune, to be cultivated by each one separately, at his own cost and risk. Thus individual holding habitually goes hand in hand with collective proprietorship. In this *mir*, apparently wholly communistic, the mainspring of effort is personal interest. In opposition to an idea widely spread abroad, nothing is so repugnant to the peasant as labor in common ; ever since he has been free he almost invariably insists on working for his own account.

The principle on which the *mir* is based is that of periodical re-allotments of the soil.* There are, in this, three points to be considered : the claims which entitle to a lot ; the epochs at which the common territory is divided ; the mode of allotment. On these three points, especially on the two first, customs and practices vary greatly according to regions.

As regards the claimants, the accepted unit is sometimes the " soul " (*dushà*) or " revision soul," *i.e.*, the taxed male head, and sometimes the household (*tiàglo*),† taking into account, as a rule, the working capacities of the different households and the proportion of tax that each can bear. The first of these modes is more generally in use among the Crown peasants, who were subject to

---

* The term *mir*, the meaning of which shall be inquired into later on, is the only one in use among the peasants. Those of "commune" or "society" (*òbsh-tchina* and *òbsh-tchestvo*), employed by Russian writers as being analogous to the *gemeinde* and *communitas* of the West, are foreign to popular speech.

† The word *tiàglo* signifies "a burden," "dues," "contribution,"—and came to be applied to those who carry that burden, who owe those dues. In the time of serfdom this term served to designate the unit of labor to be supplied by each "household," technically meaning a man, woman, and horse. A married couple is most generally understood ; but the meaning undergoes singular changes in different localities. Therefore the divisions made on this basis vary a great deal.

only one tax—capitation ; the second, among the former serfs, who used to distribute their dues to their landlords by households (*tiàglo*), and naturally pursued the same system in distributing the land which he ceded to them.

The lot awarded each family is in proportion to the number of its male members or of its adult and married members.   It is easy to see what encouragement such a system gives to the increase of population.   Each son, when born, or when he arrives at man's estate, brings to the family an additional lot.   So that a numerous offspring, instead of lessening the paternal resources, increases them.   Juridically, the women have no claim whatever to land.*
In practice they have about as great a share of it as the men ; for since, under the *tiàglo* system, a lot is given to each couple, it is the woman who really holds the key to landed property.   Hence Russia is, of all European countries, that where marriage is most in honor and most prolific.   Owing to this twofold superiority, the average of births is nearly double that in France.   The rigor of the climate, the hard life, and above all the mortality among children, are the only hindrances to a marvellously rapid increase of the rural population.

This very increase compels periodical re-allotments.   To supply the new-comers with lots, without every time rehandling the whole land, many communes, especially among the Crown peasants, keep on hand reserve lands.   These they let for the *mir's* benefit, or else make use of as commons, for pasture.   The growing denseness of the population, the smallness of many of the lots ceded to the peasants at the time of the emancipation, deprive most villages of this resource.   The new-comers, then, can enforce their right only by means of a re-allotment.   This would be necessitated anyhow by the fundamental principle on which communal life is based, for otherwise, families increasing unequally, the common property would soon be unequally divided.   In this

---

* Yet in certain regions the division by "head" or "mouth," independently of age or sex, is beginning to come up.

they have to deal with one of the difficulties which beset communism of any type, which, left to itself, inevitably tends to self-destruction, absolute equality being an impossibility, unless continually kept up by watchful re-division. Of course, the more frequent the re-allotments, the more faithfully the principle is maintained, but the more agriculture is hampered and general prosperity hindered.

For meadow-lands, the system of annual re-allotment still prevails ; there even are, in the government of Tambôf, communes which proceed to it twice a year. In others again, the haymaking is done in common and the hay divided afterward.* There are districts where cultivated lands are subject to the same system of annual re-allotment ; they are only too numerous in the governments of Sarátof, Oriòl, Kalúga, Nijni-Nòvgorod, Vorònej, etc.; in that of Perm such was the widely spread custom down to 1872. Such a system is too manifestly disturbing, too much opposed to the husbandman's interest to be general. The re-allotments mostly take place every three years, in conformity to the most popular mode of culture, that by triennial rotation. In places this period of three years is doubled, tripled, quadrupled. In others again, as in some communes of the government of Moscow, a decennial period has been fixed upon ; and yet in others, as with the Great-Russians of Vorònej, they wait till a new " revision " or census takes place. From documents published in 1880, such appears to be the rule among the Crown peasants of the government of Kazàn. These " revisions," which should not be confounded with what is known in the West under the name of general census, occur at irregular intervals of (until now) over twelve or fifteen years. Since 1719 there have been but ten, the last having taken place in 1858. In the communes which proceed to general re-allotments only at revision time, none have taken place yet

* The facts and cases here mentioned are mostly taken from the agricultural inquests or the statistics kept by the various ministerial departments and the *zémstvos.*

since the abolition of serfdom, and there may be none for some time to come—perhaps never, the tax on males having been suppressed by the Emperor Alexander III., which measure did away with the necessity for " revisions " on the old line.

Triennial re-allotment was justified by the mode of culture ; re-allotment timed by " revisions " was based on the system of taxation. From one " revision " to the next, the number of " souls," or male peasants subject to the poll-tax, remained unchanged, no matter how many had been the deaths and births. The commune was mutually responsible before the fisc ; so that, each family, at each new " revision," receiving a lot in proportion to the burdens it bore or the number of hands it disposed of, the tax which, after the letter of the law, bore on the persons, was made indirectly to bear on the lands.

The fatal effects of frequent divisions of the soil scarcely need pointing out. On this point, opinions are all but unanimous. The peasant does not grow attached to a piece of ground which he does not expect to keep and only strives to draw from it the greatest possible immediate profit, without a thought for the morrow. His care and his foresight he reserves for the house-lot (*usàdba*) around his *izbà*, which cannot be taken from him. The adversaries of the *mir* do not fail to make this point in favor of their theory of the advantages of fixed and individual proprietorship over collective land tenure. The husbandman who tills a communal field is unwilling to undertake labor and expenses which are to benefit somebody else. The absolute lack of manure or fertilizer of any kind in so many Great-Russian villages is generally ascribed to this want of interest in the husbandman. Hence the unavoidable impoverishment of the soil and constant aggravation of bad crops. To this evil there formerly was a remedy, or at least a palliative : an exhausted tract of land was abandoned to seek new, sometimes virgin, lands. Nowadays the increase of population and the extension of husbandry render this remedy more and more difficult to apply and less and less efficient.

33

Is this an irreparable evil, a curse naturally inherent to collective property holding? An impartial mind must needs reply : not proven. Some few communes in the governments of Penza and Simbirsk have hit on the expedient of imposing on the peasants obligatory manuring, with the alternative of keeping the same lot at the next distribution. This is an example that might be followed, and the communal authorities, being always on the spot, would be better qualified than a non-resident to see that such conditions be complied with. There is, moreover, a still simpler and easier way : to put off the re-allotments. And that is precisely, on the showing of the agricultural inquests, what has been done more and more since the emancipation, and almost everywhere, now of their own accord, now at the suggestion of some intelligent functionary. Annual re-allotment, at least for cultivated fields, has actually become an exception and even the triennial period is growing rare. Periods of ten, fifteen, twenty, even thirty years are getting more and more frequent. In some districts, the peasants, made wise by experience, have recourse to a new distribution only at the last extremity.

For that frequent re-allotments are an evil, the most determined advocates of the *mir* are the first to acknowledge. It is, therefore, not to be wondered at, in a country always inclined to look to the State for interference, if more than one voice endowed with authority has expressed the wish that law and administration should regulate this vital matter. Some defenders of communal institutions, seeing their pet theories endangered before public opinion by the abuse of the right of re-allotment, have besought the government to hasten to the *mir's* assistance by protecting it against itself, strangely unconscious that, by such an appeal to official interference, they run the risk of striking a mortal blow at a system of which the main strength lies in the popular customs, in tradition, in its living spontaneity.

These evils are far from belonging exclusively to communal lands. Private landed property is not free from them. Many estates are leased for short terms to the peasants of a commune, and they proceed to divide and cultivate them in the same manner as their own lands. "What difference," on this occasion remarks one of the advocates of the *mir*, "between personal property leased out every year, as is customary with so many noblemen's estates, and collective property, re-divided each year? It is more difficult to bring the noble landlords to lengthen the term of their leases than the peasants to put off their re-allotments. If a law is needed to regulate the latter, why not the former?"

The Minister of Crown Demesnes is said to have lately proposed for study the question of a minimum term to be fixed for the use of arable lands ; but official measures have already been forestalled and may be rendered unnecessary by the spontaneous resolutions of several rural communes. Thus the natural course of things brings its own remedy to one of the chief evils of collective tenure. The beneficial effects of this reform already make themselves felt. In the governments of Tula and Kursk, manuring and crops have increased in consequence. And it has been noticed that the wealthiest communes are those that are most backward with rehandling their lands. A further good effect is the delay and limitations imposed on family divisions of land. Young men or young couples can either stay at home or go out to work for a salary until a new division gives them a lot of the communal land.

The manner of allotment is not of less importance nor does it entail less inconvenience than the time of it. Here also the damage is greater in proportion as the communistic spirit and practices are more strictly adhered to. The principle of the *mir* demands that, each lot bearing an equal part of the tax, each should be strictly equal to the next one. This principle the Russian commune usually conforms to with servile punctiliousness. It strives to make the pieces of ground equal both in area and value, then lots are drawn for them. This twofold equality cannot, as a rule, be arrived at by giving to each one compact lot. So each peasant receives a bit each of as many kinds of soil as there are in the commune. The village surveyors begin by marking off the lands of the different categories, then, in each of these blocks, as many small lots are cut out as there are members to be supplied. When the lands are all of the same quality, a thing which, thanks to the homogeneousness of the Russian soil, is fortunately less rare than in Western Europe, the unequal distance from the village still makes them of unequal value to the peasant. One of the consequences of the community of landed property is, indeed, the agglomeration of the dwellings. Isolated houses, dispersed farms, presuppose permanent ownership. To be within reach of the lot which may fall to him, each member of the community must be settled near his brethren, in the centre of the common domain.

Thus in Great-Russia, peasant houses crowd together into large villages, holding, many of them, several thousands of inhabitants. The log-houses stand on two long straight lines, on both sides of a disproportionately wide street (to obviate the spreading of fire), disposed, if possible, along a stream. The *izbàs*, which never touch, usually present to the street one of their lateral faces, often sporting a balcony, or merely carved wood ornaments. In front of the *izbà* is a yard with stables and barns ; back of it the enclosed " house-lot " (*usàdba*), exempt from divisions. This manner of clustering together, in harmony with the mode of land tenure, is also justified by the climate and the nature of the Russian soil. In the south and east, where it is most fertile, water is scarce and springs are few ; all over the land communications are impeded in spring, at thaw-time, and in autumn, not to mention the fear of robbery and assassination. These huge villages are at present one of the chief obstacles to the establishment of individual property which, under this system of agglomerated dwellings, cannot enjoy all its advantages. Husbandry, in fact, is nearly as dependent on the manner of residence as on that of tenure. In a country where population is not dense, and distances are great, individual proprietorship can have a fair chance and full play only if the husbandman, with his stock and implements, resides in the middle of his land. Now in Great-Russia, farms with isolated farmhouses (*khùtor*) are almost unknown ; they are rare even where the peasants have purchased land for their own. They are met with scarcely anywhere but in Little-Russia, where manners are very different in this respect, and lands, even where the communal system prevails, are divided more by the "house" or "yard" (*dvor*) than by the "soul" or household labor unit (*tiàglo*).

A goodly portion of the evils ascribed to the communal land system really is caused by that of rural agglomerations. Now it would not be sufficient to abolish collective land tenure in order to substitute isolated farms to the large villages, to what the Germans call *das Dorfsystem*. Such a substitution is everywhere a difficult thing and a costly, demanding much time too ; in Russia it would prove so perhaps more than anywhere else. It has been now and then proposed to use the frequent fires as a pretence for scattering the dwellings more. The greater distance between the houses would reduce the losses which the country endures through the yearly burning down of thousands of villages. Unfortunately manners, clime, soil, and the eminently sociable nature of the Russian people, are not the only obstacles to such plans. The Emancipation Act has raised one more : the "house-lot" adjoining the *izbà* and given to the owner thereof in full permanent possession. This little enclosed patch, exempt from the control of the *mir*, means simply this : that, should the lands now owned by a village in common, be to-morrow distributed finally among the families, each would remain where it now lives, and be a fixture in the village for a long time to come. Even then it would take centuries, most likely, to transform the present mode of residence, and in the meantime Russia would remain subject to all the disadvantages which are entailed on agriculture by the remoteness of the husbandman's residence, and which make themselves the more felt at present, the larger the villages and the more extensive the territory, increasing by just so much the waste of time, the cost of transportation, and the difficulty of returning to the soil in manure or fertilizers what is taken from it in crops.   This again, however, is one of those evils of collective property from which private property is far from being always exempt.   Many of the old estates, disproportionately vast even yet, are still less within reach of the hands that are to work them.

Under the system of division generally in force, the commune's territory is usually divided into three concentric zones or fields, in conformity to the practice of triennial rotation.   From the centre, occupied by the village, start as many rays as there are claimants, and the sections thus obtained represent the lots to be awarded each one of them.   These lots, therefore, frequently assume the wedge-shape ; but sometimes they take that of long and narrow parallel strips.   The drawing of lots is arranged in such a manner that each claimant must receive a portion of all the three fields of each category, without any thought being taken to join together the portions allotted to the same family.   Thus each lot (*nadiêl*) is mostly composed of bits of land, separated from one another and wedged in in other lots.   The portion of one "soul" or one *tiàglo* can be made up of scraps scattered in six, seven, eight, nine, ten distant places, sometimes more.   To get an idea of the exceeding smallness of each such particle of land, it is sufficient to keep in mind that the average allowance was from seven and a half to ten acres per male head, and that, the peasants having in many cases redeemed only the legal minimum, the share of each falls much short of that average.   In the communes which, while bearing a large population, are ill provided with land, this parcelling of the communal domain leads to an actual trituration of the soil.   The agricultural inquest mentions communes in the government of Kursk where fractions of lots have been found measuring not quite seven feet in width.   Under the system of individual tenure this infinitesimal parcelling is rarely equalled.   Thus the system now in force adds the defect of individualism, chief among which is the excessive parcelling of the land, to those of communism, which weakens the attachment to the soil and the energy in labor.*

With such scraps of land rational cultivation is impossible. Then, as they are distant sometimes several miles from one another, the peasant wastes a large portion of his time and strength in useless journeys, so that it is not unusual for the remoter ones to be simply given up by their temporary owner. Again, a great deal of land is lost in boundaries, and large quantities of grain in seed. Lastly they are so entangled that they leave no room for turning round in and no facility of access, so that, from their narrowness, they are exceedingly difficult to plough and harrow. This places the husbandmen in a state of mutual dependence which is fatal to individual enterprise. Neighbors, being unable to act singly, are compelled to combine, and this leads to the so-called "compulsory culture" (*flurzwang*) of the Germans. It becomes necessary to leave the commune to decide as to the time, if not always as to the nature of the work to be done. Mathematical impartiality thus really destroys the free enjoyment of the land and brings about, indirectly, a sort of common, or at least simultaneous, cultivation, which might be made profitable by improved proceedings, but which, with the routine at present prevailing, becomes an additional hindrance to progress.

Faults such as these cannot be corrected without giving up the deceptive theory of absolutely identical lots and the puerile practice which, by a grossly material interpretation, seems bent on presenting each claimant with a clod of earth exactly like his neighbor's. It would be better to make up well rounded lots,

---

* The difficulties and disadvantages of communal allotment are sometimes attenuated by dividing the land, and the taxes along with it, among larger and smaller groups, which then subdivide it among the single members. These preliminary divisions by fractions of villages are usually preferred in the larger communes, where direct division, by the "soul" or *tiàglo*, would prove too complicated.

well balanced in value, of sizes varying according to the quality of the soil and the distance from the village. Yet even this reform would not remove the evil. In the poorer communes, the lots still would be disproportionately small, and would become smaller still from generation to generation, along with the increase of the population.*

As a remedy for this evil, one of the most serious that threaten the *mir* in the future, the usual panacea has of course been proposed : the intervention of the State. It has been proposed to establish a legal minimum, below which no lot or fraction of lot should be allowed to descend. Such measures would not only have against them the theoretical principle on which communities are based and according to which each member holds an equal right to the land,—they would stumble against serious practical difficulties and would find it hard to triumph over the great diversity of local conditions. It must not be forgotten, moreover, that the excessive parcelling of land is not a fault belonging exclusively to the collective system. Under that of individual property, family divisions can lead to similar results. We see something of this in the West, in certain parts of France for instance. In Russia itself, this evil is encountered, among others, in Lithuania, where the individual system is predominant. From the moment that the peasant is to be a landholder, it cannot be avoided under any system. In one way the collective system even has one indubitable advantage : it would, in case of need, allow of having recourse to uniform culture on a large scale—a thing which, keeping pace with the progress of instruction and agriculture, might prove as favorable to the productiveness of the soil, as to the interests of the joint proprietors.

* On the Isle of Java, where collective land tenure also prevails, similar causes have produced similar effects. The rapid increase of the population has reduced the lot of each laborer to particles far more infinitesimal than in Russia. Then also there is a general demand for interference to set a limit to the parcelling of the soil, or, better still, for the substitution of individual and hereditary tenure for that at present in use. See **De Laveleye** : *De la Propriété et de ses Formes Primitives.*

BOOK VIII. CHAPTER IV.

The *Mir* in Theory and Practice—The Material Equality of the Lots does not Always Imply Equitable Distribution—Division according to the Working Capacity or Resources of the Laborers—Story of One Commune—"Soulless" Families; Strong, "Half-Power," Weak Families —The *Mir* as a Providence—Arbitrariness and Injustice—Usury—The Vampires or "*Mir*-Eaters"—Rural Oligarchy—Landless Peasants and Rural Proletariate.

THE system of strict material equality is far from implying invariable equity in the distribution of the lands. As a rule, there is nothing fixed and regular about the proceeding, certainly nothing mathematical. The *mir* deals with its members more paternally, *i.e.*, more arbitrarily : it does not consider merely the number of persons that dwell in a house, but also their ages, their state of health, their resources ; it takes into account natural or accidental inequalities, weighs the strength and capacity of each member, and treats each according to his needs or faculties.

It would be a great mistake to see in this effort at compensation only a humanitarian instinct or an unconscious socialism, bent on levelling everything in despite of nature. No ; the peasants obey very different promptings, more positive, more practical, as is their nature.

Community of lands stands, as already indicated, in closest relation to solidarity before the fisc. For centuries the two things have been so intimately connected, that it was very possible for a certain school to consider collective property as simply a consequence of that solidarity. In a country where taxes of all kinds have always been very heavy, where the possession of the soil might always have been regarded more as a burden than as a privilege, where the sum-total of taxes and dues even now frequently exceeds the normal income from the land, it was but natural that, in distributing the communal domain, the peasants' prime object should always have been the payment of the taxes. Since the emancipation this question controls the entire life of the *mir* as it did before, and, in distributing the communal *ager*, it considers less each individual's claim to the land than his paying capacity. Each lot, as a rule, corresponds to a proportionate share of the taxes, and the quantum of land adjudged to each household is in proportion to the burdens it can bear. The distribution of the communal lands is but another form of the distribution of the communal taxes.

The endowment of families varies not only with the number, but also with the strength and ages, of their members. The most robust and prosperous receive a larger share of the land because they contribute a larger portion of the taxes. Only those communes where the income from the land regularly exceeds the annual payments need not give way to such preoccupations but are able simply to divide their fields by the male head or by the household.

What need to point out all the complications and difficulties of such a system? The proceedings in use can scarcely be comprehended without the help of an example or a sort of diagram. We will here find it convenient to borrow Mr. Le Play's system of monographs, though not without warning the reader that such a method can only give the particular facts in a given case, from which it were imprudent to generalize. The Russian *mir*, we must remember, knows of no uniform laws or rules, the customs vary with the regions, the districts, even the villages, each community being free to regulate these matters to please itself, so it pays the taxes imposed on it.

An economist, Mr. Trirógof, seeing in the village communities the organic cells of the great body politic, resolved to investigate one closely; so to speak, under the microscope. At the end of a few years of patient observation, he gave to the world, in two successive, most curious papers, the results of this sort of socio-histological study. The commune chosen by him is named Aráshin and is situated in the government of Sarátoi. It is in no wise different from its neighbors.

When Mr. Trirógof began his investigation, Aráshin numbered 493 inhabitants of both sexes, who formed 87 families, dwelling in the same number of houses. The "souls," as established by the last "revision" and subject to the poll-tax, were 212 in number. The communal territory covered 846 *dessiatínas* (about 2,327 acres, at about 2¾ acres to the *dessiatína*) of arable land, not including the vegetable gardens and hemp patches immediately adjoining the village. The arable lands, divided, as usual, in three fields, were broken up into 212 lots, the same number as that of the tax-paying "souls," of about 4 *dessiatínas* (11 acres) each, every lot comprising a portion of each of the three communal fields. To the distribution of the property corresponds that of the burdens. All contributions and dues, be they personal or land taxes, charged by the State to the commune of Aráshin, the *mir* merged into one mass, with no distinction as to name, origin, or destination. The taxes, thus blocked, are then divided into a number of quotas equal to that of the "revision souls" and the corresponding lots. The sum-total of taxes and dues amounted for Aráshin to 2,607 roubles and 30 copecks, which gives 12 roubles and 30 copecks by "soul" and lot.

If, in conformity with theory and legal fictions, the unit of distribution had been the "revision soul," every such "soul" would have had its 4 *dessiatínas* and paid its 12 roubles. But Aráshin does not operate per "soul" or "head," nor even by the household. While one family would receive only one lot and pay the 12 roubles and 30 copecks thereto pertaining, another would be put in possession of five and a-half lots and assessed at over 73 roubles a year. The most singular thing about it is that the portion of land and of taxes allotted to certain families fluctuates every year, according as the laboring power of their members increases or decreases. Thus the house of one Vassíli Fedótof held, in 1874, four and a-half lots, five in 1875 and five and a half in 1876. Why this yearly augmentation of half a lot, *i.e.*, of two *dessiatínas?* Because Vassíli Fedótof's children were growing up, and the family, therefore, was able to bear an increase of labor and payment. Ivan Fedótof's share, on the other hand, had, from three lots, fallen to two within the same span of time, because the head of the house was growing old and the laboring power of the family was steadily decreasing.

It appears from this that, where the commune wishes to keep an account of all the changes brought on by age, sickness, or infirmity, it is compelled to divide the land anew each year— unless, as is frequently done, a lot or half lot is simply transferred from one family to another, without touching the whole. At Aráshin the distribution is continually fluctuating according to the means of families, the age and health of their members. In this respect the paternal, if not disinterested, solicitude and caution of the Aráshin *mir* goes very far ; it investigates all the phases of domestic life, it enters into individual differences. Thus a certain family by the name of Maxímof, which, by the "revision lists," should have received four lots and paid for four "souls," had only two and a half and paid in proportion, because one of its members was afflicted with bad eyes and another with a chronic throat trouble.

Age and physical strength are not the only standards of assessment ; the *mir* also considers the resources, the means of labor of each house or "yard" (*dvor*), what economists call "the plant." Thus the *mir* of Aráshin classes the families into four categories. The first comprises those which, from lack of adult laborers or agricultural implements, are unable to cultivate land profitably and to bear the least part of the communal burdens. Out of eighty-seven families, three were in this condition. They got no land and were exempt from taxes ; in technical jargon, "they had no souls." Next to these "soulless" families come, in the classification adopted by Aráshin, the "half-power families," *i.e.*, such as do have one valid laborer, but are unprovided with the laborer's indispensable helpmate—a horse. There were some ten such families ; they received each one lot, and were taxed accordingly. To the third class, by far the most numerous (45 out of 87), belong the families which have only one laborer, but one or two horses ; they paid each for two "souls" and got two lots. Lastly came thirty families more numerous or wealthier than the others, each of which had charge of more than two lots, most of them having three or four, some five and even five and a half, and naturally taxed in proportion.

It appears from the above that, in the commune of Aráshin, the "soulless" and the "half-power" families, and those having only one laborer, the joint number of which amounted to fifty-seven, *i.e.*, over two thirds of the whole, held, together, less than half the communal lands, while the remaining third, composed of the richer families, held between them more than half the lots—112 against 100, —and paid more than the other fifty-seven put together—1,377 roubles and 60 copecks against 1,230 roubles on a total of 2,607 roubles and 60 copecks.

A rather unexpected deduction is forced on us by this mode of distribution, which is that, with these seemingly wholly communistic proceedings, it is in reality not so much the personal strength of the laborer as the resources he disposes of which constitute a claim to the land. In a *mir* like that of Aráshin, it might almost be said to be—*capital !* Land is preferably awarded to those who have most means to get something out of it. It is less the demand for produce which is considered than the means of production.

This uneven distribution, whether by "the soul" or the "household" (*tiàglo*), in accordance with the number of able-bodied laborers in each house and their aptitude to work, is adduced by certain Russian writers of note, such as Yúri Samárin and Prince Vassíltchikof, as the distinctive characteristic of the *mir*, the essential trait by which the Great-Russian commune differs from all agrarian associations or communities, whether of ancient or modern times. They delight in presenting this mode of division as a solution of the property question especially belonging to the Russian people, and radically different from all more or less analogous institutions. As a matter of fact it may be so to-day, but from the historical standpoint the correctness of this assertion is questionable. This manner of distributing land seems to be derived, not from a particular conception of property as such, but simply from the application to property of the mode of distributing the taxes. The truth of this position is proved by the fact that in certain urban communities the produce of the communal lands is distributed among the inhabitants in proportion to the figure of taxes paid by each of them.*

Such a standard—the working capacity of the husbandmen—could hardly suit any but a country where the use of the soil was, for the laborer, less a right than a burden. Take it all in all, the cultivation of the soil may be regarded as a sort of public service, —an obligatory service incumbent on every able-bodied man, and from which only age or sickness exempts. It is a fact that in most communes where the income from the land runs short of the dues, the men, from the age of twenty to that of sixty, are accounted as laborers, and, as such, obliged to take their share of the land and of the taxes. In the poorest villages this sort of service begins at eighteen, or even sixteen ; and no one can ask to be freed from it until he is sixty, or fifty-five, at the very least.

Should the antiquity of the *tiàglo* as labor unit be established, it would go far to confirm, at least in part, the views of Mr. Tchi-

* A large number of cities own cultivated lands. Some let them to farmers, others divide them after the manner of the rural *mir*. The system mentioned in the text is found to exist in Mológa, a district city in the government of Yaroslàvl. The inhabitants are divided into eleven *sòtnias, i.e.,* " hundreds," and the meadows belonging to the city into as many lots, which each *sòtnia* mows by turns. The produce, instead of being distributed by the " head " or family, is divided among the members of each *sòtnia*, in proportion to the quota of their respective taxes.

tcherin and the school which regards the Russian commune as having sprung out of the Moscovite fiscal system. In that case the mode of division and onerous taxation would also mainly account for the general adherence to the communal system. In a state where the fiscal system, through centuries, made of the possession of land as much an obligation and burden as a privilege and right, the reasons which elsewhere urged to the dissolution of communities could not have much weight. Why proceed to a final division when it frequently was more in the taxpayer's interest to reduce his lot than to extend it? It is quite possible the *mir* may have stood its ground through so many centuries because of the burdens which were heaped on it, the individuals dreading to take on their own responsibility the load which it was for the community to bear.

This lumping and distribution of lands and taxes, in conformity with each member's resources, constitutes what the ingenious investigator of Aráshin calls " the popular tax apportionment," and in his opinion there is not much need of any other. It little matters what is taxed, or how the state or provinces distribute the direct taxes. The peasant does not care to know whether he pays for the land, or for "souls" or families; poll-tax, land-tax,—in his eyes it is all one. All he cares for is the sum-total of the dues and the manner in which the *mir* distributes it among the members.[1] So that it was almost an idle trouble to substitute a land-tax or income-tax for the capitation-tax; any kind of reform is bootless unless it lightens the mass of the peasant's liabilities. On the other hand, the taxes, heavy as they are, do not crush him as utterly as is usually supposed, the assessment in each individual case being proportioned to the taxpayer's means and strength.

Aráshin shows us the exact nature of what may be called the commune's fiscal solidarity and the almost sovereign power with which it invests the *mir*. This power, the apologists of the village communes assure us, the *mir* almost invariably uses for the greater

[1] Does not this practically amount to " single-tax " ?

good of all its members, striving with the strictest equity, the most scrupulous earnestness, to balance all unevenness, to avoid all unfairness. Conceived of thus, the *mir* would be to the peasant a sort of earthly providence ; the commune, a mother ever watchful lest any of her children should be taxed beyond their powers. A village like Aràshin appears to our enraptured eyes in the guise of a living rural Utopia, where ignorant boors have been, for several centuries, converting into realities the most daring dreams of the thinkers of the West. To make of these communes veritable Edens, all that were needed, it would seem, is to lighten the taxation.

Many writers since Herzen have extolled the peasants' sense of solidarity, their good faith and sound judgment in their dealings with one another and matters pertaining to all those delicate questions of measurement and partition. These praises are, on the whole, deserved. But, were they *always* so, the *mujik* would not be human. Such proceedings lend themselves too easily to abuses of all sorts for the *mir* to be quite free from them. Accordingly the detractors of the communal principle are not at a loss for flaws and elements of disturbance.

Fiscal solidarity, which, in a model village like Aràshin beams on us as the beneficient *mir*-fairy, frowns in others as a tyrant whose yoke is unbearable. To rid themselves of it, many peasants of those who are better off try to go out of the community. The discretionary powers of distribution, admired by some as the master stroke of popular genius, is regarded by many even of the advocates of the *mir* as an ingenious but dangerous piece of machinery, which, in order not to degenerate into an abuse, stands in need of being regulated by the State.*

The fact is that arbitrariness has opened the way for intrigue and corruption into this system, apparently so strictly equitable.

---

* Thus Prince Vassìltchikof, a great admirer of the system—not perceiving how difficult and, perhaps, inefficient any legislation in such a matter would be.

The agricultural inquests have, in this respect, become the vehicle of plaints which come indeed from functionaries or proprietors foreign to the *mir* but should not therefore be made light of. These small self-governing democracies are exposed to two opposite evils : the tyranny of the crowd and that of individuals. At one time it will be the mass, the poor, who will lay down the law to the rich, forcing on them supplementary lots and thus compelling them to pay more than their share of the dues. In the north, where the peasants frequently make their living chiefly by industry and trade, it is no rare thing for a commune to let in a particularly skilled artisan or a more than usually successful tradesman for two lots, *i. e.*, for a double quota of taxes, which is but another way of taxing capital or income. At another time, it will be the rich who, through corruption or bullying, will lay down the law to the majority, gain possession of the best lands, and create in the very midst of the *mir* a sort of oppressive oligarchy. This latter abuse, although apparently the least reconcilable with the constitution of the *mir*, appears at present to be the more frequent of the two ; at least it is more complained of in the depositions made before the great agricultural inquest. There are in these Russian villages men who would be called in the West *exploiteurs*, vampires : enterprising, clever men, who fatten themselves at the cost of the community. The *mujik* has for them the frightfully expressive name of "*mir*-eaters" (*miro-yèdy*). In many governments—those of Kalúga, Sarátof, and others—most villages are pictured as being under the control of two or three wealthy peasants, who beguile the commune out of its best lands "for a song"—or for no compensation at all. To achieve this there is no need either of dealing unfairly at the partitions or of cheating at the drawing of lots.

In these villages as in ancient Rome, it is usually through debt that the poor fall into the power of the rich.* The vampire

* It must be admitted that in this respect the peasant is wronged not by his brethren alone, but also by middlemen of all sorts, by speculators, either urban or rural, and generally known under the designation of "fists,"

34

extends to the peasant reduced to want through improvidence, sickness, or accident, loans beyond his power of repayment. The frequent failures of crops in the southeast are a standing danger to the needy, a standing opportunity for the unscrupulous rich. The insolvent debtor is compelled to give up to his creditor, often for a nominal price, a lot which he has no longer the means of tilling. Liquor is the bait most freely used, and the keeper of the *kabàk* (saloon-keeper) the habitual "*mir*-eater." Usury is the ulcer that gnaws at the peasants' vitals, and collective land tenure is not free from blame in this.

Property being common, the *mujik* cannot mortgage his share of it. Even the *usàdba*, or house-lot, which is exempt from communal handling, cannot, so long as the redemption operation is not completed, be alienated to anybody not of the *mir* without the latter's consent. So that among the Russian peasants, as among the Arab tribes of French Algeria, there is no landed, but only personal, credit ; the consequence is—the *mujik* pays for the " *mir*-eater's*" money at the rate of 10 % *a month*, often as high as 150 % a year.* The administration, the press, the local assemblies have been, for the last twenty years, cudgelling their brains to find a way of coming to the peasant's relief ;—popular banks have been started by the State and by private enterprise,—in vain. The thorny problem of agricultural credit, so complicated everywhere, remains harder to solve in Russia than elsewhere. The peasant

(*kulakì*), *i.e.*, monopolizers. There even are cases, if we are to believe the denunciations of a portion of the press and the revelations brought about by certain trials (for instance the affair with Count Bòbrinsky's peasants, February, 1891), when former serfs, hopelessly in arrear with their rents for lands farmed by them from their former lords, are actually reduced to a semi-servitude, until they have acquitted themselves in full, by the "counting-houses" of great landholders.

* See reports of the " Inquest " ; also the writings of Prince Vassìltchi-kof and A. V. Yákovlef. The Russian "land-banks," whose bonds are in great demand in the west of the empire, usually lend only to individual landholders—*pomièsh-tchiks*,—and, owing to the improvident thriftlessness of many of the latter, these advances, meant to support large-scale agriculture through the crisis of emancipation, became for numbers of the former serfholders the cause or means of total ruin.

remains the quarry of Jewish usurers in the west, of vampires and close-fisted speculators in the north, centre, and southeast. Accordingly, penury is frequently met with among these husband-men, who boast the title of landowners. The tendency of a great mass of testimony—which, it is true, one should beware of accepting literally—is to show that since the emancipation there are only two classes of peasants left : the rich and the poor. The middle class would seem to have vanished along with serfdom, which, by bending all heads under a uniform yoke, maintained an artificial kind of level, to fall below which was almost as difficult as to rise above it. The restraint of nobiliary tutelage once removed, free play was left to individual qualities and vices, to industry and laziness, so that, in spite of the common ownership of the soil, one of the first effects produced by liberty was to increase inequalities.

The picture which results from the investigations of the great agricultural inquest is not attractive. The greater part of the depositions goes to show that the soil is being impoverished from lack of fertilizing, in consequence of the too frequent partitions ; the effort to achieve absolute equality in the allotments leads to an absurd and inconvenient parcelling of the land, which is, so to speak, frittered into dust, while the object is not attained, for all this minuteness cannot maintain even an average semblance of well-being in the families. Undivided property, the commission's report concludes, is an insuperable obstacle to agriculture, a fetter to individual liberty, a hindrance to all spirit of enterprise, a premium to carelessness and indolence. The great advantage of the communal system, the great argument put forward by its advocates, is that, by making the holding of land open to all, it does away with proletariate ; and now, if its opponents are to be credited, it already threatens to do in Russia what it has done in Java : to transform the entire rural population into proletarians.

What is true, in Russia as well as elsewhere, is that the bare owning of land is not much without the means of bringing out its value. Now the commune, while it distributes the land to its members, gives them neither working funds, nor livestock, nor agricultural implements.   Therefore we often see peasants who, having sold their right in the land—" sold their souls " is the technical expression—live as day-laborers on wages upon the land assigned them by the *mir*. The guaranty against proletariate lies less in the even partition of the soil than in the diffusion of capital.

Besides, even as matters stand now, it is not strictly true that each man has his share of the soil. The universal right admitted by theory cannot always be carried out in practice. Not content with spreading through the cities, where there is nothing to check it, proletariate gradually sneaks into the villages, guarded as they seem to be by that solid rampart, the commune. Numbers of peasants at the present day have not a foot of land to their name : some because they have given up their share, to take up trade or a vagrant's life ; many because their communes, having no reserve lands and putting off the allotments more and more, have not yet given them their share ; others again because they became orphaned before they were of age and the commune, their legal guardian, has taken from them their father's lot, fearing lest, through their inability or inadequate strength, the commune should be left to pay the dues with which every lot is burdened.

Popular speech has a special name for these *mujiks* despoiled of land : it calls them *bobylï*. Provincial statistics supply some instructive figures on this subject. In 1871, only ten years after the emancipation which had given them land, thousands of peasants already were without any, in the rich Black-Mould regions as well as in the meagre ones of the north. In the government of Kostromà alone there were 98,000 such peasants, 94,000 in that of Tambòf, and 77,000 in that of Kursk.* This evil, moreover, can

* In this latter government $\frac{1}{100}$ of the peasants are said to be landless, and almost as many more reduced to the small hereditary "house-lot" (*usàdba*). Adding to these the people of various classes settled in the villages, it was found that in this government alone over 200,000 persons, *i. e.* over $\frac{12}{100}$ of the rural population, had no part in the landed property.   In that of Kostromà the proportion rose to $\frac{15}{100}$.

only increase, since the families that once have gone out of a community cannot return into it except they buy back their forfeited membership, not to mention the fact that re-allotments are becoming more and more rare, the lots smaller and smaller as a natural effect of the increase of the population.*   Thus collective tenure stands doubly convicted of inefficiency : first in being unable to really secure a share in the land to every one ; second, in being unable to protect from penury such families as it does provide with land.

---

* Rural proletariate would already be a much more numerous class than it is, were it not for the resource opened to it by colonization. (See end of this volume.) The greater part of the peasants who go off into Asia are driven to emigrate by lack of land.   Out of each 100 emigrants going to settle in Siberia who passed through the government of Tomsk in 1887, 62 owned no land, or very little.   Out of a total of 780 families, 479 declared they had left their communes from lack of land, and 278 from lack of work. So it appears that, in spite of the *mir*, the causes that lead to emigration are much the same in Russia as in the West. In 1890 the number of emigrants who had gone to Siberia was estimated at 40,000 annually. Emigration was regulated by law only in 1889. Until then it had been going on almost at random.

BOOK VIII. CHAPTER V.

Partisans and Opponents of the Communal System—Frequent Exaggerations in Both Camps—Are the Faults most justly Imputed to the *Mir* All Inherent to Collective Tenure?—How Many are Due to Communal Solidarity and to the Fiscal System—Situation Created for the Communes by Emancipation and Redemption—The Extent of Peasant Lots—The *Mir* does not yet really Own the Land—The Village Communities will be in a Normal Condition only after they have done Paying the Redemption Annuities.

AT the present day, as in the days of serfdom, the Russian commune generally has two kinds of partisans : the Slavophils, defenders of the national traditions, and the radical democrats, more or less avowed followers of the West. The former see in it a Slavic and patriarchal institution, destined to preserve Russia from the revolutionary throes of the West ; the latter insist on seeing in it a survival of the primeval joint land tenure, and a precious germ of the popular associations of the future. Between these two schools, so different in spirit, and starting from such different premises,—orthodox Slavophilism and cosmopolitan radicalism,—their common liking for the agrarian commune forms a connecting link. On this neutral ground many conservatives, with more or less national and sometimes aristocratic tendencies, are willing to make gracious advances to socialism and radicalism with their levelling propensities, and affect to deplore, as incurably tainted, the social conditions of the most thriving Western states, hinting that Russia is the only country where property is organized on rational principles, and, not content with proclaiming that landed property is the indispensable consummation and accompaniment of liberty, to indorse the revolutionary sophisms about paid labor being only another form of serfdom.*

This queer combination, not unusual in Russia, of the Slavo-phil spirit and socialistic vagaries, is not as unnatural as may seem at first sight. Between these two seemingly diametrically opposed tendencies,—between the socialistic innovator, who is nothing if not cosmopolitan and unbelieving, who dreams of annulling political boundaries as well as pulling down private landmarks, and the orthodox Slavophil, austerely in love with the national traditions, sensitively jealous of his country's glory and suspicious of all things foreign,—between these two there is, as we have seen,† a hidden link : contempt for modern civilization which both anathematize,—an aversion, common to both against European society, against the *bourgeois* science and political economy of the West, which one party attacks in the name of an unrealizable utopian future, and the other in that of traditions belonging to an almost as chimerical past.

The Russian commune's enemies are the habitual opponents of the Slavophil tendencies and socialistic dreams, devoted to Western institutions and anxious for their country's complete assimilation with Europe ; the economists, who take thought, first and foremost, for material production, and are opposed, in the

---

* See in the *Revue des Deux Mondes* of March 1st, 1879, my study entitled : *Le Socialisme Agraire et la Propriété Foncière en Europe (Agrarian Socialism and Landed Property in Europe).* One of the journalists who have most brilliantly debated these delicate questions, the late Prince A. Vassíltchikof, wrote the following lines in a letter with which he honored me, in reply to the above-mentioned paper : " The communal system having been introduced in Russia centuries ago, it is very natural that, in discussing it, we should meet on common ground with the socialists of the West, and that, in upholding this traditional institution in our country, we should, to a great extent, reproduce the arguments by which the socialists are striving to force it into the Western societies. . . . It is an undoubted fact that, in several social and agrarian questions, we trespass on theories reputed radical and revolutionary in Europe. . . ." (This letter was published in the *Revue des Deux Mondes* of July 15th, 1879.)

† See Book IV., Chap. I.

north as everywhere else, to anything that interferes with individual and free competition. Besides these, are arrayed against the *mir* the greater number of landed proprietors and professional agriculturists, these two classes being more nearly concerned in its practical defects than any other. As an offset, however, the majority of desk-and-library-men, the journalists and writers of both capitals, won over by the theoretical advantages of the communal principle, hold fast to the *mir*, and are fond of presenting it as Russia's anchor of salvation. Is this always a tribute to the *mir's* own intrinsic merits? Perhaps not quite. In their pæans on collective tenure, the writers least suspectable of Slavophilism are prompted by another idea, which unconsciously becomes the main one : that of dealing with an institution essentially national, Russian, Slavic—or reputed such.* That is how, in a country sick of imitation, patriotic self-consciousness asserts itself and becomes excited to exaltation at sight of an undoubtedly original feature. That is how we can account for the almost religious enthusiasm and fervent partisanship with which collective land tenure inspires so many of the most distinguished Russian writers, such men as Samárin, Kavélin, Vassìltchikof, of the latter of whom it has been ingeniously remarked by one of his countrymen that, under the socialist's working-man's blouse shows the velvet *kaftàn* of the Moscovite *boyàr.*

In the conflict which was raging all round it, since the middle of the reign of Nicolas, the Russian commune, up to the Bulgarian war, seemed rather to be losing than gaining ground. Public prejudice, which had been in its favor, seemed on the point of turning against it. By temporarily raising to high honor all that was Slavic in name or appearance, the last Oriental war

* In spite of all the proofs at present accumulated against this system, Prince Vassìltchikof, for one, strives at great length to demonstrate that the form of property in use in the *mir* is peculiar to the Slavs, and, at the same time, that it has been in general use among all the peoples of this race who were preserved from Teutonic influences.

revived the waning popularity of the *mir*. The nihilistic agitation at the end of the reign of Alexander II. may also have indirectly contributed to strengthen the village communities, by removing from the administrative mind, for a considerable time, any latent notion of altering the traditional agrarian system, as such a course might have supplied the foes of public order with a dangerous weapon.

The reckless exaggerations in which the advocates of the commune at times indulge may have repeatedly given rise in the opposite camp to speculations and delusions no less excessive. There are few Russians but have a fixed, determined, and absolute opinion on this complex question. It has often struck me that on no other point dogmatism is so rampant ; on no other do the Russians find it so difficult to keep to the critical point of view. I confess that both the commune's friends and enemies impress me frequently as overrating, respectively, its qualities and faults. The lack of moderation, of impartiality, which prevails in this wordy war is easily accounted for by the vital importance of the issues at stake and by the excitement of battle.

Prior to the emancipation, all social vices, all economic plagues, used to be ascribed to serfdom. Now there are Russians who would throw every blame on the collective tenure system. If the great reform has not given to agriculture and production all the impetus that might have been expected—the fault, to hear them, is the commune's. The temptation is great to create to oneself a scapegoat, that can be made to answer for all one's mistakes or disappointments. Such is the part assigned to the rural commune by many Russians. Public opinion lays on it the heavy load of unavoidable errors and unrealized hopes ; it is charged with all that the liberated peasant is blamed for : with the backwardness of agriculture ; the *mujik's* improvidence or drunkenness; the dearth or high price of labor ; the bad crops ; the premature exhaustion of the soil ; even the famines that visit periodically certain portions of the empire, become so many texts for homilies against the

Slavophils' pet national institution. If we are to believe certain detractors of the *mir*, all there is to do in order to doom Russia to irretrievable decadence is to treasure this legacy of barbarous ages ; while, to open to agriculture and production an era of unexampled prosperity, it would be sufficient to rid property of the communal swaddling-clothes.* Even did the present system merit all these attacks, such views and hopes would still be dangerous ; for those who gather and merge into one all the evils under which agriculture and rural production are suffering, prepare terrible disappointments for the day when the sore from which they derive them all will be closed—if it ever is.

The Russian commune is most frequently and justly found fault with in the name of agriculture on one side, of individual enterprise on the other. We have discussed the harm to agriculture in describing the mode of allotment. It can be summed up under two heads : short term of usufruct and, in consequence, carelessness of the husbandman and exhaustion of the soil ; excessive parcelling of the land and dispersion of the lot fractions, rendering rational culture impossible. The sad effects of the system are mentioned in all the inquests. So in certain districts of the government of Simbirsk, for instance, the rent of communal lands is said to be about half that of private lands. So too, the yield of wheat, oats, rye, is said to be generally one or two *tchèt-verts*—between six and twelve bushels—per *dessiatína* greater on private than on communal lands.

Supposing all this to be correct, reply the advocates of the commune, it is so under the system of division in force up to the latter years ; but these methods can be changed—they are chan-

---

* Thus a gentleman farmer from the south, denouncing, in a most spirited pamphlet, the idolatrous infatuation of the men who, from their libraries, place the commune on a pedestal, actually dared to assert that, were the communal system suppressed, *production would be doubled forthwith*, and all demand for police or prisons against the nihilists, communists, anarchists, would be done away with ! (Deltof, *The Crisis of Ignorance,* Khàrkof, 1879.)

ging already. This system can be modified to suit the demands of modern improved modes of culture, in proportion as the greater number of inhabitants, the opening of new outlets, or the impoverishment of the soil—so lately almost virgin soil—make such alterations desirable. Why should the rural communities be more impermeable to progress than the individuals of an ignorant and conservative class in the matter of personal inheritances ?

And the barriers to individual endeavor, retort the detractors of the collective system, are they not the communes' doing? Who else discourages all original enterprise, taking the sinew out of labor and making the soil barren ? Does not the very security which the peasant derives from the certainty of always having a lot, countenance idleness, incline him to drunkenness and improvidence ?

That may be true, again reply the apologists of the *mir*, but such habits, long fostered by serfdom, are to be met with in other countries, under a property system as well as a climate wholly different from those of Russia. The remedy, with us as well as in the south of Italy or Spain, lies not so much in a change in the mode of tenure, as in the development of public instruction, of the consumers' demands, in the progress of general well-being. In what way does undivided proprietorship rob the husbandman of that indispensable incentive—personal interest ? From the moment that the distribution has taken place, proprietorship virtually becomes personal, and there is nothing that betokens the application of that most deadening principle : equal remuneration of the laborers independently of each one's efforts and deserts ; every worker is compensated according to his works, every man is free to make savings. Why is it necessary that, to apply all his care and all his powers to the culture of the soil, he should own it, and that not merely personally, but hereditarily ? Is it not enough that the usufruct of it is assured him for a space of time sufficient to enable him to gather all the fruits of his labors ? By lengthening the terms of allotment the commune peasant becomes, virtually, a long-lease farmer.* Between these two men, or these two conditions, where is the difference? There is only one, all to the peasant's advantage, which is that, the last instalment of the redemption debt once acquitted, he will have no other rent than the tax to pay for his land. If, with a usufruct of ten, fifteen, or twenty years, there are costly works and improvements, wholly with a view to a distant future, which the temporary holder of the land may not dare to undertake, does not the same difficulty exist under the farming system which is in force in the most flourishing agricultural regions of Europe? Would not, indeed, an equitable solution of this delicate problem be easier with Russian collective than with English individual tenure? because, in the former case, the proprietor being a body of men, the individual's interests are identical with those of all the others, so their triumph is assured in the end.†

To an impartially minded observer one thing is clear : that many of the drawbacks to the present system are by no means inherent to it. They frequently depend on local circumstances which react in exactly the same way on individual property : want of instruction, lack of capital, the agglomeration of villages, and the great distances from them to the lots,—lastly the condi-

---

* The analogy between the temporary usufructuary of a communal lot and the long-lease farmer of a private property is too obvious to need demonstrating. Certain defenders of the commune have made it the theme of their arguments in favor of the *mir*. Others, more uncompromising, like Prince Vassiltchikof, refuse to admit this analogy, proscribe renting land on lease as an irrational form of farming which must fatally impoverish the soil, and invite the State to forbid or restrain by laws this pernicious Western custom, not perceiving that most of these arguments also condemn the temporary use of land in force in the *mir*. (See *Socialisme Agraire*, etc, *Revue des Deux Mondes*, March 1st, 1879.)

† This question of improvements made by the tenant and the compensation to which they entitle him at the expiration of his lease is one of those that must preoccupy the English agronomists and economists. Prince Vassiltchikof, more logical on this point, would like the peasants to be given the right to demand an indemnity from the commune for money spent on improving the soil.

tions created for the commune by law and the fisc. Many among the worst faults of the rural *régime* come from the administrative and financial *régime*. They should, in part at least, be imputed to the State, which, finding it handy to make use of the *mir* in the capacity of tax collector, has in many ways converted it into a tool of oppression. The taxation itself is partly responsible, as, by loading down the common property under an inordinate weight, it has become an instrument of grinding and torture. In short, collective property in Russia is placed in conditions which, far from helping it to work easily and profitably, have completely warped and clogged its action.

There is one universal fact which is admired too unconditionally—the solidarity in the matter of taxes. All the holders of communal land are equally and mutually responsible for them. That is a thing which disheartens individual endeavor and slackens labor as surely as brief lot-terms, for it is all profit to the idle and ignorant. This solidarity, so highly extolled even by some Western would-be reformers, is too often the *mir's* scourge and the greatest hindrance to economic progress. The industrious and well-to-do peasant does not care to work for the good of some lazy, drunken neighbor, who does not get out of the soil enough to pay his quota, which, sooth to say, is often out of proportion to the yield of it. Hence we see in Russia a renewal of the heart-rending sight so familiar in pre-revolutionary France—that of peasants purposely making themselves outwardly poor and miserable to avoid being sold out for taxes.* Prosperous husbandmen have been known to rid themselves of this solidarity by renouncing all claims to communal lands, or even by purchasing for cash their dismissal from the commune. It is nothing unusual for lots

---

* The agricultural inquest reports that some well-to-do peasants in the government of Smolensk hide their money instead of spending it on livestock, out of fear that the animals may be seized for their neighbors' arrears. In many villages, besides, there is a large class of tax-payers who have fallen behind and, not unfrequently, become the *mir's* insolvent debtors.

to be offered to any one who will engage to pay the taxes—and for no one to be found willing to take them on the terms.   Or, a lot will be let for half the amount of the taxes it is assessed at.*   Live-stock is taken for arrears of taxes, and sometimes even the work-ing implements, to the great detriment of the land, which has to do without manure or fertilizer of any kind.   Thence an evil greater still : the dependence on the communal authorities of the members, and the embargo laid on the first and simplest of liber-ties—that of coming and going.   The *mir*, being responsible for all, cannot consent to the temporary absence of its members, unless they have acquitted their dues or given security for them.   All this further indirectly results in handicapping intellectual and moral as well as material progress, blunting the sense of responsi-bility, smothering originality, invention and enterprise.

If the principle of solidarity were applied to a normal land-tax, taking from the soil only a portion of its yield, there would not be much harm in it ; but we know, unfortunately, that such is far from being the case everywhere, owing : first, to the excessive burden laid on the peasant in the shape of taxes ; and, second, to the still heavier burden of the redemption dues, which will weigh him down through nearly the half of a century, so that he really is called "landowner" very prematurely.   When we examine into the condition of the rural communities, we must not lose sight of the fact that they will fall into a regular normal state only after the last instalment of the redemption indemnities will have been paid. At present everything in them is precarious, temporary, so it is hardly possible to form a definite judgment.

The emancipation itself, far from improving the *mir's* condi-tion, has temporarily made it worse : in a general way, by tight-ening the bond of solidarity ; and, in a special, local way, by

* The number of peasants who voluntarily go out of communes seems to be on the increase.   In the government of Vladímir there have been as many 2,266 in fifteen years—390 for the first five years, 739 for the second, and 1,137 for the last.

imposing a rate of redemption out of proportion to the yield of the soil, or by awarding them an insufficient allotment of land. Of the two latter abuses, the first is unfortunately the most frequent, and it distorts the principle of land community, by transmuting it into a form of servitude.

In some regions, and sometimes they are the most fertile ones, where the peasants have gone in for the "quarter lot," they have received one half or one third of the land of which they had the use in the times of serfdom. In such communes the lot awarded to each family is quite insufficient for that family's support, and, worse still, cannot be placed under regular cultivation. They suffer already now from the evils with which other communes are only threatened in view of increased population. Unable to exist on the land allotted him, the peasant is forced to seek a living in some industrial craft or to go elsewhere to hire himself out as laborer. The inadequacy of the communal funds—where such exist—is so notorious that already under Alexander II. several provincial assemblies—those of Tver and Tauris among the number—were driven to make advances to the communes, to enable them to enlarge the lots, while, under Alexander III., the State itself, and for the same purpose, founded a special real-estate bank.

The complaints against the exiguity of the peasant lots have become almost universal. Mr. Ianson, professor of statistics at the University of St. Petersburgh, has made himself the main organ of them, until they have become, in the Petersburgh press, a sort of commonplace. It has gone so far as to assert that the peasant's hopes had been raised by imperial promises only to be dashed ; that, while he had been promised a lot sufficient to ensure his sustenance and enable him to take care of himself, the lot actually given him is generally too small to meet the needs of his family.

Now all such complaints are based on a misunderstanding. The instigators of the charter, as we have seen, were everywhere desirous of so extending the territorial endowment, that the peasants, when free, should own a quantity of land not lesser than that of which they had the usufruct as serfs. But not even those members of the Drafting Commission who most favored the peasant ever dreamt of giving him land enough to make it unnecessary for him to work outside of his own lot. What would, in that case, have become of the estates left to the nobility? By whose hands would they have been cultivated? And where would trade, industry, large-scale agriculture, have taken the hands they need? As it is, and in spite of the smallness of the endowment, in spite of the taxes which drive the peasants to look outside for work, complaints of the lack of hands come from nearly all parts of the empire, and, it should be noted, they are often loudest where the *mujik's* lot is smallest.

There is still another obstacle to an extension of the peasants' territorial endowment as urged by some journalists who, it seems, would fain demand new agrarian laws, and that is that in many provinces—precisely, too, in the richest, comprising nearly the whole of the Black-Mould belt, which is under regular cultivation—there is not enough land to cut out for every peasant what the Petersburgh press calls "a normal lot," and there will naturally be even less in twenty years from now. Such a demand is knocked on the head by a physical impossibility, against which all the agrarian laws in the world can avail nothing.

In reality, many Russian writers, when indulging in speculations on the proper dimensions of the peasants' lots, unconsciously start from a principle, too thoughtlessly erected into an axiom : that, under the collective tenure system, nothing should be easier than to ensure a competence to everybody. At the first glance it seems only a question of distribution ; one forgets that collective tenure increases neither the extent nor the bearing capacity of the soil ; that capital and science alone can extract from the earth all that it is capable of yielding.

If, in some parts of the country, the endowment has been manifestly insufficient to lend itself comfortably to the communal system, such, certainly, was not the case everywhere. The communal lot conceded to much the greater part of the peasants would be accounted considerable in any other country. Statistics give an average of 16 or 17 *dessiatínas* (about 45 to 48 acres) per *dvor* or family for the entire empire. True, this average is naturally much lowered in the richer and more fertile regions of the Black-Mould belt. There as elsewhere the Crown peasants, being endowed with State lands, almost the whole of which (at least of the arable lands) was made over to them, were placed in more favorable conditions than the former serfs who had to share the land with the masters, and moreover frequently elected the gratuitous minimum authorized by the law, so as to liberate themselves from all payments and dues.* In those rich provinces, Vorònej, Tambòf, Kursk, Penza, the average still oscillated between 15 and 10 *dessiatínas* (42 and 28 acres) per family, without descending noticeably below the latter figure ; † but we must remember that, since the agrarian laws of 1861 were promulgated the increase in the population has been considerable, and has reduced each "soul's" or family's lot by just so much.

* To relieve this class, which numbers about 600,000, it has been proposed to revise the Statute of 1861, and give such peasants a chance to redeem, even yet, with the assistance of the State, the lands which they had foolishly renounced.

† On the latest showing, the communes of Crown and Appanage peasants situated in the eight governments of the central agricultural zone, and making up between them an actual male population of 2,901,000 souls, of whom 2,318,000 are entered on the " revision " registers, have received 11,092,000 *dessiatínas* (over 30,000,000 acres). To the communes of private noblemen's serfs, with an actual male population of 2,929,000 souls, of whom 2,456,770 registered, only 6,539,000 *dessiatínas* (about 18,000,000 acres) have been given. Which means that the private serfs have, on an average, about 3 *dessiatínas* ($2\frac{9}{10}$) per " soul " to the Crown peasant's 5 or thereabouts ($4\frac{8}{10}$.) But, owing to the rapid increase of the population, that average is at the present writing reduced to $2\frac{2}{10}$ for the former and to less than 4 ($3\frac{8}{10}$) for the latter. Even so the average is still, for the former, of $7\frac{1}{2}$, and for the latter, of 13 *dessiatínas* per family. (These figures are taken from official statements, published in 1880, in St. Petersburgh, by the Central Committee of Statistics.) The *dessiatína*, as already stated, is equal to about $2\frac{3}{4}$ acres.

35

Still, when all is said and done, one cannot consider as fatally doomed to destitution peasants who own, on an average, from thirty-eight to fifty acres of land ; who, even in the wealthiest and most populous provinces, still can call some twenty-five acres their own ; whose labor is at a premium in an extensive neighborhood. The insufficiency of the peasant's endowment can hardly be held alone or chiefly responsible for the evil plight of the villagers and of agriculture. Of the advocates of the *mir*, several—and not the least enlightened—do not hesitate to admit so much. Not there is the root of the evil : if the peasant's lot so often seems insufficient, it comes half the time from the imperfection of the agricultural methods in use. Ignorance and penury, the lack of intellectual and material capital, the lack of livestock and the necessary implements,—these are the things which debar the freedman from making more out of his piece of ground ; and this penury of man and impoverishment of the soil are, in a great measure, directly caused by excessive taxation.* There in very truth lies the main sore, the root of the agrarian trouble : in the disproportion between the extent or value of the lands allotted to the peasants, and the burden laid on them ; and the evil is such, that all the measures of relief already effected or promised by the Emperor Alexander III. are inadequate to cope with it. Not only was the land he tills not received by the liberated serf as a free gift, but he is paying for it, in the shape of every manner of taxes and dues, a most exorbitant price. So long as he labors for the fisc and not for himself, the question of tenure is a secondary one. Had the peasants initiated the uniform principle of individual ownership, they would have been beggared all the same.

The communes, such as the emancipation has left them, are traversing a crisis. We cannot possibly judge of what they can be from what, at present, they are. Before we can do so,

* Mr. Ianson (1881) gives most doleful figures in this respect, in which the Russian journalists of all the different schools have been compelled most unwillingly to acquiesce.

fairly, they would have to be relieved of their fiscal fetters, of the heavy and demoralizing load of fiscal solidarity—and that will not be easy, even after the suppression of capitation and the final winding up of redemption accounts will have made the commune really owner of its lands.* Then, and then only, it can be put to the test and experience pronounce the verdict. The redemption dues figure for nearly sixty per cent. in the burdens borne by the former serfs, and this terrible ransom, distributed over forty-nine years, will not be acquitted before the twentieth century has seen its first quarter wane. It is not likely that the state of the imperial finances should allow of liberating the peasants before the expiration of the originally appointed term. It is a great thing gained already, that the Emperor Alexander III. should have been able, without prolonging that term, to alleviate ever so slightly the weight of the annuities paid by the former serfs.

* Capitation has been abolished by the Emperor Alexander III., not so the redemption dues. Besides, were fiscal solidarity officially suppressed, it might be, in the practice, upheld for a long while still by habit and by the *mir's* authority. The government has more than once initiated the study of ways and means for the modification of the system of tax-collecting in rural districts. Unfortunately the calls on the imperial budget are so heavy as to make such reforms hardly practicable ; arrears in the payment of taxes might increase unconscionably in the hands of a collector less **watch**ful or less interested in the matter than the commune itself.

BOOK VIII. CHAPTER VI.

The Manner of Dissolving a Community—The Peasants of any Village are Always Free to Suppress the *Mir*—Why they don't Do it more Frequently—What they Think of the *Mir*—How the *Mir* has No Objection Whatever to Individual Property, even though it Usually Upholds the Communal System—Purchases of Land by Peasants—Distribution of the Arable Lands between the Communes and Other Proprietors—Utility and Functions of Personal Property—Can Both Modes of Tenure Co-Exist Some Day?

WHAT is the ultimate fate of the rural communes to be? and shall a decision on this head be postponed until they are free from all the encumbrances which crush them, and have become real and full proprietors of the land allotted them—or, do the difficulties that at present beset them make it desirable to come to a decision at once and to cut down at the root that gigantic growth of centuries, the *mir*, without first attempting to trim it down and to rid it of the parasitical plants which choke it?

Few are those who demand the immediate abrogation of the *mir*, but many those who wish for measures that should prepare and ensure its gradual disparition. Even now village communes are not indissoluble. The law, while upholding them, leaves to the members the privilege of abolishing them by instituting a final division of the communal domain between themselves. Nothing more is needed for that than a resolution passed by the assembled community, by a majority of not less than two thirds.* The an-

* More than that: the Statute, doubtless with a view to safeguard the quondam serf's right of choosing the mode of tenure which best suits him, has an article—Art. 165 of the Redemption Regulation—which empowers single peasants to withdraw their lot from the common domain, provided

tagonists of collective tenure would like to leave the fate of the communal lands to an absolute majority, in the hope that this would accelerate the suppression of all these agrarian associations. To this demand, at first sight moderate and legitimate, there is one main and weighty objection : the dissolution of the community is not the only question which, under the existing law, the *mir* is not allowed to settle by a majority of not less than two thirds. The same rule applies to all questions of any importance. It is the case with all questions that concern the division of land, and this restriction is not without a good reason. It is a useful curb, a wise precaution against the impulsiveness of ignorant villagers, who need to be restrained and protected against their own blunders all the more that, in its own sphere of action, the commune is all-powerful and paramount. To leave to an absolute majority the most important decision there is for the *mir* to take, would be to make light indeed of dissolution, to renounce, for any administrative or economic measure, the wholesome protection awarded by an obligatory majority of two thirds.

Even with this restriction, the Russian law as it actually is, opposes less barriers than almost any other to the alienation or partition of communal lands. In France, where they still take up one eleventh ($\frac{1}{11}$) of the national territory, the communal domains are far more efficiently protected against any sudden whim in the way of selling or dividing them. The law leaves to the communes the faculty of making certain purchases, but forbids their alienating any land without being authorized thereto by the central power. The jurisprudence of the State Council, indeed, is wholly opposed to any kind of division among the villagers. In England, where they enjoy so large a share of self-government, communes cannot alienate their lands without the approbation of the

they personally pay into the treasury the whole of the redemption sum which falls on that lot. Several among the partisans of the *mir* wanted to have that article recalled, but it does not seem to have had the effects they dreaded, as few peasants ever were in a position to take advantage of this concession.

government. Were the system now in force in Russia introduced in France, and were two thirds of the votes sufficient to cut up the communal domains and divide them among the members, they would soon have vanished, to round up the field of Peter and defray the expenses of Paul. The wonder is how common property has not yet crumbled away in Russia, with so little protection from the law.

It has often been asserted that there are instances of lands divided long ago among the serfs by the masters, and reconstituted by the former into a communal domain after the emancipation, while there is no instance on record of the opposite proceeding. This is a mistake. Final partitions are rare, exceptional, but they occur. The agricultural inquest mentions several as having taken place in various governments of Great-Russia. There even are districts where such cases are comparatively numerous, showing signs of a turn in the tide of popular feeling, favorable to individual property and principally caused, aside from the wish to escape from fiscal solidarity, by the fear that the increase of population, by making the lots smaller all the time, may at last deal a mortal blow to the communal system, unless some way is found of substituting some other method for the system of periodical reallotment.*

The instances we have of such dissolutions are, in any case, sufficient to show that the law even now is far from opposing an insurmountable barrier to such operations. They occurred very

* Thus, in one district of the government of Nijni Nòvgorod, 49 villages out of 190, and in a district of Mohilef, 25 out of 344, had given up the communal system. These, however, were exceptional cases. In many villages, in many governments even, only one or two final partitions occurred out of hundreds and thousands of villages (in the government of Kursk, for instance, 2 out of 3,591). It is to be noticed that these resolutions, sometimes suggested by a functionary or by a private landholder who is not of the *mir*, are not always carried out. In the government of Simbirsk some communes are said to have passed such a resolution, only that a few wealthy peasants should be enabled to redeem their individual lots, as provided by Art. 165 of the Regulation ; the rest kept to the old way. In other places sham resolutions are passed—just to get rid of fiscal solidarity.

rarely in the first years, but have been much more frequent of late. The peasants in many cases were ignorant of their rights in this respect, but now that they have found them out they are beginning to make use of them.* With the law as it stands, the fate of the collective system is in the hands of the peasants themselves ; the day on which the *mir* will have against it a considerable majority it will fall at one voting.

The moment has not yet come for that. Setting aside custom and tradition, which have a great hold on the *mujik's* mind, sundry reasons and prejudices militate against a final division of lands. To begin with—the crowding of dwellings, which makes every man fearful of being given a lot at too great a distance from the village where all live together. Then—the fear of drawing a bad lot, without the chance there is now of better luck at the next drawing. Another objection lies in the communistic tendencies of the *mir*. The peasants dread the unequal increase of families, which, in the course of two generations at most, would mix up everything. Lastly, where the taxes exceed the income, they are afraid of being burdened with too large a lot ; in this case what they dread is not the inequality of possession resulting from the unequal increase of families, but, on the contrary, an excess of it, resulting from deaths or sickness in families. " Bad as it is now," a village elder replied to the questions put to him by the inquest commission, " it would be much worse if the land were not at times re-divided ; the man whose family grew smaller could not at all till his land and pay the taxes." In short, the greater part of the peasants are still attached to the old way, even though they often acknowledge its shortcomings. Of the noble land-

---

* In the course of the nine or ten years that followed on the emancipation, there were probably not a hundred communes that renounced collective tenure. But since that, on the showing of the *Materials* published in 1880 by the Ministry of Crown Demesnes, 140 communes were found to have taken this step in only three districts of the government of Tula alone, and analogous facts are reported of other provinces, that of Tver, for instance.

lords questioned on the subject by the commission, several declared that they had tried in vain to get their peasants' consent to
a final partition. I myself have heard the same assertion from
men who are strongly opposed to the present system.

It is, moreover, difficult to find out, with any degree of certainty, what the peasants really think on this subject, which so
nearly concerns them. Who, in the *mir*, are the advocates of
communal tenure? Are they the idlers, the drunkards, the improvident, or are they, on the contrary, the industrious and well-
to-do? On this point the most opposite assertions are found in
the reports of the agricultural inquest commission, and elsewhere.
The peasants are represented as divided into two classes, without
an intermediate class : the rich and the poor. Towards which
opinion does each incline? The rich, who have been enriched
by the actually subsisting system, are usually considered as its
opponents, while the poor, who have reaped from it nothing but
penury, are said to be its warmest adherents. Which would
mean that the more prosperous, being the most industrious and
hard-working, advocate the system which would best ensure to
them the fruits of their labor, while the more improvident or
indolent hold with that which guarantees them the easiest
existence.

Yet, on the commission's own showing, this distribution is
far from universal. For one witness—a governor of Kursk
among others—who testifies that the more well-to-do are those
who want the communities to be dissolved, and even sometimes
petition the government in this sense, there will be numerous
landlords who say and repeat that a few wealthy peasants are the
only ones to benefit by the communal system ; that these village
oligarchs, who hold the *mir* under their thumb, exert their
authority to uphold it, because it enables them to squeeze their
fellow-members dry. One witness, a Mr. Yereméyef, even goes so
far as to aver that, owing to these "vampires," only a power
placed above the community can pronounce the sentence of abro-

gation. A commission chosen out of the nobility of St. Petersburgh recently proposed, as a means to facilitate the dissolution,
that ill-behaved members, and such as are in arrear with their
taxes, should be excluded. To this a writer in Moscow replied
that those were precisely the most inclined to a final partition, the
most desirous of having a lot all their own, to sell for money or
drink, as they pleased !

When the Russians themselves, who know the *mujik* best,
give us such contradictory information, a foreigner would find it
hard indeed to make a choice and would be overbold to draw a
conclusion. Such divergences can be accounted for only in one
of two ways . either the peasant puts this big question to himself
but rarely as yet, or he has not yet formed a fixed opinion regarding it. In the meantime, the greater portion cling to the old
customs and the ways of their fathers. The facts nevertheless
show that he begins to revolve the question in his mind and that
his verdict is not always favorable to the *mir*. It should not be
forgotten either, that a not inconsiderable number of communes,
without actually going over to individual tenure, have not proceeded to re-allotments since the emancipation. In such villages
it is not impossible that the change may be effected without any
harsh revulsion, in a manner almost insensible.

One thing is certain—that the Russian peasants, even while
upholding, as a rule, collective tenure where it exists, do not feel
that instinctive, unreasoning aversion against the opposite system,
with which Herzen and the Russian socialists credit them. They
by no means see in communal tenure the only natural and legitimate form of landholding, and in personal proprietorship a monstrous and iniquitous usurpation. Those who can, are fond of
purchasing a piece of land for their very own. The liking which,
in common with all the peasants in the world, they have for the
soil, the earth as such, is counterbalanced in them only by the
national taste for trading. All the reasons that seem to carry
them along towards the dissolution of the commune, prompt them

to begin at once acquiring personal property. The liberated serfs buy land, but of their former lords, outside the jurisdiction of the *mir*. This appetite for property has been noticed of all since the emancipation. The merchants also buy up many lands long in the possession of noble families, but it is usually with a view to reselling to the peasants in small lots. The demand on the latter's part is such that this speculation has become quite remunerative ; the margin of profit is very considerable. In the single government of Kursk the communal peasants had acquired land for two million roubles in one year. This transfer movement, which the agricultural inquest commission pointed out in 1872, has steadily increased since. In the government of Tver the peasants, during the last years of Alexander II., bought up near on 1,250,000 acres, in Tauris 430,000 *dessiatínas* (about 1,180,000 acres), over 300,000 (825,000 acres) in that of Samára, over 200,000 (550,000 acres) in that of Sarátof, and over 150,000 (413,000 acres) in that of Khersòn. And now, since Alexander III. came to the throne, the Peasants' Bank has loaned them, for the purpose of purchasing lands, sixteen millions of roubles in 1886, thirteen in 1887, the average purchase price being, in 1887, 41 roubles 73 copecks per *dessiatína*. True, the purchase is generally made in bits, by some one peasant who has somehow made money ; still, sometimes an *artèl* will be formed ; at other times again the communes become purchasers. Vast estates, of thousands of acres, have been known to pass into the hands of peasants' associations in this way. Sometimes they keep the land undivided, as common property ; but more frequently they divide it among themselves finally, which gives one argument at any rate to the opponents of collective tenure. In this way, many *mujiks* are at the same time usufructuaries of a communal lot, and full proprietors of a piece of land bought with their pence.*

* In the government of Tver, for instance, out of 469,000 *dessiatínas* (1,290,000 acres), 115,000 (317,000 acres) have been bought up by communes, 105,000 (289,000 acres) by *artèls* or associations, and 248,000 (682,000 acres)

There is plenty of room for such operations. For the whole Russian territory is far from belonging to the rural communities. There are the Crown lands, there are the estates of the noble landlords, there are many domains of vast extent, some of them colossal, often badly cared for, if not quite uncultivated, which the owners would be only too glad to alienate or reduce to reasonable proportions.*

It were highly interesting to have an exact and detailed diagram of the proportion in which lands are divided between the various classes, and especially between individual and collective tenure. Now, on this latter point, we are reduced to estimates which are as yet incomplete. Moreover, the general estimates covering the area of a territory in great part unsuited for agriculture, the averages deducted from them, could give only a very misleading idea of the real importance of that or the other mode of tenure.

The peasant is shown to possess at the present moment an agricultural domain at least twice as extensive as the entire European territory of France. Of this vast area the greater part, probably more than two thirds, is subject to communal tenure, which, so

by individual peasants, in the number of 12,600, so that each buyer comes in, on an average, for a little over 50 acres. In the government of Sarátof, out of 308,000 *dessiatínas* (847,000 acres), 187,000 (542,000 acres) have been bought by individuals and 121,000 (332,000 acres) by communes. It is to be noted that even when these purchases are made by a commune or an *artèl,* the land is seldom left undivided. The new property is usually divided among the purchasers' families, in proportion to the sums contributed by each.

* There still are in Russia numerous estates of 10,000, 20,000, 40,000 *dessiatínas* and more, the *dessiatína,* as already mentioned, being equal to about 2¾ acres. The great landlords, *i. e.* those who own over 1,000 *dessiatínas,* still hold, according to the latest information, 53 per cent. of the entire territory on personal tenure in the most fertile agricultural zone. In the eight governments which compose the central agricultural region, where land is the most valuable, official statistics reported 1,800 landlords with from 1,000 to 5,000 *dessiatínas;* 141, with from 5,000 to 10,000 *dessiatínas;* lastly 82 owning each more than 10,000. The number of large estates is probably very much greater in most other regions.

far, prevails in the whole of Great-Russia. Setting aside the Crown lands, which comprise many inaccessible forests and barren tracts, the peasant already holds more than half the totality of arable lands, and the proportion is still more in his favor if we take into consideration the exceptional value of the Black-Mould belt.

In this region, according to Mr. Ianson, the statistician already mentioned, the lands belonging to the peasant cover from 70 to 90 % of the governments of Vorònej, Kazàn, Orenburg, Ufà, Viatka, and something over 50 % in the middle region of the Black-Mould. According to Mr. Semiònof and the Central Committee of Statistics, the rural communes already owned, in the eight agricultural governments of the centre, 56 % of the entire extent and 66 % of the arable part, while only 37 % of the entire extent and 31 % of the arable lands, *i. e.* less than half as much, was owned on individual rights, in the same region. Which shows that, in the most fertile portion of Great-Russia, the greater part of the cultivated lands is held by communal tenure.

Vast as the peasant's possessions are, they are steadily increasing, and, to do so, they have not waited for the foundation of the real-estate banks specially created under Alexander III. to quicken that increase. The transfer movement by which the lands are fast passing into the hands of those that till them is so rapid and powerful, that various agricultural societies and a few nobiliary assemblies have already evinced some uneasiness and looked around for ways to forestall the destruction with which the *mujik's* suddenly developed acquisitiveness threatens large land-holding.

In the face of these continual encroachments, is there not, indeed, reason to dread an impending expropriation of the nobility for the benefit of a peasantry, ignorant and unprovided with capital, or of tradesmen who have no affection for rural life, who take no interest in the soil, and only hasten to exhaust it by means of proceedings justly stamped with the name of ''agricultural brigandage''? Here lurks a question of ominous bearing on the economic development of the empire, and one which many Russians, in their natural desire for the extension of the people's domanial territory, lose sight of. This revolution, which curtails the rural possessions of the nobility, is not all gain for the country and its culture, especially since the peasant, no longer content with occasional bites out of the loaf of huge estates belonging to a few over-wealthy families, is setting his teeth deeper every day into the middling and small landed properties.

When we speak of " culture" suffering from this sort of gradual elimination of the nobility in certain parts of Great-Russia, we do not mean, or not only, that of general civilization—intellectual, literary, and scientific culture, of which the old time *pomiêsh-tchik*, with all his faults and all his frivolity, was, after all, the only representative in the rural districts,—but material culture, the culture of the soil, which is seriously endangered ; production, the soil itself, which runs the risk of falling into hands too poor, too ignorant, or too routine-bound, to extract from it all that it ought to yield.

Exaggerated or premature as such apprehensions may appear, they hardly can be said to be baseless. In the actual stage of the Russian people's development, if private property were to vanish to-morrow and leave the field to the village communities ; if the *mujik's* new acquisitions were to become merged in the lands of the *mir*, Russia, it is to be feared, would have little cause for self-gratulation on having allowed the bulk of the empire to pass under the control of a lot of small rustic democracies, unlettered and superstitious.

To an impartial mind it is very doubtful whether it would be for the good of the State, to hand over, in the near future, all the arable lands to communes and peasants, whether under collective or individual tenure. Here more than in other countries, the rural masses being so lately liberated and so backward still in development and education, the great and lesser landholders have an economic part to play, a local mission to discharge. It is through them—through the *pomiêsh-tchik* preferably to the peasant —that belated agronomy is to enter on its career of progress. If too many of the private estates are not in much better condition than the *mujik's* acres, it is among them, on the other hand, that we occasionally encounter the soundest and most rationally conducted farming. For many long years to come, until the intellectual level of the rural masses is greatly elevated, the communities and the peasants cannot be counted on to improve farming. Were the entire territory in their hands, under any form of tenure, the State would find itself compelled, rather than abandon national production to semi-stagnation, to take the direction of farming interests into its own hands, to confide the tutelage over the agrarian communities to a special administration,—in a word, it would be driven to call in the doubtful and costly assistance of bureaucracy. Far better that there should be enough private landholders left to lead with their example, to give the needed impulse, to propagate and acclimate the new methods and sound farming practices. Neither the wealthy urban tradesman nor the well-to-do peasant is at present, as a rule, fit for this mission of enlightenment ; such men, as yet, are to be found only in the ranks of the old landholding nobility.

The fact is, this knotty property problem has two sides, and we should not let one blind us to the other. The social question must not make us lose sight of the economic question, nor must the seeming interests of the husbandman blind us to the no less essential interests of the soil and of agriculture. Of the two, neither can, with impunity, be sacrificed to the other. If certain nations, like England, seem to have taken thought too exclusively for culture and production, certain Russians sometimes seem ready to fall into the other extreme. Between the two errors, the latter is possibly the worse, for the husbandman's interests cannot, for any length of time, be separated from those of the soil and production. If, in a wealthy country, the wealth can become concentrated in too small a number of hands, a poor and badly farmed one cannot place wealth or competence within reach of the greater number.

Russia presents this sad and instructive anomaly : a people of which the bulk is at the same time landholding and poor. The reason is simple—it lies in the ignorance of the people and the excessive taxation ; even more, perhaps, in the lack of capital, without which production can never take a soaring flight. Instead of playing as much land as possible into the peasant's hands, his friends might be better employed, perhaps, in thinking out means that would help him to make more out of what he already has.

This is a vital question for Russia ; one which makes itself more and more urgently felt, and which American competition will not suffer to be ignored. If, owing to the export trade of the United States and the other trans-oceanic countries, the farming interests of old Europe are just now traversing a hard crisis, the ordeal is not less hard on Russian agriculture, which is threatened with expulsion from all the markets of the West by a rival richer in virgin lands, and especially in capital—a rival beyond comparison better stocked and less burdened with taxes and hindrances of all sorts. To the great rural empire whose agriculture is far and away its main resource, and whose soil, in places, already seems prematurely exhausted, this should be matter for serious reflection. What makes the superiority of the United States of America is not so much their fertility and the extent of their arable lands,—Russia also has her Far West (or rather, Far East) in the southern stretch of Siberia, which can easily be linked on to Europe by means of railroads and canals ; what makes Russia's inferiority is not so much the imperfection of her tools and communications,—it is, above all, the ignorance and poverty of the people, and to remedy these it is not enough—let us repeat it again and again—to increase the peasants' territorial endowment or facilitate for them the purchase of land. Unless Russia is prepared to live entirely in and on herself, to renounce all exchange with the West, and to give up borrowing from it the capital of which she stands so much in need, the *mujik* and the *pomiêsh-tchik* of the Don and the Volga must not leave the farmer of the Mississippi out of their calculation. This American competition, added to the bad crops and the famines of these latter years, is a new danger that threatens the superannuated agrarian system, the *mir* and the commune, which many Russians incline to hold responsible for the defeats inflicted on their national agriculture.

And yet, with the ideas and prejudices so widely spread among the people, the immediate abolition of the rural commune would scarcely improve matters much, because it would make hardly any change in the farming methods. Whatever we may think of collective tenure, it is not by modifying this or that system that production will be increased, but by changing the husbandman, the man. And such a change—of manners, customs, agricultural and general notions—cannot, in such huge rural masses, be accomplished in a few years. The schools themselves, even could they be multiplied to meet the demand for them, would be powerless to achieve, alone, such a transformation. To accomplish this, there must surge up from the very bottom of the people, from the midst of the lately liberated peasants, a new class, a comparatively well-informed, well-to-do class, capable of profiting by the light and examples shed from above and to propagate and spread them around. In the villages there must form, what is lacking in the country still more than in the cities, a sort of third estate, a real middle class, to fill the gap between the former serf-holders, now isolated, and the crowd of *mujiks*, as yet unlettered. The creation of such a rural class is not less necessary from a political point of view, if Russia means to have a free government, than from an economic one, if she means to raise her agricultural production to the level of her natural resources. Now it rather looks as though Russia has the germ of such a future rural burgherdom in the prosperous few among the peasants who are buying land on individual titles. Another new element, too, has of late years made its appearance in rural districts, one that seems to have a a considerable future before it.*   It will become the nucleus of a rural middle class composed of mixed proprietors, interested in both tenures and better qualified than anybody to appreciate the strong and weak points of both.   This new class, to which alone, with pecuniary ease, instruction will gradually come, will become for the *mir*, wielding powers until now centred in the hands of poor and ignorant men, a principle either of dissolution or renovation.   Under its influence, which will naturally increase, the commune will have to alter its usages, to admit new ideas and new methods, or else, should it turn out incapable of so doing, succumb under the onslaught of individualism.   Until matters have gone so far, the abolition of the communal system, before the *mujik* is in a condition to ameliorate his agricultural proceedings, would not only present few economic advantages, but might be fraught with considerable political danger.

It is the peasant's own business to experiment anent the comparative merits and demerits of both tenures.   Vast as are to-day the communal domains, the prosperous and enterprising peasant can still find land enough to achieve personal proprietorship without being necessarily compelled to abrogate the *mir's* collective proprietorship.   Russia is not called on to make an immediate choice between the two systems, both consecrated by time, both equally suited to the national habits.   Each of the two has its

* Notwithstanding their repeated purchases, the total number of peasants who have attained to individual proprietorship is still very small, but is steadily increasing. In the eight governments of the central agricultural zone the number of peasants holding land on individual tenure did not yet reach, toward the end of the reign of Alexander II., as high as 57,000, not much more than double that of noble landowners (25,000). If we take the extent of landed property, we find that four fifths of it (80 per cent) still belong to the nobility, 11 per cent. to the merchant, 2 per cent. to the *mièsh-tchánié* (townsmen of average means), and only 7 per cent to the peasants. Of these latter none as yet were classed under the head of " great proprietors," but several already came under that of "average proprietors," which means that they owned anywhere from 100 to 1,000 *dessiatînas*. The average extent of each peasant's personal property was, in this region, not quite forty acres. (Statistics of 1880.)

adepts, each may have its advantages,—social, moral, economic. Thanks to the extent of the Russian territory, both rival forms still can co-exist, whether to mutually complete and correct one another, or for one some day finally to triumph over the other, after both have had their fair innings.

BOOK VIII.   CHAPTER VII.

The Communal System and the Struggle between " Great " and " Small "
Landed Property—The *Mir*, the Peasant's Entail—Transformations
which the Agrarian Commune might Undergo—Can this System be
Adapted to Modern Manners?—What is Legislature to Do with Regard
to Collective Tenure?—Can we See in the *Mir* a Palladium of Society?
—Illusions on this Subject—The Communal System and the Population
Problem—Collective Tenure and Emigration—Village Communities
and Agrarian Socialism.

THE competition between personal and collective tenure will
be made more complicated in Russia by the habitual competition
between " great " and " small " property, " great " and " small "
culture.   There is not only the question as to which mode of
tenure, but also that as to which mode of culture is finally to
carry the day.   Habit and succession laws are not alone to regulate the extent of the land to be owned or tilled by one individual ;
the structure of the soil, its agricultural aptitude and that of the
climates also have their say.   There are localities cut up, slashed
into strips by nature herself, which seem meant for small farms.
There are cultures, that of the vine, for instance, which demand
division of labor, and consequently call for division of the soil.
The question is, what system, from this double point of view,
would be the most remunerative and the most natural to the
country ?   If any spot on earth seems to be made on purpose for
wholesale culture carried on by machinery, is it not those immense
tchernoziòm plains, where there is nothing to hinder the machines ?
or those boundless steppes where flocks sometimes have to be
taken miles to water ?   True, just now the great landholders are

selling and the peasants are buying.   It is a fact, but perhaps a
fact dependent on transitory rather than permanent and natural
economic conditions.   There is nothing to warrant that a reaction
will not set in after a while ; that, as capital becomes more plentiful, population denser, farming more scientific, property and
culture on a large scale will not rapidly regain the upper hand.
There, as in everything pertaining to the economic world, lies a
question of competition.   On the day that large farming will
prove more productive, more remunerative, small property will
find itself seriously endangered, and not more fit to hold its own
against such rivalry than are small workshops and small shops to
stand competition with the large factories and immense bazaars.

But the danger is not here yet, and the peasant might lose the
artificial shelter of the *mir* without fear of other encroachments
than those of his own brethren and of the " vampires,"—and it
would take these long to reconstruct large property.   Under
present circumstances, with the special conditions in which
Russian agriculture is situated, and those created for European
agriculture by American competition ;—with the inheritance laws
which, at every generation, cut up the land anew, the fall of the
village communities could not result in Russia, as it did in England, in the expropriation of the greater part of the peasants.
There is no doubt of that ; still, the defenders of the *mir*, in spite
of their exaggerations, have good cause to ask whether, if a
change did come, the *mujik* would not be glad to find one day in
his commune a barrier against the invasion of large domains.

For one of the village communities' most salient characteristics
is that they afford the rural population a substantial protection
against competition from the outer world, against the urban and
industrial classes, against what, in Russia as well as elsewhere, is
generally designated as the tyranny of capital.   The *mir* is an
impregnable stronghold for small proprietors.   Common property
is inalienable and so constitutes a sort of entail, with this difference that, whereas family entail ensures the future of only the

first-born of the family, communal inheritance provides for all the members of the community. In both cases the guaranties are of the same kind ; in both cases unborn generations are protected against the thriftlessness of the living, the children against the father's wrongdoing or improvidence. There is a degree of destitution or disaster below which a father cannot drag down his descendants or himself. To the disinherited the *mir* offers a shelter. This is the light in which the peasants themselves regard the matter, and that is why those of them who have achieved competence and become individual landholders, hesitate to go out of the commune. If they cannot attend to their lot, they let it or give the use of it to others, looking on the communal lands as a safety plank for their children or for themselves, should their private fortunes ever be wrecked.*

In this sense it is that Mr. Kavélin, one of the most enlightened and moderate defenders of the present system, could say that communal tenure was, for the rural population, a species of insurance trust. It gives each family the certainty of having a bit of land and a hearth. Without it, the former serf might be tempted to alienate his lot, to eat or drink away his children's patrimony. There is no doubt but that the *mujik*, so recently emancipated, will ofttimes still need this protection against himself, as proven by

---

* This is—to give an instance—what the peasants of the government of Moscow replied at an inquest by the provincial assembly : If the lots should become personal property, they would frequently be sold to the detriment of the holders or their descendants. A peasant dies, leaving infant children ; the head of a household is called off to the army,—an occurrence by no means rare under the prevailing custom of early marriages ; the widow or the young married woman cannot till the land all by herself, she has not enough to pay a laborer, nor can she often let the lot, on account of the taxes it is burdened with. In such a case, were sales allowed, the lot of course would be sold, whereas now the *mir* just takes it away to give to a family numbering more laboring hands, and when, in due time, the man returns from the army, or his children, if he died, come of age, they are sooner or later once more provided with land. The same thing happens, say the peasants, in case of sickness, of fire, loss of cattle, etc.

the fact that, in spite of this shielding system, it is no unusual thing for him to fraudulently mortgage to the "vampires," or "*mir*-eaters" the lot he cannot sell. Even should the most enterprising leave the commune to settle on land of their own, or devote themselves in the cities to trade or industry, it would still remain a refuge to the poor, the weak, or the timid. Side by side with a great development of wealth, it might still subsist,—as a sort of national agricultural *poorhouse*, one of its detractors says,—freely managed by its members and not dependent upon charity, either public or private.*

Far from lowering it to so humble a function, the progress of wealth and population may some day strangely transform the use of undivided property and reveal to it a very different vocation. As things are now, the communal lands, as opposed to the extensive domains of the former lords, represent small culture as well as small property. Should the peasants go on breaking crumbs off the large estates by their small purchases, it would not be impossible for the two kinds of property, great and small, to change places some day. Each has its advantages and each its drawbacks. If, from the social standpoint, one is inclined to favor the latter, it is difficult not to give the preference to the former in certain regions, from an agronomic point of view, from that of production. Now communal property has one singular faculty, that of adapting itself equally well to culture on a small and on a large scale, of combining the agricultural advantages of the one with the social advantages of the other. There is no reason why, some day, the temporary allotments to families should not be supplanted by wholesale culture or large farms let on leases by the communities. That would, indeed, be a transformation which would spoil the *mir* in the eyes of many of its

---

* Such might, indeed, be the ultimate fate of the communal lands, were they not so vast. But in a country where they take up the greater part of the arable lands, the State hardly could suffer them to become an endowment for the destitute and incapable. That would be the death of progress and production.

partisans ; yet it may be found some day, should collective tenure persist so long, that this is the only means to keep it alive and to justify its existence. In this respect it really has undoubted advantages over individual small property. In a country of wide plains, and in an age of steam-engines, would it not lend itself better to rational and scientific farming ? Formed into a sort of permanent syndicate, members of an agricultural association, in which they would be both shareholders and laborers, the peasants would find in their communal lands a field open to farming on the largest possible scale.

Even under the system of periodical re-allotments, outside of all these remote hypotheses, the community, which is apparently a constant barrier to progress of any kind, still could at times afford facilities towards the improvement of the lands and the habitual farming methods. The authority of the *mir* has already, in some few villages, introduced more rational methods. Communes are mentioned as having, upon formal deliberation, abandoned the traditional triennial rotation system, others as having declared manuring to be obligatory. As school-learning progresses, could not this concentration of rural forces be utilized ? It would seem as though association alone is capable of drawing out all the Russian soil's resources and of forestalling its natural defects. How can we contradict the advocates of the commune when they assert that it is better able than the isolated husbandman to undertake the vast labor needed to bring out the full value of the national territory, such as draining the marshes of the north and west, irrigating and restocking with trees the steppes of the south and east ?

It must be admitted that, in the *mujik's* present state of ignorance and poverty, all these improvements which seem to be the natural mission of the commune are manifestly beyond him. It will take generations for these collective proprietors to comprehend their interests and their duties in this respect, to learn how to form, at need, associations of several communes, the better to fight the climate and the defects of the soil, both frequently made worse by man's own carelessness. This spirit of enterprise and initiative will probably not descend on the peasant communes for a long time to come, and the antagonists of the present system may not be so entirely wide of the mark when they contend that it has killed the germ of that spirit in peasant and commune both.

For my own part, I would not, on the whole, venture to affirm that the form of land tenure bequeathed by primitive ages is absolutely incapable of being adapted to the demands of modern times. Only, of all objections brought out against it, the strongest in my eyes is precisely that which is founded on its antiquity.

If communal land tenure was good for the people and is conformable to natural law, how comes it that it has almost entirely disappeared from the wealthiest and most civilized countries? This cannot be attributed to chance. When an institution, which, once on a time, existed in vast regions, vanishes and leaves behind mere vestiges of its existence, in isolated localities, is not one tempted to think it unreconcilable with the development of human societies? This is, no one can deny it, a serious point against a belief in the future of collective land tenure. Yet this objection, however plausible, is not decisive. There is nothing to prove that an economic proceeding dating from the infancy of social life is incapable of being renovated and adapted to the spirit of a mature civilization. Would it not be easy to discover in many a law or custom of modern Europe—in the trial by jury for example—sundry traits descended from the barbarians? And even were it not so, would it not be somewhat presumptuous to forbid human societies all advance aside from beaten tracks, or to assume that all nations must necessarily travel the same stages?

In the modern world, ever since the French Revolution, a great struggle is going on. Two hostile principles, tricked out in various names and titles and which would centre all things, one in the individual, the other in the community, wage a war the issue of which is not to be foreseen. At an epoch when the talk is all of association and co-operation, when millions of human beings dream of reciprocity and solidarity, the law-maker must hesitate long before he strikes out a form of property which partly realizes what in other countries is accounted an absolute Utopia. By bequeathing to Russia collective land tenure, the past has imposed on her an experiment which, once it is given up, cannot be resumed again without a violent revulsion. The more vital its object, the more complete, the more patient the experiment must be. Russia owes it to civilization. One of the great boasts of the modern world is the variety, the individuality of its nations. The various states are, with regard to civilization, so many workshops, so many laboratories, rivalling and differing from one another ; each nation is an artificer, with a genius and tools of his own, and it is profitable to all that all should not work out the same pattern, should not continually copy one another. Great as is this variety on all other points—political, juridical, religious, —on one point it scarcely exists at all, that point being the regulation of property. Alone in the entire Christian world, the Slavs show some originality in this respect ; surely they may well pause before they decide that they will, in this also, discard it for the sake of prematurely imitating Europe. Alone among the nations of both worlds, Russia is enabled and qualified, by her traditions and the extent of her territory, to conduct parallel experiments with both forms of property. The Slavs of the south— *Yugo-Slavs* —cannot be counted on for that, because they are less advanced in civilization or already bound hand and foot by Teutonic and Latin influences. If the communal tenure of the soil is to be tested outside of Utopia and the revolutionary Icarias, it can be only in Russia and if the test is to be conclusive, it must be carried on at least until the final clearing of the peasants' lands from all encumbrances.

In the meantime, the attitude indicated for the government and legislature towards this question which causes such passionate controversy, appears to me the simplest and easiest in the world. Between the two modes of tenure, so extolled by one side, so reviled by the other, the government has not to decide; it is not the judge in the case so tumultuously tried before it. It is for the country, for the people, aided by time, to render the final verdict. The governing power has nothing to do but to keep strictly neutral, showing favor to neither combatant, but leaving both to fight it out between themselves. If, on the plains of Russia, collective tenure and individual tenure cannot live side by side, custom, the facts of the case, the needs of the country, the husbandman's personal interests, will naturally win the battle for the stronger, more serviceable, more productive of the two rivals. If the *mir* has not sufficient suppleness to lend itself to the progress of agriculture and the demands of modern life—the *mir* will gradually dissolve of itself, with the free consent of the communes, without interference from either law or State

There is no need of new laws against village communities. Under the law as it stands, they are much easier to destroy than to build up. Indeed this will be a great point against them in the coming struggle. If anything, it will be in favor of communal lands that laws will have to be made in, say, half a century from now, to protect whatever of them may then have survived, as is done in France.* Till that time comes, and it is still far enough, judging by the *mujik's* present disposition in the matter, the best thing to do, is to trust to time and nature, to the progress of instruction and the free play of interests—in a word, to free competition which, better than anybody, is able to decide between the various modes of tenure. At the risk of equally displeasing both the advocates and the detractors of the *mir*, of butting against prejudices and economic traditions, I must confess

---

* Already the partisans of the *mir* should like the law to interfere and put difficulties in the way of the dissolution of communes ; several even insist that the communal domains should be declared inalienable, as a safeguard against the encroachments of personal tenure, and virtually be erected into a perpetual endowment fund for the peasant class.

that, to my mind, here or never the old economists' "let-things-alone" principle may properly be applied.

Supposing that collective tenure should come out victorious from the present contest, could it become acclimated among nations the extent of whose territory and the density of whose population stand to each other in relations entirely different from what they do in Russia? Could it be transplanted on old Europe's soil after having been extirpated thence almost entirely centuries ago? On this question even the Russians most enthusiastically in love with the Moscovite commune rarely indulge in any self-delusion : very few believe that their pet institutions ever could be imported into the West. Not perceiving any other anchor of salvation for foreign nations, many sincerely bewail the fact that they should be so wedded to a radically wrong system which must, sooner or later, bring about the fall of the most flourishing of states.

Those who would, as do so many Russians, see there the complete and rational solution of what is known as "the social problem," are manifestly mistaken. It might be, perhaps, in a primitive country, all rural and agricultural still, such as Russia has been so long. With modern nations, where labor is evenly divided between agriculture and industry, between cities and country, the case is different. What modicum of land should be allotted to the millions that live in the capitals? Where is the endowment fund to come from for the families crowded into the cities? and, owing to industry and commerce, owing to the growth of prosperity, the cities will go on sucking into their walls a larger percentage of the entire population. The principal sore of Western Europe, almost the only one with which France is plagued, is the urban factory proletariate, and the Russian remedy, offered as a sort of social panacea, is a purely rural one.

And besides, can collective tenure, in Russia itself, attain the lofty destinies which are the dream of so many patriots? Is it possible that, in the old Slavic empire, preserved from Occidental contagion by its historical and geographical isolation, the Moscovite *mir* should become the foundation of a new and original civilization, exempt from the vices of the classical civilization, untainted with proletariate, pauperism, and the wages question?

For certain Russians would have us believe that all Russia has to do is to remain true to her history and her rural commune, in order to bring forth a society as brilliant, as prosperous as those of the West, and incomparably more harmonious and healthy,—a society unencumbered with class strife, free from all those morbid principles which, they aver, threaten the European nations with premature dissolution.

To what amounts this claim, of founding, with the assistance of a different agrarian system, a new civilization, unsullied with the taints of Western societies? In reality it comes to this: can there be a high-grade civilization, a high-grade culture, without large industries, a large commerce, large cities? Can there be, in Russia or elsewhere, a prosperous and indefinitely progressive society if—as is actually the case in Russia—the urban element should remain forever comparatively insignificant and subordinate? If, with the help of collective tenure and the *mir*, it should be possible to erect a new society on a wider and more firmly established basis, it could be only an exclusively agricultural and eminently rural one.

But even as a rural nostrum, is this social panacea of the Slavophils and their followers an absolutely infallible one? Who does not see that, to work to best advantage, the system of collective tenure needs unbounded space? In order that each inhabitant, each adult couple, may have a recognized claim to land, the first requisite is that there should *be* land, free land and a great deal of it. The Russian communes, at least those that are territorially well endowed, have reserve lands, which are kept for new claimants. That is really the only means of satisfying all those who are entitled to a share, as they appear on the labor stage; but such a system presupposes vacancies, either in the commune or in the lands. It is a banquet at which it is easy to place the first guests;

but it soon becomes a problem how to make room for later comers without crowding out the early ones. As the number of guests goes on increasing while the table does not stretch, will it not end in their all feeling cramped and being cut down to insufficient rations ? This is perhaps the worst that threatens collective tenure in the future.

One thing has been ascertained, and indeed is easy to understand : it is that the *mir* system encourages marriage and increase of population, since each family is entitled to land in proportion to the number of laborers it musters. On the other hand, the communal system, by setting, so to speak, a premium on large families and partly relieving parents from the cares that children bring, is apt indirectly to foster proletariate,—in other words, the supply of land being limited, the population, under this system, is apt to increase faster than the means of subsistence or comfort.* On this point collective land tenure is at odds with individual, hereditary tenure. The latter, at least under the system of equal division, tends to limit, in each family, the number of children who are to share the paternal loaf. Indeed, this is, in our eyes, about the weightiest objection to it. Thus it is that, under the property question, the population problem is found to lurk.†

Not quite a hundred years ago, Arthur Young, the English traveller in France, wrote that, at the rate at which property was being subdivided, the country must soon be converted into a rabbit warren. Facts have shown how vain his fears were. But

---

* It is this consideration,—although it would strike with full force only were the family to be unpossessed of either working implements or capital apart from its share of the territorial endowment—which made John Stuart Mill, among others, so bitter an opponent of communal tenure with periodical re-allotments.

† Some are of the opinion, not unfounded, that in this lies one of the causes which render population nearly stationary in France. Analogous circumstances have been shown to result in the same phenomenon in other countries also. In Belgium, for instance, Mr. E. de Laveleye has observed that the two provinces in which property is most subdivided—the Flanders —are those where the increase of population is least rapid. Switzerland might give occasion to similar observations.

then the French law set a limit to the excessive increase of the population by agrarian regulations which prevent indefinite parcelling of the soil. Now, in many parts of Russia, anything but dense as the population is, even in the most populous governments, the effects of this natural law already make themselves felt. In numbers of communes the peasants feel cramped and ill at ease ; the lots awarded to them at the time of the emancipation are already noticeably reduced, and grow smaller at each new division. And village communities—partly, it must be admitted, owing to bad farming—are stifling on lands which, in the West, would support twice or three times the number of mouths. If it has come to this not twenty-five years after the emancipation and the territorial endowment, what will it be in a hundred years from now—or in two, or in three hundred ?

In an empire such as Russia, where the vacant acres are counted by hundreds of millions, both in its European and Asiatic territories, where vast wildernesses vainly wait for somebody to settle on them, there is no occasion for uneasiness on the score of lack of land, say the advocates of the *mir*. In such a state it is easy to make up for the injustice of nature and society ; easy to solve the problem, unsolvable by the old states of the West, of a fair partition of the soil and of wealth. In Russia there is enough room, there are enough natural resources to smooth out as much as possible social inequalities, to suppress proletarianism without interfering with the rights of individual property, of the rural communes, and of the Exchequer. All there is to do is to regulate emigration, or rather internal colonization, to direct and locate the thousands of peasants who each summer leave their native communes in gangs, going forth to seek vacant lands, frequently on the faith of false rumors or lying emissaries.*

Russia, indeed, resembles, on a large scale, one of her own wealthy communes, endowed with land enough to form vast terri-

---

* Historically, this is probably the manner in which the *mir* both preserved itself and spread—by colonization—over the plains of Great-Russia.

torial reserve funds for the coming generations. The steppes of the south, certain regions of the Ural and Caucasus, especially Southern Siberia, are there, ready, for a greater or lesser number of years, to receive the excess of population of the village communities in the interior. It is the State's business to make use of these resources to the best advantage and, under Alexander III., it has given serious attention to the matter.* These reserve lands, however vast, will be exhausted some day, probably much sooner than those patriots imagine who allow the immensity of the areas comprised in the empire to mislead them. However remote it seems, that day will come in Russia with collective tenure, as it has come in America with individual tenure, and on that day the two systems will stand face to face, on their own intrinsic merits and demerits, with no possibility for either to call emigration to its aid. Then the critical hour will strike for collective tenure (if it survives so long), cornered as it will be by the increase of population, charged with failing more and more to do what is expected of it—to place landed property within everybody's reach. For there is no getting round this : that no matter what form of tenure is adopted, men cannot be largely provided with land, unless there be a great deal of land and few men.

I shall close this most unprejudiced study, with a last remark. In Petersburgh and Moscow men flatter themselves that, by preserving the peasant's communal domain side by side with the noble's or merchant's hereditary one, Russia will steer clear of the class conflicts which disturb the West. This has become, with many Russians, an uncontested axiom ; but it is to be feared that, on this point also, they are deceived. If there is not in Russia at this day conscious and declared antagonism between the

* The emigration question has been debated more especially by the assemblies of experts convoked by Alexander III. ; moreover, it has made real progress owing to the creation of colonization agencies and to the law of 1889.

"boss" and the working man, between capital and labor, the cause lies not so much in the existence of the *mir* as in the condition of the people,—social, religious, intellectual. Should the day come when the revolutionary crop sown by so many youthful hands should rise, on that day the form of tenure so extolled of the Slavophils would prove to Russian society a feeble palladium indeed. For the *mir*, such as it exists at present, with a whole class of landed proprietors outside of it, has a great social fault— that of dividing the rural population as well as landed property into two categories, two clearly defined classes. While in France there runs from the largest to the smallest holder of land a continuous and graded chain of proprietors, of every variety of rank and fortune, in Russia the holder of large estates—the *pomiêsh-tchik*— who stays outside of the *mir*, is entirely separate from the peasant communes, and that makes him an object of envy to them, if it does not some day arouse their cupidity against him. A great defect of the Russian commune, which is held up to us as the most certain preventive to the division of society into hostile classes, is precisely that it does cut the rural population into two classes having different if not opposite interests.

This would be a substantial danger, but for the fact that, through the land-purchases made by peasants, an intermediate class of small landholders is slowly forming between the *pomiêsh-tchik* and the *mujik* of the communes, a class that is in touch with both. These peasants, who are at the same time members of the *mir* and independent of it in their capacity of individual landholders, on the same footing as the former lord and the city tradesman,—these peasants who, in their person, embody both forms of tenure, will be the very link indicated to connect the two now widely separated classes. Without this intermediate group, which is with every year becoming more numerous, Russia would not long remain free from the class feuds which the revolutionists are working hard to provoke. Even now, when he as yet turns a deaf ear to all the "nihilistic" preachings, is not the *mujik* inclined to think himself despoiled in favor of the *pomiêsh-tchik*, to dream, for himself or for his children, of new distributions of lands ?

So that, instead of closing forever the door of the villager's *izbà* against the revolutionist, the *mir* may very well some day open it for them.* It will be in the name of the *mir*, represented to us as the safeguard of society, that the peasant will be invited to "round up" his lot, to gather all the lands into the communal domain.† The Russian commune, such as it exists in ancient Moscovia, is in fact an easy means of gaining possession of the soil on behalf of the masses; it is the only practical proceeding known, so far, for applying to the soil the theories of even distribution, without seeing inequality reappear out of the distribution itself. In all other countries, the main obstacle to any attempt at agrarian communism lies in the popular customs and manners; in Russia, thanks to the training imparted by the *mir*, this obstacle does not exist.

Must we then, from the fact that, at a given hour, the village communities serve as tools or bait to the revolutionists, conclude that they should, on shortest notice, be abolished by the law, as being noxious to society ? By no means, in our opinion, for there would be, in such precipitate prevention, great risk of increasing the evil. What can, at a certain moment, give the anarchist propaganda a hold on the peasant, is not so much the *mir* itself as the vague notions set afloat among the people by the customs born of the *mir;* and these ideas, these vague aspirations cannot be smothered by an *ukàz* for the suppression of village communities. So long as the ancient form of tenure retains the sympathies of the peasantry, the government cannot lift its hand

* In this respect the village communities offer much more hold to the revolutionary spirit than the family communities of the *Yugo-Slavs*, as these latter maintain much more clear the notion of property.

† Since these lines were first printed (*Revue des Deux Mondes*, May 15, 1876), more than one political trial has shown that these and similar apprehensions were far from fanciful.

37

against the *mir* without doing violence to the people's customs and their juridical conscience, and, consequently, without laying itself open, some day, to perilous retrospective demands.

The Russians are fond of representing collective tenure as a paramount remedy, an infallible nostrum against socialism and communism. If the *mir* really has this property, it must be in accordance with the theory which, in order to preserve an organism from a disease, inoculates it. It would be more correct to say. that, through her communal system, Russia was inoculated with communism, or rather with agrarian socialism ; that, thanks to the *mir*, it circulates, unbeknown to herself, in her veins and in her blood. Will the virus, at this dose, remain forever harmless ? Will it prove a preservative against contagion from abroad, or will it, on the contrary, call out some day, in the social organism, unexpected disorders and serious disturbances ? Time will show. In the meantime this is a treatment which no prudent counsellor will advise other societies to try, for fear of their taking the disease in good earnest.

Even now, when he keeps his ear closed against revolutionary preaching, the *mujik* is not always content patiently to wait for the tsar's bounty, in the form of new land allotments. As he passes by the lands of his neighbor, the *pomiêsh-tchik*, he cannot help squinting a little that way.* Sometimes, indeed, in his collisions with riverside landlords, he tries to extend the domain of the *mir* at their expense. Under the Emperor Alexander III., who, at his coronation, had the loyalty to warn the delegates

---

* "What will be done with the waste lands?" a peasant inquired of a certain Mr. Prugàvin.—"What waste lands?"—"Why, those that the rich people are keeping from us ; are n't they coming to us? Is there not going to be a division?"—"It is said there will be one," put in another ;—"that we are to get a little more."—"And where is the land to come from for another distribution?"—"Sure enough! Where *is* it to come from? There are the rich though   .   .   .   just a little, now, so every one gets a bit?"—"Would it be just to take from some, to give to others?"—"No, indeed."—Then after a pause : "They do say the lords would be given money instead." (*Revue des Deux Mondes*, January 1, 1883.)

of the peasantry that the property question was settled for good and all, there have been agrarian riots in various provinces. More than once the military had to be called in to repress them; the authorities took advantage of the laws issued against the revolutionists to send the leaders before a council of war. These things are hushed up as much as possible; the papers have strict orders to keep silence on all affairs of the kind. Thus in 1886, there was a riot in the government of Penza; in 1887, in that of Riazàn; in 1888, in that of Kazàn. Each time the troops were compelled to charge, and the ringleaders were tried by military commissions, so that, notwithstanding the abolition of the death penalty, they were condemned to death, and hung, it is averred, twelve or fifteen at a time. With less severity, it might have been difficult to maintain social peace.

As to the belief which makes of collective tenure a sure antidote against the revolutionary poison, warranted to keep Russia safe from all political epidemics, that is a prejudice, the fallacy of which has been too clearly demonstrated by the innumerable plots and audacious attempts of the last years of Alexander II. Mines and bombs, nitro-glycerine and dynamite have undertaken to undeceive the most confiding. Against the slow mining process of nihilism and revolutionary explosions, the Moscovite *mir* is manifestly an insufficient insurance. After the assassination of the Liberator of the serfs, no Russian can assert that all the periodical troubles which harass the West come from the Occidental form of land tenure; that social questions are the only ones that breed revolutions; that, in order to escape violent commotions, Russia only has to place the land within the reach of all.

APPENDIX TO BOOK VIII.

The following brief selection from Vladímir Dahl's famous collection of popular sayings, proverbs, adages, riddles, etc., may not be unwelcome, as setting forth, after the terse and pointed fashion of their kind, the people's own estimation of their principal national institution. It will be noticed that it is by no means one-sided or exclusively admiring.

What the *mir* has settled, is God's own judgment.

As the *mir* has resolved, so it shall be.

The *mir* will stand up for itself. You can't be the winner in a suit against the *mir*.

If the *mir* gives a whoop, the forests shall groan and bend.

The *mir* is subject to no jurisdiction but God's.

God alone can judge the *mir*.

The *mir* is inviolable, but the *mir*-members get thrashed.

A man of might is the *mir*. None may gainsay it.

Should the *mir* heave a sigh, it will reach the Tsar's ears.

If the *mir* goes mad, it can't be put in a strait-jacket (literally—"chained up").

There is no guilt in the *mir* : how should the guilty be picked out in the crowd?

All for one and one for all : that 's the *mir*.

When the *mir* comes together, it is ready to fight that minute ; when it separates, all it does is to lie on the stove-bench.

The *mir* is mighty as water and silly as a babe.

One or other *mujik* may be wise, but the *mir* is a fool.

It was the people's voice that condemned Christ.

INDEX.